AF693749

THE ESSENTIAL GUIDE TO
TIMEX/SINCLAIR
HOME COMPUTERS

The Only Book You'll Ever Need to Become an Expert at the Timex/Sinclair 1000 and 2000

by
PETER MORSE, IAN ADAMSON
BEN ANREP and BRIAN HANCOCK

A TOUCHSTONE BOOK
Published by Simon & Schuster, Inc.
NEW YORK

We are grateful to Sinclair Research for their cooperation
This book was published in England under the title *The Century Computer Programming Course*
Copyright © 1983 by Eosoft
All rights reserved
including the right of reproduction
in whole or in part in any form
A Touchstone Book
Published by Simon & Schuster, Inc.
Simon & Schuster Building
Rockefeller Center
1230 Avenue of the Americas
New York, New York 10020
Published by arrangement with Century Publishing Company, England
TOUCHSTONE and colophon are registered trademarks of Simon & Schuster, Inc.
Manufactured in the United States of America
10 9 8 7 6 5 4 3 2 1 Pbk.

Library of Congress Cataloging in Publication Data
Main entry under title:

The Essential guide to Timex/Sinclair home computers.
(A Touchstone book)
British ed. published as: The century computer programming course.
1. Timex 1000 (Computer)—Programming. 2. Timex Sinclair 2000 (Computer)—Programming. 3. Basic (Computer program language) I. Morse, Peter (Peter L. R.) II. Title.
QA76.8.T48E77 1983 001.64'2 83-9090
ISBN 0-671-47069-8 Pbk.

IMPORTANT NOTE FOR ALL READERS

This book uses the Sinclair version of single keystroke BASIC as featured on the ZX81 and Spectrum microcomputers. In the States the ZX81 has been marketed as the Timex/Sinclair 1000 and the Spectrum is known as the Timex/Sinclair 2000. American readers should note that throughout the text we refer to these machines by their UK names. There are a few minor differences between the UK version of the ZX81 and the US TS 1000. The first is that the TS 1000 has more 'on board' memory (2k) than its UK equivalent. However, this is still insufficient for the scope of this text, and the majority of the programs occurring in the book will require a 16k RAM pack. The second difference is that two keys, which do exactly the same thing, are labelled differently. Thus, NEWLINE and ENTER are equivalent on the ZX81 and the TS 1000, as are RUBOUT and DELETE. On each occasion that these commands occur in the text, readers will find either NEWLINE (ENTER) or RUBOUT (DELETE).

For the sake of clarity we have used the ZX81/TS 1000 version of BASIC as the foundation of the book, and have noted those instances where Spectrum (TS 2000) BASIC differs from that used by the ZX81 (TS 1000). Functions and commands exclusive to the Spectrum (TS 2000) BASIC superset are fully explained at the end of the book (Units W2 and W3).

In short, the book has been designed to enable its readers to learn how to program using any of the Sinclair machines.

Users of the Spectrum should note that all programs are listed in capital letters throughout. To get program results and listings that look identical to those given here the capital letter (CAPS) mode must be used on the Spectrum for all letters input or printed. The first two Units of Part One deal only with the ZX81. The Spectrum user should read instead Unit W1 (page 439) of the Spectrum dedicated Section which forms Part Five of this text.

CONTENTS

PART FIVE

COVERING THE WHOLE SPECTRUM 437

APPENDICES 477

INTRODUCTION

The central conviction behind this book is that programming computers to solve problems is essentially a language independent activity. This means that there is no reason why Sinclair BASIC should not be learnt in exactly the same way as other high level languages: that is, with the fundamentals of problem solving and structured programming introduced at an early stage. For the majority of readers, Sinclair BASIC will be their first introduction to computing. We would like to think that many will use it as a stepping stone to more advanced study and application. Good problem solving and programming habits will make both applications programming in BASIC and learning a different *structured* language like PASCAL (which has a richer programming environment than BASIC), much easier. We are convinced that bad programming habits acquired early on are extremely difficult to throw off; thus, this book has been designed to introduce readers to the elements of computer programming in a systematic manner, with the emphasis on correct rather than merely adequate techniques.

Although we intend the text to be a serious treatment of Sinclair BASIC, as an introduction to computing it assumes no prior knowledge of computers and only a minimal understanding of mathematics. (Without the maths you will still be able to make your way through the book, but if you don't know what SIN and COS are, you won't be able to write programs using them!) Before all else, we intend to give readers a full introduction to the essential control and modular structures present in truly structured computer languages and the way in which they operate in Sinclair BASIC. Once again, we hope that with this behind them, readers will be able to go on to tackle more sophisticated computer languages with a clear understanding of the essentials of good programming in any language. This approach also ensures that the reader who stays with his Sinclair machine will be able to maximise its potential. As it runs on the world's most popular microcomputers, there can be little doubt that Sinclair BASIC will become one of the most commonly used computer languages. This, coupled with the fact that more and more software is becoming available for the machines, makes it all the more important that users attain a sound understanding of the language. Most published programs in books and magazines have little in the way of documentation. Debugging them, normally a tedious and difficult task, becomes much easier if the techniques to do so are known.

This book introduces readers to three main sets of computer rules:

1 The rules of using your computer system.
2 The rules of the Sinclair BASIC programming language.
3 The rules of problem solving and structured programming using Sinclair BASIC.

WHY DID WE WRITE THIS BOOK?

The sheer availability of the Sinclair machines demands that they be treated seriously as a means of teaching progamming methods to a large number of people. The programmer of a personal computer must understand the characteristics of the machine, the high level language (in this case BASIC), by which it is used and controlled and the problem solving techniques to which it should be applied.

The first rush of books on the Sinclair machines has been, to put it kindly, disappointing. Certainly none can be considered a serious text on Sinclair BASIC. We felt that a book was needed which gave the first time user a worthwhile home tutor on computing. So we decided to write one!

WHO IS THE BOOK FOR?

The book has been written for the home user or school user who has just bought a ZX81 or Spectrum and wants to learn how to program it from scratch. Experience has shown that most Sinclair users will buy more than one book on the subject of programming their machine. This book will clear up a few misunderstandings and confusions presented by other texts and will take you further into programming techniques.

The text has also been designed as an aid to Sinclair BASIC programmers who are having trouble designing error free programs and are attempting some serious application.

HOW IS THE BOOK STRUCTURED?

As a self-study text, this book should be worked through with your computer in front of you, so that programs and examples can be keyed in as and when they arise.

The book has twenty-three Sections and is divided into five Parts.

Part 1: FIRST STEPS in which, after a brief introduction to the machine and system (the first two units are ZX81 specific, and Spectrum users should go immediately to the Spectrum specific units – W1 on page 439 – before returning to start the main text at Section C) you are told how to set it up correctly and start to write and run simple BASIC programs.

Part 2: FUNDAMENTALS OF BASIC PROGRAMMING, which first introduces the reader to the fundamentals of problem solving and structured programming in BASIC. The properties and implementation of important language CONTROL STRUCTURES – decisions, loops, and subroutines – are introduced, together with the use of arithmetic, functions, strings, and how to print and plot information on the screen.

Part 3: ADVANCED BASIC PROGRAMMING contains further sections on programming methodology, as well as details of debugging, testing and documenting programs. Interactive graphics is introduced, together with the use of logical operators. Lists and arrays and methods to sort and search them (vital subjects for applications programming) and a treatment of how the computer uses its memory are fully covered.

Part 4: APPLICATIONS PROGRAMMING AND GAMES focuses the fundamental programming skills acquired in the earlier parts of the book in the study of specific examples, linked to some further discussion of programming technique.

Part 5: COVERING THE WHOLE SPECTRUM is the portion of the book dedicated to the Spectrum. The first Unit of this Section, dealing with the Spectrum system and keyboard, replaces the ZX81 specific Sections A and B, since there are major differences in the arrangements of the two machines which require separate treatment. The two following Units in this Part of the book deal with additional features of the Spectrum not covered in the main text. It is intended that, after using the first Unit to acquaint him or herself with the Spectrum, the reader should defer reading these Units until the main body of the text has been worked through. For the Spectrum user, this starts at Section C.

The book is detailed and thorough. Remember that programming is learned most effectively through experience. You should work through the text systematically using your computer. Key in each example in the text and run it. Some further programs to key in are available in Appendix VI.

The exercises which appear at regular intervals throughout the book are meant to give you practice in programming methods and to further illustrate the function and application of the Sinclair BASIC language constructions. Attempt most of them, but don't ever allow yourself to become discouraged. If you get stuck, go back through the relevant section again.

We hope that you find learning BASIC programming with this book a successful, enjoyable and useful experience, and that the knowledge and programming skills obtained will be a step on the path to a more advanced use of your Spectrum or ZX81 for real applications and enjoyment.

PART ONE

FIRST STEPS

Important Note: The first two units of this part are specific to the ZX81. Spectrum users should ignore these pages and directly GOTO the first Spectrum specific section (W1 on page 439) before returning to the main text (Section C on page 19).

SECTION A: ZX81 MICROCOMPUTER SYSTEM

A1: ZX81 Description

We assume you have in front of you the components of your ZX81 computer system.

It consists of:

1 The ZX81 microcomputer with its touch-sensitive keyboard.
2 The Sinclair 16k RAM pack (Random Access Memory) or a RAM pack of at least 16k produced by one of the other manufacturers for the ZX81.
3 The ZX power supply, with a lead and plug, for connection to the a.c. power supply, and the lead, ending in a jack-plug, to connect the power supply unit to the ZX81.
4 The ZX printer and its connector socket.
5 A domestic UHF TV set to be used as a TV monitor.
6 A mono cassette recorder, with power supply lead if not battery powered.
7 The aerial cable which connects the ZX81 to the TV monitor.
8 A pair of cassette recorder leads fitted with 3.5mm jack-plugs on each end.

These components make up a complete system. As far as this text is concerned, the least crucial component is the printer. Without it you can simply ignore the printer-related portions, and will be able to work through the book and learn the BASIC programming techniques just as well. However, it is extremely useful to have a printer both for hard-copy printouts of results, and more importantly for program listings for documentation purposes.

There are a large number of 'add-ons' and accessories available for the ZX81. None of these are of any interest as far as this book is concerned, and most should be considered only when you have absorbed the text and are going to write programs for specific purposes, which might require the facilities provided by some of these units. A noteworthy exception is a workstation to hold the components of the system securely. There are types available which have on/off switches for the d.c. power supply from the power supply unit, which saves a lot of plug pulling and re-insertion, since pulling the power plug out of the ZX81 is the only way to re-set the computer if it 'crashes' (i.e. will not respond to keyboard commands).

What *is* vital is enough memory. RAM memory is measured by kilobytes ('k'). The basic ZX81 has only 1k of RAM built in (2k on the Timex/Sinclair 1ØØØ), and, without an add-on, RAM memory has very little space available for programs. Computers are essentially devices which store and manipulate data, and since programs, data, and the manipulations all take up memory space, an add-on RAM

Figure 1

ZX81 SYSTEM DIAGRAM

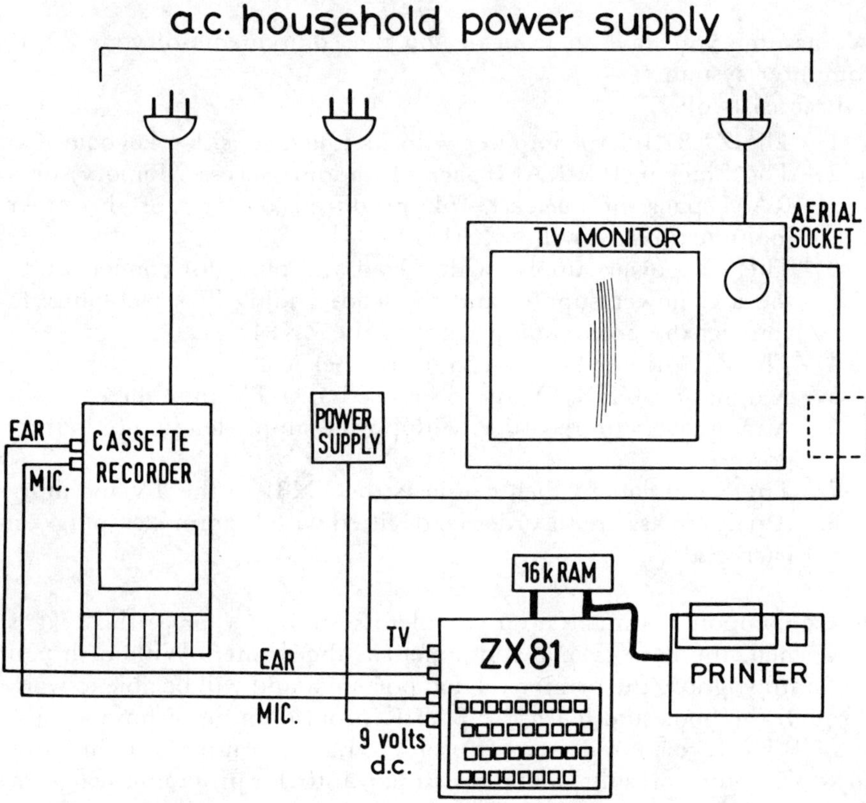

NOTE: U.S. USERS MAY HAVE ANTENNAE ON/OFF SWITCH FITTED IN AERIAL LEAD, SHOWN AS DOTTED BOX IN DIAGRAM.

memory is needed. RAM memory of up to 48k is available for the ZX81, but 16k is more than enough for our purposes. Independently produced RAM packs are usually just as good as those produced by Sinclair.

The cassette recorder should be mono, since stereo tape deck recording heads can cause problems, even used on one channel only. The cheaper recorders work somewhat better (due to the less sophisticated audio circuits being better for handling the crude form of the computer's signals) than more expensive ones, but try to get one with a tape counter, as finding programs without one can be irritatingly time consuming. You should always use the same recorder, as problems can be encountered when playing back tapes recorded on a different machine. Battery-operated recorders actually avoid some potential problems, but must always have good batteries, to keep tape speed constant. The cheapest solution to this in the long term (especially since if you're not sure about the state of the batteries you have to put in new ones) is to buy nickel-cadmium batteries and a charging unit. All recorders have automatic level controls for recording, but some cause problems with their continual variation around the correct level ('hunting'). Get a model that has been shown to be compatible with the Sinclair computers.

Having a TV for exclusive use with your computer system is a good idea, to avoid having to unplug and move around elements of your system (it also avoids arguments with non-computing members of the family!).

Some problems can interfere with the operation of your computer (leaving to one side things like spilling coffee on it or otherwise abusing it!). The first is overheating. After the computer has been on for some time, it may heat up to such an extent that it 'whites out' and wipes out the program you have just finished, except for that last line. This is very irritating, to say the least. Some ZX81s seem to suffer from this more than others. If it is a persistent problem, it can be helped by placing a fairly hefty chunk of metal on top of the case to radiate heat away more effectively. It should be approximately 3 × 2 inches and 0.5 inch deep, have a flat surface to sit on the ZX81 case, and should be placed on the case, above the keyboard, on the left-hand side of the case.

The corollary to this problem is that you should SAVE a long program being developed or keyed in at intervals, and/or take listings from the printer, to avoid a total loss if you do get a white out. The same problem can also be caused by two other factors, and this procedure will protect against the worst results from these problems as well. The first is that household power supplies are sometimes interrupted, or occasionally have brief large voltage fluctuations. Computers are sensitive to such things, and a crash may be caused. Other than buying a stabiliser which will continue to supply power during such an interruption (of very short duration, but computers work fast!) we cannot protect against a.c. supply fluctuations, but similar results can sometimes be caused by appliances connected to the same local power circuit switching on and off, and this should be investigated if the problem is frequent.

The other main source of problems is the connector to the RAM pack and printer via the edge connectors at the back of the ZX81. Movement can be caused in this connector by flexing the system whilst keying in programs. This can be minimised by always pushing the connectors home firmly before switching on, but a better solution is to attach the components to a board, fixing them down to a suitably rigid base with 'Blu-Tack' or the double sided adhesive pads that are now available. Fix the printer down as well – the process of tearing off printout can move printer and connector if you are not careful. Note that the method of fixing cannot be permanent, which is why Blu-Tack or a similar plastic fixative is recommended.

The edge connectors themselves are gold plated, but they connect to the printed circuit board edges which may become oxidised, causing circuit problems (not necessarily white-outs or crashes – the keyboard may cease to work, or the printer miss lines, for example). Proprietary (non-abrasive) contact cleaners should be used to ensure clean contacts.

Other than the problems above, the only maintenance that should be needed is the brushing away of the dust that accumulates in the printer from the burnt-off particles of paper. After removing the paper holder, use a soft small brush (e.g. a small paint brush) to clear away the dust. Pay particular attention to the slot in which the electrode runs, but if, as sometimes happens, the electrode is visible, do not disturb it. (The electrode is a small piece of wire which is normally not visible, but if BREAK has been used it can be left in the middle of the printer slot.)

A2: Function of Components

This is a programming text, not a manual on computer architecture or computer science. However, we thought it might be useful to provide you with a brief rundown of the functions of each of the components of your microcomputer system.

Device	*Function*
ZX81 computer board (inside case)	Data processing and control of information handling. Input from keyboard or cassette. Output to TV screen and printer.
Keyboard	Input of information. Programs, data and commands are keyed in. On-line control.
TV set	Used as V.D.U. (visual display unit) monitor. Provides on-line output of information – visual display of programs, results (data, graphs, pictures) and control commands.
Cassette recorder	Off-line storage of information. Program data are stored (written) as coded electromagnetic

	impulses on cassette tapes. They can be played back (loaded) at any time for use again. The computer reads the data from the tape.
ZX printer	Output device, to provide a permanent printed record of the screen display, program listings or information in the computer memory. Prints on electrosensitive paper.
16k RAM pack	Add-on memory enabling large programs to be stored and run. K stands for kilobyte. One *byte* is eight *bits*, which are the *bi*nary digi*ts* (Ø and 1, represented by on-off switches in the computer) computers work with. A kilobyte is roughly 1ØØØ bytes, hence the name. (It is actually $2^{1Ø}$, 1Ø24).
Power supply	Supplies the d.c. current (9 volts at 1.2 amps) to run the computer, RAM pack and printer, from the household power supply.
Cables	To interconnect the devices which make up the system. The printer uses the same socket as the memory pack and has an extension socket to allow this.

The printed circuit board inside the ZX81 holds and connects the IC (integrated circuit) microchips which provide the computing facilities. These are:

1 Z8ØA CPU (**C**entral **P**rocessing **U**nit) microprocessor chip which is the heart of the system. It is used in many other microcomputers, and performs the arithmetic manipulations.

2 ROM (**R**ead **O**nly **M**emory) chip holds the 8k BASIC interpreter which translates BASIC instructions into the machine code instructions that the Z8ØA operates with. The data in this chip is fixed, hence the name, and also stable – it remains when the power is switched off.

3 RAM (**R**andom **A**ccess **M**emory) chip provides a 1k* memory store. When the memory pack is fitted it blocks off this memory and substitutes its own 16k of memory. This memory is *volatile* – the data is stored as electrical impulses and is lost when the power is switched off. This memory stores the BASIC programs, the values of variables (including some *system variables* that the computer uses to organise its own affairs), a memory picture of the TV screen display, and the *stacks* which hold the numbers whilst they are being manipulated. This is covered in more detail in Section U.

4 The Logic chip co-ordinates the operation of the other chips.

Also mounted on the board are: the stabiliser for the 5 volt supply the computer takes from the power supply, the TV signal modulator and the sockets for the connecting cables to the TV and cassette recorder.

*2k on the TS 1ØØØ.

SECTION B: GETTING TO KNOW THE ZX81

B1: Connecting Up

1 Lay out the ZX81 system devices on your work area as on page 2. It is far better to have an area where the system can be set up permanently. Failing this, a board can be used to mount the components.

2 Place the a.c. power supply plugs of the power supply, TV and tape recorder next to the sockets. A plug board with multiple sockets mounted on it is better than an extension socket fitting.

3 Connect the printer socket into the 23 pin edge connector at the back of the ZX81. Get the slot in the ZX81 board and the block in the printer socket aligned and push in gently but firmly.

4 Connect the 16k RAM pack socket into the extension connector at the back of the printer socket in the same way. This is better done with the ZX81 flat on the table to avoid too much stress on the connectors, which might occur if you are holding up the ZX81.

5 With both connectors inserted, push the RAM pack firmly in to ensure the connectors are fully seated home.

6 Connect the power supply cable into the socket marked DC on the left-hand side of the ZX81.

7 Connect one end of the twin jack-plug leads, placing one jack-plug into each of the MIC and EAR sockets on the cassette recorder.

Place the other jack-plugs into the ZX81 sockets. It is very useful to have the EAR and MIC sockets marked on the *top* of the ZX81 case, where the marks can be seen. Use sticky labels of some type to mark which is which, and also the exact centre of the plug socket. This will save much probing of sockets (there are no guides to ensure you get the socket) and peering at the markings on the side of the ZX81, which are scarcely visible when the ZX81 is flat on a surface.

The yellow banded plugs should go to both MIC sockets. You can also mark the other jack-plug with E or EAR as a helpful aid. Push the jack-plugs gently in, making sure the tips are in the sockets (which has to be done by feel) until a resistance is felt, then push until they click into place. Waggle them slightly to ensure they are well-seated.

8 Connect the aerial lead into the TV aerial socket at the rear of the TV and into the TV socket on the ZX81. A slight twisting motion may be needed if the fit is tight.

US Users will find that the TV connects to the antenna lead with standard terminals, and an antenna ON/OFF switch is fitted between the antenna lead and the antenna lead that plugs into the

Timex/Sinclair 1000 version of the ZX81. This switch must of course be ON.

9 Straighten the interconnecting cables on your work area at this point. Make sure that the cassette leads are not in contact with any a.c. power leads.

SWITCHING ON

1 Ensure that the TV receiver is off and that no cassette recorder keys are depressed.
2 Plug the power supply, TV, and cassette recorder plugs into the a.c. power supply.
3 Switch on the a.c. power sockets (if they have switches).
4 There are no ON/OFF switches on the ZX81 or on most cassette recorders – they are now powered up.
5 Switch on the TV.
6 Turn the volume control on the TV to zero.
7 Turn the brightness control to MAXIMUM.
8 Turn the contrast control to MINIMUM.
9 Tune in the TV. With a rotary tuning control, turn to channel 36. Otherwise select a channel, using the pushbutton or other channel select switch, and tune this channel in. When the TV is at the right setting, a small black square with a white K inset appears. This is the K-cursor, and appears on the bottom left-hand side of the screen.

U.S. Users should note that the Timex/Sinclair 1000 version of the ZX81 has a channel select switch for Channel 1 or Channel 2 fitted underneath the case. Choose whichever channel is not transmitting in your area, and select this channel on the TV and the computer.

10 Adjust the tuning, brightness and contrast until the cursor is distinct, and the white K clear.
11 Check that the cassette recorder keys function. Insert a blank cassette, and try all the controls.
12 Insert a roll of silver printing paper into the printer and press the button on the right-hand side of the printer to feed some paper through. Check the paper does not rub on either side of the printer as it comes through.
13 Press the [COPY] key and then the [NEWLINE (ENTER)] key. The printer will start to copy what is on the screen. About 3 inches of paper will be fed through. There will be nothing printed on it as there is nothing on the screen. A message 0/0 will appear at the bottom of the screen.

N.B. The bottom two lines of the screen are never printed and are used for keying in program lines and commands. These program lines, when correct, are transferred into an area of memory reserved for the programs by pressing the NEWLINE (ENTER) key. The program lines will then appear on the printer when the COPY command is given.

14 Press characters at random on the keyboard. They will appear at the bottom of the screen. Press [SHIFT] and [EDIT] keys together to clear the screen.

15 If the [K] cursor will not appear on the screen switch off the power supply and adjust the 16k RAM pack and printer connections. Switch on the power supply again and retune the TV.

N.B. Never adjust or pull out the RAM pack when the power supply is ON, you may damage it.

16 Other components failing to work will probably be caused by plugs not switched on, or fuses blown. Alternatively, it could be that some connections are not being properly made. You should remove and re-insert jack-plugs and connectors.

17 On leaving your computer:
   a Leave it connected up
   b Switch OFF a.c. power supply plugs and TV
   c Disconnect plugs from sockets.

B2: The Keyboard

The ZX81 keyboard has 40 touch sensitive keys arranged in 4 rows of 10 keys.

At first sight it looks like a typewriter keyboard, but a closer look reveals that some keys have five functions or characters written on them. In fact:

***Six* different characters can be obtained from some keys!**

The keyboard contains:

(1) The digits 0 to 9
(2) The letters of the alphabet printed in upper case
(3) The complete BASIC language
   – instructions
   – commands
   – arithmetic, conditional and logical operators
   – arithmetic functions
(4) Grammatical signs and symbols
(5) Special control keys
(6) Graphics symbols

These are all called *characters*.

Notice that words like PRINT, RUN, SLOW, LET, INKEY$ are

written on the keys and are printed on the screen when we press that key in the correct mode.

The facility of complete words in the BASIC language being printed at the press of a single key is called

SINGLE KEYSTROKE BASIC

On most other computers you have to key in each letter of, for example, the instruction PRINT. This is inefficient. The ZX81 is very powerful in this respect.

The keyboard contains most of the characters in the ZX81 character set and a few special keys. Some 202 different characters are available. Some print on the screen, others are non-printing, e.g. RUBOUT (DELETE).

Each of the different types of character is described in Section B4.

The ZX81 keyboard layout is reproduced in the diagram on the next page.

B3: Cursors

[K] [L] [G] [F] [S] [>]

Cursors indicate what operational *mode* the computer is in and what symbol or name should be typed in next. They appear in inverse video (a white letter in a black square).

[K] **Keyword mode.**
ZX81 expects a command
a line number
or a keyword
Keywords are the symbols printed on the keyboard *above* the keys (see keyboard). SHIFTed keys also function in this mode.

[L] **Letter mode.**
Occurs at most other times.
ZX81 expects a letter
a number
an operator
or a special command
SHIFTed keys function in this mode.

[F] **Function mode.**
Obtained by pressing FUNCTION key (SHIFT, NEWLINE/ENTER).
The functions obtainable are printed under each key in white.

Figure 2

ZX81 KEYBOARD

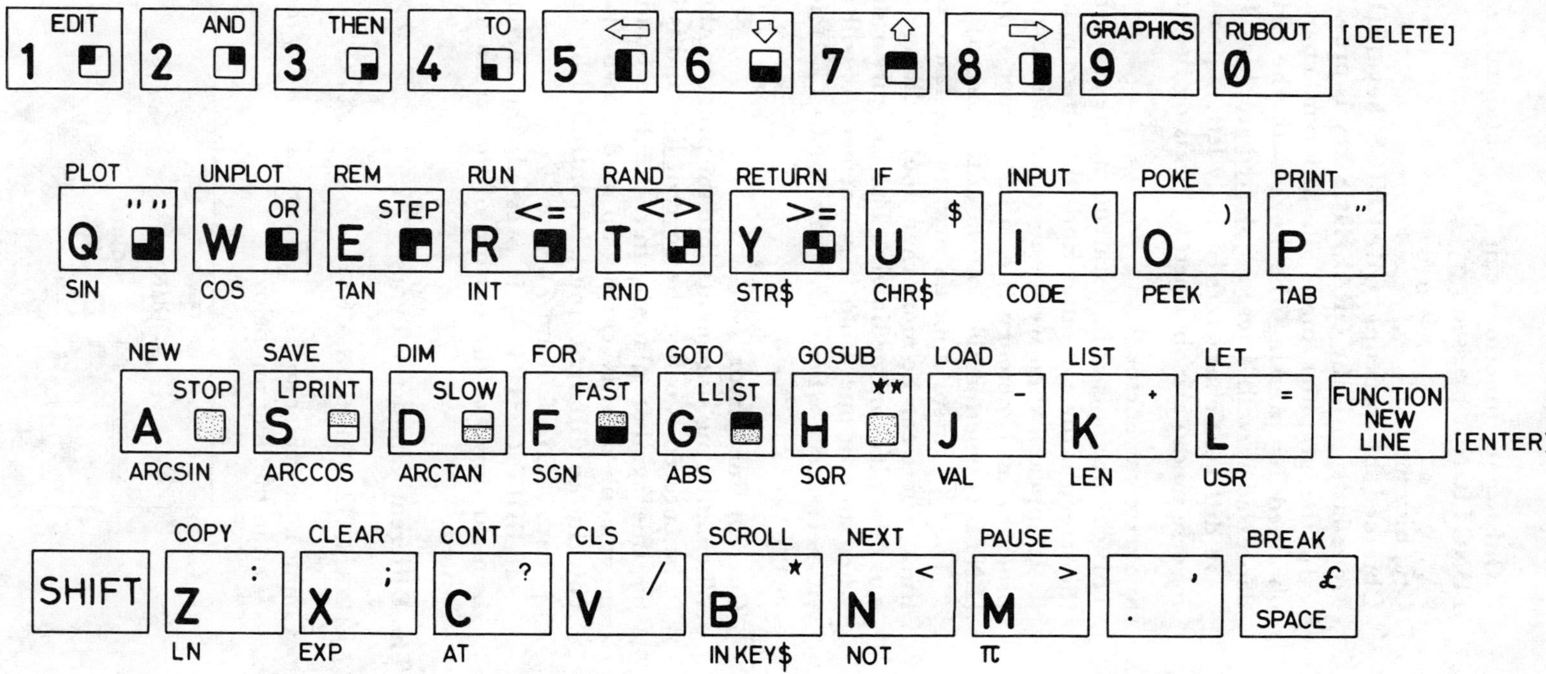

Only one function can be obtained each time **FUNCTION** is pressed.

[G] **Graphics mode.**
Obtained by pressing **GRAPHICS** key (**SHIFT**, 9). Mode lasts until the **GRAPHICS** key is pressed again.

In the graphics mode 36 different characters are obtained by pressing the keys with the **SHIFT** key depressed as well. These are shifted graphics characters.

38 different characters (mainly letters printed in the inverse mode) are obtained by pressing the keys.

[S] **Syntax error cursor.**
This cursor appears in a statement line at the bottom of the screen if the computer finds that there is an error in it. It appears when we try to enter an incorrect line of program into memory (i.e. after we press **NEWLINE** (**ENTER**) when at the bottom of the screen).

The [S] cursor appears next to the last error in the line. (There can be more than one). Editing on the line can take place immediately. The [S] cursor disappears when an edit operation is performed. It will re-appear (if necessary) when **NEWLINE** (**ENTER**) is pressed again.

[>] **Current line cursor.**
When entering statements into the program the last line to be entered is called the current line and is indicated by this symbol placed after the line number. The movement of this cursor up and down the screen, pointing to different lines, is controlled by the ↓ and ↑ keys (**SHIFT** 6 and 7).

If **EDIT** (**SHIFT** 1) is pressed, the current line is brought down to the bottom of the screen and can be edited.

B4: The Different Character Types

THE 6 CHARACTER TYPES ON A KEY

If we examine a particular key, say [R] , we can classify the 6 character types, as seen in the diagram below.

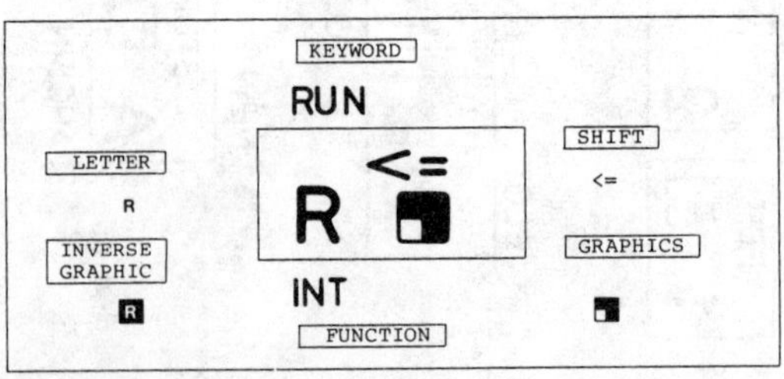

KEYWORD

On top of the R key is the word RUN. This is a KEYWORD character.

All characters printed on the keyboard in this position are KEYWORDS. KEYWORDS will be printed on the screen if the desired key is pressed when the ZX81 is in KEYWORD MODE (i.e. the [K] cursor is on the screen).

Exercise

If the [K] cursor is at the bottom left-hand side of the screen then enter a keyword. Press the [PRINT] (P) key. Notice that PRINT appears on the screen but the [K] cursor has changed to an [L] cursor and the computer is in the letter mode. This means that it is expecting a letter to be keyed in next, e.g. A.

If we try to key in another keyword, e.g. [PLOT] , the keyword PLOT does not appear. Instead the letter Q is printed. So the rule is:

No two keywords may be entered in succession.

To clear the screen and return to [K] mode press [SHIFT] [EDIT] keys together. Try it. Print different keywords on the screen. Which one does not print?

LETTER

The LETTER characters (or QWERTY characters as they are sometimes called) are the bold type letters on each key. They are identical to those on a typewriter keyboard. It is worth trying to memorise these. Do it by lines, and in groups of five.

Letter characters may be keyed in when the computer is in the letter mode and the [L] cursor appears in the entered program line, or at the bottom left-hand side of the screen. Certain letters may be entered in the [K] mode as *default* when there is no keyword on that key, e.g. the digits Ø-9 and the full stop [•] [BREAK] is also an exception. A space is printed in the [K] mode.

Exercise

Key in PRINT to obtain the L̇ mode. Then key in the letters, starting from 1 .

What happens with NEWLINE (ENTER) and SPACE ?

SHIFT

There are 39 SHIFT characters on the keyboard. These may be obtained in the K or L modes, i.e. when K or L is on the screen.

To obtain these characters or symbols e.g. <= in our diagram, press the SHIFT key and the desired CHARACTER key at the same time.

Exercise

Start keying in the SHIFT characters starting with EDIT on the top line of the keyboard.

Notice what happens with:

EDIT
THE ARROW KEYS (↑ ↓ ← →)
GRAPHICS
RUBOUT (DELETE)
FUNCTION

GRAPHICS

There are two types of graphics characters, the characters like ▜ as in our diagram below, and the letter and shift characters printed in INVERSE (i.e. white letter on black background) on the screen (R).

Exercise

To print the graphics characters on the screen key in:

Keys to Press	What happens on the Screen
—	K
PRINT	PRINT L
SHIFT "	PRINT " L
SHIFT GRAPHICS	PRINT " G
SHIFT R	PRINT " ▖ G
R	PRINT " ▖ R G
SHIFT GRAPHICS	PRINT " ▖ R L
SHIFT "	PRINT " ▖ R " L
NEWLINE (ENTER)	▖ R at top of screen
	0/0 at bottom of screen
NEWLINE (ENTER)	K (clears screen)

Notice the mode cursor changes.

Note that to come out of the G mode, you need to press SHIFT GRAPHICS again, to get the L cursor back. To clear the screen press NEWLINE (ENTER) .

Repeat the exercise and obtain all the graphics characters. Where no graphics character is printed on the key then the inverse of the shift character is obtained by default. Test this out.

INVERSE GRAPHICS

These characters are the inverse video letter characters, and are obtained in the GRAPHICS mode, i.e. G cursor on the screen, when the desired key is pressed.

Exercise

Key in the characters as before, but this time only press the letters and not the shift characters when in the [G] mode.

What happens when you press [SPACE] ?

FUNCTION

There are 24 Function characters that are obtained only in the Function mode, when the [F] cursor is on the screen. The [F] cursor is obtained by pressing the [SHIFT] and [FUNCTION] keys together. Only one Function character may be entered. The mode changes to [L] after entry. To input another Function character we need to get back to the [F] mode again.

Exercise

Get into the FUNCTION mode and key in all the function characters.

Key in – [PRINT]
[SHIFT] [FUNCTION]
[π]
[NEWLINE (ENTER)]

What happens? Press NEWLINE (ENTER) again to clear the screen.

HOW TO OBTAIN THE DIFFERENT CHARACTER TYPES

Character Type	Number of Chars.	Mode	To Obtain the Mode:	To Obtain the Character:
KEYWORD	26	[K]	Automatic	[CHARACTER]
SHIFT	39	[K] [L]	Automatic	[SHIFT] [CHARACTER]
LETTER	39	[L] [K] (sometimes)	Automatic	[CHARACTER]
GRAPHICS	36	[G]	[SHIFT] [GRAPHICS]	[SHIFT] [CHARACTER]
INVERSE GRAPHICS	38	[G]	[SHIFT] [GRAPHICS]	[CHARACTER]
FUNCTION	24	[F]	[SHIFT] [FUNCTION]	[CHARACTER]

Exercise

Using the above table, obtain all the modes and key in example character types.

ALPHABETIC CHARACTER/KEY TABLE

The following table locates the letter or number key which provides each character (keyword, function, or symbol) on the keyboard. Use this table when entering programs until you are familiar with the placing of all the commands. An * indicates a non-printing character.

BASIC Word	Keyword (K), Function or Shift and Key to Press	BASIC Word	Keyword (K), Function or Shift and Key to Press
ABS	Function G	LPRINT	Shift S
ACS	Function S	NEW	(K) A
AND	Shift 2	NEXT	Shift N
ASN	Function A	NOT	Function N
AT	Function C	OR	Shift W
ATN	Function D	PAUSE	Shift M
CHR$	Function U	PEEK	Function O
CLEAR	(K) X	PI (π)	Function M
CLS	(K) V	PLOT	Function Q
CODE	Function I	POKE	Function O
CONT	(K) C	PRINT	Function P
COPY	(K) Z	RAND	Function T
COS	Function W	REM	Function E
DELETE	Shift Ø *	RETURN	Function Y
DIM	(K) D	RND	Function T
EDIT	Shift 1 *	RUBOUT	Shift Ø *
EXP	Function X	RUN	Shift R
FAST	Shift F	SAVE	Shift S
FOR	(K) F	SCROLL	Shift B
FUNCTION	Shift NEWLINE(ENTER)	SGN	Function F
GOSUB	(K) H	SIN	Function Q
GOTO	(K) G	SLOW	Shift D
GRAPHICS	Shift 9 *	SQR	Function H
IF	(K) U	STEP	Shift E
INKEY$	Function B	STOP	Shift A
INPUT	(K) I	STR$	Function Y
INT	Function F	TAB	Function P
LEN	Function K	TAN	Function E
LET	(K) L	THEN	Shift 2
LIST	(K) K	TO	Shift 4
LLIST	Shift G	UNPLOT	Function W
LN	Function Z	USR	Function L
LOAD	(K) J	VAL	Function J

SYMBOLS

Symbol	Cursor and Key	Symbol Meaning
	K or L, Full stop or decimal point (Separate key)	
,	K or L, shifted Full stop.	Comma
;	K or L, shifted X.	Semicolon
:	K or L, shifted Z.	Colon
?	K or L, shifted C.	Question mark
‘‘	K or L, shifted P.	String quote
‘‘ ’’	K or L, shifted Q.	Quote image
(	K or L, shifted I.	Open bracket
)	K or L, shifted O.	Close bracket
£	K or L, shifted SPACE.	Pound
$	K or L, shifted U.	Dollar
+	K or L, shifted K.	Plus
−	K or L, shifted J.	Minus
*	K or L, shifted B.	Times
/	K or L, shifted V.	Divide
**	K or L, shifted H.	To power
=	K or L, shifted L.	Equals
>	K or L, shifted M.	Greater than
<	K or L, shifted N.	Less than
<=	K or L, shifted R.	Less than or equal to
>=	K or L, shifted Y.	Greater than or equal to
<>	K or L, shifted T.	Not equal to
←	K or L, shifted 5.	Cursor left
↓	K or L, shifted 6.	Cursor down
↑	K or L, shifted 7.	Cursor up
→	K or L, shifted 8.	Cursor right

SECTION C: BASIC BASIC

C1: The BASIC Language

This book is all about BASIC, which is the world's most commonly used computer language. Just as English is a natural language used to communicate with people, BASIC is a formal language used to communicate with COMPUTERS. Like natural languages BASIC has grammatical rules which, although they are fairly simple, must be strictly followed to ensure that the computer understands exactly what it is being instructed to do.

BASIC stands for **B**eginners **A**ll-Purpose **S**ymbolic **I**nstruction **C**ode. It was invented in 1964 in the USA and is a combination of simple English and algebra. BASIC is the language we will use throughout this book to write PROGRAMS. Programs instruct the computer what to do, and the sequence in which particular operations are to be performed.

BASIC is a *high-level programming language*. The instructions we write in BASIC are *interpreted* by a built-in program into the *low-level* programming language (the MACHINE CODE) that directly controls the switching of the electrical impulses inside the MICROCHIPS which store and manipulate the data. High-level languages like BASIC are far easier to write programs in than the low-level languages, and the simple language and structure of BASIC was designed to be easy to learn. The Sinclair version of BASIC also has single-keystroke entry of BASIC words, which makes mistakes in spelling impossible.

C2: A Simple Program

A sequence of BASIC statements is called a PROGRAM. Here is an example of a program:

```
10  INPUT A
20  INPUT B
30  LET S = A + B
40  PRINT S
```

The simple program above adds two numbers keyed in on the keyboard and prints the results on the screen. A program is keyed (or typed or input or entered) into the computer by you, the programmer, line by line, from the keyboard.

Before we key a program in we design it to make the computer do exactly what we want. We first write a program down line by line on a piece of paper. This is called CODING.

After coding the program we key it into the computer and RUN it. To RUN it we give the computer a COMMAND to RUN the program to see if it works. It probably won't work the first time, unless it's as simple as our example. A program which doesn't work as intended is said to contain ERRORS or BUGS.

If we have asked it to do something it can't do, or forgotten to include an instruction the computer will tell us what is wrong and give us an ERROR MESSAGE. If the program runs without error messages but doesn't do what we wanted it to then it is the programmers' fault. In either case we need to correct or EDIT or DEBUG the program. We do this whilst the program is in the computer, using the editing facilities of the computer.

Editing or revising a program is called PROGRAM DEVELOPMENT. When the editing is finished and the program works we take a LISTING of the program on the PRINTER. We can also SAVE a copy of our program on cassette tape and STORE it so that we can LOAD it back into the computer.

The complete exercise of designing, coding, developing and documenting a program is called PROGRAMMING.

C3: A Statement

This is a BASIC statement:
1Ø INPUT A

A statement is also called a LINE. A statement can:
(1) instruct the computer to do something
(2) state something

A statement is composed of: a **line number**, e.g. 1Ø
an **instruction**, e.g. INPUT
some **variables**, e.g. A

Statements are either: **Executable** – those which specify a program action, as with our INPUT A, or **Non-Executable** – those which provide information for the user of the program.

All variables (e.g. A in our example) must be **initialised** to a start value before being used in a program. In this case the statement:

1Ø INPUT A

tells the computer to request the user to input a value for the variable A from the keyboard.

C4: Statement Numbers

Each BASIC statement or line must begin with a statement number, as with 2Ø in this example.
2Ø INPUT B

The number 2Ø is called a statement number or line number. The statement number is chosen by you, the programmer. It may be any number from 1 to 9999 inclusive. The computer uses the numbers to keep the statements in order. Each statement has a unique statement number. If you use the same statement number twice, the second line will replace the first.

Statements may be keyed in via the keyboard in any order. The computer sorts them into the correct sequence. Statements are usually numbered in tens so that additional statements are easily inserted later. For example:

```
10  INPUT A
20  INPUT B
25  INPUT C      (Inserted line)
30  LET S = A + B
```

The computer runs the program in order of statement numbers.

C5: Instructions

A statement gives an *instruction* to the computer. In this example it is LET.

30 LET S = A + B

Instructions are called *statement types* because they identify a type of statement. In our example the statement is a LET statement. It tells the computer to let the *variable* S have a value equal to the sum of the values of *variable* A and *variable* B.

C6: Numeric Variables

A numeric variable is the name given to a storage location which holds a number in the computer's memory.

A numeric variable can have a name which is:

A letter from A-Z
or **A letter followed by a number**
or **A group of letters and numbers**

Variable names *must* start with a letter.

Examples of numeric variables: A
NUMBER 1
B2
X136
TOTAL

Numeric variables are used to represent numbers inside the computer. We can give (or *assign*) different values to a variable. The numbers we give to variables are used in calculations.

Variables are symbols or names given to parameters or quantities. They represent the VALUE of the parameter, i.e. the number stored in the named memory location. We can use variable names which remind us of the parameter concerned, but they should not be too long or you will find them tiresome to key in (which is why single letters are usually used).

For example, we could use:

S – Speed
PRICE – Price of fish
SUM 1 – Sum of the first set of numbers
R3 – Resistor Three

In our program the statement

```
10 INPUT A
```

sets up a variable in the computer's memory with the symbolic name A. We could have called it NUM1, or even FIRSTNUMBER.

The statement tells the computer to ask us to input a value for A when we run the program. If we key in the number 3 the memory cell allocated to A will contain the number 3. This value is then used in all calculations involving A until we change its value.

In the statement:

```
30 LET S = A + B
```

S, A and B are the variables in the algebraic equation S = A + B. S is our 'unknown' and will take the sum of the values of A and B. The computer will work out the value of A + B and put the result in the memory cell it has allocated to the variable S. The computer will not let us input LET A + B = S (it will give us a syntax error), because the variable to be given a value must come first. A + B is not a valid variable name.

Variables are so-called because their values can vary or change, according to the values we input, or in the course of a program, when we instruct the computer to do something which causes the value to change. For CONSTANTS, which are quantities which do not change their value, we set up a variable in the same way, by giving it a name and a value with a LET statement and let it keep the same value – a variable that doesn't vary!

Variable names may be of any length, but they must start with a letter, and must only contain the *alphanumeric* characters (the letters A to Z and the numbers 0 to 9). They can have spaces included, but this is unwise, as it is easy to key in PRICE1, for example, when you initialised a variable as PRICE 1. The computer will consider them to be two different variables. The inverse video (white on black) characters also cannot be used in variable names.

C7: Strings and String Variables

STRING

A STRING is a group of characters enclosed by quotation marks.

The following are examples of strings:

"PETER"
"12345"
"JANUARY 1ST, 1982"
"! $,."**
"REF:A2"

As well as numbers, computers can also handle text or groups of characters. To define a group of characters as a string, we have to place quotation marks at the beginning and end. This tells the computer, for example, that the string "TOTAL" means the characters T,O,T,A,L, and not the numeric variable TOTAL, which is a number.

Strings can contain any character which prints on the screen, plus spaces, but a string cannot contain quotation marks, because the computer thinks it has got to the end of the string when it gets to the second quotation mark.

Now that you know what a string is, we can tell you that strings can be handled by string variables, just as numbers can be manipulated with numeric variables.

STRING VARIABLE

A string variable is used to store strings. It consists of a single letter (A to Z) followed by the $ sign. For example:

A$, Z$, M$

We allocate (or assign) strings to string variables with LET statements, as with numeric variables. For example:

```
10  LET A$ = "STRING 1"
20  PRINT A$
```

The memory store allocated to A$ will contain the string 'STRING 1' (line 10).

When we RUN the program the computer will print the contents of memory store A$ on the screen (line 20), i.e. STRING 1. Note the string is printed without the quotation marks. The string is just the characters inside the quotes.

C8: Operators and Operands

OPERATORS

Operators perform arithmetic, logical or conditional operations on variables or numbers.

In our program the line:

30 LET S = A + B

uses the two arithmetic operators

= and +

OPERANDS

Operands are the variables or numbers which are manipulated (i.e. operated on) by the operators.

In the line:

30 LET S = A + B

the variables S, A and B are operands.

C9: Format of Statements

BASIC is a 'free format' language. The computer will ignore extra blank spaces in a statement.

The following statements are equivalent:

```
10  INPUT A
10  INPUT         A
10           INPUT        A
```

The computer will automatically leave spaces after each line number and a space after keywords. It will list programs with all the other spaces you include between instructions and variables. It will ignore them when you run the program.

C10: Keying in a Statement

Statement to be keyed in:

10 INPUT A Press **[NEWLINE (ENTER)]**

If your computer system is set up and ready for use (see Section B1) the [K] cursor will be in the bottom left-hand corner of the screen. You can now key in the first statement.

Character or instruction to key in	Cursor	Keys to Press	What appears on the Screen
1	[K]	1	1 [K]
Ø	[K]	Ø	1Ø [K]
INPUT	[K]	I	1Ø INPUT [L]*
A	[L]*	A	1Ø INPUT A [L]*
	[L]*	NEWLINE (ENTER)	[K] Entered line is transferred to top of screen

* [C] on Spectrum in CAPS mode

PRESS NEWLINE (ENTER) AFTER EACH STATEMENT

The [NEWLINE (ENTER)] key must be pressed after *each* statement has been entered.

10 INPUT A [NEWLINE (ENTER)]
20 INPUT B [NEWLINE (ENTER)]
30 LET S = A + B [NEWLINE (ENTER)]
40 PRINT S [NEWLINE (ENTER)]

Pressing the [NEWLINE (ENTER)] key informs the computer that the statement is complete. The computer checks the line for mistakes then transfers the statement to the top of the screen and returns the [K] cursor to the left-hand side of the screen, ready for us to enter the next program line.

Notice that the line at the top of the screen now contains the CURRENT LINE CURSOR:

[>]

This indicates the last program line entered and accepted by the computer. It appears immediately after the line number:

10 [>] INPUT A

C11: Correcting Errors

RUBOUT (DELETE)

The RUBOUT (DELETE) key acts as a backspace, deleting the character symbol or keyword immediately preceding (to the left of) it.

As we type in a line we may press the wrong key. For example, we might get:

10 INPUT S [L]

where we pressed S instead of A. To correct this we press RUBOUT (DELETE) and we get:

10 INPUT [L]

We may now continue and type in A.

[← →]

The horizontal arrow keys move the cursor one character or keyword to the left or right along a line as indicated.

For obvious reasons, these keys are also referred to as cursor control keys.

To correct an earlier mistake on a line

(a) Use the arrow keys to move the cursor to a position immediately to the right of the character to be changed.
(b) Press RUBOUT (DELETE) to delete the incorrect character, and key in the correct character.
(c) Use the arrow key to return the cursor to the end of the line, if you have more to key in. Otherwise, you may press NEWLINE (ENTER) immediately. It does not matter if the [L] cursor is in the middle of the line.

To delete a complete line

This can be done by using the → key to get the cursor to the end of the line, if you are not there already, and then using RUBOUT (DELETE) repeatedly until the line is completely deleted and just the [K] cursor remains. This is tedious on a ZX81, without the Spectrum's repeat key, especially on a long line. A better way is:

(1) Press EDIT
(2) Press NEWLINE (ENTER)

If you are keying in the first line of a program and there are no existing lines at the top of the screen, pressing EDIT will clear the line.

If there are program lines at the top of the screen, pressing EDIT clears the current line and brings down the program line marked with the [>] cursor. Pressing NEWLINE (ENTER) sends this line up again and clears the current line.

Exercises

1 Start keying in the first line of the program. Don't press NEWLINE (ENTER).
   Play around with the cursor control keys and RUBOUT (DELETE).
2 Delete the complete line.
3 Key in the first line and press NEWLINE (ENTER).
   Key in the second line.
4 Delete the second line using EDIT and NEWLINE (ENTER).
5 Key in the third line to read: Key in the second line. Key in the third line to read:
   30 LET X = A + B. Press NEWLINE (ENTER)
   Use EDIT to bring this line down again. Use the cursor control keys to put the cursor to the right of X and delete it. Insert S. Leave the cursor where it is, and press NEWLINE (ENTER) to send the line to the top of the screen.
6 Key in the complete program.

C12: Commands

COMMANDS are direct instructions to the computer. They are executed immediately. They do not need line numbers, as they are not part of a program.

Commands give us direct control over the computer. Examples are:

RUN
LIST
BREAK
SAVE

To execute a command, we key it in. If it is a command that is printed, it will appear on the bottom line of the screen. This area of the screen must be empty. Then press [NEWLINE (ENTER)]. Some commands are executed instantly, without pressing NEWLINE (ENTER) (e.g. BREAK), and are not printed on the screen.

Most commands are also used as instructions in programs. Some of the commands that can be used as direct commands are not actually very useful in this role. Equally, some that could be used in programs never are. However, each command has a key role to play in the

BASIC language and we will deal with the individual commands as we encounter them in the text.

You have already met the NEWLINE (ENTER), RUBOUT (DELETE), ← and → commands, and the mode commands (GRAPHICS and FUNCTION). Together with EDIT, RUBOUT (DELETE) and BREAK, plus the ↑ and ↓ arrow keys, these are the commands that don't print, and act instantly. All the others need NEWLINE (ENTER) to be activated.

C13: Editing the Program

EDIT

The EDIT command copies the program line indicated by the [>] cursor at the top of the screen, to the bottom of the screen, replacing any current line. The line brought down can then be edited or changed.

EDIT may also be used for entering lines that are similar where only the line number changes:

(1) Key in the line.
(2) Press NEWLINE (ENTER) – line goes to top of screen.
(3) Press EDIT – line copied to bottom of screen.
(4) Use RUBOUT (DELETE) to delete the line number.
(5) Key in new line number.
(6) Press NEWLINE (ENTER) – new line goes to top of screen.

The same procedure can also be useful with lines which only vary slightly, i.e. perhaps only the line number and a variable are different. If you can save keystrokes by bringing down a line and revising it, then do so. The technique is as above, but after (5) you must use the cursor control keys to shift the L-cursor along the line and use RUBOUT (DELETE) to erase the variable (or keyword) that needs to be changed. Insert the new character, and press NEWLINE (ENTER).

[↑ ↓]

These commands move the [>] cursor in the entered program at the top of the screen from one line to another. This enables us to then copy down any line in the program for editing using [EDIT].

Deleting a line in the entered program

To delete a given program line which has been entered and is at the top of the screen just type the line number and press NEWLINE (ENTER).

For example:

10 [NEWLINE (ENTER)]

will delete line 10 in the program. You will see it disappear from the screen.

C14: Listing a Program on the Screen

LIST

The program has been entered into memory. To produce a listing on the screen of all lines accepted by the computer key in:

[LIST] [NEWLINE (ENTER)]

LIST is a command that prints on the screen. It appears on the bottom of the screen, and is executed when NEWLINE (ENTER) is pressed.

LIST N

Will list a program starting from program line N.
For example, if we key in:

LIST 30 [NEWLINE (ENTER)]

our program will be listed from line 30.

We key in LIST, then the line number we want the listing to start at. If we have a program that is longer than will fit on the screen, we use the LIST (line number) command to display successive screenfuls of the program. If the bottom line on the first screen is 210, for example, we would use LIST 220 to get the next set of program lines. Listing a program on the Spectrum which is larger than a screenful produces a SCROLL? prompt. Answering this with anything other than 'N' or BREAK scrolls the listing up so that the next screenful of statements can be seen.

C15: Running the Program

Our simple program has been keyed into the computer line by line and entered into memory.

Let's see if it works. We give the computer the command RUN.

RUN

RUN NEWLINE (ENTER)

The RUN command starts execution of a program at the lowest numbered statement.

Run is a command and is keyed in. It appears at the bottom of the screen. It will not be executed until NEWLINE (ENTER) is pressed. When we do this the program starts operating. The screen will go blank and the L-cursor will appear at the bottom. (This will be a C-cursor if you are using a Spectrum in CAPS (capital letter) mode, using CAPS LOCK as we advised.) The computer is now running the program and asking us to input a number for the variable A.

Key in the number 3 and press NEWLINE (ENTER). The L-cursor appears again at the bottom of the screen. The computer requests another number, to be assigned to the variable B. Key in the number 5 and press NEWLINE (ENTER).

Our *result* (the number 8) is printed at the top left of the screen. Notice the message that appears on the bottom of the screen. We can also run the program from a line other than the first program line:

RUN N

RUN (Line Number)

This command starts execution of the program from the specified statement (line) number.

RUN 2Ø

will start a program at line 2Ø.

Note that when the RUN N command is used all statements before the specified statement number (N) will be ignored and any variables defined in these statements will be considered by the computer to be undefined because it has not RUN the lines. The program will not work and an **error message** will result. All values of variables are wiped out by the RUN command.

We can RUN the program as many times as we wish:

Key in RUN NEWLINE (ENTER) again

If the program has been run once and the message is at the bottom of the screen, to rerun the program key in RUN. This overwrites the message and pressing NEWLINE (ENTER) starts the computer operating the program. The L-cursor appears to prompt for an input again (C-cursor for Spectrum in CAPS mode).

The screen is now blank. We can get the program listing back very easily:

Press NEWLINE (ENTER)

After running the program, the program listing re-appears at the top of the screen if the NEWLINE (ENTER) key is pressed. The program can now be edited if necessary.

C16: Error Messages

Our computer tells us it has finished running the program by giving us a message. On the ZX81 this will be:

Ø/4Ø

at the bottom of the screen. The Spectrum gives an expanded version of the message:

Ø OK, 4Ø:1

This tells us that no errors were found and the program finished at line 4Ø (the last line). The number after the colon can be ignored in most Spectrum error messages, as it refers to multiple-statement lines. We shall not use these in this text. There is one case where it is 2, as we shall see later.

These special diagnostic messages appear at the bottom of the screen every time a program is run. If the program does not work a message appears with the form:

E/N

E is a number or a letter indicating the type of error that has caused the program to stop, and N the line number where the program halted due to the error. The Spectrum adds a message briefly stating the cause of the error.

We look up the meaning of E in the list of Error Codes in Appendix II. This helps us to correct or debug the program, since we know what sort of problem has occurred and which program line it happened at.

Exercises

1 Run the program on page 19 a number of times keying in different values for A and B.
2 Press NEWLINE (ENTER) to get the listing. Change line 3Ø to read:

```
3Ø   LET S = A + C
```

Now RUN the program.

The error message 2/3Ø (on the ZX81) appears. On the Spectrum we get 2: Variable not found 3Ø;1. So we have a type 2 error and the program stopped at line 3Ø. A type 2 error means we have forgotten to define a variable. We are now using the variable C instead of B, but we have not yet given C a value, and the computer could not complete the operation of line 3Ø due to insufficient information.

Insert a new line:

25 INPUT C

and run the program again. It now works.

Why did the program originally stop at line 3Ø?

Why do we now have to key in 3 numbers to make it work?

3 Add an extra line at the beginning of the program. Key in:

5 PRINT "PROGRAM ADDS 2 NUMBERS"

RUN the program, starting from different lines by using:

RUN
RUN 1Ø
RUN 15

Why do you think RUN 15 does not work?

4 Edit the program to obtain the original version.

C17: How the Program Works

1Ø INPUT A

Line 1Ø tells the computer that a number must be input and given the name A, (i.e. assigned to the variable A). The computer reads the line and prints an [L] at the bottom of the screen,* reminding us to input a number. The computer will wait until we key in a number. The number is then stored in memory cell A. The computer goes to the next line.

2Ø INPUT B

Line 2Ø tells the computer that another number, to be assigned to the variable B, must be input. [L] appears at the bottom of the screen* and the computer waits until we key in a second number, which is stored in memory cell B. The computer goes to the next line.

3Ø LET S = A + B

Line 3Ø tells the computer that a variable S is to be assigned the value of the sum of the variables A and B. The numbers in cells A and B are added

*This will be a C-cursor if using a Spectrum with the CAPS LOCK facility used, as Spectrum users must do throughout this text to get program listings which appear the same as the ones in the text. Use the CAPS SHIFT and CAPS LOCK keys simultaneously on switch-on, and remember that the C-cursor will appear instead of the L-cursor. We will not mention this again.

and placed in cell S. The computer goes to the next line.

Line 4Ø instructs the computer to output the value of S to the screen. The computer looks for the next line. **4Ø PRINT S**

The computer can find no more statements to execute in the program and gives a message Ø/4Ø on the screen telling us that the program finished with zero errors at line 4Ø. The Spectrum gives the same message, in the form Ø OK, 4Ø:1.

The computer now waits for more commands.

C18: Naming the Program

5 REM "NAME"

Programs are named in a REM statement. The program name is enclosed in quotation marks. The program is usually named in the first statement in the program.

We need to give our program a *name* in order to:

(1) Differentiate it from other programs
(2) Store it permanently on cassette tape (SAVE it)
(3) Put it back into the computer from cassette tape in order to run it (LOAD it).

The program name can be any combination of characters and any length on the ZX81. On the Spectrum, program names for use with the SAVE and LOAD instructions *must* start with a letter, and can *only* have 1Ø characters in the name.

It is sensible to keep the program name short and relevant to the type of program, although some programmers name programs after themselves:

"PETER 1"
"PETER 2" etc.

Programs which undertake various kinds of statistical analysis could be named:

"STATS1"
"STATS2" etc.

Programs which perform calculations for experiments in the laboratory could be named:

"OPTICS 3"
"FRICTION"
"TITRATION" etc.

If spaces are used in program names, it is easy to misread them, or forget that there should be a space. If the program name is not one word, we can use an asterisk:

"PETER*1"
"FOCAL*LENGTH" etc. ("FOCAL*LEN" for the Spectrum)

Program names and cassette tape codes should be recorded in a DIRECTORY which enables us to access a PROGRAM LIBRARY of programs stored on tape.

We need to name our program: List the program and add a line which names the program. For example:

5 REM "SUMPROG"

or 5 REM "PROG*1"

could be used. We will call our program "ADDER", so key in

5 REM "ADDER"

SECTION D: SAVING, LOADING AND LISTING

D1: Saving the Program on Cassette Tape

We need to save programs on to cassette tape (the *off-line storage medium* the Sinclair computers use) because when the power supply is switched off (or disrupted – variations in the mains supply can affect the computer) the RAM memory and the registers in the CPU are cleared and we lose the program. The memory is said to be *volatile*. This means we have to key it in again – not too bad for a 5 line program, but a 5Ø liner will take you an hour!

If we had made a copy of the program on to magnetic cassette tape using the SAVE command we could have reloaded it into the computer quickly, using the LOAD command. Tape storage is not the quickest or most reliable method used for off-line storage, but it works, and has the advantage of low cost. The ZX81 reads and writes tape fairly slowly in computer terms, and a large program will take some minutes to LOAD or SAVE. The Spectrum loads programs several times faster. Software (programs) stored on tape is available for use when needed, making it PERMANENT.

Software also has to be PORTABLE. Programs we write can be used by other people with the same computer, or software available on cassette can be bought.

SAVE

SAVE "NAME"

The SAVE command outputs the program and variables to the cassette recorder. If the cassette recorder is in record mode then a copy of the program will be made on the tape.

Spectrum users please note that the program name for SAVEing must be 1Ø letters or less. The name can be in either upper or lower case (or a mixture) but exactly the same name must be used to LOAD. It is safer to choose to use capitals only.

SAVING THE PROGRAM

1 **Check that the cassette recorder is plugged in (or has good batteries).**
2 **Ensure it is connected to the computer, with the MIC-MIC sockets being connected. See the important Spectrum note below.**

3 Set the **TONE** control on the cassette recorder to **HIGH**.
4 Set the volume control on the cassette recorder to 3/4 of MAXIMUM.
5 Insert a new C12 computer cassette tape into the recorder. Short cassettes are more convenient than long ones for our purposes.
6 Run the tape through on FAST FORWARD and then REWIND to ensure equal tension.
7 Set the tape counter to zero and run the tape forward five revolutions (about 20 or 30 seconds).
8 List the program on the screen and printer.
9 Check the program is named (e.g. "ADDER") in a REM statement.

ZX81 Sequence

10 Type SAVE "ADDER" *don't* press NEWLINE (ENTER) yet.
11 Press RECORD and PLAY buttons on the recorder.
12 Press [NEWLINE (ENTER)].
13 Watch the screen.
   a) For five seconds it will be grey inversed by diagonal white lines and if the sound on the TV is turned up it will be a monotone.
   This is the SILENT LEAD IN
   b) For ten seconds a horizontal striped pattern appears on the screen. This is the program going in. A warbling sound is first heard, then half second pulses.
   c) The screen goes white and the message 0/0 appears, telling us the computer has transmitted the program to the cassette recorder.
   The ZX81 does not know whether the recording is successful.
   We can only tell by later loading the program back in.
   Stop the recorder
14 Note the counter reading at the end of the program.
15 Run the tape forward five more revolutions of the counter, ready for the next program.

Spectrum Sequence

IMPORTANT NOTE: YOU MUST ALWAYS TAKE THE JACK-PLUG OUT OF THE EAR SOCKET OF THE SPECTRUM BEFORE ATTEMPTING TO SAVE A PROGRAM.

10 Key in SAVE "ADDER".

11 Press ENTER. The Spectrum will print a message on the screen which tells you to 'Start tape', i.e. press RECORD (or record and play, depending on your cassette recorder), and 'then press any key'. Do so.

12 Blue and red lines (black and grey on a black and white TV) will scroll up the *border* area of your TV screen. This happens twice as the name of the program is recorded. When the program is copied, narrow yellow and blue/black lines roll up the *border* area. When the recording is complete an 'Ø OK' report appears on the screen. Stop the recorder. Note the tape counter reading. Your program should now be correctly recorded.

13 On the Spectrum, you can check this without wiping out the program in memory first. Connect the EAR lead from the Spectrum to the cassette player EAR socket. Rewind the cassette to before the start of your recorded program. Get into the E mode, and key in VERIFY, then enter the program name between quotes. Press ENTER and start the cassette on PLAY. The Spectrum displays on the screen any other programs before the specified one that it finds on the tape, printing their names on the screen.

14 When the program has finished playing back, an 'Ø OK' message means the program was correctly SAVEd, and 'R Tape loading error' means the recording is faulty and you should SAVE the program again.

15 Run the cassette on five more revolutions of the tape counter, ready for the next program.

The sequence above assumes a tape counter on your cassette recorder. Without a counter, the process of finding a program is more difficult. To place a voice message on the tape, so that the tape is searched for the voice giving the program name, will prevent the tape being searched automatically by the computer, but it is one possible method. If used, you should record your voice (most cassette machines have a built-in microphone) stating the program name several times, then the program name should be spelt out, the name stated again, and some cue statement ('saving starts now') to let you know that after that point only computer-generated noises exist. This will make finding the program much easier, as the voice cues occupy a larger length of tape than a single statement of program name.

The other alternatives are to place only one program on each tape (a bit uneconomical!) or to leave very large gaps between tapes (3Ø seconds at least), so that you can search using fast forward/reverse and are unlikely to miss the gap. This has the advantage that you can set the computer to search through the tape program by program if you do miss it. Larger programs should be placed if possible on a side of a cassette by themselves. Short length cassettes are available (5 minutes a side) to make this a viable option.

Exercises

1 Try a *dummy run* first. Do not press the recorder keys. Turn up the sound on the TV until you can hear a hum. Awful, isn't it! Key in SAVE "ADDER" and press NEWLINE (ENTER). (Press a key in response to the message if using a Spectrum). Watch the screen and listen to the different sounds. When the screen clears and the Ø/Ø message appears (Ø OK, Ø:1 on a Spectrum), key in LIST NEWLINE (ENTER) to get the listing back.
2 Now SAVE the program on to the tape.

D2: Deleting the Program from Memory

A sure way is to switch off the power – this is *not* recommended. This should only be done if the computer needs to be *re-set* because it will not respond to commands keyed in. It is much better to use the command NEW.

NEW

The NEW command deletes any current program and variables from the computer and clears the screen.

We use the NEW command before we LOAD a program into the computer from cassette tape, to erase old programs and data from memory. It is also used to do the same thing, if we have a program in the computer and wish to clear it out to enter another.

There is another command that only affects the *variables* store, and not both this store and the program store, as NEW does.

CLEAR

The CLEAR command erases all the variables in the current memory.

CLEAR can be used as an instruction in a program, as can NEW, but since NEW would merely wipe the program its use would be self-defeating. Try it, if you like the idea of a program that self-destructs!

CLEAR is similarly useless in the middle of a program – we would merely have to re-define all variables.

With our program, if we RUN it, at the end of the run it will have in the variables store the values of A, B and S. If we then SAVE it, these values are SAVEd also. In our case this is irrelevant, since the INPUTs will change them when it is used but often it is useful. We can store data as variables in a program, and not have to re-input values (as long as certain procedures are followed, as we will see later). This enables us to have, for example, a telephone directory stored in variables. We might then use CLEAR to wipe one list, and re-input new data or use CLEAR before SAVEing the program to send to a friend for his use. CLEAR acts slightly differently on the Spectrum (see page 458), but for our purposes at this point the difference is insignificant. The major function is the same. It is very easy to key CLEAR by accident on the Spectrum, so be careful!

Exercises

1 RUN "ADDER". Enter [CLS] [NEWLINE (ENTER)] to clear the screen. Enter GOTO 40, then press NEWLINE (ENTER). The computer will print the value of S. Now enter [CLEAR] [NEWLINE (ENTER)] and then GOTO 40 (NEWLINE/ENTER) again. We then get an error message 2/40 (2 variable not found, 40:1 on the Spectrum) indicating an undefined variable, because the computer has wiped the value of S. We will deal with GOTO in due course. Just follow the instructions for now.

2 LIST the program "ADDER" on the screen. Press [NEW] and [NEWLINE (ENTER)]. The listing will disappear and the [K] cursor appears. On the Spectrum, when NEW is followed by ENTER, the screen will go black for a moment then become white, with the words '© 1982 Sinclair Research Ltd' at the bottom of the screen.

3 Press [LIST] and then [NEWLINE (ENTER)]. What happens? Why?

4 Key in the first line of the program and press NEWLINE (ENTER). Switch off the power supply (by pulling out the jack-plug). Switch it on again (by re-inserting the jack-plug). What happens?

5 Re-enter "ADDER".

D-3

D3: Loading the Program from Cassette Tape

LOAD "NAME"

The command LOAD "NAME" waits for the cassette to play the portion of tape with the program called "NAME" and copies the program, with its variables into the computer's memory.

This means that we can start the tape, give the command LOAD "NAME", and the computer loads nothing into its memory until the signal it recognises as NAME appears on tape. We can thus search a tape for a program. The Spectrum will print on the screen the names of any programs it finds on tape, before it encounters the specified program.

LOAD " "

The LOAD " " (nothing between the quotes) command LOADs the first program it finds on the tape.

LOADING PROCEDURE ON THE ZX81

1. **Place the tape with the desired program in the cassette player.**
2. **Position the tape via the counter to just before the location of the required program.**
3. **Clear the computer's memory using the NEW command if there's a program in memory.**
4. **Set the TONE control on the tape recorder to nearly Maximum (High), and the VOLUME control to ¾ Maximum.**
5. **Key in LOAD "ADDER" or the appropriate name. Don't press NEWLINE (ENTER).**
6. **Depress the PLAY key on the cassette recorder.**
7. **Press NEWLINE (ENTER).**
8. **A thin diagonal pattern will appear on the screen with a single tone sound.**

   The pattern changes to broad horizontal stripes with thinner diagonal stripes and half second sound pulses are heard as the program is loaded in.

   The screen clears and a 0/0 message indicates the loading is a success.
9. **STOP the recorder.**

10 LIST and RUN the program.
11 Remove the tape when finished.

LOADING PROCEDURE ON THE SPECTRUM

1 Place the tape with the desired program in the cassette player.
2 Position the tape via the counter to just before the location of the required program.
3 Clear the computer's memory using the NEW command if there's a program in memory.
4 Set the TONE control on the tape recorder to nearly MAX (High), and the VOLUME control to ¾ MAX.
5 Key in LOAD "ADDER", but *don't* press ENTER yet.
6 Press the PLAY button on your cassette recorder.
7 Press ENTER.
8 When the Spectrum has found a program it will scroll blue and red bands of colour up the border area. The name of the program will be printed to the screen and then the blue and red lines repeated again. If the correct program has been located, then it will LOAD with a finer set of blue and yellow lines scrolling up the border area. If not, the border area will flash blue and red alternately as it carries on to the next program on the tape.
9 When the program is correctly loaded, the phrase:

Ø OK, Ø:1

will appear at the bottom of the screen to indicate that all is well.
10 Stop the recorder.
11 LIST and RUN the program.
12 Remove the tape when finished.

CAUSES OF FAILURE TO LOAD

1 Volume too low.
2 Volume too high.
3 Tone too low.
These indicate that the program has been played at the wrong settings. New volume and tone adjustments will have to be made. Some indications of these problems are visible on the screen display of the ZX81, although systems vary in their response. Appendix IV has a procedure for adjusting tone and volume settings for the ZX81, as well as some general hints on tape use. Experiment and get to know the patterns produced during LOAD on your ZX81.

4 Loading started in the middle of the program. If a mistake has been made with the start position, rewind the tape completely and let the computer search for the program name.
5 The program is not on the tape. Check your directory, and the writing on the cassette.
6 The program name is incorrect. Try again, making sure you have spelt it correctly in the LOAD instruction. If you fail again, run through the tape using the LOAD " " command. This will load the first program each time. Stop the cassette player after each load and LIST the program to check. (This is not necessary on the Spectrum.) If it's not the program you want, repeat for the next program on the tape. The Spectrum will print the name of all programs on tape if you use a LOAD "ZZZ" instruction, i.e. a name that does not exist as a program name.
7 Pick up from stray electromagnetic fields.
This will show as violent interference on the screen, distorting the patterns together with excessive hum on the sound. It could originate from the TV itself, feedback between the recorder and the computer or an external field. Switch off any radio that is in the vicinity. Take out the jack-plug from the MIC socket of the cassette player, as this will break the feedback loop that can exist between the computer and the cassette player.

The Spectrum has fewer LOADing problems than the ZX81. It will accept a much greater variation in both the volume and tone of the signal. However, it is worth noting that if there are great differences between the recorder the tape was recorded on and the one it is played back on (variations in tape-head azimuth is often the main source of the problem), then LOADing can be almost impossible, even on the Spectrum.

As we noted at the beginning of the book, the Spectrum, unlike the ZX81, offers a choice of upper and lower case letters. Ensure that if you have used lower case ones in the program's name, then you use them again in the LOAD "xxx" command. The same applies if you use upper case letters to name a program. Thus, a program named "MATHS" will *not* LOAD with the statement: LOAD "maths".

Some further information concerning the use of cassette tapes, and advice for the ZX81 if problems are encountered is given in Appendix IV.

Exercises

1 Load the program "ADDER". LIST and RUN it.
2 Delete it from memory, using NEW.
Try loading it with different volume and tone setting. Estimate the volume and tone ranges for which it will not load. If you have a ZX81, you can do this by watching how the screen

patterns change when you change the settings while the program is loading. Read Appendix IV.

D4: Listing the Program on the Printer

LLIST

LLIST lists the program currently in the computer memory on the printer, starting from the first program line.

LLIST N

LLIST N lists the program on the printer starting from line N.

We can stop the listing by pressing [BREAK] (BREAK needs CAPS SHIFT on the Spectrum). This stops the listing with an error message D/line number on the ZX81 and D BREAK – CONT repeats Ø:1 on the Spectrum.

It is important that you keep a listing or printed record of all the programs you write or use. The listings are a great help in debugging programs (both under development and if there are problems discovered later). We can key the program back in from this listing, if necessary.

Printouts also form part of the documentation for a program and should be pasted into a notebook. Printed records of program results can also be kept using the COPY command.

Exercises

1 LLIST the program "ADDER" on the printer.

2 Try stopping the listing with the BREAK key. The listing *cannot* be continued by pressing CONT (try it). On the Spectrum, despite what it says, this doesn't work. The screen just goes blank. Don't worry. Press BREAK again.

3 List the program on the screen. Use the COPY command to list the program on the printer.

What is the difference between the two listings obtained with LLIST and COPY?

D5: Program Libraries and Directories

LIBRARY

A collection of programs stored on cassette tape. For example:
COMPUTERLAB PROGRAM LIBRARY
or Your own program library.

Notice that programs can also be stored on magnetic discs and in ROM memories.

DIRECTORY

The list of program names in the library together with important information about them. Another name for a directory is CATALOG.

You should keep, in your notebook, or a special book, a directory of all programs you have entered and saved on tape. This will seem a bit pointless when you only have a dozen or so, but you will appreciate the need to be systematic when you accumulate a large number.

PROGRAMS YOU WRITE

Each program you write should be

1. **Named.**
2. **Saved on a cassette tape.**
3. **Listed on the printer.**
4. **Documented.**
5. **Catalogued into the Directory of your own program library.**

DOCUMENTATION

The complete collection of information about the program or file, written on paper. The information should include:

1. **What the program does.**
2. **How it does it.**
3. **A listing.**
4. **A flowchart.**
5. **How to use it.**
6. **When it was written and by whom.**

We will introduce flowcharts in Section G.

DIRECTORY LAYOUT

A typical layout for the Directory Section of your notebook would be:

Program Name:	**MOONLANDER**
Cassette Name:	**GAMES 3**
Location:	**1ØØ-12Ø**
Program Length:	**3Ø lines**
Date Created:	**18.5.82**
Author:	**PAUL NIXON**
Function:	**Lands a spaceship on the moon**

WRITING ON THE CASSETTE

There is a label on each side of the cassette. Write on each side:

1) Cassette name or code.

2) Date.

3) Program names as they are copied into it. Make sure these are correctly spelt!

Your directory should provide you with the more detailed information, such as precisely where the program is to be found.

E1: Adding Comments

REM

The REM statement is used for adding comments to a program. All REM statements are ignored by the computer when the program is RUN.

These comment statements are for the users' benefit only. They contain information in the text of the program which explains what the program is doing. For example:

REM **THIS PROGRAM ADDS TWO NUMBERS KEYED IN AND PRINTS THE RESULTS**

Notice the use of the asterisks to separate the text from the instruction.

100 REM **END OF PROGRAM**

The complete program including all REM statements appears on the screen or printer when using the LIST and LLIST commands.

Our saved program so far looks like this:

```
5  REM "ADDER"
10 INPUT A
20 INPUT B
30 LET S = A + B
40 PRINT S
```

Let us add some additional REM statements:

```
6  REM **THIS PROGRAM ADDS TWO NUMBERS
   KEYED IN AND PRINTS THE RESULT**
60 REM **END OF PROGRAM**
```

Key these extra statements in. LIST the program and RUN the program.

Do not worry about the line numbers not being in intervals of 10. We will renumber the program when we have added all the extra lines.

E2: Using the Print Statement

PRINT

In our simple program we will use the PRINT statement:

a) To print messages and instructions to the user on the screen:

7 PRINT "INPUT TWO NUMBERS"

The message INPUT TWO NUMBERS is a string, and will be printed without the quotes.

b) To print the numbers keyed in and the result:

4Ø PRINT A; " + ";B;" = ";S

A and B are the names of the variables to which the numbers keyed in are assigned, and S is the variable that stores the sum of A and B, i.e. the result. Variables do not need quotes to be printed.

The semicolons (;) tell the computer that we want close printing, with each *print item* (character or variable) directly after the last, with no spaces between. The inverted commas (quotes) enclosing the symbols + and = means we want those symbols printed.

c) To leave spaces between lines printed on the screen:

8 PRINT

The PRINT instruction used on its own prints an empty line on the screen.

Note that we have changed line 4Ø from what it was previously. Our program now looks like this:

```
 5  REM "ADDER"
 6  REM **THIS PROGRAM ADDS TWO NUMBERS
    KEYED IN AND PRINTS THE RESULT**
 7  PRINT "INPUT TWO NUMBERS"
 8  PRINT
1Ø  INPUT A
2Ø  INPUT B
3Ø  LET S = A + B
4Ø  PRINT A;" + ";B;" = ";S
6Ø  REM **END OF PROGRAM**
```

Key in the new lines and RUN it.

E3: Adding a Loop

GOTO N

The statement GOTO N transfers program execution to the specified line number, N. For example:

5Ø GOTO 7

When we insert line 5Ø into our program we can see that, after printing the result on the screen, line 5Ø sends the computer back to line 7 to execute the program again from that line, and as soon as the computer reaches line 5Ø again it is sent back to line 7 once more.

We have constructed a LOOP. The program is going to carry on looping forever unless we can pull out of it.

Our program now is:

```
 5  REM "ADDER"
 6  REM **THIS PROGRAM ADDS TWO NUMBERS
    KEYED IN AND PRINTS THE RESULT**
 7  PRINT "INPUT TWO NUMBERS"
 8  PRINT
1Ø  INPUT A
2Ø  INPUT B
3Ø  LET S = A + B
4Ø  PRINT A;" + ";B;" = ";S
5Ø  GOTO 7
6Ø  REM **END OF PROGRAM**
```

Key in line 5Ø. RUN the program. When you are tired of inputting numbers, read on.

E4: Stopping the Program

We need to know how to get out of the input loop between lines 7 and 5Ø. The program will wait for an input of a number at line 1Ø INPUT A. The [L] cursor will appear on the screen.

To pull out or stop the program at this stage key in [STOP] [NEWLINE (ENTER)]. STOP is a command we input directly, like RUN.

STOP

On the ZX81 the STOP command stops a program with the message: D/line number, and on the Spectrum we get H STOP in INPUT (Line number):1.

The line number refers to the program line the computer was executing when it was stopped.

Our program will give D/1Ø as the message (H STOP in INPUT 1Ø:1 on the Spectrum). We can cancel the STOP command and continue the program with the CONT command.

CONT

The CONT command used after the STOP command will continue the program from the line the program was stopped at.

Key in [CONT] [NEWLINE (ENTER)] to continue the program. Note the Spectrum prints CONT in full as CONTINUE.

Exercise

Run the program "ADDER".
STOP the program when the first [L] cursor appears.
CONTinue the program, and input a value for A.
STOP the program when the second [L] cursor appears. Note that the line number is different in the message that appears on the bottom of the screen.
CONTinue the program.

E5: Testing for a Condition

In a program we can make decisions which will affect what the computer does next. A decision is made on the basis of whether a CONDITION is true or false.

CONDITION

A condition has the form (X) (condition) (Y) where X and Y are numbers, variables or expressions and the condition is a <u>conditional operator</u>. We shall use only the = (equality) operator for the moment. The following are all conditions:

X = Y
A = 23
B = 2*3

Conditions are tested and the next action determined by the result of the test with the IF and THEN statements used together.

IF – THEN

An IF – THEN statement has the form:
IF (condition) THEN (instruction)
For example: IF A = B THEN PRINT "EQUAL"
IF A = Ø THEN LET A = 3
The instruction can be any valid instruction. The statement means:
IF (the condition is TRUE) THEN (perform as instruction).
IF (the condition is FALSE) the computer ignores the instruction after THEN and goes to the next line of the program.

In our simple program we can use the IF – THEN statement to insert in the program a conditional test which will stop the loop, without using the direct commands which we used in the last Unit. To STOP the program in the same way as with a direct command we can insert another line:

15 IF A = Ø THEN STOP

This tells the computer that IF A = Ø (if it is TRUE that A is equal to Ø) THEN it should STOP. IF A is any other value (if it is FALSE that A = Ø) it ignores the THEN STOP instruction and moves to line 2Ø. Enter this line into the program. RUN the program.

Enter different non-zero values for A to see that if A is not zero then the program continues as before. Enter .ØØØØØØØØ1 to see that only if A is *exactly* zero will the STOP instruction be executed. Input 2 for B, and notice that the result is given as 2. This is due to the fact that calculations are only performed to a certain degree of accuracy.

Enter .ØØØØØØ1 for A, and input B as 2. The computer returns 2.ØØØØØØ1 as the value of S – the number is within the limits of accuracy.

Now enter Ø for A. The program will stop, just as when we entered STOP as a direct command. Notice, however, that the message at the bottom of the screen is different. We get the message 9/15 on the ZX81 (a STOP statement, 15:2 on the Spectrum).* The message is different because STOP in a program means 'if the CONT command is received, proceed with the *next* program line', since if it continued with the same line it would just STOP again! As a direct command, however, STOP means 'if the CONT command is received, start with the *same* program line', so that the computer does not miss out a program line.

Now we have some extra control over the program, but it is still not satisfactory. We used IF A = Ø because in this program it is not a value we are interested in seeing added to B (a value used in this way is known as a DUMMY or SENTINEL VALUE – a value just used as a signal to the computer which would not need to be entered in the course of normal inputs). This stops the program and we can continue it, but the program just goes back into the loop. We need a method of proceeding out of the loop to end the program, or continuing with more program lines.

We can do this with a STRING CONDITION. The conditional operators can also be used to express relations between strings – either string variables or simple strings.

We insert the following lines:

```
50  PRINT "RUN PROGRAM AGAIN ?(YES/NO)"
55  INPUT A$
56  IF A$ = "YES" THEN GOTO 7
```

*On the Spectrum, the statement after the THEN in an IF – THEN statement is treated as the second statement in the program line. This is why we get 15:2, meaning line 15, statement 2. This is the only instruction used in the main text of this book (before Unit W2) where the statement number will not be 1 in an error message.

When the program gets to line 50 it will print out the message, and then put the [L] cursor at the bottom of the screen. Because it has been told that a string input is to come, the cursor has quotes either side: "[L]". There is no need to type quotes. Whatever characters are typed in will be stored as A$. The string is entered by pressing NEWLINE (ENTER) after keying in the characters. Line 56 tells the computer to check if the characters in A$ are the same as the characters of the string "YES". If they are it goes to line 7. If they are not the program will continue to line 60. Notice that any string other than "YES" will cause the program to continue to line 60.

Exercises

1 Delete line 15 in our program, which we no longer need.
2 Insert the new lines 50, 55 and 56.
3 RUN the program. Enter "YES" in response to the string input cursor and see that the program loops back to line 7.
4 Next enter "NO" to see that the program goes to line 60 and gives the message 0/60 (0 OK, 60:1 on the Spectrum). Run the program again. This time enter anything other than "YES" or "NO", to see that the program goes by default to line 60 if anything other than "YES" is entered.
5 Experiment with the string input. What happens if you press NEWLINE (ENTER) without inputting anything? What happens if you try to key in quotes around the string?
6 LLIST the program on the printer. The development of our program is complete, and we have run it to see that it works. It remains to renumber the lines, and this is easier to do if we have a listing.

E6: Final Edit and Saving

Our program "ADDER" is complete and works. We need, however, to renumber the lines. The procedure for this is as follows:

1) Using the listing from the printer, renumber the statement lines in tens at the side of the old number. You can also count the number of lines in the program on the screen display, and multiply by ten to get the new highest line number. For our program, this will be 120.
2) a) List the program on the screen.
   b) Use the ↑ and ↓ cursor control keys to bring the current line cursor [>] to line 60 (the bottom line of the program).
   c) Press EDIT and pull line 60 down to the bottom of the screen.
   d) The new HIGHEST line number is 120.
   e) Change 60 to 120.

f) Press NEWLINE (ENTER). Line 6Ø remains, but it is duplicated by the new line 12Ø.
g) Delete the old line 6Ø by entering 6Ø and pressing NEWLINE (ENTER).
h) Change each line number in this way, going from highest to lowest.
i) Lines that contain other line numbers must have these changed to their new numbers. In our program we must remember to change line 56 to:

   9Ø IF A$ = "YES" THEN GOTO 3Ø

   where 3Ø is the new line number corresponding to the old line 7.
j) Rename the program "ADDER2", at the same time as you change the line number of line 5 to 1Ø. This program is different from the original version, and must be given a different name both for our reference, and the SAVE and LOAD operations.
k) Run the program to check that it still works, and that we have all the lines, with any GOTO (line number) statements correctly renumbered.
l) LIST and LLIST the program.
m) SAVE "ADDER2".
n) Write the name of the program on the tape cassette, along with the tape counter readings.
o) Put details of the program in your directory.
p) Stick the listing of the program in the notebook you are using for documentation.

SECTION F: A GAME INTERLUDE

F1: The Program Library

In addition to the many programs and subroutines in the main body of the text, there are additional applications and games programs in the Program Library (Appendix VI). Our main objective is to enable you to write your own programs, and the programs in the text have been used to illustrate the use of techniques. Some are functional (do something significant) and some are just illustrative. You don't have to key *all* the programs in the text into the computer, but you *must* understand them. However, you should key in all the shorter programs since it's important to see how different types of program operate in practice. Analysing the longer programs is vital, even if you don't key them in. The use of flowcharts (to come in Lesson G) is helpful for this. There are also suggestions for programs you should write, to get practice in writing programs to perform tasks, after units dealing with specific techniques.

The programs in the library are examples of applications and games programs, plus a number of subroutines for some of the manipulations commonly required in programs. You can key these in at any time if you want to see how the program works, find the program useful, or want to play the game. Once keyed in you can SAVE them on cassette and LOAD them back in quickly. None of the programs are very long, since it is difficult to analyse long programs, and this is what we want you to do. Keying in a program from a listing doesn't teach you anything about programming, nor does running it. Writing or modifying a program does! We hope you find the programs entertaining or useful, but please treat them as a source of ideas and illustrations about programming, not as a fixed set of optimum solutions. Programs can always be improved!

Be careful when keying in programs, especially if you don't understand how they work. (It might be better to work this out first – because, to labour the point, that way you'll learn something.) The S-cursor will mark some errors in lines for you and stop you entering them, but there are always other problems you can introduce. Check through your listing for errors and missing lines (surprisingly easy to do, even with numbered lines) before you run the program.

You must also be careful to check that any necessary alterations have been made to the program if you are going to run it on a Spectrum, as noted in Unit W2. These are mostly minor but can be crucial.

F2: A Game to Key In

You have now spent a lot of time working through the essentials of your computer system and its BASIC, and you probably have the feeling that thus far you haven't seen anything to persuade you that computers are particularly exciting machines. Far from being impressed by their capabilities, you may well be thinking, 'What's so good about a computer if you need to do all this to get it to do something that I could do in my head when I was six?' Well, the following program may not be earth-shattering, but it does in fact reveal a fairly complex set of computer operations, as well as providing amusement. The program is called "BUG" and it enables you to play a game that consists of dropping bricks from a height to squash the 'spider' (an asterisk) scurrying along below. If you have a militaristic or SF streak in your nature, or are an arachnid lover, feel free to change the name to "BOMBER" or whatever (in line 5). Whether you will enjoy it more by pretending you're napalming Venusians is your affair. It won't alter how the program works!

To play the game, however, you first have to key it in. You won't understand at this point how it works (and won't for a few chapters yet), so you have to rely on keying it in *exactly* as listed. Like all the programs in the text, this one will look somewhat different on the screen or in a printer listing, since for clarity we have not reproduced the printer listings exactly, since printouts tend to contain broken words (when one line on the screen is full and the computer runs on to the next) and other possible confusions. Check each line carefully before you press NEWLINE (ENTER), and pay special attention to the punctuation. Notice that there are 2 spaces before the asterisk (spider) in line 5Ø, and 3 spaces either side of the <=> (brick dropper/intergalactic space hod) in line 6Ø. If you have any difficulty finding the right modes and keys for the characters you need, refer to the list in Section B (ZX81) and Unit W1 (Spectrum). It is very easy to end up typing a keyword instead of inputting it directly when you are keying in a listing (typing T,O instead of inputting TO, for example). If you do this it is not clear why you get the S cursor indicating an error, since the line *looks* the same as the listing, so be warned.

ZX81 Users' Notes

The graphic character in line 16Ø is an *inverse* asterisk, (SHIFT B in Graphics mode) and in line 19Ø the characters are the SHIFTed graphic on the T key, the asterisk again, and the SHIFTed graphic on the Y key. The comments in square brackets are intended to be helpful, *not* to be entered!

Spectrum Users' Notes

Line 6Ø has an inverse video asterisk. To get this, key CAPS SHIFT and the 4 key to get INV. VIDEO. Then input the asterisk. Use CAPS SHIFT and the 3 key to get TRUE VIDEO, i.e. normal black on white, back. If you don't return to normal video, the quotes will be in inverse, and so will everything after it.

Line 190 has the unshifted G mode graphic on the 6 key, and then the CAPS SHIFT graphics on the 8 key and the 6 key as the graphics string.

```
  5 REM "BUG"
 10 LET S=0
 20 LET B=10
 30 FOR N=1 TO 12
 40 LET C=3
 50 PRINT AT 20,C-2;"  *"           [2 Space,*]
 60 PRINT AT 0,B-3;"   <=>   "       [3 Sp,<=>,3 Sp]
 70 IF INKEY$ ="6" THEN GOTO
     150
 80 LET B=B+(3 AND INKEY$ ="8"
    AND B<28)-(3 AND INKEY$ =
     "5" AND B>3)
 90 LET C=C+ INT ( RND *2+1)
100 IF C<30 THEN GOTO 50
110 CLS
120 NEXT N
130 PRINT "YOU SCORED ";S;        [SCORED,Sp & Sp,OUT]
    " OUT OF 12"
140 STOP

150 FOR F=4 TO 20 STEP 4
160 PRINT AT F,B+1;"■"; AT         [Inverse *]
    F,B+1;" "
170 NEXT F
180 IF B+1 <> C THEN GOTO 50      [ <>  is one character]
190 PRINT AT 20,C-1;"▀▄▀"; AT
     21,C-2;"SPLAT"
200 CLS
210 LET S=S+1
220 GOTO 120
```

When you've got it all keyed in, LIST it to check it through again. Check the first screenful, then (on a ZX81) LIST 170 to get the rest of the program (with a line that was on the first screenful to keep your place). LLIST it on the printer.

Key RUN then NEWLINE (ENTER) to play. The keys 5 and 8 move you left and right respectively across the top of the screen. They are chosen for the direction of the arrows printed on them. Key 6 will drop the brick. If you hit the spider it goes splat and you score a point. You have to hold the keys down to ensure that the computer will read the keys and perform the right operations. This is because it reads the keys only once in each pass through the loop (lines 50 to 100), and might miss the input otherwise.

When you've played the game a few times, SAVE it on to tape and catalogue it.

PART TWO

ESSENTIALS OF BASIC PROGRAMMING

SECTION G: PROGRAMMING METHODS I

G1: Programming

Now that you can operate your computer and have written a short program we must look in greater detail at the activity we call PROGRAMMING and study how:

COMPUTERS SOLVE PROBLEMS

To enable them to do this we engage in the two main activities of programming:

1. **PRODUCE THE METHOD FOR SOLVING THE PROBLEM**
2. **PRODUCE A WORKING PROGRAM**

The method for solving our problem is called an ALGORITHM. An algorithm is like a cookbook recipe, and is written down in steps in a brief English style we call PSEUDOCODE, and the method by which we arrive at the recipe is called STRUCTURED PROGRAMMING.

We break the problem up into smaller sub-problems or sub-tasks in a step by step, modular fashion, starting from the simple initial statement of the problem and working down to lower levels of greater complexity (i.e. in a TOP DOWN manner). As we refine our problem our steps become more like the operations the computer can perform. Our final description of the lower level of the algorithm will be in terms of the control and other *structures* of the language.

To help us produce the algorithm we use STRUCTURE DIAGRAMS. The simplest of these is a TREE diagram. The pseudocode description of the algorithm is easily written down from the descriptions of tasks in the tree diagram. We cannot key the pseudocode description of the algorithm into the ZX81 or Spectrum because it will not understand it, and there is no means of doing it anyway. We have to translate each section of the pseudocode into its equivalent in the BASIC language, which the computer understands, to produce a PROGRAM.

For the computer to be able to run the program successfully and produce the results we require, there has to be a LOGICAL FLOW to the program. This is often difficult to see from the structure diagram, and so we use another diagrammatic technique to illustrate the flow of control through the program, i.e. determine the order in which the program modules or sub-programs are processed and the order of coding the specific instuctions within a module.

This technique uses FLOWCHARTS. These are important for documentation purposes and are in common use. We will describe them shortly.

Producing a working program involves running and DEBUGGING (correcting errors in) our first effort. We then have to TEST the program with sample data and finally DOCUMENT it. In this first section on methodology we shall consider problem solving and coding the algorithm in BASIC in more detail.

You will see that the first half of the activity we call programming is LANGUAGE INDEPENDENT. Having produced our problem solving method – the algorithm – we can code it into any computer language we wish. We need to know the language thoroughly and how the fundamental programming structures we have used in the algorithm – decisions, loops, subroutines, subprograms, functions – can be implemented in that version of the language which runs on the computer we are going to use.

In this book we are using the ZX81 or Spectrum computers. The versions of BASIC are slightly different. All that this means is that whilst the algorithms to be coded for both machines will be the same, the final programs may be slightly different.

Our algorithms and their representation in pseudocode and flowchart form are thus PORTABLE from one machine and language to another.

Good coding habits are also important. There are good and bad ways of turning the solution to a problem into a working program. Style, presentation, ease of understanding, modularity, efficiency are all important. Throughout our book the emphasis will be on correct problem solving techniques and good programming practice, while you gain a thorough knowledge of BASIC.

Here is our first rule of programming:

PROGRAM CORRECTLY FROM THE START

Remember – bad habits die hard!

The material in this Section may initially appear dense and difficult to follow. Work through the text carefully, and refer back to this Section as often as you feel necessary, when each of the topics covered in the following Sections (dealing with the essential groundwork of the BASIC language) has been introduced. The exercises given in the text should be used to put into practice both the specific techniques involved and the general approach to programming presented here.

G2: Problem Analysis

Producing the algorithm, or method of solving the problem, is often the most difficult part of programming because it involves the most work. From the start careful planning and organisation are absolutely essential. The task is simplified when a structured design method is used, coupled with a diagrammatic representation of the algorithm using a structure diagram or flowchart. The actual coding of the program in BASIC using the available language instructions is then a straightforward matter.

To produce the Algorithm we must:

1.1 STATE THE PROBLEM
1.2 RESEARCH THE PROBLEM
1.3 DESIGN THE ALGORITHM
1.4 DESCRIBE THE ALGORITHM IN PSEUDOCODE AND FLOWCHART FORM

Let us now consider each of these steps.

1.1 State the problem fully

1.1.1 STATE THE PROBLEM
1.1.2 UNDERSTAND *WHAT* IS TO BE DONE

To solve any problem we must know what the problem is and what is to be done. We later work out *how* to do it. A complete statement of the problem should include:

(i) What information or data is to be input.
(ii) What answers or results are to be output.
(iii) What operations are to be performed on the data.

At this stage a precise description of (iii) may not be available.

<u>EXAMPLES</u>

Problem: Write a program which will print out the sum and average of five numbers input at the keyboard.
Problem: Using the computer produce a telephone directory to contain up to fifty entries, which may be updated and assessed in an enquiry mode.

In the first problem the input data, output data and operations are easy to see. The second is much more complex and needs more researching and information.

What we are trying to do in 1.1.1 and 1.1.2 is to initially specify the problem as exactly as possible. When we analyse the problem further we may have to go back and ask for more information i.e. a more detailed specification.

1.2 Research the problem

1.2.1 RESEARCH AND ANALYSE THE PROBLEM TO SEE HOW THE COMPUTER CAN HANDLE IT
1.2.2 IDENTIFY ALL FORMULAE AND RELATIONS INVOLVED
1.2.3 IDENTIFY ALL DATA INVOLVED

Here we start to determine how the computer may solve the problem. We need to find out and write down:

(i) What formulae and expressions are to be used.
(ii) What kinds of data are involved – numeric, string, etc.
(iii) What functions are involved.
(iv) What is input and output data.
(v) What is the form of this data.
(vi) How much data there is.
(vii) What processing is to be done and how many times.

It is useful at this stage to start to create a *data table* (a table of variables, constants and counters), to record how we are going to store the data. Other questions we will ask when we are a little more experienced are:
Have I solved a problem like this before?
Can I use my solution or modify it?
Has anyone else solved it?
Where can I find their algorithm or program?

ALL THE FACTS OBTAINED FROM RESEARCHING THE PROBLEM SHOULD BE JOTTED DOWN

We can now begin to design the algorithm in a structured manner.

1.3 Design the algorithm using structured methods

1.3.1 BREAK THE PROBLEM DOWN INTO SUB-PROBLEMS
1.3.2 USE A STRUCTURE OR TREE DIAGRAM TO HELP
1.3.3 CLASSIFY MODULES OR PART MODULES AS
– INPUT
– PROCESSING
– OUTPUT
1.3.4 USE FUNDAMENTAL CONTROL STRUCTURES
1.3.5 SET UP A DATA TABLE
1.3.6 REFINE THE ALGORITHM UNTIL CODING INTO BASIC IS AN OBVIOUS EXERCISE

Structured programming means designing the algorithm in a top down, modular fashion, with step by step refinement of the solution starting from the single statement of the problem which we place at the highest level. We break the problem into sub-problems at successive lower levels. Each sub-problem or module is one that can be solved individually. Structure diagrams or tree diagrams are useful as a representation of this refinement process.

G3: Structure diagrams

These enable us to break down the problem into distinct tasks and sub-tasks which eventually become simple enough to be coded directly in BASIC instructions. One form of these diagrams is TREE DIAGRAMS. The tree diagram has its trunk at the top of the page. We call this BOX 1 and give it the title: TASK TO BE DONE. We could have called it 'problem to be solved'.

For example, make a cup of tea or find the average of five numbers.

We next break down the task into things to do. These are sub-tasks and each has its own box. For example:

BOX 1.1: First thing to do
BOX 1.2: Second thing to do

Each sub-task is broken down into further sub-tasks: 1.1.1, 1.1.2 etc, each with their own boxes, the things to do placed in them becoming progressively more exact and simple.

Breaking down a task into a tree diagram:

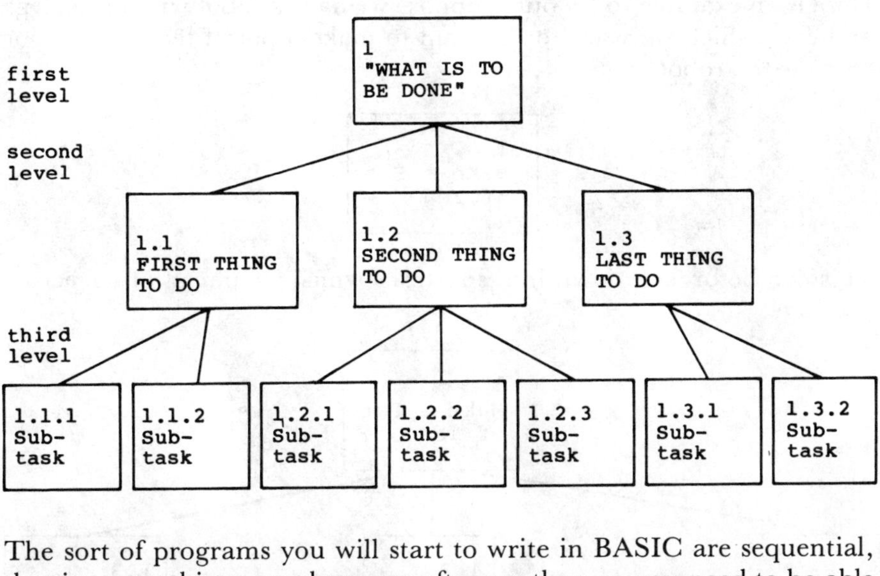

The sort of programs you will start to write in BASIC are sequential, that is to say things are done one after another, so you need to be able to indicate that the program should first do one thing, then a second, then a third . . . and so on. You do this by drawing the boxes which contain the tasks to be done in a straight line across the page next to each other for example:

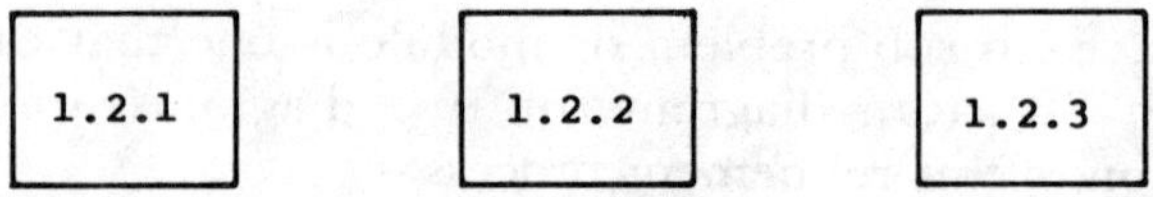

The numbers contained within each box identify where the box is placed on the tree. Take 1.2.3 for example:

The first digit shows it comes from the first level 1 'What is to be done'.

The second digit '2' shows it has come from the second level box 1.2 'Second thing to be done'.

The third digit '3' shows this box 1.2.3 is the third sub-task in the sequence derived from 1.2 which in turn is derived from 1 . Into the boxes go brief statements of the actions needing to be performed. These are general statements at the top of the tree, e.g. 'Get Sum of numbers', but become more specific at each lower level, so that 'Get Sum' is broken down in the operations needed to produce the result 'Get Sum', e.g. 'Input first number', 'Input second number', 'Add the two numbers'. Finally the instructions become detailed enough to form our English language 'pseudocode' which can be written out, ready to be translated into BASIC instructions.

AN EXAMPLE OF TREE DIAGRAM DESIGN

Here is an example to try out. Suppose we have a robot with arms, legs and eyes which we want to program to make a pot of tea. Our major task for the robot is:

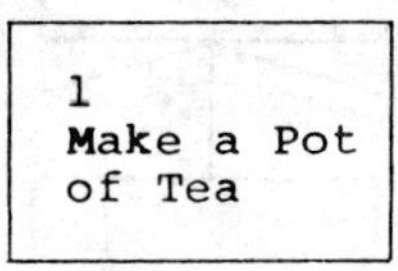

This can be broken down into sub-tasks which we put in order across the page:

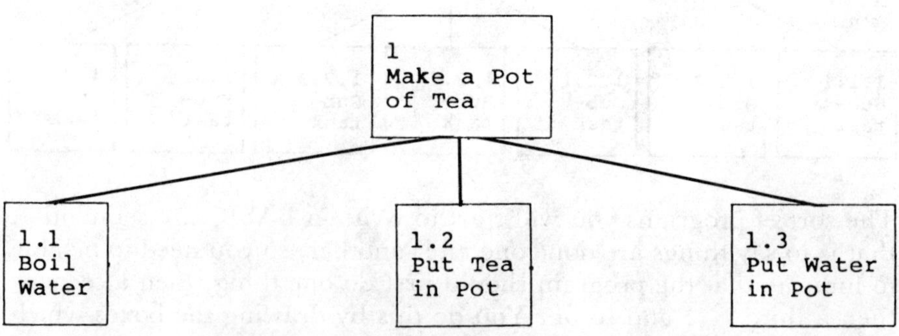

Each of these sub-tasks is still far too complicated for our robot to do. We must break the problem down further. Breaking down 1.1 into sub-tasks we get:

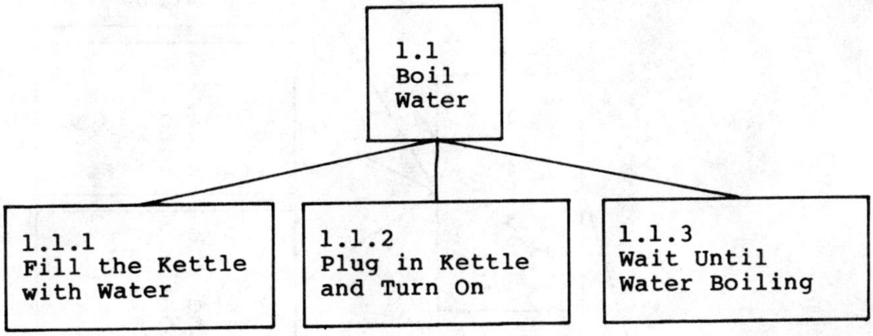

The robot also needs to be told how to fill the kettle so we break this down as:

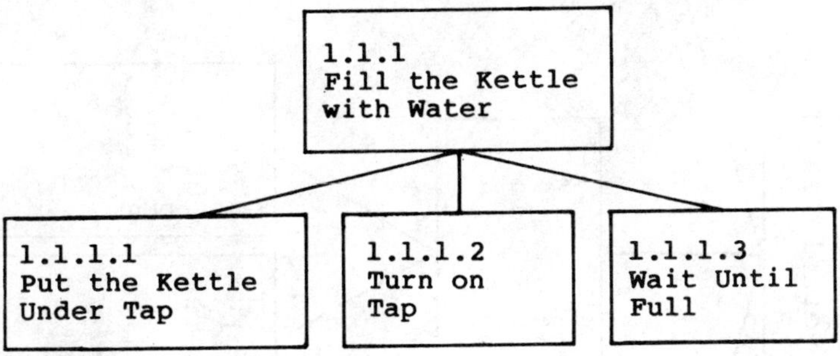

On the next page is a complete tree diagram. Certain things are still wrong with this algorithm for our robot, but it does show you how a problem can be broken down.

G4: Classifying Program Modules

Most computer programs involve:

INPUT
PROCESSING
and OUTPUT

activities.

As we are designing our programs and forming modules, it becomes evident from our pseudocode description of the algorithm which of the above functions the modules should have. Depending on the problem and the result of our algorithm design, modules may be separately

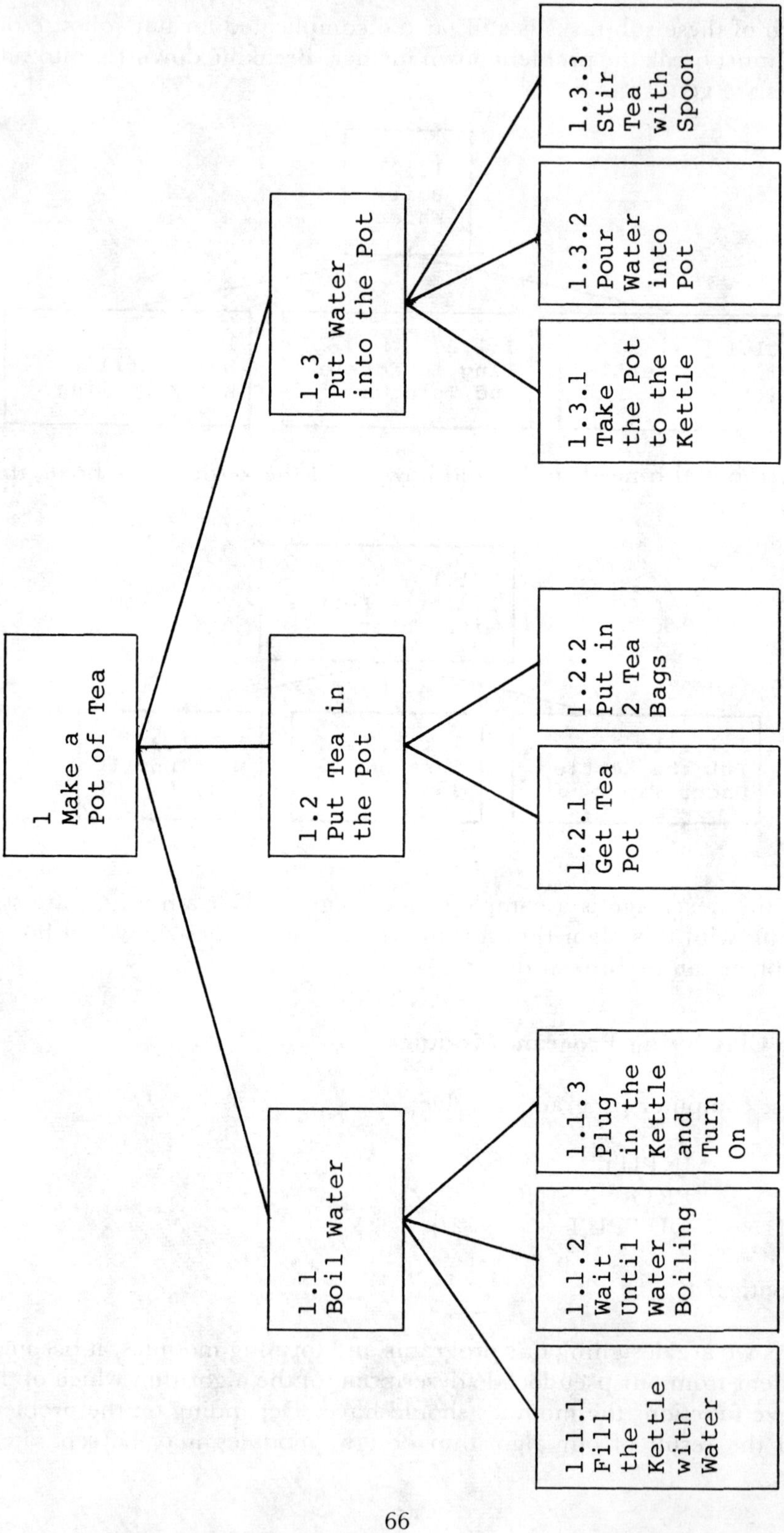
1 Make a Pot of Tea
1.1 Boil Water
1.2 Put Tea in the Pot
1.3 Put Water into the Pot
1.1.1 Fill the Kettle with Water
1.1.2 Wait Until Water Boiling
1.1.3 Plug in the Kettle and Turn On
1.2.1 Get Tea Pot
1.2.2 Put in 2 Tea Bags
1.3.1 Take the Pot to the Kettle
1.3.2 Pour Water into Pot
1.3.3 Stir Tea with Spoon

designated input, processing, and output functions or may have these functions nested as sub-modules.

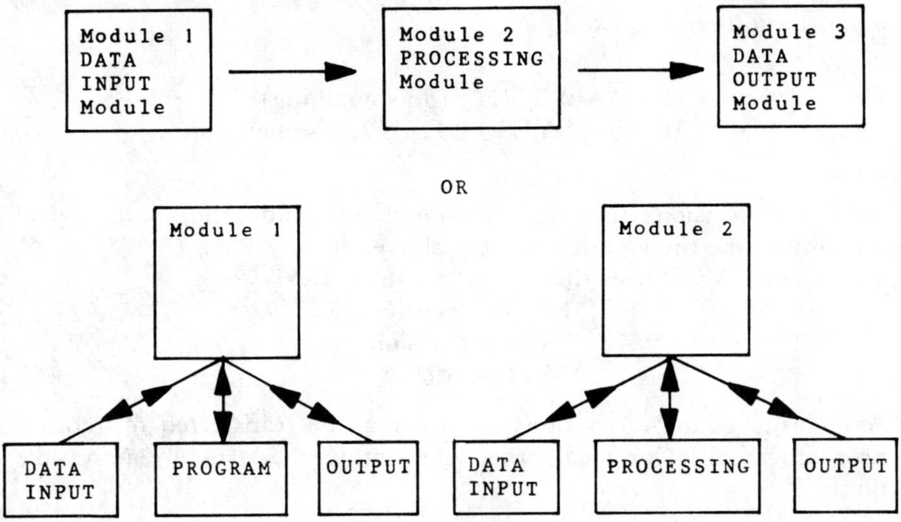

G5: Control Structures

Control structures are the statements or groups of statements (modules) in a program and algorithm by which the order of processing is controlled. Using them properly is the most important part of programming.

BASIC is a line numbered language. The order of processing in a program is from the lowest line number in the program sequentially through to the highest, *unless* this is changed by using a control structure. Control structures link the different modules in a program together and are themselves modules. They will be dealt with in depth in the remainder of this section.

To make our algorithm **language-independent** we can write them using a standard notation in pseudocode for the particular control structure together with its flowchart description. When we code the structures into the BASIC language the instructions used and the order of statements in the structure may be slightly different according to the version of BASIC and how 'structured' it is (i.e. how easily it accommodates these control structures). The structures we will study in BASIC are:

(i) **DECISION STRUCTURES**
(ii) **TRANSFER STRUCTURES**
(iii) **LOOPS**
(iv) **SUBROUTINES**
(v) **NESTED STRUCTURES**
(vi) **SUB-PROGRAMS**

DECISION STRUCTURES

Computers make decisions by comparing the value of one variable against another. For example:

IF A = Ø THEN (do something)
IF A$ = "YES" THEN (do something)

To make decisions they use relational (or conditional) and logical operators, like the equals operator above.

Sinclair BASIC uses three decision structures:

Simple decision
Double decision
Multiple decision

As a result of these decisions control may be transferred to another program module, or local processing within the structure may take place.

TRANSFER STRUCTURES

These structures involve:

(i) UNCONDITIONAL TRANSFER

which is a direct transfer of control using a GOTO (line number) statement. Transfer is to another program statement or a module consisting of a group of statements. GOTO is a very powerful structure and must be used with care.

(ii) CONDITIONAL TRANSFER

in which transfer of control to another segment is made as the result of a decision: i.e. IF (condition is true) THEN GOTO (line number).

These program structures are discussed further in Section H.

LOOPS

The need for the repetition of simple tasks is one of the fundamental reasons computers exist. Loop structures are incorporated in most computer programs. A loop is a sequence of repeated steps in a program. This repetition must be controlled. We shall see in Section L that repetition is controlled by:

(i) COUNTING
(ii) TESTING FOR A CONDITION

There are three common loop structures:

(i) **Repeat** (the process) **forever!**
(ii) **Repeat** (the process) **until** (a condition is met).
(iii) **While** (a condition holds) **repeat** (the process).

Structure (i) is of little use, except that we have to note it and make sure it does *not* occur.

In structure (ii) the condition is tested *after* processing.

In structure (iii) the condition is tested *before* processing.

Sinclair BASIC uses a convenient and powerful set of statements for controlling repetition by counting called:

FOR – NEXT Statements

SUBROUTINES

Structured programming involves breaking down a complicated problem into subproblems which can be worked on separately.

SUBROUTINES are such separate independent program modules. They are distinct from SUBPROGRAMS which have similar properties in that they are routines or groups of program statements that are repeated more then once during a program run.

Subroutine modules have a unique address and can have a name (like a person who lives in a house). Transfer of control to the subroutine from the MAIN PROGRAM, when the program runs is by reference to the subroutine address through a special SUBROUTINE CALL INSTRUCTION. This is the GOSUB (address of subroutine) statement.

A return of control to the main program to carry on processing from where it left off is through a special instruction: RETURN.

Subroutine structures in Sinclair BASIC are explained in Section N.

NESTED STRUCTURES

These are program modules or structures that lie entirely embedded within each other (like a set of Russian dolls).

A simple nested structure is

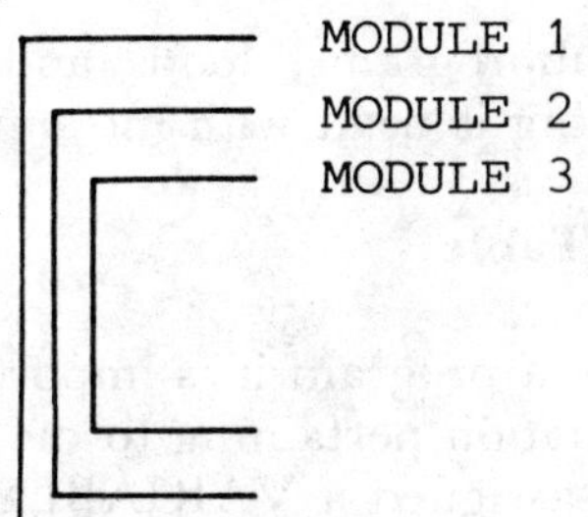

In terms of program statements this would look like:

```
        module 1
      1Ø_______
      2Ø_______
                    module 2
                  4Ø_______
                  5Ø_______
                  6Ø_______
                              module 3
                            7Ø_______
                            8Ø_______
                 1ØØ_______
                 11Ø_______
                 12Ø_______
                 13Ø_______
     14Ø_______
```

The flow of control is:

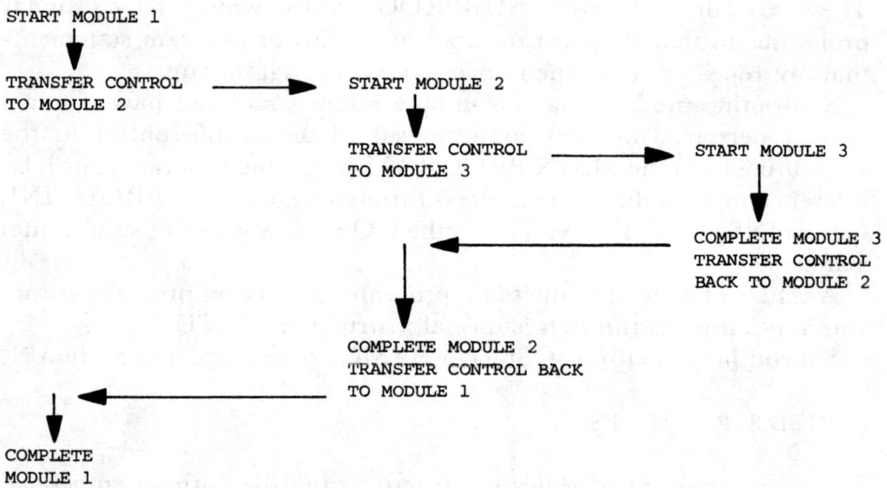

Subroutines, subprograms, loops and decisions may be nested in programs. Nesting is dealt with more fully in Sections H, L and N.

G6: The Data Table

When designing a program it is important that our knowledge of the data and information pertaining to the problem is complete. All data will need to be assigned a VARIABLE name, unless it is a numeric constant used in a formula.

The variable type will be either:

NUMERIC	– numbers	– A, N1, COUNT, A(I,J)
STRING	– characters	– A$, A$(I,J)
LOGICAL	– numbers or characters	– A, A$, NOT B

Numeric variables will be integers, fractions, real and imaginary numbers.

Strings will be names, characters and symbols.

Logical variables will be the values TRUE or FALSE, 1 or Ø as appropriate to their use. Logic is dealt with in Section R.

We also require to know whether our data is:

INPUT
OUTPUT
or INTERMEDIATE

Intermediate data is used in the body of the program, e.g. the value of a loop counter, or the intermediate result of a calculation. Intermediate data is useful for testing and debugging purposes when running the program or algorithm, using machine or hand traces.

The equations, functions and expressions that will use the variables will need to be known. When dealing with equations, functions and expressions the units of the variables or parameters concerned must be known and should be stated.

The first and simplest data table to construct is a descriptive list of variables to be used in the program. This is important for documentation purposes. For example:

VARIABLE	*DESCRIPTION*	*TYPE*
A	First number	Input
B	Second number	Input
SUM	Sum of A and B	Output
A$	User response to 'RUN AGAIN?'	Input

For program design purposes the value ascribed to each variable at different points through the programs can be added. This forms a data table that is useful for checking the algorithm before and after coding it into BASIC, and is also a way of analysing errors in your own program, and understanding how other programs work.

ALGORITHM STEP NUMBER	VARIABLES						
	A	B	S	COUNT	A$	etc	etc
MODULE 1 1.1 1.2							
MODULE N N.1 . . .							

Loop counters are included in the list of variables. If their values are used for calculation inside the loop, this should be stated. There are some examples of this type of data table in the text.

REFINING THE ALGORITHM

The tree diagram should be further broken down and refined until the final sub-modules correspond to recognisable BASIC statements and structures. As you get more experienced, you will recognise more complex structures, and the solution to a problem will become apparent at an earlier stage.

G7: Describe the Algorithm

1.4.1 WRITE OUT YOUR METHOD OF SOLVING THE PROBLEM (THE ALGORITHM) IN STEPS IN A SIMPLE ENGLISH STYLE (PSEUDOCODE).

1.4.2 DRAW A FLOWCHART SHOWING HOW THE PROGRAM WILL RUN FROM START TO FINISH.

1.4.3 TEST THAT THE ALGORITHM WILL WORK BEFORE CODING IT INTO BASIC.

Having broken our problem down into distinct things to do, or subproblems, to a stage where we are able to write a BASIC program, we need to do at least two things before we code. These enable us to write programs that work and that other users can understand.

The algorithm description in pseudocode or flowchart form is an important point of the documentation of your programs. This is not written as part of the program but as a separate document which will also include a listing of the program. This is important for other programmers who may want to modify your program or use it as part of a larger program, and for you yourself if you come back to it after a period of time and cannot remember how you designed it! The program listing alone is often not enough, if the algorithm is complex, to show how the program works.

G8: The Pseudocode Description

In the structure or tree diagram – which we draw out in rough on a piece of paper as we design our solution – each block or module right down to the lowest level has an English description of the task to be done inside it. (The very lowest level tasks will be described in sentences that are very similar to the BASIC program statements themselves, as you will see in Programming Methods II.)

Our algorithm will be written out, in a step-by-step fashion, and will include all the descriptions in the boxes. The highest or first level description (simple box) will be the algorithm and program title. The second level will be the titles of the program sections. Each of these major sections will encompass a further group of modules, all of which will be named in our description of the solution.

The lowest level of our tree diagram will be the specific instuctions the computer has to perform. These will be translated into the BASIC language on an almost one to one basis, and will contain the important and easily recognised language structures, for making decisions, branching and jumping, and repetition that we have previously mentioned. (A summary of pseudocode descriptions of some control structures and their flowcharts with BASIC program equivalents is given in Section 0, Programming Methods II.) If you imagine turning the tree diagram on its side and taking away the boxes, the descriptions that are left constitute a pseudocode description of the algorithm.

As an example, let's look at the tree diagram and the algorithm description for the problem of asking our robot to make a pot of tea.

Using our tree diagram we can write down our algorithm for making a pot of tea as a sequence of instructions (to be coded later into a computer language). We use the English language as our pseudocode and our program is written directly from the sub-tasks in the bottom line of boxes in the tree diagram.

We use the boxes at higher levels in the tree to define distinct modules. Comments or REMARK statements identify each module and explain what is being done in each algorithm section:

```
Remark * * Algorithm for robot to make pot of tea * *
Remark *   Boil water – task 1.1*
      1.1.1   Fill the kettle with water
      1.1.2   Wait until the water is boiling
      1.1.3   Plug in the kettle and turn it on
Remark *   End of task 1.1*
Remark*    Module – Put tea in the pot – task 1.2 *
      1.2.1   Get toe pot
      1.2.2   Put 2ØØ tea bags in the pot
```

Remark* End of task 1.2*
Remark * Module – Put water in the pot – task 1.3 *
  1.3.1 Take pot to kettle
  1.3.3 Stir tea with spoon
  1.3.4 Put lid on tea pot
Remark * End of task 1.3 *
Remark * * End of Algorithm – tea is made * *

You can see that the tree diagram shows why each part of your algorithm is included and why it is in the particular position in which you have placed it on the tree.

The tree diagram contains information about three things:

(1) The problem broken down into different levels of detail starting from the general concept of what is to be done down to the specific activities and instructions which will enable the problem to be coded.
(2) The order in which instructions must be performed.
(3) The comments which must be included to explain what the program is doing.

Exercises

1 Our algorithm has the following mistakes in it:
  a) Some instructions are wrong. They are spelt incorrectly and the robot will not be able to recognise them.
  b) Some instructions are in the wrong order.
  c) Some instructions are missing in the algorithm.
  d) Some instructions are missing on the tree diagram.
  Find the mistakes!
2 Correct the tree diagram and the algorithm.
3 Expand the tree diagram and the algorithm to a further sub-task level. For example:

  1.1.1 Fill the kettle

  becomes

  1.1.1.1 Put kettle under tap
  1.1.1.2 Turn on tap

  etc.
4 Draw a tree diagram and write the algorithm in pseudocode for a robot to set up and switch on your microcomputer system.

G9: Flowcharts

Flowcharts are a second graphical method used in designing programs. They consist of linked boxes of different shapes. Each shape has a different use and, as with tree diagrams, each contains a brief description of what the program should do at a particular point.

It is harder to *design* programs using flowcharts than with tree diagrams. Their power comes from using them to help make visible and describe the flow of control in the algorithm and the resulting program. They are used to help code the program into BASIC instructions, and later form an important part of the DOCUMENTATION of a program. Note that flowcharts express the important control structures used in programming in diagram form.

We give a selection of standard flowchart symbols here. There are additional ones, but their usage varies. The conventions of use should be followed if you wish other people to understand your flowcharts. For your own use, in analysing programs, you may be less exact, but not less systematic. Flow in a program *can* be illustrated by a selection of blobs and rectangles only, given that the lines of flow are correctly given, and the right words are written in the blobs! Doing this is all right for yourself, but not if your flowcharts are to be comprehensible to others.

FLOWCHART SYMBOLS

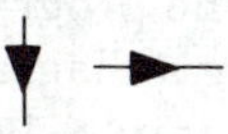

Flow lines. These connect the program blocks. The arrows show the direction of flow, and are very important.

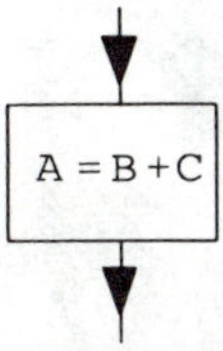

This symbol represents any kind of processing function, that is general Programming Statements, i.e. "Purchase Tea" or LET A = B + C.

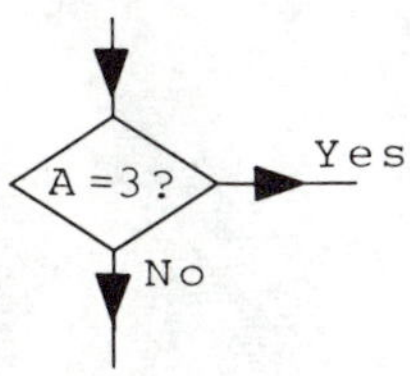

This represents a decision, with a Conditional test, e.g. "Is there another shop open" or IF A = 3 THEN ... It has a Yes/No branch, according to whether the condition is True or False, which determines the program flow.

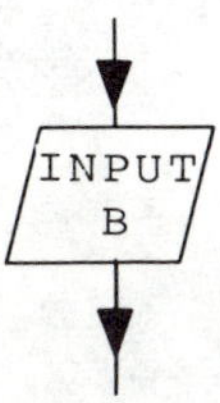

This represents either Output in the program to the screen or printer, or Input from the keyboard, e.g. PRINT "HAVE YOU A PACKET OF TEA?" or INPUT B.

This represents a named process that is specified elsewhere, e.g. Subroutine GOSUB 1ØØØ. The subroutine would have a separate flowchart.

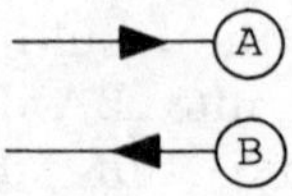

This represents an exit to or entry from another part of the flowchart, allowing one part of the chart to be connected to another part. Used when another direct line link would be confusing, or to connect to a separate page.

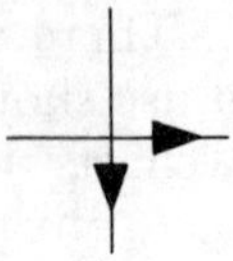

This represents the <u>Crossing</u> of two Flow Lines. They are *not* connected.

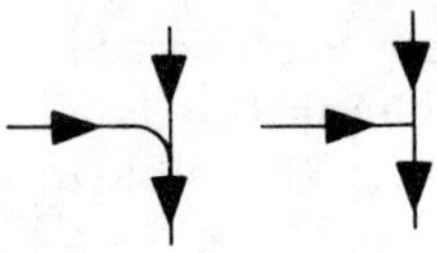

This represents the <u>Junction</u> of Flow Lines. The two lines of flow join.

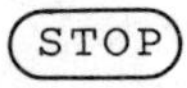

Terminal Point, e.g. Start, Stop, Pause.

A flowchart does not branch out like a tree diagram. It always converges to the stop point. It has a direct relationship to the program it describes. Writing down a flowchart is rather like drawing a diagram of the program itself. Below are some examples of simple flow structures, with the program and the flowchart.

FLOWCHART PROGRAM

1. Simple sequences

```
10 LET X = 5
20 INPUT Y
30 PRINT X,Y
```

FLOWCHART PROGRAM

2. Decision and program branch

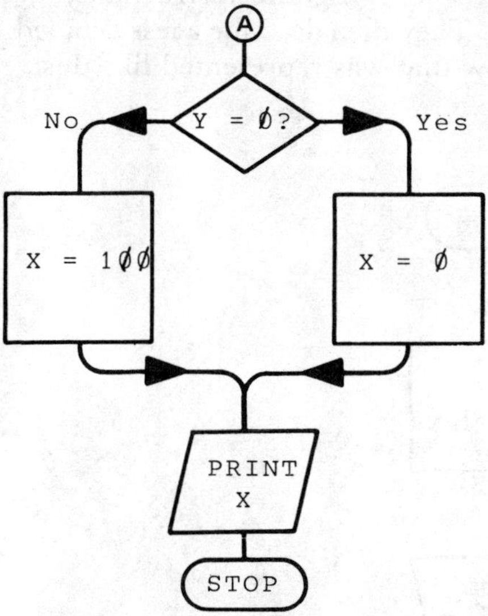


```
4Ø IF Y=Ø THEN GOTO 7Ø
5Ø LET X=1ØØ
6Ø GOTO 8Ø
7Ø LET X=Ø
8Ø PRINT X
9Ø STOP
```

Notice that we have omitted a flowchart symbol for line 6Ø. This GOTO is indicated by the flow lines. The same is true of the GOTO in the conditional statement of line 4Ø.

3. Loop

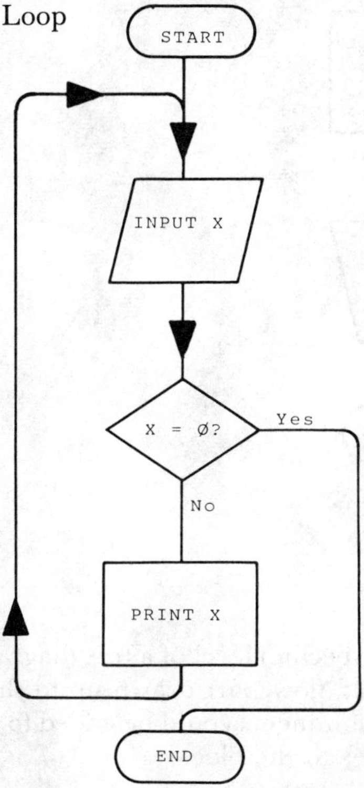


```
1Ø INPUT X
2Ø IF X=Ø THEN GOTO 5Ø
3Ø PRINT X
4Ø GOTO 1Ø
5Ø REM **END**
```

Notice that the above flowcharts represent the programs line by line. Flowcharts can also be less detailed, and the flowchart symbols used to represent program blocks (sequences of program instructions) or modules rather than one or two lines. They then describe a less detailed flow structure. We might have a flow that was represented like this:

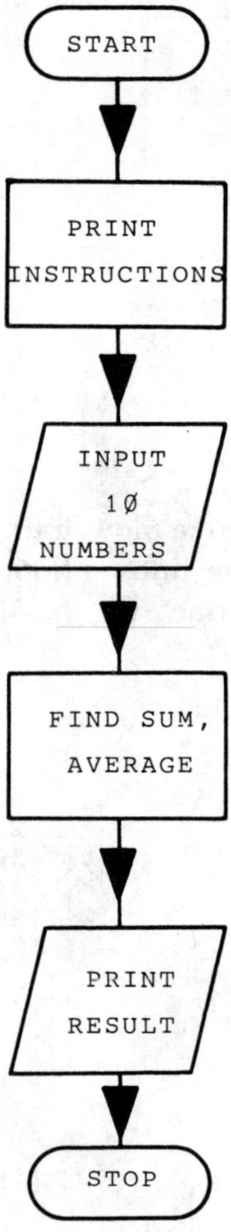

This is like a flowchart of a higher (less specific) level of a tree diagram. Each section could have a more detailed flowchart drawn up to show the individual lines of the program, or comments could be added to the blocks above, relating the program lines to the blocks:

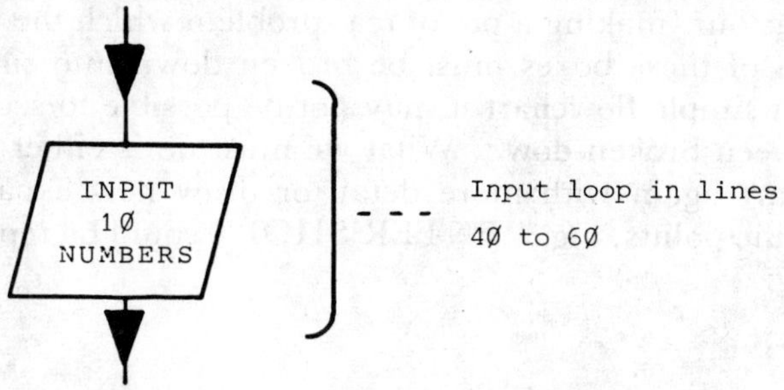

You will soon start to write short programs, and should draw up flowcharts with each program line or instruction indicated separately. Later, for longer programs with large numbers of lines, the flowcharts must be condensed *where the sequence is simple to follow in the program*, to keep them of manageable size. Any *complex* manipulations should still be included in full.

EXAMPLES

(1) Here is a flowchart for our robot. We are going to ask it to buy a packet of tea.

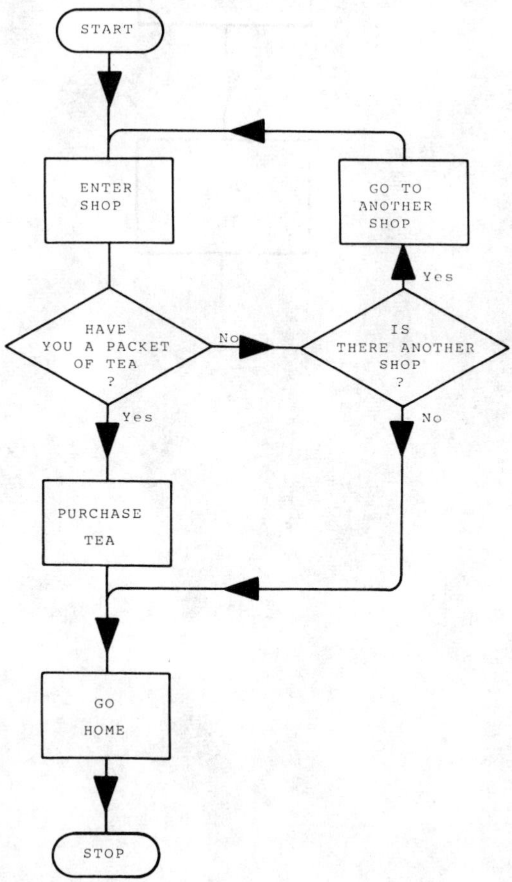

In the same way as our 'making a pot of tea' problem which the robot has to solve, each of these boxes must be broken down into simpler instructions. On a simple flowchart it may not be possible to see how the problem has been broken down. What we must do is either draw the whole flowchart again with more detail or draw new expanded flowcharts at specific points, e.g. "ENTER SHOP" could be replaced with the following:

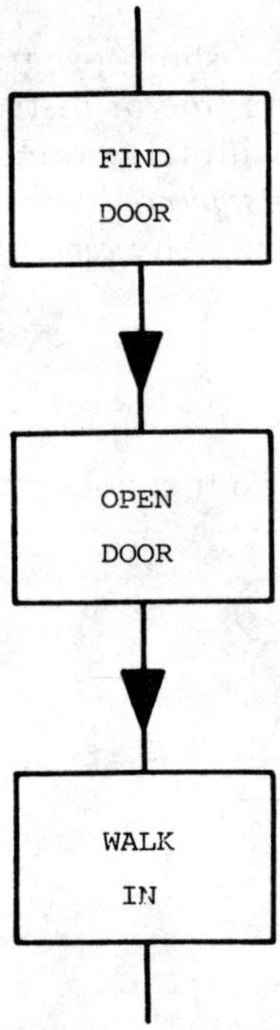

(2) Here is a flowchart of a program to input two numbers, output the sum, and ask you if you want to run the program again.

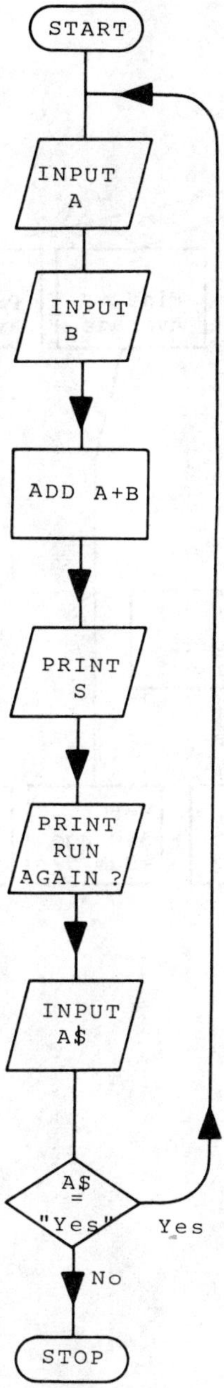


```
10  INPUT A
20  INPUT B
30  LET S = A + B
40  PRINT S
50  PRINT "RUN AGAIN?
    (YES/NO)"
60  INPUT A$
70  IF A$ = "YES" THEN
    GOTO 10
80  STOP
```

AN EXAMPLE OF STRUCTURED DESIGN

Problem: Find the average of five numbers:

(1) *TREE DIAGRAM*

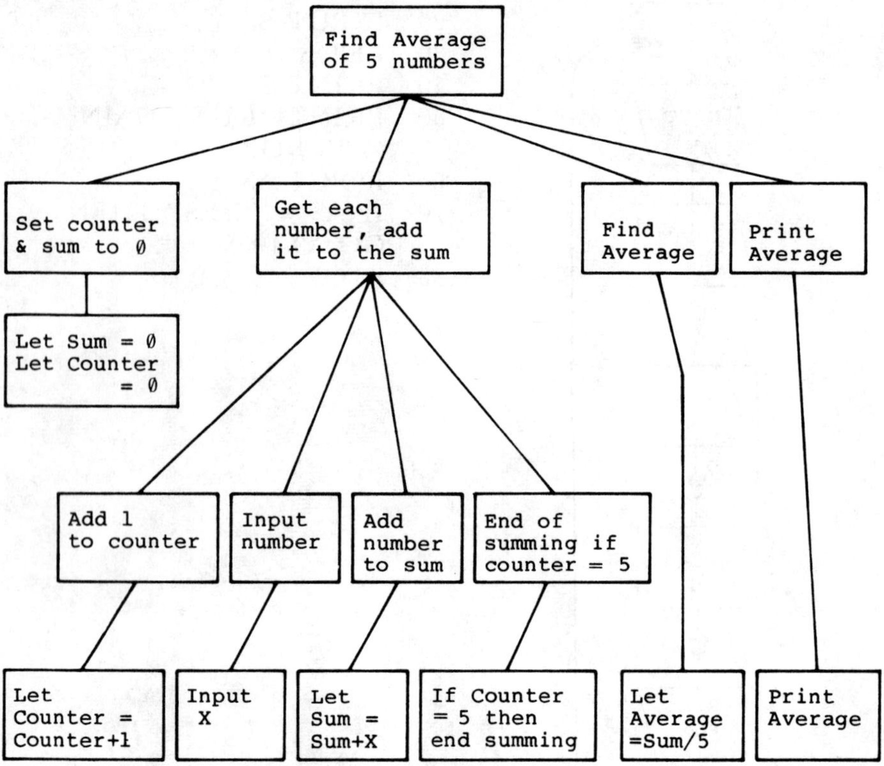

(2) *FLOWCHART*

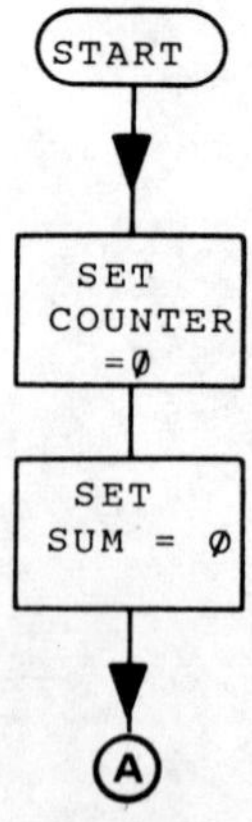

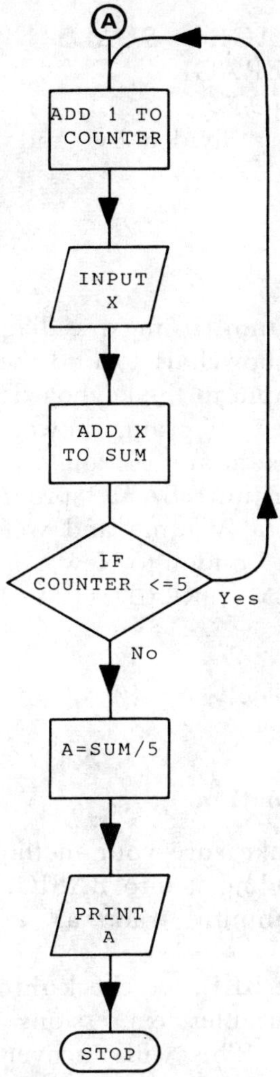

Note that the flowchart and program test whether the counter value is *less than 5*, using the < symbol.

(3) *PROGRAM*

```
10  REM "AVERAGE"
20  REM ** PROGRAM FINDS AVERAGE OF FIVE
    NUMBERS INPUT **
30  REM ** START **
40  LET SUM = Ø
50  LET COUNTER = Ø
60  LET COUNTER = COUNTER + 1
70  INPUT X
80  LET SUM = SUM + X
90  IF COUNTER < 5 THEN GOTO 6Ø
```

```
100  LET AVERAGE = SUM/5
110  PRINT AVERAGE
120  REM ** END **
```

The operand '/' means 'divided by' and is equivalent to the '÷' symbol.

Exercises

1 Design an algorithm (using tree diagram) and write a BASIC program with a flowchart to find the sum and average of ten numbers to be input at the keyboard.
2 Produce the tree diagram, flowchart and program which calculates the area of any rectangle.
3 Design the algorithm, BASIC program and flowchart which calculates the total volume and weight of three boxes to be airfreighted from London to New York. Use the following data:

BOX	LENGTH CM	BREADTH CM	HEIGHT CM	WEIGHT KG
1	20	4	2	2
2	40	3	6	3.5
3	70	10	15	20

Test that it works!

G10: Testing the Algorithm

It is always best to make sure your method of solving the problem actually works *before* coding it into BASIC. This pre-coding check is known in the programming trade as a DRY RUN or WALK THROUGH.

Using the DATA TABLE, we check through, module by module, the values of all the variables, expressions and counters step by step through the algorithm. This will uncover errors in the logic and method and will save time when debugging the finished product later on. Professional programmers always do this as they have to work to very tight time schedules, and by doing things properly at the start they save time later on. We would like you to try a few walk throughs on the simple programs you will be designing at first, just to get the hang of the idea.

We have now covered the first essential steps in designing a program and have seen a simple coding process. We have talked about methods and concepts and introduced some new terminology. After concepts we go to detail.

The algorithm is ready to be coded into a BASIC program. In doing this we are going to put into the program the fundamental programming tools, which are language structure and control structures. We have to know what these structures or tools are before we can use them. This requires a look at how Sinclair BASIC, through small groups of instructions, enables decisions to be taken, branching and jumping to different parts of the program to happen, repetition of parts of the program to take place and how separate modules called subroutines and sub-programs can be called into action where necessary – these are the language structures.

Let's go and meet them!

SECTION H: CONTROL

H1: Control in Programs

The statements which make up a BASIC program are numbered. BASIC is thus called a LINE NUMBERED LANGUAGE. Control in all BASIC programs is carried out by reference to these line or statement numbers. The ZX81 and Spectrum will normally run a program from the lowest numbered statement through to that with the highest number *unless instructed to do otherwise.* This is exactly what concerns us here, and thus we need to recognise that we can control the order in which program statements are executed by using four important instructions in Sinclair BASIC:

- GOTO (for direct transfer)
- IF-THEN (for decisions and branching)
- FOR-NEXT (for loops (repetitions))
- GOSUB-RETURN (for accessing program modules called subroutines)

These instructions are used singly or combined together with other instructions to form groups of program statements called CONTROL STRUCTURES. There are four principal control structures:

- DECISION AND BRANCH
- LOOPS
- SUBROUTINES
- NESTED STRUCTURES

In this Section we will discover how to take decisions and branch to other parts of the program. We will study the remaining structures later in Part Three. The most important property of a computer is that it can be programmed to make decisions, by using the relational or conditional operators of BASIC.

H2: Condition Testing

CONDITIONAL OPERATORS

Conditional operators are also called relational operators as they determine the logical relationship between two expressions, numeric or string, as:

Equality:	=
Inequality:	<>
Greater than:	>
Less than:	<
Greater than or equal to:	>=
Less than or equal to:	<=

The *priority* of conditional operators is 5. Priority will be explained in Section J.

They are executed in order left to right across a statement unless in brackets.

We often need to use the complements or opposites of these operators in decision making. The complements are:

Operator	*Complement*
equality =	inequality <>
greater than >	less than or equal to < =
greater than or equal to > =	less than <

The reverse operations are true in each case.

H3: IF-THEN

IF-THEN

Conditional operators are used with:
IF-THEN statements

IF (CONDITION IS TRUE) THEN (PERFORM AN INSTRUCTION).

For example:

```
40 IF (A = B) THEN GOTO 10
50 IF C < = 6 THEN STOP
60 IF J > K THEN PRINT "J"
```

The format of the statement is:
IF (CONDITION) THEN (INSTRUCTION)

Any BASIC instructions can be used in this kind of statement, although a number are unlikely to be useful (e.g. NEW, CLEAR). In general if the condition in the program line is TRUE then the instruction following the condition is obeyed. If the condition is not TRUE (FALSE) then control passes to the next line.

This powerful facility enables us to branch and transfer control to another line in the program.

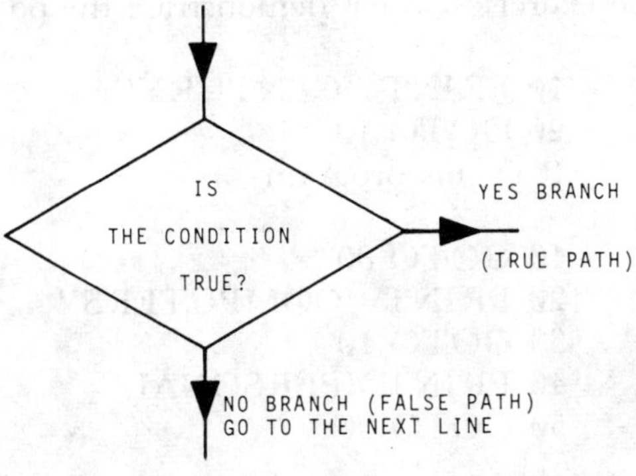

H4: GOTO Instructions

GOTO

The normal control sequence in a program is via numbered statements – from the lowest to the highest. GOTO (line number) switches control to the line number specified:

100 GOTO 20
200 GOTO (B + C)

As a *command* GOTO 30 executes a program from line 30. Unlike RUN, with this method variables are *not* cleared before execution.

The Spectrum includes a space between GO and TO when printing this instruction.

Exercises

Key in and run this program which checks that only positive numbers are input and gives a bad data error message as well as prompting for the next input. Notice the use of IF-THEN and GOTO. INPUT both positive and negative numbers.

```
10 REM*INPUT CHECK*
20 INPUT A
30 IF A>0 THEN PRINT A
40 IF A<=0 THEN  PRINT "BAD IN
   PUT"
50 PRINT "HAVE YOU ANOTHER NUMB
   ER? ANSWER YES OR NO"
60 INPUT A$
70 IF A$ ="YES"THEN GOTO 20
80 STOP
90 REM*END INPUT CHECK*
```

Now try these exercises which demonstrate the power of GOTO:

1

```
10 PRINT "CENTURY";
20 GOTO 10
```

Run this program

2

```
10 GOTO 80
20 PRINT "COMPUTERS";
30 GOTO 10
40 PRINT "PERSONAL";
50 GOTO 20
```

```
60 PRINT "SINCLAIR";
70 GOTO 40
80 GOTO 60
```

Key it in and sort it out!

This is called 'spaghetti programming'. Structured programming techniques have been designed to avoid the excessive use of GOTO statements.

3

```
10 INPUT A$
20 PRINT A$;
30 GOTO 10
```

INPUT some graphics characters and watch the patterns!

4 Key in and run this example:

```
10 INPUT A
20 IF A = 1 THEN FOR I = 1 TO 10
30 PRINT "CENTURY"
40 IF A = 1 THEN NEXT I
50 STOP
```

Line 10 asks you to input a number.

Line 20 examines if it is equal to 1. IF this condition is TRUE then a FOR-NEXT loop is set up to print "CENTURY" ten times. If it is not TRUE then control passes to the next line.

Line 30 "CENTURY" is printed once.

Line 40 the condition is tested again. If TRUE the loop continues and CENTURY is printed again. If not then control passes to line 50.

Line 50 stops program execution.

Can you understand it? If not wait until you have read the section on LOOPS.

H5: Decision Structures

DOUBLE DECISIONS

The simplest decision involves the evaluation of a LOGICAL CONDITION – i.e. a condition that may have the value of either TRUE or FALSE. A result of this evaluation decides which part of a program is executed next. These parts of the program are called TRUE TASK and FALSE TASK.

The flowchart for the Double Decision STRUCTURE is:

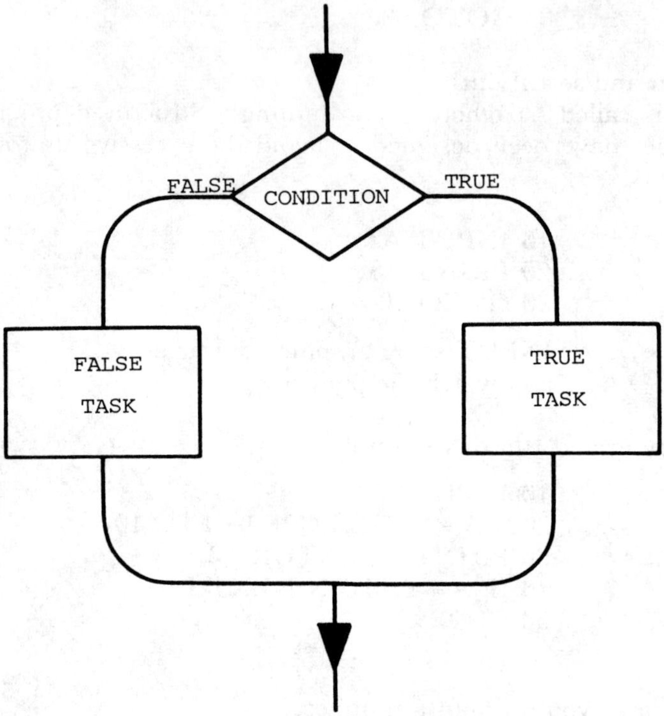

It is called a *double* decision as there are two alternative modules that can be performed.

In the flowchart, if the indicated condition is true, then the program section representing the True task is carried out, otherwise the program section representing the False task is performed. Only one of the paths from the condition test is taken, and the program will continue at the statement represented by the arrow at the bottom of the flowchart.

Each task can be a single instruction or a statement or a group of instructions.

The Double Decision Structure is known by the general name of the "IF-THEN-ELSE Decision Structure". Its general form is:

IF (condition) THEN (true) ELSE (false)

This means: IF the condition tested is True THEN perform the True task, and IF the condition is *not* true perform the False task.

Our algorithm description of it would look like:

1. Decision Module.
1.1 Do the test. If result is True then
1.2 Do True task
1.3 Otherwise do False task

We can write this formally in pseudocode as:

```
module – decision
            if condition
            then True Task
            else False Task
            end if
 end module
```

End if and end module are *bounds* to the structure. In Sinclair BASIC we code it as:

```
10 IF (cond) THEN (branch to True task)
20 (False task)
```

Note that in this case the only literal equivalent of BASIC from the pseudocode is with the use of IF and THEN.

The branch to the true task is made with a GOTO instruction. For example:

```
 1Ø IF A>Ø THEN GOTO 1ØØ
 2Ø REM * FALSE TASK *
 3Ø ...
    ...
 9Ø GOTO 12Ø
1ØØ REM * TRUE TASK *
11Ø PRINT A
```

If we did not branch to the true task starting at 1ØØ and used:

```
1Ø IF A>Ø THEN PRINT A
2Ø REM FALSE TASK
```

in line 1Ø, the true task would be processed and control would then pass to line 2Ø – the false task. In other words, both tasks would be processed! Watch out for this.

EXAMPLE: Input two names as strings. The program compares them and prints them out in alphabetical order:

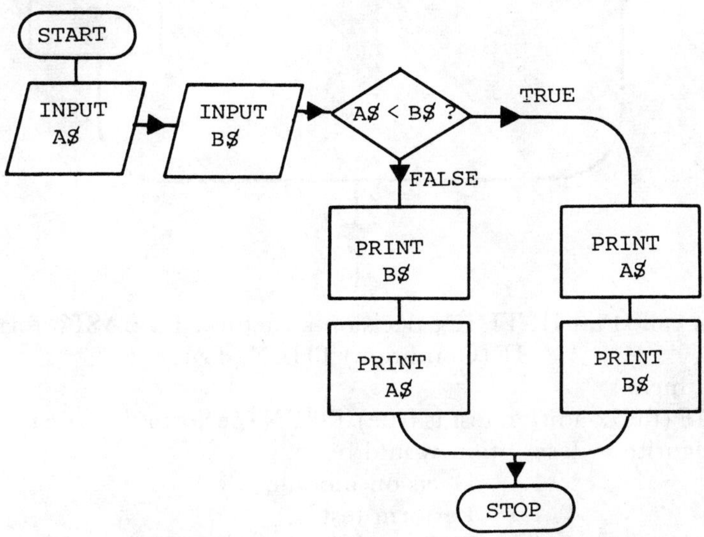

```
              10   REM * ALPHA *
              20   INPUT A$
              30   INPUT B$
              40   IF A$<B$ THEN GOTO 80
--------------------------------------------
FALSE         50   PRINT B$
TASK          60   PRINT A$
              70   GOTO 100
--------------------------------------------
TRUE          80   PRINT A$
TASK          90   PRINT B$
             100   STOP
             110   REM * END ALPHA *
```

THE SINGLE DECISION

This is a special case of the double decision structure in which there is only one task to perform – the True task.

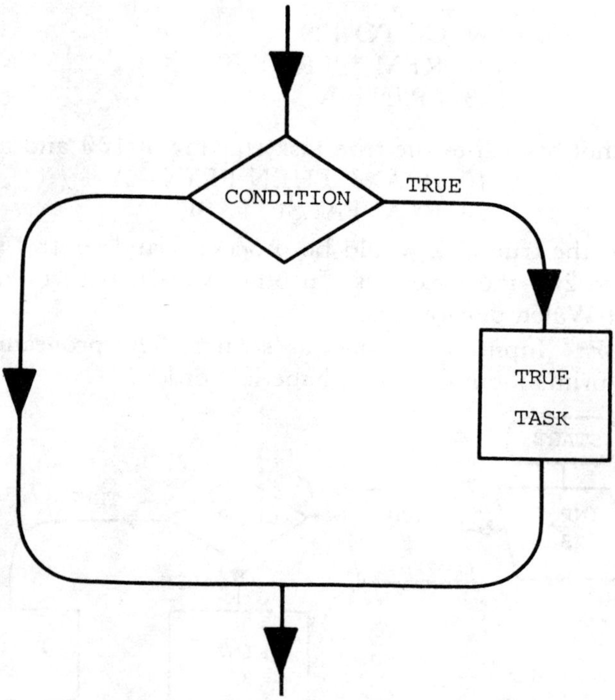

This is called an IF-THEN decision structure. Its BASIC form is:

IF (Condition) THEN (True)

Which means:

IF (the condition test is true) THEN (perform the true task)

Our algorithm description would be:

1. Decision module
1.1 Perform test
1.2 If True, process true task

A brief formal pseudocode description is:

```
mod – Decision
      if Condition
            Then P
      end if
end mod
```

Our BASIC statement is:

IF (condition) THEN (TRUE)

EXAMPLE: Input numbers and stop if a number greater than 1Ø is input:

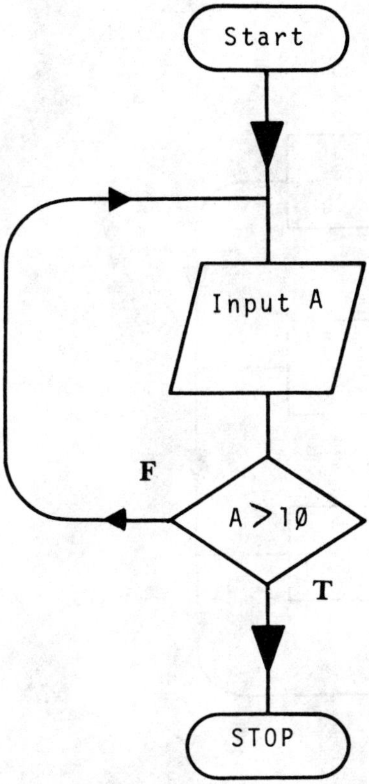


```
1Ø INPUT A
2Ø IF A>1Ø THEN STOP
3Ø GOTO 1Ø
```

Note the abbreviation of True to T and False to F.

MULTIPLE DECISIONS

There is often the need in programs to perform several tasks based on the result of a set of conditions. To solve these problems we use a multiple decision structure. This kind of structure is especially useful in breaking up larger tasks into smaller ones.

Multiple decisions are most conveniently handled by multiple logical operations. This is covered in Section R. We will consider the conventional way of handling them.

As an example of multiple decisions consider a food vending machine. You put a coin in and press the respective button of the article you wish to be delivered to you. Another example would be a set of arithmetic testing programs, with questions in each. The computer would ask you which set of tests you required, you would key in the reply and, from several alternatives, the required program would run.

The flowchart for such a structure is:

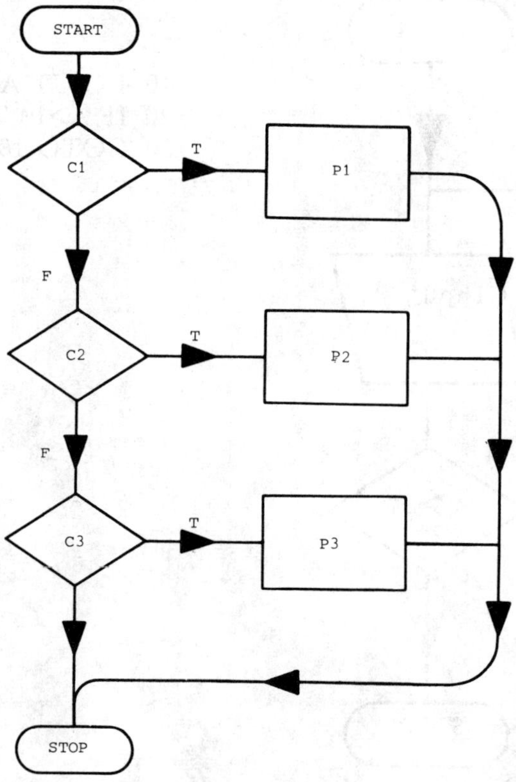

Where C1, C2, C3 are the conditions and P1, P2, P3 are the True tasks.

EXAMPLE: Input any of three letters A, B, C and print out a corresponding reply.

```
 5 PRINT "ENTER A,B OR C"
10 INPUT A$
20 IF A$="A" THEN GOTO 60
```

```
30 IF A$="B" THEN GOTO 80
40 IF A$="C" THEN GOTO 100
50 STOP
60 PRINT "YOU INPUT A"
70 STOP
80 PRINT "YOU INPUT B"
90 STOP
100 PRINT "YOU INPUT C"
110 STOP
```

The Pseudocode description of this structure is:

	BASIC
mod	
case	
if C1	
then P1	1Ø IF (C1) THEN (P1)
if C2	
then P2	2Ø IF (C2) THEN (P2)
if C3	
then P3	3Ø IF (C3) THEN (P3)
endcase	
endmod	

PROGRAMMING WITH GOTO

When programming in BASIC take great care in how you use the GOTO statement. It takes two main forms. Used on its own it is called an unconditional GOTO and when used with IF-THEN it is called a conditional GOTO.

GOTO enables you to jump around in a program like a flea on a blanket – don't do it! Try and code your program to execute in sequence and avoid it becoming a bowl of spaghetti. Excessive use of GOTO makes programs difficult to refine and debug. Relationships between the program paths become difficult to follow. However – do not take the other extreme and write awkward complicated code to try and avoid GOTOs!

Ideally, unconditional GOTO statements should only be used to skip over code and not to repeat code sections (i.e. they should only be used to transfer control *forward* in a program).

Do not put an unconditional GOTO inside a loop or subroutine to jump out of it. Do not jump inside a loop or subroutine, because you'll find that jumping in and out of loops can cause unpredictable results.

Do not jump to another GOTO. For example:

```
1ØØ GOTO 2ØØ
2ØØ GOTO 3ØØ
```

or else:

```
100 GOTO 100 !
```

Exercises

1 Write a program to input integer numbers and stop if zero is input.
2 Write a program to input integers and count the number of times zero is input.
3 Write a program to input integers and calculate the percentage of zeros input.
4 Write a program which prints out the result of dividing any two numbers' input and gives a "bad data – try again" message if any of the input values is zero.
5 Write a program which will print out on request a lunch menu for the different days of the week.

H6: Logical Operators: AND/OR

We will only introduce you to simple logical operations here. Logic is dealt with fully in Section R.

Use of the AND and OR statements enables us to combine conditional statements in powerful ways to make more complex decisions in programs.

AND

AND combines relations so that the expression:
(condition 1) AND (condition 2)
e.g. (A = B) AND (B>1)
is TRUE when BOTH conditions are TRUE.
It is FALSE when *one* or *both* conditions are FALSE.

OR

OR combines relations so that the expression:
(condition 1) OR (condition 2)
e.g. (A = B) OR (B<>1)
is TRUE when EITHER condition is TRUE.
It is FALSE when *both* conditions are FALSE.

The expressions formed by the use of AND and OR are used with IF...THEN statements. For example:

```
20  IF X>1 AND X<10 THEN PRINT
      "BETWEEN 1 AND 10"
```

```
5Ø  IFX<>2 AND X<>3 THEN PRINT
    " X NOT EQUAL TO 2 OR 3"
4Ø  IF A = B OR B = C THEN LET F = F + 1
```

The first example will be true if X is greater than 1 and X is also less than 1Ø, and the message will be printed. If X was 11, the first condition would be true, but the second false. The whole expression would then be false.

Notice the danger with the second example, in that we say in English 'not equal to 2 *or* 3', but we must key in an expression using AND. It is clear once you realise that two conditions are to be tested – 'not equal to 2 and not equal to 3'. If, for example, X were 3 when this line in the program was reached, then the second condition would be false in this expression, and the whole expression would also be false.

The third example would be true if *either* A was equal to B *or* if B was equal to C. It is also true if both these conditions are true.

We can also combine more than two conditions:

```
2Ø IF A = B AND B = C AND C = 2Ø THEN STOP
```

will stop if all three conditions are *true.* If *one* or more is false then the whole expression is false.

Similarly:

```
2Ø IF B = 2 OR B = 3 OR B = 4 THEN LET B = 1
```

will make B = 1 if B is equal to 2 or 3 or 4.

It is also possible to use combinations of AND and OR:

```
3Ø IF (A = B AND B>2) OR (A = 2 AND B = 3) THEN GOTO 6Ø
```

The expressions in brackets are evaluated first. The first expression in brackets will be true if B is greater than 2 and equal to A. The second expression will be true if A is 2 and B is 3. The program will pass control to line 6Ø if either expression in brackets is true.

To summarise: where T1, T2 etc. are true conditional expressions and F1, F2 etc. are false conditional expressions:

(T1) AND (T2)	TRUE
(T1) AND (F2)	FALSE
(F1) AND (T2)	FALSE
(F1) AND (F2)	FALSE
(T1) OR (T2)	TRUE
(F1) OR (T2)	TRUE
(T1) OR (F2)	TRUE
(F1) OR (F2)	FALSE

Each condition may also be another AND or OR expression.

Exercises

Work out what will be printed by these programs, then key in and run them to check. The operator "/" means "divided by" (÷) and "*" means "multiplied by" (*).

1

```
10 LET A=2
20 LET B=3
30 LET C=10
40 LET X=15
50 IF X/B=A AND C/A=5 THEN PRINT
   "LINE 50 TRUE"
60 IF X/B=A OR C/A=5 THEN PRINT
   "LINE 60 TRUE"
70 IF X/B=C/2 AND X>=15 THEN PRINT
   "LINE 70 TRUE"
```

2

```
10 LET A=20
20 LET B=150
30 LET X=7.5
40 LET Y=2
50 LET S=B/20
60 IF S=X AND X*A=B AND Y=2 THEN
   PRINT "LINE 60 TRUE"
70 IF X=B OR X<20 OR X>2 THEN
   PRINT "LINE 70 TRUE"
80 IF (X=7.5 OR Y=10) AND (A/Y=1
   0 AND B=150) THEN PRINT "LINE
   80 TRUE"
```

Make sure you have got the programs correct before you run them. Work out both sides of each expression using a relational operator first. Then, giving each expression a T or F value, work out the bracketed AND/OR expressions. This gives you a T or F value for the whole bracket. Then work out whether the whole expression will be true or false.

3 Write some similar programs for yourself to experiment with all the relational operators used with AND and OR.

I1: PRINT LPRINT

PRINT

The PRINT statement is used to output information by displaying it on the screen.

It can take many forms. For example:

10 PRINT A	prints out the value of numeric variable A
20 PRINT B$	prints out string variable B$
30 PRINT "YOUR NAME?"	prints out whatever is included within the quotes (inverted commas)
40 PRINT (B**2 – 4*A*C)	prints out the calculated value of the expression
50 PRINT	leaves a blank line

LPRINT

The LPRINT statement is used to output information by printing it out on the printer.

The LPRINT statement is used in exactly the same way as the PRINT statement, but produces printer and not screen output. If the printer is not attached LPRINT statements are ignored.

The screen size for printing is 22 PRINT lines down the screen, and each line is 32 columns (character spaces) wide. The actual screen size is 24 lines by 32 columns, but the bottom two lines are reserved for commands and operating messages. The lines are numbered 0 to 21 down the screen and the columns 0 to 31 across.

The PRINT statements shown above each commence at the left-hand side of the screen, and each PRINT statement moves the printing position to the start of the next line after it prints whatever it was told to. Lines of greater than 32 characters will go on to the next line automatically.

To clear the screen of printing we use the CLS (Clear Screen) statement.

CLS

CLS erases all printing on the screen, and sets the new print position at the start of the top line of the screen.

I2: Spacing Items on the Screen

;

A semicolon (;) between two items causes the printing of the second item immediately after the first.

For example:

```
10  PRINT A;B$
20  PRINT "AVERAGE";C
```

Try the following program:

```
10  LET A = 6.89
20  LET B = 87.6
30  PRINT A;B
40  PRINT "AVERAGE";(A + B)/2
```

The display is:

```
6.8987.6
AVERAGE47.245
```

This does not give a very satisfactory display since values run into each other. One simple way to overcome this is shown below.

```
10  LET A = 6.89
20  LET B = 87.6
30  PRINT A;"    ";B
40  PRINT "AVERAGE   ";(A + B)/2
```

The display now becomes:

```
6.89 87.6
AVERAGE 47.245
```

,

A comma (,) between two items causes the print position to be shifted on (at least one place) to either column 16 or to the next line column 0.

For example:

```
10  PRINT A,B
20  PRINT A$,B$
30  PRINT "AVERAGE",C
```

Try the following program:

```
10  LET A = 7.65
20  LET B = 8.67
30  PRINT "AVERAGE",(A + B)/2
```

```
40  PRINT
50  PRINT "NUMBER1","NUMBER2",
    "AVERAGE"
60  PRINT A,B,(A + B)/2
```

The display is:

```
AVERAGE          8.16
NUMBER1          NUMBER2
AVERAGE
7.65             8.67
8.16
```

Clearly the comma is useful if we wish to print a table with two columns, but is unsuitable if we wish to have a table with more than two columns.

It is important to remember the screen size when deciding the form of your output. For your output the effective screen is 22 lines each 32 columns wide.

TAB

TAB C; **moves the print position to column C. If this would involve back-spacing it moves on to the next line.**

The following program (with printout) indicates how the TAB function can be used to improve the presentation of results.

```
10  LET A$ = "A.B.JONES"
20  LET B = 65
30  PRINT "NAME";TAB 6;A$;TAB 19;"AGE";
    TAB 23;B;TAB 27;"YEARS"
```

```
NAME  A.B.JONES  AGE  65  YEARS
```

Note the semi-colons between TABs and print items. It is important to remember that each line has 32 columns, numbered 0 to 31.

The next program shows a simple way of tabulating results.

```
10  PRINT "NO.";TAB 4;"SQUARE";TAB 12;
    "CUBE";TAB 20;"RECIP"
20  INPUT N
30  PRINT N;TAB 4;N*N;TAB 12;N*N*N;
    TAB 20;1/N
40  GOTO 20
```

NO.	SQUARE	CUBE	RECIP
1	1	1	1
2	4	8	Ø.5
3	9	37	Ø.33333333
4	16	64	Ø.25
5	25	125	Ø.2
6	36	216	Ø.16666667
7	49	343	Ø.14285714
8	64	512	Ø.125
9	81	729	Ø.11111111
1Ø	1ØØ	1ØØØ	Ø.1

It is important to remember that numbers are output with up to 8 figures and allow the appropriate space. An alternative is to decide how many figures you want and use the INT function (see Section J).

I3: PRINT AT

AT L, C moves the print position to line L and column C.

For example:

10 PRINT AT 1Ø,12;"CENTRE"

will cause the string specified to be printed starting at line 1Ø, column 12, i.e. roughly in the centre of the screen – since L goes from Ø to 21, counting down the screen, and C goes from Ø to 31, counting left to right.

EXAMPLE

The program below sets up a symmetrical pattern using the character of your choice. Note the use of the command CLS to clear the screen of your input.

```
 1Ø PRINT AT 5,4;"WHICH CHARACTER?"
 2Ø INPUT A$
 3Ø CLS
 4Ø LET L=INT (RND*1Ø)+1
 5Ø LET C=INT (RND*15)+1
 6Ø PRINT AT 11+L,16+C;A$
 7Ø PRINT AT 11-L,16-C;A$
 8Ø PRINT AT 11+L,16-C;A$
 9Ø PRINT AT 11-L,16+C;A$
1ØØ GOTO 2Ø
```

Try adjusting the parameters in lines 6Ø-1ØØ.

The important feature to remember is:

Number of character cells is 32 horizontally by 22 vertically, i.e. 32 × 22 altogether.

The TAB function uses C = 0 to 31 *only*.
The AT function uses L = 0 to 21
and C = 0 to 31.

You should have noticed that the PRINT commands reinforce each other, and provide alternative ways of achieving the aim of placing characters, character strings or numbers at the desired positions on the 22 line, 32 column screen display.

For example, these three programs:

```
10 LET X = 3
20 PRINT X,,,,
30 PRINT X*X

10 LET X = 3
20 PRINT X
30 PRINT
40 PRINT X*X

10 LET X= 3
20 PRINT X,TAB 32;" ";TAB 32;X*X
```

would give the same printout on screen. The number of keystrokes (count them) is what determines which statement usage is efficient in any instance. You will soon come to recognise which to use if you experiment.

PRINT AT instructions will overprint anything already printed at the position specified. We can use this to replace on the screen one set of data, or one string, by another.

```
10  INPUT X
20  PRINT AT 0,0;X
30  GOTO 10
```

overprints one X by the next X each time. If we input 1,2,3...10 it works fine. But if we input 10,9,8...1 we get:

```
10
90
80
70
```

etc.

Similarly,

```
10  PRINT AT 10, 10; "ZX81"
20  .......
30  ......
40  PRINT AT 10, 10; "SINCLAIR"
```

works, but not if we swap the two strings around – we end up with ZX81LAIR, and we have the same problem with numbers, which can be between one and eight digits long.

We can blank out something on the screen by overprinting an empty string. For the simple problems above, the addition of appropriate strings will work; we add 4 spaces after "ZX81", so that line 1Ø becomes:

```
10  PRINT AT 10,10; "ZX81    "
```

and for numbers, we can use:

```
20  PRINT AT 0,0;X; "       "
```
(7 spaces)

Using LPRINT also requires care.

For the LPRINT instruction, TAB works exactly as PRINT TAB.
LPRINT AT L,C is converted to LPRINT TAB C, and the line number is ignored.

This is because the printer cannot go back to a previous line. Try this program. Input 1,2,3,4,5.

```
10  INPUT X
20  LPRINT AT X,X;X
30  GOTO 10
```

will print 12345, as if line 2Ø had read LPRINT TAB X;X.
For any programmed screen format that is not a simple sequence of print lines, it is better to use COPY to produce output on the printer, once all the data is on the screen.

COPY prints the entire current screen display on the printer.

If used as direct command, we can COPY less than a whole screen by pressing BREAK before completion, but if used in a program, the whole screen will be copied.

I4: The Graphics Characters on the ZX81*

The ZX81 character set includes a set of graphics characters, and you were told how to access them in Section B. To recap:

Graphics characters are accessed by using [Graphics] to get the [G] cursor. Repeat to return to [L] cursor. *Unshifted* keys then produce inverse video characters. (e.g. key Q gives Q .) *Shifted* keys produce graphics cells, if shown on the keys: e.g. SHIFT R gives ▜ .If no graphics cell is shown, result is *inverse video* form of normal shifted character (e.g. SHIFT U gives $).

The inverse video characters and graphics cells can be used for enhancing displays and drawing bar charts, diagrams and pictures. They are manipulated as strings, by putting quotes round them, e.g. PRINT " ▒" or PRINT " A ".

* The Spectrum offers more extensive graphics facilities than the ZX81, and Spectrum owners should refer to Unit W3 for details. The Spectrum has the solid graphics characters of the ZX81, but not the shaded characters, on keys 1 to 8 in graphics mode. Read through this section bearing this in mind.

Put your computer in graphics mode and run through the keyboard, noting the unshifted and shifted versions of each key. Note that RUBOUT (DELETE) works with the [G] cursor, but the cursor control keys do not, and that the [L] cursor must be on screen for them to work.

By the time you fill one line and move on to the next, you will see that all these graphics characters join up, with no gaps between the cells. The difference between the grey cells on the A and K keys is that they join up with the half-shaded graphics cells on the S, D, F and G keys in different ways. Experiment with these. If they join up properly, you cannot see the join. If they do not, the join is visible as a chequered pattern. To check the characters across the screen, use the bottom lines of the screen directly. To check the vertical joins, enter this program:

```
10  INPUT A$
20  PRINT A$
30  GOTO 10
```

Change the [L] cursor to [G], then input the graphics character. You have to then press NEWLINE (ENTER) twice; the first time to change [G] to [L], the second to input the character.

We can use the graphics characters to draw (crude!) pictures, enhance printout on the screen – by printing prompts in inverse video for example – or putting titles inside surrounds, and use them in diagrams or moving graphics. You'll have to wait a few more chapters before we can do anything interesting, but here are a few things to try: Here's a program to put a border round a word in inverse video. Notice we store the graphics in string variables. This gives us better manipulative power than if we just used literal strings. On the ZX81 the graphics characters in A$ are the shift graphic on the E key, 11 times the one on the 7 key and the one on the R key. If you are using a Spectrum, the relevant keys are '4', '3' and '7'. You can work the other lines out for yourself.

```
  5 REM **BLOCK**
 10 LET A$="▛▀▀▀▀▀▀▀▀▀▀▀▜"
 20 LET B$="▌   [illegible]   ▐"
 30 LET C$="▙▄▄▄▄▄▄▄▄▄▄▄▟"
 40 LET X=0
 50 LET Y=0
 60 PRINT AT X,Y;A$;AT X+1,Y;B$
;AT X+2,Y;C$
```

Notice the combined PRINT AT statements in line 60.

The production of inverse characters on the Spectrum (white characters on a black background, unless colour is being used) can be done in different ways. You can use CAPS SHIFT and the 4 key to put an INVerse VIDEO control character before a letter or other character, but this will make *all* characters thereafter into their inverse forms unless CAPS SHIFT and 3 is used to restore NORMAL VIDEO. The alternative is to use INVERSE as part of a program statement. INVERSE is obtained using SYMBOL SHIFT and the M key in E mode. To get inverse video this must be followed by 1, so that to print HELLO in inverse video we key in:

```
10  PRINT INVERSE 1;"HELLO"
```

This will appear normally in the program listing, but in inverse when the instruction is carried out.

Now add the following lines, and you will see why the use of string variables, and variables for the line and column numbers, can be useful.

```
 70  LET X = X + 1
 80  LET Y = Y + 1
 90  CLS
100  GOTO 60
```

Run the program, and you see we have a crude moving display. CLS makes the screen 'flash' a bit, but we could avoid this by overprinting. Revise the program to erase by overprinting empty strings.

We can use the graphics characters for pictures. Try this:

```
10 PRINT AT 0,9;
20 PRINT AT 1,8;
30 PRINT AT 2,8;
```

(it's supposed to be a car).

Change the program to allow you to input a value for Line and Column numbers, so that you can place the car in different places. Then add a GOTO loop to allow multiple cars on the screen.

Exercises

1 Write a program that puts:

NAME:
AGE:
ADDRESS:

on the screen, then prompts for inputs on line 20 (INPUT NAME etc), and prints the responses on the screen.

Each prompt should overprint the previous one. Allow four separate lines for the address. Blank out the last prompt, then have the screen copied on the printer.

2 Add a routine to LPRINT name, address and age, without the borders or titles, on the printer after deleting the COPY instruction.
3 Input names, ages and occupations of three friends and arrange them to be tabulated in a suitable form.
4 Experiment with ways to make the car move across the screen.

SECTION J: ARITHMETIC AND FUNCTIONS

J1: Arithmetic Operations

A prime function of the computer is to evaluate formulae and expressions similar to those used in standard mathematical calculation.

Algebraic EXPRESSIONS are written in BASIC using the following OPERATORS with a set of variables or numbers as the OPERANDS.

ARITHMETIC OPERATOR			*EXAMPLE*	
SYMBOL	*NAME*	*PRIORITY*	*BASIC*	*MATHS*
**	**exponentiation (raising to a power)**	**1Ø**	**A**3**	**A^3**
[↑]	**(on the Spectrum)**		**A↑3**	**A^3**
–	**negation**	**9**	**–A**	**–A**
*	**multiplication**	**8**	**A*B**	**A × B (a.b)**
/	**division**	**8**	**A/B**	**A ÷ B $(\frac{a}{b})$**
+	**addition**	**6**	**A + B**	**A + B**
–	**subtraction**	**6**	**A – B**	**A – B**

Note that negation operates on *one* operand – a *unary* operation (i.e. makes a variable negative, e.g. – A) and that the subtraction operator uses *two* operands, e.g. A – B, a *binary* operation.

J2: Priority

1 All arithmetic, conditional and logical operations are assigned a *priority* number from 1Ø to 1. High priority is 1Ø, low priority is 1. The priority numbers for the arithmetic operators are as shown in the previous Unit.

2 The priority of an operation determines the order in which it is evaluated in a complex statement in which more than one operation is to be performed. High priority operations are performed earlier.

3 Brackets (parentheses) are used in BASIC algebraic expressions. Brackets clarify which expressions constitute separate values to be operated on. Expressions inside brackets are evaluated first *before* the quantity is used in further computation. With multiple (nested) brackets the evaluation proceeds from the innermost bracketed expression to the outermost.

4 For operations of equal priority in the same statement, evaluation is from *Left* to *Right*.

Brackets can often be omitted when the sequence of evaluation is understood, but there is no harm in using them to ensure correct evaluation. Expressions may be tested by using PRINT as a direct command, to check that you have them correct. For instance key in PRINT (8*2.6/5)*2/3 and press NEWLINE (ENTER). The result will be printed on the screen. If a sequence of direct assignments of values to variables is keyed in first (using LET A = 4 (NEWLINE/ENTER), LET B = 3 (NEWLINE/ENTER), etc.) then variable expressions may be evaluated.

Using this facility you should experiment with a variety of expressions until you feel confident that you have understood the way in which expressions are evaluated, and the way you have to formulate an expression in BASIC to ensure it returns the desired result.

EXAMPLES

1 Evaluation of $a + b - c$

In BASIC: A + B – C

Operators have equal priority;

(1) Left to Right A + B

(2) L → R (A + B) – C

2 Evaluation of $\frac{a.b}{c}$, $(a \times b) \div c$

In BASIC A*B/C

* has same priority as /

(1) L → R A*B

(2) L → R (A*B)/C

3 Evaluation of $a.(\frac{b}{c})$, $a \times (b \div c)$

In BASIC A*(B/C)

(1) Brackets first (B/C)

(2) Multiplication A*(B/C)

But notice we could write the expression *without brackets* in BASIC as B/C*A

This is evaluated:

(1) L → R (B/C)

(2) L → R (B/C)*A

which gives the correct result.

4 Evaluation of $(b^2 - 6c)^2 + 5$

In ZX81 BASIC notation: (B**2 – 6*C)**2 + 5

(1) Inside bracket; exponentiation B**2

(2) Inside bracket; multiplication 6*C

(3) Inside bracket; subtraction (B**2) – (6*C)

(4) Exponentiation ((B**2) – (6*C))**2
(5) Addition (((B**2) – (6*C))**2) + 5

In Spectrum BASIC notation: (B ↑ 2 – 6*C) ↑ 2 + 5
(1) Inside bracket; exponentiation B ↑ 2
(2) Inside bracket; multiplication 6*C
(3) Inside bracket; subtraction (B ↑ 2) – (6*C)
(4) Exponentiation ((B ↑ 2) – (6*C)) ↑ 2
(5) Addition (((B ↑ 2) – (6*C)) ↑ 2) + 5

5 Computer evaluation of $a.b - \dfrac{c^3}{d} + \dfrac{(e-f)}{g}$

In ZX81 BASIC notation: A*B – C**3/D + (E – F)/G
(1) brackets E – F
(2) exponentiation C**3
(3) multiplication/ division L → R A*B C**3/D (E – F)/G
(4) addition/ subtraction L → R (A*B) – (C**3/D) + (E – F)/G

In Spectrum BASIC notation: A*B – C ↑ 3/D + (E – F)/G
(1) brackets E – F
(2) exponentiation C ↑ 3
(3) multiplication/ division L → R A*B C ↑ 3/D (E – F)/G
(4) addition/ subtraction L → R (A*B) – (C ↑ 3/D) + (E – F)/G

6 Evaluation of $-7\emptyset + 2 \times 4^2 \times 3 - 3 \times 7$

In ZX81 BASIC notation:	– 7Ø + 2 * 4**2 * 3 – 3 * 7
Priority 1Ø	4**2
	16
Priority 9 Negation	– 7Ø
Priority 8 L → R	2 * 16 * 3 3 * 7
	96 21
Priority 6	– 7Ø + 96 – 21
Result	5
In Spectrum BASIC	– 7Ø + 2 * 4 ↑ 2 * 3 – 3 * 7
Priority 1Ø	4 ↑ 2
	16

Priority 9 Negation	– 7Ø			
Priority 8 L → R		2 *	16 * 3 96	3 * 7 21
Priority 6	– 7Ø	+	96	– 21
Result			5	

Exercises

1 Write the order in which the following BASIC expression is evaluated:

– A + ((B**3/C) – (A**2/D))*(E + F)/G (ZX81)
– A + ((B ↑ 3/C) – (A ↑ 2/D))*(E + F)/G (Spectrum)

2 Write down the BASIC expressions for:

(i) $(u^2 + 2as)^{½}$
(ii) $ut + \frac{1}{2} at^2$
(iii) $\frac{b + (4ac)^{½}}{2a}$
(iv) $(X^a)^{1/6}$

Work out the order in which each of the expressions is evaluated. Test your results on the computer.

J3: Number

A positive or negative decimal number whose magnitude is between an approximate *minimum* of:

$$\pm 3 \times 1Ø^{-39}$$

and an approximate *maximum* of:

$$\pm 2 \times 1Ø^{38}$$

Zero is included in this range.

The smallest number the computer can handle is

$$2.9387359 \times 1Ø^{-39}$$

The largest is:

$$1.7Ø14118 \times 1Ø^{38}$$

The computer stores and calculates numbers internally to an accuracy of nine or ten digits, but prints out the results of calculations to eight significant figures only, rounding where necessary.

J4: The E Notation

The E or EXPONENT or scientific notation is the notation computers use for input and output of numbers having a large

number of decimal digits. E should be taken to read: 'times ten to the power of'. For example:

1.73 E5

is

1.73 times 10 to the power of 5
= 1.73*105 (1.73*10 ↑ 5 in Spectrum notation)**
= 173000.

Similarly:

3.8 E – 7

is

3.8 times 10 to the power of – 7
= 3.8*10 – 7 (3.8*10 ↑ – 7 in Spectrum notation)**
= .00000038.

The computer will accept any number keyed-in in this form and will print out numbers in this notation when their values are outside a certain range.

For large positive and negative numbers the E notation is automatically used by the computer for numbers

$$>= 10^{13}$$

Numbers up to this figure are first rounded to 8 significant figures and trailing zeros are added until 10^{13} is reached.

Key in and run this program:

```
10  LET A = 9.9999993E12
20  PRINT A
30  LET A = A + 1E5
40  GOTO 20
```

Change line 20 to read:

```
20  LPRINT TAB 10;A
```

to get a listing of the result on the printer.

For small positive and negative numbers the E notation is automatically used for numbers:

$$<= 10^{-6}$$

To see this in action, key in and run the program below:

```
10  LET A = 1.000001E – 5
20  PRINT A
30  LET A = A – (1E – 12)
40  GOTO 20
```

Change line 20 to:

```
20  LPRINT TAB 10;A
```

if you want a printer listing of the changeover.

Exercises

1 Key in and run the following simple program, which illustrates how numbers are printed, the E notation and the largest number which may be obtained.

```
10  LET A = 1
20  LET A = A*10
30  PRINT A
40  GOTO 20
```

With the ZX81 press CONT and NEWLINE (ENTER) when the screen becomes full, and the message 5/30 appears on the bottom of the screen to indicate no more room on the screen. The Spectrum will display the 'scroll?' prompt.

Notice the change to the E notation. Note that the program finally stops itself on the ZX81 with the error message '6/20', which indicates an arithmetic overflow (error code 6) as a result of line 20, i.e. the number is too large for the computer to handle. The Spectrum's response is more precise; the error code in this instance will read: '6 Number too big, 20:1'.

2 Change line 10 of the program to each of the following and run the program each time.

a) 10 LET A = 1.000000000
b) 10 LET A = 1.1111111
c) 10 LET A = 1.7
d) 10 LET A = 1.7014118
e) 10 LET A = 1.71

What conclusion do you draw?

3 To show that negative numbers behave in the same way, change line 10 to the following and run the program.

a) 10 LET A = − 1
b) 10 LET A = − 1.7
c) 10 LET A = − 1.7014118
d) 10 LET A = − 1.71

4 To show how small numbers are handled by your computer a similar program divides a number (A) by increasing powers of 10.

Key in the program and run it.

```
10  LET A = 1
20  LET A = A/10
30  PRINT A
40  GOTO 20
```

Note the change of notation.

Notice that after 1E − 38 the computer prints zeros indefinitely, i.e. it has reached the smallest number it can register.

5 Change line 10 to

a) 10 LET A = 3
b) 10 LET A = 2.9

and re-run the program each time.

Notice that 2.9387359E − 39 is the smallest number before zero.

Write this number out in full.

Can you think of any applications for very large and very small numbers?

6 Change the values of A in the program to negative values and confirm that small negative numbers behave in the same way.

PROGRAMS TO SAVE IN YOUR TAPE LIBRARY

The following two programs should be keyed in, run, listed and saved for your tape library. They both do what the previous programs did but in addition give a printed copy of the results.

```
10 REM "LARGE NUMBERS"
20 REM** PROGRAM MULTIPLIES +
   AND - NUMBERS INPUT FROM
   THE KEYBOARD BY POWERS O
   F 10 **
30 REM **KEY IN VALUES FOR A O
   F +-1.,+-1.1111111,+-1.7, +
   -1.7014118,+- 1.71.**
40 INPUT A
50 LET N=0
60 PRINT A*(10**N)
70 LPRINT TAB 10;A*(10**N)
80 LET N=N+1
90 GOTO 60
```

For the Spectrum, replace ** by ↑ in lines 60 and 70.

```
10 REM "SMALL NUMBERS"
20 REM**PROGRAM SHOWS PRINTING
   OF SMALL NUMBERS**
30 REM**INPUT VALUES OF A AS +
   -1, +-2.9,+-3.**
40 INPUT A
50 LET N=0
60 PRINT A*(10**N)
70 LPRINT TAB 10;A*(10**N)
80 LET N=N-1
90 GOTO 60
```

J5: Rounding

ROUNDING UP

The computer will print out computed values to an accuracy of 8 significant figures, ignoring leading zeros.

Digits after the 8th significant one will be rounded up. For example, if we key in (as a direct command, followed by NEWLINE/ENTER):

PRINT Ø.111111111 + Ø.888888888

the answer on the screen is 1.Try

PRINT Ø.ØØØØ111111

showing 1Ø digits can be held exactly.

Adding a one on the end forces the use of the E notation.

ROUNDING DOWN

The INT function returns the nearest integer of the expression X, which is < = X, i.e. it rounds down.

e.g. INT 3.9 = 3
INT – 2.8 = – 3
INT (4 – 8.7 + Ø.8) = – 4

Try printing these functions. Notice that for negative numbers – 6 is *less* than – 5, and so on. To round to the *nearest* integer add Ø.5 to the number first:

e.g. INT (3.9 + Ø.5) = 4
INT (2.4 + Ø.5) = 2
INT (– 1.7 + Ø.5) = – 2
INT (– 2.3 + Ø.5) = – 2

Notice this assumes that Ø.5 rounds to 1.

INT (1.5 + Ø.5) = 2
INT (– 1.5 + Ø.5) = – 1

Notice we don't have to enter the zero before the decimal point on the computer (though it doesn't matter if we do), it's in that form here for clarity.

J6: How Numbers are Handled

All computers perform their arithmetic and processing using the BINARY NUMBER SYSTEM

In the binary system only two digits are used, 1 and Ø. A group of 8 *b*inary dig*its* (bits) is called a BYTE, and we communicate with the computer in Decimal Notation. This is rather more convenient than using Binary. Conversion from Decimal to Binary and vice versa is thus necessary and occurs inside the computer.

One BYTE is equivalent to a single character of the computer's character set. A byte represents a number between Ø and 255 (decimal). This is why the character codes are in this range (see Section P). A group of 8 zeros and ones can have 2^8 (= 256) different states.

A digit or number is represented by one or several bytes according to its context in the computer.

A character input to the computer or output to the screen or printer is held in one byte. Program line numbers, which are whole numbers 1 to 9999, are held in two bytes.

Numbers are held in a form which occupies five bytes. The point to be noted here is that conversion from decimal to binary and back is involved in the operation of the computer, and this conversion is not always exact. This must be allowed for in certain circumstances, especially where the computer is asked to check whether two numbers are equal. A difference in the binary form of the number, *however small*, will cause the computer to decide they are not equal. In testing two numbers for equality, therefore, if non-integer values have been utilised, and the value of one number arrived at by calculation, the equivalence check should be replaced by assessing the *difference*. A statement such as:

```
IF ABS(A - B) < 1E - 4 THEN...
```

which checks that the difference between the numbers is less than .ØØØ1, can be used instead of IF A = B THEN...., if either A or B has been calculated.

The forms in which numbers are held in the computer are considered in detail in Section U – the Computer Memory.

J7: Function

We define a FUNCTION as

Y = F(X)

'Y equals some function of X, F(X)'

A function is the mathematical relationship between two variables X and Y such that for each value of X there is a unique value of Y.

Y takes the function value and is the DEPENDENT VARIABLE.

X is the ARGUMENT – the INDEPENDENT VARIABLE.

F is the function NAME, e.g. square root, sine, natural logarithm.

In a program statement we write, for example:

```
100 LET Y = SQR(X)
```

The argument X can be a single variable, a number or an expression. If X is a single variable or a number it does not need brackets. If it is an expression it requires brackets so that the expression is evaluated before the function is applied to it (so that SQR 9 + 7 gives 1Ø, whilst SQR (9 + 7) gives 4). For example:

```
100 LET Y = SQR 9
100 LET Y = SQR(B**2 - 4*A*C)  (B↑2 on the Spectrum)
```

We see that a function is a mathematical operation which gives a number. It is treated in BASIC as a numeric expression, with priority 11.

The standard mathematical and trigonometric functions are important timesavers for programmers. They are the same as the function keys on scientific calculators. Other functions (utility functions) control or monitor the handling of data by BASIC rather than perform mathematics.

If the functions were not available in BASIC we would need to write separate programs to undertake their tasks every time we had need of them!

J8: List of Functions used in Sinclair BASIC

In this list of functions X is the argument. X is a variable, a number or an expression. If an expression, X must be in brackets. Each of the individual functions will be discussed in more detail later in this section.

1. Standard Mathematical Functions:

ABS (X) – gives the absolute value of X
EXP (X) – gives e^X, value of e raised to the power X
INT (X) – gives the largest integer <= X, i.e. rounds down
LN (X) – gives natural logarithm (value of $\log_e X$)
SQR (X) – value of $\sqrt{X}$ or $X^{1/2}$ (X positive)
PI – 3.14159265 i.e. value of π, PI, which is how it prints on screen
SGN (X) – gives sign of X, i.e. whether X is +ve, –ve or zero.

2. Trigonometric Functions

SIN (X) – value of sine X (X in radians)
COS (X) – value of cosine X (X in radians)
TAN (X) – value of tangent X (X in radians)
ACS (X) – angle in radians whose cosine is X – arccosine X(–1 <= X <= 1)
ASN (X) – angle in radians whose sine is X – arcsine X (–1 <= X <= 1)
ATN (X) – angle in radians whose tangent is X – arctangent X

3. Special Mathematical Functions

RND A random number generating function; gives the next pseudo random number N from a fixed series of random numbers (Ø <= N < 1).
RAND (= RAND Ø) starts the sequence of random numbers in an unknown position.
RAND N (Ø <= N <= 65535) makes RND always return to the same value, if N is the same.

4. Character and String Functions

CHR$(X) — Ø<=X <=255 returns the single character whose code is X.

CODE A$ — When applied to the string A$, it returns the code of the first character in the string or Ø if the string is empty (null string).

LEN A$ — Returns the number of characters in the string.

VAL A$ — Turns a string in number representation into *the* number for calculation (e.g. A$ = "12.4", VAL A$ = 12.4).

STR$ N — Turns the number N into the string "N".

5. Printing Functions used in the form PRINT F(X)

TAB (X) — Places the print position in column X. If X>32 then column number is the remainder when X is divided by 32. If it involves back spacing, goes on to next line. Rounds X to nearest integer.

AT (X), (Y) — Starts printing at line X, column Y
Ø <= X <= 21   Ø <= Y <= 31
Rounds X and Y to nearest integer.

6. Special Functions

INKEY$ — No argument. Reads keyboard and senses what key is being pressed at that time. Returns key being pressed as a string, e.g. "A" or "8". If no key is pressed the null string is returned.

PEEK X — Ø <= X <= 65535 Returns the value of the byte at address X in RAM or ROM memory.

USR N — Returns the contents of a pair of CPU registers after running a machine code program from address N.

N.B. For the Spectrum's additional functions, see Section W. The above functions, common to both the ZX81 and the Spectrum, are the ones used in the main body of the text.

J9: The Function Characters

Each of the functions in Sinclair BASIC is represented on the keyboard as a single character word.

You don't have to type the function name letter by letter (if you try to it won't work), just press the particular function key.

Each function character has a special character code and is part of the computer's character set. Each of the Function

characters on the ZX81 is situated at the same position on each key, i.e. bottom outside.

To obtain the function the ZX81 must be in FUNCTION MODE, with the F-cursor on the screen.

On the Spectrum, all functions are obtained in the Extended mode with the E-cursor on the screen (for further details see Section W1). All FUNCTIONS treated here are in green above the key on the Spectrum, with the exception of ASN, ACS, ATN which are in red below the associated SIN, COS and TAN functions, although they are still obtained in the E-mode.

The FUNCTION/EXTENDED MODE only lasts for one function. To obtain successive functions this mode must be repeatedly entered.

J10: The Function Character Set

Character	Code (ZX81)	Code (Spectrum)
SIN	199	178
COS	200	179
TAN	201	180
INT	207	186
RAND	64	249
STR$	213	193
CHR$	214	194
CODE	196	175
PEEK	211	190
TAB	194	173
ASN	202	181
ACS	203	182
ATN	204	183
SGN	209	188
ABS	210	189
SQR	208	187
VAL	197	176
LEN	198	177
USR	212	192
LN	205	184
EXP	206	185
AT	193	172
INKEY$	65	166
NOT	215	195
π (PI)	66	167

These are the function characters as represented on the ZX81 keyboard. NOT is dealt with in Section R and INKEY$ in Section K. Note that ARCSIN, ARCCOS and ARCTAN are used on the ZX81 keyboard but print as ASN, ACS, ATN, and π prints as PI.

J11: The Standard Mathematical Functions

ABS (X)

Returns the absolute value or modulus of the value X. X may be a number, variable or expression.

ABS(X) gives us the positive value of X. For example:

10 PRINT ABS(– 3.7) gives 3.7

10 PRINT ABS (4) gives 4

Exercises

Key in and run this program:

```
10  INPUT A
20  INPUT B
30  PRINT TAB 3;A; TAB 10;B
40  PRINT TAB 3; ABS (A – B)
50  GOTO 10
```

Input positive and negative values for A and B.

Now change line 40 to:

```
40  PRINT TAB 3; ABS (A*B)
```

and input some more values. Try replacing the * with ** (↑ Spectrum), or using ABS (SQR A).

N.B. ABS (– 3**3) , or expressions in similar form will *not* work as the ** (↑ Spectrum) operator only works for *positive* first operands.

EXP (X)

Where X is a number or an expression EXP (X) gives the value of the constant e raised to the power of the value of X

e = 2.7183

e.g. 10 PRINT EXP (3.4)

i.e. 10 PRINT (2.71833.4) (2.7183 ↑ 3.4 on Spectrum)**

The function EXP is the inverse to LN.

Exercises

1 Using log tables write a program to check the values of e^x given in the log tables.

2 Write a program which will calculate Q from the expression:

$Q = Qo.e^{-t/rc}$ (In BASIC Q = QO* EXP(– T/R*C))

If you know anything about electricity, you might recognise this expression.

3 Key in this program. It calculates a value for e from the formula:

e = (1 + 1/N)**N (↑ N on Spectrum)

where N is very large. Spectrum users should replace ** by ↑ in lines 3Ø and 4Ø.

```
1Ø  REM "VALUE OF E"
2Ø  LET I = 1
3Ø  LET N = 1Ø**I    [ ↑ Spectrum]
4Ø  LET E = (1 + 1/N)**N
5Ø  PRINT TAB 1;N;TAB 12;E
6Ø  LET I = I + 1
7Ø  IF I = 5 THEN STOP
8Ø  GOTO 3Ø
```

LN (X)

Gives the value of the natural logarithm.

LN (X) = $\mathbf{Log_e}$ (x)

Note that $\mathbf{log_{1Ø}}$ (X) (common logarithm)

= (LN(X))/(LN 1Ø)

The LN function is the inverse of EXP

So: If EXP (X) = Y

Then (X) = LN(Y).

LN (Y) is the natural logarithm of Y. The antilog is EXP(LN(Y)). The normal log operations can be used if appropriate, as with common logs. For example EXP(LN (X) + LN (Y)) gives the product of X and Y.

Exercises

1
```
1Ø  LET Y = 1
2Ø  PRINT TAB 3;Y; TAB 1Ø;EXP (LN Y)
3Ø  LET Y = Y + 1
4Ø  GOTO 2Ø
```
Key in and run this program which proves the relationship between the EXP and LN functions.

2 Change 3Ø to: 3Ø LET Y = Y*1Ø and run again.

SQR (X)

The function SQR returns the square root of (X), √(X) or $\mathbf{X^{0.5}}$. For example:

```
PRINT SQR 9              gives 3
PRINT SQR 23             gives 4.7958315
PRINT SQR (19 + 17)      gives 6
PRINT SQR (ABS  - 25)    gives 5
```

SGN (X)

SGN (X) returns + 1 if (X) is positive, Ø if (X) is zero, – 1 if (X) is negative.
SGN is short for Sign or Signum (Signum doesn't sound like Sine). For example:

```
SGN 23                 gives   1
SGN  - 5               gives - 1
SGN (3 - 3)            gives   Ø
SGN 1                  gives   1
SGN (25 - (2*23))      gives - 1
```

π PI

π (which prints on the screen as PI) is a function which has no argument. It returns the value of π as 3.1415927.

3.1415927 is what prints on screen for PI. How would you test whether the computer held any more digits of PI in memory? What happens when you take away 3 from PI?

J12: Trigonometric Functions

SIN COS TAN

The functions SIN (X), COS(X) and TAN(X) give the value of the sine, cosine, and tangent of the number or expression X, which is an angular measure. X must be in RADIANS.

We normally express angles in DEGREES.

$$1 \text{ DEGREE} = \frac{\text{PI}}{18\emptyset} \text{ RADIANS } \left(1^\circ = \frac{\pi}{18\emptyset} \text{ radians}\right)$$

To convert degrees to radians multiply by PI/18Ø. For example, if Y is our measure of angle in *degrees* then:

SIN (Y*PI/18Ø)

gives the correct value of Sine Y.

Exercises

1 Generate a table of values for SIN (X), COS (X) and TAN (X)

for every 2Ø degrees in the range Ø – 36Ø degrees.

2 Write a program to verify the trigonometric formula:

$$SIN^2(X) + COS^2(X) = 1$$
$$1 + TAN^2(X) = SEC^2(X)$$

3 Write a program to calculate the area of a triangle from a knowledge of the length of 3 sides and an angle.

ACS ASN ATN

The functions:

ACS (X), ASN (X), ATN (X)

give the arc cosine, the arc sine and the arc tangent, respectively, of (X).

The returned value is the angle in RADIANS for which the cosine, sine or tangent would be given by the value of (X).

To get the angle in degrees multiply by 18Ø/PI e.g. Y = 18Ø/PI*ACS(X) gives arcsin (X) in degrees.

Notice these functions print as above, but appear on the ZX81 keyboard as ARCSIN, ARCCOS, ARCTAN.

J13: Special Functions

Random number generators are useful for games and simulation in statistics. The numbers generated are part of a very long sequence of numbers (there are 65536 of them) and are in fact only 'pseudo-random', but good enough for our needs.

RND

RND gives a random number greater or equal to zero but less than one.

1Ø LET A = RND

assigns a number in the range Ø < = N <1 to the variable A.

Notice RND has no argument.

If we key in PRINT RND we get a number like .ØØ112519Ø4 or Ø.43715682 which is eight or ten digits long and is not much use to anybody in this form.

We need to be able to generate random numbers within a useful range, according to our purposes:

1. <u>To obtain a Random Number Ø – 9</u>

To obtain a random number from Ø – 9 we must multiply our

function by 1Ø and take the integer value.

i.e. PRINT INT (RND*1Ø)

RND*1Ø gives random numbers between Ø.ØØØØØØØØ and 9.9999999. INT( ) will round these values down to integers Ø to 9.

2. Numbers 1-1Ø

Although Ø to 9 gives us ten values the range 1 to 1Ø would be more useful. This is obtained by adding one to the RND function:

PRINT INT (RND*1Ø + 1)

Suppose we wanted random numbers generated for simulating a dice roll, we would use:

PRINT INT (RND*6 + 1)

3. Random Numbers for a Card Game

There are 4 suits, with 13 cards per suit = 52 cards. So if we used:

PRINT INT (RND*52 + 1)

we could select cards at random.

Think about how you could identify the suits and not deal the same card twice.

4. Tossing a Coin

There are two outcomes, head or tails, so:

```
1Ø  LET A =  INT(RND*2 + 1)
2Ø  IF A = 1 THEN GOTO 5Ø
3Ø  PRINT "TAILS"
4Ø  GOTO 1Ø
5Ø  PRINT "HEADS"
6Ø  GOTO 1Ø
```

This program will toss coins until we use BREAK.

RAND N

RAND is a keyword and is used for controlling the randomness of RND.

The computer has a fixed sequence of 65536 jumbled up numbers. RAND N will start RND reading numbers from the Nth number in the sequence.

Key in and run this program to prove the above:

```
1Ø  RAND 7
2Ø  LET C = 1
3Ø  PRINT RND
4Ø  LET C = C + 1
```

```
50  IF C<6 THEN GOTO 30
60  GOTO 10
```

Not amazingly random after all!

Exercises

1 Write a program which throws three dice and prints the values thrown across the screen.
2 Write a program to check that the number generated by RND using RAND N is given by RND = (75*(N + 1) – 1/65536).
3 Modify the coin tossing program to count the number of times heads or tails have come up (you need one variable for each). When you've stopped the program by pressing BREAK, you can then access the values by keying in PRINT HEADS, or whatever your variable name is, as a direct command.
4 Write a program to print four groups of three random numbers in the range 1 to 52.

SECTION K: STRINGS

K1: Strings

A string is a set of characters enclosed by quotation marks, e.g. "THIS IS A STRING" or the null string (no characters "").

Typical Strings: "BALL OF STRING"
"JANUARY 1ST 1982"
"URGHH!"
"FAB ** – + /!3"
"   " (String of spaces)
"1234"
"" (Null string)

Computers handle two kinds of DATA:

NUMERIC – numbers

ALPHANUMERIC – names or TEXT.

The way a computer deals with text is called STRING HANDLING. Strings deal with ALPHANUMERIC information.

The sequence of alphanumeric characters is handled in a string as a single unit of data.

Characters are defined as LITERALS when placed inside quotes " ". They are taken literally to represent themselves. Strings are therefore literals.

Characters are IDENTIFIERS where they are not enclosed in quotes. Thus, for example, A represents or identifies a numeric variable and A$ identifies a string variable.

Strings can either be of FIXED LENGTH – e.g. always 1Ø characters long – or VARIABLE LENGTH. The fixed length is determined by the string dimension instruction:

DIM A$ (N)

where N is the length in characters.

Characters which cannot be used in strings

A string cannot contain a character that is a line terminator: NEWLINE (ENTER) or TAB. Nor can it contain any of the following:

EDIT
GRAPHICS
RUBOUT (DELETE)
FUNCTION
BREAK
"   (single quotes)

All other characters in your computer's character set can be used. Run the program which checks this:

```
10  INPUT A$
20  PRINT A$
30  GOTO 10
```

Now try and input some of the above characters.

Examples of the sort of text we may want the computer to handle are:

- a telephone directory
- names and addresses
- a timetable
- expenses details

Computers store all this textual information as strings.

String manipulation by the computer would, for our first example, need to deal with:

creating the telephone directory
sorting the names and numbers into the correct order
searching the directory for somebody's number
revising the directory, i.e. updating or adding an entry
printing out the directory in whole or part.

K2: Quotes and Quote Image

QUOTES

All strings are enclosed in quotes "" when:
(1) They are to be INPUT from the keyboard, as in a program line such as: 10 INPUT A$. When the line is run the [L] cursor on the screen appears already enclosed in quotes "[L]". You key in just the characters wanted in the string.
(2) When used in programs with the PRINT instruction, e.g. 20 PRINT "STRING".
(3) When assigned in a program to a string variable, e.g. 30 LET A$ = "STRING".

THE QUOTE IMAGE KEY ON THE ZX81

The QUOTE IMAGE is a special single character on the shift keyboard of the ZX81.

""

It is used to write ordinary quotes in the middle of a string.

e.g. 10 PRINT "SAY ""HELLO"" TOO"

When the line is run the double quotes will be printed on the screen as single quotes:

SAY "HELLO" TOO

A special character is needed as two single quotes won't work.

Key in and try to run each of the following lines:

```
10  PRINT " SAY "HELLO" TOO"
10  PRINT "SAY"; "HELLO"; "TOO"
10  PRINT " SAY """HELLO""" TOO"
```

The Spectrum has no QUOTE IMAGE character. Instead, you must put two quotes for every one you want printed. For example, to obtain double quotation marks you type in PRINT""""" """""". Single quotes are obtained with PRINT"""" """". Program listings look the same for both machines.

K3: String Input

On running 10 INPUT A$ the letter cursor appears at the bottom of the screen with quotes round it, prompting you to key in characters for the string

" [L] "

On the Spectrum this can also be the C-cursor – " [C] ".

STOPPING STRING INPUT

When keying in the characters for the string to be input notice that BREAK and STOP have no effect.

To escape (1) Use the ← key to get [L] outside the quotes.
(2) Press STOP, NEWLINE (ENTER)
or
press [RUBOUT (DELETE)] [STOP] [NEWLINE (ENTER)].

There is a special form of string input, using the INKEY$ instruction:

INKEY$

When INKEY$ is encountered by the computer it reads the keyboard to determine if a key is being pressed. It *does not wait* for input like the INPUT instruction. If a key is being pressed it returns the string containing the [L] mode character of the key being pressed. If no key is being pressed it returns the empty string "".

The Spectrum returns the [C] mode character with INKEY$ if in the CAPS mode.

We can spend as long as we want before we input a string with the INPUT command, since the cursor will remain on screen. If we want to take advantage of the fact that, unlike INPUT, INKEY$ does not require NEWLINE(ENTER) to be pressed, we must arrange a delay.

Try this program:

```
1Ø   PRINT "PRESS A KEY WHEN READY"
2Ø   IF INKEY$ = "" THEN GOTO 2Ø    (no spaces)
3Ø   LET A$ = INKEY$
4Ø   PRINT "YOU PRESSED ";A$
```

Line 2Ø sends the program back to the beginning of line 2Ø as long as no key has been pressed. Line 3Ø makes A$ the single character string returned by INKEY$ when a key is pressed.

Due to a design error the Spectrum has far less predictable keyboard scanning using INKEY$ than the ZX81. If you type in the program as above on the Spectrum it will work about half of the time. The rest of the time it will skip over line 3Ø. This program will work every time though:

```
1Ø   PRINT " PRESS A KEY WHEN READY"
2Ø   PAUSE Ø
3Ø   PRINT "YOU PRESSED ";INKEY$
```

Experiment with the two versions to see this problem in action. The action of PAUSE Ø is to stop until a key is pressed. The first key pressed will be the INKEY$. PAUSE will be dealt with later, but remember this quirk of the Spectrum, and this method of dealing with it. The rule is to use PAUSE Ø immediately before INKEY$ is used in a program line, to wait for input.

Now enter and run this program:

```
1Ø PRINT "PRESS 6"
2Ø IF INKEY$ = ""
   THEN GOTO 2Ø (on the Spectrum 2Ø PAUSE Ø)
3Ø IF INKEY$ = "6" THEN GOTO 6Ø
4Ø PRINT "FOLLOW INSTRUCTIONS"
5Ø GOTO 2Ø
6Ø PRINT "ENDING PROGRAM NOW"
7Ø STOP
```

Line 2Ø does the same as before, but line 3Ø now checks that the right key has been pressed. Notice the 6 must be enclosed in quotes, because INKEY$ returns a *string*. If 6 was pressed, the program goes to line 6Ø. If any other key was pressed, it goes to 4Ø, prints the message, and then is sent back (line 5Ø) to line 2Ø, which waits for another key to be pressed.

Games programs, which require interaction, often use INKEY$ in a loop, so that every time the program loops, it checks which key, if any, is being pressed.

K4: Length of a String

LEN

The length of a specified string A$ is obtained by using the function: LEN A$. The length is given as the *number* of characters and is the *current* length of the string.

Spaces are included in the length of a string.

EXAMPLES

1 10 LET A$ = "SINCLAIR"
  20 PRINT LEN A$
  Check that the result is 8.
2 10 LET A$ = "A   B" (9 spaces between A and B)
  20 PRINT A$
  30 PRINT LEN A$
  Key in and run.
3 10 LET A$ = "PRINT"
  20 PRINT A$
  30 PRINT LEN A$

Key in the program first with PRINT formed from separate keys, and then change line 10 so that PRINT is formed by pressing the [PRINT] key.

Why are the answers different?

4 10 INPUT A$
  20 PRINT A$, LEN A$
  30 GOTO 10

K5: Null Strings

A string with no characters is called a null string. For example:

LET A$ = ""

The length of the string is 0.

A string which contains *spaces* is *not* a null string. A space is a *character* obtained by pressing [SPACE]. The null string is returned by INKEY$ if no key is being pressed.

Exercises

1 Key in and run the following program:

10 LET A$ = ""

```
20  PRINT A$
30  PRINT LEN A$
```

2 Key in and run this program:

```
10  LET A$ = "    "
20  PRINT A$
30  PRINT LEN A$
```

K6: String and String Array Variables

A$

is a *string variable* used to store strings. It consists of a *single letter* (A to Z), followed by the dollar sign.

Twenty-six variables of this type are thus possible.

The Spectrum accepts upper and lower case letters, but treats, e.g. k$ as the same string as K$.

A$(N)

is a *string array variable* or *string list variable* where N refers to the number of strings in the list. String lists must be dimensioned as an array before the string array variable can be used, by the DIM (DIMension) instruction.

Using the array notation, an unlimited number of string variables are possible.

Again, the Spectrum accepts upper and lower case letters, but does not differentiate, e.g. b$(N) and B$(N) are the same.

Caution: A$(N) can have two meanings in a program.
(1) It can refer to the N'th *character* in a string A$.
(2) It can refer to the N'th *string* in a list or array of strings. In this case *the string array must previously have been dimensioned* with a DIM A$(N) instruction.

K7: String and String Array Dimension

STRING DIMENSION

DIM A$(N)

sets a fixed length of N characters for the string. For example:

```
10  DIM A$(6)
```

sets a length of 6 characters for the string A$.

If strings of length <N (less than N characters) are assigned or input, then space characters are added to make up the complete string of length N. Spaces do not show up on the screen when they are printed! (To check they are in the string we can ask for their character set code to be printed using the CODE instruction. We'll get to this later.)

If more characters than the number allowed in the DIM A$(N) statement are assigned from INPUT or LET statements they are ignored. If strings are not dimensioned their length is effectively unlimited.

The DIM statement fixes the length of a string until changed by another DIM statement. LEN is thus not useful when strings are dimensioned.

STRING ARRAY DIMENSION

The DIM statement for string arrays has the form:

DIM A$ (N,L)

where N = number of strings and L = the fixed length of each string. A may be any single letter A to Z, but must NOT be the same as a simple string variable. Each string is set to contain L spaces initially.

For example, DIM A$(3,4) will reserve storage space for 3 strings, A$(1), A$(2), A$(3), each of length 4, in the string array A$.

K8: String and String Array Assignment

STRING ASSIGNMENT

Strings are assigned to string variables using the LET or INPUT instructions. For example:

LET A$ = "A STRING"

or INPUT A$

This establishes a value for the string.

As we shall see later, the value may be a literal value in quotation marks, or a string or substring value.

STRING ARRAY ASSIGNMENT

```
 5 DIM A$(3,9)
10 LET A$(1) = "SINCLAIR"
20 LET A$(2) = "COMPUTING"
30 LET A$(3) = "COURSE"
```

assigns 3 strings to the string array variable A$(3).

We can also use an INPUT instruction:

```
10 INPUT A$(1)
20 INPUT A$(2)
30 INPUT A$(3)
```

Exercises

1 Key in and run this program:

```
10 DIM A$(2,9)
20 LET A$(1) = "PERSONAL"
30 LET A$(2) = "COMPUTING "
40 PRINT A$(1), A$(2)
```

2 Now key in and run this. Input different strings of varying length. The string length is set at 8 in line 10.

```
10 DIM A$(3,8)
20 INPUT A$(1)
30 INPUT A$(2)
40 INPUT A$(3)
50 PRINT A$(1)
60 PRINT A$(2)
70 PRINT A$(3)
```

3 Key in and run this program:

```
10 DIM A$(6)
20 INPUT A$
30 PRINT A$
40 PRINT LEN A$
50 PRINT A$;"END"
60 GOTO 20
```

line 10 sets a length of 6 characters for A$
line 20 asks you to input a string
line 30 prints the string
line 40 prints the size of the string in terms of characters
line 50 prints END starting directly after the 6th character in the string
line 60 loops us back to input another string

a) INPUT less than 6 characters.
   See that the remaining characters are spaces. Notice that LEN A$ always gives 6 even though different numbers of characters are input for A$.

b) INPUT 8 characters.
   Notice the extra characters are ignored.

K9: Substrings and String Slices

A SUBSTRING or a STRING SLICE is any set of consecutive characters taken in sequence from the parent string. For

example, for the string – "ABCDEFG":

a substring is "CDEF"

or "ABC"

or "G"

A substring can be a single character.

SPECIFYING SUBSTRINGS

A$(P TO Q)

or

"ANYSTRING" (P TO Q)

where P is the first character and Q the last character of the substring wanted in the strings A$ or "ANYSTRING".

SUBSTRING ASSIGNMENT

Any substring is itself a string. We can assign a string to a substring:

```
10  DIM A$(12)
20  LET A$ (1 TO 4) = "JOHN"
30  LET A$ (6 TO 10) = "SMITH"
40  PRINT A$
```

This program assigns strings to substring variables.

EXAMPLES

1 10 PRINT "SINCLAIR" (2 TO 5) prints INCL

2 10 PRINT "SINCLAIR" (TO 3) prints SIN, since 1 is assumed if it is omitted at the start.

3 10 PRINT "SINCLAIR" (3 TO) prints NCLAIR (omitting the character after TO means the last character in the string is assumed).

4 10 PRINT "SINCLAIR" (3 TO 3) prints N.
This is more conveniently written as

```
10  PRINT "SINCLAIR"(3)
```

or

```
10  LET A$ = "SINCLAIR"
20  PRINT A$(3)
```

which prints the 3rd character in A$, exactly as with a literal string.

5 10 PRINT "SINCLAIR" (1 TO 0) prints " "
i.e. gives the null string (no characters).

6 Here is a program that uses names and numbers in single strings:

```
10 LET A$="NAME AGE"
20 LET B$="TOM  16"
30 LET C$="BILL 14"
40 LET D$="JANE 17"
50 PRINT AT 1,6;A$(1 TO 4); AT
     1,14;A$(6 TO 8)
60 PRINT AT 4,6;B$(1 TO 4); AT
     4,14;B$(6 TO 7)
70 PRINT AT 7,6;C$(1 TO 4); AT
     7,14;C$(6 TO 7)
80 PRINT AT 10,6;D$(1 TO 4);
    AT 10,14;D$(6 TO 7)
```

Notice how we spread the print out using substrings.

K1Ø: String Concatenation

A$ + B$

Concatenation means chaining strings together. It is derived from the word catenary meaning a chain. What the computer does is to 'add' them together to form a new string.

"COM" + "PU" + "TER" = "COMPUTER"

```
1Ø   LET A$ = "COM"
2Ø   LET B$ = "PU"
3Ø   LET C$ = "TER"
4Ø   LET T$ = A$ + B$ + C$
5Ø   PRINT T$
```

Note that the + operator is used for string concatenation.

We cannot subtract, multiply, divide strings or raise them to powers, because they are not numbers. Although the 'adding' of concatenation uses the same symbol it is not an arithmetic operation.

Key in and run the example program given above.

Add some DIM statements to the program:

```
2    DIM A$(6)
4    DIM B$(6)
6    DIM C$(6)
```

Run it. You will notice that although the strings are chained they are far apart. Why is this?

Now try this program:

```
1Ø INPUT A$
2Ø INPUT B$
3Ø PRINT A$,B$,A$+B$
```

```
40 LET A$ = A$+B$
50 PRINT A$
60 LET A$=A$+A$
70 PRINT A$
```

Notice in line 40 we have incremented the string by adding B$ on to A$. This gives us a new A$ made up of the old A$ plus B$. The statement in line 60 is equivalent, in string terms, to having a line which for numeric variables says LET A = A + A.

K11: Comparing Strings

The conditional operators:

=   <>   < =   <   > =   >

may be used between strings and string variables using the IF... THEN instructions. For example:

IF A$ = "YES" THEN GOTO ....
IF N$ = B$ THEN PRINT ....
IF A$< = B$ THEN GOTO ....

When the computer compares strings of characters it does so by comparing the codes of each of the characters in sequence. A string is found to be less than another if it comes first in alphabetic order. If the strings contain numbers we should remember that numeric codes are less than alphabetic (letter) codes. This affects comparisons. (See Section P for the character codes.)

Strings are compared in order of characters from left to right. For example:

"A"< "B"
"AB"< "AZ"
"A"< "AA"
"2"< "5"
"A3"< "A4"
"6"< "Q"
"3X"< "4A"

Key in and run the next program. Input the strings above plus others you want to try and it will print out their relative alphabetic orders.

```
 10 INPUT A$
 20 INPUT B$
 30 IF A$<B$ THEN GOTO 70
 40 IF A$=B$ THEN GOTO 90
 50 PRINT A$;">";B$
 60 STOP
 70 PRINT A$;"<"; B$
 80 STOP
 90 PRINT A$;"=";B$
100 STOP
```

This gives us a method for putting names into alphabetic order, like in a telephone directory. We also have a method of searching it, since we can check whether any name in the list is equal to the desired name.

We have already used string equality, but here's another example of string comparison:

```
10 PRINT "DO YOU UNDERSTAND STRINGS?"
20 PRINT "ANSWER YES OR NO"
30 INPUT A$
40 IF A$ = "YES" THEN GO TO 70
50 PRINT "THEN READ THE SECTION AGAIN!"
60 STOP
70 PRINT "YOU ARE A GENIUS!"
80 STOP
```

Key it in and run it. *Do* you understand?

The above assumes the use of capital (upper case) letters only on the Spectrum. For lower case letters, these are all *after* upper case letters in the ordering of strings. So on the Spectrum:

AA<Aa
Z<a
Z1<z1
SMITH<Smith

So any ordering of strings must take this into account. For this text we assume the use of capitals throughout.

Exercises

1 The "TELEPHONE" program sets up a telephone directory with names and telephone numbers. It will search through its lists to find the telephone number corresponding to a given name. Run and analyse the program to find out how it works.

```
 10 REM "TELEPHONE"
 20 REM **PROGRAM SETS UP A TEL
    EPHONE DIRECTORY AND USES IT**
 30 PRINT "HOW MANY NAMES DO YO
    U WISH TO ENTER INTO THE DIRECTO
    RY?"
 40 INPUT N
 50 PRINT
 60 PRINT "INPUT ";N;" NAME (20
    LETTERS) AND NUMBER(8 FIGS) PAIR
    S"
 70 DIM A$(N,20)
 80 DIM B$(N,8)
 90 DIM D$(20)
100 PRINT
```

```
110 PRINT
120 PRINT "NAME";TAB (22);"NUMB
    ER"
130 PRINT
140 FOR F=1 TO N
150 INPUT A$(F)
160 PRINT A$(F);
170 INPUT B$(F)
180 PRINT TAB (22);B$(F)
190 NEXT F
200 PRINT
210 PRINT
220 PRINT "TO CLEAR THE SCREEN
    TO USE THE DIRECTORY PRESS CONT
    AND NEW LINE KEYS"
230 STOP
240 CLS
250 PRINT
260 PRINT "WHAT NAME?"
270 INPUT D$
280 REM **NEXT PART OF THE PROG
    RAM SEARCHES FOR THE NAME**
290 PRINT
300 PRINT D$;
310 FOR F=1 TO N
320 IF A$(F)=D$ THEN GOTO 370
330 NEXT F
340 PRINT
350 PRINT "NAME NOT FOUND"
360 GOTO 260
370 PRINT TAB (22);B$(F)
380 PRINT
390 PRINT
400 PRINT "ANOTHER NAME?(Y/N)"
410 INPUT Q$
420 IF Q$="Y" THEN GOTO 240
430 PRINT
440 PRINT "TO KEEP YOUR DIRECTOR
    Y AFTER SAVING, USE ""GOTO 240""
    WHEN RUNNING THE LOADED PROGRAM
    , NOT ""RUN""."
450 PRINT
460 PRINT "BYE FOR NOW"
470 STOP
```

2 Modify "TELEPHONE" to create your own directory with your friends' names and addresses or birthdays or telephone numbers.

a) Redesign the program
b) Document it
c) Key it in
d) SAVE it
e) Debug it
f) LLIST it
g) SAVE the working version
h) Put it in your personal tape library
i) Enter details in your notebook

K12: Strings and Numbers

In addition to the handling of strings as strings, there are instructions which enable us to convert strings to numbers, numbers to strings, and to usefully manipulate various numerical values of strings and their characters. We have already dealt with LEN. The other available string functions are dealt with here. The first two instructions cover the character set which is dealt with in Section P.

CODE A$

When applied to a string A$ CODE returns the character set code number of the *first* character in a string. For example:

```
10 LET X = CODE "MOTHER"
```

On the ZX81 X becomes 50, the code for M (CODE "M"). When applied to a single character substring, it returns the code of the substring:

```
e.g. 10 LET A$ = "CODE"
     20 PRINT CODE A$(3)
```

prints 41, the CODE for D (CODE "D").

The Spectrum uses a different code to the ZX81 (called ASCII, an international standard). Thus, CODE "MOTHER" is 77, and CODE A$(3) in the above is 68 (= CODE "D").

CODE A$ (M,N)

When applied to a string array CODE returns the character code of the N'th character in the M'th string. For example:

```
10 DIM A$(10,10)
20 LET A$(1) = "SINCLAIR"
30 LET A$(2) = "BASIC"
40 PRINT CODE A$(2,3)
```

will print 38 (CODE"S") on the ZX81, whilst on the Spectrum the 'S' in ASCII code is 83 (there is no significance in one being the reverse of the other!).

CODE A$(2), applied to a string array as above, would return the CODE of the first character in A$(2), just as when applied to a literal string or string variable.

CHR$

When applied to a *number* N, CHR$ N gives the single character *string* in the computer's character set whose code is the number N.

For example, on the ZX81:

CHR$ 49 is "L"
CHR$ 12 is "£"

whilst on the Spectrum CODE "L" is 76 and CODE "£" is 96, so CHR$ 76 gives "L" on the Spectrum, and CHR$ 96 gives "£".

We can treat these characters as elements in a string and make up a word by concatenation. Try this on the ZX81:

```
10  LET A$ = CHR$ 63 + CHR$ 61 + CHR$ 36 + CHR$ 29
20  PRINT A$
```

or this on the Spectrum:

```
10  LET A$ = CHR$ 83 + CHR$ 80 + CHR$ 69 + CHR$ 67
      + CHR$ 84 + CHR$ 82 + CHR$ 85 + CHR$ 77
20  PRINT A$
```

VAL A$

Applying VAL to a string containing only numeric characters and arithmetic or logic operators, returns the result of the arithmetic inside the string.

For example:

```
10  PRINT VAL "1 + 2 + 3"
    prints 6

10  LET A$ = "3"
20  LET B$ = "4"
30  PRINT VAL (A$ + B$)
    prints 7
```

All recognised arithmetic functions can be used:

```
10  PRINT VAL"SQR 16"
    (prints 4)

10  PRINT VAL "ABS  - 29"
    (prints 29)
```

An interesting use of VAL is where alphabetic and numeric information in a string can be treated as substrings. Arithmetic can then be performed on the numeric substring. For example, try this program which gives the total ages of three people in a group.

```
10 LET A$="SMITH  23"
20 LET B$="JONES  34"
30 LET C$="WEST   17"
40 LET T= VAL A$(8 TO 9)+ VAL
   B$(8 TO 9)+ VAL C$(8 TO 9)
50 PRINT A$
60 PRINT B$
70 PRINT C$
80 PRINT ,,"TOTAL AGE ";T;
   " YEARS"
```

STR$

STR$ (N) returns the value of (N), a numeric expression, as a string. For example:

STR$ 3.4 gives "3.4"
STR$ (3*31) gives "93"
STR$ (SQR 4) gives "2"

STR$ is the complementary or opposite function to VAL

To see STR$ in operation, and the complementary functions of VAL and STR$, try this program:

```
10 LET X=3
20 LET Y=0.5
30 LET A$= STR$ (X/Y)
40 PRINT A$, VAL A$
50 LET B$=A$+ STR$ X
60 PRINT B$, VAL B$/2
70 LET C= VAL ( STR$ ( VAL A$+
   VAL B$))
80 PRINT C
```

Exercises

1 Write a program which inputs a number of strings and calculates the total number of characters in each, and the total number of characters in all the strings.
2 Write a program which calculates the total price of items in a shopping list, after receiving and printing out the string inputs of each item and its cost.
3 Write a program which will print a calendar for any month of next year. Key in the month names and lengths as a string in the program.

SECTION L: LOOPS

L1: Loops

A loop is a block of instructions that the computer executes repeatedly until a terminating condition is met.

The usefulness of loops can be seen by considering three forms of a program to print out the first one hundred positive integers.

```
  10  PRINT 1
  20  PRINT 2
  30  PRINT 3
      .....
      .....
      .....
1000  PRINT 100
```

This program, which *does not use a loop*, is 100 statements long. This next program uses a *conditional jump loop* which does the same thing and uses only five statements.

```
10  LET C = 0
20  LET C = C + 1
30  PRINT C
40  IF C < 100 THEN GOTO 20
50  STOP
```

The third program uses a *FOR – NEXT loop* which is the commonest method of looping in BASIC, and the most economical in program lines.

```
10  FOR F = 1 TO 100
20  PRINT F
30  NEXT F
40  STOP
```

All loops have four characteristics:

1. **Initialisation (start value of counter)**
2. **BODY of loop**
3. **Modification of counter**
4. **Exit condition.**

Loop structures may be properly formed in two ways:

1. CONDITIONAL GOTO STATEMENT LOOPS
2. FOR .... NEXT LOOPS

Loops are extremely useful. They allow repeated procedures to be performed, and the values of the counters, which are modified each time the program passes through the body of the loop, may also be used in calculations, if care is taken.

L2: Counters

Here are two examples of the use of the conditional GOTO loop:

```
10 LET C=0
20 LET C=C+1
30 PRINT "COUNTING"
40 IF C <= 10 THEN GOTO 20
50 PRINT "FINISH"
```

```
10 LET C=0
20 LET C=C+1
30 INPUT A
40 PRINT A
50 IF C<10 THEN GOTO 20
60 PRINT "END OF NUMBERS"
```

The variable C is used as a counter in these programs, adding 1 every time the program loops. *If* the value of C is less than the value set *then* the GOTO statement is executed and the program loops. If it is greater then control passes to the next program line. This enables us to control the number of times the program lines within the loop are executed.

Our procedure for using counters in the example programs above is:

1 Initialise the counter
2 Increment the counter (add 1)
3 Do the task
4 Check the counter. If it has not reached the final value then go back to item 2. If it has then program exits from the loop.

Note that we can perform the incrementation of the counter in a different place:

1 Initialise
2 Do the task
3 Increment counter
4 Check the counter. If less than specified value, GOTO 2. If more than specified value, program exits from the loop.

We must be careful to set the conditions properly to achieve our desired result (the correct number of passes through the loop). Look at the first two simple programs above again. How many times will each of them pass through the body of the loop? Which is wrong if we wanted to loop exactly ten times? If you don't see the answer, key them in and run them.

The GOTO statement in the program below enables the program to loop continuously between lines 50 and 80. This would continue indefinitely so it is important to get out of the loop at the appropriate point. This is achieved by line 60 utilising the IF (condition) THEN GOTO (line-number) statement. Notice that the value of the counter (N) is used inside the loop:

```
10 REM "SIMPLE1"
20 PRINT "SEVEN TIMES TABLE"
30 PRINT "UP TO TIMES 20"
40 LET N=0
50 LET N=N+1
60 IF N>20 THEN GOTO 100
70 PRINT N,7*N
80 GOTO 50

100 REM **END**
```

Notice that the counting procedure in this program is set up differently again. Line 50 increments the counter. Line 60 checks the counter value. In this case, the IF – THEN statement has the effect of transferring control *out* of the loop *if* the counter exceeds 20, with the GOTO 100 statement.

The procedure in this case is:

1 Initialise
2 Increment
3 Check counter. If greater than specified value, jump to program end.
4 Body of loop
5 Return to 2.

Key in the program. Run it to check it loops exactly twenty times. Then EDIT line 60, to insert:

75 IF N> 20 THEN GOTO 100

and delete line 60. Now run it. It is surprisingly easy to miss the desired number of loops, if you are not careful with the structure of the loop, and the exit conditions. (Change N>20 in line 75 to N> = 20 and the program will loop the correct number of times).

Different procedures using counters give different program structures. Look at the flowcharts of different counter procedures. Remember that the conditional test can put to use the >, <, > = , < = , = operators, as appropriate.

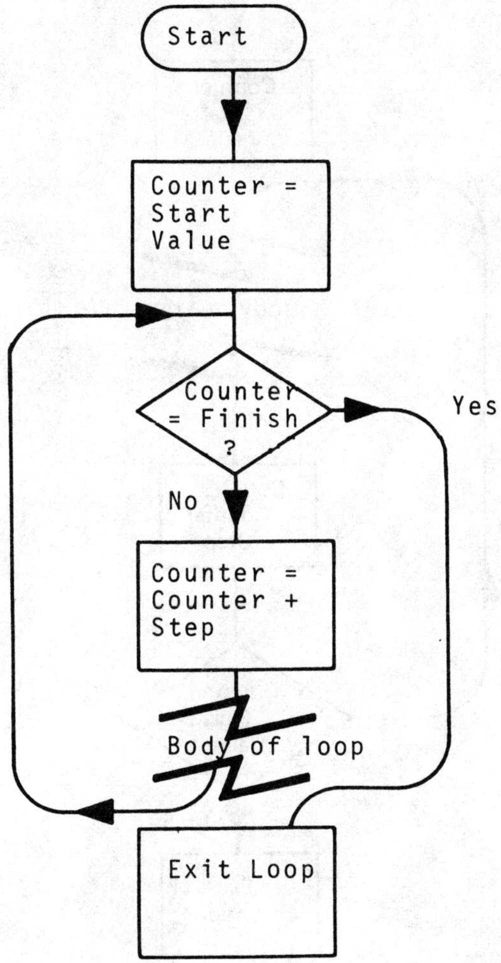
Start
Counter =
Start
Value
Counter
= Finish
?
Yes
No
Counter =
Counter +
Step
Body of loop
Exit Loop

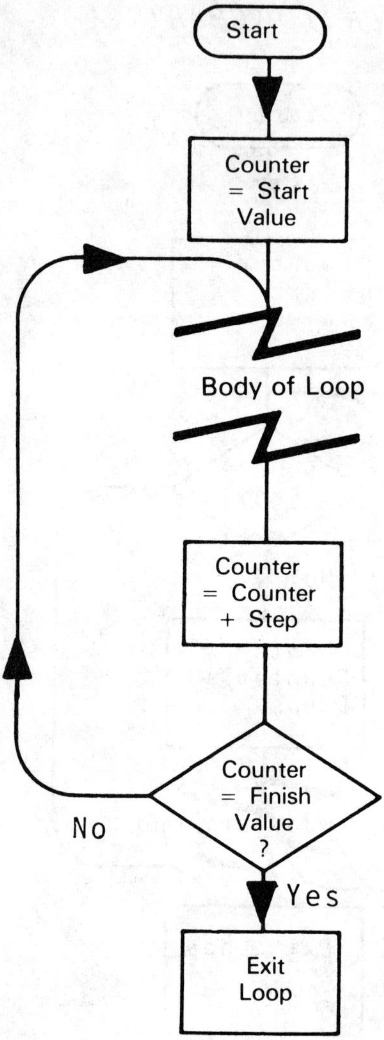

Exercise

Consider a simple program to work out the squares of the first 2Ø integers.

```
10 PRINT "NUMBER", "SQUARE"
20 LET N=0
30 LET N=N+1
40 IF N>20 THEN GOTO 70
50 PRINT N,N*N
60 GOTO 30
70 REM*END OF PROGRAM*
```

The GOTO statement in line 6Ø will cause the program to loop continuously between lines 3Ø and 6Ø.

This would continue indefinitely but line 4Ø is inserted so that the program jumps out of the loop when N>2Ø.

N is used as a counter. Line 2Ø initialises N and line 3Ø increments N by 1 each time the program goes round the loop.

Write a program which calculates and prints the square and the cube power of even numbers between 1Ø and 3Ø. The counter will need to be incremented by 2 each time the loop is executed by a GOTO statement.

Write a program which loops 1Ø times (counter 1 to 1Ø) but uses *another* counter to print the squares of the ten numbers 5.25, 5.Ø, 4.75 ..... 3.Ø.

L3: For – Next Loops

This is a more convenient way of having a program loop. The loop is set up with the FOR... TO ... STEP and NEXT instructions used in combination. The loop goes from the first value to the last value, counting by adding the defined STEP value every time it loops until the exit condition is met.

FOR (variable) = (first value) TO (last value) STEP (step)
FOR C = (N) TO (M) STEP (X)
where C is the counter variable or control variable of the loop and (N), (M) and (X) are numeric expressions.

C can be any single letter A to Z. It must not be the same as a single letter numeric variable. It is initialised at value (N). (N), (M) and (X) may take any values, positive or negative, as long as repeated additions of (X) to (N) will reach (M). If STEP is omitted, + 1 is assumed. NEXT C indicates last line of the loop. It adds (X) to C and loops back if the total is less than (M). The program loops back to the line after the line with the FOR – TO – STEP instruction.

The FOR – NEXT loop has a fixed procedure, unlike loops formed with conditional GOTO instructions.

We form a FOR – NEXT loop in a program like this:

```
1Ø   FOR F = Ø TO 1ØØ STEP 2
.....)
     )Body of loop
.....)
4Ø   NEXT F
```

The FOR statement initialises the loop.

Ø is the start value
1ØØ is the stop value
F is the counter variable and is initialised as Ø
STEP 2 is the increment.

NEXT F is the last line of the loop and increments the counter F by the STEP value.

We can also *decrement* the counter (decrease it). For example:

10 FOR F = 100 TO 0 STEP −2

(where the *decrement* is 2)

The loop will be exited in the first example when F>100 and in the second when F<0. F will take values 0, 2, 4 .... 98, 100 in the first case, and 100, 98 .... 4, 2, 0 in the second. Any program lines in the body of the loop will be repeated each time the program loops.

Try these simple examples:

```
10 FOR F=2 TO 4 STEP 1.3
20 PRINT F
30 NEXT F

10 FOR F=4 TO -1 STEP -1
20 PRINT F
30 NEXT F

10 FOR F=-2 TO 4 STEP 2
20 PRINT F
30 NEXT F
40 PRINT
50 PRINT "F EQUALS ";F;" ON EXIT"
```

Convince yourself that this *doesn't* work:

```
10  FOR F = 2 TO 4 STEP -1
20  PRINT F
30  NEXT F
```

The next one is an interesting example of the inaccuracies in the computer's arithmetic:

```
10  FOR F = 1.2 TO -0.3 STEP -0.2
20  PRINT F
30  NEXT F
```

The only reason for using F as the control variable is that it is convenient: FOR F can be entered just by pressing the F key twice. You can use any letter, but it is good personal programming practice to use the same letters consistently, and not use these for single letter variables. 'I' is often used by programmers as a control variable (I for Integer) but can be confused in program listings.

This next example uses N:

```
10  FOR N = 1 TO 15 STEP 1
20  PRINT N,N*N
30  NEXT N
```

We can use the value of the control variable in calculation within the loop. Edit STEP 1, so that line 10 reads:

```
10  FOR N = 1 TO 15
```

and run it again. STEP may *only* be omitted for a STEP of +1.

In the program, line 1Ø allows N to go from 1 to 15 with a step value of 1. That is to say, N takes the values, 1, 2, 3, 4, 5, 6, 6, 8, 9, 1Ø, 11, 12, 13, 14, 15 each time performing the calculations within the loop.

The next program illustrates the use of different values for the step. The value can be positive or negative, integer or non-integer. In the case of decimal increments or decrements there is the possibility of rounding errors if the loop is executed many times – it is therefore advisable to use integer values for the step and divide by the appropriate power of ten, if the loop variable is to be used in calculations. If this were done in the program below, lines 13Ø and 14Ø would read:

```
130   FOR N = 1Ø TO 56 STEP 7
140   PRINT N/1Ø; TAB 8; (N/1Ø)**2;
       TAB 16; (N/1Ø)**3                    (↑ on Spectrum)
```

The program calculates squares and cubes for:

1, 4, 7, ... 31 (line 2Ø)
12Ø, 115, 11Ø, ... 6Ø (line 7Ø)
1, 1.7, 2.4, ... 5.6 (line 13Ø)

Once again, Spectrum owners should remember that their machine uses the 'up-arrow' (↑) rather than the ZX81's stars (**) to represent 'to the power of'.

```
  5 REM "MULTILOOP"
 1Ø PRINT "NUMBER"; TAB 8; "SQ
    UARE"; TAB 16; "CUBE"
 2Ø FOR N=1 TO 31 STEP 3
 3Ø PRINT N; TAB 8; N**2; TAB 1
    6; N**3
 4Ø NEXT N
 45 PRINT "TYPE CONT KEY"
 5Ø STOP
 6Ø PRINT "NUMBER"; TAB 8; "SQU
    ARE"; TAB 16; "CUBE"
 7Ø FOR N=12Ø TO 6Ø STEP -5
 8Ø PRINT N; TAB 8; N**2; TAB 1
    6; N**3
 9Ø NEXT N
1ØØ PRINT "TYPE CONT KEY"
11Ø STOP
12Ø PRINT "NUMBER"; TAB 8; "SQU
    ARE"; TAB 16; "CUBE"
13Ø FOR N=1 TO 5.6 STEP .7
14Ø PRINT N; TAB 8; N**2; TAB 1
    6; N**3
15Ø NEXT N
```

In this next program the total is represented by T which is initialised equal to zero (line 1Ø). Each time the program goes through the loop the INPUT number is added to T (line 4Ø) so that when the loop (lines 2Ø to 5Ø) is exited T represents the sum of the ten numbers input. The program evaluates the average by dividing the total by the number of numbers input.

```
 5  REM "AVERAGE"
1Ø  LET T = Ø
2Ø  FOR N = 1 TO 1Ø
3Ø  INPUT X
4Ø  LET T = T + X
5Ø  NEXT N
6Ø  PRINT "AVERAGE = "; T/1Ø
```

This program illustrates a loop used to print a table. In this case a heading is given (line 7Ø) and this must be outside the loop as it is only required at the beginning. We require all names and ages to be tabulated so the print statement doing this (lines 14Ø, 15Ø) must be within the loop. Finally, we require the average age, which is to be printed underneath, and so the print statement (lines 17Ø, 18Ø) is inserted after the loop has been completed.

```
 1Ø REM "LOOPS3"
 2Ø PRINT "THIS PROGRAM PRINTS
    OUT THE NAME AND AGE OF A
    GROUP OF PEOPLE AND WORKS
    OUT THE AVERAGE AGE"
 3Ø PRINT
 4Ø PRINT "INPUT NUMBER IN GROU
    P"
 5Ø INPUT X
 6Ø LET T=Ø
 7Ø LPRINT "NAME", "AGE"
 8Ø FOR N=1 TO X
 9Ø PRINT "INPUT NAME"
1ØØ INPUT N$
11Ø PRINT "INPUT AGE"
12Ø INPUT A
13Ø LET T=T+A
14Ø PRINT N$,A
15Ø LPRINT N$,A
16Ø NEXT N
17Ø PRINT "AVERAGE AGE="; T/X;"
    YEARS"
18Ø LPRINT "AVERAGE AGE"; T/X;"
    YEARS"
```

The flowchart of a FOR – NEXT loop would be drawn like this, if we used the standard set of symbols as presented in the unit on programming:

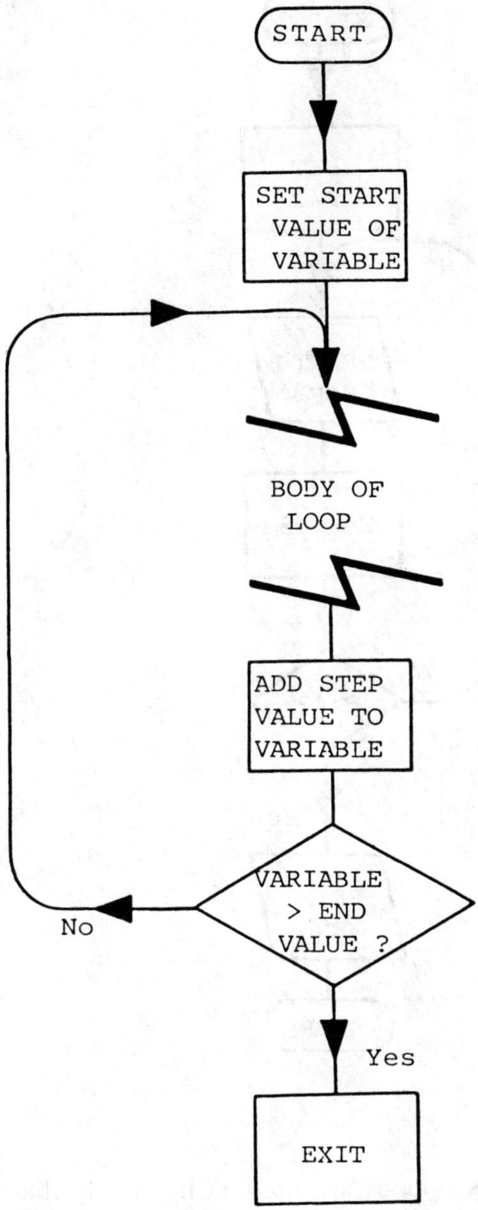

So for a program like the following:

```
10  FOR F = 2 TO 4 STEP .5
20  PRINT F*F
30  NEXT F
40  PRINT "END"
```

the flowchart would be like this:

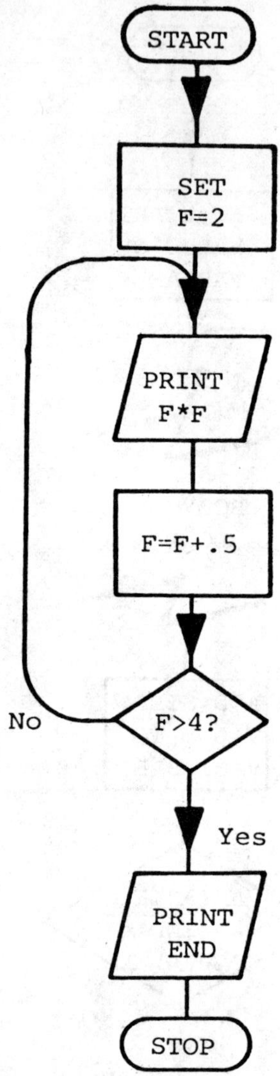

However, FOR – NEXT loops are used so frequently that this is a somewhat inefficient way of representing a loop of this type. There is another symbol often used, although it is not a standard symbol, which condenses all the required information. This has the form:

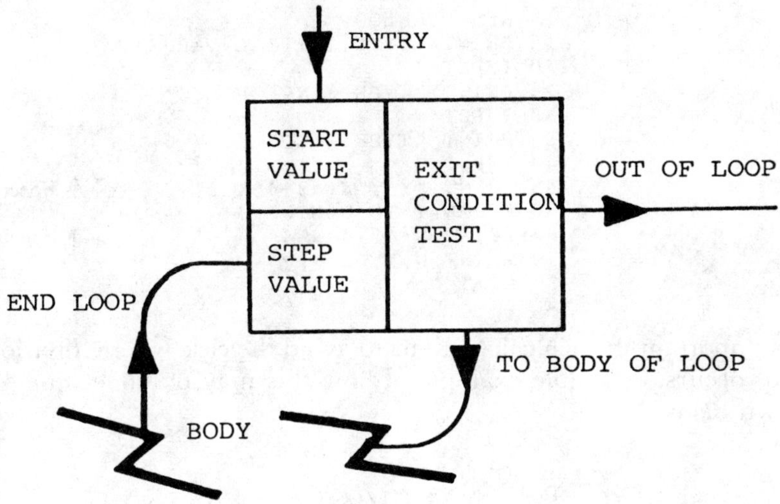

Our example program would be represented like this:

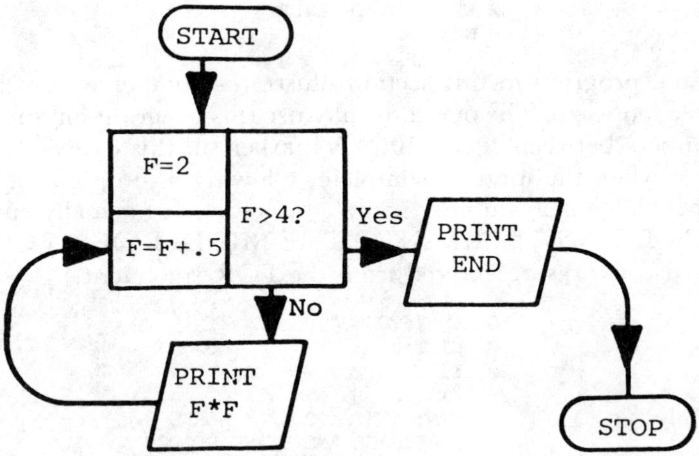

L4: Loops of Variable Length

The first value, final value and step of a loop may have any values (including variables which may be specified using INPUT). The first example shows a simple program which allows all conditions in the FOR statement to be specified using the INPUT statement.

```
1Ø REM "VARLOOP"
15 PRINT "TYPE INITIAL VALUE"
2Ø INPUT I
25 PRINT "TYPE FINAL VALUE"
3Ø INPUT F
35 PRINT "TYPE STEP"
4Ø INPUT S
45 PRINT "X","X**2+4*X-3"          [ ↑ Spectrum]
5Ø FOR N=I TO F STEP S
6Ø LET Y=N**2+4*N-3                [ ↑ Spectrum]
7Ø PRINT N,Y
8Ø NEXT N
```

It is important in such calculations to avoid the case where 'division by zero' occurs. A simple example of how this may be done (line 4Ø) is shown below:

```
 5 REM "DIVZER"
1Ø PRINT "X","1/(X-3)"
2Ø PRINT
3Ø FOR N=-9 TO 15 STEP 3
4Ø IF N-3=Ø THEN GOTO 8Ø
5Ø LET Y=1/(N-3)
6Ø PRINT N,Y
7Ø GOTO 9Ø
8Ø PRINT N,"INFINITY"
9Ø NEXT N
```

The final program in this section illustrates another way of having a variable loop size. The operator may use this program for any number of numbers between 1 and 1ØØ. A marker (in this case − 1) is set to indicate when the input is complete, allowing a jump out of the loop (line 69). This is a 'dummy value' – a value not normally entered.

(**N.B.** DO *NOT* JUMP INTO THE MIDDLE OF A LOOP i.e. a loop must **always** be entered from the FOR statement.)

```
  5 REM "STDDEV"
 1Ø LET T=Ø
 2Ø LET S=Ø
 3Ø LET C=Ø
 4Ø PRINT "THIS PROGRAM WORKS O
    UT AVERAGE AND STANDARD DEV
    IATION OF A SET OF NUMBERS"
 5Ø PRINT
 6Ø PRINT "TYPE NUMBERS ONE AT
    A TIME,TO FINISH TYPE -1"
 7Ø FOR N=1 TO 1ØØ
 8Ø INPUT X
 9Ø IF X=-1 THEN GOTO 14Ø
1ØØ LET T=T+X                       [ ↑ Spectrum]
11Ø LET S=S+X**2
12Ø LET C=C+1
13Ø NEXT N
14Ø PRINT
15Ø PRINT "AVERAGE IS ";T/C
16Ø PRINT "STANDARD DEVIATION I
    S ";SQR (S/C-(T/C)**2)          [ ↑ Spectrum]
```

The procedure used in this program can confuse the flow of a program and must be used with care. It is useful on occasion, but it is preferable to have only *one* entry and *one* exit from a loop. In this program, the loop may be exited from line 9Ø in addition to the normal termination, when N>1ØØ.

L5: Nested Loops

We can place one loop inside another loop, so that every time the program goes through the outside loop, it will perform the inner loop sequence. The inner loop must be entirely within the outer loop. Loops are said to be NESTED one inside the other. Loops can be nested to any depth, i.e. we can have as many loops as we wish, as long as they're correctly arranged.

```
30  FOR A = 1 TO 6      ─────────────────────┐
40  FOR B = 1 TO 3      ──────────┐          │
...............                   │          │
...............            Inner Loop        │
                                  │      Outer Loop
80  NEXT B              ──────────┘          │
..........                                   │
120 NEXT A              ─────────────────────┘
```

To have a third loop correctly placed, it would have to be inside the B (Inner) Loop, or outside the A (Outer) Loop.

Be careful to avoid crossing the loops:

```
10  FOR A = 1 TO 6    ────────┐
20  FOR B = 1 TO 3    ────────┼──────┐
    ........                  │      │
    ........                  │      │
60  NEXT A            ────────┘      │
    .......                          │
80  NEXT B            ───────────────┘
```

Programs with wrongly arranged loops will run, without giving an error message, but won't give you the correct answers!

To illustrate the use of nested loops, here are two programs. The first evaluates and prints out the squares, cubes and fourth powers of the first ten integers. Each number (N = 1 TO 1Ø) is to be raised to the appropriate power (E = 1 TO 4). Note that the loops are correctly nested.

```
┌──────────  20  FOR N = 1 TO 1Ø
│    ┌─────  3Ø  FOR E = 1 TO 4
│    │           ............
│    └─────  5Ø  NEXT E
│                ...........
└──────────  7Ø  NEXT N
```

```
 5 REM "NEST1"
10 PRINT "NUMBER";TAB 7;"SQUAR
   E";TAB 14;"CUBE";TAB 21;"4T
   H POWER"
20 FOR N=1 TO 10
30 FOR E=1 TO 4
40 PRINT TAB (E-1)*7;N**E;   [↑Spectrum]
50 NEXT E
60 PRINT
70 NEXT N
```

You will get a printout that starts off like this:

NUMBER	SQUARE	CUBE	4TH POWER
1	1	1	1
2	4	8	16
3	9	27	81
4	16	64	256

The flowchart for the "NEST1" program, using the flowchart symbol for FOR – NEXT loops we have introduced, will look like this:

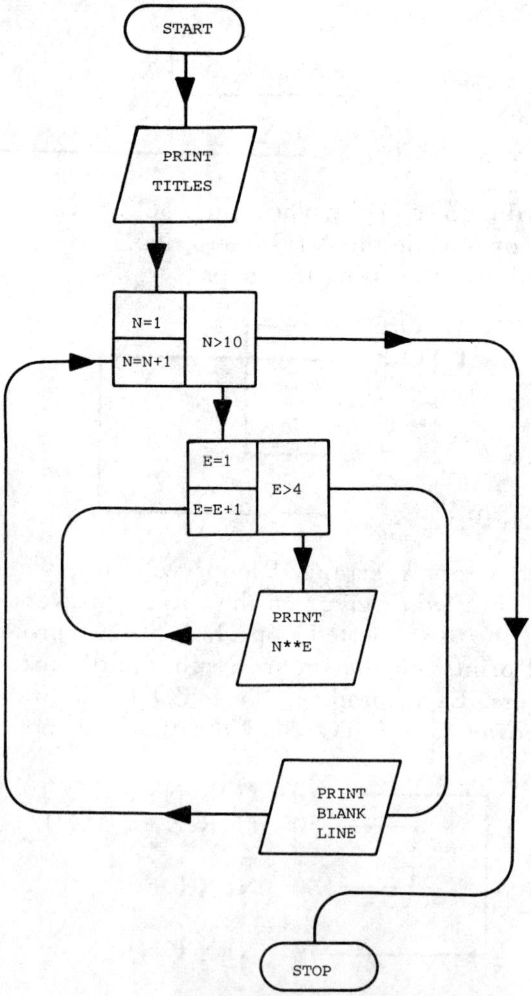

We can see the sequence of operations by tracing the program.

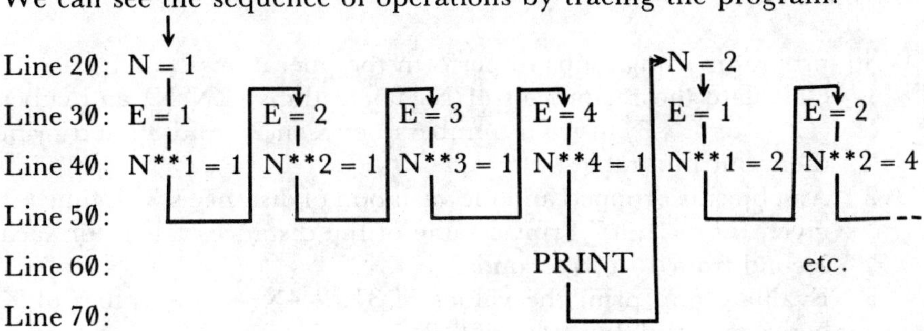

This table uses the ZX81 symbol for exponentiation. Notice how line 40 uses the value of E to format the output.

The second example assumes that a company employs three salesmen who keep sales figures for each week. At the end of four weeks the company requires a summary of sales to be printed. Each salesman S (1 TO 3) has weekly takings W (1 TO 4). Notice again that the loops are nested within each other.

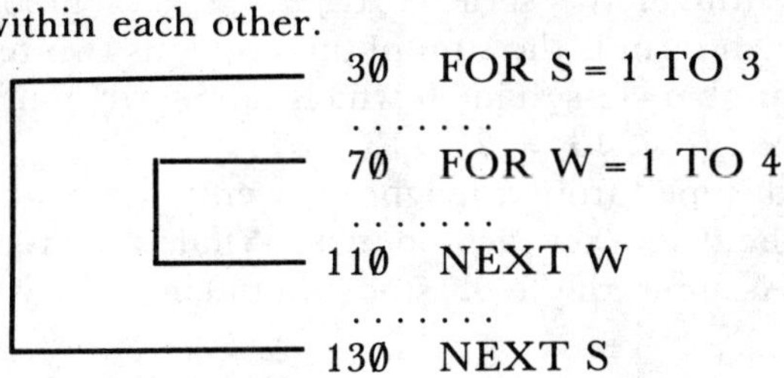

NAME	WEEK1	WEEK2	WEEK3	WEEK4
JONES	12	16	19	13
BROWN	23	26	29	21
SMITH	31	4	6	39

```
  10 REM *NESTED*
  20 LPRINT "NAME"; TAB 6;"WEEK1
"; TAB 13;"WEEK2"; TAB 20;"WEEK3
"; TAB 27;"WEEK4"
  30 FOR S=1 TO 3
  40 PRINT "INPUT SALESMANS NAME
"
  50 INPUT N$
  60 LPRINT N$;
  70 FOR W=1 TO 4
  80 PRINT "TYPE WEEK ";W;" SALE
S"
  90 INPUT X
 100 LPRINT TAB (7*W-1);X
 110 NEXT W
 120 LPRINT
 130 NEXT S
```

Exercises

Write programs using loops to perform the operations stated:

1. Calculate the reciprocals (1/N), logarithms (LN N) and cubes (L**3 or L ↑ 3) of even numbers between 2Ø and 36 and print them out in a table.
2. An object is dropped and the variation of distance s with time t is given by $s = 4.9t^2$. Print a table of the distances fallen for each second from 1 to 15 seconds.
3. Evaluate and print the values of $3X^2 + 4X - 7$ for values of X between 6 and 8 in steps of Ø.25.
4. Evaluate SIN X for values of X from Ø° to 36Ø° in intervals of 1Ø°. Remember you must convert from degrees to radians. Print out the results in two columns.
5. Print a table of the discount at 5%, 1Ø%, 15%, 2Ø% on articles from £1ØØ to £2ØØ in steps of £1Ø.
6. Find the sum of all odd numbers between 39 and 75.
7. Find the sum of the series 1,1,2,3,5,8,... (Fibonacci) to 2Ø terms. (Each term is the sum of the previous two terms.)
8. Find all numbers less than 5Ø which can be written as the sum of two squares. (e.g. $13 = 2^2 + 3^2$)
9. A ball is dropped from a height of twenty metres and rebounds one-half the height on each bounce. What is the total distance it travels? Assume the ball stops bouncing on its hundredth bounce.

SECTION M: PLOTTING

M1: Plot and Unplot

The screen size is the same on both the ZX81 and the Spectrum. It is divided into 24 × 32 character cells in the same way for printing on the screen. The bottom two lines are reserved for use by the computer. However, the plot screens of the ZX81 and Spectrum differ. The principle is the same, that of dividing up the screen into small squares, each of which can be blacked in separately, but the Spectrum has a higher resolution plot screen than the ZX81. This means that the screen is divided up into smaller squares (called *pixels*, short for *pic*ture *el*ements) on the Spectrum. The Spectrum has extra graphics commands not available on the ZX81 which make use of these pixels, some of which are mentioned in this Unit, but are dealt with fully in Section W. The commands are also different on the two machines, so we will describe the two separately before dealing with some of the uses of these commands.

Spectrum users should note the principles of plotting as presented here (even where we note that a particular process is easier using one of the Spectrum graphics commands, since it is the principles that are important, and can be extended to more complex tasks), and not just feel superior to the ZX81 user, who has no access to CIRCLE or DRAW!

On both machines each pixel is specified by X,Y co-ordinates. Thus, on the ZX81 (Ø,Ø) is the bottom left-hand corner and (63,43) is the top right-hand corner. There are 4 pixels in each character cell.

PLOT X,Y – blacks out the picture element (pixel) with co-ordinates X,Y.
UNPLOT X,Y – blanks out the pixel with co-ordinates X,Y.
The PLOT co-ordinates run from Ø to 63 across the screen left to right (X co-ordinates) and from Ø to 43 up the screen bottom to top (Y co-ordinates).

As a memory aid, remember that X is 'a cross', and X before Y.

It is a simple matter to print horizontal and vertical lines. This program plots a horizontal line across the screen:

```
10  FOR N = Ø TO 63
20  PLOT N,2Ø
30  NEXT N
```

See if you can write a program that plots a rectangle.

Each of the character cells on the Spectrum's screen has 8 × 8 = 64 pixels, and there are thus 176 in any column up the screen and 256 in any line across the screen. Once again specifying each pixel with X and Y co-ordinates, Ø,Ø is the bottom left-hand corner and 255,175 is the top right-hand corner.

Whilst PLOT X,Y on the Spectrum blacks in the pixel element in exactly the same way as on the ZX81, there is no UNPLOT statement on the Spectrum. To erase the dot again the OVER 1 facility is used. Thus, to erase at X,Y you must enter a multiple statement line.

OVER 1: PLOT X,Y – blanks out the pixel at co-ordinates X,Y

Although it is perfectly possible to plot a horizontal line to the screen using a program similar to that used on the ZX81:

```
10  FOR N = 0 TO 255
20  PLOT N,20
30  NEXT N
```

it is far simpler on the Spectrum to use the following type of formulation:

```
10  PLOT 0,20: DRAW 255,0
```

It is also possible to get some semblance of motion. The program below moves a dot across the screen:

On the ZX81

```
10  FOR N = 0 TO 63
20  UNPLOT N - 2,20
30  PLOT N,20
40  NEXT N
```

On the Spectrum

```
10  FOR N = 0 TO 255
20  PLOT OVER 1; N - 2,20
30  PLOT N,20
40  NEXT N
```

It is possible to construct simple shapes using PLOT. Here is a ZX81 routine to draw a (somewhat stylised) dog:

```
 10 LET X=0
 20 LET Y=10
 30 PLOT X,Y
 40 PLOT X+1,Y-1
 50 FOR N=2 TO 4
 60 PLOT X+2,Y-N
 70 NEXT N
 80 PLOT X+3,Y-2
 90 PLOT X+4,Y-2
100 FOR N=1 TO 4
110 PLOT X+5,Y-N
120 NEXT N
130 PLOT X+6,Y
140 PLOT X+7,Y-1
```

It can sometimes be worth remembering that the PLOT pixels are not exactly square. The visible variation from square will depend on the type of plotting being done, and the particular TV screen in use. It is worth drawing what should be a square on the screen, and simply measuring the variation with a ruler. Try running this program, and do this for different areas on the screen, so that you can check if the variation is constant. Note the double loop, which is often useful in PLOT routines.

On the ZX81

```
10  FOR F = 10 TO 30
20  FOR L = 10 TO 30
30  PLOT F,L
40  NEXT L
50  NEXT F
```

On the Spectrum

```
10  FOR F = 10 TO 100
20  FOR L = 10 TO 100
30  PLOT F,L
40  NEXT L
50  NEXT F
```

The variation from square on the screen is typically in a ratio between 1.1:1 and 1.2:1 (across screen/down screen). This means a 'square' that looks square will need to be 10 pixels across and either 11 or 12 pixels down.

Most PLOTting is done utilising loops. To PLOT a circle we need to choose a suitable STEP value for a loop that runs either from 0 to 360 (degrees), or 0 to 2 PI (Radians). We also have to set a centre to give us a circle where we want it, and a radius such that it will fit the screen. For a circle in degrees, code in this program:

On the ZX81

```
10  FOR D = 0 TO 360 STEP 10
20  LET R = D*PI/180
30  LET X = 30 + 20* COS R
40  LET Y = 20 + 20* SIN R
50  PLOT X,Y
60  NEXT D
```

On the Spectrum

```
10  FOR D = 0 TO 360 STEP 2
20  LET R = D*PI/180
30  LET X = 120 + 80* COS R
40  LET Y = 80 + 80* SIN R
50  PLOT X,Y
60  NEXT D
```

Line 20 converts to radians, in which all the trigonometric functions of the computer work. Line 30 calculates the horizontal component, and line 40 the vertical. The SIN and COS functions are multiplied by 20 (80 on the Spectrum) to give a radius of 20 pixels. The centre is set for the ZX81 at pixel 30, 20, and for the Spectrum at pixel 120, 80. In most cases, it is convenient to consider the PLOT screen to be 60 × 40 pixels (ZX81), rather than 64 × 44, in order to set scales and position plots on the screen, and 240 × 160 similarly for the Spectrum.

Having set the basic values, we can introduce variations within the loop into the above program. We can calculate the radius value and get a spiral plot. Alter the program to:

For the ZX81

```
10  FOR D = 0 TO 360 STEP 10
20  LET Z  =  D*PI/180
30  LET R = Z*3
40  LET X = 30 + R*COS Z
50  LET Y = 20 + R*SIN Z
60  PLOT X,Y
70  NEXT D
```

For the Spectrum

```
10  FOR D = 0 TO 360 STEP 2
20  LET Z = D*PI/180
30  LET R = Z*10
40  LET X = 120 + R*COS Z
50  LET Y = 80 + R*SIN Z
60  PLOT X,Y
70  NEXT D
```

Calculating additional values, all within the loop, and using the loop values as a basis, provides complex shapes fairly easily. Alter the first three lines of the program:

For the ZX81

```
10  FOR D = 0 TO 360 STEP 5
20  LET Z = D*PI/180
30  LET R = 20*SIN(Z*4)
```

For the Spectrum

```
10  FOR D = 0 TO 360
20  LET Z = D*PI/180
30  LET R = 60*SIN(Z*4)
```

RUN it. From a simple circle, we now have the basis for a polar graph plot and can identify a scale of values for PLOTting that will fit the screen. Similarly using parametric equations for the ellipse on the ZX81, X goes from 10 to 50 as COS goes from – 1 to 1 and Y from 10 to 3Ø as SIN goes from –1 to 1 round the circle. Notice this uses radians directly (2*PI radians = 36Ø degrees). Spectrum plot points are multiplied by 4.

For the ZX81

```
1Ø   FOR N = Ø TO 2*PI STEP PI/2Ø
2Ø   PLOT 3Ø + 2Ø*COS N, 2Ø + 1Ø*SIN N
3Ø   NEXT N
```

For the Spectrum

```
1Ø   FOR N = Ø TO 2*PI STEP PI/18Ø
2Ø   PLOT 12Ø + 8Ø*COS N, 8Ø + 4Ø*SIN N
3Ø   NEXT N
```

Try altering the multiplication factors in line 2Ø for different ellipses. Alter the STEP value to get a continuous line.

Of course, on the Spectrum a simple CIRCLE statement enables us to achieve the same result demonstrated in our first example much more quickly. For instance:

```
CIRCLE 128,88,5Ø
```

will draw a circle of radius 5Ø pixels with its centre in the middle of the screen. This is included with the additional Spectrum functions in Section W. Note however that the calculated circles are more accurate than the ones drawn using CIRCLE, but a lot slower to PLOT!

Exercises

1 PLOT the extreme corner pixels, measure the rectangle and use the computer in command mode to calculate the proportions of a pixel rectangle on your screen.
2 PLOT a circle, using radians directly, without a degree conversion, with another circle, half the radius, inside.
3 PLOT a more accurate circle with allowancc made for the pixels being non-square, by altering the multiplication factors for either COS or SIN.
4 Change the spiral routine to produce a double spiral (i.e. going round the circle twice).
5 Experiment with the rosette producing program. Alter the values of R in line 3Ø by changing the factor by which Z is multiplied. Try Z**2 (Z↑2 on Spectrum) and similar expressions.

M2: Graph Plotting

Simple graphs may be plotted using the PRINT functions already encountered. The following program illustrates its use for drawing a histogram. Lines 2Ø to 7Ø allow twelve values to be input and make Z the largest value input. Lines 9Ø to 15Ø plot out the histogram allowing the maximum value (i.e. Z) to be 25 columns long and all the others are drawn in proportion.

```
 10 REM "HISTO"
 20 DIM M(12)
 30 LET Z=0
 40 FOR N=1 TO 12
 50 INPUT M(N)
 60 IF M(N) > Z THEN LET Z=M(N)
 70 NEXT N
 80 REM **PLOT**
 90 FOR N=1 TO 12
100 PRINT N;TAB 4;
110 FOR L=1 TO M(N) STEP Z/25
120 PRINT "*";
130 NEXT L
140 PRINT
150 NEXT N
```

Result:

```
 1   *********************
 2   ****
 3   ***************
 4   ********
 5   ***********
 6   *************************
 7   *
 8   ***********
 9   *******
10   *********************
11   ****
12   ***************
```

The STEP value in the program above is a SCALE FACTOR. The use of a suitable scale factor is needed in most graphical routines. Here is another version of a barchart program that identifies the scale factor and uses it to multiply the values to be plotted out using the asterisks. (The graphics characters can be put to use to draw solid bars, where the asterisk is used here.)

```
 10 REM *BARCHART*
 20 PRINT "ENTER MAX VALUE"
 30 INPUT M
 40 LET SCALE=25/M
 50 PRINT "ENTER VALUES (MAX 2
    0) ENTER -1 TO FINISH"
 60 PAUSE 150
 70 CLS
 80 FOR F=1 TO 20
 90 PRINT AT 21,0;"INPUT VALUE ";F
100 INPUT V
110 IF V=-1 THEN GOTO 190
120 PRINT AT F,0;V
130 PRINT AT F,5;
140 LET V=V*SCALE
150 FOR T=1 TO INT (V+.5)
160 PRINT "*";
170 NEXT T
180 NEXT F
190 PRINT AT 21,0;"              "
```

The identification of scale factors to produce the best plot possible within the available X,Y values on the screen is vital in all plotting routines. The plotted functions have to be plotted on the biggest scale that will enable them to fit the screen. This program fits the screen without any problem:

ZX81

```
10  FOR X = Ø TO 6Ø
20  PLOT X,SQRX
30  NEXT X
```

Spectrum owners should bear in mind that each pixel you can PLOT on the Spectrum is a quarter as wide and a quarter as high as those on the ZX81. Thus, as a general rule, you should allow for a factor of four when working with ZX81 scales, as shown in this discussion of scaling factors. In the program above, for example, the first line would read FOR X = Ø TO 24Ø.

The program above does not give the best illustration of the shape of the curve, although it has the X,Y scales the same (one pixel = 1). Changing line 2Ø to:

```
2Ø  PLOT X, 2*SQRX
```

gives a better graph. It is obvious, in this instance, that we could increase the scale factor – in this case the number by which we multiply SQR X to get the Y value – to 5, and the graph would still fit the screen.

But if we try this program (do!):

ZX81	*Spectrum*
1Ø FOR X = Ø TO 6Ø	1Ø FOR X = Ø TO 24Ø
2Ø PLOT X, X*X	2Ø PLOT X,X*X
3Ø NEXT X	3Ø NEXT X

we would only get a few points plotted before the computer stops with an 'integer out of range' error code. It is obvious that the maximum value in this case will bc 6Ø × 6Ø = 36ØØ (ZX81) and 24Ø × 24Ø = 576ØØ on the Spectrum. So if we used:

2Ø PLOT X, X*X/1ØØ	2Ø PLOT X, X*X/4ØØ

the highest value for the Y pixel would be 36 on the ZX81, which makes use of most of the screen. (For the Spectrum it would be 144.) In most cases, however, it is not so easy to see what the scale factors should be. We have a 44 × 64 screen to use on the ZX81 and a 256 × 176 screen on the Spectrum, and so in general, for positive values only, suitable scale factors are given by:

	ZX81	*Spectrum*
(X axis)	$\dfrac{63}{\text{Largest value of X}}$	$\dfrac{255}{\text{Largest value of X}}$
(Y axis)	$\dfrac{43}{\text{Largest value for Y}}$	$\dfrac{175}{\text{Largest value for Y}}$

For a full range plot of a function that takes positive and negative values, for example SIN, we have to set a scale factor which refers to the screen available for use above and below the pixel Y value taken as zero. To give an example, for a SIN function, taking values between +1 and −1 we set the zero line as Y = 2Ø (ZX81) or Y = 8Ø (Spectrum). We then need to find a scale value such that the Y values vary between 2Ø above and 2Ø below this line (8Ø above and below for Spectrum) as SIN varies between +1 and −1. Again, it is obvious that we need to use a line like:

ZX81	*Spectrum*
2Ø PLOT X, 2Ø + 2Ø*SIN X	2Ø PLOT X, 8Ø + 8Ø*SIN X

To get a single full range curve we need X to vary from Ø to 2PI radians, so we can use:

```
1Ø  FOR X = Ø TO 2*PI STEP 2*PI/6Ø
2Ø  PLOT X, 2Ø + 2Ø*SIN X          [8Ø + 8Ø*SIN X on Spectrum]
3Ø  NEXT X
```

for full screen use. (Remember 2PI radius = 36Ø°.)

Up to now, although you have been told about the co-ordinates of the PRINT and PLOT screens, we have treated the use of PRINT and PLOT as two separate areas.

Since the PRINT and PLOT co-ordinate systems refer to the same screen, the two may also be used in concert, but care must be taken. Confusion is likely to arise between the numbering systems, not so much in the numbering across the screen, but in the Y plane, where pixels count Ø-43 (Ø-175 on the Spectrum) *upwards*, and the print lines Ø-21 *downwards*. Pixels are coded X,Y, *across* and *up*, print positions L,C, *down* and *across*. The screen grids for printing and plotting are reproduced here for both the ZX81 and Spectrum.

THE ZX81 PRINT AND PLOT SCREEN

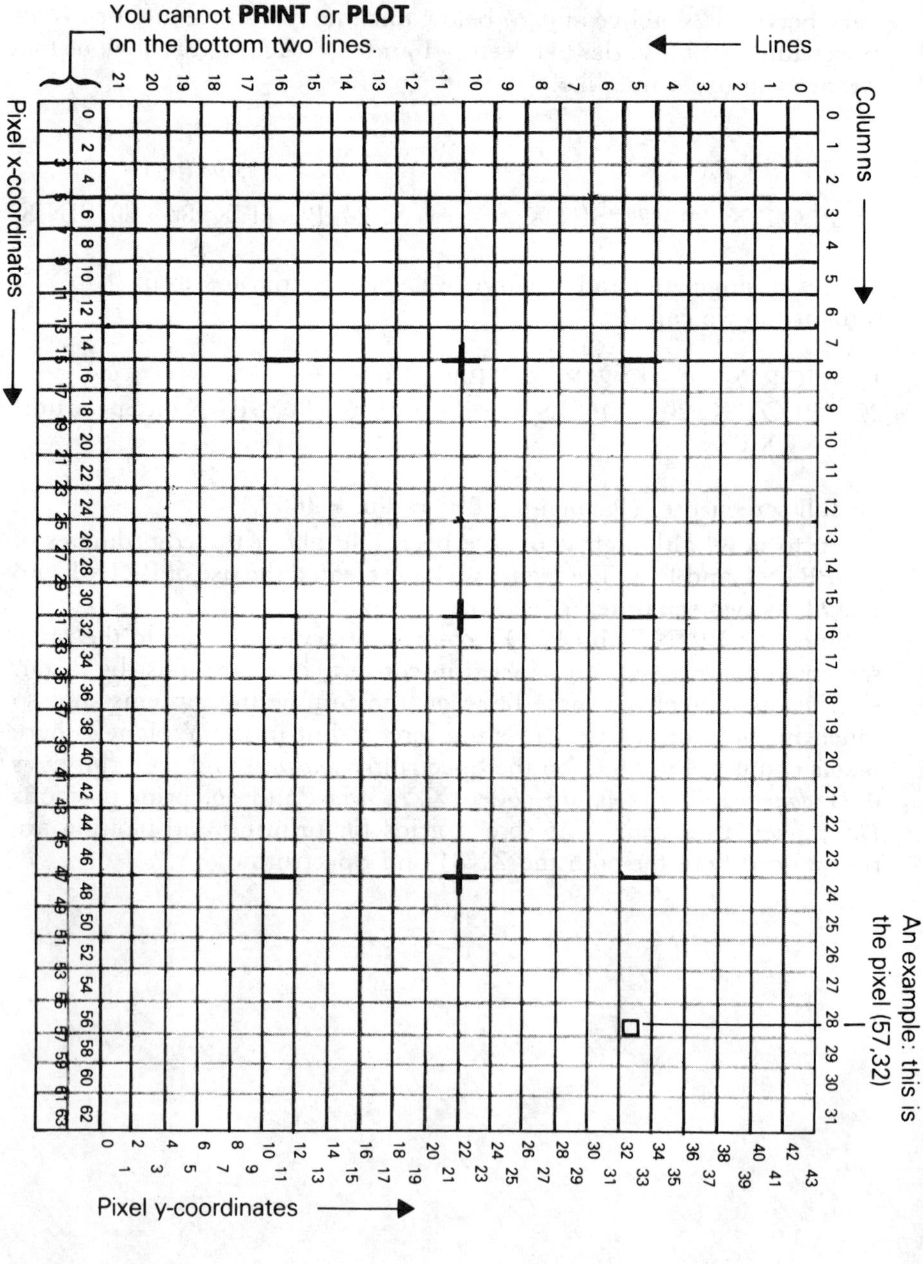

THE SPECTRUM PRINT & PLOT SCREEN

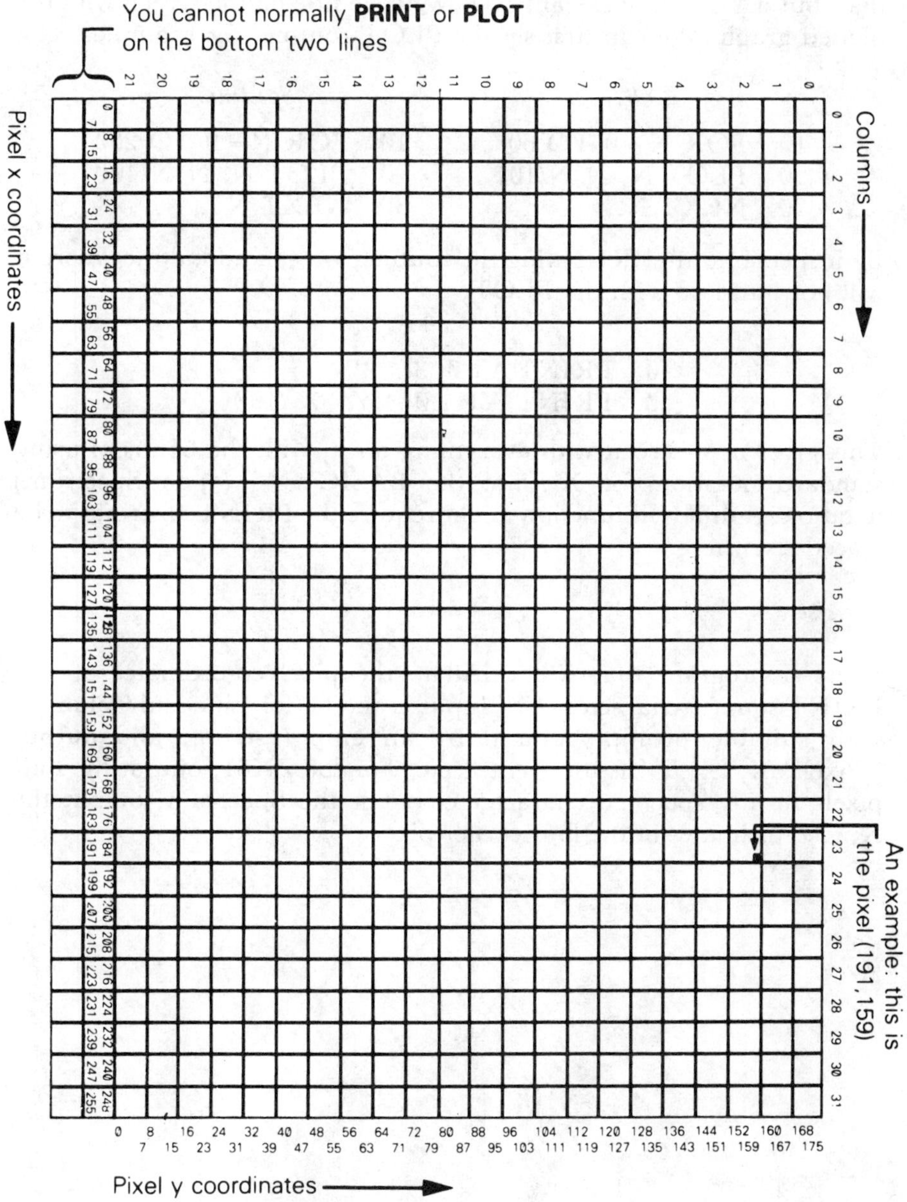

It is useful, when both PRINTing and PLOTting on the screen, to work with one screen grid first, and then add the other grid. As an example, consider graph titles. We could, to get a title for a printout of a graph, use a direct command: PRINT "GRAPH OF Y = X**2/100", then use COPY, BREAK the COPY routine after the first lines printed, then PLOT the graph with our program and COPY that, but it's not very elegant. We want the title on the screen with the plotted graph. We can first set the PLOT routine, for example:

ZX81	*Spectrum*
10 FOR N = 0 TO 60	10 FOR N = 0 TO 250
20 PLOT N, N*N/100	20 PLOT N, N*N/400
30 NEXT N	30 NEXT N

By inspection, after RUNning the routine, we can add a title where it will not interfere with the PLOT.

```
40  PRINT AT 0, 3; "2"
50  PRINT AT 1,0; "Y = X /100
```

This gives us a screen with everything on it, with the bonus of using standard notation for X^2, not the BASIC's ** (↑ on Spectrum) notation. A different function might require the PRINTed strings to be placed elsewhere.

Exercise

Write a program that will calculate the pixel co-ordinates of any PRINT square (character cell). Input L and C (for Line and Column), with suitable prompts erased by an empty string, and output "Pixel";X;",";Y;"is top right", etc. For the ZX81, output the four pixels in any specified character cell. For the Spectrum, output the X,Y co-ordinates of the four corner pixels.

SECTION N: SUBROUTINES

N1: Subroutines

A subroutine in BASIC is a program module performing an allotted task and is entered using a GOSUB statement. The section of program is completed and exited by a RETURN statement which sends the computer back to the line following the GOSUB statement. A subroutine must only be entered via a GOSUB statement and exited by a RETURN statement.

Two instructions are used to create subroutines.

GOSUB (line number)	**– transfers control to the specified line number**
RETURN	**– leaves subroutine and returns control to the line immediately after the GOSUB instruction which transferred control to the subroutine.**

Spectrum users have probably noted that their machine prints GO SUB with a space.

Here is an example of the program structure for these instructions:

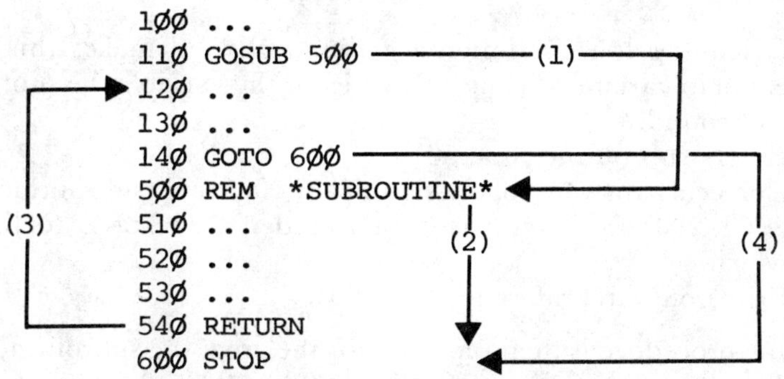

(1) GOSUB – goes immediately to line indicated (5ØØ)

(2) Continues program (lines 5ØØ-54Ø) until RETURN reached

(3) Program returns to line 12Ø (line immediately after GOSUB statement).

(4) It is vital to ensure that a subroutine is not entered accidentally when writing the program. Note that line 14Ø does this by using a GOTO statement to bypass the subroutine. Line 6ØØ may continue the program, or be a statement such as REM*END OF PROGRAM*. It is a useful practice to end a program at the highest line number, which indicates successful completion of the whole program. The alternative, stopping the program with a line 14Ø STOP, could also be used.

Subroutines are often used for repeated procedures and may be thought of as separate program structures:

```
     MAIN ROUTINE                        SUBROUTINE
100
110  GOSUB 500 ──────►  ┌500  REM * SUBROUTINE *             ┐
120             ◄────── │510                                 │
130                     │520                                 │
140  GOSUB 500 ──────►  │530  REM * END OF SUBROUTINE *      │
150             ◄────── │540  RETURN                         │
160                     └                                    ┘
```

The computer stores the line number of the GOSUB instruction (whereas it doesn't with a GOTO). The RETURN instruction transfers control back to the line number after the *latest* GOSUB. As shown above, this means we can enter a subroutine repeatedly in the course of a program.

N2: Subroutine Example

The example program given below evaluates the circumference and area of a circle, and has a subroutine to round the results to two decimal places. The program works as follows:

(i) Calculates the circumference (line 40), and makes this figure equal to variable Z (line 45), which is the variable the subroutine will round.

(ii) Enters subroutine (line 50).

(iii) Corrects answer to 2 significant figures (subroutine lines 200 – 230), and returns with rounded value of Z to line 60, which:

(iv) Prints out circumference (line 60).

The same procedure is then repeated for the area, the subroutine being entered (*called*) again in line 90. Lines 200 to 230 of the program are then executed again, but the RETURN statement this time returns control to line 100 (the next line after the last GOSUB statement).

It is *essential* to have line 110, which prevents the subroutine being entered accidentally when the calculation is complete.

```
10 REM "CIRCLE"
20 PRINT "TYPE RADIUS"
30 INPUT R
40 LET C=2*PI*R
45 LET Z=C
50 GOSUB 200
60 PRINT "CIRCUMFERENCE IS ";Z
70 LET A=PI*R**2                    [ ↑ Spectrum]
80 LET Z=A
90 GOSUB 200
```

```
100 PRINT "AREA IS ";Z
110 GOTO 300
120 REM *MUST NOT ENTER A SUBROUTINE
    EXCEPT BY A GOSUB*
200 REM **SUBROUTINE TO CORRECT TO
    TWO DECIMAL PLACES**
210 LET Z=INT (100*(Z+.005))
220 LET Z=Z/100
230 RETURN
240 **END OF SUBROUTINE**
300 REM **END OF PROGRAM**
```

The second example is a program to evaluate the sum of the series $1 + 1/2! + 1/3! + .. + 1/10!$ to 6 decimal places. (The exclamation mark (!) means 'factorial'. Factorial 5 (5!) is $5 \times 4 \times 3 \times 2 \times 1$, etc.).

In this program there are two separate subroutines. The subroutines are both entered repeatedly. The first is to evaluate the factorial and the second corrects the answer to 6 decimal places. Although it is not essential to use subroutines in such a program it does improve the structure and make it considerably easier to follow the sequence of operations.

```
 10 REM "FACTORS"
 40 LET S=0
 50 FOR Z=1 TO 10
 60 GOSUB 200
 70 LET T=1/X
 90 LET S=S+T
100 PRINT Z;" TH TERM IS ";T
110 NEXT Z
120 GOSUB 300
130 PRINT
140 PRINT "SUM OF SERIES ";V
150 GOTO 400
200 REM **SUBROUTINE FACTORIAL**
210 LET X=1
220 FOR N=1 TO Z
230 LET X=X*N
240 NEXT N
250 RETURN
300 REM **SUBROUTINE 6 D.P. **
310 LET V=INT (1E6*(S+5E-7))
320 LET V=V*1E-6
330 RETURN
400 REM **END**
```

Results on screen:

```
 1 TH TERM IS 1
 2 TH TERM IS 0.5
 3 TH TERM IS 0.16666667
 4 TH TERM IS .041666666
 5 TH TERM IS .0083333333
 6 TH TERM IS .0013888889
 7 TH TERM IS .0001964127
 8 TH TERM IS .000024801587
 9 TH TERM IS 2.7557319E-6
10 TH TERM IS 2.7557319E-7
   SUM OF SERIES 1.7182862
```

Trace the program through for the first two terms to ensure that you can follow the flow.

N3: Nested Subroutines

This technique is similar to nested loops in that a subroutine is entered from another subroutine.

In the simple example given the program enters the first subroutine (line 3ØØ) and from within this calls up the second subroutine (line 32Ø calls up subroutine at line 4ØØ) which is completed and returns (line 42Ø) to the first subroutine which is then completed. See the diagram below of the program flow.

Hand trace this program to discover the result of running it. (N.B. This program is only used to illustrate nested subroutines and the calculation carried out clearly can be done more easily without their use.)

```
 1Ø REM "SUBROUTINE1"
 2Ø LET M=5
 3Ø GOSUB 3ØØ
 4Ø PRINT M
 5Ø GOTO 5ØØ
3ØØ REM ****1ST SUBROUTINE****
31Ø LET M=M+1
32Ø GOSUB 4ØØ
33Ø REM **RETURN TO MAIN PROGRAM**
34Ø RETURN
35Ø REM **********************
4ØØ REM ****2ND SUBROUTINE****
41Ø LET M=M* (M+1) **2              [ ↑ Spectrum]
42Ø RETURN
43Ø REM ***********************
5ØØ PRINT "END OF PROGRAM"
```

The diagram illustrates the procedure in the above program for two nested subroutines.

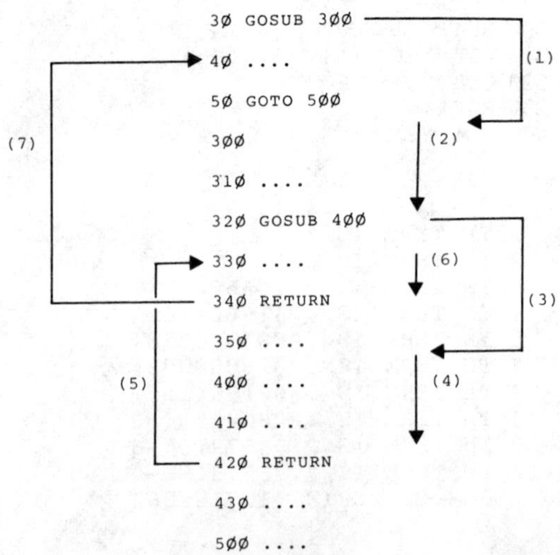

(1) Subroutine 1 is called at line 3Ø.
Enter first subroutine at line 3ØØ.
(2) Start executing first subroutine.
(3) Subroutine 2 is called at line 32Ø.
Enter second subroutine at line 4ØØ.
(4) Execute second subroutine.
(5) RETURN at line 42Ø returns program to line 33Ø (line following GOSUB call).
(6) Continue execution of first subroutine.
(7) RETURN at line 34Ø returns program to line 4Ø (line following GOSUB call).
(8) Statement to avoid entering subroutines accidentally.

The second example is typical of a computer games program. The nested subroutine ensures that the computer's move is printed out each time before the player makes his move.

```
 1Ø REM "NESTSUB"
 2Ø REM **PART OF GAMES PROG**
 3Ø LET X=3
 4Ø GOSUB 6ØØ
 45 PRINT
 5Ø PRINT "YOUR MOVE WAS ";M
 6Ø PRINT "COMPUTERS MOVE ";X
 7Ø STOP
6ØØ REM **SUBROUTINE PLAYER**
61Ø GOSUB 7ØØ
62Ø PRINT "YOUR MOVE?"
63Ø INPUT M
64Ø RETURN
7ØØ REM **SUBROUTINE COMPUTER**
71Ø PRINT "COMPUTERS MOVE ";X
72Ø RETURN
```

Note that it would make no difference if the nested (called from a subroutine) subroutine were to start at a lower line number than the subroutine which called it. Subroutines are always discrete program modules, wherever they are located in a program.

N4: Recursive Subroutines

A **recursive** subroutine is a subroutine that calls itself. This facility is not available in some versions of BASIC used on other computers. For some purposes this can be a very useful program structure. From within a subroutine, a GOSUB instruction is used to transfer control so that the program re-enters the subroutine. The computer stores each GOSUB call, with the line number to RETURN to, just as if the GOSUB call had been made to a different subroutine. The RETURN instructions are executed in reverse sequence to the order in which the GOSUB instructions were encountered.

The example program below evaluates the factorial of any number N, input as an integer less than 3Ø. First the program, then the explanation:

```
 10 REM "RECSUB"
 20 PRINT "TYPE NUMBER<30"
 30 INPUT N
 40 IF N>30 THEN GOTO 200
 50 GOSUB 100
 60 PRINT F
 70 GOTO 210
 80 REM
 90 REM ******************
100 REM ****SUBROUTINE****
110 IF N <> 1 THEN GOTO 140
120 LET F=1
130 GOTO 180
140 LET N=N-1
150 GOSUB 100
160 LET F=F*(N+1)
170 LET N=N+1
180 RETURN
185 REM ****ENDSUB**
190 REM
200 PRINT "OBEY INSTRUCTIONS.PR
ESS RUN AND NEWLINE/ENTER"
210 REM **END**
```

To help us decipher the program flow, we can insert PRINT statements and add a counter, in order to code the GOSUB and RETURN instructions with a number to indicate the sequence in which the recursive calls are performed. Add the following lines to the program:

5 LET C = Ø	(sets counter to count GOSUB calls)
35 PRINT N	(prints first value of N)
45 LET C = C + 1	(first GOSUB call from main program)
55 PRINT "RETURN TO MAIN PROGRAM"	(final RETURN executed)
145 LET C = C + 1	(increments counter each time GOSUB is used recursively)
146 PRINT "GOSUB CALL ";C	(prints each time GOSUB is used recursively)
147 PRINT "N = ";N	(value of N before each recursive GOSUB call)
155 PRINT"RETURN CALL ";C	(prints each RETURN call as made, corresponding to the GOSUB call of the same number)
156 LET C = C – 1	(decrements counter as each RETURN is executed)
165 PRINT "F = ";F	(value of F at each stage)
175 PRINT "N = ";N	(value of N at each stage)

Then run the program for N = 3. The resulting 'machine trace' screen display is:

```
3
GOSUB CALL 2
N = 2
GOSUB CALL 3
N = 1
RETURN CALL 3
F = 2
N = 2
RETURN CALL 2
F = 6
N = 3
RETURN TO MAIN PROGRAM
6
```

If we draw up a trace using the data from this display (as below), we will see that the GOSUB at line 15Ø is executed for *each* value of N from 1 to N. The RETURN calls are then made for each value from 1 to N, calculating F each time (line 16Ø) and incrementing N (line 17Ø), so that the value of factorial N is calculated as 1 × 2 × 3... × N. The flowchart of this program is quite simple, but the algorithm is not clear unless the sequence of GOSUB and RETURN calls is understood.

The computer stores each GOSUB call in sequence in a portion of memory called the GOSUB stack, and each RETURN instruction removes one of these stored GOSUBs, passing control to the line after the GOSUB call. Confusion is possible with recursive subroutines because the RETURNs are made to the same program line each time (line 16Ø in this case).

"RECSUB" – Trace for N = 3:

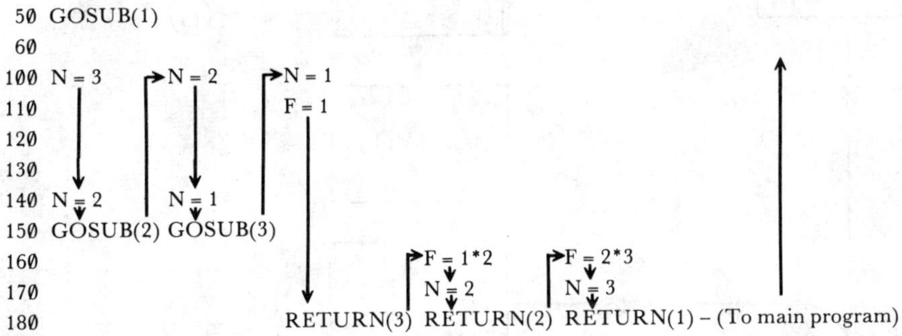

Flowchart – "RECSUB"

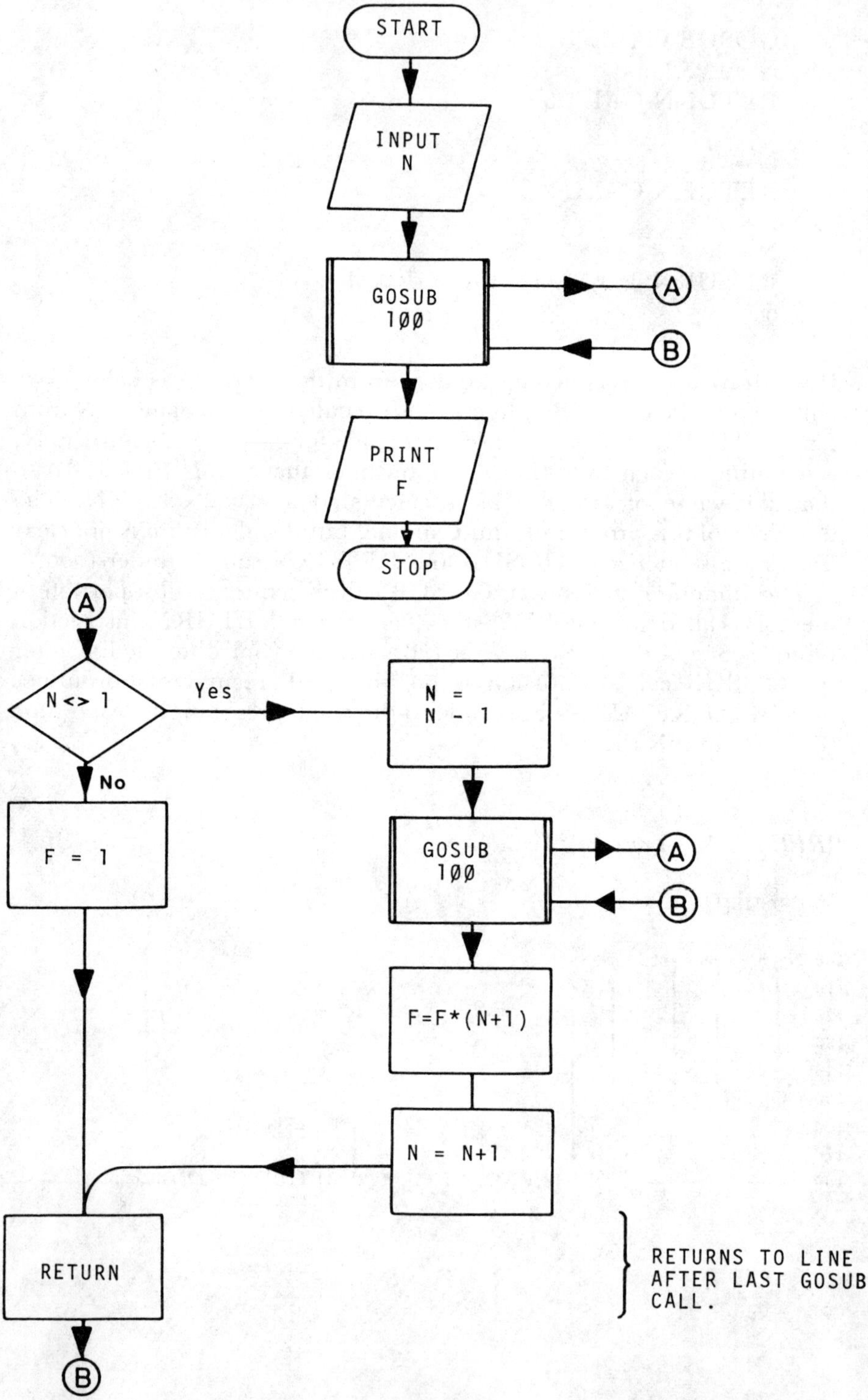

Notice that line 130 passes control to the RETURN statement of line 180. Check for yourself that line 130 could be a RETURN instruction and the program would still run correctly. This is likely to result in a less visible flow in the program, however.

The next program has a subroutine (starting at line 100) which calls itself in line 150. As for the previous program, insert suitable PRINT statements to print out the values of the variables and the number of GOSUB calls made. Hand trace the program for suitable integers, e.g. 15 and 25. The program evaluates the highest common factor of the two numbers input. Note that in this case there are no processing statements between the GOSUB call in line 150 and the RETURN instruction of line 160. The sequence of RETURNs will be executed by control going repeatedly to line 160 (the line after the GOSUB call), which does the next RETURN, until the last stored GOSUB is encountered, which will pass control back to line 50 of the main program.

```
  5 REM "HCF"
 10 PRINT "TYPE TWO POSITIVE INTEGERS"
 20 INPUT M
 30 INPUT N
 40 GOSUB 100
 50 PRINT "ANSWER IS";P
 60 GOTO 220
100 REM **SUBROUTINE**
110 LET P=N
120 LET N=M-N*INT (M/N)
130 LET M=P
140 IF N=0 THEN GOTO 160
150 GOSUB 100
160 RETURN
200 REM **ENDSUB**
210 REM
220 REM **END**
```

N5: Computed Gosubs

The line number N in a GOSUB N program instruction may be a computed expression: it is permissible to have any expression as the numeric value for a line number.

We can make use of this in programs where we want to give the user some options of operations. Since we would write the program with these options as subroutines, a suitable choice of line numbers can allow us to present a *menu* to the user. Here are two (useless) examples to illustrate the principle:

1)

```
10 PRINT "MAIN PROGRAM"
20 PRINT "INPUT 1 OR 2"
30 INPUT X
40 GOSUB X*100
50 PRINT "MAIN PROGRAM ENDS"
60 PRINT "NOW BACK TO MENU"
70 PRINT
80 GOTO 10
```

```
 100 PRINT "FIRST SUBROUTINE"
 110 RETURN
 200 PRINT "SECOND SUBROUTINE"
 210 RETURN
```

2)

```
  10 REM *NESTED SUBS FOR MENU**
  20 REM **INITIALISE MENU GOSUB**
  30 LET MENU=1000
  40 REM **MAIN PROGRAM**
  50 PRINT "MAIN PROGRAM"
  60 REM ....
  70 PRINT "NOW TO MENU"
  80 PRINT
  90 GOSUB MENU
 100 PRINT "MORE MAIN PROGRAM"
 110 PRINT "MENU OR END PROGRAM?"
 120 PRINT "INPUT M OR E"
 130 INPUT N$
 140 IF N$="M" THEN GOSUB MENU
 150 GOTO 9999
1000 PRINT TAB 3;"MENU"
1010 PRINT ,,"1. OPTION 1",,"2.
OPTION 2"
1020 PRINT "INPUT 1 OR 2"
1030 INPUT M
1040 GOSUB (M*1000)+100
1050 RETURN
1100 REM ****SUB 1******
1110 REM ***************
1120 PRINT "SUB 1 COMPLETED"
1130 PRINT
1140 RETURN
2100 REM ****SUB 2******
2110 REM ***************
2120 PRINT "SUB 2 COMPLETED"
2130 PRINT
2140 RETURN
9999 STOP
```

Notice the use of a variable (“MENU”) to hold the line number (1000) of the Menu subroutine (Lines 20 and 30). This technique can be useful as a mnemonic in longer programs, and can help the user identify which program module has been called.

This technique can be combined with the use of INKEY$ to give an instantaneous jump to the required subroutine. The program waits for a key to be pressed and then jumps to the required subroutine.

```
  10 PRINT "PRESS 1 FOR SUB 1","
PRESS 2 FOR SUB 2"
  20 IF INKEY$="" THEN GOTO 20
  30 LET A$=INKEY$
  35 IF A$="1" OR A$="2" THEN GO
TO 60
  40 PRINT "KEYS 1 OR 2 ONLY PLE
ASE"
  50 GOTO 10
  60 GOSUB VAL A$*100
  70 PRINT "BACK TO MENU"
  80 GOTO 10
```

```
100 PRINT "***************"
110 PRINT "SUBROUTINE ONE"
120 PRINT "***************"
130 RETURN
200 PRINT "***************"
210 PRINT "SUBROUTINE TWO"
220 PRINT "***************"
230 RETURN
```

Spectrum users should replace line 2Ø with

20 PAUSE Ø

N6: Subroutine Use: Example

As an example of the use of subroutines, here is a guess-the-number game. The program has three subroutines, one to get the number (lines 15Ø – 19Ø), one to check the guess (lines 21Ø – 3ØØ), and one for the success message (lines 35Ø – 41Ø), which sets the marker MARK to tell the main program, which is the loop between lines 5Ø and 14Ø, whether the number N (computer's number) is the same as G (the player's guess). This defines whether the success subroutine has been called as a result of the conditional test in line 11Ø.

```
  5 REM "GUESSNUM"
 10 LET MARK=0
 20 LET TRIES=0
 30 PRINT "GUESS MY NUMBER.",,,
"NUMBER IS BETWEEN 1 AND 99"
 35 REM ** GET NUMBER **
 40 GOSUB 150
 50 LET TRIES=TRIES+1
 60 PRINT ,,"ENTER YOUR GUESS"
 70 INPUT G
 80 CLS
 85 REM ** GOSUB CHECK **
 90 GOSUB 200
100 REM ** GOSUB SUCCESS **
110 IF DIFF=0 THEN GOSUB 350
120 REM ** CHECK MARK **
130 IF MARK=1 THEN GOTO 500
135 REM ** LOOP BACK **
140 GOTO 50

150 REM *********************
160 REM **  GET NUMBER SUB  **
165 REM *********************
170 LET N= INT ( RND *99)+1
180 RETURN

190 REM **   ENDSUB         **
195 REM *********************
200 REM
205 REM *********************
210 REM **  CHECK SUB       **
220 REM *********************
230 LET DIFF= ABS (G-N)
240 IF DIFF>50 THEN PRINT ,,"FR
EEZING"
```

```
 250 IF DIFF>25 AND DIFF <= 50 T
HEN PRINT ,,"COLD"
 260 IF DIFF>10 AND DIFF <= 25 T
HEN PRINT ,,"*WARM*"
 270 IF DIFF>4 AND DIFF <= 10 TH
EN PRINT ,," ** HOT ** "
 280 IF DIFF>0 AND DIFF <= 4 THE
N PRINT ,," ** *BOILING* ** "
 290 RETURN

 300 REM **     END CHECKSUB **
 310 REM *********************
 320 REM
 340 REM *********************
 350 REM **    SUCCESS SUB    **
 360 REM *********************
 370 PRINT AT 5,5;"$$$$$$$$$$$";
 TAB 5;"$ SUCCESS $"; TAB 5;"$$$
$$$$$$$$"
 380 PRINT AT 10,5;"IT TOOK ";TR
IES;" TRIES."
 390 LET MARK=1
 400 RETURN

 410 REM ** END SUCCESS SUB **
 420 REM *********************
 430 REM
 480 REM *********************
 490 REM **  END/RERUN MOD    **
 495 REM *********************
 500 PRINT ,,"ANOTHER GO? INPUT
Y OR N"
 510 INPUT A$
 520 CLS
 530 IF A$="Y" THEN GOTO 40
 540 PRINT ,,"OK,BYE"
 550 STOP

 560 REM ** ** END ** **
```

The structure of the program is thus:

Module 1:

1. Initialise success marker MARK and variable to store number of guesses made (TRIES)
2. Print Instructions
3. Call GET NUMBER Subroutine

Module 2 (Main program loop):

1. Increment TRIES
2. Input guess
3. Call CHECK Subroutine
4. Check if Guess equals Number. If it is, then call SUCCESS Subroutine
5. Check marker. If Success subroutine has been called (MARK = 1), then GOTO END/RERUN module
6. Loop back to Input guess again (1)

Module 3 (GET NUMBER Subroutine):
1. Define random number 1 – 99 as number N
2. Return

Module 4 (CHECK Subroutine):
1. Set variable DIFF equal to ABS difference of guess and number
2. Check value of DIFF, print appropriate message
3. Return

Module 5 (SUCCESS Subroutine):
1. Print success message, number of guesses made
2. Set MARK equal to 1
3. Return

Module 6 (END/RERUN module):
1. Print prompt for input
2. Input response to Another go? (A$)
3. If replay required (A$ = "Y") then GOTO Module 1,3
4. If A$ not "Y" then print end message
5. Stop

Notice that (although this is a program that has been modularised rather artificially to demonstrate the principles in a short program) the program consists of an introductory section, then a main program loop with both conditional and unconditional calls to subroutines, within a short main program loop. This makes the structure of the program clear, and minimises the use of GOTO statements, which would be required in profusion if the program were written in a linear, rather than modular fashion. It is perfectly possible to write the program in this linear manner, but the structure will not be as visible.

You should also note that the END/RERUN module is not a subroutine, but uses GOTO to pass control to this section from the main program, with a conditional GOTO to pass control back to the main program if required. Conditional GOTOs are preferable program structures to unconditional GOTOs, and whilst the END module could be a subroutine, RETURNing to the main program loop, further conditions would need to be inserted to pass control to Module 1 for a new number to be defined. The subroutine would also need to be exited by a GOTO for the program to stop. There is another solution, however, involving a nested subroutine, which we will set as an exercise.

Exercises

1 Rewrite "GUESSNUM" with the END/RERUN module as a subroutine. The procedure should be as follows:

END/RERUN SUB

i. Prompt for player input, and get response, as before.

ii. If RERUN not required, bypass 3 and 4 below, by a GOTO the RETURN line.
iii. GOSUB to GETNUMBER subroutine. This is a nested subroutine. The new value of N will be set by this operation.
iv. Re-initialise TRIES as Ø and MARK as Ø.
v. Return.

The main program loop is then returned to. The main program must then test whether it is to exit (rerun not required) or continue (new game started). We could set another marker to test this, but in effect we have done this by re-setting MARK if a rerun is required.

Rewrite the main program loop, so that on return from the END/RERUN subroutine, the program loops back *only* if MARK = Ø. If MARK = 1 then the program will not loop back and you can either insert a GOTO to bypass all the subroutines to an end program procedure, or STOP the program before the subroutines.

2 Insert an additional subroutine which prints 1;"ST",2; "ND",3;"RD", and then "TH" for other numbers into the "FACTORS" program (Unit N2).

3 Write a program which determines how many rolls of a die are required to produce a total score greater than 1ØØ. Use subroutines to produce the random numbers for the die rolls and to print out the results.

4 Let the computer choose a four digit number with no two digits alike. You try to guess the number chosen. The computer indicates H (too high), L (too low) or R (right) for each digit in turn and determines how many guesses are required to get the correct number. Use subroutines to create the number, input the operator's guess and give the response to each guess.

PART THREE

ADVANCED BASIC PROGRAMMING

SECTION O: PROGRAMMING METHODS II

O1: Résumé

Before we enter the arena of advanced BASIC programming let us recap on what we have examined and accomplished so far.

The method to design the solution or algorithm to a computational problem using 'top down' analysis has been explained. We have seen how to break our problem up into sub-problems which form our program modules (using tree diagrams). We know how to describe the algorithm in concise English sentences that we call pseudocode and how to determine and illustrate the flow of control in the problem solution by drawing a flowchart. When designing our solution we recognise the need to use the fundamental programming tools of:

(i) decision making
(ii) branching as a result of decisions
(iii) direct transfer from one point in the algorithm to another
(iv) repetition

These control structures, as they are called, which are present in all computer languages, have been discussed in some depth, together with other important BASIC language fundamentals. The techniques of:

(i) decision making
(ii) numeric processing
(iii) character handling with strings
(iv) looping through counting and condition testing
(v) handling of output by printing and plotting

and the realisation of modular techniques in programming by using subroutines have all been covered.

<u>WHAT'S NEXT?</u>

We must now consider the second phase of the programming method – producing the program itself.

It is important to do so at this stage in the book, so that our programming tool kit is complete enough to investigate and use the more sophisticated information handling facilities to be introduced later in this section:

(i) logical operations on data
(ii) character codes
(iii) moving graphics
(iv) graph plotting
(v) constructing and searching lists and data arrays
(vi) how to sort information into order

Once these skills have been mastered our complete programming expertise can then be applied to real applications.

Let's now see in this section of the text how to code our algorithms into BASIC language programs, and then debug, test and document them.

Further important design rules will be given, and finally a summary of our complete programming method will be provided with a flowchart and worked example.

O2: Producing the Program

We now consider the method by which a well designed, tested and fully documented program is produced.

Given our algorithm – which we have written out in steps in a description we call pseudocode – together with our flowchart – which shows how the steps of the solution are combined in sequence for the computer to solve the problem – we must now:

1. **CODE THE ALGORITHM IN SINCLAIR BASIC**
2. **DEBUG AND TEST THE PROGRAM**
3. **DOCUMENT THE PROGRAM**

O3: Coding and Design

CODE ON A ONE TO ONE BASIS

If the description of the algorithm is correct then coding on an almost one to one basis from statements in the pseudocode or the flowchart is possible. If you cannot code from the flowchart or pseudocode then further refinement of the algorithm is necessary.

Pseudocode descriptions in formal mode of the BASIC language control structures for decisions and loops are given later in this section. You will notice that the description itself is indented and concise, with the terms almost the same as BASIC statements. This is not unusual as BASIC was designed to do this very thing and is English-like in its syntax.

To be able to code at all you must of course:

KNOW THE BASIC LANGUAGE AND ITS RULES

Hopefully it is the right language for the job. On the ZX81 and Spectrum you don't have much choice! Actually it is a question of ease of programming specific applications that generates different languages. Most things can be done in BASIC, although perhaps not efficiently or elegantly. It is often useful to identify the kind of processing that will be required. When designing the algorithm consider whether the problem is a scientific or a business application, whether extensive calculations will be performed or large amounts of list processing done, whether the data is extensively numeric or string and whether the program will be interactive with much user dialogue.

When coding, avoid spelling and formatting mistakes. Sinclair BASIC is powerful in that it is one of the few available single keystroke

BASICs, hence you cannot make spelling mistakes on instructions or commands because the whole instruction is keyed in at once. However, mistakes can still be made when assigning variable names and in PRINT and REM statements.

DEFINE AND CONTAIN EACH MODULE WITH REM STATEMENTS

For example:

```
100  REM * SORT MODULE *
200  REM * THIS MODULE SORTS STRINGS *
.
.
.
500  REM * END SORT *
```

TERMINATE YOUR PROGRAM PROPERLY

You may have noticed that Sinclair BASIC does not need a special end-of-program statement. We can, however, put one in using a REM statement. For example:

```
500  REM * END OF PROGRAM *
```

The ZX81 and Spectrum do not process but only note REM statements. When the above line runs, the program will finish elegantly with a Ø/5ØØ message.

We can also stop a program with the STOP statement. Main modules should finish like this with subroutines programmed at higher line numbers terminated with a REM * END * statement. When terminated with STOP a message 9/line number (a 9 Stop (Line number): 1 statement on Spectrum) will be given.

```
  5  REM * NAME OF PROG *
 10  REM * MAIN MODULE *
 20  GOSUB 500
 30  STOP
 40  REM * END MAIN *
500  REM * SUBROUTINE *
600  RETURN
700  REM * END SUBROUTINE *
800  REM * END OF PROGRAM *
```

We could also use a GOTO 8ØØ at line 3Ø to terminate execution on the last program line.

ALWAYS CODE ACCORDING TO THE LOGICAL ORDER OF PROCESSING

This is usually ensured if you code from a flowchart, with your flowchart structured into modules, i.e. flowchart groups for the modules in the program.

Take care with the control structures and avoid unnecessary branching, especially with GOTO instructions. Try to make your programs both readable and efficient – but *first* make them *readable*!

USER FRIENDLY PROGRAMS

Design your programs with the user in mind – and that includes you! Directions to users should be concise and as few as is necessary, both in the program and in the user guide if your program is large enough to merit one.

Where the user needs a number of instructions to operate the program then these can be built into an optional 'help' module or subroutine.

```
100    REM * USER INSTRUCTION *
110    REM * DIRECTS USER TO HELP SUBROUTINE *
120    PRINT " FOR INSTRUCTIONS TYPE HELP
       OTHERWISE TYPE C "
130    INPUT A$
140    IF A$ = "HELP"THEN GOSUB 1000
150    REM * END USER INST *
. .    . . . . . . . .
1000   REM * HELP SUBROUTINE *
. .    . . . . . . . .

. .    . . . . . . . .
1200   RETURN
1210   REM * END HELP *
```

Users usually require to know:

- how to run the program
- what form of input data is required
- what output is produced

Your program should check on the range and type of input data. If the input data is out of range or incorrect the program should not stop with an error, but continue with a message to input correct data.

After you have designed a program to do a specific task it may be worthwhile to change it to be as general as possible – i.e. do several similar tasks. As you become more skilled and confident in programming you will be able to generalise and write a subroutine that enables users to select options from a menu. This is exactly similar to the exercise you have seen in multiple decision structures. See the "CASSFILE" program in Section V, for a "menu-driven" program. More "user-friendly" tips are given in the section on documentation, and some useful routines in Unit V2.

You must make your program readable. The program design will be modular and contain specific identifiable segments, subroutines and modules. These should be labelled in the design of the algorithm and transferred in the coding process.

(1) EACH MODULE SHOULD BE TITLED AND LABELLED TO INDICATE ITS FUNCTION. FOR EXAMPLE:

```
 10  REM "AVERAGE"
 20  REM * PROGRAM AVERAGES ANY NUMBERS
     INPUT *
 30  REM *
 40  REM * USER ROUTINE *
 50  REM * CHOICE OF NUMBERS INPUT *
 60  PRINT "HOW MANY NUMBERS DO YOU WISH
     TO AVERAGE"
 70  INPUT N
 80  DIM A(N)
 90  REM * INPUT ROUTINE *
100  REM * NUMBERS INPUT TO ARRAY *
110  PRINT "INPUT NUMBERS"
120  FOR I = 1 TO N
130  INPUT A(I)
140  NEXT I
150  REM
160  REM * PROCESSING ROUTINE *
170  REM * COMPUTES AVERAGE *
180  LET SUM = 0
190  FOR J = 1 TO N
200  LET SUM = SUM + A(J)
210  NEXT J
220  LET AVERAGE = SUM/N
230  REM
240  REM * OUTPUT ROUTINE *
250  PRINT "THE AVERAGE OF"
260  FOR K = 1 TO N
270  PRINT A(K);" ";
280  NEXT K
290  PRINT "IS "; AVERAGE
300  REM
310  REM * END AVERAGE *
```

(2) DESIGN YOUR PROGRAM SO THAT RELATED STATEMENTS ARE TOGETHER

For example, input – processing – output statements:

(i) All input statements will be at the beginning of a simple sequential program, processing in the middle, and output normally at the end.

(ii) For a modular program, input, processing and output routines will be separate modules or groups of statements within a single module.

(iii) Subroutine modules will usually be placed separately at the end of a program.

(3) INSERT REM STATEMENTS BETWEEN PROGRAM MODULES AS SEPARATORS
Program modules are then easily identified. Use blank REM lines or lines of asterisks.

(4) PLAN YOUR PROGRAM LAYOUT BEFORE CODING
The printed listing of your program is important. Choose a maximum line width. Break longer lines into shorter ones in REM statements by using spaces. Compensate for overrun. For example:

```
10 REM * AAAAA
         AAAAA
         AAAAA *
```

You will not be able to do this with other BASIC statement lines.

(5) YOUR LAYOUT SHOULD TRY TO REFLECT THE MODULAR STRUCTURE OF YOUR PROGRAM

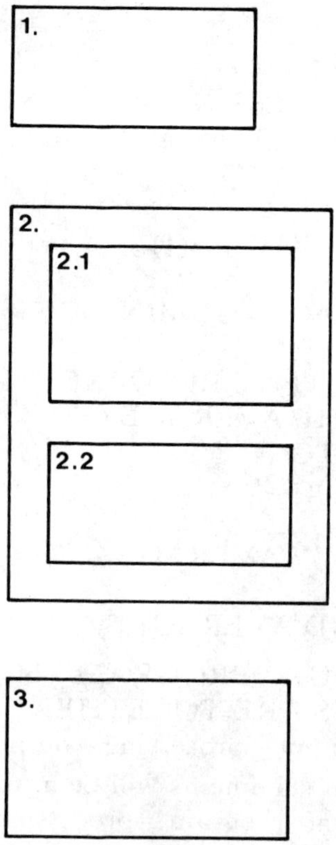

Indented statements are not possible on the ZX81 or Spectrum, unfortunately!

DESIGNING PROGRAM OUTPUT

For the user the output is the most important part of the program. Take time planning it. The output instructions in Sinclair BASIC are: PRINT, PRINT AT, PLOT, LPRINT, COPY, TAB, plus graphics commands.

(i) RESULTS SHOULD BE OUTPUT WITH RELATED TEXT.
Label all your numerical output:
e.g. [YEAR] 1974 [NET INCOME] £5678.65
instead of 1974 5678.65
e.g. AVERAGE AGE OF BOYS IS 15 YRS 3 MONTHS
rather than 15 3

(ii) DISPLAY LARGE AMOUNTS OF OUTPUT AS A TABLE, HISTOGRAM OR GRAPH, AND GIVE TITLES.
For example:

TABLE 1: NET INCOME FOR B. JONES
FOR YEARS 1978-80

YEAR	NET INCOME
1978	£2018.45

Box your tables if possible.

The user should not have to look up the program listing to see what the numbers in the output mean.

(iii) DESIGN YOUR OUTPUT TO BE EASY TO READ
Plan it to be attractive to any user of your program and, of course, yourself. Graphics is a powerful tool for this.

(iv) ALIGN, SPACE AND JUSTIFY THE OUTPUT
Plan your output with reference to the screen size and divisions.
For tables – align information central to the heading
align signs
right justify numbers
left justify characters.
(There are routines in the text for doing this). For example:

STUDENT CODE	NAME
876-340	JIM SMITH
27-210	HUNG FO
453-003	SARAH JAY
1-025	DRACULA

NUMBERS
15.003
815.231
- 4.000
- 100.100

Fill in with zeros to get decimal placing correct.

(v) USE SPACE CAREFULLY

Sinclair computers use expensive printer paper! Print output horizontally wherever possible. For example:

TABLE OF POWERS OF 2
2
4
8
16
32 etc

should be:

TABLE OF POWERS OF 2				
2	4	8	16	32
64	128	256	512	1024

(vi) DO NOT OVERDO EXPLANATIONS

Be succinct!

(vii) MAKE YOUR ABBREVIATIONS CLEAR

x = 25
NDTC = 25
NUMBER OF DAYS TO CHRISTMAS = 25

(viii) DISPLAY INPUT DATA AS AN OPTION

Allow checking of input data before processing.
Make your program check for incorrect or bad input data.

MODULAR DESIGN

We break problems down into sequences of steps to produce programs in which different kinds of activities are separated out. These distinctive program modules are our SUBROUTINES or SUB-PROGRAMS. Each module has its own name and address, but in BASIC we usually refer to program modules by address only, as with:

GOTO 100 and GOSUB 3300

where the address is the line number of the first statement in the module.

We can address sub-programs or modules by name by assigning the name and address of the module at the start of the program. For example:

```
10  REM * ASSIGN MODULE NAMES *
20  LET INPUT DATA = 1000
30  LET PROCESSING = 2000
```

```
  40  LET OUTPUT DATA = 3000
  50  REM * END MODULE ASSIGN *
  60  REM
  70  REM * MAIN *
  80  GOTO INPUT DATA
  90  GOSUB PROCESSING
 100  GOTO OUTPUT DATA
 110  STOP

1000  REM * INPUT DATA MOD *
. . . . .

. . . . .
1500  GOTO 90
1600  REM * END INPUT *
2000  REM * PROCESSING SUBROUTINE *
. . . . .
2500  RETURN
2600  REM * END PROCESSING *
3000  REM * OUTPUT DATA MOD *
. . . . .
3500  GOTO 110
3600  REM * END OUTPUT MOD *
4000  REM * END PROG.*
```

There are good reasons for modular design and the use of subroutines and sub-program modules. The logic of the program, i.e. its flow, is easier to follow. The clarity of the structure of the main program is improved whilst program design is proceeding by referring to the number or name of the module initially, instead of starting to write out the code of the module at that point. The module can be coded as a separate entity.

Independent testing of modules is possible, but care must be taken that all variables have been declared and have their correct values at the start of the module. Debugging is simpler with this approach, since the module is isolated. You can leave the coding of a module until a later stage, but you must know what it will do when coded.

If a module has to be used several times in a program from different places it need only be written once and called (into action) from these points by reference to its line number or name.

Program modules can be designed to run sequentially:

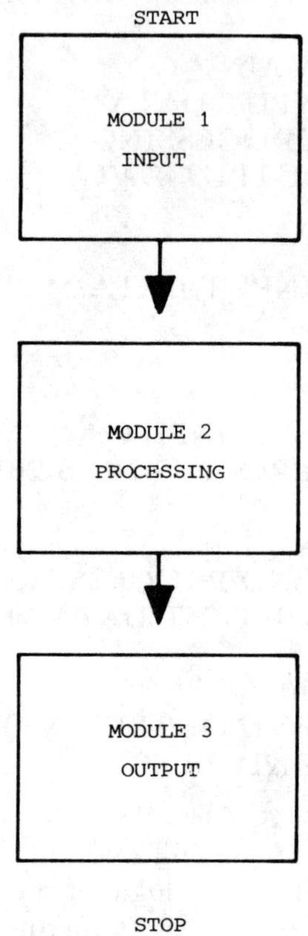

This structure is convenient for simple programs. However, programs can be structured in terms of subroutines and sub-programs being called from a short and simple main program module.

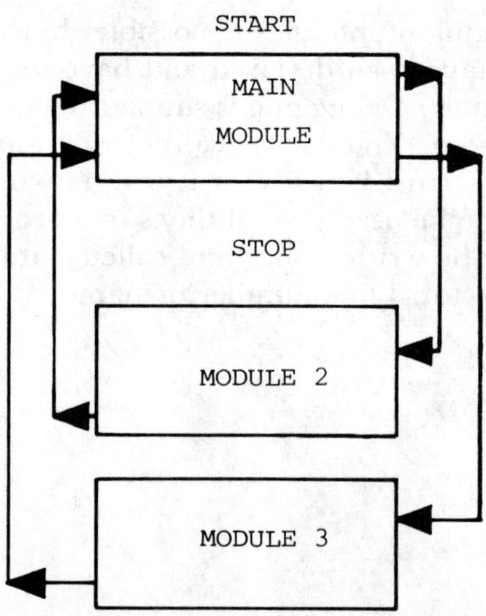

This structure is convenient for longer, more complicated, programs with many modules and nestings.

Subroutines automatically return to the next line in the main program through the RETURN statement. Other modules are <u>called</u> by GOTO (line number) and <u>return</u> by GOTO (line number) instructions. GOTO MUST BE USED WITH THOUGHT AND CARE AND NOT EXCESSIVELY. Use a GOSUB unless a return to a different point in the main module is needed or a multiple return is possible as a result of a decision to be made within the module.

Nested modules can be treated as other modules and called from within the subroutine or sub-program, by GOSUB and GOTO instructions. Nested loops <u>must</u> be contained within the same module, however.

CONTROL STRUCTURES IN SINCLAIR BASIC

(1) Each <u>control</u> <u>structure</u> is a <u>program</u> <u>module</u>.
(2) A formal pseudocode description of each structure is given of the general form of the control structure.
(3) A flowchart description is given of the general form.
(4) The BASIC version is given of the general form.
(5) A simple example illustrates the BASIC form of the control structure.
(6) Structures will be written in indented form in the pseudocode version for clarity. You cannot indent in Sinclair BASIC program listings. REM statements must be used to show the start and stop lines for program modules.
(7) P is a <u>processing</u> <u>operation</u>. It can be a single instruction, a statement or a group of statements.
(8) In the formal pseudocode each structure will commence with the title <u>module</u> (abbreviated to <u>mod</u>), and end with the statement <u>endmodule</u> (abbreviated to <u>endmod</u>).
(9) In BASIC each structure will be bounded by REM*STARTMOD* and REM*ENDMOD* statements.
(10) Flowcharts will be bounded by START and STOP symbols.

The structures summarised are:

A) *Decision Structures*
- (i) Single decision
  IF-THEN structure
- (ii) Double decision
  IF-THEN-else structure
- (iii) Multiple decision
  Case structure

B) *Loop Structures*

(i) repeat-forever loop structure
(ii) repeat-until structure
(iii) while-do structure
(iv) FOR-NEXT structure

The names of the structures are implemented as actual programming language structures in other languages and some forms of BASIC. The FOR-NEXT structure is a special form of the while-do loop, given a specific implementation in BASIC.

A. DECISION STRUCTURES

(i) SINGLE DECISION: The IF-THEN structure
Meaning: IF (condition is true) THEN (do something)

Pseudocode

```
mod
  if (condition)
      then P
  endif
endmod
```

Flowchart

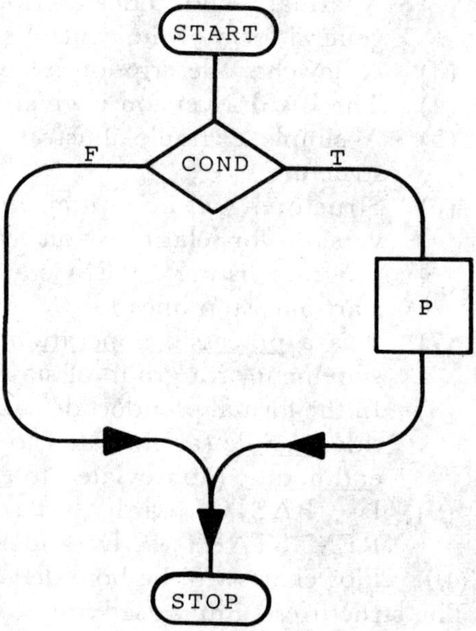

BASIC

```
10  REM*START MOD*
20  IF (COND) THEN P
30  REM* ENDMOD*
```

Example

Input a number and if it is positive, print it.

Pseudocode

```
mod
  input A
    if A > 0
      then print A
    endif
endmod
```

BASIC

```
10  REM*START MOD*
20  INPUT A
30  IF A > 0 THEN PRINT A
40  REM*END MOD*
```

(ii) DOUBLE DECISION: The IF-THEN-else structure

Meaning: IF (condition is true) THEN (do something) otherwise (if condition is false) do something else.

Pseudocode

```
mod
  if (cond)
    then P1
    else P2
  endif
endmod
```

Flowchart

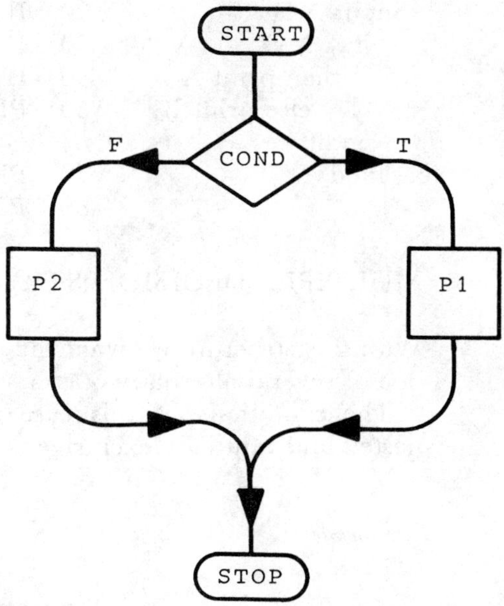

BASIC

```
1Ø  REM*START MOD*
2Ø  IF (COND) THEN GOTO 5Ø
3Ø  (FALSE TASK P2)
4Ø  GO TO 6Ø
5Ø  (TRUE TASK P1)
6Ø  REM*ENDMOD*
```

To perform the true task (P1 in the pseudocode) first, the BASIC implementation of the structure would test the complement of the condition, so that in the program below, for example, A>B would be replaced by A<B, and lines 5Ø and 7Ø swapped. Note the standard form of complement would be B< = A, but we have defined the input numbers as unequal in this case.

Example

Input two unequal numbers and print the largest.

Pseudocode

```
mod
  input A,B
    if A > B
      then print A
        else print B
    endif
endmod
```

BASIC

```
1Ø  REM*STARTMOD*
2Ø  INPUT A
3Ø  INPUT B
4Ø  IF A > B THEN GOTO 7Ø
5Ø  PRINT B
6Ø  GOTO 8Ø
7Ø  PRINT A
8Ø  REM*ENDMOD*
```

(iii) MULTIPLE DECISION STRUCTURE: The case structure

With this structure we want the program to select and perform one of several alternative tasks.

The conditions in this case structure are sequential, not nested and mutually exclusive.

Pseudocode

```
mod
  case
    if (condition 1 is true)
    then P1
    if (condition 2 is true)
    then P2
    if (condition 3 is true)
    then P3
  end case
endmod
```

Flowchart

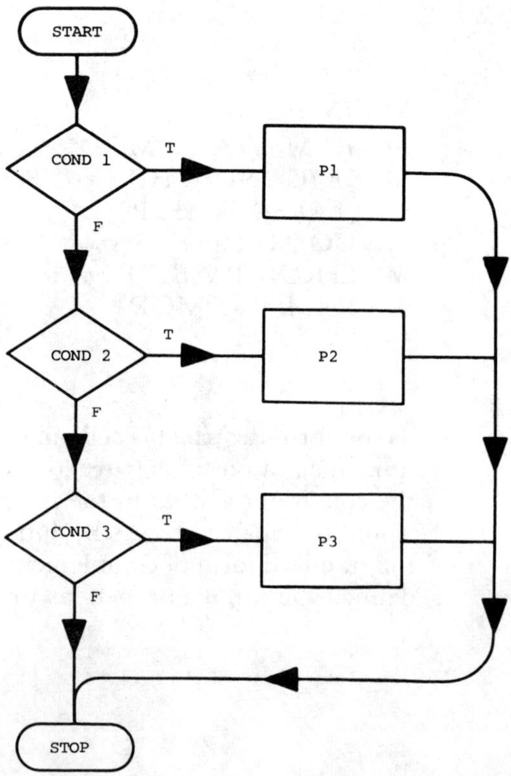

BASIC

```
10  REM*STARTMOD*
20  IF C1 THEN P1
30  IF C2 THEN P2
40  IF C3 THEN P3
50  REM*ENDMOD*
```

Example

Test whether a number input is positive, zero, or negative, and print the result.

Pseudocode

```
mod
  input A
  case
    if A<Ø
      then print "NEGATIVE"
    if A = Ø
      then print "ZERO"
    if A>Ø
      then print "POSITIVE"
  endcase
endmod
```

Flowchart

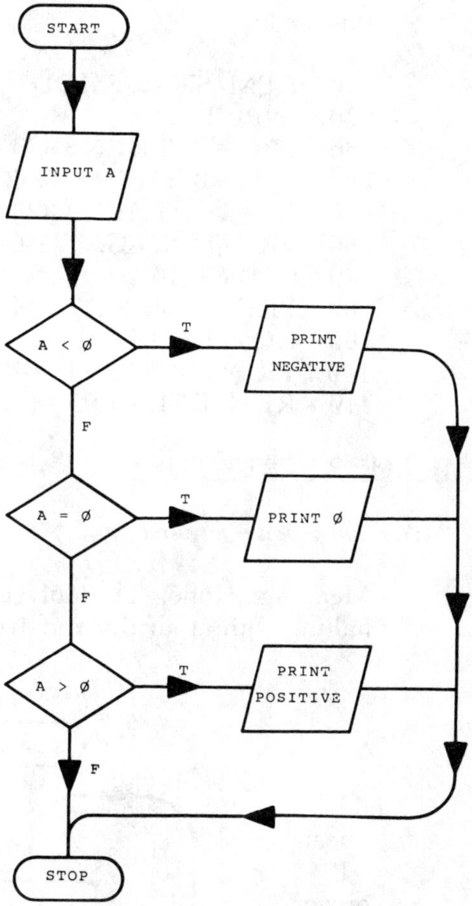

BASIC

```
10  REM*STARTMOD*
20  INPUT A
30  IF A < 0 THEN PRINT "NEGATIVE"
40  IF A = 0 THEN PRINT "ZERO"
50  IF A > 0 THEN PRINT "POSITIVE"
60  REM*ENDMOD*
```

Alternatively, we can use conditional and unconditional GOTO statements to implement this structure. This would be appropriate if the processing section of a program after the decision were several statements long, rather than the single instruction available on the ZX81. Spectrum users can add more instructions on the same line. They should be restrained in using this facility.

```
 10  REM*STARTMOD*
 20  INPUT A
 30  IF A < 0 THEN GOTO 60
 40  IF A = 0 THEN GOTO 80
 50  IF A > 0 THEN GOTO 100
 60  PRINT "NEGATIVE"
 70  GOTO 110
 80  PRINT "ZERO"
 90  GOTO 110
100  PRINT "POSITIVE"
110  REM*ENDMOD*
```

B. LOOP STRUCTURES

(i) *The repeat – forever loop*

Meaning: None. The only conceivable result is the program halting with an arithmetic overflow report.

Pseudocode

```
mod
  repeat
    P
  forever
endmod
```

Flowchart

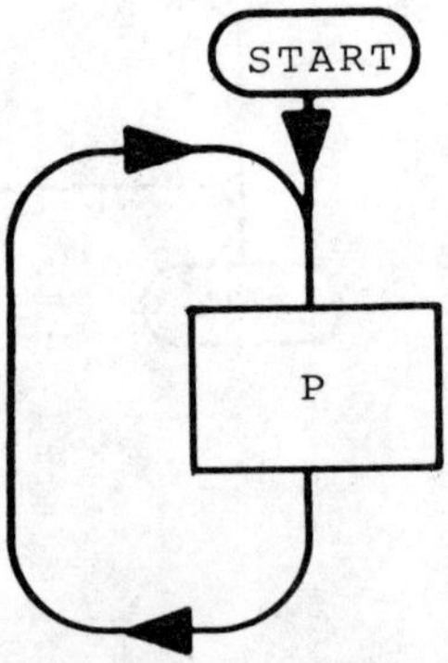

BASIC

```
10  REM*STARTMOD*
20  P
30  GOTO 20
40  REM*ENDMOD*
```

This structure is for demonstration only. Avoid using it in programs! It can sometimes occur in error. Use BREAK if you suspect your program has entered such a loop (because nothing happens).

(ii) *The repeat – until loop*

Meaning: Repeat processing until a condition is true.
These structures loop until a specific termination condition is met, for example until a counter reaches a certain value or until a dummy or sentinel value is input. The important characteristic of this loop structure is that the repeat test (or exit test) is at the bottom of the loop, after the processing 'body'. The program lines making up the body of the loop (P) will be executed *at least* once. The repeat condition can use any conditional operator *or* its complement (reverse).

e.g. equals ⟷ not equal
= <>

Use of the complement often leads to a more elegant program.

Pseudocode

```
mod
  repeat
    P
  until (condition is true)
endmod
```

Flowchart

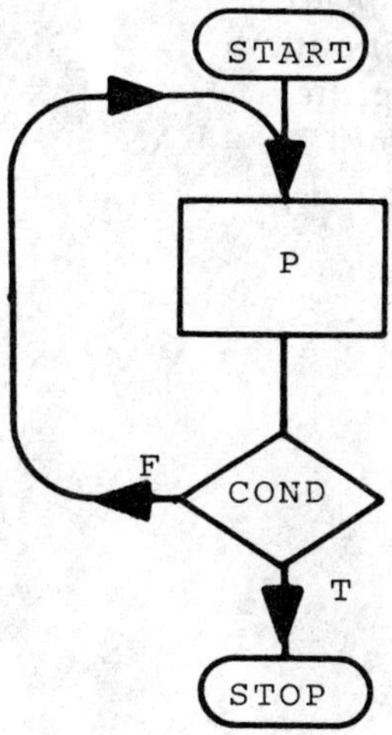

BASIC

```
10  REM*STARTMOD*
20  P
30  IF (COND) THEN GOTO 50
40  GOTO 20
50  REM*ENDMOD*
```

BASIC using complement

```
10  REM*STARTMOD*
20  P
30  IF (COMP COND) THEN GOTO 20
40  REM*ENDMOD*
```

Exit requires no specific instruction.

Example

Input and print strings until the sentinel value "LAST" is input.

Pseudocode

```
mod
   repeat
      input A$
      print A$
   until A$ = LAST
endmod
```

Flowchart

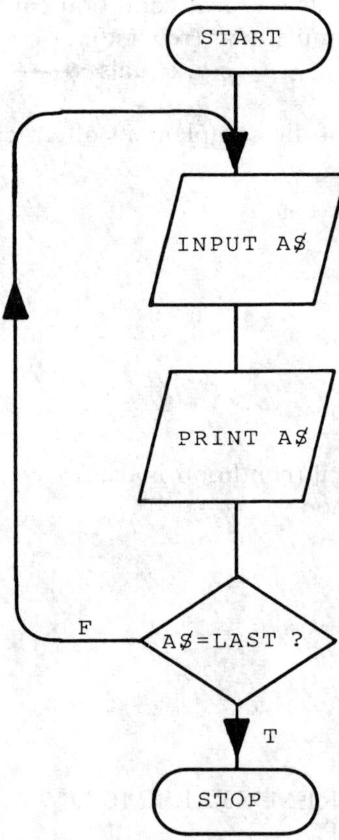

BASIC

```
10  REM*STARTMOD*
20  INPUT A$
30  PRINT A$
40  IF A$ = "LAST" THEN GOTO 60
50  GOTO 20
60  REM*ENDMOD*
```

Complement Version

```
10  REM*STARTMOD*
20  INPUT A$
30  PRINT A$
40  IF A$<>"LAST" THEN GOTO 20
50  REM *ENDMOD*
```

(iii) *While – do structure*

Meaning: While a condition holds (TRUE) keep repeating the process until the condition is broken (FALSE).

The condition can be, for example, that a loop-counter variable value is not equal to its final value (IF N<10 THEN..). The process will then repeat until it is. The condition may also be set so that a sentinel value has not occurred (IF N<>6 THEN). These conditions are set so that the true pathway is the process task, and the false is the exit.

The While – do loop is characterised by having the repeat test carried out prior to the body of the loop (i.e. at the top). No processing will happen if the repeat test is false at the first encounter, i.e. the body of the loop is never entered.

Pseudocode

```
mod
  while (condition is true)
    do P
  endwhile
endmod
```

Flowchart

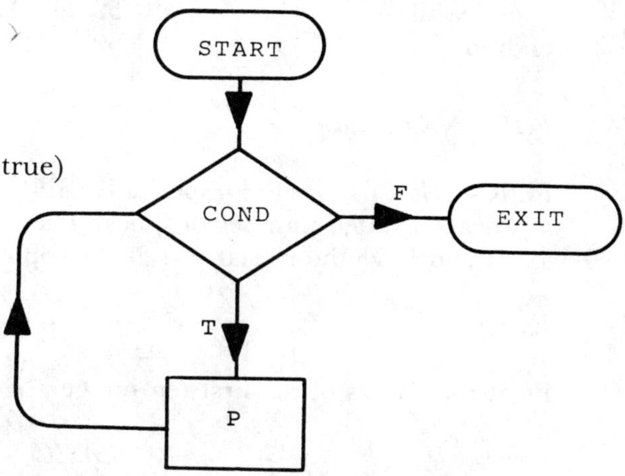

BASIC

```
10  REM*STARTMOD*
20  IF (COND) THEN GOTO 40
30  GOTO 60
40  P
50  GOTO 20
60  REM*ENDMOD*
```

Using the complement of the repeat condition gives a neater program.

Complement Version

```
10  REM*STARTMOD*
20  IF (COND) THEN GOTO 50
30  P
40  GOTO 20
50  REM*ENDMOD*
```

Example

While the value of the square of consecutive integers is less than 100, print them on the screen.

Pseudocode

```
mod
  n = 1
  while n*n< = 100
     do print n*n
     n = n + 1

  end while
endmod
```

BASIC (complement)

```
10  REM*STARTMOD*
20  LET N = 1
30  IF N*N>100 THEN
    GOTO 60
40  PRINT N*N
45  LET N = N + 1
50  GOTO 30
60  REM*ENDMOD*
```

(iv) *FOR – NEXT Loops*

FOR – NEXT loops are a special BASIC structure for repeating a process a stated number of times. They are in fact While – do loops and have the repeat test at the top of the loop.

Example

Print the values of the first ten integers.

Pseudocode

```
mod
  n = 1
  While n < = 10
    do print n
    n = n + 1
  end while
endmod
```

BASIC

```
10  REM*STARTMOD*
20  FOR N = 1 TO 10
30  PRINT N
40  NEXT N
50  REM*ENDMOD*
```

FOR – NEXT loops have their own special flowchart symbol, because they are used so extensively in BASIC:

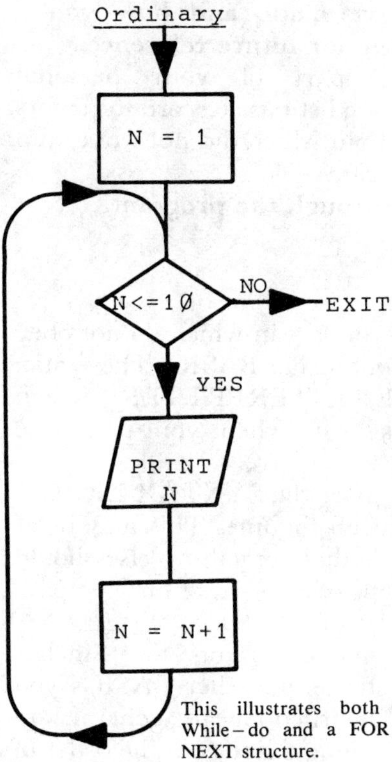

This illustrates both a While–do and a FOR–NEXT structure.

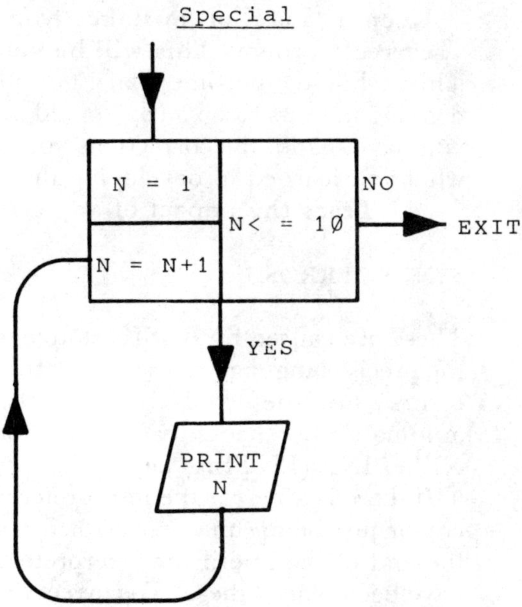

This is a condensed version. It groups together the FOR – NEXT – STEP instruction elements, which the standard form separates.

O4: Program Development

Program Development involves the activities of DEBUGGING your program of errors, TESTING to see if it behaves as specified and gives the desired results, and DOCUMENTATION which tells users how to run the program.

DEBUGGING

The Sinclair machines have good editing facilities and error messages. Those on the Spectrum have brief statements of the error type, those on the ZX81 have just a number or letter.

Although it is inefficient to correct errors one at a time (because there is seldom only a single error since programming mistakes tend to compound one another), error messages on the machine are produced singly, since an error stops the computer from running. Thus we must deal with the errors as they occur in the program sequence. You may notice a number of errors on carefully looking through the listing. Any you spot should be edited out at once.

GET TO KNOW YOUR COMPUTER ERROR CODES

This will happen automatically in time (as you make mistakes!), but it is worthwhile studying the codes. They define the ways in which 'run-time' errors occur, and an understanding of them will help you avoid bugs.

Keep a note of mistakes you have made and how you corrected them. This will be valuable for future reference.

This should become an automatic part of your personal documentation. Keep a copy of old program listings. Record the errors you have made, the corrections you tried but which did not work, and what you learned in developing the program.

Trace the impact of any error through the program.

SYNTAX ERRORS

These are caused by BASIC statements you key in which do not obey the precise language rules (syntax rules) of Sinclair BASIC. The syntax errors are detected by the LINE INTERPRETER which automatically checks each line you key in when you press the NEWLINE (ENTER) key.

If there is an error the interpreter will place the SYNTAX ERROR cursor just before the first error it detects on the line. This may be at the end of the line if the interpreter finds that something else should have been placed there. To correct this type of error you must compare the syntax you have written with the rules of BASIC.

Typing instructions incorrectly cannot occur on the Sinclair computers as the BASIC is single key-stroke. In other BASICs you must type P,R,I,N,T, for PRINT. Instructions in general are automatically placed in the correct order along a line (i.e. the order of line number – instruction – operand), since they are taken care of by the mode controller which sets the cursors in the correct sequence.

Errors which can occur are:

1 Omission of line number
2 Line number too large (>9999)
3 Line number negative
4 Line number non-integer
5 Omission of delimiters:
    brackets (must be paired)
    commas
    semicolons
    quotes
    colons (on the Spectrum)
6 Typing in of improper variable names
7 Incorrect logical expressions

There can be more than one error per line. The S-cursor will re-appear in the line when you try to enter it into memory. The line edit facility is comprehensive and easy to use on the ZX81 and Spectrum.

You must correct your mistakes, and keep trying to 'compile' the line into correct BASIC syntax (to be entered into memory). When successful, the program line will appear at the top of the screen.

The syntax error check ensures no nonsense lines (from the computer's point of view) are entered. It cannot help you in coding correct sequences of program lines, or prevent logical errors.

PROGRAM LOGIC ERRORS

These are the effect of bad logical design of the program. They can be avoided if care is taken in the design and coding of the program. If a program produces incorrect results then there is an error in the flow of logic in the program. This may only occur with certain values of data.

If each program section or module has been tested independently then the linking of the modules is incorrect. We can test program sections as follows:

1) Insert a temporary breakpoint into the program, at the appropriate point.
2) Print out values of intermediate results, to the screen or printer.
3) It is most important to print out the values of variables used in making a decision and those used in loops, either counter loops or FOR – NEXT loops.
4) Go back to the pseudocode or flowchart and modify the steps which are in error. 'Walk through' the algorithm, using a flowchart, to check the step sequence, and hand trace the program with selected values of data and/or variables. Be careful! Often changes in one part of the algorithm cause changes in the others. It is no use solving one problem if it causes another!
5) Change the documentation if necessary. Note down the changes you have made, or lines you have deleted. Keep program listings.
6) Re-test the complete program, using a variety of data.

Each testing statement in a complex program should be headed by a remark statement.

```
1ØØØ   REM – DEBUG
  –
  –
  –    (Testing Statements)
  –
  –
  –
  –    REM – END DEBUG
```

These temporary REM statements are later deleted by keying in their line numbers, as are the testing statements. It is very easy to leave in test instructions unless they are marked.

INSERTING BREAK POINTS

We can stop a program at any point and obtain the values of variables, expressions, etc. to test calculations or check for errors. We do this by inserting a group of statements which will output the values we want and then stop the program.

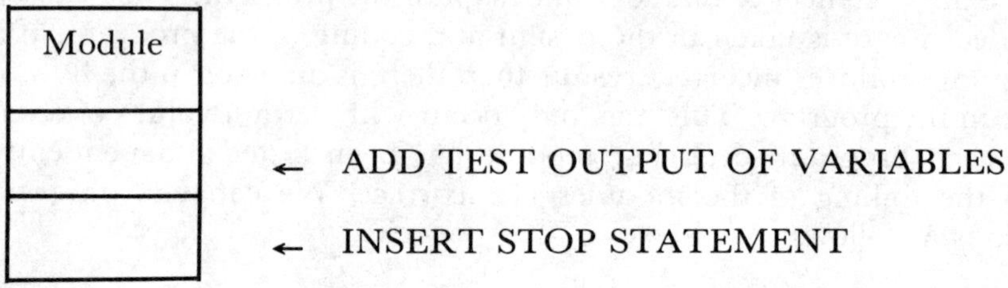

CONT will restart the program.

Individual modules or sections of program can be tested this way. We do, of course, have to RUN the program from the *required* module line number. Care should be taken when this is done that variables needed in the module have been declared properly and that the values of parameters passed to the module are as required. Remember that you can INPUT the values of variables directly if necessary, using the command mode, and using LET statements:

LET X(2) = 2Ø, etc.

The value of any variable at the point the program crashed can also be obtained by keying a statement without the line number, and again using the computer in command mode:

```
PRINT A$
LPRINT X(3)
```

The commands RUN N (where N is the line number we wish to run the program from) and GOTO N enable us to run the program starting at any point. Using GOTO N does not negate the initialisation of variables that occurs *if* the program has already run. For example, if we input:

```
1Ø  LET  A = 1
2Ø  LET  B = 2
3Ø  PRINT  A,B
```

and then key in GOTO 3Ø, we get the error report '2/3Ø' (ZX81) or '2 Variable not found 3Ø:1' (Spectrum) meaning an undefined variable was found. If we RUN the program, we can then use GOTO 3Ø, and the program signals successful completion.

RUN-TIME ERRORS

These are a result of programmer carelessness and do not prevent the interpreter from translating the program. They make the program crash when you attempt to run it, that is they prevent the program from running to completion. Common run-time errors are:

1) undeclared or unidentified variables
2) arithmetic overflow
3) lack of data for processing

4) failure to complete loop increment and subroutine section statements
5) subscript out of range
6) memory full
7) screen display file full
8) integer out of range

As we have seen, run-time errors cause diagnostic system messages to be printed. These appear at the bottom of the screen and are called:

ERROR CODES

These errors can then be traced through the type of error given by the code and the line number at which the program stopped.

ERROR CODES

Error codes or Report codes are presented on the screen when a program stops for any reason, either as a result of successful completion (no more program lines), an instruction or command (STOP, BREAK), or a run-time error.

On the ZX81 the codes have the form E/N, where E is the code for the type of error and N is the line number where the program was stopped (STOP or BREAK), or where an error occurred. N is Ø for a direct command. This is an example of an error code on the ZX81 which is printed on the screen when an arithmetic overflow (number larger than about $1Ø^{38}$ generated) occurs in line 6Ø of the program:

6/6Ø

The Spectrum gives an extended error report code, with a brief statement in the form:

E Statement   N:S

where E is the report code, the statement is the reason for stopping (with BREAK or STOP or program completion) or type of error. N is the line number, but since the Spectrum can have multiple line statements, the S number indicates which statement on the line the report code refers to. We are not using multiple line statements in this text, so S will always be 1, meaning the first (and only) statement on the line, unless after the THEN in an IF. . . THEN statement, which is treated, like a colon, as a statement separator.

The Spectrum's version of the example given above (the ZX81's arithmetic overflow error code) is:

6 Number too big 6Ø:1

Report codes are crucial aids to debugging programs. Without them we would know only that we had an error, but not where it occurred or what type of error it was. The error reports indicate both of these items of information.

It is important to understand that the *cause* of an error may come earlier in a program than the line where the program stopped. For example, a code 2 error (variable not found), occurring in line 1ØØ of a program might be caused by a mis-spelt variable name in line 1ØØ (not the same as the variable you meant it to be – putting GUES when you meant GUESS, for example). It could also be the result of not having assigned the variable *earlier* in the program. If the error causing the program to halt is not apparent from the line given in the error report, the program flow must be traced backwards to find the prior cause. In some cases this can be extremely difficult to track down – for example, where a numeric value wrongly defined or generated by the program causes another expression to cause an arithmetic overflow. Tracing techniques must be used.

Lists of Error codes and their meanings for the ZX81 and Spectrum are given in Appendix II.

TESTING AND VERIFICATION

Verify that your program works by testing it with Test Data

Testing comes after debugging a program. Its purpose is to ensure that the program is logically correct, produces correct answers and meets the specification of its purpose.

1 First test each module separately

Each procedure and subroutine should be treated as if it were a separate program.

Test for (i) good data – the expected type and range of inputs.
(ii) bad data – out-of-range and incorrect type inputs.

Try to ensure each procedure 'fails softly'. For bad data (particularly in any data entry module) following each input a check routine or procedure should be used to give an error message if range is incorrect or check type of input and correct syntax. This is best done with strings, which are more flexibly handled. See Unit V which deals with input checks at length.

2 Combine the modules and test the complete program

If there is a logical error (i.e. program does not produce the intended results) insert additional test statements which will:

(i) Output intermediate results.
(ii) Output values of variables at each stage.
(iii) Output results of expressions at each stage.
(iv) Output values of the loop counter at each pass.
(v) Output results of array manipulation after each operation.
(vi) Output values of parameters before and after subroutines entry and return.

3 Handle exceptions

(i) Test all data in the program.
(ii) Screen all data.
(iii) Process only good data.
(iv) Output bad data saying why it was bad.

4 Let your program stop elegantly

(i) When there is no data input or data available, the program should tell you so.

(ii) Sinclair BASIC programs are interactive. The user can control program continuation with:

```
910  PRINT "PROCESSING ENDED – MORE
     DATA? ANSWER YES OR NO"
920  INPUT A$
930  IF A$ = "YES" THEN GOTO 100
940  PRINT "GOODBYE"
950  STOP
960  REM PROGRAM END
```

5 Rewrite the program until you are satisfied with it

Remember the program should be – structured
– easy to read
– easy to understand
– handle exceptions
– be as efficient as possible
– documented

and it must solve the problem as specified!

6 Put clarity before efficiency

To be good a program algorithm does not have to be clever, difficult to understand or run super-fast. If you do not understand how the algorithm works do not use it – rewrite and re-design or use another method.

Programs will work correctly if the rules of the language are obeyed, and the program will work to specification if the algorithm is properly designed.

DOCUMENTATION

ANNOTATE AND DOCUMENT YOUR PROGRAM AND CREATE A READABLE PROGRAM

1 Write an explanation for each program module or segment. At the beginning of each segment provide suitable comments which explain:

(1) the purpose of the algorithm

(2) the variables and their significance (the values they store)

(3) the results expected.

2 Use comments only where necessary:

(1) don't comment each program line

(2) don't explain the obvious

(3) at the beginning of the program provide a block of

comments that explain the program at each module and provide a comment which explains what the module does in relation to the program.

3 Clear comments should appear separated from program code. The clearest comments are framed. For example

```
10  REM  *    *    *    *    *    *    *    *
20  REM  *       SUBROUTINE TO              *
30  REM  *    CALCULATE N TO 2 D.P.         *
40  REM  *                                  *
50  REM  *    *    *    *    *    *    *    *
```

Lines of asterisks provide visible dividers between sections of program.

4 Use comment in the program and in the output to the screen or printer.

Use blank REM lines as separators in the program.

5 For large programs write a reference document:
- (i) Describe the algorithm you used. If it is not original you should include a note of its source, author, version, and type of computer it was written on.
- (ii) Explain how you wrote the program, the reasons for writing it, the type of computer used and memory required.
- (iii) Make a note of areas that may need improving, or could be modified for different purposes.
- (iv) Which modules are general (menus, subroutines), and which require specific kinds of input.
- (v) Explain the scope and limitations of the program.
- (vi) Include your name, and the date of production.

6 List the tests you made and data used. Reproduce some of the results of the tests.

7 List performance tests (e.g. how long it takes the program to run).

8 Give user instructions and reproduce the output of a run and explain to the user how he uses the program.

9 Give the program characteristics. Explain any abnormal behaviour of the program (e.g. response to bad input).

10 Write a brief USER GUIDE. This is *not* for the computer expert. It should explain:
- the purpose of the program
- the algorithm
- how to run the program
- what input is needed
- what results are printed
- how to use the menu (if included)

O5: THE COMPLETE PROGRAMMING METHOD

SUMMARY: THE STRUCTURED PROGRAMMING METHOD

1. PRODUCE THE ALGORITHM

1.1 *State the Problem fully*

- 1.1.1 State the problem
- 1.1.2 Understand *what* is to be done

1.2 *Research the Problem*

- 1.2.1 Research and analyse the problem to see *how* the computer can handle it
- 1.2.2 Identify all formulae and relations to be used.
- 1.2.3 Identify all data involved

1.3 *Design the algorithm*

Use top down structured methods:

- 1.3.1 Break the problem up into sub-problems or modules.
- 1.3.2 Use a structure diagram or tree diagram to help in breaking down the problem.
- 1.3.3 Start classifying modules or parts of modules as:
  INPUT
  PROCESSING
  OUTPUT
- 1.3.4 Utilise the fundamental control structures in the modules
  - Decision structures
  - Transfer structures
  - Loops
  - Subroutines
  - Nested structures
  - Subprograms
- 1.3.5 Set up a DATA TABLE in which all data types are classified as
  Variables
  Constants
  Counters
  Functions – if using a Spectrum and the DEF FN instructions
- 1.3.6 Define the algorithm further until coding it into a BASIC language program is an easy and obvious exercise.

1.4 *Describe the algorithm in Pseudocode and Flowchart form*

- 1.4.1 Write out the final algorithm (now in modular form) in small steps in an abbreviated English style called Pseudocode.
  Each module should be treated separately and labelled.
- 1.4.2 Illustrate the logical flow of control in the algorithm by constructing a flowchart.
- 1.4.3 Test the algorithm, if necessary using a hand trace or walk through.

2. PRODUCE THE PROGRAM

2.1 *Code the Algorithm in SINCLAIR BASIC*

2.1.1 Code on a direct basis from the pseudocode or flowchart description in line numbered BASIC statements, module by module.

2.1.2 Implement the fundamental control structures, used in their SINCLAIR BASIC versions.

2.2 *Debug and Test the Program*

2.2.1 Debug the Program. Check the program variables against your algorithm test. Correct syntax, run time, and logical errors.

2.2.2 Test the program for further logical errors. Run the program with sample data.

2.3 *Document the Program*

For a full documentation, you should:

2.3.1 Produce a *programmers'* guide consisting of:
pseudocode
flowchart
variable table or data table
program listing
test results or sample printout.

2.3.2 Detail the steps that producing the program involved.

2.3.4 Write a *user* guide.

PROGRAMMING: SUMMARY OF METHOD IN FLOWCHART FORM

This provides a diagrammatic version of the summary of structured programming:

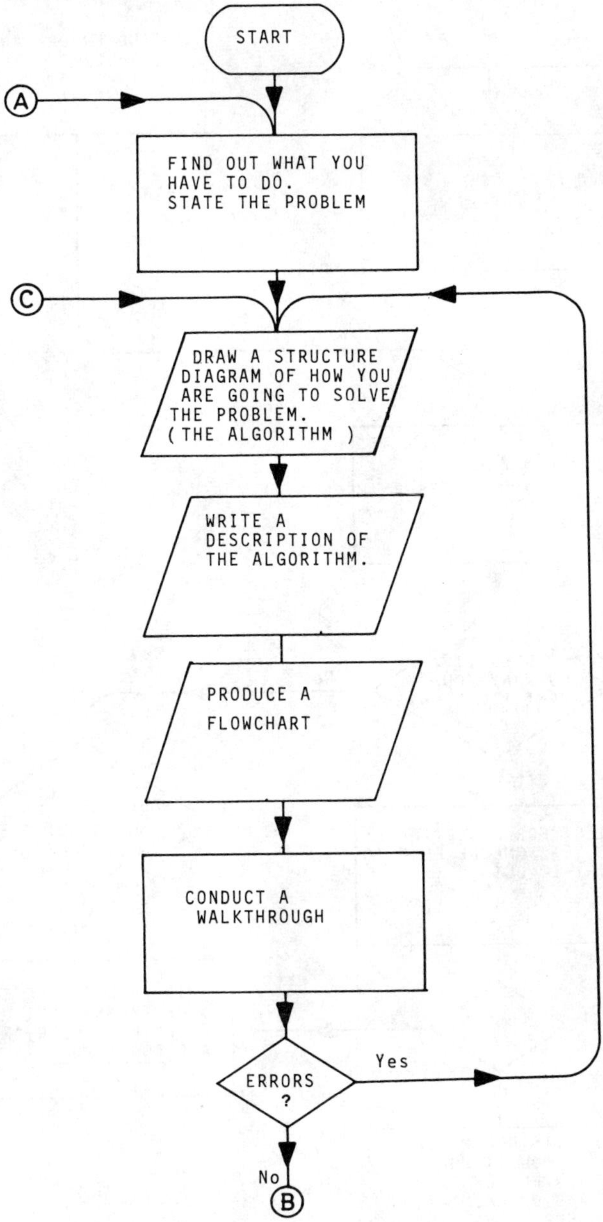

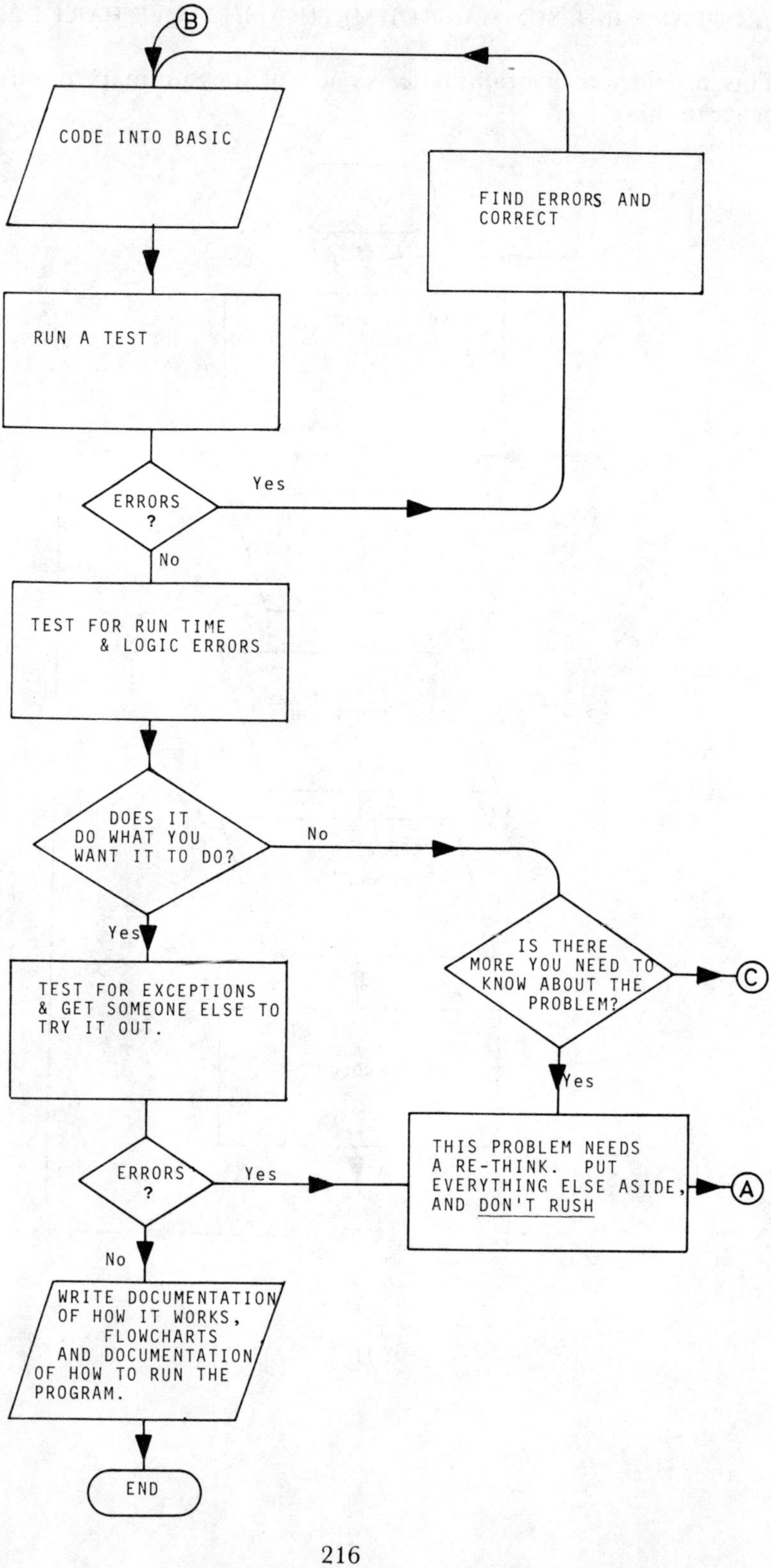
B
CODE INTO BASIC
FIND ERRORS AND CORRECT
RUN A TEST
ERRORS ?
Yes
No
TEST FOR RUN TIME & LOGIC ERRORS
DOES IT DO WHAT YOU WANT IT TO DO?
No
Yes
IS THERE MORE YOU NEED TO KNOW ABOUT THE PROBLEM?
C
Yes
TEST FOR EXCEPTIONS & GET SOMEONE ELSE TO TRY IT OUT.
ERRORS ?
Yes
THIS PROBLEM NEEDS A RE-THINK. PUT EVERYTHING ELSE ASIDE, AND DON'T RUSH
A
No
WRITE DOCUMENTATION OF HOW IT WORKS, FLOWCHARTS AND DOCUMENTATION OF HOW TO RUN THE PROGRAM.
END

1. Problem Statement

Write a program that computes and prints the Average or Mean (M) and Standard Deviation (S) of a collection of N data items.

To compute S use the formula:

$$\text{Standard Deviation} = \sqrt{\frac{\text{(Sum of Squares of Items)}}{N} - (\text{Mean})^2}$$

2. Find out what we have to do (research the problem)

We are given most of the information in the question but we are missing some. It does *not* tell us how to compute the Mean or Average. This is given by the formula:

$$\text{Mean} = \frac{\text{(Sum of all numbers)}}{N}$$

We now have all the information, we need to start designing the algorithm.

3. What is involved in this problem

The outline procedure we can now define:

a) We have to INPUT the numbers, and
b) Perform two calculations on these numbers. First we calculate the Mean and then use the Mean value to calculate the Standard Deviation, then
c) Output the results.

4. Design the algorithm

This gives the detailed procedure for the steps needed to solve the problem:

a) INPUT
   The numbers are going to be input into an array because they will be needed twice in the calculation module.
b) 1. Calculate: the Mean –
      Add all the numbers in the array and divide by N.
   2. Calculate: the Standard Deviation –
      Total the squares of all the numbers in the array.
      Use the formula to calculate S.
c) Output: the Results –
   The results will be printed on new lines with the words MEAN = and STANDARD DEVIATION =
   followed by their values.

5. The Tree Diagrams

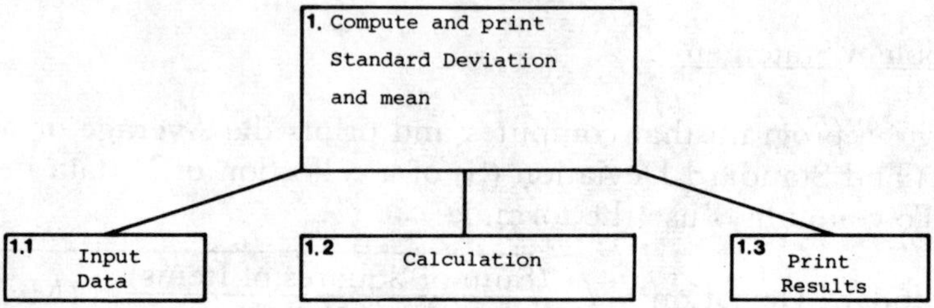

Each of modules 1.1, 1.2 and 1.3 will be subroutines. These will be called in the appropriate sequence by the main program module.

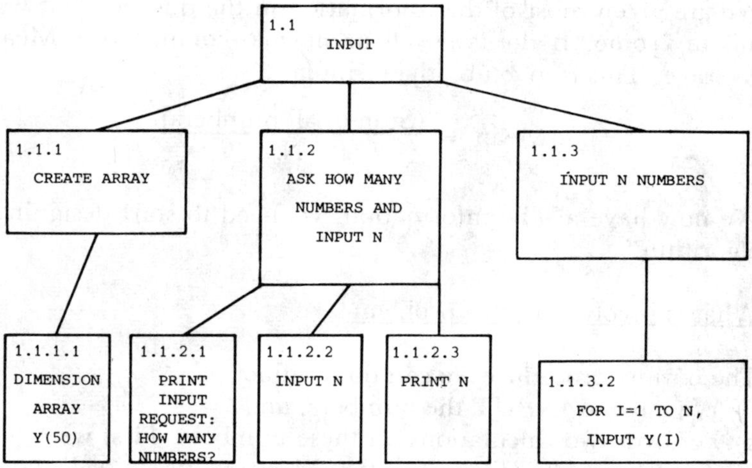

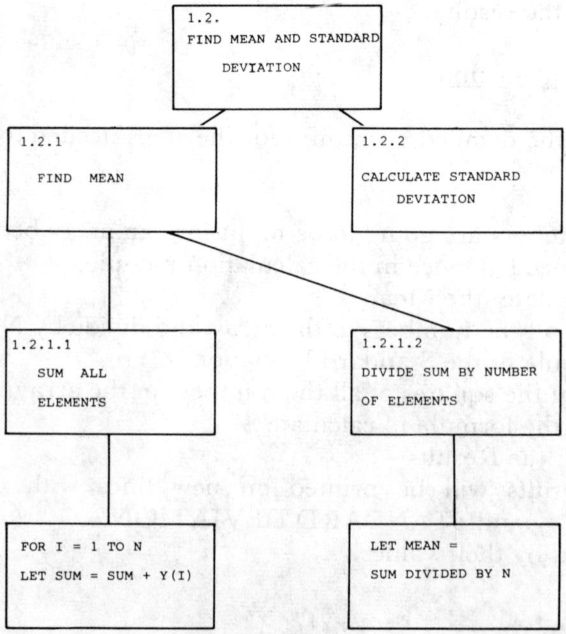

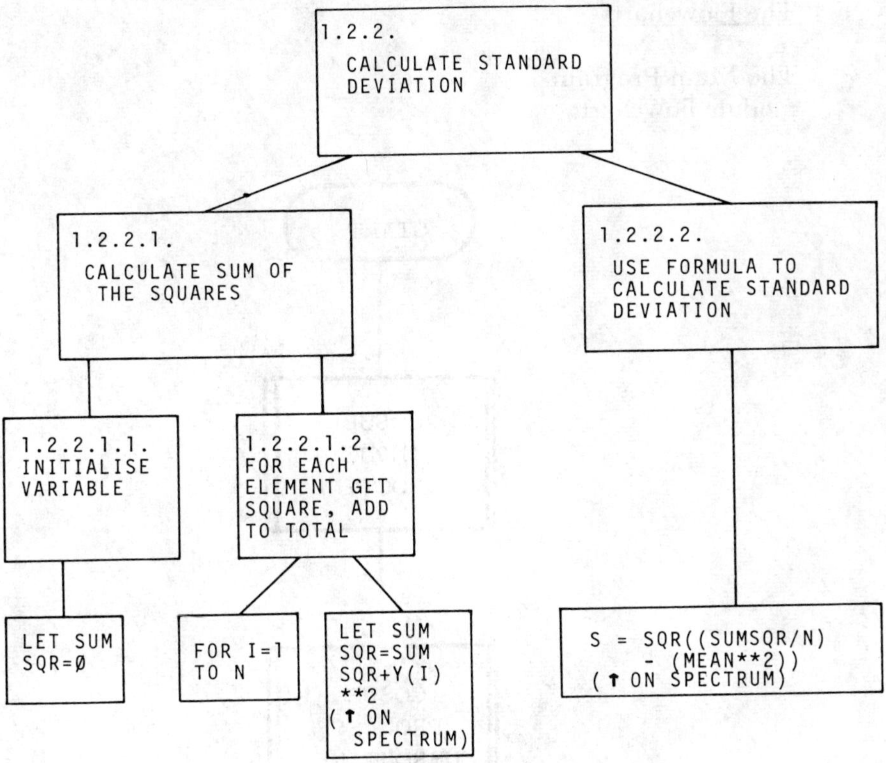
1.2.2.
CALCULATE STANDARD DEVIATION
1.2.2.1.
CALCULATE SUM OF THE SQUARES
1.2.2.2.
USE FORMULA TO CALCULATE STANDARD DEVIATION
1.2.2.1.1.
INITIALISE VARIABLE
1.2.2.1.2.
FOR EACH ELEMENT GET SQUARE, ADD TO TOTAL
LET SUM SQR=Ø
FOR I=1 TO N
LET SUM SQR=SUM SQR+Y(I) **2
(↑ ON SPECTRUM)
S = SQR((SUMSQR/N) - (MEAN**2))
(↑ ON SPECTRUM)

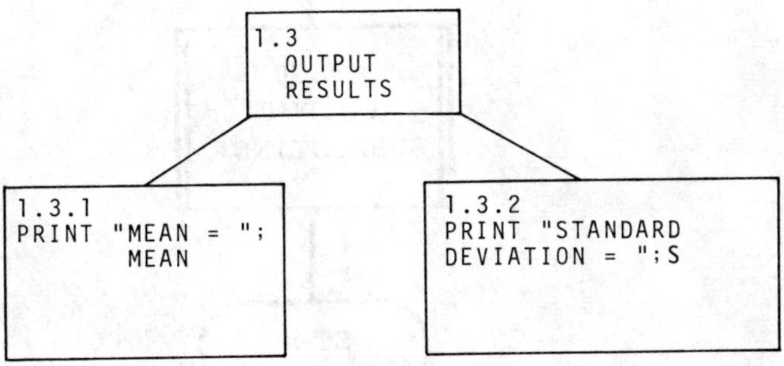
1.3
OUTPUT RESULTS
1.3.1
PRINT "MEAN = "; MEAN
1.3.2
PRINT "STANDARD DEVIATION = ";S

6. <u>The Flowcharts</u>

The Main Program
module flowchart:

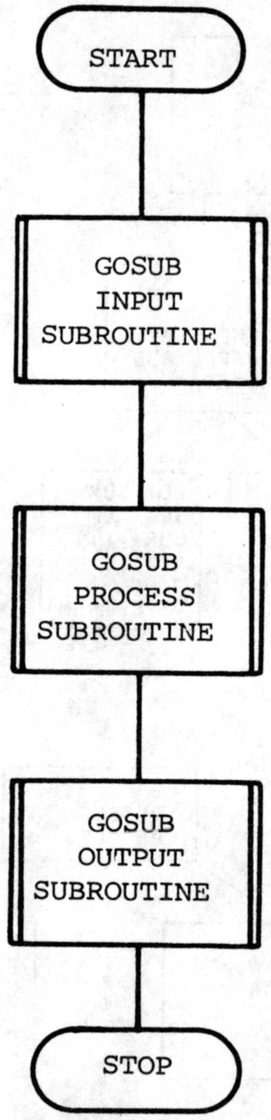

The Input Subroutine flowchart:

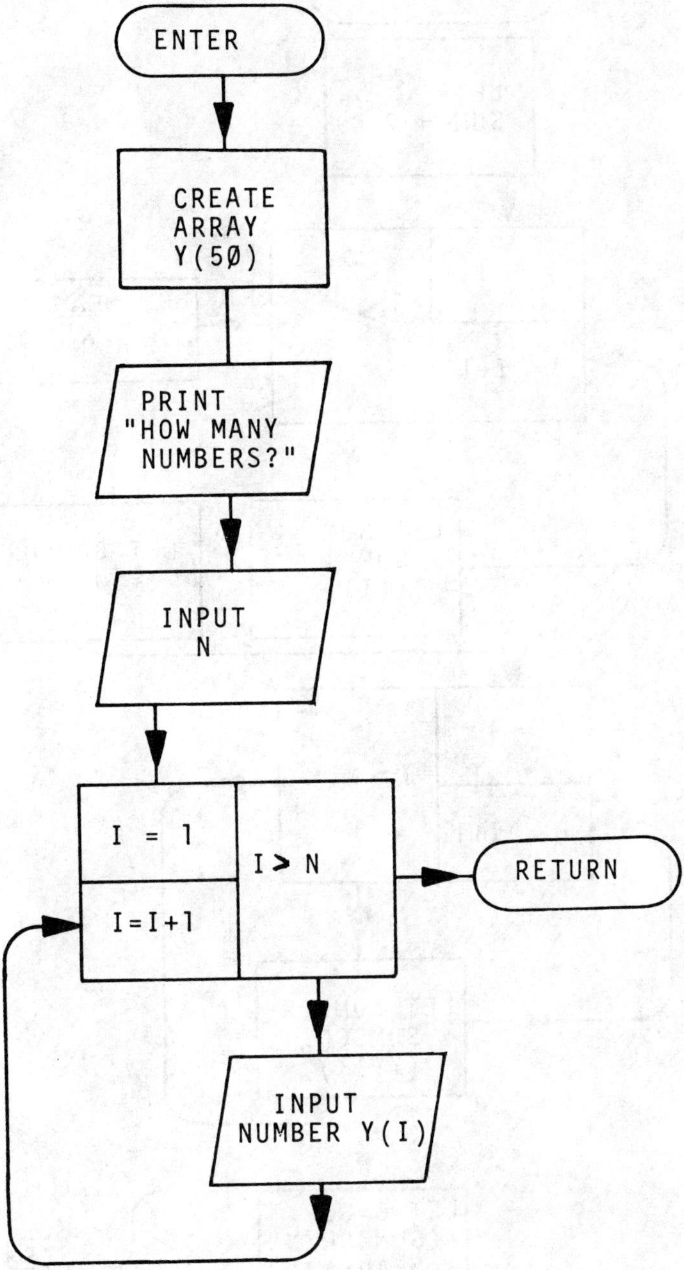

The Processing
Subroutine flowchart:

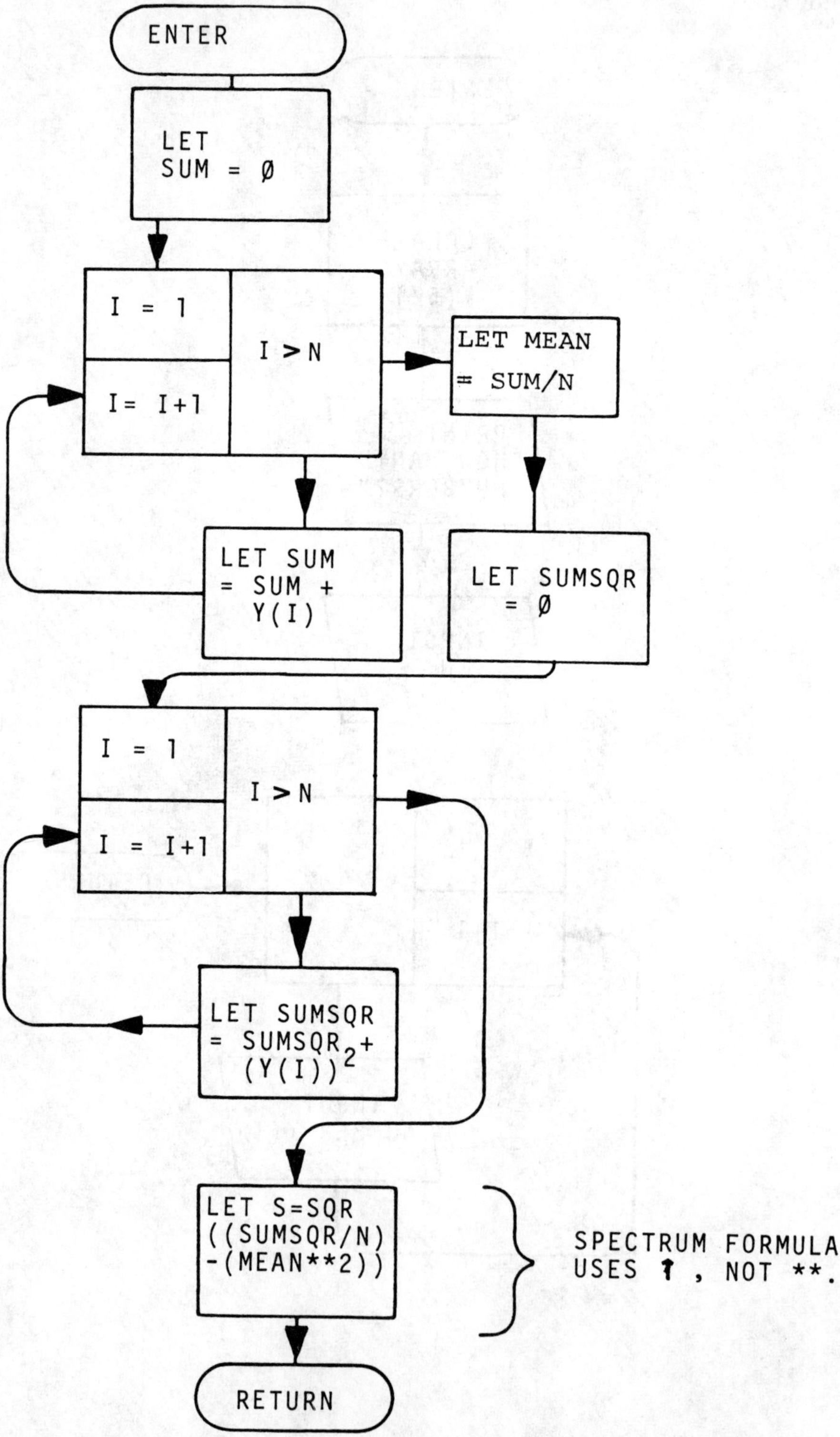

The Output
Subroutine flowchart:

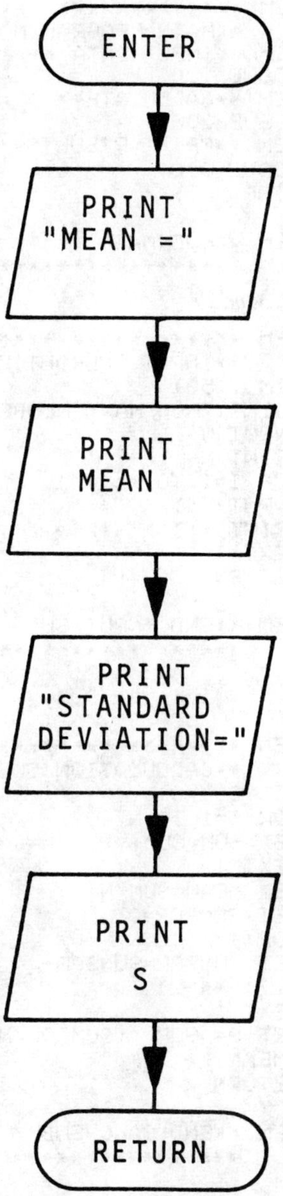

7. The Program

7.1 *The Main Program Module*

```
  5 REM "SDEVIATION"
 10 REM **********************
        **MAIN PROGRAM MOD   **
 20 REM **INPUT DATA **
 30 GOSUB 100
 40 REM **CALCULATE**
 50 GOSUB 200
 60 REM **PRINT RESULTS**
 70 GOSUB 400
 80 STOP

 90 REM **END MAIN           **
        **********************
```

7.2 *The Input Subroutine Module*

```
 95 REM **********************
        **INPUT SUBROUTINE   **
100 DIM Y(50)
110 PRINT "HOW MANY NUMBERS?";
120 INPUT N
130 PRINT N
140 FOR I=1 TO N
150 INPUT Y(I)
160 PRINT Y(I);" ";
170 NEXT I
180 RETURN

190 REM **END INPUT SUB      **
        **********************
```

7.3 *The Calculation Module*

```
200 REM **********************
        **CALCULATION SUB    **
210 LET SUM=0
220 FOR I=1 TO N
230 LET SUM=SUM+Y(I)
240 NEXT I
250 LET MEAN=SUM/N
260 LET SUMSQR=0
270 FOR I=1 TO N
280 LET SUMSQR=SUMSQR+
   (Y(I) ** 2)                  [ ↑ Spectrum]
290 NEXT I
300 LET S= SQR ((SUMSQR/N)-
    (MEAN ** 2))
310 RETURN

320 REM **END CALC SUB       **
        **********************
```

7.4 *The Output Module*

```
400 REM **********************
        **OUTPUT SUBROUTINE **
410 PRINT
420 PRINT "MEAN=";MEAN
430 PRINT
```

```
440 PRINT "STANDARD DEVIATION
    =";S
450 RETURN

460 REM **END OUTPUT SUB     **
        **********************
```

8. Documentation

1) This program will compute and print the Mean and Standard Deviation of a collection of data items (numbers).
2) It allows for a maximum of 5Ø items to be entered. You can increase the size of array Y if you wish to deal with more data.
3) The numbers can be of any size, positive or negative, to the limit of the computer's handling capacity. This is large – you will not exceed it.
4) To run the program key in RUN, and enter numbers one at a time, pressing NEWLINE (ENTER) after each one has been keyed in.

Sample run to find Mean and Standard Deviation of 3Ø, 31, 32, 5, 6, 7, 1Ø, 13, 27, 3:

```
HOW MANY NUMBERS ? 1Ø
3Ø 31 32 5 6 7 1Ø 13 27 3
MEAN = 16.4
STANDARD DEVIATION = 11.456Ø3
```

Exercise

The example program to compute and print the standard deviation of a set of data items does not include a pseudocode description of the algorithm, and the documentation process is incomplete in other ways too. Complete the programming procedure by doing the following:

1. Write out a pseudocode description of the algorithm.
2. Perform a pre-coding walk through, checking the values of the variables, counters and expressions for each subroutine module.
3. Key in the program and debug it.
4. Insert breakpoints in each subroutine and perform a program trace. Insert PRINT statements to print out values of variables, counters and expressions.
5. Obtain a program listing from the printer and run the program for a sample set of data. Keep a copy of the printer output.
6. Document the program fully in your notebook.

P1: The ZX81 Character Set and Codes

CODE	CHR$	CODE	CHR$	CODE	CHR$
0		49	L	98	
1	▘	50	M	99	
2	▝	51	N	100	
3	▀	52	O	101	
4	▖	53	P	102	
5	▌	54	Q	103	NOT
6	▞	55	R	104	USED
7	▛	56	S	105	
8	▒	57	T	106	
9	🮏	58	U	107	
10	🮎	59	V	108	
11	"	60	W	109	
12	£	61	X	110	
13	$	62	Y	111	
14	:	63	Z	112	↑
15	?	64	RND	113	↓
16	(	65	INKEY£	114	←
17	)	66	PI	115	→
18		67		116	GRAPHICS
19		68		117	EDIT
20	=	69		118	NEW LINE (E
21	+	70		119	RUBOUT (DE
22	–	71		120	K/L Mode
23	*	72		121	FUNCTION
24	/	73		122	
25	;	74	NOT	123	NOT
26	,	75	USED	124	USED
27	.	76		125	
28	0	77		126	NUMBER
29	1	78		127	CURSOR
30	2	79		128	█
31	3	80		129	▟
32	4	81		130	▙
33	5	82		131	▄
34	6	83		132	▜
35	7	84		133	▐
36	8	85		134	▚
37	9	86		135	▗
38	A	87		136	▒
39	B	88		137	🮑
40	C	89		138	🮒
41	D	90		139	inverse "
42	E	91		140	inverse £
43	F	92		141	inverse $
44	G	93		142	inverse :
45	H	94		143	inverse ?
46	I	95		144	inverse (
47	J	96		145	inverse)
48	K	97		146	inverse >

CODE/CHR$	
147	inverse <
148	inverse =
149	inverse +
150	inverse −
151	inverse *
152	inverse /
153	inverse ;
154	inverse ,
155	inverse .
156	inverse 0
157	inverse 1
158	inverse 2
159	inverse 3
160	inverse 4
161	inverse 5
162	inverse 6
163	inverse 7
164	inverse 8
165	inverse 9
166	inverse A
167	inverse B
168	inverse C
169	inverse D
170	inverse E
171	inverse F
172	inverse G
173	inverse H
174	inverse I
175	inverse J
176	inverse K
177	inverse L
178	inverse M
179	inverse N
180	inverse O
181	inverse P
182	inverse Q
183	inverse R
184	inverse S
185	inverse T
186	inverse U
187	inverse V
188	inverse W
189	inverse X
190	inverse Y
191	inverse Z
192	""
193	AT
194	TAB
195	(NOT USED)
196	CODE
197	VAL
198	LEN
199	SIN
200	COS
201	TAN
202	ASN

CODE/CHR$	
203	ACS
204	ATN
205	LN
206	EXP
207	INT
208	SQR
209	SGN
210	ABS
211	PEEK
212	USR
213	STR$
214	CHR$
215	NOT
216	**
217	OR
218	AND
219	<=
220	>=
221	<>
222	THEN
223	TO
224	STEP
225	LPRINT
226	LLIST
227	STOP
228	SLOW
229	FAST
230	NEW
231	SCROLL
232	CONT
233	DIM
234	REM
235	FOR
236	GOTO
237	GOSUB
238	INPUT
239	LOAD
240	LIST
241	LET
242	PAUSE
243	NEXT
244	PI
245	PRINT
246	PLOT
247	RUN
248	SAVE
249	RAND
250	IF
251	CLS
252	UNPLOT
253	CLEAR
254	RETURN
255	COPY

Of the non-printing characters, those that *are* used, but print a question mark, are the following:

116-121 inclusive
126-127 inclusive

(NOTE: 5 is *the* question mark.)

192 is the Quote image character, which prints a single quote. The character set is coded with the numbers Ø to 255. This, you may recall, is the number of values held in a single byte. The characters can thus be accessed with a single byte identification code. This is also the reason why some codes are listed, but have no character associated with them. The same is true of the Spectrum character set, which follows.

P2: Spectrum Character Set and Codes

Code	*Character*	*Code*	*Character*	*Code*	*Character*
Ø		35	#	7Ø	F
1		36	$	71	G
2		37	%	72	H
3	not used	38	&	73	I
4		39	'	74	J
5		4Ø	(	75	K
6	**PRINT** comma	41	)	76	L
7	**EDIT**	42	*	77	M
8	cursor left	43	+	78	N
9	cursor right	44	,	79	O
1Ø	cursor down	45	– (minus sign)	8Ø	P
11	cursor up	46	.	81	Q
12	**DELETE**	47	/	82	R
13	**ENTER**	48	Ø	83	S
14	number	49	1	84	T
15	not used	5Ø	2	85	U
16	**INK** control	51	3	86	V
17	**PAPER** control	52	4	87	W
18	**FLASH** control	53	5	88	X
19	**BRIGHT** control	54	6	89	Y
2Ø	**INVERSE** control	55	7	9Ø	Z
21	**OVER** control	56	8	91	[
22	**AT** control	57	9	92	/
23	**TAB** control	58	:	93	]
24		59	;	94	↑
25		6Ø	<	95	—
26		61	=	96	£
27	not used	62	>	97	a
28		63	?	98	b
29		64	@	99	c
3Ø		65	A	1ØØ	d
31		66	B	1Ø1	e
32	space	67	C	1Ø2	f
33	!	68	D	1Ø3	g
34	"	69	E	1Ø4	h

Code	Character	Code	Character	Code	Character
105	i	159	(p)	213	**MERGE**
106	j	160	(q)	214	**VERIFY**
107	k	161	(r)	215	**BEEP**
108	l	162	(s)	216	**CIRCLE**
109	m	163	(t)	217	**INK**
110	n	164	(u)	218	**PAPER**
111	o	165	**RND**	219	**FLASH**
112	p	166	**INKEY$**	220	**BRIGHT**
113	q	167	**PI**	221	**INVERSE**
114	r	168	**FN**	222	**OVER**
115	s	169	**POINT**	223	**OUT**
116	t	170	**SCREEN$**	224	**LPRINT**
117	u	171	**ATTR**	225	**LLIST**
118	v	172	**AT**	226	**STOP**
119	w	173	**TAB**	227	**READ**
120	x	174	**VAL$**	228	**DATA**
121	y	175	**CODE**	229	**RESTORE**
122	z	176	**VAL**	230	**NEW**
123	{	177	**LEN**	231	**BORDER**
124			178	**SIN**	232	**CONTINUE**
125	}	179	**COS**	233	**DIM**
126	~	180	**TAN**	234	**REM**
127	©	181	**ASN**	235	**FOR**
128		182	**ACS**	236	**GO TO**
129	▝	183	**ATN**	237	**GO SUB**
130	▘	184	**LN**	238	**INPUT**
131	▀	185	**EXP**	239	**LOAD**
132	▗	186	**INT**	240	**LIST**
133	▐	187	**SQR**	241	**LET**
134	▚	188	**SGN**	242	**PAUSE**
135	▜	189	**ABS**	243	**NEXT**
136	▖	190	**PEEK**	244	**POKE**
137	▞	191	**IN**	245	**PRINT**
138	▌	192	**USR**	246	**PLOT**
139	▛	193	**STR$**	247	**RUN**
140	▄	194	**CHR$**	248	**SAVE**
141	▟	195	**NOT**	249	**RANDOMIZE**
142	▙	196	**BIN**	250	**IF**
143	█	197	**OR**	251	**CLS**
144	(a)	198	**AND**	252	**DRAW**
145	(b)	199	<=	253	**CLEAR**
146	(c)	200	>=	254	**RETURN**
147	(d)	201	<>	255	**COPY**
148	(e)	202	**LINE**		
149	(f)	203	**THEN**		
150	(g)	204	**TO**		
151	(h)	205	**STEP**		
152	(i)	206	**DEF FN**		
153	(j)	207	**CAT**		
154	(k) user	208	**FORMAT**		
155	(l) graphics	209	**MOVE**		
156	(m)	210	**ERASE**		
157	(n)	211	**OPEN #**		
158	(o)	212	**OPEN #**		

There is an important point to be noted with regard to the Spectrum character set, which does not apply to the ZX81. Among the Spectrum character set, codes 16 to 23 are control characters which are used to specify certain attributes of the character cell for printing purposes. These require arguments within a certain range (Ø to 9 for colours, or Ø and 1 for on or off, etc.). Codes 6 to 14, 22 and 23 are also control characters for printing and editing. The problem with using CHR$ with these control characters is that they *can* be used in programs, and are then called by inserting, e.g. CHR$ 2Ø, followed by the argument. This means that a simple call to PRINT one of these CHR$ will cause the computer to think it is being given an instruction, and the syntax demands an argument. If this is not forthcoming after the CHR$, or the argument is in the wrong range, an error message results when the Spectrum cannot do what it thinks it is being asked to do.

Some of these control characters, however, for colour (dealt with in Section W), and also for print control can be usefully placed in programs. If we take CODE 8, which is a *cursor control character*, we can write a program like this:

```
1Ø  PRINT "SIN";
2Ø PAUSE 5Ø
3Ø PRINT CHR$ 8;CHR$ 8;"ACRED"
```

The CHR$ 8 instructions in line 3Ø backspace the cursor twice, resetting the PRINT position, so that "ACRED" overprints "IN". The upshot of this is that we cannot print out the character set of the Spectrum completely, but must start from CODE 24, after the control characters. This is no great loss, since they print (or *would* print, *if* you could get them to!) either a space or a question mark. Remember these control characters, though, as they can sometimes be useful in a program, although mostly it is far more convenient to use the BASIC instructions. For example, we can use CHR$ 23 instead of TAB:

```
1Ø PRINT CHR$ 23;1Ø; "TAB CONTROL"
```

This is not an advantage over using TAB! However it does show how these characters are used by the computer – it inserts them into program listings where the control function (e.g. TAB), has been used. TAB itself does not have a *control* function, and needs CHR$ 23 placed after it to work.

P3: Characters

The ZX81 and Spectrum have a character alphabet consisting of 256 items which include numeric characters, alphabetic characters, keywords, instructions, commands, operators, graphics and inverse graphics symbols and other symbols. As

seen in the tables in the previous Units, of these 256 items some are not used at all, and some are non-printing (i.e. control characters).

In Appendix III the ZX81 character codes are laid out by character type and their position on the keyboard. Spectrum codes are referenced alphabetically in Unit W1.

The CODE (occupying a single byte) identifies each character uniquely for input/output purposes – i.e. input from the keyboard and output to the screen or printer.

The ZX81 has a non-standard character set unique to the machine. The Spectrum has a character set in which the characters used have the codes of the ASCII character set (an internationally agreed standard) for the most part. Non-standard ASCII characters are the symbols for £ and ©, and the graphics characters.

P4: CHR$ and Code

The purpose of the instructions CODE and CHR$ is to convert from the code to the character and vice versa. The ZX81 and Spectrum have different character sets and codes, but the instructions work in the same way.

CODE

CODE is a function that takes a character or string and gives as a result the numeric code that the character (a single letter string, or first character in a string) corresponds to. For example:

CODE S gives 56 on the ZX81, 83 on the Spectrum

CODE "ABCD"	**gives CODE A, 38 on the ZX81, 65 on the Spectrum**
CODE X$	**gives the code of the first (or only) character in X$**
CODE D$(3)	**gives the code of the third character in D$.**

CHR$

CHR$ (N), where N is a numeric expression with a value Ø < = N < = 255, is a function that gives as a result the single character whose code is N. CHR$ does the opposite of CODE. For example:

CHR$ (A + B + C)
CHR$ (X/Z)
CHR$ (INT(RND * 255))
CHR$ 36 gives 8 on the ZX81, $ on the Spectrum

To see the inverse relationship of CHR$ and CODE, key in the following as direct commands:

PRINT CHR$ 50	will print M on the ZX81, 2 on the Spectrum
PRINT CODE "2"	will print 30 on the ZX81, 50 on the Spectrum
PRINT CODE CHR$ 50	will print 50
PRINT CODE "A"	will print 38 on the ZX81, 65 on the Spectrum
PRINT CHR$ 38	will print A on the ZX81, & on the Spectrum
PRINT CHR$ CODE "A"	will print A

The next program will print out all the characters used on the ZX81.

```
10 FOR F=0 TO 255
20 SCROLL
30 PRINT F, CHR$ F
40 NEXT F
```

For the Spectrum, as noted above, we must miss out some CHR$ and line 20. Line 10 must read FOR F = 24 TO 255. Key it in and run it. Add:

```
35 LPRINT F; TAB 6; CHR$ F
```

to get a printer listing. A better program (since it uses less printer paper!) but one with an expression you won't understand until we cover logic, is this one:

```
10 REM **CHARACTER SET**
20 LPRINT "CODE/CHR$"; TAB 10;
"CODE/CHR$"; TAB 20;"CODE/CHR$"
30 FOR F=0 TO 85
40 LPRINT F; TAB 4; CHR$ F;
 TAB 10;F+86; TAB 14; CHR$
 (F+86); TAB 20;(F+172 AND
 F+172<256); TAB 24; CHR$
 (F+172 AND F+172<256)
50 NEXT F
```

Use these lines for the Spectrum version:

```
30 FOR F=24 TO 77
40 LPRINT F; TAB 4; CHR$ F;
 TAB 10;F+77; TAB 14; CHR$
(F+77); TAB 20;F+154; TAB 24;
  CHR$ (F+154)
```

Exercises

1 Key in and run the following programs. You may find some surprising results, due to the control characters, on the

Spectrum. No harm will be done.

(a)
```
1Ø FOR F = Ø TO 255 (Spectrum: FOR F = 24 TO 255)
2Ø PRINT CHR$ F;
3Ø NEXT F
```
Notice that the word characters print with the spaces that your computer automatically inserts in program lines.

(b)
```
1Ø RAND
2Ø PRINT CHR$ INT (128* RND + 128)
3Ø GOTO 2Ø
```

(c)
```
1Ø INPUT A$
2Ø PRINT A$, CODE A$
3Ø GOTO 1Ø
```

(d)
```
1Ø PRINT "INPUT STRING OF 6 CHARACTERS"
2Ø INPUT A$
3Ø FOR F = 1 TO 6
4Ø PRINT A$(F), CODE A$(F)
5Ø NEXT F
```

(e)
```
1Ø RAND
2Ø IF INT (RND*2) = 1 THEN PRINT CHR$ INT
   (RND*128)
3Ø IF INT (RND*2) = Ø THEN PRINT CHR$
   (INT(RND*128) + 128)
4Ø GOTO 2Ø
```

(f)
```
1Ø RAND
2Ø LET A$ = CHR$ INT (RND* 255)
3Ø SCROLL
4Ø PRINT CODE A$, A$
5Ø GOTO 2Ø
```
In this last program, Spectrum owners can omit line 3Ø and simply respond to the Scroll? prompt by pressing ENTER.

2 Write a program that given a number (code), will check that Ø < = code < = 255, and will print out the character. On the Spectrum, the program should print "CONTROL CHARACTER" if the CODE is between 6 and 23.

3 Write a program that when given an alphabetic character as an input will print out the next in the alphabet. If the character input was 'Z' then 'A' should be printed.

SECTION Q: GRAPHICS

Q1: More Printing

Since we dealt with the PRINT instructions, you have been introduced to other statements that can be used with the PRINT statements for format and manipulation.

Loops are of use in printing. For instance we can set up an empty string with 32 spaces and use it to clear different areas:

```
20 LET A$ = "(32 spaces)"
30 .......
40 .......
100 FOR X = 11 TO 21
110 PRINT AT X, 0; A$
120 NEXT X
```

will clear the bottom half of the screen, and we could use it repeatedly, as a subroutine, if we wished. We then avoid using CLS, which would mean re-printing anything that we wanted to keep on the screen.

Except for numbers, anything we wish to print must be in the form of a string, either between quotes, a string variable, part of a string array, or a CHR$(X) instruction.

Obviously any operations or functions used with strings may be useful, and in the same way as:

```
10 PRINT (1 + 3)
```

prints 4, we can use:

```
20 PRINT A$ (X TO Y)
```

to extract the desired characters of A$.

Enter and run this program

```
10 LET A$="ABRACADABRA"
20 LET L= LEN A$
30 FOR X=1 TO 6
40 PRINT TAB 10+X;A$(X TO
   L+1-X)
50 NEXT X
```

Remember that numbers can always be treated as strings, and vice versa, using VAL and STR$. This is often useful for formatting numbers. For example, with a number X, this program:

```
10 LET A$="0000"
20 LET B$= STR$ X
30 FOR F=1 TO 4
40 IF LEN B$<F THEN GOTO 70
50 LET A$(F)=B$(F)
60 NEXT F
70 PRINT A$
```

will print the first four digits of any number, or follow the number with zeros if less than 4 digits. Change the zeros to spaces, and you have a number string that will overprint any other string however many digits are in the original.

Code the program in with A$ = ‘‘(4 spaces)’’ and try it. As it is, you will have to enter X as a direct command (LET X = 123, then NEWLINE/ENTER) and then use GOTO 1Ø, since RUN would clear the variables (in this case, the value of X you have just entered).

This principle can be expanded. Here is an example of a subroutine used to justify numbers and print them in the position required for the decimal places to be in the same column:

```
  10 REM "FORMAT"
  20 REM *FORMAT SUBROUTINE FOR*
         *NUMBERS               *
  30 REM *COLUMN NUMBER FOR    *
         *DECIMAL PLACE        *
  40 LET C=12
  50 REM *INITIALISE GOSUB*
  60 LET FORMAT=9000
  70 REM *NUMBER*
  80 INPUT N1
  90 REM *INITIALIZE NUMBER*
 100 LET N=N1
 110 GOSUB FORMAT
 200 REM *MORE NUMBERS*
 210 FOR L=1 TO 4
 220 INPUT N
 230 GOSUB FORMAT
 240 NEXT L
8980 GOTO 9999

8990 REM **********************
         **SUBROUTINE        **

9000 LET N$= STR$ N
9010 LET P=0
9020 FOR F=1 TO LEN N$
9030 IF N$(F)="." THEN LET P=F
9040 NEXT F
9050 IF P=1 THEN LET N$="0"+N$
9060 LET P=P+(P=1)
9070 IF P=0 THEN LET P= LEN N$+1
9080 PRINT TAB (C-P+1);N$
9090 RETURN

9100 REM **ENDSUB**************
9999 STOP
```

Lines 1Ø to 24Ø are a main program to initialise and provide numbers for the subroutine. Notice it adds a Ø if the number is a decimal. Line

9030 sets a marker for a decimal point in the first letter of the number string, and adding a 0 is done in line 9050. 9060 uses the *logical value* of (P = 1) to add 1 if a zero was added, i.e. if P = 1 is true. This will be explained in the Section on Logic, but the line is equivalent to IF P = 1 THEN LET P = 2. Check this by trying both versions of the line. Line 9070 adjusts the length of the string if there is no decimal place found (i.e. if the number was an integer). 9080 prints the number in the correct column.

The next program shows a simple way of tabulating results, using a loop:

```
10 PRINT "NO.";TAB 4;"SQUARE";TAB 12;
   "CUBE";TAB 20;"RECIP"
20 FOR N = 1 TO 10
30 PRINT N;TAB 4;N*N;TAB 12;N**3;     (↑ on Spectrum)
   TAB 20;1/N
40 NEXT N
```

NO.	SQUARE	CUBE	RECIP
1	1	1	1
2	4	8	0.5
3	9	27	0.33333333
4	16	64	0.25
5	25	125	0.2
6	36	216	0.16666667
7	49	343	0.14285714
8	64	512	0.125
9	81	729	0.11111111
10	100	1000	0.1

It is important to remember that numbers are output with 8 figures and allow the appropriate space. An alternative is to decide how many figures you want and use the INT function.

For example, we can replace 1/N in line 30 by INT(1E4*(1/N) + .5)/1E4 , and get a printout like this:

NO.	SQUARE	CUBE	RECIP
1	1	1	1
2	4	8	0.5
3	9	27	0.3333
4	16	64	0.25
5	25	125	0.2
6	36	216	0.1667
7	49	343	0.1429
8	64	512	0.125
9	81	729	0.1111
10	100	1000	0.1

Using the E notation allows easy definition of the number of decimal places, without the possibility of missing a zero as, for example, if we used INT(1ØØØØ*(1/N) + .5)/1ØØØØ, since using 1E4 gives four d.p., 1E3 three d.p., etc. In using this, be careful with the bracket placing, as INT(1E4*(1/N)) + .5/1E4 will *not* round! Try both the correct and incorrect versions in the program.

You should note that:

With PRINT TAB C; or PRINT AT L,C instructions L and C can be dependent or calculated variables. For example:

PRINT TAB (X*2)/3;
PRINT AT 1Ø, 2Ø/X;

Try these:

```
10 FOR X = 1 TO 5
20 PRINT AT X, X * 2;X
30 NEXT X
```

```
10 FOR X = 1 TO 5
20 PRINT TAB X * 2;X
30 NEXT X
```

An automatic INT function operates with PRINT AT instructions.

For PRINT AT (L), (C); if (L) and (C) > n and < n + 1, (L) and (C) = n

For example:

PRINT AT 3/2, 1Ø.5;"..."
equals PRINT AT 1,1Ø;"..."

Try this:

```
10 FOR X = 1 TO 10
20 PRINT AT X, X/2; X
30 NEXT X
```

The AT function rounds down, exactly as if we had used PRINT AT X, INT (X/2);X as line 2Ø.

PRINT TAB(N), where N is non-integer, rounds to the *nearest* integer.

TAB N, where N is between X and X + 1, gives TAB X if N< X + .5 and TAB X + 1 if N> = X + .5. For example

TAB (1.3) = TAB 1
TAB (1.5) = TAB 2

To see the difference, RUN both these programs, use COPY to get a printout, and compare the results.

```
10 FOR X=0 TO 10
20 PRINT TAB X/2;X
30 NEXT X

10 FOR X=0 TO 10
20 PRINT TAB INT (X/2);X
30 NEXT X
```

You must also watch for arithmetic mistakes in calculating the PRINT position. For instance:

```
10 FOR X=0 TO 10
20 PRINT TAB 20/X;X
30 NEXT X
```

is not going to get past line 2Ø the first time round! Why?

This next example illustrates the use of PRINT AT to give changing display.

A die is rolled and we wish to display its value for each of a series of throws. In addition we require cumulative values after each throw. Thus each time line 9Ø is reached it overprints line 7Ø and vice versa. Similarly line 12Ø overprints itself after each throw.

```
  5 REM "DICEROLL"
 10 PRINT "NUMBER OF THROWS?"
 20 INPUT X
 30 DIM N(6)
 35 CLS
 40 PRINT AT 8,6;"CUMULATIVE VA
LUES"
 50 PRINT AT 10,4;"1***2***3***
4***5***6"
 60 FOR M=1 TO X
 65 PRINT AT 1,8;"THROW"; TAB 1
4;"VALUE"
 70 PRINT AT 3,10;"*","*"
 80 LET A= INT (6* RND +1)
 90 PRINT AT 3,10;M,A
100 LET N(A)=N(A)+1
110 FOR B=1 TO 6
120 PRINT AT 12,4*B;N(B)
130 NEXT B
140 NEXT M
```

(**N.B.** Choose a relatively small value for X (say 24) or the program will take a long time to run.)

Exercises

1 Modify the FORMAT subroutine to round the number to 3 decimal places before determining the print position.
2 Modify your result for the exercise above to print zeros for any decimal place not filled.
3 Write a program that displays the result of throwing three dice, displaying the result for each die, and the total value for each throw. Overprint the last result with each new one, and store the total values resulting. After the specified number of throws, derive the average value for a throw.

Q2: More Plotting

Although the definition of the graphics on the ZX81 is low, the computer has the capacity to draw useful graphs, and most graphics processes can be illustrated. This is a program that draws a line between two specified points:

```
 10 INPUT X1
 20 INPUT Y1
 30 INPUT X2
 40 INPUT Y2
 50 LET X=X(2) -X(1)
 60 LET Y=Y(2) -Y(1)
 65 LET A=(X AND ABS X>=ABS Y) +
    (Y AND ABS X<ABS Y)
 70 LET DX=0
 80 LET DY=0
 90 FOR F=1 TO ABS A
100 PLOT DX+X(1), DY+Y(1)
110 LET DX =DS+X/ABS A
120 LET DY=DY+Y/ABS A
130 NEXT F
```

The logic in line 65 checks which is the greater of the distances to be covered between the points, and makes A equal to that, since the smaller value will be in a false statement, and will be evaluated as 0. You will have to wait until we deal fully with logical operations for the explanation of the reason this works. The program library has an expanded version of this program ("LINE").

Spectrum owners should relish the fact that their machine's ability to accept a simple DRAW X,Y statement makes this entire program redundant. Study the principle, however.

Subroutines can be used for plotting. If you recall our dog-plot, here is an example of a subroutine used to fill the screen with dogs. The subroutine for this is between lines 300 and 430 and is based on a grid (8 horizontal by 5 vertical):

```
10 REM "DOGS"
20 FOR X=0 TO 50 STEP 10
30 FOR Y=10 TO 40 STEP 10
40 GOSUB 300
```

```
 45 NEXT Y
 50 NEXT X
 60 GOTO 700
300 REM **DOG PLOT**
310 PLOT X,Y
320 PLOT X+1,Y-1
330 FOR N=2 TO 4
340 PLOT X+2,Y-N
350 NEXT N
360 PLOT X+3,Y-2
370 PLOT X+4,Y-2
380 FOR N=1 TO 4
390 PLOT X+5,Y-N
400 NEXT N
410 PLOT X+6,Y
420 PLOT X+7,Y-1
430 RETURN
700 REM **END**
```

With plots of functions where the values of Y are not visible by inspection, we can use the computer to ascertain them and derive the appropriate scale factor.

For a function producing positive values of Y, we can use a routine as below. We set A and B as the values of X between which we want to plot the value of Y, and store the largest number encountered in a variable MAXY. The routine is for the ZX81. Spectrum users would need to use 240 in place of 60 (line 40), and 160 instead of 40 (line 80).

```
10 LET A=(MINIMUM VALUE OF X)
20 LET B=(MAXIMUM VALUE OF X)
30 LET MAXY=0
40 FOR X=A TO B STEP (B-A)/60
50 LET Y=(FUNCTION OF X)
60 IF Y>MAXY THEN LET MAXY=Y
70 NEXT X
80 LET SY=40/MAXY
```

Adding the following lines gives us the plot:

```
 90 FOR X=A-A TO B-A STEP (B-A)
/60
100 LET Y=X*X
110 PLOT X*60/(B-A),Y*SY
120 NEXT X
```

Spectrum: 240 not 60 in line 90.

Notice that all the function values are calculated twice. It would be neater to set up either two lists, or a two dimensional numerical array (X(60) and U(60) or X(2,60)), and store the values the first time round. Try this when we have dealt with numerical arrays. Run the program, using different values of X in lines 10 and 20 and some different equations in line 50 (and the same one in line 100). Try X**2 + 3X, X**3 – 6X + 2, etc. (↑ in place of ** if using Spectrum). Revise the program to allow inputs in lines 10 and 20.

Q3: Movement and Timing

We can deal with the two topics of time and motion together. We will introduce and illustrate the new functions concerned, and then look at them in combination.

The first new commands (which *only* apply to the ZX81) are FAST and SLOW. If the screen display is to be continuous, the ZX81 has to read and print on screen the contents of the display file fifty times a second (sixty times a second in the U.S.). It can then only compute in the gaps between doing this. Up to now, we have used this continuous compute and display mode exclusively. This is SLOW mode on the ZX81. The Spectrum works in the equivalent of the ZX81 FAST mode, and displays the screen at the same time:

> **SLOW allows a continuous screen display. Computations are performed in the intervals between reprinting the screen. SLOW may be used as a direct command or in a program line.**
>
> **FAST blanks out the screen, and the ZX81 computes faster, not needing to break off to display the screen. Screen display is restored when**
> **(i) the program ends**
> **(ii) the program stops to await input**
> **(iii) the program goes into SLOW mode**
> **(iv) the program is instructed to PAUSE.**
> **The screen display is updated during FAST, but only printed at a break in the program.**

FAST mode is used whenever it is necessary to perform a large number of calculations on the ZX81, and a screen display is not vital. To illustrate the two modes, enter and RUN this program:

```
10  SLOW
20  FOR X = 1 TO 20
30  LET Z = X*X**X/X**X
40  PRINT Z;
50  NEXT X
```

Line 10 is redundant, the ZX81 will already be in SLOW mode. But now change it to:

```
10  FAST
```

and RUN. Change it back and, by counting, see what the difference in timing is between the two modes. You can also delete line 10, and shift between the modes by using direct commands. Note the flash of the screen when you input lines from the keyboard in FAST mode. This makes it easy to tell which mode you are in. The ZX81 computer is always in SLOW mode at switch on, and if you are shifting between the two modes, using direct instructions, then the characteristic flash will let you know if FAST is the current mode.

PAUSE

PAUSE causes the execution of a program to halt for the time specified. The screen display is shown on the screen during the PAUSE. Pressing a key during a PAUSE will cut the PAUSE short and the program will continue.

PAUSE N gives a delay of N/5Ø seconds (N/6Ø seconds in the U.S.)

PAUSE 15Ø gives a delay of 3 seconds (2½ seconds in the U.S.)

If N>32767 the PAUSE will continue until a key is pressed on the ZX81.

If N = Ø the PAUSE will continue until a key is pressed on the Spectrum.

PAUSE allows us to insert a specific delay in a program. It also allows us to cause the program to wait for a key to be pressed before the program will continue. The following program illustrates both these functions:

```
 1Ø PRINT "PROGRAM START"
 2Ø PAUSE 1ØØ
 3Ø PRINT "2 SECONDS"
 4Ø PAUSE 1ØØ
 5Ø PRINT "4 SECONDS"
 6Ø PAUSE 2ØØ
 7Ø PRINT "8 SECONDS"
 8Ø PRINT "NOW PAUSE UNTIL KEY PRESSED"
 9Ø PAUSE 4ØØØØ
1ØØ PRINT "END"
```

Spectrum users must enter line 9Ø as 9Ø PAUSE Ø.

PAUSE is useful in programs run in FAST mode on the ZX81, since the display file is shown on the screen during a PAUSE, and we can use this directly to get a screen display for a specified time.

PAUSE used the system variable FRAMES to count in units of 1/5Øth of a second (1/6Øth second in the U.S.). This is set by the a.c. power supply frequency to the TV monitor, which governs the number of times a second the screen display is refreshed, which is why the timing varies in different countries.

When a PAUSE commences on the ZX81 the screen 'flashes'. This can be irritating. It can be avoided by use of an empty FOR...NEXT loop, which does not produce this effect. The time delay is less precise, but for non-timing functions – providing a delay whilst instructions are read, for example – it is easily modified to suit.

```
10 PRINT "START"
20 PRINT "2SECOND DELAY"
30 PAUSE 100
40 PRINT "FOR...NEXT LOOP"
50 FOR X = 1 TO 150
60 NEXT X
70 PRINT "END"
```

The next instruction can be used in a program line by the ZX81 only. It does not exist for the Spectrum. The definition and discussion apply only the the ZX81, but the method of achieving the same effect on the Spectrum is given below.

SCROLL

SCROLL moves the whole screen up one line, deleting the top line, and sets a new PRINT position at the start of the new bottom line.

To see this work, try this program:

```
10  FOR X = 1 TO 10
20  PRINT X
30  IF X>5 THEN SCROLL
40  NEXT X
```

We can use SCROLL to clear printout on the top of the screen, but we must remember that if we use SCROLL the print position changes. We can, however, use PRINT AT instructions to avoid the bottom line print position. Delete line 20 in the above program and insert:

```
35  PRINT AT X, 0; X
```

Notice that we have to be careful of where we put SCROLL, and when we use it. We can use it to prevent a 'screen full' error message, but unless we want all lines rising from the bottom of the screen we have to specify when to use it.

We can set a line to use SCROLL at the correct place:

```
10  FOR X = 1 TO 50
20  PRINT X
30  IF X>21 THEN SCROLL
40  NEXT X
```

Scrolling on the Spectrum is automatic, the 'scroll?' prompt appearing when the screen is full. When any key other than BREAK and 'N' is pressed, the screen scrolls to display the next screenful of information. To get the same effect as is produced by the ZX81

SCROLL instruction in a program, which can be useful, the procedure on the Spectrum is as follows:
1. The value of – 1 must be POKEd into a system variable at memory address 23692. This is done with a program line 'POKE 23692, – 1'.
2. Something must be printed on line 21. This can be just a space, or it may be the first thing you wish to print in a sequence that will have all printing coming up from the bottom of the screen.
3. Scrolling will then occur, one line at a time, whenever another PRINT instruction is given.

A simple program illustrates this:

```
10  POKE 23692, – 1
20  PRINT AT 21,0;"PRINT HERE TO CAUSE SCROLL"
30  PAUSE 50
40  PRINT "SCROLL"
50  PAUSE 50
60  PRINT "SCROLL AGAIN"
```

The PAUSE instructions merely cause a delay to enable you to see the process properly. The PRINT item in line 20 could be a space, as long as it is something printed on the bottom line. Try this program:

```
10  POKE 23692, – 1
20  PRINT AT 21,0;" "              (Single space)
30  FOR F = 1 TO 10
40  PRINT "PRINT"
50  NEXT F
```

We can use SCROLL, or the Spectrum equivalent, to create a moving screen display. Try this:

For the ZX81

```
10  FOR X = 0 TO 30 STEP .3
20  LET L = 15 + 14*SIN X
30  PRINT TAB L; "ZX"
40  IF X>6.3 THEN SCROLL
50  NEXT X
```

For the Spectrum

```
10  FOR X = 0 TO 30 STEP .3
20  LET L = 15 + 14*SIN X
30  PRINT TAB L; "ZX"
40  POKE 23692, – 1
50  NEXT X
```

Spectrum users please note also that the POKE instruction will work if it is given as line 5 in the program, and line 40 deleted. Try it.

Try this for a rocket launch:

```
10 PRINT AT 18,17; "A"
20 PRINT ,"▯██▯"
30 PRINT ,"▯██▯"
40 PRINT ,"▙▄▄▟"
50 FOR C=10 TO 0 STEP -1
60 PRINT AT 1,1;C;" "
70 NEXT C
```

```
 80 PRINT "BLASTOFF"
 90 FOR X=1 TO 22
100 SCROLL
110 PRINT ," V"
120 NEXT X
```

Spectrum users need to delete line 1ØØ, and insert 85 POKE 23692, – 1.

Whilst on the subject of scrolling, here is a routine that scrolls a line of text across the screen from left to right. Input a name (inverse characters look better), or a line of text, and fill out the line with some graphics characters. Lines 2Ø, 5Ø and 6Ø fill up the line to 32 characters with black squares. The technique can be used with several lines of text, but is too slow to be useful if dealing with a full screen:

```
 5 REM *INPUT A NAME*
       *(NICER IN INVERSE)*
 6 REM *REPEAT IF LINE NOT*
       *FILLED*
10 INPUT A$
20 IF LEN A$<32 THEN GOTO 60
30 PRINT AT 10,0;A$
40 LET A$=A$( LEN A$)+A$(1 TO
    LEN A$-1)
50 GOTO 30
60 LET A$=A$+"■"
70 GOTO 20
```

When you have keyed in the program, try deleting "AT 1Ø,Ø," in line 3Ø. This gives an effective full-screen display.

Games programs often utilise interactive graphics, via the INKEY$ function. A SKETCH program as below shifts the PRINT position around. Note that on the Spectrum, INKEY$ is not totally reliable. Add PAUSE Ø to ensure it works.

```
10 LET X=10
20 LET Y=10
30 PRINT AT Y,X;"*"
40 LET X=X-( INKEY$ ="5" AND
  X>0)+( INKEY$ ="8" AND X<31)
50 LET Y=Y-( INKEY$ ="7" AND
  Y>0)+( INKEY$ ="6" AND Y<21)
60 GOTO 30
```

This uses logical values to do a multiple operation in lines 4Ø and 5Ø, which both adds or subtracts 1 to the values of X and Y, *and* keeps the character within the screen limits. This could be done less efficiently by the following:

```
4Ø  IF INKEY$ = "5" AND X>Ø THEN LET X = X – 1
5Ø  IF INKEY$ = "8" AND X<31 THEN LET X = X + 1
6Ø  IF INKEY$ = "7" AND Y>Ø THEN LET Y = Y – 1
7Ø  IF INKEY$ = "6" AND Y<21 THEN LET Y = Y + 1
8Ø  GOTO 3Ø
```

In lines 4Ø to 7Ø both conditions have to be true to execute the change in the values of X or Y. In the original example, these logical tests are combined (in the brackets) and use is made of the fact that the computer uses 1 for TRUE and Ø for FALSE. These logical values are used to change X and Y appropriately, according to which keys are pressed, but only if the values of X are within Ø – 31 and the values of Y are within Ø – 21 (i.e. within the PRINT AT range).

If, for example, X is equal to Ø, then in line 4Ø above, the combined conditions of INKEY$ = "5" (true, if it is being pressed) AND X>Ø (not true) will be false. The instruction following THEN will not be executed. Similarly, in the line LET X = X – (INKEY$ = "5" AND X>Ø) + (INKEY$ = "8" AND X<31) each of the bracketed expressions is evaluated for truth/falsity. Only one of the bracketed expressions can be true, and if, for example, the first is true, X will become X – (1(true)) + (Ø(false)). Logical operations, which are of great importance, are fully covered in Section R.

We could add:

```
35   PRINT AT Y,X;"   "
```

to get a single character rather than a line of characters, but our character flickers and is not on the screen very long.

A better way is to put the values of X and Y into two other variables, and use these to store the position where a space is to be printed, overprint as late as possible in the loop.

```
10 LET X=10
20 LET Y=10
30 PRINT AT Y,X;"*"
35 LET A=Y
36 LET B=X
40 LET X=X-( INKEY$ ="5" AND
  X>0)+( INKEY$ ="8" AND X<31)
50 LET Y=Y-( INKEY$ ="7" AND
  Y>0)+( INKEY$ ="6" AND Y<21)
55 PRINT AT A,B;" "
60 GOTO 30
```

To get automatic movement, we need to use loops. Try this:

10 FOR X = 25 TO Ø STEP – 1
20 PRINT AT 11,X;" 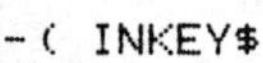 ";AT 12, X;" "
3Ø NEXT X

PAUSE 1Ø could be inserted as line 25 on the Spectrum to slow things down a bit.

Our car moves, but it leaves bits of itself behind. Add a space after each of the print strings, and the trail is automatically wiped out, overprinted by the spaces.

```
10  FOR X = 25 TO 0 STEP -1
20  PRINT AT 11,X;"▄▟▓▓▓▓▙▄";AT 12,X;"▀▣▀▀▀▀▣▀"
30  NEXT X
```

The alternative, which is slower (and harder on the eyes), is to use CLS, and reprint the screen. To see the effect, just add:

```
25 CLS
```

Or try this (which includes, to a rather distorted scale, a gravity effect) and imagine you are Galileo:

```
  1 REM GRAVITY DROP
 10 LET T=0
 20 LET H=0
 30 PRINT AT 0,5;"████"
 40 PRINT AT 21,1;"----------- "
 50 IF H>21 THEN GOTO 110
 60 PRINT AT H,10;"*"
 70 LET T=T+.25
 80 LET H=INT 32*T*T/10
 90 CLS
100 GOTO 30
110 PRINT AT 21,7;"*SMASH*"
```

The next program utilises graphics to illustrate the principle of the base current flow through an NPN transistor. The flow of the main current is indicated by a moving black graphic, and the flow of the base current by a grey square. Study the program and analyse it so that you can follow it. The string manipulation is quite complex. By now Spectrum owners should have mastered converting ZX81 programs for their own machines. Remember that the values PLOTted on the Spectrum should typically be four times larger than on the ZX81 in order to get a picture of a similar size. Apart from this, 'Transim' should not present any problems:

```
   5 REM "TRANSIM"
  10 PRINT "SIMULATION OF CURREN
T FLOW IN","+VE BIASED NPN TRANS
ISTOR"
  20 PRINT ,,"PRESS S TO SWITCH
OFF BIAS","CURRENT FLOW IN BASE"
,,,"PRESS R TO RECONNECT "
  30 PRINT ,,"GRAPHICS SHOW ELEC
TRON FLOW",,,"HIT A KEY TO START
"
  40 PAUSE 4E4
  50 CLS
  60 FOR F=9 TO 49
  70 PLOT F,9
  80 PLOT F,12
  90 IF F>26 THEN GOTO 120
 100 PLOT 27,F+3
 110 PLOT 30,F+3
 120 NEXT F
 130 UNPLOT 20,12
```

```
 140 UNPLOT 29,12
 150 PRINT AT 0,5;"* NPN TRANSIS
TOR *"; TAB 5;"*****************
*"
 160 PRINT AT 5,17;"BASE"; AT 7,
17;"CURRENT ON"; AT 14,2;"COLLEC
TOR"; TAB 22;"EMITTER"
 170 PRINT AT 5,10;"+VE"; AT 18,
0;"+VE <N*N*N*N><P><N*N*N*N> -VE
"
 180 REM **GRAPHIC STRINGS**
 190 LET A$="□■□■□■□■□■□■□■□■□■"
 200 LET B$="□□□■□■□■□□□■□■□■□"
 210 LET S$="▟ ▗ ▟▄▙"
 220 FOR N=1 TO 15
 230 REM **GRAPHICS LOOP**
 240 FOR F=1 TO 8
 250 IF F=1 THEN PRINT AT 7,14;"
■"
 260 PRINT AT 16-F,14;"■"
 270 PRINT AT 16,4;B$(F TO F+9);
A$(F TO F+10)
 280 PRINT AT 7,13;S$(1 TO 3);
 290 IF F=8 AND INKEY$ ="S" THEN
 GOSUB 400
 300 PRINT AT 7,14;" "; AT 16-F,
14;" "
 310 NEXT F
 320 NEXT N
 330 PRINT AT 21,0;"PROGRAM HALT
ED.RESTART?(Y OR N)"
 340 INPUT R$
 350 IF R$ <> "Y" THEN GOTO 440
 360 PRINT AT 21,0;"
                              "
 370 GOTO 220

 395 REM **********************
          **BASE CURRENT OFF SUB**
 400 PRINT AT 5,10;"   "; AT 7,1
3;S$(4 TO ); AT 7,25;"OFF"
 410 IF INKEY$ <> "R" THEN GOTO
410
 420 PRINT AT 5,10;"+VE"; AT 7,1
3;S$(1 TO 3); AT 7,25;"ON "
 430 RETURN

 435 REM ** ENDSUB          ****
         **********************

 440 CLS
 450 REM **END PROGRAM **
```

Spectrum modifictions: PAUSE Ø in line 4Ø.
The program uses the 'chunky' ZX81 plot squares to draw the outline (lines 6Ø to 14Ø). Spectrum plot points could be used, but strings of the graphics characters on keys 1 to 8 would be better. Refer to the screen diagrams in Unit M2 for the positions on screen requiring printing.

Exercises

1. For ZX81 users: Computer performance in terms of speed is compared by benchmark tests. Write a program that loops 500 times, performing a calculation each time. Run it in FAST and SLOW modes, and time it.
2. Revise the left to right scroll to work right to left.
3. Write a program that draws a ship and moves it backwards and forwards across the screen, automatically.
4. Revise the program to move the ship in response to INKEY$ input from the keyboard.
5. Write a program that uses PAUSE to display minutes and seconds. Check the clock against a watch and improve the accuracy.

Q4: The Display File

In order to talk about the display file, we must introduce some new concepts, which are dealt with more fully in a later section of the book (Section U).

The DISPLAY FILE is the memory picture of the screen display stored in a sequence of memory locations or addresses in the computer RAM.

BYTE. Each memory location in the computer stores an 8 bit (digit) binary number which has a decimal value between 0 and 255.

To interact with the computer's memory, we use PEEK and POKE. We are concerned here not with the general instructions (which are dealt with in Section U) but with some specific uses for these commands. We will give a definition of PEEK and POKE here, and then discuss the use of these only in terms of some simple techniques connected with the screen display that can be of use in graphics.

PEEK (M) returns the contents of the memory address (M) (a binary number) in decimal form.

POKE (M),(N) inserts the value N (0 to 255) into the specified memory address, M.

The display files of the ZX81 and Spectrum are organised very differently. That of the Spectrum is much more complex, due to the high-resolution PLOT screen and colour on the machine. We will deal with the ZX81 display file in some depth below, and then describe the Spectrum display file. Spectrum users should GOTO page 257, and omit the ZX81 specific section below, unless they find it interesting for general information. It is useful to know the ZX81 display file system if you are interested in converting ZX81 programs for the Spectrum, as some programs use the techniques described below.

On the ZX81:

Each address of the display file stores in a byte a character code, corresponding to the character to be printed on the screen.

The display file memory location differs according to the program length, since it starts where the portion of memory occupied by the program ends. For any given program the start location is constant.

The DISPLAY FILE start address is stored in the system variable D-FILE, at memory locations 16396 and 16397.

For the display file memory locations:

PEEK M gives a number (in decimal) which corresponds to the character code located in the memory address M.

POKE puts into one of these memory locations a character code.

POKE M, N puts the number (character code) N into memory address M

The ZX81 has done away with much of the use of POKE in connection with the display file, because the PRINT AT function actually uses a routine in the computer that finds out where the display file starts and then POKEs to it the required characters at the correct position.

To illustrate the work this saves, here is a program that puts ZX at line 1, column 1Ø, on the screen.

```
1Ø  LET D = PEEK 16396 + 256*PEEK 16397
2Ø  LET Z = D + (32 + 1 + 11)
3Ø  POKE Z, 63
4Ø  POKE Z + 1,61
```

Note that, even though we could write the routine above more compactly (by missing out line 2Ø and using POKE D + 44, POKE D + 45 as lines 3Ø and 4Ø) it is still rather more complicated than:

```
1Ø  PRINT AT 1,1Ø;"ZX"
```

Thus we will not use it unless we have good reason. But let's run through what we are doing. Do not worry if you cannot fully understand all of this, you can return to this Section later, when the memory has been covered.

Line 1Ø sets D to the values of the 'D-FILE' *system variable*, which stores the memory location of the start of the display file. The address is always stored in two bytes (16396 and 16397) of memory and the second is the more significant byte (i.e. stores the higher value). Hence the *256 before the second memory location.

PEEK 16396 + 256 * PEEK 16397 returns the value of the memory location of the NEWLINE (ENTER) character at the start of the display file.

Line 2Ø counts along the screen to the position required. The value of 44 has been broken down to show the principle. The D-FILE address contains the NEWLINE (ENTER) character, which is always present at the start of the first line. We count 32 for the spaces in line Ø, and then there is another NEWLINE (ENTER) character, marking the end of line Ø. We want the eleventh position (column 1Ø) along the next line, so we count 11. This gives us a value for the memory location corresponding to the desired print position. Using this, line 3Ø prints Z by POKEing the corresponding character code into this location and similarly line 4Ø puts X in the next position along.

Notice that the display file has no correspondence to line and column numbers, it merely numbers in sequence:

	Start Newline (Enter) Character	Column Ø	1	2	3.....	31	Newline (Enter) Character
(Line Ø)	1	2	3	4	5.....	33	34
		35	36	37	38.....	66	67
		1Ø1	1Ø2	....	....	....	....
		....	....	....	....	....	....
(Line 21)		....	....	....	....	.726	727
(Line 22)		728	729	....	....	.759	76Ø
(Line 23)		761	762	....	....	.792	793

So to use this technique we only need to find the start location of the display file once, and allocate a variable to it (D in the program above), or arrange to re-use a program line with the PEEK commands.

To try to make things a little clearer, try the following program:

```
1Ø  LET DFILE = PEEK 16396 + 256*
    PEEK 16397
2Ø  PRINT "DISPLAY FILE START ADDRESS
    IS", "MEMORY LOCATION  "; DFILE
3Ø  FOR M = DFILE - 8 TO DFILE + 8
4Ø  PRINT M;TAB 1Ø; PEEK M; TAB 18;CHR$ PEEK M
5Ø  NEXT M
```

Line 1Ø PEEKs the D-FILE memory locations, which store the number of the address in which the first NEWLINE (ENTER) character of the display file is located.

If you have entered the program *exactly* as shown – including the space after "Memory Location" – line 2Ø will print:

```
DISPLAY FILE START ADDRESS IS
MEMORY LOCATION 16694
```

This is followed by a printout like this:

```
16686   118   ?
16687   Ø
16688   5Ø    M
16689   3     ■
1669Ø   Ø     ⬒
16691   243   NEXT
16692   5Ø    M
16693   118   ?
16694   118   ?
16695   41    D
16696   46    I
16697   56    S
16698   53    P
16699   49    L
167ØØ   38    A
167Ø1   62    Y
167Ø2   Ø
```

This shows a memory address (16686) then the character code it contains (118) and its character string (in this case 118 is NEWLINE (ENTER), and prints a '?'). Address 16687 is a space (character code Ø) and a space is printed. 16688 contains the *number* 5Ø, which is the line number of the last program line, and prints M. Then there is a 3 stored (which is the number of characters in the program line) and which prints the graphic character, then NEXT (character code 243), and M again, this time representing the *variable* M, not the number 5Ø. Then there is a NEWLINE (ENTER) character (118) marking the end of the program. The next NEWLINE (ENTER) is at 16694, the start of the display file, and then there are the codes and characters for DISPLAY (the first words to be printed on the screen).

To illustrate the use of PEEK and POKE with the display file, here is a program to draw on the screen. This does essentially the same thing as the sketch program we met earlier, but it uses the technique of POKEing characters to the display file directly, instead of via the PRINT AT function. We give a full listing here, but in fact to run it, you need only enter lines 19Ø to 29Ø.

```
10 REM "ARTIST"
20 PRINT "DRAWS A PICTURE BY M
   OVING A CHARACTER IN 8 DIRE
   CTIONS"
30 PRINT "TO MOVE IN THE FOLLO
   WING DIRECTIONS PRESS THE C
   ORRESPONDING KEY"
40 PRINT TAB 10; "NORTH--W"
50 PRINT TAB 10; "SOUTH--X"
60 PRINT TAB 10; "EAST--D"
70 PRINT TAB 10; "WEST--A"
80 PRINT TAB 10; "NORTHEAST--E"
90 PRINT TAB 10; "SOUTHEAST--C"
100 PRINT TAB 10; "SOUTHWEST--Z"
110 PRINT TAB 10; "NORTHWEST--Q"
120 PRINT
130 PRINT
140 PRINT "TO CHANGE THE CHARAC
    TER PRESS S THEN THE CHARAC
    TER THEN NEWLINE"
150 PRINT
160 PRINT "DON'T GO OVER THE ED
    GE OF THE SCREEN"
170 PAUSE 400
180 CLS
190 LET T=120
200 LET A$="*"
240 POKE PEEK 16396+PEEK 16397*
    256+T,CODE A$
250 IF INKEY$="" THEN GOTO 250
270 LET B$=INKEY$
280 LET T=T+(32 AND B$="Z")+(33
    AND B$="X")+(34 AND B$="C"
    )-(34 AND B$="Q")-(33 AND
    B$="W")-(32 AND B$="E")+(
    1 AND B$="D")-(1 AND B$="
    A")
290 IF B$="S" THEN INPUT A$
300 GOTO 240
```

The complex looking line 280 (be careful to input it correctly) uses the same logic as was mentioned with the "Sketch" program. If you inspect it, after we've dealt with logic properly, you will see that each key that is pressed gives a different value. The equivalent lines without this technique would be:

```
280 IF B$="Z" THEN LET T=T+32
281 IF B$="X" THEN LET T=T+33
282 IF B$="C" THEN LET T=T+34
283 IF B$="Q" THEN LET T=T-34
284 IF B$="W" THEN LET T=T-33
285 IF B$="E" THEN LET T=T-32
286 IF B$="D" THEN LET T=T+1
287 IF B$="A" THEN LET T=T-1
```

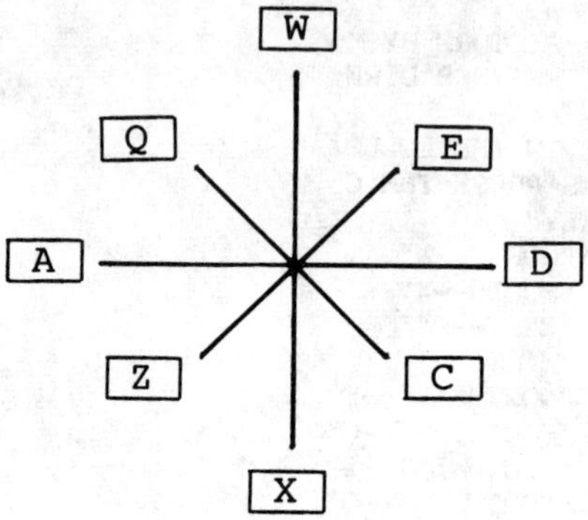

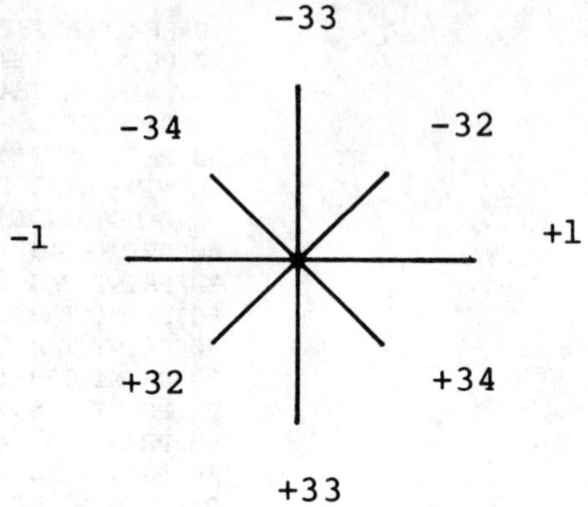

If you look at the diagram above and the numbering of the display file, you will see how it works. – 1 or + 1 move the position along a line, – 34 moves it up one line and to the left etc. All this numbering is within the display file. Line 240 PEEKs the D-FILE memory locations, adds the display file position number and POKEs into the result (a memory address in the display file) the character code for A$. Notice the speed of this program. This gives us one reason to use PEEK and POKE: to provide speed of display.

Notice the warning about the edges of the screen in the program listing. When you have decided you have played with the program enough, try going off the edge of the screen. The results will not harm the ZX81, but you will probably have to switch the power off to reset the computer. All manipulations of the display file must be done with great care so as not to interfere with the NEWLINE (ENTER) characters marking the end of each line. If these are altered the computer cannot keep track of where everything should be, the display will go crazy and the program will crash. Be warned! (And be *careful* in your programming!)

It is possible to increase the screen size of the display to give the capability to PRINT or PRINT AT on the bottom lines of the screen. The system variable (DF-SZ) at memory location 16418 holds the number of lines in the bottom half of the screen, and is normally set at 2. If we use POKE 16418,Ø, the bottom two lines can be used to PRINT AT. Try this program.

```
1Ø  POKE 16418,Ø
2Ø  FOR L = Ø TO 23
3Ø  PRINT "LINE NUMBER" ;L
4Ø  NEXT L
5Ø  FOR X = 1 TO 3ØØ
6Ø  NEXT X
```

Notice that, after the delay caused by the FOR...NEXT loop, the Ø/6Ø message appears on the bottom line as usual, and that the next command from the keyboard clears the bottom two lines. This is because DF-SZ returns to its normal value on completion of a program. If we use COPY it will also not print the bottom two lines – it is only set for a normal screen size of 22 lines.

We may also restrict the screen size. Key in this program:

```
10 POKE 16418,20
20 PRINT "TOP LINE"
30 PRINT "SECOND LINE"
40 PAUSE 150
50 PRINT "NOW SCROLL"
60 FOR X=1 TO 4
70 SCROLL
80 PRINT "SCROLLED ";X
90 NEXT X
```

The SCROLL instruction now operates from the bottom line of a screen which is only 4 lines deep. This can be used to clear just the top part of the screen, leaving the rest undisturbed.

Try this next program, which uses both these techniques together. (You don't need to input the text in lines 70, 90 and 110. Just PRINT 1, 2 and 3 instead).

```
 10 POKE 16418,0
 20 FOR L=0 TO 23
 30 PRINT "LINE NUMBER ";L
 40 NEXT L
 50 POKE 16418,21
 60 SCROLL
 70 PRINT "THESE LINES"
 80 SCROLL
 90 PRINT "NOW CLEARED AND "
100 SCROLL
110 PRINT "REST OF SCREEN LEFT
    AS IS"
120 FOR X=1 TO 300
    NEXT X
```

If entered as above, the top portion of the screen would look like this:

THESE LINES NOW
CLEARED AND REST OF
SCREEN LEFT AS IS
LINE NUMBER 3
LINE NUMBER 4
LINE NUMBER 5
LINE NUMBER 6

Unfortunately, we cannot choose a screen section in the middle of the screen (e.g. lines 6, 7 and 8) to do this with, and must use PRINT AT "(32 spaces)" with the lines we want to clear, or overprint directly, or POKE spaces into the relevant positions, as in this program:

```
10 FOR F= 1 TO 9
20 PRINT "LINE NUMBER ";F;"
   (16 SPACES) END"
30 NEXT F
```

```
40 PRINT "LINE NUMBER TO BE
   CLEARED ?"
50 INPUT LINE
60 LET DFILE=PEEK 16396+256*PE
   EK 16397
70 FOR X=1 TO 32
80 POKE (LINE-1)*33+DFILE+X,0
90 NEXT X
```

Note that if we put:

70 FOR X = 32 TO 1 STEP – 1

we get a reverse line clearance (right to left), and

70 FOR X = 32 TO 30 STEP – 1

clears END, but leaves the rest of the line.

Another useful system variable concerned with the ZX81 display file is the DF-CC address, locations 16398 and 16399. This holds the address of the current print position in the display file. If this address is found by using PEEK 16398 + 256* PEEK 16399 then it can in turn be PEEKed, and will give the code of the character present at the current print position. Note that the current print position is the *next* position to be printed. A line like

10 PRINT TAB 8; "A"

leaves the current print position set at the start of the next line of the display, and

10 PRINT TAB 8;"A";

gives as the current print position the next position after the A. To illustrate, here is a variation on the basic screen movement program we derived from SKETCH which uses the DF-CC variable.

```
10 LET X=10
20 LET Y=10
30 PRINT AT Y,X;
40 LET D=PEEK 16398+256*PEEK 16399
50 PRINT "*"
60 LET X=X-(INKEY$="5" AND X>0)
   + (INKEY$="8" AND X<31)
70 LET Y=Y-(INKEY$="7" AND Y>0)
   + (INKEY$="6" AND Y<21)
80 POKE D, 0
90 GOTO 30
```

Instead of setting two variables as equal to X and Y before their values are altered (before line 50) in order to identify where to print the space which blanks the "*", we use variable D to store the location of the print position (line 40) and then POKE a 0 (space) into it to overprint (line 80).

Notice lines 3Ø and 4Ø. We must *set* the PRINT AT position in line 3Ø, *then* PEEK the DF-CC addresses, *then* PRINT the "*".

The ASTEROIDS program in the program library uses the technique of PEEKing the next PRINT position to determine whether a black square occupies this position. The relevant lines are

```
13Ø  PRINT AT 5,C;
14Ø  IF PEEK (PEEK 16398 + 256*PEEK
     16399) = 128 THEN GOTO 25Ø
15Ø  PRINT "*"
```

Look up the program and work out how these lines relate to the rest of the program. If you find line 14Ø confusing, remember that the ZX81 evaluates expressions in brackets first. It gets the value stored in the 16398/9 addresses, which returns the address of the PRINT position, *then* PEEKs this address.

We will now deal with the Spectrum display file, which does not have the straightforward structure of that of the ZX81, and to which PEEK and POKE techniques have little application.

SPECTRUM DISPLAY FILE

The Spectrum display file is organised in a very different way to that of the ZX81. This is a consequence of the high-resolution screen display on the Spectrum (256 * 176 points are plotable), compared to the 'chunky' graphics of the ZX81, with only 64 * 44 plot squares. The pattern of squares in any character cell on the ZX81 can be defined as a character code. On the Spectrum each individual point of the 8 by 8 grid of a character cell must be individually specified.

The Spectrum display file is fixed in memory, and does not vary its location. There is no need to PEEK a system variable to find its position, as the start address is always 16384, and it is a fixed length of 6144 bytes, occupying the memory addresses up to 22527.

The complex method of organisation means that it is not possible (as it is with the ZX81 and other computers), to POKE character codes to the screen and have the character specified by that code appear. Similarly, we cannot PEEK the screen to find out what character, if any, occupies a given location. Both these operations are theoretically possible, with much calculation, but not practicable. However, the speed of the Spectrum's operations takes away much of the advantage of using PEEK and POKE on the ZX81, and we can use PRINT AT instructions to place characters on the screen, and two special Spectrum functions for finding out what is on the screen. Before introducing these instructions, here is a description of the way the Spectrum display file is organised:

Each character cell has an 8 by 8 dot matrix of points, which may be 'set' (blacked or inked in) or not. These patterns of dots make up the characters. We'll treat this in more detail later. For plotting, each point must be specified individually, and this means that the characters available in the character set do not cover the whole set of possibilities for each cell. To cope with this, the Spectrum stores each pattern of points along a 32 character cell line on the screen in a sequence of bytes. However, these are not stored in sequence down the screen. The top point sequence of each of the first eight rows of characters (lines) are stored one after the other. The second line of points in each of these 8 lines of characters is then stored, and so on until the first eight lines of the screen display have been defined. The next eight lines on the screen are then stored in the same way, followed by the bottom eight lines of the 24 line screen.

To make this clearer, key in the following program and run it:

```
10  FOR A = 16384 TO 22527
20  POKE A, 85
30  NEXT A
```

This puts into each byte the binary form of 85 (01010101), giving alternate plotted and unplotted ('set' and 'unset') points. You will see that the top line of points for each of the top eight lines on the screen appears, in sequence top to bottom, then the second line of points for each of these eight PRINT lines, and so on. When this sequence has finished, it repeats for the next block of eight lines, and then again for the bottom eight.

You should now see why it is not easy to define a particular sequence of POKEs to the display file to get a character on screen! This is best done using PRINT AT on the Spectrum in all cases. Pixels can also be plotted, of course, and in Section W the user-defined graphics available on the Spectrum are dealt with, which enables any character cell pattern of 8*8 plot points to be defined and treated as a character which can be placed on the screen with a PRINT AT instruction.

To find out what is on the screen at a particular place we use SCREEN$ (instead of PEEKing the display file) on the Spectrum.

SCREEN$

SCREEN$ is a Spectrum specific function. It returns the single-character string of the character printed at the specified line and column co-ordinates. It has the form:

SCREEN$ (L,C)

PRINT SCREEN$ (2, 6) returns the character printed at Line 2, Column 6 on the screen. The brackets cannot be omitted. SCREEN$ will return the true video form of any inverse character. It does not recognise either the true video or inverse video forms of the Graphics characters.

Note the restriction on what SCREEN$ will recognise. The chunky graphics characters on keys 1 to 8 are *not* recognised. An empty string is returned. Run the following program to see SCREEN$ in action. After you've tried other characters, try the graphics characters and inverse video. Input PRINT LEN SCREEN$(1Ø,1Ø) as a direct command to see that the null string (no characters) is returned.

```
1Ø  INPUT A$
2Ø  PRINT AT 1Ø, 1Ø; A$
3Ø  PRINT SCREEN$ (1Ø,1Ø)
```

There is another Spectrum specific instruction that can be used to find out what is currently on the screen. This is POINT.

POINT

POINT returns 1 if a specified PLOT pixel is inked in ('set'), Ø if it is not. It has the form

POINT (X,Y)

where X and Y are the PLOT screen co-ordinates of the point to be checked.

To see the action of POINT to check if a plot pixel has been inked in, key in the following:

```
1Ø  PLOT 128,88
2Ø  PRINT POINT (128,88)
3Ø  PRINT POINT (128,89)
```

POINT returns 1 for line 2Ø (pixel plotted), and Ø for line 3Ø (pixel not plotted, or 'unset'). Notice that the brackets must be placed around the X and Y expressions. Both POINT and SCREEN$ will, of course, work with calculated values. POINT can be used to give information about inverse characters that SCREEN$ will not provide. We can illustrate this simply. Key in this program:

```
1Ø  PRINT "↑"
2Ø  PRINT POINT (Ø,175)
3Ø  PRINT AT 1Ø,1Ø;"█"
4Ø  PLOT OVER 1;84,9Ø
5Ø  PRINT POINT (84,9Ø)
6Ø  PRINT POINT (85,9Ø)
```

Line 2Ø checks the upper left corner pixel of the character cell with the exponentiation sign printed in inverse video. This returns 1, since the pixel is set. Line 3Ø prints an inverse square (CAPS SHIFTed graphic

8), which SCREEN$ will not recognise. Line 4Ø unplots 1 pixel, using the OVER 1 statement, and line 5Ø checks this plot point, returning Ø, since it is unplotted, and line 6Ø checks roughly the centre point of the black square, which returns 1. This offers us a way of checking inverse characters. You must, of course, make the correct calculations for the transfer from the PRINT to PLOT screens.

You should notice two points for future use, after Section W has introduced the other Spectrum functions not dealt with in the main body of the text. One is that we referred to POINT returning 1 if the pixel was set or inked in, and when you start using colour, you should remember that POINT checks for the currently specified INK colour. For our purposes, this is black. The other is that the colour attributes that refer to a character cell when colour is used can be another source of information about the screen display. (This uses the ATTR function. See Unit W3.)

R1: Logic Values and Numeric Values

When using the logical capability of Sinclair BASIC we must distinguish between *logical* values and the *numeric* values produced by logical evaluation. We have touched upon this earlier in the book, but deferred a full explanation until now.

LOGICAL VALUE is the value of an expression using the criteria:

any *non-zero* value of the expression = "TRUE"
a *zero* value of the expression = "FALSE"

When an expression is logically evaluated it is assigned one of two *numeric* values:

"TRUE" 1
"FALSE" Ø

R2: Boolean Operators: The <u>AND</u> Operator

AND ∧

Examples
```
100 IF (A = 10) AND (B<>3) THEN GOTO 60
200 PRINT (A AND B)
```

The AND operator (symbol ∧) forms a logical conjunction between two expressions involving conditional operators.

If both expressions are "TRUE" the conjunction is "TRUE".

If one or both are "FALSE" the conjunction is "FALSE".

The numeric value of "TRUE" is 1.

The numeric value of "FALSE" is Ø.

All non-zero values are "TRUE".

In line 1ØØ, if the relation A = 1Ø is "TRUE" *and* the relation B<>3 is "TRUE" then control will pass to line 6Ø. If either or both of the relations is "FALSE" then control passes to the next line.

In line 2ØØ the computer will *not* print A + B. It will print the value of A or Ø depending on the values of A and B.

Remember: All non-zero values are "TRUE".

So if

A = 15 and B = 6

A = "TRUE" B = "TRUE"

So the relation (A AND B) is ("TRUE" AND "TRUE").

So the result is logically "TRUE".

15 is printed.

If A = 16 ("TRUE") and B = Ø (zero value – *logically* "FALSE").

Then (A AND B) is ("TRUE" AND "FALSE") = "FALSE" = Ø.

So Ø is printed.

We will explain this in more detail later.

Truth Table for AND

A	B	A AND B
TRUE	TRUE	TRUE
TRUE	FALSE	FALSE
FALSE	TRUE	FALSE
FALSE	FALSE	FALSE

A and B are conditional expressions.

R3: The OR Operator

OR ∨

Examples 100 IF (A>1) OR (B = 0) THEN STOP
200 PRINT (C OR D)

The Boolean operator OR (symbol ∨) forms the logical disjunction of two expressions involving conditional operations.

If either *or* both of the expressions is "TRUE" the OR disjunction is "TRUE".

If both expressions are "FALSE" the OR disjunction is "FALSE".

In line 100 if either of the expressions (A>1) and (B = 0) are "TRUE" the program will STOP.

If both are "FALSE" control passes to the next line.

In line 200 if C = 10 = "TRUE" and D = 0 = "FALSE"
C OR D = "TRUE" OR "FALSE" = "TRUE"
10, the value of C is printed.
If C = 0 = "FALSE" and D = 0 = "FALSE"
C OR D = "FALSE" OR "FALSE" = "FALSE"
So 0 is printed.

Truth Table for OR

A	B	A OR B
TRUE	TRUE	TRUE
TRUE	FALSE	TRUE
FALSE	TRUE	TRUE
FALSE	FALSE	FALSE

A and B are conditional expressions.

R4: The NOT Operator

NOT ¬

Examples 20 IF NOT A THEN STOP
30 IF NOT (A = B) THEN STOP
100 PRINT NOT A

NOT (symbol ¬) logically evaluates the complement (reverse) of a given expression.

In line 2Ø, if A = 1Ø then A = "TRUE" and NOT A = NOT "TRUE" = "FALSE".

So in line 2Ø if A is 1Ø, NOT A is "FALSE" and control passes to the next line.

If A = Ø ("FALSE") then NOT A = NOT "FALSE" = "TRUE" and the program stops.

In line 3Ø if (A = B) is "FALSE", NOT (A = B) = NOT "FALSE" = "TRUE", so program stops.

In line 1ØØ if A = Ø = "FALSE" then NOT A = "TRUE" = 1

So 1 is printed.

If A = 29 then A is "TRUE" and NOT A = "FALSE", and Ø is printed.

Truth table for NOT

A	NOT A
TRUE	FALSE
FALSE	TRUE

A is a conditional expression.

R5: Conditional Operators

There are two ways to use conditional operators in logical evaluations.

1. To check the numeric value of an expression

Examples **1ØØ IF A = 3 THEN GOTO 6Ø**
2ØØ IF B<>C THEN STOP

The numeric value produced by the logical operation is not important. We are concerned only with the truth or falsity of the condition indicated in the IF...THEN statement, which determines whether the instruction is executed. When the specified condition is present ("TRUE"), the statement after THEN will be carried out.

2. To check on the numeric value produced by logically evaluating an expression

In this case we want the numeric values, where "TRUE" = 1 and "FALSE" = Ø

Examples **2ØØ PRINT A<B**
3ØØ PRINT A = 3

The PRINT statement used as above will give the numeric values produced by logical evaluation.

Line 2ØØ is evaluated as a logical expression, so that if it is TRUE that A is less than B, 1 will be printed, and if A is equal to or bigger than B, the expression is false and Ø will be printed.

Line 3ØØ is interpreted by the BASIC as: "Print 1 if A = 3, Ø if A does not equal 3."

The numeric value of the logical evaluation is distinct from the logical value of the expression.

R6: Logic Operations on Conditional Expressions

IF (CONDITION) [AND / OR] (CONDITION) THEN...

IF [NOT] (CONDITION) THEN...

The effect of the logical operators AND, OR and NOT on conditions which are TRUE or FALSE gives a result which is TRUE or FALSE and on which the IF...THEN instruction acts accordingly.

EXAMPLES:

```
100  IF (A>10) AND (B = 0) THEN GOTO 20
200  IF (A = 0) OR (B = 0) THEN STOP
300  IF NOT (A = B) THEN PRINT "A<>B"
```

These all mean:

IF [combined result is TRUE] THEN (do it)

IF [combined result is FALSE] go to the next line of the program.

Using logical operations is a way of *combining* conditional operators in a statement. For example:

IF [(condition 1) AND (condition 2) AND (condition 3)] evaluates as TRUE or FALSE] THEN...act accordingly.

```
60 IF ((A>B) AND (C>A) AND (D>C)) THEN STOP
```

AND

IF (CONDITION 1)	AND (CONDITION 2)	THEN (RESULT)
TRUE	TRUE	TRUE
TRUE	FALSE	FALSE
FALSE	TRUE	FALSE
FALSE	FALSE	FALSE

EXAMPLE:

Condition 1 – My age is > 12 years

Condition 2 – My age is < 2Ø years

Result – I am a teenager.

IF (my age > 12 years) AND (my age < 2Ø years) THEN (I am a teenager).

Program

```
10  PRINT "INPUT AGE"
20  INPUT A
```

```
30  IF (A>12) AND (A<2Ø) THEN GOTO 6Ø
4Ø  PRINT "YOU ARE NOT A TEENAGER"
5Ø  STOP
6Ø  PRINT "YOU ARE A TEENAGER"
```

OR

IF (CONDITION 1)	**OR (CONDITION 2)**	**THEN (RESULT)**
TRUE	**TRUE**	**TRUE**
TRUE	**FALSE**	**TRUE**
FALSE	**TRUE**	**TRUE**
FALSE	**FALSE**	**FALSE**

<u>EXAMPLE</u>:

Condition 1 – I earn wages
Condition 2 – I get pocket money
Result – I have money

IF (I earn wages) OR (I get pocket money) THEN (I have money).

<u>Program</u>

```
1Ø  PRINT "INPUT AMOUNT OF WAGES AND POCKET
    MONEY YOU GET"
2Ø  INPUT W
3Ø  INPUT P
4Ø  IF (W>Ø) OR (P>Ø) THEN GOTO 7Ø
5Ø  PRINT "YOU HAVE NO MONEY"
6Ø  STOP
7Ø  PRINT "YOU HAVE";W + P;"POUNDS"
```

NOT

IF [NOT (CONDITION)]	**THEN (RESULT)**
TRUE	**FALSE**
FALSE	**TRUE**

<u>EXAMPLE</u>:

CONDITION – I have money
RESULT – I do not have money

IF [NOT (I have money)] THEN (I don't have money)

<u>Program</u>

```
 5  PRINT "ARE YOU A LIAR?"
1Ø  PRINT "INPUT AMOUNT OF MONEY"
2Ø  INPUT M
3Ø  IF NOT (M>Ø) THEN GOTO 6Ø
4Ø  PRINT "APPARENTLY YOU DO NOT HAVE MONEY"
5Ø  STOP
6Ø  PRINT "YOU DO HAVE MONEY REALLY ?"
```

R7: Multiple Logic on Conditions

Multiple logical operations on conditions are often useful. They take the form:

$$\textbf{IF } [(\text{C1}) \begin{bmatrix}\text{AND}\\ \text{OR}\end{bmatrix} (\text{C2})] \begin{bmatrix}\text{AND}\\ \text{OR}\end{bmatrix} [(\text{C3}) \begin{bmatrix}\text{AND}\\ \text{OR}\end{bmatrix} (\text{C4})] \textbf{ THEN...}$$

Where C1 = Condition 1
C2 = Condition 2
C3 = Condition 3
C4 = Condition 4

e.g. IF [(C1 AND C2) OR (C3 AND C4)] THEN...
The above statement means that:

IF conditions 1 AND 2 are obeyed
OR conditions 3 AND 4 are obeyed

then the combined expression is TRUE, and the instruction will be executed, i.e. either pair of conditions being both TRUE will give the result.

IF [(C1 AND C2) AND (C3 AND C4)] THEN

In this statement all four conditions must be true to give the result.

What do the following imply?

IF [(C1 OR C2) AND (C3 OR C4)] THEN...
IF [(C1 OR C2) OR (C3 OR C4)] THEN...

Notice the importance of brackets in the statements.

Their placing gives a clear logical meaning to an expression. Any bracketed expression will be evaluated first. The result ("TRUE" or "FALSE") obtained from the bracketed expression will be used in evaluating the whole expression.

A practical example of multiple logical operations on conditions would be obtaining a loan. The relevant conditions could be:

C1 = Husband is over 21 years old
C2 = Husband's salary is over £5,000 per year
C3 = Wife is over 21 years old
C4 = Wife's salary is over £5,000 per year.

We can write a statement which indicates whether the bank will grant the family a loan to buy a car:

IF [(C1 AND C2) OR (C3 AND C4)] THEN loan granted.

Exercises

1. Key in and run the program which illustrates this:

```
10 PRINT "INPUT AGE OF HUSBAND"
20 INPUT HA
30 PRINT "INPUT AGE OF WIFE"
40 INPUT WA
50 PRINT "INPUT P.A. INCOME OF HUSBAND"
60 INPUT IH
```

```
 70 PRINT "INPUT P.A. INCOME OF WIFE"
 80 INPUT IW
 90 IF (HA>21 AND IH>= 5000) OR
    (WA>21 AND IW>= 5000) THEN GOTO 120
100 PRINT "NOT ELIGIBLE FOR LOAN"
110 STOP
120 PRINT "LOAN AVAILABLE"
```

2. Write a program which inputs four numbers and outputs a message if any of them are zero.

R8: Logical Operations on Numbers

The logical operations AND, OR, NOT when applied to numbers return a number as the result. The rules for the operations on two numbers X and Y are given in the following truth tables. Non-zero values may be either positive or negative.

AND

X	Y	X AND Y
X	<>Ø	X
X	Ø	Ø

i.e. X AND Y returns X if Y is non-zero
Ø if Y is zero.

OR

X	Y	X OR Y
X	<>Ø	1
X	Ø	X

i.e. X OR Y returns 1 if Y is non-zero
X if Y is zero.

NOT

Y	NOT Y
<>Ø	Ø
Ø	1

i.e. NOT Y returns Ø if Y is non-zero
1 if Y is zero

<u>EXAMPLES</u>:

7 AND 3 = 7
7 AND Ø = Ø
5 OR 2 = 1

5 OR Ø = 5
NOT 8 = Ø
NOT Ø = 1

Exercises

1 Key in the examples given above as direct commands, and verify the rules of logical operations on numbers.
2 Key in and run the following programs:

LOGIC 1:

```
 5 REM "LOGIC 1"
10 INPUT A
20 INPUT B
30 PRINT "A=";A,"B=";B
40 PRINT "A AND B=";A AND B
50 PRINT "A OR B=";A OR B
60 PRINT "NOT B=";NOT B
70 GOTO 10
```

Results:

A = 77 B = 45
A AND B = 77
A OR B = 1
NOT B = Ø

A = 77 B = Ø
A AND B = Ø
A OR B = 77
NOT B = 1

LOGIC 2:

```
 5 REM "LOGIC 2"
10 REM **THIS PROGRAM TESTS THE LOGICAL OR
   OPERATOR ACTING ON A NUMBER AND A
   CONDITION TOGETHER**
30 PRINT "Y=10*(7 OR A=3)"
35 PRINT
40 PRINT "INPUT A VALUE FOR A PLEASE"
45 PRINT
50 INPUT A
55 LET Y=10*(7 OR A=3)
60 PRINT "IF A=";A,"THEN Y=";Y
65 PRINT
70 PRINT "WHAT ARE YOUR CONCLUSIONS??"
75 PRINT
80 PRINT
90 GOTO 30
```

LOGIC 3:

```
 5 REM "LOGIC 3"
10 INPUT A
20 PRINT 77+(10 AND A=3)
30 GOTO 10
```

R9: Priority

OPERATOR	PRIORITY
=, <>, <, <=, >, >=	5
NOT	4
AND	3
OR	2

Priority rules are strictly obeyed. If brackets are not used properly when logical operators act on conditions the desired result will not be achieved. For example:

NOT ("FALSE" AND "FALSE")
gives NOT "FALSE"
= "**TRUE**"
<u>BUT</u>
NOT "FALSE" AND "FALSE"
gives "TRUE" AND "FALSE"
= "**FALSE**"

Completely the opposite!

Exercises

1 Key and and run this program, which checks priority.

```
10  LET A = 1
20  LET B = 1
30  PRINT NOT (A = Ø AND B = Ø)
40  PRINT NOT A = Ø AND B = Ø
```

2 What result would the following give?

PRINT 5 AND 3 OR Ø OR NOT 7 AND 4

3 Key in and run program "LOGIC 4", which tests priorities:

```
 5 REM "LOGIC 4"
 7 REM **THIS PROGRAM TESTS MU
   LTIPLE LOGIC OPERATORS**
10 LET A=5 AND 3 OR Ø OR NOT 7
   AND 4
20 PRINT "5 AND 3 OR Ø OR NOT
   7 AND 4="; A
30 PRINT
40 PRINT
50 LET B=((4 AND 2) AND NOT (Ø
   AND 3)) OR ((3 OR Ø) AND (4
   OR Ø))
60 PRINT "((4 AND 2) AND NOT (
   Ø AND 3)) OR ((3 OR Ø) AND
   (4 OR Ø))=";B
```

R1Ø: Logical Operations with Strings

1 **Logical operations using AND, OR and NOT may be performed on conditional string expressions. For example:**
1Ø IF (A$ = B$) AND (C$ = D$) OR (D$ = E$) THEN...
5Ø PRINT NOT A$ = B$.

2 **The AND operator may be used directly between a string and a number. For example:**
PRINT (A$ AND N)
The result of this operation is given by the truth table.

A$	N	A$ AND N
A$	<>Ø	A$
A$	Ø	" "

i.e. A$ AND N returns A$ if N is non-zero
and a null string if N is zero.

3 **Two strings cannot be directly operated on by any logical operator because strings cannot have logical values. For example:**
A$ AND B$, A$ OR B$, NOT A$
are meaningless expressions.

Exercises

1 Key in PRINT NOT "A" = "B"
and PRINT "A" = "B" AND "B" = "C" OR "G" = "E"
to test the rules of logical string operation. Try other combinations.

2 Write a program which requests a name and then checks to see if it corresponds to several strings stored in the program, printing out a message to say if the word was found.

3 Write a program to test the truth table for A$ AND N.

R11: Logical Operations Between Strings and Conditions

Only the AND operator may be used.
The rule is the same as for strings and numbers.

A$	C	A$ AND C
A$	TRUE	A$
A$	FALSE	" "

A$ AND C gives A$ if C is "TRUE"
A$ AND C gives a null string if C is "FALSE"
C can be either a string condition or a numeric condition.

EXAMPLES:

PRINT "A" AND 3 = 3 gives A
PRINT "A" AND 3 = 4 gives the empty (null) string
PRINT "A" AND "B" = "B" gives A
PRINT "A" AND "B" = "C" gives the null string

Exercises

1 Key in and run LOGIC 5, which illustrates string and condition use.

```
  5 REM "LOGIC 5"
 10 LET X$="AB"
 20 LET Y$="AC"
 30 PRINT (2 AND X$>Y$)
 40 PRINT (7 AND X$<Y$)
 50 PRINT (5 AND X$=Y$)
 52 PRINT
 54 PRINT
 60 LET P$="1"
 70 LET Q$="2"
 80 PRINT (33 AND P$>Q$)
 90 PRINT (66 AND P$<Q$)
100 PRINT (99 AND P$=Q$)
102 PRINT
110 PRINT "SO""AB""<""AC"""
112 PRINT
120 PRINT "AND ""1""<""2"""
```

Results:

```
0
7
0

0
66
0

SO "AB"<"AC"

AND "1"<"2"
```

2 Alter the values of X$,Y$,P$ and Q$ and run the program again each time.
3 Alter the program to allow various strings and numbers to be input, and print out the relationships.

R12: Logical Operations Between Numbers and Conditions

N AND C

N OR C

Where N is a number
and C is a condition:
either a string condition e.g. A$ = "A"
or a numeric condition e.g. B = 7

N	C	N AND C	N OR C
N	TRUE	N	1
N	FALSE	Ø	N

These are the same rules as with logical operations between numbers.

N AND C gives N if C is "TRUE"
N AND C gives Ø if C is "FALSE"
N OR C gives 1 if C is "TRUE"
N OR C gives N if C is "FALSE"

Exercises

1 Analyse, key in and RUN the following statements, and confirm the rules.

```
PRINT 7 AND "A" = "A"
PRINT Ø AND "A" = "A"
PRINT 7 AND "A" = "B"
PRINT Ø AND "A" = "B"
PRINT 7 OR "A" = "A"
PRINT Ø OR "A" = "A"
PRINT 7 OR "A" = "B"
PRINT Ø OR "A" = "B"
```

2 Key in and run this program.
Input B as 3 and 5.

```
1Ø  INPUT B
2Ø  PRINT 7 AND B = 3
3Ø  PRINT 7 OR B = 3
4Ø  GOTO 1Ø
```

R13: Applications of Logical Operators

1 **Simple conditional tests**
2 **Multiple conditional tests**
3 **Multibranch GOTO and GOSUB**
4 **Finding maximum and minimum values**
5 **Checking characters input**
6 **Checking input values**
7 **Testing for zero**
8 **Default values**

1 Simple Conditional Tests

IF (Logical Operation) THEN (statement).

If the logical operation is TRUE the statement is executed.

AND, OR and NOT operators are used.

2 Multiple Conditional Tests

IF [(Condition 1) AND (Condition 2) OR (Condition 3)] THEN (statement).

If the multiple logical operations are TRUE the statement is executed.

AND, OR and NOT are used.

3 Multibranch GOTO Routines

Using this technique, control may be transferred to any of a number of statement lines.

Here we use the AND routine, whose default value is zero:

GOTO (100 AND C1) + (200 AND C2) + (300 AND C3)

C1, C2 and C3 are three conditions.

Control is transferred to line 100 if C1 is TRUE
200 if C2 is TRUE
300 if C3 is TRUE.

Similarly:

GOSUB (100 AND C1) + (200 AND C2)

Control is transferred to:
the subroutine at line 100 if C1 is TRUE
200 if C2 is TRUE
300 if C1 *and* C2 are TRUE
and the next line, if neither are true.

Key in and run this program:

```
 10 INPUT A
 20 INPUT B
 30 GOTO (100 AND A=0)+(200 A
    ND B=0)
 40 PRINT A+B
 50 STOP
100 PRINT "A=0.INPUT A AND B
    AGAIN"
110 GOTO 10
200 PRINT "B=0.INPUT B AGAIN"
210 GOTO 20
300 PRINT "BOTH ZERO.INPUT A
    AND B AGAIN"
310 GOTO 10
```

4 Finding Maxima and Minima Values

We use the AND operator to find the maxima and minima of two numbers X and Y.

```
10 INPUT X
20 INPUT Y
30 PRINT "MAX IS";(X AND X>=Y)
   +(Y AND Y>X)
40 PRINT "MIN IS";(X AND X<=Y)
   +(Y AND Y<X)
```

or we could program this as

```
30 IF X >= Y THEN GOTO 60
40 PRINT "MAX=";Y;" MIN=";X
50 STOP
60 PRINT "MAX=";X;" MIN=";Y
```

Which do you think is the best method?

Finding the largest number in a list is another application. We have a list of numbers A(1) to A(N). We can compare the first two, A(1) and A(2), and put the largest of these into a variable L by the statement:

LET L = (A(1)AND A(1)> = A(2)) + (A(2)AND A(2)>A(1))

We compare this value of L with the next number A(3) and make L take the larger value of the two and so on through the list.

LET L = (L AND L> = A(3)) + (A(3) AND A(3)>L)

The program asks us to input how many numbers will be in our list (N). We then input the numbers A(I). These are printed on the screen together with the largest value. Two loops are used, the first to input the numbers and the second to perform the comparisons.

```
 10 REM "LARGEST"
 20 PRINT "INPUT HOW MANY NUMBE
    RS"
 30 INPUT N
 40 PRINT N
 50 DIM A(N)
 60 FOR I = 1 TO N
 70 INPUT A(I)
 80 PRINT A(I);" ";
 90 NEXT I
100 LET L =(A(1)AND A(1)>=A(2)
    )+(A(2)AND A(2)> A(1))
110 FOR I = 3 TO N
120 LET L = (L AND L>=A(I)) +
    (A(I)AND A(I)> L)
130 NEXT I
140 PRINT "LARGEST NUMBER IS "
    ;L
```

Key in and run the program.

This is an appropriate place to emphasise the care needed in programming logical operations. There are two things that cause problems. The first is the setting of conditions, and the second is the grouping of these conditions in a logical sequence that will produce the *required* result. Any line the computer does not reject because of a syntax error will produce *a* result. Care is needed to get the *right* result.

This can be illustrated by the question of deriving the larger of two numbers, using AND. The problems of non-rigorous use of the logical and relational operators can be illustrated by considering the following problem. We have two numbers X and Y. We know that AND can be used so that if we code a program line as LET M = X AND X>Y it will return the value of X if the condition is true. We want to use this to get the value of a maximum. The line above will produce zero if the condition is not true. So we can combine two such tests in one line to get our maximum. We key in this sort of program (do it):

```
10  INPUT X
20  INPUT Y
30  LET MAX = X AND X>Y + Y AND Y>X
40  PRINT MAX
```

Input some numbers and check the results.

Something is wrong. Looking at the program, we see we need some brackets. As it stands, line 3Ø is actually a sequence of three conditions, joined by two AND operators. It reads 'give MAX the logical value of (X) AND (X>Y + Y) AND (Y>X)'. Since all three conditions have to be true for the whole expression to be true, and since (X>Y + Y) and (Y>X) cannot both be true, we get zero.

We make the expression more sensible, we hope, by changing line 3Ø to read: LET MAX = X AND (X>Y) + Y AND (Y>X).

Key in this as a new line. Now try some inputs.

If X is smaller than Y we get the value of X printed, and if X is greater than Y we get zero. We haven't got the brackets right. There are still three conditions joined by two ANDs. We've changed the meaning, but not to what we actually want. If X and Y are non-zero, (X) is true, ((X>Y) + Y) is zero for smaller X, one (TRUE) for larger X, added to Y. This is non-zero, so is TRUE. If the last condition is TRUE (i.e. Y>X) then the combined expressions give X as the result. If it's FALSE then the whole expression is FALSE and prints Ø. Now we see what's wrong, we can put some more brackets in.

Edit line 3Ø to read: LET MAX = (X AND(X>Y)) + (Y AND (Y>X)).

Now try some inputs. The greater of the two numbers is returned, which *is* what we wanted. If we now look at our working line, we can see (or should) that there are brackets we don't need, although they don't do any harm. Edit line 3Ø to read LET MAX = (X AND X>Y) + (Y AND Y>X) and check the greater value is still returned. So we're finished – or are we? Only if you didn't consider what happens if the numbers X and Y are *equal*. Input the two numbers as the same value and see what result you get. Both expressions are FALSE if the numbers are equal, so we get zero printed.

The line should read: 3Ø LET MAX = (X AND X> = Y) + (Y AND Y>X). Just in case you're not convinced of the problems you can get into if you are not careful, enter the line as above and check that it works. Then edit it to read: LET MAX = (X

AND X> = Y) + (Y AND Y> = X) and input values with X>Y, Y>X and X = Y.

This sort of problem is only avoided by carefully thinking out the result required in the case of *all* inputs, and checking the logic before you code it in. If there are these possible problems in a four-line program, think of the potential pitfalls in a complex one!

5 Checking Characters Input

Control in a program can be achieved using the INKEY$ statement and checking which character is keyed in using combined conditional logic operations. We have seen this used in programs earlier in the text.

The following program enables the numbers on the keyboard to be used as a joystick, allowing you to move a dot in any direction on the screen.

To move the dot in the following compass directions press the desired key.

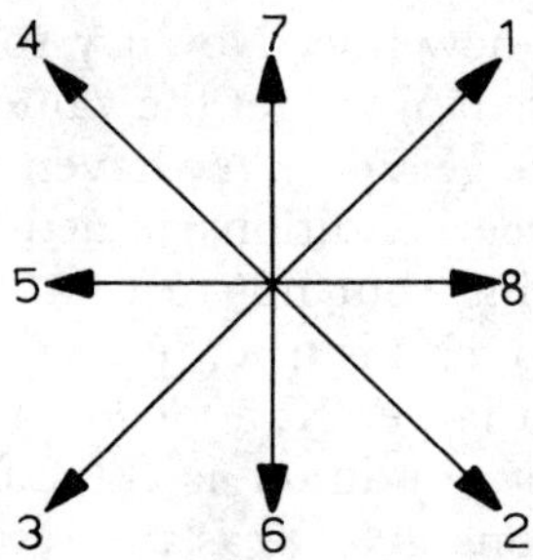


```
   5 REM "JOYSTICK"
  10 REM *SPECTRUM:X=120,Y=80
  20 LET X=30
  30 LET Y=20
  40 PLOT X,Y
  50 IF INKEY$ ="" THEN GOTO 50
  60 LET A$= INKEY$
  65 REM *SPECTRUM:
          70 OVER 1:PLOT X,Y
  70 UNPLOT X,Y
  75 REM *SPECTRUM:X<255
  80 IF X<63 AND (A$="8" OR A$="
1" OR A$="2") THEN LET X=X+1
  90 IF X>0 AND (A$="4" OR A$="3
" OR A$="5") THEN LET X=X-1
  95 REM *SPECTRUM:Y<175
 100 IF Y<43 AND (A$="7" OR A$="
4" OR A$="1") THEN LET Y=Y+1
 110 IF Y>0 AND (A$="6" OR A$="2
" OR A$="3") THEN LET Y=Y-1
 120 GOTO 40
```

Analyse the program.
Key it in and run it.
Change the program to move the dot in larger jumps.
Change the program to move the dot in sixteen different directions.

6 Checking Input Values

The OR operator can be used to check that values keyed into a program are in range. For example, we are asked to input values for variables in the following ranges:

A range Ø – 9
B range 1Ø – 99
C range 1ØØ – 999

Here is a program that checks values input:

```
 1Ø INPUT A
 2Ø IF A<Ø OR A>9 THEN GOTO 1ØØ
 3Ø INPUT B
 4Ø IF B<1Ø OR B>99 THEN GOTO 2
    ØØ
 5Ø INPUT C
 6Ø IF C<1ØØ OR C>999 THEN GOTO
    3ØØ
 7Ø PRINT AT 1,1;A; AT 1,8;B;A
    T 1,15;C
 8Ø STOP
1ØØ PRINT "INPUT A OUT OF RANGE"
11Ø GOTO 1Ø
2ØØ PRINT "INPUT B OUT OF RANGE"
21Ø GOTO 3Ø
3ØØ PRINT "INPUT C OUT OF RANGE"
31Ø GOTO 5Ø
```

7 Testing for Zero

We can use the NOT routine to check for zeros in a list of numbers.

NOT (N) = Ø when N<>Ø
NOT (Ø) = 1

Here is a program which sets up a counter C, initialises it, and requests numbers to be input. If a zero is input NOT Ø = 1 and C is incremented by LET C = C + NOT (A(F)).

```
 5 DIM A(1Ø)
1Ø LET C=Ø
2Ø FOR F = 1TO1Ø
3Ø INPUT A(F)
35 PRINT A(F);" ";
4Ø LET C=C+NOT (A(F))
5Ø NEXT F
6Ø PRINT "THERE ARE";C;"ZEROS"
```

Key in and run the program.

8 Default Values

The default value of AND is zero. AND is therefore extremely useful in the *addition* of logical operations. For example:

6Ø GOTO (1ØØ AND A = Ø) + (2ØØ AND A>Ø).

The default value of OR is 1. OR is thus useful in the *multiplication* of logical operations.

For example, the following program asks you to input any three digits in the range 0 – 9. The computer will generate three digits at random.

You win £10, £100 or £1000 depending on how many digits you guess correctly.

```
   5 REM "GUESSANUM"
  10 DIM A(3)
  20 DIM B(3)
  30 PRINT "INPUT 3 DIGITS IN TH
E RANGE 0-9 ONE AT A TIME"
  40 FOR F=1 TO 3
  50 INPUT A(F)
  60 PRINT A(F);" ";
  70 LET B(F)= INT ( RND *10)
  80 NEXT F
  90 PRINT
 100 PRINT B(1);" ";B(2);" ";B(3
)
 110 LET Z=(10 OR (A(1) <> B(1))
)*(10 OR (A(2) <> B(2)))*(10 OR
(A(3) <> B(3)))
 120 IF Z=1 THEN LET Z=0
 130 PRINT "YOU WIN ";Z
 140 INPUT A$
 150 IF A$="Y" THEN GOTO 30
 160 STOP
```

SECTION S: LISTS AND ARRAYS

S1: Dimension

The dimension statement DIM is used to reserve storage space for a LIST or ARRAY to contain numbers. DIM A (N) sets up an array A with space for N numbers.

A may be any single letter A to Z. The Spectrum will accept both upper and lower case letters, but a(N) will signify the same array as A(N).

N may be a number, a numeric variable or an expression.

A dimension statement must be declared before the array can be used. This is usually done at the beginning of a program, unless the value of N is to be set equal to an expression or variable which will be calculated later in the program.

There may only be one DIM statement on a line for the ZX81. These statements in a program:

```
10  DIM A(10)
20  DIM B(15)
30  DIM C(30)
```

will reserve storage for a list A containing 10 numbers, a list B containing 15 numbers and a list C containing 30 numbers. The values of each ELEMENT (number) in an array are automatically set (initialised) as zero.

Error code 4 ('out of memory' on the Spectrum) will be displayed if there is no room for the array, i.e. if N is too large.

S2: Index Variable

The index variable N is used to locate a member of a list.

We use the form A(N) to locate the N'th number of a list A(L), where 1< = N< = L.

If N = 5, then A(N) refers to A(5), the fifth number in the list.

The program below establishes a four element list, so that:

A(1) = 1
A(2) = 4
A(3) = 9
A(4) = 16

and then prints out the second and fourth element.

```
10  DIM A(4)
20  FOR N = 1 TO 4
30  LET A(N) = N*N
40  NEXT N
50  PRINT "SECOND ELEMENT IS   "; A(2)
60  PRINT "FOURTH ELEMENT IS   "; A(4)
```

S3: Lists

Many types of problem involve a set of values and it is convenient to store such items in a list. The next program illustrates the idea. We assume a list of the squares of the first 2Ø integers is required. It is necessary to reserve storage for the twenty numbers (1, 4, 9 etc., up to 4ØØ) and this is done in line 2Ø. The loop (lines 3Ø to 5Ø) puts A(1) = 1, A(2) = 4...A(2Ø) = 4ØØ and it is thus possible to use any item of this list at a later date, using the index variable.

Line 6Ø prints out 4 16 36 and the loop (lines 8Ø – 1ØØ) will print out the complete list of numbers.

```
10 REM "LIST"
20 DIM A(20)
30 FOR N=1 TO 20
40 LET A(N)=N*N
50 NEXT N
60 PRINT A(2);" ";A(4);" ";
  A(6)
70 PRINT
80 FOR N=1 TO 20
90 PRINT A(N)
100 NEXT N
```

S4: Examples of Lists

We give below some example programs illustrating the use of lists.

1 Simple allocation of elements in a list. Look at the program. What will be printed out when the program is RUN? Check by entering and running the program.

```
10 REM "LIST1"
20 DIM A(4)
30 LET A(1)=10
40 LET A(2)=58
50 LET A(3)=72
60 LET A(4)=20
70 PRINT A(1)*A(3)
80 PRINT
90 PRINT A(3)-A(2)
```

2 Allocation of values to the elements in a list using a loop and the INPUT statement. The value of the control variable (N) of the loop is used to specify each element of the list in turn. Again, work out the results of the program, then check by keying it in and running it.

```
10 REM "LIST2"
20 DIM A(4)
30 FOR N=1 TO 4
40 PRINT "TYPE A(";N;")"
```

```
50 INPUT A(N)
60 NEXT N
70 PRINT A(1)*A(3)
80 PRINT
90 PRINT A(3)-A(2)
```

3 All lists used in a program must be dimensioned, with each dimension statement on a separate line. Hand trace this program and decide what the 1Ø elements in list B(N) are. Check by entering and running the program.

```
  5 REM "LIST3"
 10 DIM A(20)
 20 DIM B(10)
 30 FOR N=1 TO 20
 40 LET A(N)=N*N
 50 NEXT N
 60 FOR N=1 TO 10
 70 LET B(N)=A(2*N)-A(2*N-1)
 80 NEXT N
 90 FOR N=1 TO 10
100 PRINT B(N)
110 NEXT N
```

4 A variable may be used in a DIM statement, provided its value is assigned before the DIM statement is reached. Enter program "LIST4". Run the program for X = 2Ø.

```
 5 REM "LIST4"
10 INPUT X
20 DIM A(X)
30 FOR N=1 TO X
40 LET A(N)= SQR N
50 PRINT A(N)
60 NEXT N
```

5 The program "OHMS LAW" illustrates the use of lists to store data from a set of electrical circuit experiments. The voltmeter and ammeter readings from each experiment are stored in the lists A(N) and V(N) as they are input. Notice that it is essential to dimension storage space for the derived list of results, R(N), (line 6Ø). The loop (lines 9Ø to 14Ø) enables the readings to be stored for use in the later loop (lines 18Ø to 22Ø), which performs the calculation and prints out the results of each experiment, giving the current in amps, the voltage in volts, and the resistance in ohms derived by the formula, R = V/I in line 19Ø.

Line 17Ø initialises a variable T which has each resistance in turn added to it. This enables line 25Ø to print the average resistance value.

```
10 REM "OHMS*LAW"
20 PRINT "OHMS LAW RESULTS"
30 PRINT "UP TO 20 PAIRS OF R
   EADINGS"
40 DIM A(20)
50 DIM V(20)
60 DIM R(20)
```

```
 7Ø PRINT "TYPE NUMBER OF SETS
    OF READINGS"
 8Ø INPUT X
 9Ø FOR N=1 TO X
1ØØ PRINT "TYPE CURRENT IN AMPS"
11Ø INPUT A(N)
12Ø PRINT "TYPE VOLTAGE IN VOLTS"
13Ø INPUT V(N)
14Ø NEXT N
15Ø PRINT "AMPS";TAB 8;"VOLTS";
    TAB 16;"OHMS"
16Ø PRINT "*******************
    ****"
17Ø LET T=Ø
18Ø FOR N=1 TO X
19Ø LET R(N) =V(N)/A(N)
2ØØ LET T=T+R(N)
21Ø PRINT A(N);TAB 8;V(N);TAB 1
    6;R(N)
22Ø NEXT N
23Ø PRINT "*******************
    ****"
24Ø PRINT
25Ø PRINT "AVERAGE RESISTANCE "
    ;T/X;" OHMS"
```

Notice that if lines 7Ø and 8Ø had come before the DIM statements, we could use DIM A(X), etc. to set the size of the arrays exactly, as in program LIST4 above.

6 A similar type of program is shown below. This shows image positions (V) and magnifications (M) for a convex lens, given the focal length of the lens (F) and the object distance (U).

```
  5 REM "CONVEXLENS"
 1Ø PRINT "THIS PROGRAM SHOWS THE POSITION AND
    MAGNIFICATION OF THE IMAGE PRODUCED BY A
    CONVEX LENS"
 2Ø PRINT "******************************"
 3Ø DIM U(12)
 4Ø DIM V(12)
 5Ø DIM M(12)
 6Ø PRINT "TYPE FOCAL LENGTH IN CM."
 7Ø INPUT F
 8Ø PRINT "TYPE OBJECT DISTANCE IN CM."
 9Ø FOR N=1 TO 12
1ØØ INPUT U(N)
11Ø LET V(N)=U(N)*F/(U(N)-F)
12Ø LET M(N)=V(N)/U(N)
13Ø NEXT N
14Ø PRINT "U";TAB (8);"V";TAB (22);"M"
15Ø FOR N=1 TO 12
16Ø PRINT U(N);TAB (8);V(N);TAB (22);M(N)
17Ø NEXT N
```

The screen display will look like this:

```
THIS PROGRAM SHOWS THE POSITION
AND MAGNIFICATION OF THE IMAGE
PRODUCED BY A CONVEX LENS
******************************
U         V            M
1Ø        -13,333333   -1.3333333
2Ø        -4Ø          -2
3Ø        -12Ø         -4
39.555    -3555.5Ø56   -89.887639
4Ø.555    2922.8829    72.Ø72Ø73
5Ø        2ØØ          4
6Ø        12Ø          2
7Ø        93.333333    1.3333333
8Ø        8Ø           1
9Ø        72           Ø.8
1ØØ       66.666667    Ø.66666667
12Ø       6Ø           Ø.5
```

S5: String Arrays

The DIM statement for string arrays has the form

DIM A$ (N,L)

where N = number of strings and L = the fixed length of each string. A may be any single letter A to Z, but must NOT be the same as a simple string variable. Each string is set to contain L spaces initially.

DIM A$(3,4) will reserve storage space for 3 strings A$(1),A$(2),A$(3), each of length 4, in the string array A$.

Each letter of each string can be accessed separately, as with a string variable. A$(2,3) will return the third character of the string A$(2). Substrings may also be allocated by a statement such as A$(2,1 TO 2), which will return the first and second characters of A$(2). For example, if A$(2) = "EFGH" then:

A$(2,2 TO 4) = "FGH"

The two programs below show these operations. Key them in and run them. Note that spaces may be included as letters, as can any other characters useable in a string.

If we have:

```
20 DIM A$(3,8)
30 LET A$(3)="ABC E* G"
```

then

```
A$(3,4)=" "
```

and

```
A$(3,5 TO 8)="E* G"
```

1)

```
 5 REM "STRING*ARR1"
1Ø DIM A$(4,3)
15 PRINT "TYPE IN LETTERS THRE
   E AT A TIME"
2Ø FOR N=1 TO 4
3Ø INPUT A$(N)
4Ø NEXT N
5Ø PRINT A$(4,3);" ";A$(3,2)
7Ø PRINT
8Ø PRINT A$(1);" ";A$(2);" "; A
   $(3)
```

2)

```
 10 REM "STR*ARR2"
 20 DIM A$(3,4)
 30 LET A$(1)="ABCD"
 40 LET A$(2)="EFGH"
 50 LET A$(3)="IJKL"
 60 PRINT A$(2,4);" ";A$(3,2)
 70 PRINT
 80 PRINT A$(2,2 TO 4)
 90 PRINT
100 PRINT A$(1,3 TO 4)
```

S6: Two Dimensional Arrays

A 2-D (two dimensional) numeric array is dimensioned by the statement:

DIM A(R,C)

where A is any letter, R is the number of Rows and C is the number of Columns.

All elements are set as zero.

The simple array is one-dimensional, and contains just a linear sequence of items. Arrays can have more than one dimension:

4	6	8
10	12	14
16	18	20
22	24	26

This is a numeric array consisting of 4 rows of numbers in 3 columns. Storage would be reserved by the statement:

10 DIM A(4,3).

In an array A(R,C) we can access any element, so that in the array above:

A(2,1) = 10   A(3,2) = 18   etc.

An array of two (or more) dimensions is also known as a MATRIX (plural matrices).

The following program establishes an array and prints out two selected elements and then the complete array:

```
 10 REM "ARRAY"
 20 DIM A(10,9)
 30 FOR R=1 TO 10
 35 FOR C=1 TO 9
 40 LET A(R,C)=R*C
 50 NEXT C
 60 NEXT R
 70 PRINT A(10,6),A(5,3)
 80 PRINT
 90 FOR R=1 TO 10
100 FOR C=1 TO 9
110 PRINT TAB 3*C;A(R,C);
120 NEXT C
130 PRINT TAB 4;
140 NEXT R
```

Line 20 allocates the appropriate storage. Nested loops (line 30 – 60) are used to allocate values to the elements in the array. Line 70 prints out two elements in the array. Nested loops (line 9Ø to 14Ø) print out the complete array.

Why is line 13Ø required?

In order to keep track of the elements of an array we need to have a system. In general it is easiest to use R to represent the Rows and C the Columns and to always access the rows before the columns.

Note the use of the TAB function to give a clear printout.

1	2	3	4	5	6	7	8	9
2	4	6	8	1Ø	12	14	16	18
3	6	9	12	15	18	21	24	27
4	8	12	16	2Ø	24	28	32	36
5	1Ø	15	2Ø	25	3Ø	35	4Ø	45

etc.

String arrays can also have more than one dimension.

2-D String arrays are dimensioned by a statement of the form
DIM A$(R,C,L)
where R is the number of Rows, C is the number of Columns and L is the length of all strings in the array.

Try this program:

```
 1Ø REM "2DSTRING"
 2Ø DIM A$(3,3,5)
 3Ø PRINT "TYPE WORDS 5 LETTERS
    OR LESS"
 4Ø FOR R=1 TO 3
 5Ø FOR C=1 TO 3
 6Ø PRINT AT 2,Ø;"ROW ";R;" COL ";C
 65 INPUT A$(R,C)
 7Ø NEXT C
 8Ø NEXT R
 9Ø FOR R=1 TO 3
1ØØ FOR C=1 TO 3
11Ø PRINT AT R*4,C*8;A$(R,C)
12Ø NEXT C
13Ø NEXT R
```

Key this in and run it. Try some appropriate entries for the rows and columns, as the routine in line 6Ø gives a cue for which entry is next. This is a useful routine for use with multiple entry INPUT routines, since it is very easy to forget which entry is next. One run of this program gave a final screen display like this:

```
TYPE WORDS 5 LETTERS OR LESS

ROW 3 COL 3

     START    2ND      THIRD


     FOUR     FIVE     SIXTH


     SEVEN    EIGHT    FINAL
```

Note also line 11Ø, where both control variables of the nested loops are used to format the printout using the PRINT AT instruction.

S7: Multidimensional Arrays

Multidimensional arrays are available for both numbers and strings, although a 3-D string array is rarely something needed in a program! The easiest way of thinking of these arrays is as follows:

A (P, R, C) is a 3 dimensional array: page, row, column

A (B, P, R, C) is a 4 dimensional array: book, page, row, column.

A 5 dimensional array would be a library, on the basis of this analogy. These arrays require DIM statements to reserve the necessary storage. A simple example of a 3 dimensional array (which needs 3 nested loops) is given below.

```
 1Ø REM "3DLIST"
1ØØ DIM A(3,2,4)
11Ø FOR P=1 TO 3
12Ø FOR R=1 TO 2
13Ø FOR C=1 TO 4
14Ø LET A(P,R,C)=P*C*R
15Ø NEXT C
16Ø NEXT R
17Ø NEXT P
18Ø PRINT A(2,1,3)
19Ø PRINT
2ØØ FOR P=1 TO 3
21Ø FOR R=1 TO 2
22Ø FOR C=1 TO 4
23Ø PRINT A(P,R,C);" ";
24Ø NEXT C
245 PRINT
25Ø NEXT R
255 PRINT
26Ø NEXT P
```

The similar program below, extended by a dimension, shows a 4 dimensional array printed out in a suitable form.

```
 10 REM "4DARRAY"
100 DIM A(2,3,4,5)
110 FOR B=1 TO 2
120 FOR P=1 TO 3
130 FOR R=1 TO 4
140 FOR C=1 TO 5
150 LET A(B,P,R,C)=B*P*R*C
160 NEXT C
170 NEXT R
180 NEXT P
190 NEXT B
200 PRINT A(1,2,3,4);" ";A(2,2,3,3)
210 PRINT
220 FOR B=1 TO 2
230 FOR P=1 TO 3
235 PRINT "BOOK";B;"/PAGE";P
240 FOR R=1 TO 4
250 FOR C=1 TO 5
260 PRINT A(B,P,R,C);" ";
270 NEXT C
280 PRINT
290 NEXT R
300 PRINT
310 NEXT P
320 PRINT
330 NEXT B
```

Here's a 3-D string version to try. Input only two letters at a time. Actually it doesn't matter, the computer will ignore any characters in excess of 2, since that is the dimensioned length.

```
  5 REM "3D*STR*ARR"
 10 DIM A$(3,3,3,2)
 20 FOR P=1 TO 3
 30 FOR R=1 TO 3
 40 FOR C=1 TO 3
 50 INPUT A$(P,R,C)
 60 NEXT C
 70 NEXT R
 80 NEXT P
 90 FOR P=1 TO 3
100 FOR R=1 TO 3
110 FOR C=1 TO 3
120 PRINT AT R*3,(P*10-10)+C*3;
    A$(P,R,C)
130 NEXT C
140 NEXT R
150 NEXT P
```

Work out how the PRINT AT expressions work.

S8: Use of Arrays

A simple example of the use of 2-D arrays is shown in the seat booking program below. A small theatre consists of 10 rows of seats with 6 seats in each row. Some seats may already be reserved. These are input when the program is run. When a new booking is made the requested seat, if available, is sold. If the seat is not available a seat in the same row is offered. If no seat in that row is available the customer is asked to choose another row.

The sections of the program are as follows:

1 Initialise an array to represent the 10 rows of 6 seats (line 30). All elements in this array are 0, and represent unbooked seats.

2 Input seats already booked (lines 40 – 130).

2.1 Input row and seat number of booked seats. If input is 0 for the row number, program goes to 2.3.

2.2 If seat already booked (array element = 1), print message to user. Seat is booked by placing a 1 in the appropriate array element.

2.3 Program prints prompt, then halts until C is input.

3 Customer request for seat is input (lines 165 – 240).

3.1 Row and seat required are input. If seat already booked (array element = 1), program goes to 4.

3.2 Seat is booked.

3.3 Menu is printed to enable user to choose to book another seat, or to view seating plan.

3.4 If seat booking is requested, program returns to 3.1. If seating plan option is chosen, program goes to 5.

4 Seat unavailable module (lines 300 – 450).

4.1 Seat unavailable message is printed, then the variable SEATS is set at zero, and the loop checks if at least one seat is free in this row, setting SEATS = 1 if a seat is free (Current Row R, checked for S(R,1) to S(R,6)).

4.2 If no seats are free in this row (SEATS = 0), program passes to line 440 and prints message, then returns to menu (3.3).

4.3 If at least one seat is free, the loop at lines 390 to 410 prints out the numbers of the seats free, and the program returns to the menu.

5 View Seat Plan Module (lines 500 – 600).

5.1 Nested loops are used to display seat plan, row 10 being at the top, as 0's and 1's.

5.2 Copy option is given, to print out seating plan.

5.3 Menu presented for end of program or return to book seats. Program goes to 3.1, or proceeds to 6.

6 Program ends. Instructions given to restart if required without using RUN and clearing the data stored in the array.

```
 10 REM "THEATRE"
 20 REM **INITIALISE ARRAY**

 30 DIM S(10,6)
 35 REM **INSERT SEATS ALREADY*
        **BOOKED             *
 40 PRINT "INPUT SEATS THAT ARE
BOOKED.","INPUT 0 TO FINISH"
 50 PRINT "ROW?"
 60 INPUT R
 70 IF R=0 THEN GOTO 130
 80 PRINT "SEAT?"
 90 INPUT C
```

```
 100 IF S(R,C)=1 THEN PRINT "ROW
 ";R;" SEAT ";C;" ALREADY","BOOK
ED"
 110 LET S(R,C)=1
 120 GOTO 50

 130 CLS
 140 PRINT "INPUT C TO PROCEED T
O BOOKING."
 150 INPUT A$
 160 CLS
 165 REM **CUSTOMER REQUEST FOR*
        **SEAT              **
 170 PRINT "TYPE ROW REQUIRED"
 180 INPUT R
 190 PRINT "TYPE SEAT NUMBER"
 200 INPUT C
 210 IF S(R,C)=1 THEN GOTO 300
 220 LET S(R,C)=1
 230 PRINT "THIS SEAT FREE. NOW B
OOKED."
 240 PRINT "ROW ";R;" SEAT ";C
 250 PRINT
 260 PRINT "BOOK ANOTHER SEAT (S
)OR VIEW","SEATING PLAN (P)?INPU
T S OR P"
 270 INPUT A$
 280 IF A$="S" THEN GOTO 170
 290 GOTO 500

 300 REM ** SEAT UNAVAILABLE **
 310 PRINT "REQUESTED SEAT NOT A
VAILABLE"
 320 LET SEATS=0
 330 FOR N=1 TO 6
 340 IF S(R,N)=1 THEN GOTO 360
 350 LET SEATS=1
 360 NEXT N
 370 IF SEATS=0 THEN GOTO 440
 380 PRINT "SEATS FREE:";
 390 FOR N=1 TO 6
 400 IF S(R,N)=0 THEN PRINT N;"
";
 410 NEXT N
 420 PRINT "."
 430 GOTO 450

 440 PRINT "NO SEATS ARE FREE IN
 ROW ";R
 450 GOTO 260

 490 REM ** SEATING PLAN **
 500 CLS
 510 FOR R=1 TO 10
 520 LET X=11-R
 530 PRINT TAB 5;"ROW ";X; TAB 1
2;
 540 FOR C=1 TO 6
 550 PRINT S(X,C);
 560 NEXT C
 570 PRINT
 580 NEXT R
```

```
 590 PRINT ,,"INPUT C TO COPY,AN
Y TO PROCEED"
 600 INPUT A$
 610 IF A$="C" THEN COPY
 620 PRINT ,,"INPUT E TO END,S T
O BOOK SEATS."
 630 INPUT A$
 640 IF A$="E" THEN GOTO 670
 650 CLS
 660 GOTO 170

 670 PRINT "PROGRAM STOPPED.USE
GOTO 170 TO","RESTART."
 680 STOP

 690 REM ** END PROGRAM  **
```

Screen display, at end of seat plan print routine (the first prompt has been responded to with a user input):

```
ROW 10 000000
ROW 9  000000
ROW 8  000000
ROW 7  000000
ROW 6  000000
ROW 5  000000
ROW 4  000100
ROW 3  100000
ROW 2  111111
ROW 1  000000

INPUT C TO COPY,ANY TO PROCEED
INPUT E TO END,S TO BOOK SEATS.
```

The variables used in the theatre booking program are as follows:

"THEATRE" – DATA TABLE

S(10,6)	Array to store 10 rows of 6 seats (value 1 when seat booked, 0 when free).
R	Current Row of array in processing.
C	Current Seat number in processing.
A$	User Input string for menu choices.
SEATS	Marker used to indicate whether seats are free in current row. Set to 0 when no seats free, 1 when seats available.
N	Loop variable. Value used in processing inside loops to check seat availability, and print seat numbers.
R	Loop variable used to print seat plan. Note this is the same name as the variable for Rows above. This name may be used in two different ways in this program because the value of the simple variable R is re-initialised by the input at line 170 on return to the seat selection routine.
X	Variable used for reverse printing of seating rows.

C Loop variable for seats in seat plan printing. As with R above, re-initialised as simple variable on return to seat selection routine.

Note that the use of variables in two ways, as with R and C in this program is only possible if the simple variables will be re-initialised *every time* they are used, otherwise problems can arise. A loop variable erases a simple variable of the same name. It would be better practice to use different names for the two types of variables.

SECTION T: SORTING SEARCHING AND STORING ARRAYS

T1: Searching and Sorting

Searching a list of numbers (or strings) for specified values can obviously be done much more efficiently if the numbers (or strings) are *sorted* according to some specified order, commonly alphabetical order or ascending numerical order. In electronic data processing groups of records (files) can be handled more efficiently if the records are pre-sorted into a specified order (e.g. by merging transaction files into a master file). Various techniques have been developed to sort data and several of the simpler methods are illustrated in this section together with two simple methods of searching lists.

There is a considerable difference in the efficiency of the various sorting techniques depending on the type and volume of data to be sorted. A technique which is good for a random list of numbers may not be appropriate for a list in which only one number is out of sequence. For random lists the Quick Sort and Shell Sort techniques are very much faster than a Bubble Sort. Deciding on which is the most suitable method is largely a matter of experience and you should experiment using the different techniques for equivalent sets of numbers, timing the sort procedures.

Many sorting algorithms exist, and we will first deal with the simplest.

The BUBBLE SORT is used for sorting numbers (or strings with appropriate alterations) into ascending or descending order. The principle of the bubble sort is to compare adjacent numbers and change positions if they are in the incorrect order. This is done for elements 1 and 2, then 2 and 3, 3 and 4...X – 1 to X at the end of which the highest number is in the Xth position. This is repeated (and the next highest number bubbles up to the X – 1th position) and repeated again, until the ordering is complete.

The following program is a bubble sort to put numbers into ascending order. The sorting routine itself is in lines 13Ø to 225.

```
 1Ø REM "BUBBLE"
 2Ø PRINT "TYPE NUMBER OF ITEMS
    TO BE SORTED"
 25 PRINT "MAXIMUM NUMBER 5Ø"
 3Ø INPUT X
 35 IF X>5Ø THEN GOTO 25
 4Ø DIM A(5Ø)
 6Ø PRINT "TYPE NUMBERS ONE AT
    A TIME"
 75 LPRINT "UNSORTED LIST"
 8Ø FOR N=1 TO X
 9Ø INPUT Z
1ØØ LET A(N)=Z
11Ø LPRINT A(N) ;" ";
12Ø NEXT N
125 LPRINT
```

```
130 REM **SORTING ROUTINE****
140 FOR N=1 TO X-1
150 FOR M=1 TO X-N
160 LET C=A(M)
170 LET D=A(M+1)
180 IF C<=D THEN GOTO 210
190 LET A(M)=D
200 LET A(M+1)=C
210 NEXT M
220 NEXT N
225 REM ******END SORT******
230 LPRINT "SORTED LIST"
240 FOR N=1 TO X
250 LPRINT A(N);" ";
260 NEXT N
```

Sample printout:

```
UNSORTED LIST
129   267   56   41   69   43   99   90   4   8

SORTED LIST
4   8   41   43   56   69   90   99   129   267
```

To illustrate the operation of the program, we'll take the first four of these numbers and see how the program sorts them:

Bubble sort for 4 numbers	A(1),	A(2),	A(3),	A(4)
input as	129,	267,	56,	41

Procedure:

(1) Go through the list comparing successive number pairs. For example:

A(1) and A(2), then A(2) and A(3).

If A(1)>A(2) then they are swapped so that A(2) becomes A(1) and A(1) becomes A(2). If A(1) <A(2) then they are left as is.

We see that the largest number in the list will finally be in the highest position, i.e. A(4).

(2) On the first pass we make three comparisons and the largest number will end as A(4).

On the second pass we make two comparisons, and the largest number will be in position A(3).

On the third pass we make one comparison. The larger number will be A(2).

No need for any more passes. Smallest number will be A(1).

There are four numbers: so X = 4

We need X – 1 passes: so N = 1 TO (X – 1)

= 1 TO 3 passes

For *each pass* we need from 1 to X – N comparisons:

so M = 1 to (X – N) comparisons

Here is a diagram in table form of the operations performed in the course of the sort:

Table of Operations

	Pass 1				Pass 2			Pass 3	
	N = 3				N = 2			N = 3	
START	M = 1	M = 2	M = 3	START PASS 2	M = 1	M = 2	START PASS 3	M = 1	FINISH
A(1) 129	129			129	56		56	41	41
A(2) 267	267	56		56	129	41	41	56	56
A(3) 56		267	41	41		129	129		129
A(4) 41			267	267			267		267

T2: Bubble Sort with Flag

```
10 REM "SORTFLAG"
20 PRINT "TYPE NUMBER OF ITEM
   S TO BE SORTED"
25 PRINT "MAXIMUM NUMBER 5Ø"
3Ø INPUT X
35 IF X>5Ø THEN GOTO 25
4Ø DIM A(5Ø)
6Ø PRINT "TYPE NUMBERS ONE AT
   A TIME"
7Ø PRINT "UNSORTED LIST"
8Ø FOR N=1 TO X
9Ø INPUT Z
1ØØ LET A(N)=Z
11Ø PRINT A(N) ;" ";
12Ø NEXT N
125 PRINT
13Ø REM **SORTING ROUTINE****
14Ø FOR N=1 TO X-1
145 LET S=Ø
15Ø FOR M=1 TO X-N
16Ø LET C=A(M)
17Ø LET D=A(M+1)
18Ø IF C<=D THEN GOTO 21Ø
19Ø LET A(M)=D
2ØØ LET A(M+1)=C
2Ø5 LET S=1
21Ø NEXT M
215 IF S=Ø THEN GOTO 23Ø
22Ø NEXT N
225 REM *******END******
23Ø PRINT "SORTED LIST"
24Ø FOR N=1 TO X
25Ø PRINT A(N);" ";
26Ø NEXT N
```

In order to ensure that the sort is completed as quickly as possible, a *flag* (in this case the variable S) is introduced to indicate if it has been necessary to swap elements in the list. S = 1 when a swap has occurred and sorting will continue until S = Ø at line 215. This prevents unnecessary sorting taking place. The procedure and program are otherwise the same as the bubble sort. The lines 145, 2Ø5 and 215 have been inserted into the "BUBBLE" program.

Exercise

Draw up the table of operations for this program, as was done for the "BUBBLE".

T3: Alphabetic Sort

The Bubble Sort (and all other sorts) may be used to sort strings by using appropriate string variables and string arrays.

```
  5 REM "ALPHASORT"
 10 PRINT "HOW MANY STRINGS"
 20 INPUT X
 30 PRINT "MAXIMUM 10 CHARACTERS"
 35 PRINT
 40 DIM A$(X,10)
 50 FOR N=1 TO X
 60 INPUT A$(N)
 70 NEXT N
 80 PRINT "UNSORTED LIST"
 90 FOR N=1 TO X
100 PRINT A$(N),
110 NEXT N
120 PRINT
130 REM **SORTING ROUTINE**
140 FOR M=1 TO X-1
150 FOR N=1 TO X-M
160 IF A$(N+1) >=A$(N) THEN GOTO 200
170 LET T$=A$(N+1)
180 LET A$(N+1) =A$(N)
190 LET A$(N) =T$
200 NEXT N
210 NEXT M
220 PRINT
230 PRINT "SORTED LIST"
240 FOR N=1 TO X
250 PRINT A$(N),
260 NEXT N
```

Some care must be exercised if the above sort is to be used on numbers entered as strings. The example given below shows that it will work *provided* one ensures that all numbers entered have the *same number* of figures.

(i) Incorrect use:

HOW MANY STRINGS
MAXIMUM 10 CHARACTERS

UNSORTED LIST

123	99
543	6
456	897
567	21
345	45

SORTED LIST

123	21
345	45
456	543
567	6
897	99

(ii) Correct use:

HOW MANY STRINGS
MAXIMUM 1Ø CHARACTERS

UNSORTED LIST

123	Ø99
543	ØØ6
456	897
567	Ø21
345	Ø45

SORTED LIST

ØØ6	Ø21
Ø45	Ø99
123	345
456	543
567	897

T4: Insertion Sort

This is another type of sort which is more efficient than the Bubble Sort and is also the basis of an even faster sort called a Shell Sort. Speed is a prime consideration when sorting large amounts of data.

Consider the list of numbers:

3 2 5 4 1

We start with the first entry in the list. Then we take the second item, compare the two, and swap if necessary. Then the second is compared with the third, a swap performed if required, and *if* a swap was made the first and second are compared again, and swapped if necessary. Then the third item is compared with the fourth, and so on. The list above will be sorted like this:

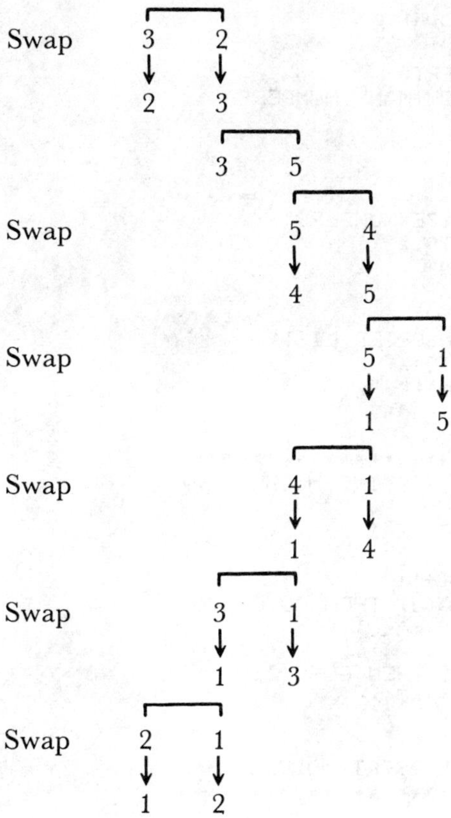

Consider the list A(1), A(2) . . . A(X). To insert item A(I + 1) in the correct position:

Let T = A(I + 1), then
if T> = A(I) no swap is necessary and no further comparisons are required.
if T<A(I) we let A(I + 1) = A(I) and we move on to A(I – 1), then
if T> = A(I – 1),we let A(I) = T and insertion is complete
if T<A(I – 1), we let A(I) = A(I – 1), and so on down the list.

The various steps we will make in the program are therefore as follows:

1) Set J = I and T = A(I + 1)
2) If T> = A(J) let A(J + 1) = T and stop
3) Let A(J + 1) = A(J)
4) Let J = J – 1
5) If J<1 let A(J + 1) = T and stop. If not, go to (2).
6) Repeat for each value of I (from 1 to N – 1) where N = number in list.

Program Listing

```
  5 REM "INSERT"
 10 PRINT "HOW MANY NUMBERS?"
 15 PRINT
 20 PRINT
 30 INPUT X
 40 DIM A(X)
 50 PRINT "TYPE NUMBERS"
 60 FOR N=1 TO X
 70 INPUT A(N)
 80 NEXT N
 90 PRINT
100 PRINT "UNSORTED LIST"
110 FOR N=1 TO X
120 PRINT A(N);" ";
130 NEXT N
140 PRINT
190 REM **********************
        **   SORTING MODULE  **

200 FOR I=1 TO X-1
210 LET J=I
220 LET T=A(I+1)
230 IF T >= A(J) THEN GOTO 270
240 LET A(J+1)=A(J)
250 LET J=J-1
260 IF J >= 1 THEN GOTO 230
270 LET A(J+1)=T
280 NEXT I
290 REM
        **END  SORT MODULE  **
        **********************
300 PRINT
310 PRINT "SORTED LIST"
320 FOR N=1 TO X
330 PRINT A(N);" ";
340 NEXT N
350 REM   **END**
```

A trace of the program, using our example list again, can be shown like this:

	I = 1	I = 2	I = 3		I = 4				
Start	J = 1	J = 2	J = 3	J = 2	J = 4	J = 3	J = 2	J = 1	J = Ø
	T = 3	T = 5	T = 4	T = 4	T = 1	T = 1	T = 1	T = 1	T = 1
A(1)=3	2								1
A(2)=2	3	3						2	
A(3)=5		5		4			3		
A(4)=4			5			4			
A(5)=1					5				

T5: Shell Sort

The procedure in this sort is to precede an insertion sort by a process which, if we consider a list of numbers to be placed in ascending order left to right, will move low values to the left and high values to the right more quickly.

Consider an 8 element list A(8), holding the values: 74, 32, 59, 46, 26, 9, 62, 42. The sort proceeds in the following stages:

1) Divide the 8 by 2 and compare elements 4 positions apart in the list, swapping if necessary:

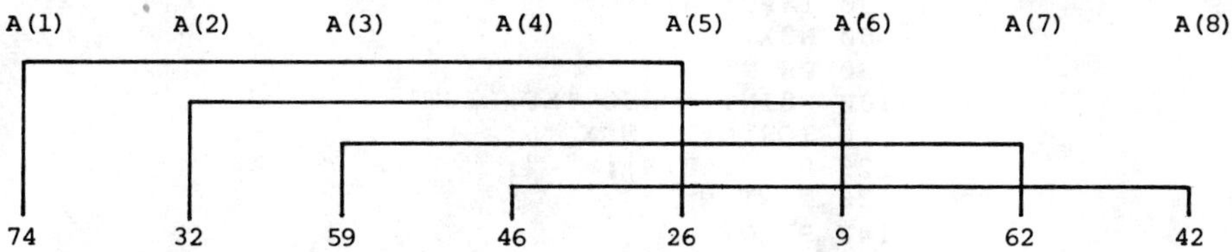

Compare	A(1) and A(5)	Swap
	A(2) and A(6)	Swap
	A(3) and A(7)	In order – leave
	A(4) and A(8)	Swap

New list:
26 9 59 42 74 32 62 46

2) Divide the 4 by 2 and compare the elements 2 positions apart in the list and swap if necessary:

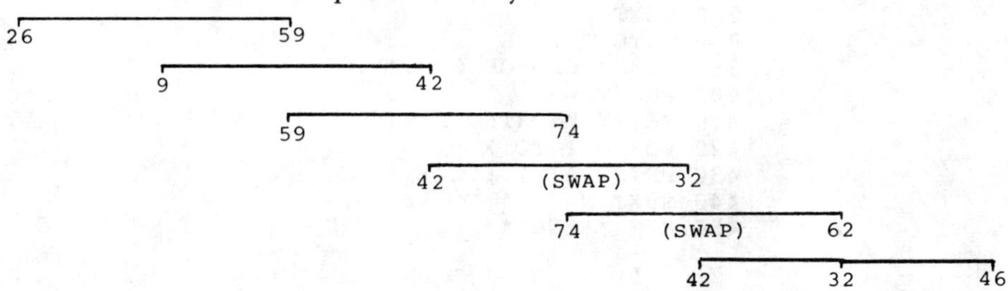

New list:
26 9 59 32 62 42 74 46

3) Divide 2 by 2 and compare elements 1 apart in the list, which is using the equivalent of an insertion sort to give the final order:
9 26 32 42 46 59 62 74

The steps we make in the program are as follows:

a) Select an integer S (number of positions apart from comparison). This is usually taken as INT (N/2) where

N = number of items in the list.

b) Sort the lists of items S positions apart, by comparing and swapping if necessary.

c) If S<1 then stop, since the list is sorted.

d) If S> = 1 then pick a new value of S (usually INT(S/2)), and repeat steps b) to d) as often as necessary.

```
  5 REM "SHELL"
 10 PRINT "HOW MANY NUMBERS?"
 20 INPUT X
 30 DIM A(X)
 50 PRINT "TYPE NUMBERS"
 60 FOR N=1 TO X
 70 INPUT A(N)
 80 NEXT N
 90 PRINT
100 PRINT "UNSORTED LIST"
110 FOR N=1 TO X
120 PRINT A(N); " ";
130 NEXT N
140 PRINT
190 REM **SORTING ROUTINE**
200 LET S=X
210 LET S=INT (S/2)
220 IF S<1 THEN GOTO 400
230 FOR K=1 TO S
240 FOR I=K TO X-S STEP K
250 LET J=I
260 LET T=A(I+S)
270 IF T>=A(J) THEN GOTO 310
280 LET A(J+S) =A(J)
290 LET J=J-S
300 IF J>=1 THEN GOTO 270
310 LET A(J+S) =T
320 NEXT I
330 NEXT K
340 GOTO 210
350 REM **END OF SORT**
400 PRINT
410 PRINT "SORTED LIST"
420 FOR N=1 TO X
430 PRINT A(N) ;" ";
440 NEXT N
450 REM **END**
```

Hand trace of Shell Sort

Consider the 8 element list 74, 32, 59, 46, 26, 9, 62, 42.
X = 8.

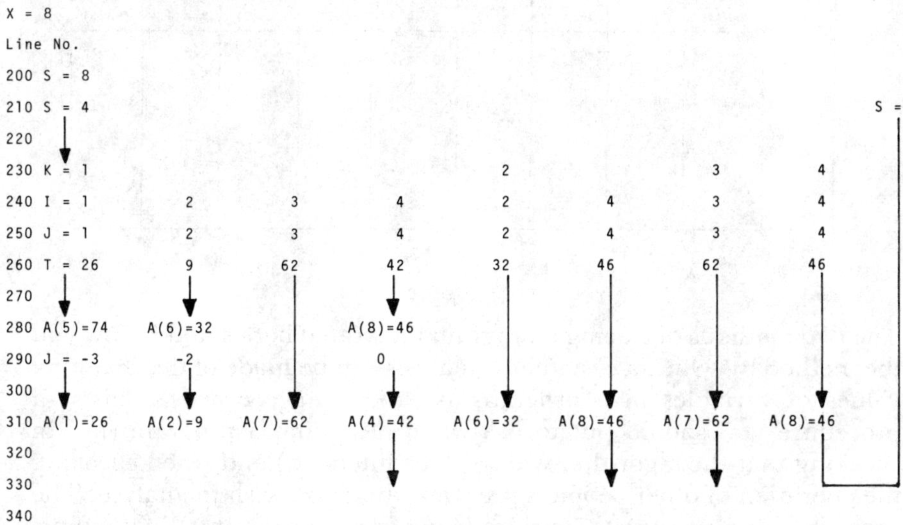

At this stage (1) the list is 26, 9, 59, 42, 74, 32, 62, 46.

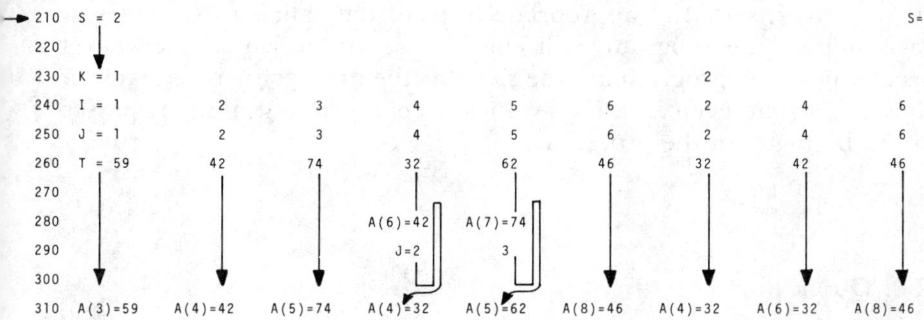

At this stage (2) the list is 26, 9, 59, 32, 62, 42, 74, 46.

The final stage is the comparison of neighbouring elements using the insertion sort technique, to which the Shell Sort routine is equivalent when S = 1. This is perhaps more easily seen if we consider the trace below of the operation of the Shell Sort program on a simple 5-item list, in which only two passes need to be made.

	Pass 1						Pass 2				
	S = INT5/2 = 2						S = INT 2/2 = 1				
	K = 1						K = 1				
	I = 1	I = 2	I = 3	I = 2	I = 2		I = 1	I = 2	I = 3	I = 4	
	J = 1	J = 2	J = 3	J = 2	J = 2	Start	J = 1	J = 2	J = 3	J = 4	Finish
	T=A(3)	T=A(4)	T=A(5)	T=A(4)	T=A(5)	Pass 2	T=A(2)	T=A(3)	T=A(4)	T=A(5)	
Start											
A(1)=2	1					1	1				1
A(2)=4		3		3		3	3	2			2
A(3)=1	2		2		2	2		3	3		3
A(4)=3		4		4		4			4	4	4
A(5)=5			5		5	5				5	5

The two methods of tracing a program illustrated here should show you the method by which a systematic analysis can be made of the changing values of variables in a program as processing proceeds. This is a procedure you should put to use when designing a program (i.e. in checking that the algorithm will work as intended) and when checking the operation of other people's programs that you wish to analyse. The procedure is also a great help in debugging a program. Break points inserted into the program (STOP commands), after which you can print the values of variables by direct commands, or PRINT statements, inserted as appropriate to print the values of variables at each step in the program, will enable you to check that the values occurring in the program are the same as the ones your trace diagram shows. You can even LPRINT values to get a printout, if many passes are to be made in the program.

T6: Quick Sort

This provides a fast sorting technique which works by subdividing the list into two sub-lists and then subdividing the sub-lists. The principle of the Quick Sort is as follows: consider a list A(X) containing X numbers. We assume as an example that X = 8 and the numbers are as shown below. The following steps are carried out:

1) Initialise two *pointers*, I and J, at opposite ends of the list. Let X(I) be the *reference number*. In our example, this is 63.

I							J
63	27	43	96	72	31	82	43

2) Compare the two numbers indicated by the pointers and swap if necessary.

I							J
43	27	43	96	72	31	82	63

3) Move the pointer opposite the reference number one place towards it.

	I						J
43	27	43	96	72	31	82	63

4) Repeat steps 2) and 3) until I = J.

		I					J
43	27	43	96	72	31	82	63

			I				J
43	27	43	96	72	31	82	63

			I			J	
43	27	43	63	72	31	82	96

			I		J		
43	27	43	63	72	31	82	96

				I	J		
43	27	43	31	72	63	82	96

				I			
43	27	43	31	63	72	82	96

When this stage has been reached the list has been split into two sub-lists. The reference number is now in its correct position in the list, and the sub-lists are the numbers to the left and right of this position.

5) One of the lists is stored for future sorting (see below) and the other is taken through steps 1 to 4 above.

[43 27 43 31]	63	[72 82 96]
continue with sub-list	↓ in correct position	store sub-list

I			J	
<u>43</u>	27	43	31	
	I		J	
31	27	43	<u>43</u>	
		I	J	
31	27	43	<u>43</u>	
New Sub-list			↓	
[31	27	43]	in correct position	
<u>31</u>	27	43		
31	27	43		
27	<u>31</u>	43		
	↓ in correct position			

6) This process is repeated, in each case storing a sub-list where necessary, and finally going back and sorting all stored sub-lists so that eventually each number is in the correct position.

The left-hand and right-hand numbers of a list are denoted by subscripts L and R respectively.

The pointer positions are denoted by I and J and a *flag* S is set to indicate the pointer at the reference number, so that:

S = 1 if reference number at pointer I
S = − 1 if reference number at pointer J

If at the end of step 4 the reference number is at I (as in our example) then the list has been split into:

sub-list	reference	sub-list
(L, . . . , I − 1)	I	(I + 1, . . . , R)

The right-hand list is remembered by setting up a *stack*, using an array S (P,2) with P initially set to zero. As each sub-list is stored, we make:

$$P = P + 1 \quad , \quad S(P,1) = I + 1 \text{ and } S(P,2) = R$$

The array S is initially dimensioned as S(X,2) for a list with X elements. P indicates the number of the sub-lists; S(P,1) the left-hand element and S(P,2) the right-hand element of the sub-list. In the example given, at step 5 we will have the first sub-list generated stored by setting:

$$P = 1, S(P,1) = 6 \text{ and } S(P,2) = 8$$

Thus each list to be stored is placed in sequence into the array, this process being known as PUSHing on to the STACK.

When the sub-list that the program continues with finally has only one number we must return to sort the stored lists. We retrieve a stored sub-list (POP a list out of the STACK) by letting:

$$L = S(P,1), R = S(P,2) \text{ and } P = P - 1$$

and continuing until all the lists are sorted.

Program Listing

```
  5 REM "QUICK"
 10 PRINT "HOW MANY NUMBERS?"
 20 INPUT X
 30 DIM A(X)
 40 DIM S(X,2)
 50 PRINT ,,"INPUT NUMBERS"
 60 FOR N=1 TO X
 70 INPUT A(N)
 80 NEXT N
 90 PRINT
100 PRINT "UNSORTED LIST"
110 FOR N=1 TO X
120 PRINT A(N);" ";
130 NEXT N
140 PRINT
180 REM ***********************
*         ** SORTING ROUTINE   **
190 LET P=0
200 LET L=1
210 LET R=X
220 LET I=L
230 LET J=R
240 LET S=-1
250 IF A(I) <= A(J) THEN GOTO 3
00
260 LET T=A(I)
270 LET A(I)=A(J)
280 LET A(J)=T
290 LET S=-S
300 IF S=1 THEN LET I=I+1
310 IF S=-1 THEN LET J=J-1
320 IF I<J THEN GOTO 250
330 IF I+1 >= R THEN GOTO 370
340 LET P=P+1
350 LET S(P,1)=I+1
360 LET S(P,2)=R
370 LET R=I-1
```

```
380 IF L<R THEN GOTO 220
390 IF P=0 THEN GOTO 450
400 LET L=S(P,1)
410 LET R=S(P,2)
420 LET P=P-1
430 GOTO 220

440 REM **  END OF SORT   **
            ******************
450 PRINT
460 PRINT "SORTED LIST"
470 FOR N=1 TO X
480 PRINT A(N);" ";
490 NEXT N
500 REM ** ENDPROG **
```

Lines 19Ø – 23Ø initialise P, and set values for L, R and the pointers I and J.

Line 24Ø sets the flag which indicates the position of the reference pointer (S = – 1).

Lines 25Ø – 29Ø make the interchange of A(I) and A(J) if necessary and reset the flag.

Lines 3ØØ – 32Ø move whichever of I and J is to be moved, according to how the flag is set.

Line 33Ø checks if I is at the end of the list, bypassing the sub-list storage routine.

Lines 34Ø – 36Ø 'push' sub-lists on to the stack.

Lines 37Ø and 38Ø check if the sub-list has more than one element, sending control back to line 22Ø if it has.

Line 39Ø sends control to the print routine if no sub-lists are stored.

Lines 4ØØ – 42Ø 'pop' sub-lists out of the stack.

Line 43Ø starts the sort routine for the 'popped' sub-list.

T7: Index Sort

When data records or files contain several items ('fields') of information we often need to sort them according to one particular item. An index sort routine will enable us to do this.

For example, we may have a series of records each containing a reference number, name, sex, age, home town and occupation:

1Ø	SMITH	MALE	21	OXFORD	BUTCHER
2Ø	JONES	FEMALE	32	ENFIELD	GROCER

Each record contains six fields. We might wish to sort these records alphabetically by name (field 2) or numerically by age (field 4). A sort of the type presented here enables this to be done for any of the fields. Since it uses string arrays to hold records and performs an *alphabetical* sort it is necessary for all numerical items in any field to contain the same number of digits. We must hence use Ø1Ø, Ø2Ø, 1ØØ, 2ØØ and not

10, 20, 100, 200, using leading zeros to maintain the value, but giving the same number of digits.

The procedure is as follows:

1. Set up an array N$ (N,L,C) containing N records, each of L fields with a maximum of C characters in any string. For example, we might use an array N$ (10,5,20), to represent 10 records, each with 5 fields, which can each contain up to 20 characters.

2. Decide on the *key field* (i.e. the field you wish to sort) – say the Jth field. We must then set up an array K$(N,C) to store it, and let K$ (R) = N$ (R,J) for the number of records (FOR R = 1 to N) so that the list K$ (N,C) will then contain the items we wish to arrange in order.

3. Sort the key field into ascending order. This is done in the subroutine starting at line 900 by counting how many times each element in the array K$ (N,C) is >= the other elements (including itself). This sort uses a numerical array X(N) to store the result of this count (P) for each element, by setting X(P) to equal N, when K$(N) is the item being checked.

   We first set P = 1 (since each item is equal to itself) and then check through the other items of K$ (lines 920 to 970), making the count by letting P = P + 1 when the element is >= another element. If the elements are equal, the original order in N$ is kept (line 960): (i.e. test first element of K$ and set X(P) = 1, reset P, test second element of K$ and set X(P) = 2, etc.)

   For example, with 10, 30, 20, 40 as our K$ list, the array X(4) would hold the values:

   10 X(1) = K$ (1)
   30 X(3) = K$ (2)
   20 X(2) = K$ (3)
   40 X(4) = K$ (4)

   Printing out K$ (X(1)) to K$ (X(4)) in order will give the sorted order of K$ elements.

4. The array N$ (X (N), L, C) will now consist of the records sorted in the appropriate order, according to the field chosen, and is printed out using the loop variables R and I to access N$ (X(R), I) in lines 290 to 340.

Program Listing

```
  5 REM "INDEX"
 10 PRINT "SORTING RECORDS"
 20 PRINT ,,"TYPE MAXIMUM NUMBE
R OF CHARACTERS IN ANY ITEM"
```

```
  30 INPUT C
  40 PRINT ,,"HOW MANY RECORDS?"
  50 INPUT N
  60 PRINT ,,"HOW MANY ITEMS IN
EACH RECORD?"
  70 PRINT
  80 INPUT L
  85 REM ***********************
       **INITIALISE $ ARRAYS**
  90 DIM N$(N,L,C)
 100 DIM K$(N,C)
 110 DIM X(N)
 120 REM **********************
       **INPUT RECORDS      **
 130 FOR R=1 TO N
 140 PRINT "TYPE ";L;" ITEMS FOR
 RECORD ";R
 150 FOR I=1 TO L
 160 INPUT N$(R,I)
 170 NEXT I
 180 NEXT R
 190 PRINT
 200 PRINT "WHICH ITEM IS SORTIN
G KEY?"
 210 INPUT J
 220 FOR R=1 TO N
 230 LET K$(R)=N$(R,J)
 240 NEXT R
 250 GOSUB 900
 260 PRINT
 270 PRINT "SORTED RECORDS ARE:"
 280 PRINT
 290 FOR R=1 TO N
 300 FOR I=1 TO L
 310 PRINT N$(X(R),I);" ";
 320 NEXT I
 330 PRINT
 340 NEXT R
 350 PRINT
 360 PRINT "DO YOU WISH TO CONTI
NUE?(Y/N)"
 370 INPUT Y$
 380 IF Y$="Y" THEN GOTO 200
 390 STOP

 400 REM **PROGRAM END         **
       ***********************
 890 REM ***********************
       **SORTING SUBROUTINE **
 900 FOR A=1 TO N
 910 LET P=1
 920 FOR B=1 TO N
 930 IF K$(A)>K$(B) THEN LET P=P
+1
 940 IF K$(A)=K$(B) THEN GOTO 96
0
 950 GOTO 970

 960 IF A>B THEN LET P=P+1
 970 NEXT B
 980 LET X(P)=A
 990 NEXT A
```

```
1000 RETURN
1010 REM **  ENDSUB         **
     ************************
```

For example, if we input a storage array of 4 records with 3 fields, maximum 6 characters in any item, and use as input data:

SMITH,	460,	OXFORD
JONES,	080	LEEDS
BROWN,	730,	YORK
WHITE,	095,	BATH

Results are as follows:

(i) *Using field 1 as key*

Sorted records are:

BROWN	730	YORK
JONES	080	LEEDS
SMITH	460	OXFORD
WHITE	095	BATH

(ii) *Using field 2 as key*

Sorted records are:

JONES	080	LEEDS
WHITE	095	BATH
SMITH	460	OXFORD
BROWN	730	YORK

(iii) *Using field 3 as key*

Sorted records are:

WHITE	095	BATH
JONES	080	LEEDS
SMITH	460	OXFORD
BROWN	730	YORK

T8: Linear Search

The most straightforward way of looking for a particular number in a list of unsorted numbers is to examine the list one by one in each case comparing with the 'wanted' number.

In this program a set of random numbers is created between 100 and 199 and it is arranged so that there is only a single occurrence of each number. This is in lines 4Ø – 6Ø. The list is printed out in lines 7Ø – 11Ø. The search routine is then carried out in lines 2ØØ – 3ØØ. Clearly a number near the beginning of the list is found quickly but one at the end rather slowly. For a 5Ø element list the average number of searches will be 25.

```
  5 REM "SEARCH1"
 1Ø DIM A(1ØØ)
 15 PRINT "TYPE NUMBER <1ØØ"
 2Ø INPUT N
 3Ø IF N>1ØØ THEN GOTO 15
 4Ø FOR M=1 TO N
 5Ø LET A(M)=INT (1ØØ*RND) +1ØØ
 52 FOR R=1 TO M-1
 54 IF A(M)=A(R) THEN GOTO 5Ø
 56 NEXT R
 6Ø NEXT M
 7Ø PRINT "UNSORTED LIST"
 8Ø FOR M=1 TO N
 9Ø PRINT A(M);" ";
1ØØ NEXT M
11Ø PRINT
2ØØ REM **LINEAR SEARCH**
21Ø PRINT "TYPE NUMBER BETWEEN"
22Ø PRINT "1ØØ AND 199"
23Ø INPUT X
24Ø FOR I=1 TO N
25Ø IF X=A(I) THEN GOTO 3ØØ
26Ø NEXT I
27Ø PRINT "NUMBER NOT IN LIST"
28Ø PRINT "AFTER ";N;" SEARCHES"
29Ø GOTO 4ØØ
3ØØ PRINT "NUMBER ";X;" AFTER ";
    I;" SEARCHES"
4ØØ REM **END**
```

T9: Binary Search

This is a much faster search technique than the linear search but can only be used for a list that has already been put in order. In many applications you will be dealing with an ordered list and under such circumstances this is the appropriate method to use.

In the program the binary search technique is in lines 5ØØ to 6ØØ. The basic idea is to compare the wanted number with the middle item of the ordered list. The wanted item is then either smaller (in which case we know it is in the first half of the list) or larger (in which case it is in the second half of the list) than the middle item, unless it is equal to it – in which case we have completed our search. The process is repeated, in each case halving the list. Consider a search for 3Ø in the following list:

1 2 4 6 8 1Ø 12 14 16 18 2Ø 24 28 3Ø 36

We first choose 14 (middle).

Our list is now:

16 18 2Ø 24 28 3Ø 36

and we choose 24 (middle).

Our list is now:

28 3Ø 36

We select 3Ø (middle).

Thus we have found the number in three searches (compared with fourteen using the linear search).

In the program the following sections occur:

(i) Setting up initial unordered list and printing out (lines 1Ø – 15Ø).
(ii) Sorting this list into order and printing it out (lines 2ØØ – 33Ø).
(iii) Binary search with printout (lines 5ØØ – 68Ø).

```
  5 REM "SEARCH2"
 1Ø DIM A(5Ø)
 2Ø PRINT "TYPE NUMBER <5Ø"
 3Ø INPUT N
 4Ø IF N>5Ø THEN GOTO 2Ø
 5Ø FOR M=1 TO N
 6Ø LET A(M)=INT (1ØØ*RND)+1ØØ
 7Ø FOR R=1 TO M-1
 8Ø IF A(M)=A(R) THEN GOTO 6Ø
 9Ø NEXT R
1ØØ NEXT M
11Ø PRINT "UNSORTED LIST"
12Ø FOR M=1 TO N
13Ø PRINT A(M);" ";
14Ø NEXT M
15Ø PRINT
2ØØ REM **INSERTION SORT**
21Ø FOR I=1 TO N-1
22Ø LET J=I
23Ø LET T=A(I+1)
24Ø IF T>=A(J) THEN GOTO 28Ø
25Ø LET A(J+1)=A(J)
26Ø LET J=J-1
27Ø LET J>=1 THEN GOTO 24Ø
28Ø LET A(J+1)=T
29Ø NEXT I
295 REM ***ENDSORT***
3ØØ PRINT "SORTED LIST"
31Ø FOR M=1 TO N
32Ø PRINT A(M);" ";
33Ø NEXT M
34Ø PRINT
35Ø PRINT "TYPE NUMBER REQUIRED"
36Ø PRINT "BETWEEN 1ØØ AND 199"
37Ø PRINT "TO FINISH TYPE 999"
38Ø INPUT X
39Ø IF X=999 THEN GOTO 7ØØ
4ØØ PRINT
```

```
410 PRINT "SEARCH ";N;" ITEM LI
    ST"
500 REM **BINARY SEARCH**
510 LET L=1
520 LET H=N
530 LET C=O
540 LET M=INT ((H+L)/2)
550 LET C=C+1
560 IF X=A(M) THEN GOTO 630
570 IF L>=H THEN GOTO 660
580 IF X>A(M) THEN GOTO 610
590 LET H=M-1
600 GOTO 540
610 LET L=M+1
620 GOTO 540
630 PRINT "NUMBER FOUND ";X
640 PRINT "AFTER ";C;" SEARCHES"
650 GOTO 350
660 PRINT "NUMBER NOT FOUND"
670 PRINT "AFTER ";C;" SEARCHES"
680 GOTO 350
690 REM **END SEARCH**
700 REM **END**
```

Results:

```
TYPE NUMBER <50
UNSORTED LIST
144   128   117   118   101   189   111   198
150   107   188   197   172   106   157   148
168   160   130   181   100   165   175   133
186   190   155   167   199   138   122   163
131   142   113   143   154   194   119   153
SORTED LIST
100   101   106   107   111   113   117   118
119   122   128   130   131   133   138   142
143   144   148   150   153   154   155   157
160   163   165   167   168   172   175   181
186   188   189   190   194   197   198   199
TYPE NUMBER REQUIRED
BETWEEN 100 AND 199
TO FINISH TYPE 999

SEARCH 40 ITEM LIST
NUMBER FOUND 198
AFTER 5 SEARCHES
```

T10: Storing a List

We can store data in an array for use in a program via INPUT loops when there is more data to be inserted than we care to put directly in the program using LET instructions. There are programs in the text that use this technique (e.g. "ELEMENT"). To illustrate the technique, here is a simple example that doesn't require you to INPUT anything. Key in and run the first program to create A(N) and fill it with random numbers. Edit the program, replacing the original lines with those of the second program. SAVE this program. LOAD it back in. If we used RUN it would clear all the variables, and wipe out the array we have stored.

Program execution must be started with a GOTO statement, in this case GOTO 10. The array will then print out.

```
10 DIM A(40)
20 FOR N=1 TO 40
30 LET A(N)=INT (100*RND)+100
40 NEXT N
```

```
10 REM "SAVED*ARRAY"
20 REM **EXECUTE PROGRAM**
30 REM **USING GOTO 10**
40 PRINT "LIST OF RANDOM NUMBERS"
50 PRINT "BETWEEN 100 AND 199"
60 FOR N=1 TO 40
70 PRINT A(N)
80 NEXT N
```

So this is the general procedure:

(1) Write an array creation program and run it, i.e. A(N) created and data inserted.
(2) Edit out lines and put in additional lines as required.
(3) SAVE the final program.
(4) LOAD program and execute using a GOTO statement.

To avoid the possibility of the user entering RUN, we can use a structure which automatically initiates the program on loading. The program below for the ZX81 also illustrates the fact that one may use a string variable as a program name.

Lines 10 to 80 create array and have the input routine. These lines could be edited out as soon as the data was input, or left in to enable (through the use of RUN) a different set of data to be input.

Line 90 onwards are the program to use the stored data.

Line 9010 requests a string input to be used as the program name. 9020 gets the string, and 9030 and 9040 give you the chance to write it down before you forget.

9050 waits for a key to be pressed, and 9070 saves the program and its variables. One of these variables stores the line the computer had got to in the program, and when loaded back it starts where it left off (9070) and goes to line 90 automatically.

```
10 REM **AUTO-RUN ROUTINE**
20 REM AUTOMATIC RUN WILL
   PRESERVE VARIABLES
30 REM    AVOID STATEMENTS
   OR EDIT THEM OUT.
40 REM ***DIMENSION/INPUT,TO
   STORE VARIABLES***
50 DIM A(20)
60 FOR F=1 TO 20
```

```
  70 INPUT A(F)
  80 NEXT F
  90 PRINT "PROGRAM TO USE DATA"
 100 FOR F=20 TO 1 STEP -1
 110 PRINT A(F)
 120 NEXT F
 130 REM ......MORE PROGRAM
 140 REM .......
8990 REM **SAVE AND AUTO-RUN**
9000 CLS
9010 PRINT "INPUT PROGRAM NAME"
9020 INPUT A$
9030 PRINT "PROGRAM NAME:";A$
9040 PRINT "READY TO SAVE.NOTE P
     ROGRAM NAME.PRESS A KEY TO
     SAVE PROGRAM","AFTER SETTI
     NG CASSETTE TO RECORD*****"
9050 IF INKEY$="" THEN GOTO 9050
9060 CLS
9070 SAVE A$
9075 REM **GOTO LINE AFTER DIM/
     INPUT ROUTINE IF NOT EDITED
     OUT**
9080 GOTO 90
```

The Spectrum has an automatic message and built in wait-for-key-press routine. It also has an automatic run-after-LOAD facility. If a line is entered in a program of the form:

9000 SAVE "program" LINE 200

and the program is saved with a GOTO 9000, the program will start running after loading by going to the line stated (200 in the example). For the Spectrum, this program needs modifying by deleting lines 9070, 9075, 9080, changing 9040 to read PRINT"NOTE PROGRAM NAME", 9050 to PAUSE 0, and 9060 to SAVE A$ LINE 90.

T11: Storing a String Array

The ZX81 program PRETTY draws a picture on the screen (slowly!) which is stored in the array A$, dimensioned in line 100. If this program is run the array A$ is created, and the screen display stored, character cell by character cell, in A$. The lines in the program can be edited out so that finally we have a program like PRETTY2. This may be SAVEd and includes the created array A$. To execute the program PRETTY2 after loading we must use GOTO 5, to avoid the use of RUN, which clears all arrays (and hence A$) before execution starts.

```
 5 REM "PRETTY"
10 FOR J=1 TO 10
20 FOR N=0 TO J*12
30 PLOT 32+J*2*SIN (N/(J*6)*PI),
   22+J*COS (N/(J*6)*PI)
40 NEXT N
50 NEXT J
```

```
100 DIM A$(704)
110 FOR I=0 TO 21
120 FOR J=1 TO 32
130 LET A$(J+32*I)=CHR$ PEEK (PEEK
    16396+256*PEEK 16397+J+33*I)
140 NEXT J
150 NEXT I
```

```
  5 REM "PRETTY2"
 10 PRINT  A$
```

Notice that we have stored the screen display in the array.

Check you understand the process of PEEKing the display file.

The Spectrum stores a screen display using a special form of SAVE. This has the form: SAVE "PRETTY" SCREEN$, where PRETTY can be any name. This is loaded back using LOAD "PRETTY" SCREEN$.

Try this procedure on your Spectrum. The program above can be revised for the Spectrum. Enter just the following lines:

```
10  FOR J = 1 TO 40 STEP 4
20  FOR N = 0 TO J*12 STEP 4
30  PLOT 125 + J*2*SIN(N/(J*6)*PI),88 + J*COS(N/(J*6)*PI)
40  NEXT N
50  NEXT J
```

Use SCREEN$ to save the picture as above. To continue with screen displays, the Spectrum can store a screenful of characters in much the same way as the ZX81 program above, using SCREEN$ to access each character in turn, placing them in sequence in array A$(704). A screenful of characters is generated at random, using the single characters from the Spectrum character set, placing these along each line.

The double loop (lines 60 to 100) uses SCREEN$ (F,N) to check each character along each line, placing it in the array A$.

```
  5 DIM A$(704)
 10 FOR F=0 TO 21
 20 FOR N=0 TO 31
 30 PRINT AT F,N; CHR$ (32+ RND
    *97)
 40 NEXT N
 50 NEXT F
 60 FOR F=0 TO 21
 70 FOR N=0 TO 31
 80 LET A$(N+1+32*F)=SCREEN$
   (F,N)
 90 NEXT N
100 NEXT F
```

Now edit out all the lines, replacing 5 with 5 PRINT A$, and RUN the program using GOTO 5.

The same program for the ZX81 needs to use PEEK to access the display file, just as in "PRETTY". Replace lines 5 to 5Ø in "PRETTY" with the following, to print a random set of ZX81 characters on the screen:

```
 5 REM "SCREENFULL"
10 FOR F=1 TO 704
20 PRINT CHR$ INT ( RND *64);
30 NEXT F
```

The same principle holds good for any string array or numeric array. Once the program has been run and the data inserted into the array, the data is safe as long as RUN is not used again, and can be accessed as required. The ELEMENT program treated in Unit W3 uses this procedure to store data required in the program.

Exercise

Write the appropriate array creation program for the following program:

```
1Ø  REM "SAVE1Ø"
2Ø  REM **THIS PROGRAM MUST BE**
3Ø  REM **EXECUTED USING GOTO1Ø**
4Ø  PRINT "MONTHS OF THE YEAR"
5Ø  FOR N = 1 TO 12
6Ø  PRINT M$ (N)
7Ø  NEXT N
```

T12: Storing Data in Strings

Strings can be used to store data, which may be accessed using the string-handling instructions. The data can also be re-assigned, or new values inserted. Numbers may be used, the STR$ and VAL instructions enabling conversion from numbers to strings and vice versa.

The first example has the data stored in A$. The names of the months are all three letters long, and can thus be accessed using the simple numeric calculation of line 7Ø.

```
1Ø REM STRING DATA STORE
2Ø REM *A$ HAS DATA*
3Ø LET A$="JANFEBMARAPRMAYJUNJ
   ULAUGSEPOCTNOVDEC"
4Ø REM *DATA INPUT*
5Ø PRINT "INPUT MONTH(1 TO 12)
   "
6Ø INPUT MONTH
7Ø PRINT "MONTH ";MONTH;" IS "
   ;A$(MONTH*3-2 TO MONTH*3)
```

The next program has the full names of the months, with varying lengths. Full stops are used to make the principle clear, but spaces between the months would be used in a practical program. (As it is, a full stop is printed after the month, rather than the useful space.) The program stops the search after the required month has been found (line 100), but is a little slow on the ZX81 unless FAST is used (line 65).

```
 10 REM STRING DATA STORE
 20 REM *A$ HAS DATA*
 25 REM **USE SPACES,NOT FULL S
    TOPS IN REAL PROGRAM**
 30 LET A$=".JANUARY.FEBRUARY.M
    ARCH.APRIL.MAY.JUNE.JULY.AU
    GUST.SEPTEMBER.OCTOBER.NOVE
    MBER.DECEMBER."
 40 REM *DATA INPUT*
 50 PRINT "INPUT MONTH(1 TO 12)
    "
 60 INPUT MONTH
 65 FAST
 70 LET P=0
 80 LET A=1
 90 IF A$(A)="." THEN LET P=P+1
100 IF P=MONTH+1 THEN GOTO 140
110 IF P=MONTH THEN PRINT A$(A+
    1);
120 LET A=A+1
130 GOTO 90
140 SLOW
150 PRINT "IS THE MONTH INPUT"
```

Spectrum users should, of course, delete the FAST and SLOW instructions, lines 65 and 140.

The next program uses a string to store numeric data. The numbers are input, and placed in the string as the STR$ string plus "*", which is used as an indicator. The data is retrieved by using the subroutine (at line 1000) to step through each number string in turn, returning the number string as Z$ when RETURN is executed on an asterisk being found (line 1020). The two data access routines (lines 110 to 140 and 150 to 180) after the initialisation of NSTRING could occur anwhere in the program. The data can be accessed in an order by suitable manipulation of the access instructions (e.g. the reverse loop in lines 150 and 180), and NSTRING can be re-initialised as zero at any point. Counting loops could be used to access an Nth item of data.

Spectrum users should note that the Spectrum has READ and DATA functions (which are dealt with in Section W), that provide a more convenient way of storing and retrieving data for many applications, but are less flexible than string storage in some cases, especially when used as illustrated below. DATA items must be keyed in within the program listing and cannot be input.

```
 5 REM *INITIALISE*
10 DIM A(10)
20 LET A$=""
```

```
  25 REM *DATA INTO STRING*
  30 FOR F=1 TO 10
  40 INPUT NUMBER
  50 LET A$=A$+STR$ NUMBER+"*"
  60 NEXT F
  70 REM .......
  80 REM .......
  90 REM .......
  95 REM *RESTORE START*
 100 LET NSTRING=0
 110 FOR F=1 TO 5
 120 GOSUB 1000
 130 LET A(F)=VAL Z$
 140 NEXT F
 150 FOR F=10 TO 6 STEP -1
 160 GOSUB 1000
 170 LET A(F)=VAL Z$
 180 NEXT F
 190 REM .......
 200 REM .......
 210 STOP
 995 REM ***READ STRING SUB***
1000 LET Z$=""
1010 LET NSTRING=NSTRING+1
1020 IF A$(NSTRING)="*" THEN RET
     URN
1030 LET Z$=Z$+A$(NSTRING)
1040 GOTO 1010
```

SECTION U: THE COMPUTER MEMORY

U1: Memory Organisation

Digital computers operate with sequences of numbers in the binary number system. Binary numbers are numbers to base 2, and our 'normal' number system is decimal (base 1Ø).

> **The BINARY system uses only two digits, Ø and 1. These are *bi*nary digi*ts* (*bits*). The computer holds a bit as a voltage level (+ 5v or Øv) in a switched pathway.**

In the decimal system, a number, for example 418, is *coded* as a number using the digits Ø to 9. The coding is based on powers of ten. 418 means: (4 times 1Ø to the power 2) + (1 times ten to the power 1) + (8 times ten to the power Ø).

$$(4 \times 10^2) + (1 \times 10^1) + (8 \times 10^0)$$
$$400 + 10 + 8 = 418$$

The binary system of coding uses powers of two in exactly the same way.
The number 13 is represented as:

(1×2^3)	+	(1×2^2)	+	(0×2^1)	+	(1×2^0)	
1		1		Ø		1	Binary number 11Ø1
8	+	4	+	Ø	+	1 = 13	Decimal equivalent

The binary number 1Ø111Ø is evaluated as:

$$(1 \times 2^5) + (0 \times 2^4) + (1 \times 2^3) + (1 \times 2^2) + (1 \times 2^1) + (0 \times 2^0)$$
$$32 + 0 + 8 + 4 + 2 + 0 = 46 \text{ in decimal}$$

Key in the following program, which converts decimal numbers to their binary representation:

```
  1 REM *DECBI*
  2 REM    CONVERTS DECIMAL TO
    BINARY NUMBERS
 1Ø PRINT "ENTER DECIMAL NUMBER
    "
 2Ø INPUT N
 3Ø PRINT N ;
 4Ø LET B$=""
 5Ø LET L=INT (N/2)
 6Ø LET B=N-2*L
 7Ø IF B=1 THEN LET A$="1"
 8Ø IF B=Ø THEN LET A$="Ø"
 9Ø LET B$=A$+B$
1ØØ LET N=L
11Ø IF L>Ø THEN GOTO 5Ø
12Ø PRINT " IS ";B$;" IN BINARY"
```

Input sequences of numbers to familiarise yourself with the binary system. The program only deals with positive whole numbers. Trace the progam to see how it works, using the examples 13 and 46 given above as inputs. Non-integer numbers are dealt with by using an exponent, as with the E notation system for decimals. Binary numbers have a *binary point*, and bits to the left of the point are binary fractions, representing the reciprocal power of two. The binary number 1.1Ø1, for instance, represents:

$$(1 \times 2^0) + \left(\frac{1}{2^1}\right) + \left(\frac{Ø}{2^2}\right) + \left(\frac{1}{2^3}\right)$$

$$1 \quad + \quad .5 \quad + \quad Ø \quad + \quad .125 \quad = 1.625$$

You may have noticed that binary numbers as seen above are all positive. Negative numbers are dealt with by using a particular form of binary representation. The method by which the ZX81 and Spectrum store numbers is described later in this Section.

In a computer, numbers are held in fixed numbers of bits. These are referred to as *words*.

A *BYTE* is a sequence of 8 bits. The sequence of 8 bits represents a number between Ø and 255 decimal, ØØØØØØØØ and 11111111 binary. The ZX81 and Spectrum use 8 bit words, i.e. 1 byte.

Memory in computers is organised as a linear sequence of addresses. Each address is a memory location or memory cell holding a single byte. The binary numbers in these locations are interpreted as numbers, characters or instructions depending on their context in the computer memory. The organisation of the memory is constant, but the space occupied by each area of memory varies according to the program and its requirements. As an obvious example, a long program takes up more space for storage than a short one.

Memory is of two types:

READ ONLY MEMORY (ROM) is fixed and cannot be altered. It contains the BASIC interpreter program, and is built-in to the computer in manufacture.

RANDOM ACCESS MEMORY (RAM) is variable, multi-purpose memory that holds the current program and all the other elements of data required to run the program.

Data can only be extracted from ROM ('read'), and is permanent. RAM memory can be both read from and written to. Inserting a value into a memory location in RAM (writing or storing) will wipe out or overwrite the existing data at that address.

Memory capacity is referred to as the number of *Kilobytes* (k) involved. Kilo refers to one thousand, but this is only approximately true, since a kilobyte is actually 1Ø24 (2^{10}) bytes. The ZX81 has 8k of ROM memory and, with the memory expansion, 16k of RAM. The

Spectrum has 16k of ROM and either 16 or 48k of RAM. The memory is organised as shown in the diagrams below (called memory maps). The ZX81 and Spectrum have somewhat different memory organisations. We will deal first with the ZX81, and then the Spectrum. Spectrum users should read through the ZX81 section, however, as definitions of the functions of various types of memory are covered in this Unit.

ZX81 MEMORY MAP

Address	Contents	
32767		
	GOSUB STACK	RAM
	MACHINE STACK	RAM
	SPARE MEMORY	RAM
	CALCULATOR STACK	RAM
	WORK SPACE (Temporary Storage)	RAM
	VARIABLES STORAGE AREA	RAM
	DISPLAY FILE	RAM
	PROGRAM AREA	RAM
16509		
	SYSTEM VARIABLES AREA	RAM
16384		
	Unused addresses. No memory space exists for this area.	
8192		
	ROM memory area. BASIC interpreter and operating system program.	
0000		

The top of memory (RAMTOP) is usually set as shown on switch-on, at 32767. The computer can be instructed to set RAMTOP at some lower value, to leave spare memory locations which can be used to store machine code programs, which are called (like subroutines) from the BASIC program with the USR instruction. Machine-code programming is outside the scope of this text.

Some areas of memory are organised in the form of a stack. This is a system such that the last item entered will be the first to be pulled off the stack. A number may only be placed on the top of the stack of existing numbers, and the only accessible number is the one on the top. This creates an ordered sequence. In the GOSUB stack this is used to ensure that the RETURN instructions are followed in correct sequence. Each GOSUB instruction causes the following line number to be added to the stack. RETURN then takes the first line number off the stack to get the correct line number to pass control of the program back.

The machine-stack memory area is used to keep track of the operation of the program. The spare memory area is that portion of the allocated area not occupied by the program and other memory areas. Although we referred to the *top* of the stack, it is more correctly the free end of the stack on to which the numbers are placed. The free end of the machine stack is at the bottom, in terms of the memory address sequence, hence the spare memory is below the machine stack in our diagram.

The calculator stack is used for arithmetic operations. The work space holds the program line being input and provides temporary storage for data being manipulated – a scratch pad.

The variables area stores all variables initialised in the course of a program. They are held in various forms, and we shall deal with the way numbers and variables are stored in the next Unit.

The display file has been covered in Section Q. The program area contains the program lines. This area always starts at address 165Ø9. All other memory areas ride on top of the program area, moving up or down as the program lengthens (has program lines added or inserted) or shortens (has lines deleted), apart from the GOSUB and machine stacks, which are always at the top of memory.

The systems variables area holds the special variables which store information concerning the state of the computer for use by the operating system. Certain of the system variables were introduced in Section Q. Like the D-FILE system variable introduced there, some of these variables hold the addresses of the divisions between the areas of memory. Other variables hold values of addresses, line numbers, characters, etc., to keep track of what state of affairs is current in the operating system. You have seen, for instance, that the DF-SZ variable stores the number of lines on the lower part of the screen. Some other system variables are dealt with in the next Unit. There are a fixed number of system variables, and their values are always held at known addresses between 16384 and 165Ø8. The names of the system variables are not recognised as BASIC variable names, but are just mnemonics for the system variable function.

On the ZX81 there is no memory corresponding to addresses 8193-16383. Addresses Ø to 8192 contain the system software in ROM which holds the BASIC interpreter and operation program in machine code.

SPECTRUM MEMORY MAP

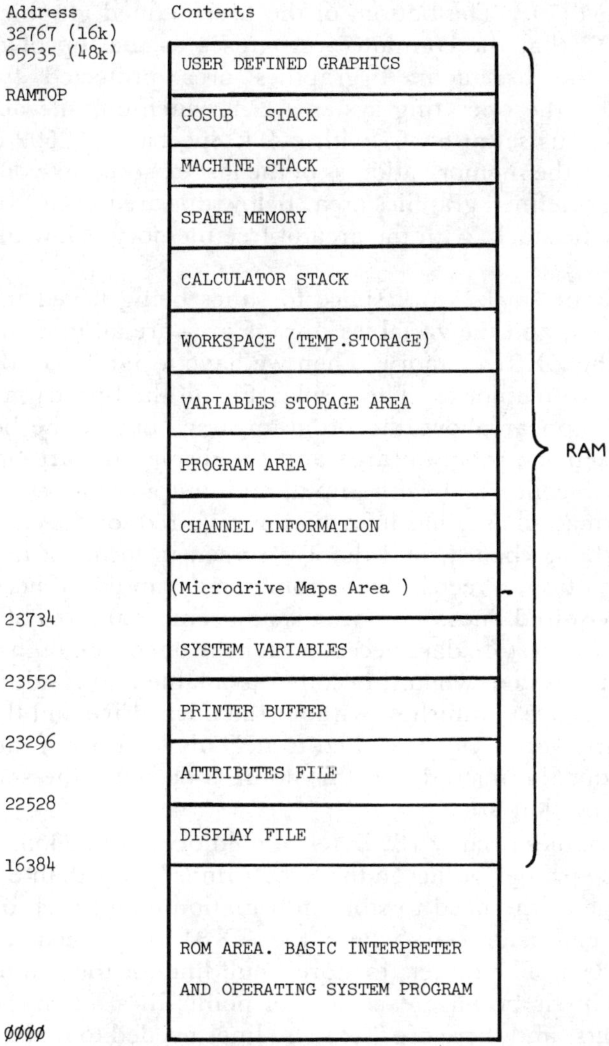

The memory map of the Spectrum memory is somewhat different from that of the ZX81. The Spectrum also comes in two versions, one with 16k of RAM, one with 48k. The ROM is also larger on the Spectrum, occupying 16k. Thus the first 16k of memory addresses (ØØØØ to 16383) are occupied by ROM on the Spectrum. A 16k version then has the next 16k of memory as RAM, up to address 32767. The 48k Spectrum uses addresses 32768 to 65535 for the additional RAM memory. Apart from the size of memory, the arrangement of memory is the same in both Spectrum versions, as shown on the diagram. The fixed memory points are given as the memory address.

The Spectrum memory requires more separate areas (reserved for the additional functions of the Spectrum), and the organisation is somewhat different. Working from the top of memory down, we notice an area set aside for user-defined graphics. This occupies 168 bytes, and is set at the actual top of the memory, which is referred to as **Physical** RAMTOP. The bottom of the user-defined graphics area is the RAMTOP that the computer recognises as the top of memory. This leaves the user-defined graphics area protected from any interference by the operating system. On switch-on, the address of RAMTOP is thus set at 65367 with a 48k Spectrum, 32599 on a 16k version. This is the memory address of the last existing byte of memory before the user-defined graphics area. Below this are the GOSUB stack and the machine stack, with the area of free memory below this, as on the ZX81.

The calculator stack, work space for lines being keyed in or data being processed, and the variables storage area are all in the sequence followed by the ZX81 memory. Then we have a significant difference between the two memories. The display file on the Spectrum is fixed, and does not appear above the program area, but at the bottom of RAM. Between the program area and the display file are Spectrum-specific areas, concerned with input and output and colour. The channel information area has information required for the operation of the printer, the keyboard, and the TV screen in terms of its division into top and bottom screens, the bottom one expanding if necessary to contain the required lines. This area is adjacent to an area of memory that will be used to store data necessary for the operation of the Sinclair microdrive disc system when it becomes available and is attached to a Spectrum. This area 'vanishes' without the microdrive and there is no sequence of memory bytes allocated to it. This area begins at address 23734. Without the microdrive, this address becomes the start of the channel information area.

System variables occupy 182 bytes of memory, from 23552 to 23733 inclusive. The printer buffer on the Spectrum is larger than that on the ZX81 because of the need to store information about each of the 8*8 points in a character cell (where the ZX81 only needed to store character codes). The buffer, to store a full line for thc printer, needs 256 bytes. This is because each line of points in a 32 character line needs 8*32 bits, and there are 8 of these lines needed to make up a line on the printer. This buffer occupies the bytes from 23296 to 23551 inclusive.

The colour attributes (see Section W for this) occupy one byte per character cell, so the storage is 24*32 bytes from 22528 to 23295. These store the information about the colour (background and printing colour), brightness and flashing characteristics of each PRINT position. This information, together with the display file, determines the screen display. The display file holds the information about the pattern of dots to be placed on the screen, and the attributes file the additional data for a colour display. The display file occupies the memory addresses from the start of RAM (16384) to 22527. This is 6144 bytes, so we can note that on a 16k Spectrum some 42% of RAM is needed for the display and attributes files only. This leaves about 9k for program and operating areas, and illustrates the fact that high-resolution graphics take up large amounts of memory.

Below 16384, the memory addresses are all ROM memory. The more complex operating system of the Spectrum demands more instructions in ROM than are required by the ZX81. There is no gap in memory at all on the 48k machine, all 64k of memory that the Z80A chip (the central processing unit) can address being used. On the 16k Spectrum, of course, the memory addresses above 32767 are unused.

U2: PEEK and POKE

The PEEK and POKE instructions have been introduced for specific purposes in connection with the display file and character storage. This should have given you some understanding of their uses. Now that you have been introduced more generally to the way memory is stored in a computer, you will notice that these instructions provide direct access to the memory of the computer.

PEEK N returns the value (in decimal notation) of the number stored in binary form in the memory byte of address N. In the ZX81, N must be in the range 0 to 8192 to return the contents of ROM memory, and in the range 16384 to 32767 to return the contents of RAM. For the Spectrum, ROM extends from 0 to 16383, RAM from 16384 to 32767 (16k version) or 65535 (48k version).

POKE M,N places into the memory address M the binary form of the decimal number N. N must be in the range 0 to 255 (to fit in a single byte). For the ZX81, and 16k Spectrum M must be in the range 16384 to 32767. The 48k Spectrum uses addresses up to 65535. ROM may not have values POKEd into it.

In general, we use PEEK to extract from memory any values useful to our program, and POKE to insert values into memory. Remember that the values (entered and returned in decimal notation) can be numbers, characters or instructions. Machine-code programming is performed by POKEing into a specified sequence of addresses the values which correspond to instructions which the Z80 central processor chip understands. This sequence of instructions is then called from within a BASIC program, in a similar fashion to calling a subroutine, and is executed. At the end of the machine-code program, a return instruction passes back control to the BASIC program.

We will use PEEK to investigate how numbers and program lines are stored in the ZX81 and Spectrum. Different types of number have different formats in which they are held. The normal number in memory is held in *5-byte floating point binary form*. Each number is stored in 5 bytes of memory.

The *line numbers* in a program are stored in 2 bytes of memory. Numbers in a program listing are stored as their printed characters, then in 5-byte form.

Enter the program below if you are using a ZX81. It PEEKs the memory locations from address 165Ø9 onwards, i.e. each address in memory from the start of the program listing, after printing out the numbers as instructed in the first three lines, and prints the address, contents of the address as a decimal number, and the character string corresponding. The corresponding program and output for the Spectrum is given after the ZX81 has been dealt with, since the character codes are different.

```
 5 REM "PROGLIST"
1Ø PRINT 23
2Ø PRINT 123E8
3Ø PRINT 123E-8
4Ø LET A=165Ø9
5Ø PRINT A;TAB 1Ø;PEEK A;TAB 1
   5;CHR$ (PEEK A)
6Ø LET A=A+1
7Ø GOTO 5Ø
```

You will get a display (use COPY to get a printer listing, and CONT to continue) that looks like this:

```
23
12300000000
1.23E-6
16509          0
16510          10    ▒
16511          10    ▒
16512          0
16513          245   PRINT
16514          30    2
16515          31    3
16516          126   ?
16517          133   ▌
16518          56    5
16519          0
16520          0
16521          0
16522          118   ?
16523          0
16524          20    =
16525          13    $
16526          0
16527          245   PRINT
16528          29    1
16529          30    2
16530          31    3
16531          42    E
16532          36    8
16533          126   ?
16534          162   █
16535          55    R
16536          72    ?
16537          198   LEN
16538          192   "
16539          118   ?
16540          0
16541          30    2
16542          14    :
16543          0
16544          245   PRINT
16545          29    1
16546          30    2
16547          31    3
16548          42    E
16549          22    -
16550          36    8
16551          126   ?
16552          109   ?
```

```
16553    37    9
16554    22    -
16555    122   ?
16556    107   ?
16557    118   ?
16558    Ø
16559    4Ø    C
1656Ø    15    ?
16561    Ø
16562    241   LET
16563    38    A
16564    2Ø    =
16565    29    1
16566    34    6
16567    33    5
16568    28    Ø
16569    37    9
```

Notice first the way the ZX81 changes the format of the numbers. 23 prints as 23, but 123E8 is printed as 123ØØØØØØØØ, and 123E-8 as 1.23E-6. The operating routines put each number into a standard format for printing to the screen. In order to present a listing of the program, which is what you've typed in, the computer must hold two forms of the number; first the literal characters and second the 5-byte floating point form.

Inspect the printout from the program. The first address printed is 165Ø9, holding zero. This is the first of the two bytes holding the line number. Notice that the *more significant byte* comes *first*. This is the other way round from normal 2-byte values (those of the system variables, for example). Since the line number is less than 255, the first byte holds zero and the second (1651Ø) holds 1Ø.

16511 holds 1Ø again. This is the number of characters in the line. 16512 has zero, since these two bytes hold the line number as (First byte value) + 256* (Second byte value), in the standard way.

16513 holds the value 245, representing the keyword character PRINT. Then come the characters 2 and 3 (codes 3Ø and 31). Bytes 16516 to 16521 hold the values 126, which indicates that the next sequence of bytes holds a number, and then 133,56,Ø,Ø,Ø. This is the 5-byte form of 23. We shall see in the next Unit the mechanics of this way of representing numbers.

Check through the rest of the listing and make sure that you understand how and why the memory addresses contain the values they do.

SPECTRUM PROGRAM LISTINGS

The program below for the Spectrum has a different form from that for the ZX81. This is a consequence of the strange results of the control characters in the Spectrum character set if used as a CHR$ (see Unit P2). We must avoid using a PRINT CHR$ instruction for these control characters. The program sets a logical condition to test the value of A in lines 6Ø and 7Ø which prints "CONTROL CHR" instead of the CHR$ form if the printing of the CHR$ would cause problems.

```
1Ø PRINT 23
2Ø PRINT 123E8
3Ø PRINT 123E-8
```

```
40 LET A=(PEEK 23635+256*PEEK
   23636)
50 PRINT A;TAB 10;PEEK A;TAB 1
   5;
60 IF PEEK A>23 OR PEEK A<15 T
   HEN PRINT CHR$ (PEEK A)
70 IF PEEK A<=23 AND PEEK A>=1
   6 THEN PRINT "CONTROL CHR"
80 LET A=A+1
90 GO TO 50
```

The results will be as follows. (Use scroll to see the full listing. To get a printout like the one here, you must BREAK the program when "Scroll?" appears, then use COPY, then CONT to get the next screenful.)

```
23
1.23E+10
1.23E-6
23755     0    ?
23756     10   ?
23757     10   ?
23758     0    ?
23759     245  PRINT
23760     50   2
23761     51   3
23762     14   ?
23763     0    ?
23764     0    ?
23765     23   CONTROL CHR
23766     0    ?
23767     0    ?
23768     13

23769     0    ?
23770     20   CONTROL CHR
23771     13

23772     0    ?
23773     245  PRINT
23774     49   1
23775     50   2
23776     51   3
23777     69   E
23778     56   8
23779     14   ?
23780     162  S
23781     55   7
23782     72   H
23783     198  AND
23784     192  USR
23785     13

23786     0    ?
23787     30   ?
23788     14   ?
23789     0    ?
23790     245  PRINT
23791     49   1
23792     50   2
23793     51   3
23794     69   E
23795     45   -
23796     56   8
23797     14   ?
23798     109  m
23799     37   %
23800     22   CONTROL CHR
23801     122  z
23802     107  k
23803     13
```

The PEEKs in line 40 set A to the value of the first memory address of the program storage area. (See the description of the System Variables in the next Unit.) Unlike the ZX81 the Spectrum program area moves around in memory.

After printing the numbers, in a revised notation, setting the exponent values to have the decimal point after the first digit (a task automatically done by the operating system) the program prints the first address (23755), which is the first byte of the program area. It then prints the value stored in this byte, followed by the character code (if it's not a control character). Codes not corresponding to a character with a printed form produce a question mark.

The first two bytes hold Ø and 1Ø. This is the line number, stored, unlike all other two-byte numbers, with the *more significant* byte first. The next two bytes hold the number of characters in the line, stored in normal fashion, with the *least significant* byte first. We then have code 245, which is the keyword PRINT, the first instruction in the line. This is followed by the *characters* 2 and 3, for printing in the program listing. This is followed by code 14, which is a control code indicating that the next 5 bytes are to be interpreted as a number. There are then five bytes storing the number 23, in the special form in which the Spectrum handles integers. We will deal with this in the next Unit. Notice that the code 14 defines for the Spectrum the way in which a character or number (stored in the same binary form in a memory byte) is to be interpreted.

After the five bytes of the number comes the ENTER character (13), signifying the end of the program line. Addresses 23772 and 23773 hold the next line number, then comes the number of character bytes in the line, and so on. Note that the number 123E8, which was input in this form, is stored as this sequence of characters, even though it prints in a different form, due to the operating system using the five-byte form to decide what number is to be printed.

Trace the program further than the third line we have included in the printout, and ensure you can follow the program line arrangement, as we will refer to this in connection with a program to renumber program lines automatically later in the text. Although the Spectrum and ZX81 character codes are different, the program line arrangement is the same.

Because we know that the address at which a program listing starts can be found, and the format of the program listing in memory, we can use PEEK to extract data from a program line. This can be useful to store data. Enter and run the program below. You should be able to see how it works. Remember that the first character after the line number (two bytes) and the line length (two bytes) will be the REM statement. The characters to be PEEKed will follow this. 5 bytes therefore need to be added to the start address of the program area.

The Spectrum user needs to use the PEEK expression to find the start of the program (the address given by M):

```
 10 REM RIALCNIS
 20 LET M= PEEK 23635+256* PEEK
23636
 30 PRINT AT 10;10
 40 FOR F=7 TO 0 STEP -1
 50 PRINT CHR$ PEEK (M+5+F);
 60 NEXT F
```

On the ZX81, the start of the program area is fixed. 5 can be added to this to give the address of the first byte of memory we are interested in (16509 + 5 = 16514).

```
10 REM RIALCNIS
20 PRINT AT 10,10;
30 FOR F=7 TO 0 STEP -1
40 PRINT CHR$ PEEK (16514+F);
50 NEXT F
```

The reverse procedure is also possible, using POKE. Try this program.
ZX81:

```
10 REM ABCDEFG
20 FOR F=0 TO 6
30 POKE (16514+F),29+F
40 NEXT F
```

Spectrum:

```
10 REM ABCDEFG
20 LET M=PEEK 23635+256*PEEK 23636
30 FOR F=0 TO 6
40 POKE (M+5+F),48+F
50 NEXT F
```

The Spectrum program again uses a PEEK to find the program area start address, and the different character codes require different values added to F to give the same result.

Run the program, then LIST it and see what has happened to the REM statement. If you want an illustration of the care needed when POKEing into programs, try setting F = Ø TO 8 and run the program again. LIST it, and then try to edit your listing. The ZX81 may crash, and if your screen blanks out or produces other strange effects you will have to reset it by pulling out the power supply plug and re-inserting it. The Spectrum is more tolerant of this sort of treatment, and will just give an error message, but the program listing is corrupt, and NEW will have to be used.

Storing information in a REM statement in this fashion, given that as you have seen it can be accessed with PEEK and updated with POKE, can provide a useful alternative to storing data in variables.

The layout of the program listing in memory, starting at a known address, enables us to write a program which will renumber the program lines. Here's the program for the ZX81:

```
   1 REM "RENUM"
   2 REM REPLACE LINE AND STEP
  30 REM VALUES IF START LINE
  45 REM OR STEP VALUE TO BE
     DIFFERENT
  50 REM RUN IN FAST MODE FOR
 121 REM LARGE PROGRAMS
1001 REM **YOU MUST REMEMBER**
1002 REM ***GOSUBS AND GOTOS***
9000 REM ***RENUMBER***
9010 LET RAM=16509
```

```
9020 LET LINE=10
9030 LET STEP=10
9040 POKE RAM,INT (LINE/256)
9050 POKE RAM+1,(LINE-256*PEEK R
     AM)
9060 LET RAM=RAM+1
9070 IF PEEK RAM<>118 THEN GOTO
     9060
9080 LET RAM=RAM+1
9090 IF 256*PEEK RAM+PEEK (RAM+1
     )=9000 THEN GOTO 9120
9100 LET LINE=LINE+STEP
9110 GOTO 9040
9120 LIST
9130 STOP
```

Modifications for the Spectrum are required as follows: Line 9010 must be edited to read LET RAM = PEEK 23635 + 256* PEEK 23636. Line 9070 must be changed to 9070 IF PEEK RAM<>13 THEN GOTO 9060.

Line 9010 sets a variable RAM equal to the start of the program area. LINE (the line number to start the new listing) and STEP (the increment of the line numbers) are both set at 10, but could take any desired values. 9040 and 9050 POKE into the first and second bytes, which hold the line number, the value 10. Into the first byte goes the line number divided by 256, the INT function turning this to an integer value. If non-integer values are POKEd into an address, they are automatically rounded, but to the nearest whole number, which does not give us the desired result if the remainder is 0.5 or greater. Into the second byte goes the line number less the value in the first byte, obtained by PEEKing the byte and multiplying by 256.

Lines 9060 and 9070 increment the address and check if the address contains the NEWLINE (ENTER) character (code 118 on the ZX81, code 13 on the Spectrum), repeating until a new line is found, which marks the end of a program line. 9080 adds 1 to RAM, giving the start address of the next program line.

Line 9090 checks the value (line number) held in this and the next byte, to see if the process has reached the start of the renumber program, passing control to 9120 for listing if it has. 9100 increments the line number by the step value and control is then passed back to line 9040, and the new line number POKEd into the first bytes of the next program line.

Notice that the program checks each byte in turn. Another way to find the address of the end of the program line, which prevents the need for this, is to use the data about line length stored in the third and fourth bytes of the program line. To do this, delete line 9080 and replace lines 9060 and 9070 as follows:

```
9060  LET LENGTH = PEEK(RAM + 2) + 256*PEEK(RAM + 3)
9070  LET RAM = RAM + LENGTH + 4
```

This finds the line length, and adds this, plus 4 for the bytes holding line number and line length, to the current RAM value, giving the address of the first byte of the next line.

Remember, to use a program like this on the ZX81, you should LOAD it before you start to program, and use RUN 9000 when you have developed your program. You will also need a STOP instruction before line 9000 to prevent your program renumbering itself every time you run it. The REM statements are not necessary to the program in the listing, of course, but do give the program something to renumber as a test. Note that GOSUB and GOTO destination line numbers are *not* renumbered, and you must edit the lines affected to suit the new numbering. Take a printer listing or note down the relevant lines *before* renumbering! On the Spectrum, a program can be MERGEd with one already in memory, and added at any time. See Unit W2 for this facility.

Loading useful programs, joined into a subroutine or sub-program toolkit, is worthwhile if you are developing a large program. This might include, for instance, a sorting routine, error message and format subroutines. As with the renumber program, which is deleted after use, any unwanted routines can be edited out.

A utility program like this should obviously have line numbers 9000 + , and the variables used should not be single letter variables, or even variables such as A9, which might be needed in the main program.

The program "TOOLS" in the program library illustrates the principle, and provides a basis for you to add further useful subroutines. It incorporates a block deletion routine (also listed separately), which enables easy deletion of any portions of the toolkit program not required to be easily edited out. This includes the facility to delete itself!

U3: System Variables

The system variables area of memory is a fixed area holding 125 bytes (ZX81) or 181 bytes (Spectrum) of system variables. These occupy either one or two bytes, generally, but exceptions include the variable PRBUFF on the ZX81 (16444 to 16476), which stores 33 characters in a line, ready for the printer (the printer buffer), the MEMBOT variable on both machines, which is a subsidiary number store used in conjunction with the calculator stack, and KSTATE and STRMS on the Spectrum, dealing with the keyboard and Input/Output respectively.

Single byte variables store a number between 0 and 255 decimal. A two-byte variable holds a number between 0 and 65535. This is because the number of bytes available is 2, hence there are 16 bits, which can store 65536 values (0 is a value). To calculate a two-byte value in decimal, which we must do because this is how values from addresses are returned by the computer, we use (value of least significant byte) + 256* (value of most significant byte). Except in the case of line numbers for program lines, the *first* byte is the *least* significant byte of any two-byte number.

The set of system variables we will look at are those variables which hold the addresses of the boundaries between areas of memory. Since some memory areas move around, the computer must know where each area starts. We can also use this information to find out what the current state of memory organisation is for use in various ways. Below are tables of the ZX81 and Spectrum memory maps with the system variables and their addresses. Note that the system variable names are just mnemonics. They are not recognised by the computer.

ZX81: MEMORY MAP WITH SYSTEM VARIABLES

Memory Area	System Variable	Addresses	Contents Returned by:
	(Fixed)	(16384)	
System Variables			
	(Fixed)	(16509)	
Program Listing			
	D-FILE	16396/7	PEEK 16396+256*PEEK 16397
Display File			
	VARS	16400/1	PEEK 16400+256*PEEK 16401
Variables			
Marker Byte	(Single byte containing CHR$ 128)		
	E-LINE	16404/5	PEEK 16404+256*PEEK 16405
Work Space			
	STKBOT	16410/1	PEEK 16410+256*PEEK 16411
Calculator Stack			
	STKEND	16412/3	PEEK 16412+256*PEEK 16413
Spare Memory			
	(Stack pointer-not accessible with BASIC commands)		
Machine Stack			
	ERR-SP	16386/7	PEEK 16386+256*PEEK 16387
Gosub Stack			
	RAMTOP	16388/9	PEEK 16388+256*PEEK 16389

The size of various portions of memory occupied on the ZX81 can be found by entering (as direct commands) the following:

Program listing: PRINT PEEK 16396 + 256*PEEK 16397-16509
Program, variables, display file and system variables:
PRINT PEEK 16404 + 256* PEEK 16405-16384
Approximate memory left for program:
PRINT PEEK 16386 + 256*PEEK 16387 – PEEK 16412 – 256*PEEK 16413

This returns only the approximate number of free memory bytes, since it does not take into account the size of the machine stack, because we cannot access the stack pointer. Actual memory is always less than the value returned.

SPECTRUM: MEMORY MAP WITH SYSTEM VARIABLES

Memory Area	System Variable	Addresses	Contents returned by:
	P-RAMT	23732/3	PEEK 23732 +256*PEEK 23733
User Defined Graphics			
	UDG	23675/6	PEEK 23675 +256*PEEK 23676
Byte with Code 60			
	RAMTOP	23730/1	PEEK 23730 +256*PEEK 23731
Byte with Code 0			
GOSUB STACK			
	Not accessible with BASIC		
MACHINE STACK			
	Not accessible with BASIC		
SPARE MEMORY			
	STKEND	26353/4	PEEK 26353 +256*PEEK 26354
CALCULATOR STACK			
	STKBOT	26351/2	PEEK 26351 +256*PEEK 26352
TEMP. WORK SPACE			
Byte with Code 13			
INPUT DATA			
	WORKSP	23649/50	PEEK 23649 +256*PEEK 23650
Byte with Code 128			
Byte with Code 13			
Current Line Keyed In			
	E-LINE	23641/2	PEEK 23641 +256*PEEK 23642
Byte with Code 128			
VARIABLES STORE			
	VARS	23627/8	PEEK 23627 +256*PEEK 23628
BASIC PROGRAM STORAGE			
	PROG	23635/6	PEEK 23635 +256*PEEK 23636
Byte with Code 128			
CHANNEL INFO.			
	CHANS	23631/2	PEEK 23631 +256*PEEK 23632
(Microdrive Maps)			
	Fixed	(23734)	

Note that various marker bytes are used to separate areas of memory, as indicated. Program length (listing only) is given by (PEEK 23627 + 256*PEEK 23628) – (PEEK 23635 + 256*PEEK 23636), i.e. VARS less PROG. Program and variables memory requirement is given by E-LINE less PROG, with the PEEKs required again as given above. All memory areas below 23734 are fixed, with their addresses being as given in the previous Unit (see the Memory Map diagram). Without the microdrive, CHANS will be fixed at address 23734. An alternative method of determining free memory left on the Spectrum is to use the following, which uses a routine in the ROM memory. The number of bytes of free memory i.e. the size of the spare memory section, is given by PRINT 65536 – USR 7962.

We can use the system variable VARS to determine how numbers are stored in the computer. Each different type of variable needs to be identifiable as the correct type, i.e. as a loop control variable, as a string variable, etc. This is done by altering the first three bits in the appropriate letter codes. (Bits in a byte are actually numbered right to left, starting from Ø. In the eight bit byte ØØ1ØØØØØ , for instance, bit 5 is set as 1. Bits 5, 6 and 7 in the byte are the ones referred to above.)

On the Spectrum, all letters in variable names are taken as lower case. These letters all have bit patterns starting Ø11. . . , codes being 97 to 122. The ZX81 letter codes all start with bits ØØ1 . . . , codes 38 to 63. Check the binary equivalents of the letter codes to confirm this. Since these three bits are always the same, the computer can alter them as a signal to indicate which type of variable is being called by a particular variable name, which may be the same as the name of some other type of variable (e.g. A as a simple variable, A(5) as an array variable, A$ as a string variable). The patterns of bytes used are as follows:

Single character variable	Ø11.....
Multiple character variable	1Ø1.....
Loop control variable	111.....
String variable	Ø1Ø.....
Numeric array variable	1ØØ.....
String array variable	11Ø.....

Because the codes for the letters have different values on the ZX81 and Spectrum, the effect on the value stored in the byte is different. After we've discussed exploring the ways variables are stored, the form for each type of variable is given, with the change in the letter code noted for both the ZX81 and Spectrum.

The next program inputs a value for the numeric variable A. This will be entered into the VARS area as the first variable stored. Line 3Ø PEEKs the value of the VARS system variable, and adds the value of the loop variable F, then PEEKs this address. The first value returned by the expression in brackets (F = Ø) is the address of the first byte of the variables store. For a numeric variable on the ZX81, this holds the name of the variable, stored as its Code + 64, if the variable name is a single character. On the Spectrum it is stored as the code of the *lower case* letter, unchanged. Key in the program and input various numbers.

```
1Ø INPUT A
2Ø PRINT "A=";A
3Ø FOR F= Ø TO 5
4Ø PRINT PEEK(PEEK 164ØØ+256*P
   EEK 164Ø1 +F)
5Ø NEXT F
6Ø GOTO 1Ø
```

Spectrum users: change the PEEK expression to:

```
40  PRINT PEEK (PEEK 23627 + 256*PEEK 23628 + F)
```

Input 1.5. The display will be like this:

ZX81		*Spectrum*	
A = 1.5		A = 1.5	
102	(= Code A + 64)	122	(= Code of lower case a)
129	(5 byte number follows)	129	(5 byte number follows)
64		64	
0		0	
0		0	
0		0	

Change the variable name in line 10 to confirm the code. The first byte of the 5-byte number is the exponent byte, the following four are the mantissa, the number the exponent acts on to get the numeric value. The Spectrum has a special form of this for integers. (See below for more on numbers.)

Change the variable name to, for example, AB5, or other variable names with more than a single letter in the name, and run the program again. You can then confirm that numeric variables are stored in these forms:

Single Character Variable

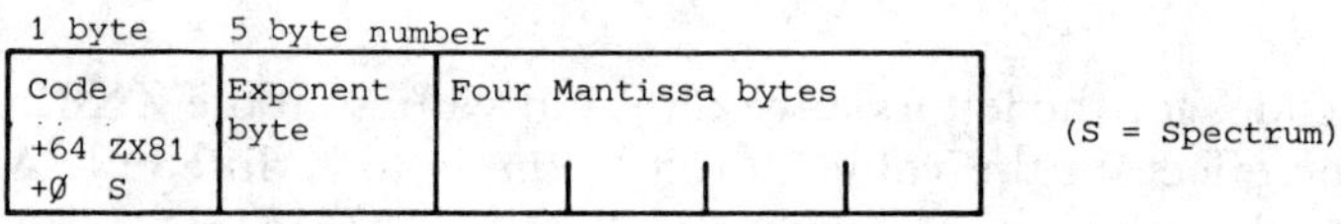

Multiple Character Name Variable

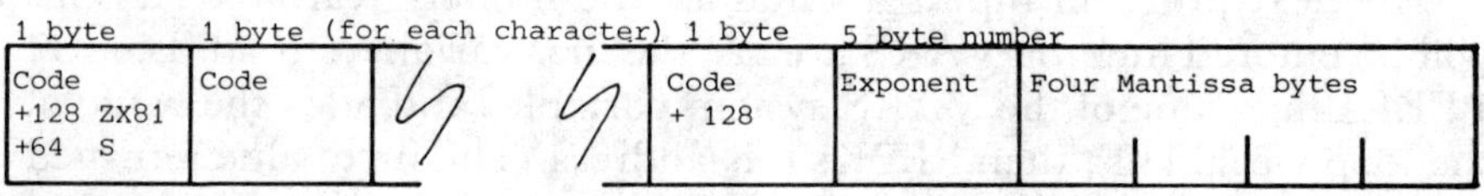

First character and last character only are stored as code plus values indicated. Other characters are stored as the standard character codes.

The other forms of variable are stored in the byte sequences shown below. Write programs to confirm these memory arrangements. You will need a loop that prints the correct number of bytes. The FOR-NEXT sequence, for example, which takes 18 bytes, can be simply programmed by deleting lines 10, 20 and 60 in the program above, and changing the loop to 0 TO 17.

Loop Control Variable

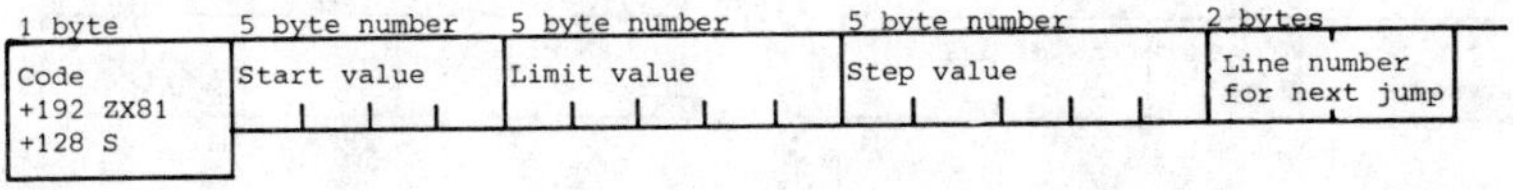

The control character is stored as code + 192 on the ZX81, + 128 on the Spectrum. The value is incremented or decremented by the step value each time the NEXT instruction is executed, and the value checked against the limit value after each such change. The line number (stored as *more* significant byte first, as are the program line numbers) is the line number of the FOR...TO instruction plus 1, as this is the destination line for the NEXT instruction to jump to.

String Variable

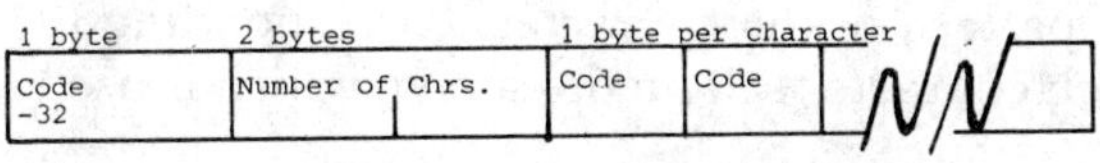

The single letter name is stored as the code less 32 on both the ZX81 and Spectrum. The number of characters is what is read by the LEN instruction. For a null string, this is zero, and no character bytes are stored.

Numeric Array Variable

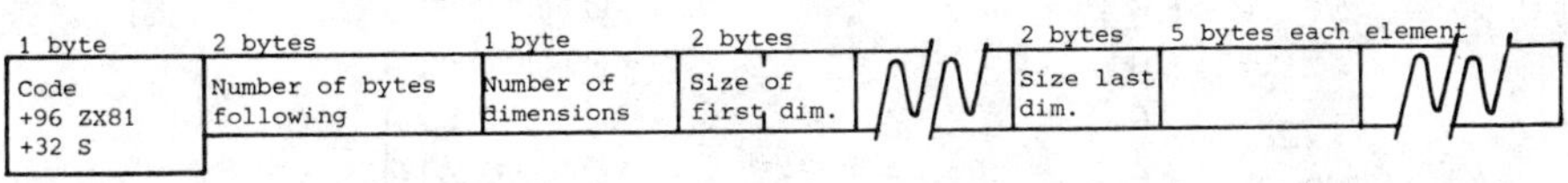

Notice that an array such as A(7) is a single dimensioned array. (It will require 1 + 2 + 1 + 2 + (7*5) = 41 bytes.) The bytes storing the size of each dimension enable the computer to keep track of a multi-dimensioned array stored in a linear sequence. For example, DIM A(3,3) sets a sequence of the eight data bytes, plus 9*5 bytes to hold:

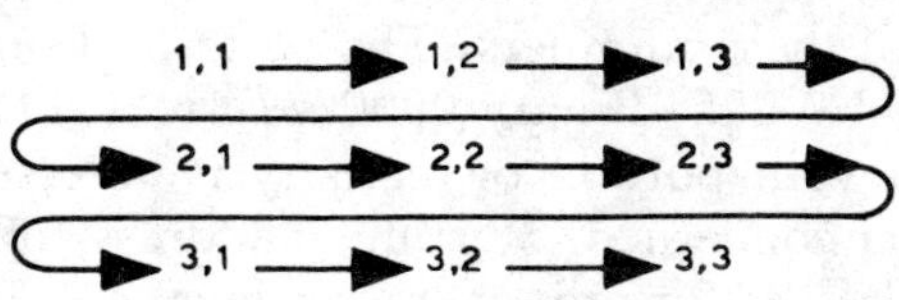

Work out how a 3-D array, say A(2,3,4) will be stored.

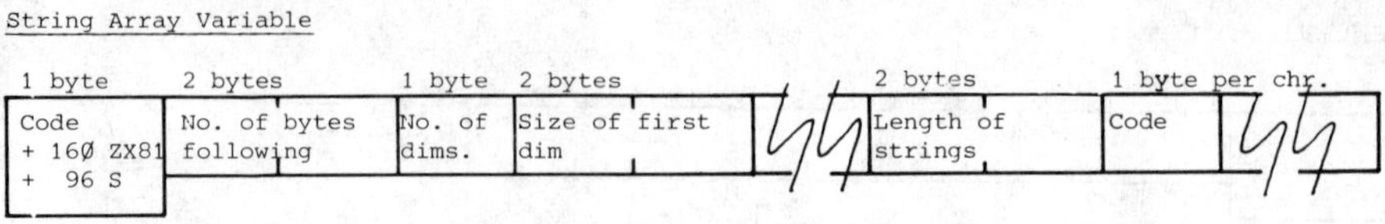

You should now see why string arrays must have fixed length strings, since otherwise the computer could not use the length of string datum to step through the linear sequence to find the appropriate set of character codes making up an element in the array.

The next manipulation we will look at concerns the way the ROM memory holds the characters to be printed on the screen.

Starting at address 768Ø on the ZX81, and at 15616 on the Spectrum, each character is held in a sequence of 8 bytes of memory. The binary number of each byte represents, in this case, a sequence of Ø's and 1's, which hold the pattern of the character, corresponding to the 8 × 8 grid of points in each character cell on the screen which is used to print a character.

If we take the letter A, for example, it is represented like this:

DECIMAL NUMBER	BINARY NUMBER
Ø	ØØØØØØØØ
6Ø	ØØ1111ØØ
66	Ø1ØØØØ1Ø
66	Ø1ØØØØ1Ø
126	Ø111111Ø
66	Ø1ØØØØ1Ø
66	Ø1ØØØØ1Ø
Ø	ØØØØØØØØ

A zero is read as an instruction to leave blank the corresponding point on the screen, and a 1 indicates it is to be blacked in.

The following program will illustrate the principles. It takes one of the 8-byte sequences of numbers stored in ROM and gives the decimal and binary forms of these numbers. The pattern of ones can be seen. Remember Decimal Ø-255, Binary ØØØØØØØØ to 11111111, is held in each byte. The relevant portion of memory is accessed by using the code of the character concerned. Starting at address 768Ø on the ZX81, the first of the addresses for any character is given by 768Ø + CODE (Character)*8. The eight addresses are then PEEKed one by one, and the decimal number given then the binary form printed out. Lines 11Ø and 13Ø convert the decimal to binary and print it.

Whilst the Spectrum characters are held at a specific address in ROM, the system variable CHARS, which is at addresses 236Ø6 and 236Ø7, holds the start address of the character memory sequence, and can be POKEd with different values to start the sequence elsewhere in memory. This can be used to define a new start point for the character set in RAM, and define a whole new character set on the Spectrum, in addition to the facility for user-defined graphics (which will be dealt with in Unit W2). CHARS returns a value which is the start address of the characters, *less 256*. The character set that is stored in ROM starts with the Space symbol (code 32) and runs in sequence to © (code 127).

To access the right sequence in ROM, we must use the start value given by CHARS, which is 15360, plus the character code multiplied by 8, just as on the ZX81. The fact that CHARS points to 256 bytes below the start of the printable character set adjusts for the fact that the first character that can be accessed has code 32 (since 32*8 = 256).

For the program below, therefore, Spectrum users need to put LET A = 15630 in line 10, which is the normal value given by PEEKing the CHARS system variable, and the right address in ROM is accessed.

```
 10 LET A=7680
 20 PRINT "INPUT A CHARACTER"
 30 INPUT A$
 40 CLS
 50 LET C=CODE A$
 60 LET D=8*C+A
 70 FOR X=0 TO 7
 80 LET L=PEEK (D+X)
 90 PRINT D+X;TAB 6;L
100 FOR Z=18 TO 11 STEP -1
110 PRINT AT X, Z;L-2*INT (L/2)
130 LET L=INT (L/2)
140 NEXT Z
150 NEXT X
```

If we add:

```
120  IF L – 2*INT (L/2) = 1 THEN PRINT
     AT X,Z + 10; "■"
```

we can print out a large version of the character. The routine will only work for the standard characters and graphics (codes 1 – 63 on the ZX81). Inverse characters and functions on the ZX81 are not held in this form. All Spectrum characters up to code 127 can be accessed.

We can use this principle to produce any size character we want, within the limits of the screen.

The next program allows a string of up to 4 characters to be printed out. You should be able to follow the same steps in this program as in the previous one – the method is essentially the same, working on a string of characters, rather than a single character, and only using the print routine. To fit 3 lines of 4 characters (which would take 24 lines) we neglect the first (top) byte, since this is blank for all the letters and numbers. This lets us fit 3 lines in, but graphics characters will look strange, since they do use the top line. A different method is used to read out the binary values for printing. To avoid complex manipulations of PRINT AT values, which would be required if we used the system in the previous program, each line of the ROM is checked for each character in turn across the line, which enables a continuous PRINT operation.

Each binary value is checked in turn to see if it is Ø or a 1 by doubling the value of X (line 18Ø), so that it is either >128 (1) or <127 (Ø). Line 15Ø takes 128 away if a 1 is found. If you do not understand this process, take any binary number and trace the operation through lines 12Ø to 19Ø.

```
  5 REM "BIGPRINT"
  6 REM *ALLOWS 3 LINES OF 4 *
        *CHARACTERS BY OMIT- *
        *TING TOP LINE(BLANK *
        *FOR LETTERS AND     *
        *NUMBERS) OF 8*8 GRID*
 10 DIM A(4)
 20 PRINT "INPUT STRING (MAX 12
LETTERS/NUMBERS)"
 25 INPUT A$
 30 CLS
 35 REM *FOR EACH LINE*
 40 FOR F=1 TO 3
 45 REM *GET CODE INTO ARRAY *
        *FOR EACH LETTER     *
 50 FOR L=1 TO 4
 60 LET A(L)= CODE A$(L)
 70 NEXT L
 75 REM *UPDATE A$*
 80 LET A$=A$(5 TO )
 85 REM *BYTES 1 TO 7 OF     *
        *CHARACTER IN ROM    *
 90 FOR B=1 TO 7
 95 REM *FOR EACH LETTER OF  *
        *LINE                *
100 FOR C=1 TO 4
105 REM *GET BYTE VALUE*
110 LET X= PEEK (7680+A(C)*8+B)
115 REM *FOR EACH BIT*
120 FOR V=0 TO 7
125 REM *IF ZERO THEN JUMP*
130 IF X<128 THEN GOTO 170
140 PRINT "■";
145 REM *DECREMENT CHECK     *
        *VALUE               *
150 LET X=X-128
160 GOTO 180

170 PRINT " ";
180 LET X=X*2
185 REM *NEXT BIT*
190 NEXT V
195 REM *NEXT LETTER OF LINE*
200 NEXT C
205 REM *NEXT BYTE OF ROM*
210 NEXT B
215 REM *NEXT GROUP OF 4*
220 NEXT F
230 REM **END**
```

Spectrum users must insert 15360 in place of 7680 in line 120.

The program, "HEADLINER" in the program library, uses the character array in ROM to print banner headlines on the printer. If you inspect this program, you will see that it has a method of enabling the inverse characters of the ZX81 to be printed by changing them into normal characters (using CHR$(CODE A$ – 128)) to access the pattern in memory, then reversing it again when it comes to print it.

RAMTOP may be set to a lower value to give memory space outside that usually used by the operating system. This has an application which is occasionally useful on the ZX81, regarding the use of CLS after SCROLL has been utilised. This does *not* apply on the Spectrum. Clearing the screen can take a long time after scrolling. Try this to illustrate:

```
10  FOR F = 1 TO 30
20  SCROLL
30  PRINT "XXXXXXXXXXXXXX"
40  NEXT F
50  CLS
```

This is due to the fact that SCROLL interferes with the way the display file is set up on a ZX81, with more than 3.25k of RAM available – with a full screen of spaces where no characters exist. A PRINT line after SCROLL is just the required length, with nothing filling up the line if there are no characters. To clear the screen, the ZX81 counts up 24 new lines, then inserts spaces to recreate a full display file. If less than 3.25k are available, an empty screen is just 24 newline characters. RAMTOP is set with 0 in address 16388 and 128 in 16389 on switch-on (0 + 256*128 = 32768, the address of the first non-existent byte).

POKEing values to set RAMTOP below 19634 (16509 + 3.25k) will set up the minimal display file and CLS will act instantly. Your program must be less than 3.25k (say 3k as returned by the commands given above). The convenient value to use is 76 poked into 16389. This sets RAMTOP as 0 (value of 16388 unchanged) + 256*76 = 19456, which is rather more convenient than POKE 16388,76 followed by POKE 16389,177 (177 + 256*76 = 19633). Insert 45 POKE 16389,76 into the program above and run it again. Note that if you NEW the program and then key in PRINT PEEK 16389, you will still get 76. RAMTOP must be re-set by POKEing the correct value (128) or by switching off and on again to re-set.

On the Spectrum, RAMTOP is moved using CLEAR. The instruction CLEAR (N) resets RAMTOP to the address given by N. RAMTOP is reset to this value, and remains at this address until reset by CLEAR (or switching off and on again.) It is *not* reset by NEW.

The procedure given below for storing data above RAMTOP is less useful than it is on the ZX81, because the Spectrum can MERGE a program with another LOADed in from tape (see Unit W2). This program can be mostly data (although it must have program lines). However, this method will work on the Spectrum, and shows the technique of moving information around in memory. If you progress to machine-code programming, this is one way in which you can store machine code.

RAMTOP may be moved so as to reserve space at the top of memory. On the ZX81, this area will not be affected by NEW or CLEAR, or the automatic NEW that occurs with LOAD. It can be used to store data for use by another program, after the data have been defined by a previous program. This procedure, available with less complications on some computers, is performed as follows on the ZX81.

i) New values are POKEd into the RAMTOP system variable, so that the system considers the top of RAM to be lower than address 32767. This reserves space above the new RAMTOP value. NEW is then used. POKEing RAMTOP has no effect until NEW has been used. How much space is reserved depends on the number of bytes of data we require to store. (Spectrum: See above for resetting RAMTOP.)

ii) The program to use the data must have been written and stored on cassette. This has instructions to copy into the variables area the data stored. It *must initialise the same variables or arrays for data in the same sequence* as the program which provides the data.

iii) The program to store the data intialises the arrays or variables for the data *first*, before any other variables. The program is then run. The required number of bytes are taken from the start of the variables area (found using VARS), and copied to the area above RAMTOP (found using RAMTOP).

iv) Program 2 is then loaded. It initialises the variables as did program 1, finds VARS and RAMTOP, and reverses the procedure, PEEKing RAMTOP and POKEing the values found into the variables area. It can then proceed to use the data.

The amount of memory needed for storage is calculated from the information given above about the method of storage of variables. As an example, let us assume we want to store an array D(2Ø) for use by another program. We will use this as a short example program. In practice, the technique will require a second program to use the data to have been written and SAVEd, but the examples are short enough to key in.

Reference to the information about variables shows us that an array D(2Ø) requires 1Ø6 bytes. On a ZX81, we must set RAMTOP as 32768 – 1Ø6 = 32662. This is the address of the first non-existent byte, and will be the address of our first storage byte. To set RAMTOP to this value, we POKE 16389,INT(32662/256) as a command, followed by POKE 16388,32662 – 256*INT(32662/256). Of course you could use the computer to work these out beforehand, and POKE the values directly. NEW the computer, then enter this program and run it. On the Spectrum, RAMTOP is set with CLEAR, and can be done simply by using:

CLEAR (PEEK 2373Ø + 256*23731 – 1Ø6)

```
  5 REM "DSTORE"
 1Ø REM **DATA ABOVE RAMTOP**
 2Ø DIM D(2Ø)
 3Ø FOR F=1 TO 2Ø
 4Ø LET D(F)=F*F
 5Ø NEXT F
 6Ø LET VARS=PEEK 164ØØ+256*PEE
    K 164Ø1
 7Ø LET RAMTOP=PEEK 16388+256*P
    EEK 16389
 8Ø FOR F=Ø TO 1Ø5
 9Ø POKE (RAMTOP+F),PEEK (VARS+F)
1ØØ NEXT F
```

The first active line (2Ø) dimensions the storage array. The loop of lines 3Ø to 5Ø merely insert some values into the array. Lines 6Ø and 7Ø find the values of VARS and RAMTOP. The loop of lines 8Ø to 1ØØ stores each byte of the variables store that contains array D above RAMTOP. Spectrum users must insert the correct PEEKs in lines 6Ø and 7Ø to get the values of the VARS and RAMTOP system variables. The same must be done with the data retrieval program below.

Now use NEW, and enter the program to retrieve the data. This reverses the procedure. After initialising D(2Ø), and finding VARS and RAMTOP, it POKEs the value of each byte stored above RAMTOP into the bytes of the variables area containing the array. Lines 7Ø to 8Ø print out the array values.

```
 1 REM "DFETCH"
 5 REM **RETRIEVE STORED DATA
       **FROM MEMORY    ******
1Ø DIM D(2Ø)
2Ø LET VARS=PEEK 164ØØ+256*PEE
   K 164Ø1
3Ø LET RAMTOP=PEEK 16388+256*P
   EEK 16389
4Ø FOR F=Ø TO 1Ø5
5Ø POKE (VARS+F),PEEK (RAMTOP+F)
6Ø NEXT F
7Ø FOR F=1 TO 2Ø
8Ø PRINT D(F)
9Ø NEXT F
```

On the ZX81 *only*, you can use CLEAR: the array will be wiped from memory, but remains safe above RAMTOP. Running the program again will retrieve the data once more. This is obviously a technique useful not only for passing data between programs, but also for allowing CLEAR to be used and still having current data (i.e. that not assigned by LET statements) preserved. This does *not* apply to the Spectrum, since CLEAR re-sets RAMTOP.

The complete list of system variables for both the ZX81 and the Spectrum is given in Appendix V. The timing variable FRAMES is used in the "REACT" program analysed in Unit V3.

MORE ON NUMBERS AND COMPUTERS

The way in which numbers are manipulated by the operating system in a computer does not concern us here, but the way numbers are held, and their form, are important in computing, even if the precise manner in which calculations are carried out is a separate topic. We will deal here with enough detail of the binary system to enable 5-byte floating point to be understood.

We briefly introduced the binary system earlier. To explain further the use of a system using powers of 2, and how any number can be represented *to a certain level of accuracy*, key in this program:

```
10 REM "POWERS OF TWO"
20 PRINT "POWERS OF TWO"
30 PRINT "-------------"
40 PRINT "2**N";TAB 10;"N";TAB
   16;"2** -N"
50 PRINT
60 PRINT TAB 6;"1   0   1.0"
70 FOR F=1 TO 16
80 PRINT TAB ( 17-LEN STR$ (2**F
   ));2**F;TAB 10;F;TAB (14+(F
   >3));2**-F
90 NEXT F
```

(Replace ** by ↑ for the Spectrum at each occurrence in the program).

You will get a display like this:

```
POWERS OF TWO
-------------
2**N      N     2** -N

     1    0    1.0
     2    1    0.5
     4    2    0.25
     8    3    0.125
    16    4     .0625
    32    5     .03125
    64    6     .015625
   128    7     .0078125
   256    8     .00390625
   512    9     .001953125
  1024   10     .0009765625
  2048   11     .00048828125
  4096   12     .00024414063
  8192   13     .00012207031
 16384   14     .000061035156
 32768   15     .000030517578
 65536   16     .000015258789
```

Notice that we have positive powers of two on the right, giving integer values, and negative powers, giving fractions which are represented as 'decimal decimals'. The emphasis in the comment above about accuracy stems from the fact that there are limits to the accuracy obtainable with *every* number system. The fraction 1/3 is never accurately represented in the decimal system, however many decimal places are used. The same goes for many numbers in both decimal and binary notation. If you study the display it should be apparent that with the binary system, only numbers equal to certain decimal values are accurately represented. Decimal .6875, equal to 1/2 + 1/8 + 1/16 is accurately represented by binary .1Ø11, for example, but with a single byte (8 bits), any number varying by .ØØ1953125 (2^{-9}) above or below the value represented in the byte will appear the same to a computer reading this byte.

To increase the accuracy of representation of numbers, a larger number of bytes is needed. This also allows larger numbers to be dealt with. The ZX81 and Spectrum use "5-byte floating point" representation of numbers. The "FLOAT" program gives the decimal value held in each byte of the five by PEEKing the variables area:

```
 1 REM *FLOAT*
 2 REM PRINTS FLOATING POINT
 FORM OF A NUMBER
10 PRINT "ENTER A NUMBER"
20 INPUT N
30 PRINT "THE NUMBER ";N;" IS
HELD","IN THE ZX81 AS:-"
40 FOR F=1 TO 5
45 REM PEEKS START OF VARIABLE
STORE (VARS) AREA IN MEMORY
50 PRINT PEEK ( PEEK 16400+256
* PEEK 16401+F);" ";
60 NEXT F
```

On the Spectrum you should change Line 5Ø to read PRINT PEEK (PEEK 23684 + 256*PEEK 23685 + F). Input only *non-integer* values (we'll explain why this is the case a little later).

If you input 2.4, you will get a screen display of:

13Ø 25 153 153 154

Try other numbers. There is no obvious pattern to the decimal values, other than the first number not varying much from around 128 unless you input very large or small numbers. This is the *exponent* byte (as with the E notation). The next program, "FIVEBYTE", displays the mantissa number (the other four bytes) in decimal and binary form, and the exponent byte in decimal form:

```
10 REM "FIVEBYTE"
20 PRINT "INPUT NUMBER"
30 INPUT N
40 PRINT "NUMBER=";N
50 LET EXP= PEEK (1+ PEEK 1640
0+256* PEEK 16401)
60 PRINT "EXPONENT=";EXP
70 LET P=EXP-128
80 IF P <> -128 THEN PRINT "2
** ";P;"=";2 ** P
90 IF EXP=0 THEN PRINT "USED F
OR ZERO ONLY"
```

```
 100 PRINT "MANTISSA BYTES:-"
 110 FOR F=2 TO 5
 120 PRINT TAB (F-2)*8; PEEK (F+
 PEEK 16400+256* PEEK 16401);
 130 NEXT F
 140 FOR F=2 TO 5
 150 LET D= PEEK (F+ PEEK 16400+
256* PEEK 16401)
 160 LET B$=""
 170 LET L= INT (D/2)
 180 REM LET A$=("1" AND D-2*L)+
("0" AND D-2*L=0)
 181 LET A$= STR$ (D-2*L)
 190 LET B$=A$+B$
 200 LET D=L
 210 IF D>0 THEN GOTO 170
 220 IF LEN B$<8 THEN LET B$="00
000000"(1 TO (8- LEN B$))+B$
 230 PRINT TAB (F-2)*8;B$
 240 NEXT F
```

(Once again, on the Spectrum change ** to ↑ at every appearance. Line 5Ø needs to be changed to read LET EXP = PEEK (1 + PEEK 23684 + 256*PEEK 23685) to give the start of the Spectrum variables area. Change 164ØØ to 23684 and 164Ø1 to 23685 in lines 12Ø and 15Ø also.)

A number stored in 5-byte floating point notation has an exponent byte, which acts, as with the decimal E notation, to shift the binary point along to the correct place.

The exponent value is stored as exponent plus 128, and can hence be negative or positive. It works in powers of two, and the value of this (exponent raised to the power of two) is given in the program. The representation of zero has a special form, such that the exponent is Ø, and the values of all the other bytes is also zero. The value stored in the exponent byte is thus between 1 and 255, giving possible exponent values between − 127 and + 127. The range of numbers covered is then what would be presented if our "POWERS OF TWO" program went on to 127 rather than just 16.

The mantissa value (represented in the next four bytes) is converted to the numeric value by multiplying it by 2 raised to the power of the exponent: $N = M*2^e$, where M is the mantissa value and e is the exponent (value stored in exponent byte less 128). This process can also be considered as moving the binary point the number of bits given by the exponent.

The mantissa bytes are considered as a single sequence of binary digits, with the binary point at the beginning. The program gives the values stored in each byte (as with the "FLOAT" program), and then converts to binary to give the mantissa sequence. Since the first bit of the mantissa sequence is always 1 (the mantissa is always between .5 decimal and 1 decimal, but never reaches 1, i.e. Ø.5< = m<1) the first bit is used as a *sign bit*. If the number is *positive*, the first bit is changed to Ø. If it is *negative*, the first bit is set to 1. This is used as a means of handling negative numbers, since all the numbers generated in the floating point notation are positive, and an equivalent to the ' – ' sign is needed to show negation.

Input Ø.75 into the computer when prompted. The display will be like this:

```
INPUT NUMBER
NUMBER = Ø.75
EXPONENT = 128
2**Ø = 1                                    (↑ on Spectrum)
MANTISSA BYTES:
64      Ø       Ø       Ø
Ø1ØØØØØØ
        ØØØØØØØØ
                ØØØØØØØØ
                        ØØØØØØØØ
```

The evaluation is as follows. The first bit is a zero in the mantissa. This indicates a positive number. The first bit is changed to a 1, and the value of the mantissa is now .11ØØØ...Ø. The trailing zeros are ignored. Binary .11 is decimal Ø.75 . The exponent value is Ø, and 2 raised to the power Ø is 1. So we have a value of Ø.75*1 = Ø.75. If you input – Ø.75, the display is identical except for the first mantissa byte (+ 128) because of the first bit now being 1, and the first mantissa bit, changed to 1 to indicate a negative number. This is left as 1, and evaluation then proceeds as before.

Now input 3.75. The exponent is 13Ø, 2**2 (↑ on Spectrum) is 4, and the mantissa bits hold the sequence Ø111Ø... The first bit changes to 1, and this gives .1111 binary, Ø.9375 decimal. 4*Ø.9375 = 3.75 . The alternative way of viewing the process is to consider the exponent as moving the binary point along. In this example, we have the sequence .1111, and since the exponent value is 2, the binary point moves the same number of places to the right, to give 11.11 , which is 3.75 in decimal. In the previous case, with Ø.75, the exponent value was Ø, so the point was not moved, and the bits were .11 . Negative exponents move the binary point to the left, adding zeros.

The Spectrum has a special representation for integers in the range + 65535 to – 65535, in which the first byte (exponent byte) is zero, as is the fifth byte. The second byte acts as a sign byte, holding Ø if the number is positive, and 255 if the number is negative. The third and fourth byte hold the number (least significant byte first). You can use the "FIVEBYTE" program to investigate this representation if you are using a Spectrum.

To illustrate rounding errors and an otherwise puzzling aspect of the representation of numbers, input 1/2 into the "FIVEBYTE" program. We get exponent byte = 128, exponent 128 – 128 = Ø, and a zero in the first bit. This changes to a 1, and we have .1ØØ.... Exponent is zero, so we don't move the binary point and get .1ØØ...., which is

Ø.5, and equal to a half. Thus far all is well. If we like, we can consider that we got .1ØØ.... and multiplied it by zero to get our half. As we said above, the two processes are identical. But now input Ø.5. This should be the same, but instead we get exponent equalling 127, and Ø111....1 (thirty-one 1's)! We seem to have an error. However it is a pretty small one, though it explains why the computer rounds its numbers. To avoid considering ½ as not equal to Ø.5 it has to take into account the fact that the decimal to binary conversions have these inaccuracies. Binary addition of two 1's causes a Ø to be placed in that byte, and a 1 is placed in the next column to the left. (If you're interested, the other rules for addition are: 1 and Ø give 1, Ø and Ø give Ø, three ones (1, 1 and a carried 1) give 1, carry 1 to next column on the left. Try a few simple sums!) This means that if a 1 is added to the least significant bit of our sequence of ones:

```
...... 1111
          1
-----------
          Ø

         1      (carry)
         Ø

        1       (carry)
        Ø
       1        (carry)
                etc
```

all the 1's will become zeros, and the last carry would put 1 in the first bit, which would make it the same representation as the ½ sequence, but this also has a 1 in it. This forces a carry to a non-existent bit to the left of the mantissa. This gives us 1.Ø as our binary, and the exponent shifts this (exponent = – 1) to .1ØØ...., which is correct. Or we can consider this as 1.Ø binary (1 decimal) multiplied by 2^{-1}(Ø.5). So the error is in the least significant bit. The size of the error is thus 2^{-33}, the value of the right-hand 1. This is fairly small! The computer rounds numbers to ensure these inaccuracies do not cause errors. It considers numbers equal if the difference between them is less than a certain amount. Rounding errors can still build up under some circumstances, however, and it is important to note that no computer performs totally accurate arithmetic, except with integer values.

You may be a little overwhelmed by numbers at this point, but before we give them a rest we should introduce you to another numbering system – Hexadecimal.

This is another numbering system much used in computing, although it has no practical application for us at present since the

Hexadecimal system (often abbreviated to Hex) is primarily used in machine-code programming which is beyond the scope of this text. Whereas binary is base 2, and decimal base 1Ø, hexadecimal is base 16. This is a convenient system for computers using 8-bit words, since $16 \times 16 = 256$. Any value which is held in a single byte can thus be represented by a two-digit hexadecimal code. The system uses the digits Ø to 9, and goes on with A, B, C, D, E and F, to represent the numbers 1 to 16. Here is how the system counts:

Decimal	Hexadecimal	
Ø	Ø	$(\emptyset \times 16^{\emptyset})$
1	1	$(1 \times 16^{\emptyset})$
–	–	
–	–	
9	9	$(9 \times 16^{\emptyset})$
1Ø	A	$(1\emptyset \times 16^{\emptyset})$
11	B	$(11 \times 16^{\emptyset})$
–	–	
15	F	$(15 \times 16^{\emptyset})$
16	1Ø	$(1 \times 16^{1}) + (\emptyset \times 16^{\emptyset})$
17	11	$(1 \times 16^{1}) + (1 \times 16^{\emptyset})$
–	–	
25	19	$(1 \times 16^{1}) + (9 \times 16^{\emptyset})$
26	1A	$(1 \times 16^{1}) + (1\emptyset \times 16^{\emptyset})$
–	–	
31	1F	$(1 \times 16^{1}) + (15 \times 16^{\emptyset})$
32	2Ø	$(2 \times 16^{1}) + (\emptyset \times 16^{\emptyset})$
–	–	
–	–	
154	9A	$(9 \times 16^{1}) + (1\emptyset \times 16^{\emptyset})$
155	9B	$(9 \times 16^{1}) + (11 \times 16^{\emptyset})$
–	–	
159	9F	$(9 \times 16^{1}) + (15 \times 16^{\emptyset})$
16Ø	AØ	$(1\emptyset \times 16^{1}) + (\emptyset \times 16^{\emptyset})$
–	–	
–	–	
25Ø	FA	$(15 \times 16^{1}) + (1\emptyset \times 16^{\emptyset})$
–	–	
254	FE	$(15 \times 16^{1}) + (14 \times 16^{\emptyset})$
255	FF	$(15 \times 16^{1}) + (15 \times 16^{\emptyset})$

As with any number system, we could go on (256 is 1ØØ hex, etc.), but the use of hexadecimal is in representing binary numbers in a more convenient form than strings of 1's and Ø's, which are difficult to read and easy to make mistakes with (unless you are a computer!).

The advantage of hexadecimal notation is that any 8-bit binary number is convertible to hex far more easily than into decimal, due to the relationship of base 2 and base 16 numbers. Base 16 is base 2^4, and this means the 8 bits of a byte can be divided into two sets of four bits (remember 1111 binary = 15 decimal = F hex) and converted to the corresponding two hex digits. For example, the number 116 decimal is in binary Ø111Ø1ØØ. Split into two groups of four bits, Ø111 and Ø1ØØ, we convert each group to a hex digit.

Ø111 binary (7 decimal) is 7 hex
Ø1ØØ binary (4 decimal) is 4 hex

The number in hex is 74. Check this: $(7 \times 16^1) + (4 \times 16^0) = 112 + 4 = 116$. Again, 93 decimal is Ø1Ø111Ø1 binary:

Ø1Ø1 binary (5 decimal) is 5 hex
11Ø1 binary (13 decimal) is D hex

The number in hex is 5D. $(5 \times 16^1) + (13 \times 16^0) = 80 + 13 = 93$

To avoid possible confusion when both hexadecimal and binary numbers are being used, a small h should be used after a hexadecimal number. Our examples above would be 74h and 5Dh. Hex numbers are grouped in twos, and the leading zero should be used for numbers less than 16 decimal, so that 12 decimal should be written ØCh, and not C or Ch.

Similarly, numbers up to 65535 decimal (held in two bytes of binary), are representable with four hex digits. 1111111111111111 binary is thus FFFF hex, 1Ø1Ø11Ø1ØØ11Ø111Ø is 1Ø1Ø (A)/11Ø1 (D)/ØØ11 (3)/111Ø (E): AD3Eh. Work out the value of this in decimal.

The program library has programs which convert decimal to hex and vice versa (''HEXDEC'' and ''DECHEX''). Analyse these programs to see how they work. The CODE and CHR$ functions are used to check the hex notation, or produce it.

Exercises

1. Alter the ''CHROM'' program to print just the large character, and then the inverse form next to it, by reversing the printing instructions for the character to be printed when a Ø or 1 is found in the binary form.
2. Using the ''BIGPRINT'' program as a basis, store the characters of each line of the large characters in an array, so that a scroll routine can be used to cause the message to disappear off the top of the screen line by line, and re-appear at the bottom.
3. Write programs to store a string array above RAMTOP, and then retrieve it. Use a three-dimensional array.

PART FOUR

APPLICATIONS PROGRAMS AND GAMES

SECTION V: APPLICATIONS PROGRAMS

V1: Programming for Applications

You have been introduced to the full set of ZX81 BASIC instructions. Spectrum users have some additional instructions in the Spectrum superset of BASIC, but we have attempted to show how all necessary operations can be performed on the ZX81 and the Spectrum merely makes some operations easier to implement. We have covered a range of operations, involving loops, lists, array manipulation, sorting, subroutines etc., and the implementation of control structures. These are the raw material of programming. The combination of what you have learned about algorithms, design, program structures, manipulations and methods with the task you wish the computer to perform produces an applications program.

There are no rules to derive algorithms. If there were, they could be coded into a master program that would write our programs for us! We have illustrated ways of thinking about a problem that can help, but each program we wish to write presents a unique problem. Familiarity with the language and control structures, and with existing solutions to a variety of problems, either other people's or your own, make it easier to program. As with most things, the art and craft of programming becomes easier with practice. The importance of keeping notes about programs you have written, and on solutions to problems you have found in analysing other programs, is that it will prevent you re-inventing the wheel. As you write more programs for yourself, you will find that you come to recognise the method (or methods – there is seldom only one way to perform a given task!) by which you can implement and code each module of your program.

Modular, structured program design methods help to break down a programming problem to these recognisable chunks, and you will recognise more aspects of a problem as having been met (and solved!) before as you gain experience.

You will also become familiar with the types of data structure required in a program to make it possible to manipulate the data efficiently, and grasp more quickly and clearly that, for example, a given set of data is more efficiently (i.e. easily) handled in a multi-dimensional array than in separate lists, or that a similar routine in different program modules could be handled by a single subroutine if suitable variables were initialised before calling the subroutine.

Experience cannot be transferred, and there is no substitute for practice, but examples can be given. After the important topic of writing user-friendly programs has been dealt with in the next Unit, we give examples of programs written to perform specific tasks, to illustrate the process of designing applications programs. Games programming is briefly dealt with in the following Units, since games are a good testing ground for problem-solving and programming techniques.

V2: Instructions and Input Checks

If you have written your own program, you know which inputs the program requires, in what form and when. You know, for example, that when "ANOTHER GO?" appears on the screen, you must press the Y key to run the program again.

Now consider what happens if someone else wishes to use the program (or if you return to it after some weeks). There is not enough information available to the user. The term *user-friendly* is applied to programs which have sufficiently clear and precise instructions to tell someone who has never seen the program running exactly what to do. We should always attempt to make our programs at least reasonably user-friendly. To continue the example of running a program again, the line:

```
60  PRINT "AGAIN?"
```

could be followed by

```
70  INPUT A$
80  RUN
```

or

```
70  IF INKEY$ = " " THEN GOTO 70
80  RUN
```

or

```
70  IF INKEY$ = " " THEN GOTO 70
80  IF INKEY$ = "Y" THEN RUN
```

or

```
70  PAUSE 40000
80  RUN
```

These need different responses. We should use for the first "PRESS NEWLINE (ENTER) TO RUN AGAIN", for the second and fourth "HIT ANY KEY TO RUN AGAIN", for the third "AGAIN? (PRESS Y OR N)" or similar instructions appropriate to the program.

We can assume that the user recognises that an input prompt requires string or numeric input, according to its form, but (as we shall see later) there may be reasons for requesting a number in string form, and in any case we must make it clear what is required. We should be careful to use, for example:

"INPUT FIRST WORD"	and not	"INPUT A$"
"ENTER A NUMBER 1 TO 10"	and not	"INPUT X"
"MONTH (1 TO 12)"	and not	"MONTH?"

since if the user does not know what A or A$ are in the context of the program he or she is unlikely to respond correctly, and might try entering JAN or MARCH for the month.

We should also avoid the use of instructions grouped together:

```
10  PRINT "INPUT CURRENT, P.D , KNOWN AND
    UNKNOWN RESISTOR"
```

```
20  INPUT A
30  INPUT B
40  INPUT C
50  INPUT D
```

```
10  DIM A(10,3)
20  PRINT "INPUT MATRIX"
30  FOR F = 1 TO 10
40  FOR N = 1 TO 3
50  INPUT A(F,N)
60  NEXT N
70  NEXT F
```

It is very easy for the user to forget which of the inputs is currently required. The information also fails to include the units of the values required, and does not print the input values on the screen. We should use a format like this:

```
10  PRINT "INPUT CURRENT IN AMPS"
20  INPUT A
30  PRINT "CURRENT = "; A;" AMPS"
40  PRINT "INPUT P.D. IN VOLTS"
50  INPUT B
60  PRINT "P.D = "; B;" VOLTS "
```

This provides both clear instructions and visible input values.

A look at any reasonably complex user-friendly program will show you that a significant portion of any application program is instructions. Instructions should be concise, but only to a degree that still provides adequate information.

Expanded instructions can form part of the documentation of a program, but the program itself must contain the basic instructions required to ensure correct input and manipulation.

The program "MATMULT" in the program library has a better approach to the array entry problem. Try to write one yourself, then compare the two routines.

The combination of good instructions and input checks is the best method of reducing user error. The human being is less reliable than the computer, and far more inaccurate results or program crashes occur due to input error than happen due to bugs in the program, assuming it has successfully completed a sequence of dry runs.

Checks to reduce the possibility of human error, or prevent bad effects from it, are the means by which a program is 'idiot-proofed' or 'mug-trapped'. Commercial programs designed for inexperienced users with no programming knowledge often have as much space devoted to input checks as to the program proper. We can assume some awareness in the users of our programs, and trust that they will enter 2 and not TWO, for example, but check routines can ensure that simple keyboard errors are not passed over. Subtle errors or straightforward mistakes are less easy to deal with.

It is a simple matter to check that an entered value is within an acceptable range:

```
10  PRINT "INPUT MONTH (1 TO 12)"
20  INPUT M
30  IF M>12 OR M<1 THEN GOTO 10
```

Since the month is to be input as an integer we could add a line to check this:

```
40  IF INT M<>M THEN GOTO 10
```

In fact one line will do it all:

```
30  IF INT M<>M OR M>12 OR M<1 THEN GOTO 10
```

Note that if there is an error, using GOTO 10 rather than GOTO 20 at least indicates to the user that something has happened by re-printing "INPUT MONTH (1 TO 12)" on the screen. If we used GOTO 20 the user would wonder what had happened, and maybe think that the year was now required. It is better to have a statement specifically stating that there was an error in input. To continue our example, we could have these lines:

```
30  IF INT M = M AND M< = 12 AND M> = 1 THEN GOTO 60
40  PRINT "INPUT ERROR:RE-INPUT MONTH"
50  GOTO 20
60  PRINT "INPUT YEAR (AS 82 FOR 1982, ETC.)"
70  ....... (Rest of program)
```

The user is informed what is wrong, and told what to do. Make sure you see why the new line 30 had to have both the relational and logical operators switched round to make the program work.

To enable re-use of check or error routines it is convenient to place them in subroutines. The following date entry routine uses a subroutine to print an error message for a few seconds (line 500) which is used if any of the checks shows an error. The routine checks the following:

i) Day of month between 1 and 31 (line 40)
ii) Month between 1 and 12 (line 90)
iii) Year between 1911 and 1998 (line 140)
iv) Whether the year is a leap year, and if it is not, that 29 February has not been entered (line 190)
v) That days which do not exist in some months have not been entered (line 210).

Check the logic used in these lines to see how it works. The lines are good examples of how multiple conditions can be combined, but for that reason they are a little difficult to follow.

```
10 PRINT "ENTER DATE"
20 PRINT "DAY?"
30 INPUT D
40 IF D>=1 AND D<=31 THEN GOTO
   70
50 GOSUB 500
60 GOTO 20
70 PRINT "MONTH? (1 TO 12)"
80 INPUT M
```

```
 90 IF M>=1 AND M<=12 THEN GOTO
    12Ø
1ØØ GOSUB 5ØØ
11Ø GOTO 7Ø
12Ø PRINT "YEAR? (AS LAST 2 DIG
    ITS)"
13Ø INPUT Y
14Ø IF Y>1Ø AND Y<99 THEN GOTO
    17Ø
15Ø GOSUB 5ØØ
16Ø GOTO 12Ø
17Ø REM *CHECK DAY US MONTH*
18Ø REM *LEAP YEAR*
19Ø IF INT (Y+19ØØ)/4)<>(Y+19Ø
    Ø)/4 AND M=2 AND D=29 THEN
    GOTO 22Ø
2ØØ REM *SHORT MONTHS*
21Ø IF NOT ((M=2 AND D>29) OR (
    M=4 OR M=6 OR M=9 OR M=11 A
    ND D=31) THEN GOTO 24Ø
22Ø GOSUB 5ØØ
23Ø GOTO 1Ø
24Ø REM .....PROGRAM
25Ø PRINT D;"/";M;"/19";Y
26Ø REM ........
27Ø REM ......
4ØØ GOTO 999
49Ø REM **ERROR NOTICE**
5ØØ PRINT "***INPUT ERROR***","
    PLEASE FOLLOW INSTRUCTIONS"
    ,"RE-INPUT REQUESTED DATA".
51Ø PAUSE 2ØØ
52Ø CLS
53Ø RETURN
999 REM*END*
```

The program "INDATE" in the program library uses much the same routines, but set up as two nested subroutines, so that it can be used in any program requiring multiple date entries, such as an accounting program.

It is also a simple matter to put in input checks that print the input, and invite the operator to check if it is correct, and to re-input if an error has been made. This is important where multiple data entries are being made, since an error would otherwise require entering everything again. As an example, here is a check routine for string input:

```
 4Ø FOR N = 1 TO X
 5Ø PRINT "INPUT STRING";N
 6Ø INPUT W$(N)
 7Ø PRINT W$ (N)
 8Ø PRINT "IF INCORRECT PRESS E
    TO RE-ENTER."; TAB Ø; "PRES
    S ANY OTHER KEY TO CONTINUE
    IF OK."
 9Ø IF INKEY$ ="" THEN GOTO 9Ø
1ØØ IF INKEY$ = "E" THEN GOTO 5
    Ø
11Ø NEXT N
```

Rather than check each value, it is sometimes better to wait until all entries have been made, and then print them out for checking. This routine does this for a list of numbers:

```
  10 REM INPUT,PRINT,CHECK AND C
ORRECT ROUTINE FOR LIST
  20 PRINT "ENTER NUMBERS"
 190 DIM A(24)
 200 FOR L=1 TO 24
 210 INPUT A(L)
 220 PRINT AT 3+L-12*(L>12),10*(
L>12);A(L)
 230 NEXT L
 300 PRINT AT 21,0;"ALL CORRECT?
(Y OR N)"
 310 INPUT E$
 320 IF E$="Y" THEN GOTO 1000
 330 CLS
 340 PRINT "EACH VALUE WILL BE P
RINTED","ENTER NEWLINE IF OK.NEW
 VALUE","IF WRONG."
 350 FOR F=1 TO 24
 360 PRINT AT 21,0;A(F)
 370 INPUT N$
 380 IF N$="" THEN GOTO 410
 390 LET A(F)= VAL N$
 400 PRINT AT 21,0;A(F);"
  "
 410 SCROLL
 420 NEXT F
1000 REM *REST OF PROGRAM*
```

Spectrum users should delete line 41Ø, inserting 41Ø POKE 23692, – 1. The virtue of using string input is that instead of stopping the program with an error message if an invalid entry is made (a letter, character that is non-numeric, or more than one decimal point), as occurs with a numeric input, the string input can be accepted whatever the characters input. The inputted string must be checked, however, or else we just get an error message when using VAL to convert to a numeric value. This requires a routine like the following:

```
  5 REM "STRINGNUM"
 1Ø PRINT AT Ø,5;"INPUT NUMBER"
 2Ø INPUT N$
 3Ø LET DP=Ø
 4Ø IF N$="" THEN GOTO 1ØØ
 5Ø FOR F=1 TO LEN N$
 6Ø IF CODE N$(F)<27 OR CODE N$
    (F)>37 THEN GOTO 1ØØ
 7Ø IF CODE N$(F)=27 THEN LET D
    P=DP+1
 8Ø NEXT F
 9Ø IF DP>=2 THEN GOTO 1ØØ
 95 GOTO 13Ø
1ØØ PRINT AT Ø,5;"ERROR IN INPU
    T"
11Ø PAUSE 75
12Ø GOTO 1Ø
13Ø REM ...REST OF PROGRAM....
14Ø SCROLL
```

```
150 PRINT VAL N$
160 GOTO 10
```

Spectrum users need to change the character code checks in lines 60 and 70. Change 27 in line 70 to 46. Change line 60 to read IF CODE N$<46 OR CODE N$ = 47 OR CODE N$>57 THEN GOTO 100. Change line 140 to read 140POKE 23692, – 1 and line 150 to read 150 PRINT AT 21,0;VALN$.

Line 20 inputs the string. Line 30 sets a variable to store the number of decimal points. Line 40 checks that NEWLINE (ENTER) alone was not pressed, and passes control to line 100 to print an error message if it was. Lines 50 and 80 set a loop for the number of characters in N$, and line 60 uses CODE to check whether characters other than numbers and the decimal point are present, and goes to 100 for an error message if they are. Line 70 adds 1 to the variable DP for each decimal point found in N$. After the loop, line 90 sends control to 100 for an error message if there is more than one decimal point. Line 95 bypasses the error routine, and line 150 uses VAL to return the number for printing. At this point, if the number were needed for calculation, a variable could be set (LET N = VAL N$) to store the value.

Note that an input error causes (line 120) the input routine to be repeated, after indicating for 1½ seconds that an error exists.

V3: Example Programs

This Unit presents some examples of applications programs of various types, as follows:

1 "REACT": Reaction time testing.
2 "BINGO": Creation, calling and checking the cards for playing Bingo on the computer.
3 "REF. INDEX": The calculation of refractive indices from the angle of deviation and prism angle data produced by spectrometer experiments.
4 "SERIES": The summing of a convergent series to a given degree of accuracy.
5 "GRAPH": Calculation and plotting of functions, with titles and scales, to give a hard-copy printout.
6 "ELEMENT": The calculation of empirical chemical formulae from the percentage composition of compounds, or the percentage composition from the numbers of atoms of each element in the molecule.
7 "CASSFILE": Cassette file storage and manipulation, with printout of cassette files and cassette label printing.

None of these programs are particularly complex (although CASSFILE is lengthy), and they deal with fairly straightforward applications. However, the principles involved are valid for any size of program, and the programs themselves demonstrate many of the techniques and procedures introduced earlier in the text. More examples of applications programs and useful subroutines are to be found in the program library provided in the Appendix, but they are not as fully annotated. The programs here are presented as problems and solutions, with some discussion of the approach to the problem. The procedure is then presented, and the derived program.

Please remember that any program can be written in different ways, even given that the algorithm is exactly the same. This variety of solutions means that there is never only one correct program.

Spectrum users should note that we have indicated some instances where the additional functions of the Spectrum can be put to use. These functions are described in the next Section. After you have explored the new functions, you should return to these programs and modify them for practice in the use of these facilities.

1. "REACT"

Problem: To use the computer to assess response times in reaction to a signal. An average should be taken of a number of timings.

Research the problem: The timing function can use the system variable FRAMES. A start signal will be required, which should be preceded by a random delay to prevent anticipation. Computing time must be allowed for in the result. The number of timings desired should be input and used to set up a loop.

On the ZX81 FRAMES is a system variable held in 2 bytes, 16436 and 16437. On the Spectrum it is 3 bytes, 23672, 23673 and 23674. The program can use both bytes on the ZX81 and the two less significant bytes (the first two) on the Spectrum (since we do not need to time hours!). This will give a timing period of up to ((256 × 255) + 255)/5Ø seconds in the U.K. and ((256 × 255) + 255)/6Ø seconds in the U.S., or about 22 and 18 minutes respectively, before the FRAMES counter, which counts backwards by decrementing by 1 every 1/5Ø (or 1/6Ø) seconds, reaches zero. This will allow the program to be used as a timer for longer periods, or modified for use as a stopwatch program.

Procedure: The program will have a loop structure, determined by the input of the number of tests required. Outside this loop will be the instructions at the beginning of the program, and the output of average reaction time.

This timing module is the core of the program. The input module (instructions, 'get ready' messages and an input for the number of timings required) and the output module (average time) are easily built around this. We may proceed to code in a version of this module, having decided our structure for the program, and test/debug the timing module, before using the editing facilities to modify this module as required and code in the input and output modules.

The timing module will require the address bytes to be set at a known value (the maximum, 255) by POKEing values in, and the values returned by PEEKing these bytes will be used to calculate the time according to the expression T – ((256*(255 – PEEK 16437)) + 255 – PEEK 16436)/5Ø. (U.S. users must use 6Ø, not 5Ø in the expression and the program.) For the Spectrum the first address will be 23673 and the second 23672.

Our procedure in this simple linear program is as follows:

1 Input Module	=	1	Give instructions
		2	Input number of tests required (A)
		3	Initialise array for timings, B(A)
		4	Initialise variable for total timings, X
		5	Initialise FOR – NEXT Loop (1 TO A)
2 Timing Module	=	1	Give "get ready" message
		2	Provide random delay to prevent anticipation
		3	Set timing function by POKEing 255 into the FRAMES addresses
		4	Give signal
		5	Wait for key to be pressed
		6	Calculate reaction time. Allow for computing time
		7	Store result as B(A)
		8	Add B(A) to X
		9	Repeat 1 – 8, A times
3 Output Module	=	1	Calculate average reaction time
		2	Print average time

The timing module could be coded, run and tested as follows:

Timing Module Program Listing

```
   1 REM REACT CORE PROGRAM
 160 PRINT "-ON YOUR MARKS-"
 170 PAUSE 75
 180 CLS
 190 PRINT "<GET SET>"
 200 FOR L=0 TO RND *500
 210 NEXT L
 220 POKE 16436,255
 230 POKE 16437,255
 240 PRINT AT 10,10;"*GO*"
 250 IF INKEY$ ="" THEN GOTO 250
 260 LET T=(255- PEEK 16436)/50+
(256*(255- PEEK 16437))/50-0.12
 270 PRINT "REACTION TIME ";T;"
SECONDS"
```

Spectrum users should note the problem with INKEY$, and the fact that we cannot use PAUSE Ø since the PAUSE instruction uses

FRAMES also. The solution is to use the ENTER key as the key to be pressed. Change line 25Ø to INPUT A$. As long as only the ENTER key is used, this works. Change .12 to .Ø3 (the time allowed for computing) in line because of the faster response of the Spectrum.

When satisfied that the timing module works, we go on to code in the rest of the program, editing any changed lines. (Only 26Ø, since we kept the same numbering.) You would have to change line numbers in developing the program, unless you coded your program accurately with line numbers before keying anything in.

For the Spectrum, modifications are required in the following lines:

```
200  FOR L = 0 TO RND * 1000
220  POKE 23673, 255
230  POKE 23672, 255
260  LET T = (256 * (255 - PEEK 23673))/50
              + (255 - PEEK 23672)/50 - .03
```

If there are problems with the INKEY$ operation on the Spectrum (as we noted earlier, it doesn't always work), the program should be modified to:

i) Instruct the user to hold his finger over, then press the ENTER key (lines 6Ø and 7Ø).
ii) Change line 25Ø to read INPUT A$. The null string will then be entered when ENTER is pressed and the program will go to the next line, to derive the reaction time.

Users in the U.S. must replace the 5Ø which appears twice in line 26Ø, by 6Ø to get an accurate timing result.

Spectrum users can use the DEF FN, FN functions for timing. See the Sinclair Spectrum manual, Chapter 18, for a good description of this method.

Flowchart "REACT"

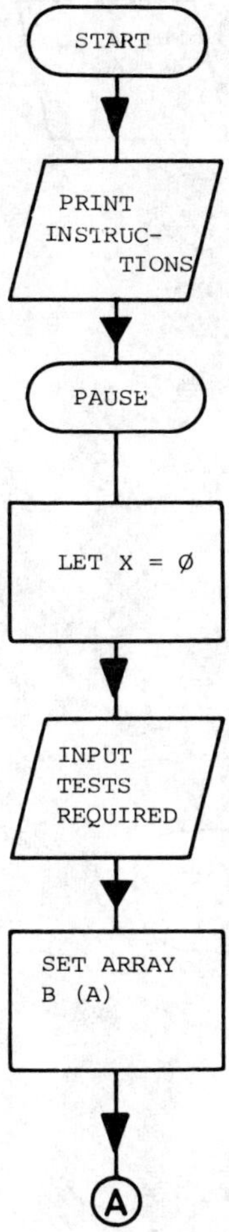

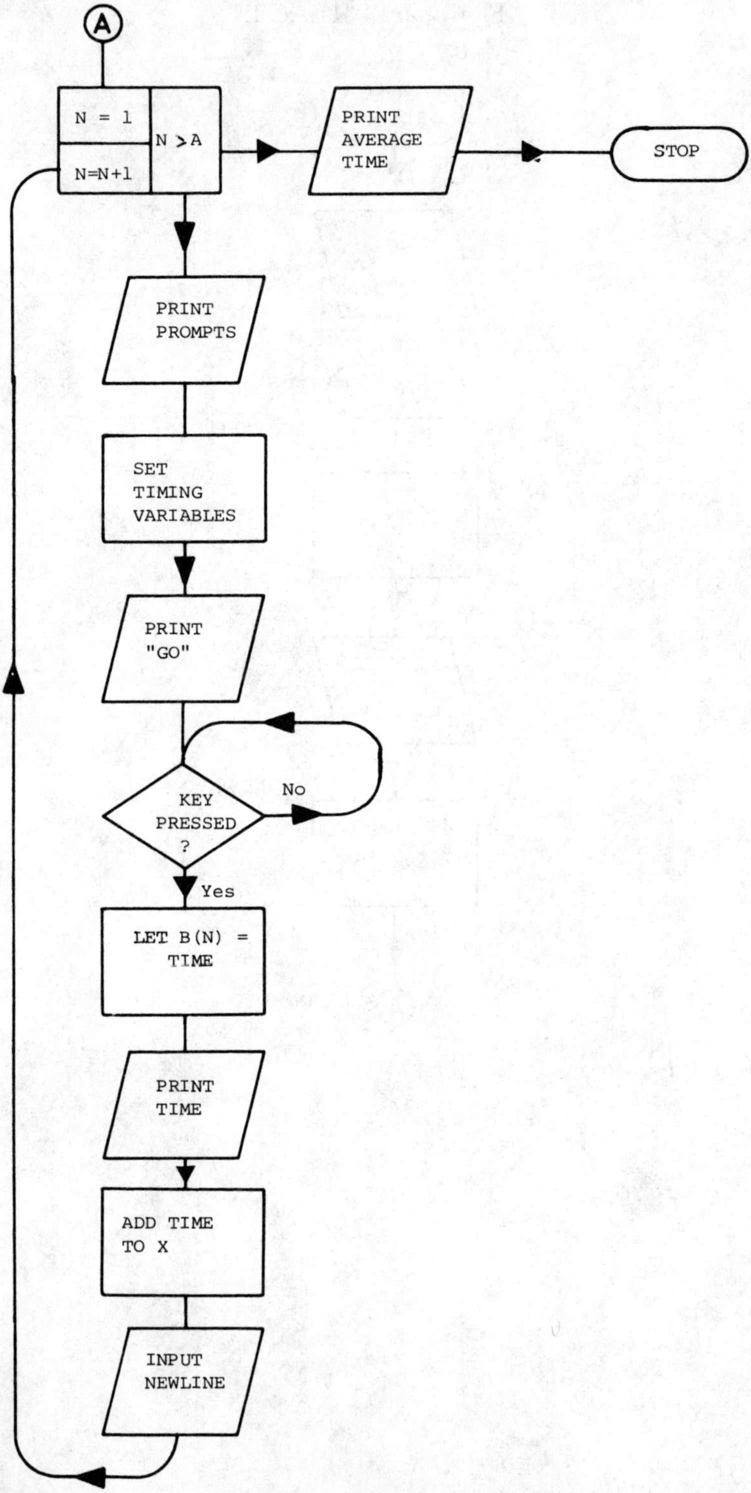
A
N = 1
N > A
N=N+1
PRINT AVERAGE TIME
STOP
PRINT PROMPTS
SET TIMING VARIABLES
PRINT "GO"
KEY PRESSED ?
No
Yes
LET B(N) = TIME
PRINT TIME
ADD TIME TO X
INPUT NEWLINE

```
■■■■
   5 REM "REACT"
  10 PRINT "REACTION TEST"
  20 PRINT "*************"
  30 PRINT
  40 PRINT "THE SCREEN WILL SHOW
 A  "" GET SET "" "
  50 PRINT "MESSAGE.PLACE A FING
ER OVER"
  60 PRINT "THE  "" R ""  KEY.WH
EN *GO* APPEARS"
  70 PRINT "PRESS R.EACH REACTIO
N TIME AND"
  80 PRINT "THE AVERAGE WILL BE
DISPLAYED"
  90 PAUSE 600
 100 PRINT ,,"ENTER NUMBER OF TE
STS REQUIRED"
 110 LET X=0
 120 INPUT A
 130 DIM B(A)
 140 PRINT
 145 REM
         **TEST LOOP**

 150 FOR N=1 TO A
 160 PRINT "-ON YOUR MARKS-"
 170 PAUSE 75
 180 CLS
 190 PRINT "<GET SET>"
 200 FOR L=0 TO RND *500
 210 NEXT L
 215 REM
        **SET TIMER BYTES**
 220 POKE 16437,255
 230 POKE 16436,255
 240 PRINT AT 10,10;"*GO*"
 250 IF INKEY$ ="" THEN GOTO 250
 260 LET B(N)=(256*(255- PEEK 16
437))/50+(255- PEEK 16436)/50-0.
12
 270 PRINT "REACTION TIME ";B(N)
;" SECONDS"
 280 LET X=X+B(N)
 290 PRINT "PRESS NEWLINE/ENTER
TO CONTINUE"
 300 INPUT A$
 310 CLS
 320 NEXT N
 325 REM
         **ENDLOOP**

 330 PRINT
 340 PRINT "AVERAGE TIME WAS ";X
/A;" SECS"
 350 STOP

 360 REM **END**
```

Comments: The use of an array (B(A)) gives us the flexibility to add further manipulations (full printout or standard deviation, for example) if we wished, by adding a further module to the program.

We could use the same principle to time other processes. The accuracy of the allowance for the delay due to computing time becomes less important as the time being measured increases. To derive a stop-watch program (timing less than 65535/50 secs – about 21 minutes in the U.K.) we would need a start and stop routine, built around the POKE and PEEK lines. Write such a program. Notice how the program is set so that the computer waits until a key is pressed in line 25Ø. Remember we cannot use PAUSE in the form of PAUSE 4ØØØØ (ZX81) or PAUSE Ø (Spectrum) since that uses the FRAMES system variables also, and would reset the timer.

2. "BINGO"

Problem: In the game of BINGO the caller shouts out the numbers between 1 and 99 in a random order and each player has a card with a set of numbers (say 15) in this range. The cards for each player contain different sets of numbers. The winner of the game is the player whose list of numbers is called first.

The program should play the game for up to four players and check the validity of the winning player's card.

Outline Procedure: Modules are required as follows:

1 Set up game   2 Play game   3 Result of game

Procedure will be as follows:

- 1.1 Write preliminary instructions
- 1.2 Set up caller's numbers
- 1.3 Set up players' numbers
- 1.4 Display players' numbers
- 2.1 Display caller's numbers (one at a time)
- 2.2 Allow interruption by player
- 3.1 Display players' numbers
- 3.2 Display numbers called
- 3.3 Check winning card

1.1 These are the <u>instructions</u> needed to start the game. At each stage in the program it is essential to give clear directions to the user on how to proceed.

1.2 The <u>caller's numbers</u> require a random list of the integers 1 to 99 (each number occurring only once) which will be put in array A(99).

1.3 The players' cards require 4 sets (cards) of 15 random integers in the range 1 to 99 (i.e. different numbers). The cards should have an ordered list of numbers and each list is a different set of numbers. These will be put into arrays Q(15), R(15), S(15) and T(15).

1.4 Display the players' cards on the screen and allow time for the players to take down the numbers.

2.1 Display the caller's numbers one at a time on the screen in large form.

2.2 Allow the display to be interrupted when a player calls 'house' (i.e. thinks that all the numbers on his card have been displayed).

3.1 Repeats 1.4 for players to check their numbers.

3.2 The numbers called (i.e. those actually displayed in 2.1) are sorted into numerical order (and put into array P(99) which contains between 15 and 99 numbers) and displayed on screen.

3.3 The 'winning' card is selected and the numbers on this card are put into the array V(15). These numbers are then compared with the numbers called [in P(99)] to check that they are correct.

Algorithm Description

1.1 This section gives the minimum instructions required to play. You may want to key in fuller details of the game of BINGO. (Lines 10 to 110 in program).

1.2 Set up caller's numbers

Flowchart:

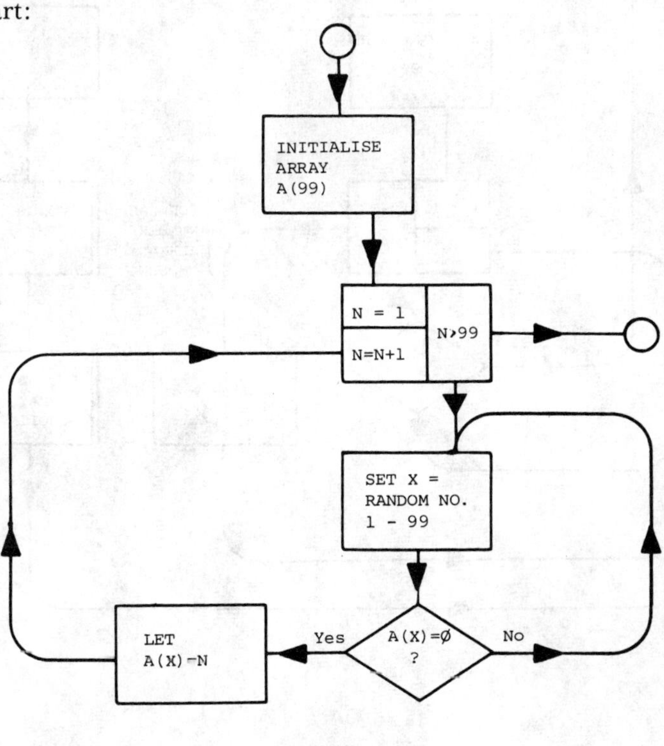

This routine starts at line 12Ø, clearing the screen and going into fast mode on the ZX81 for the calculation. The above routine is contained within the caller's numbers subroutine (lines 25ØØ to 259Ø), but note this could be a subprogram sequence as part of the main program as it is only executed once.

1.3 Setting up (the BINGO cards)

Flowchart:

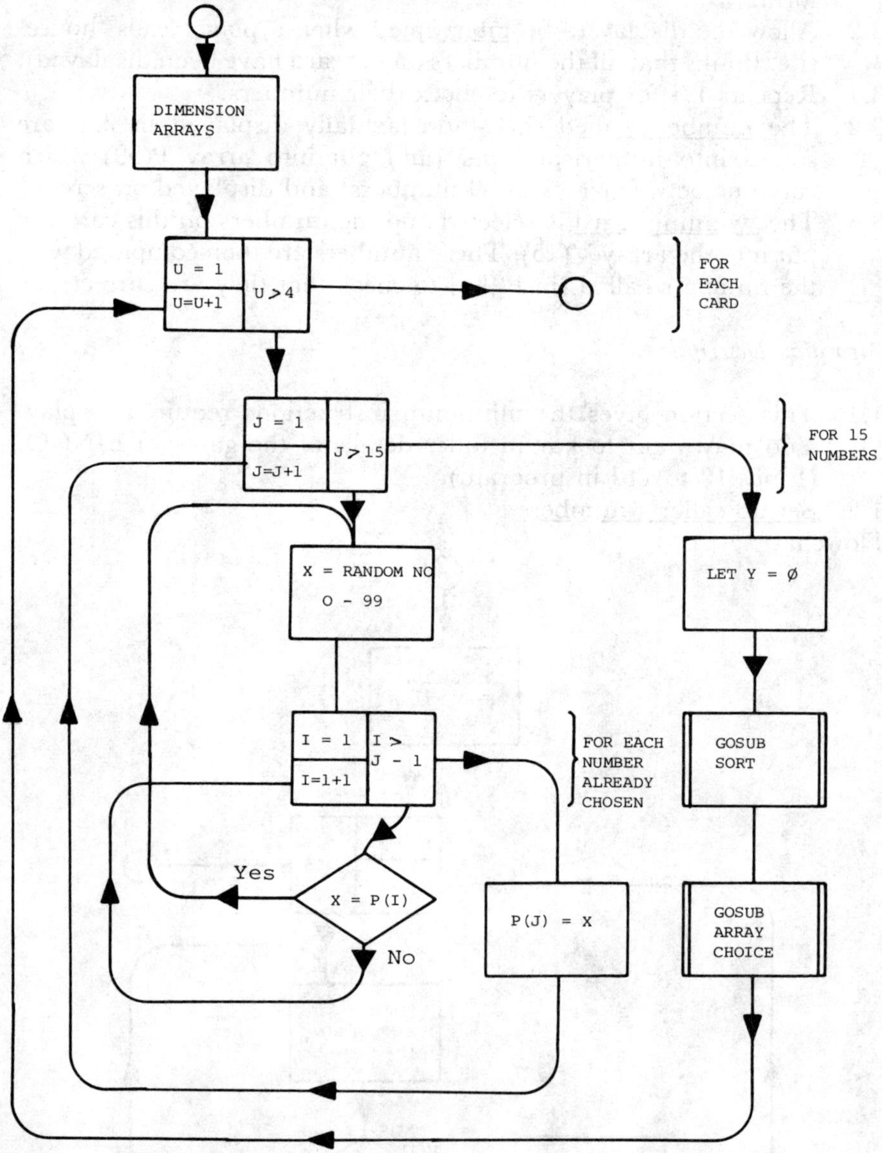

In the program this routine begins at line 320. Note array P(99), which is used in the sorting routine (although containing only 15 numbers) and is then used again later for the caller's numbers.

Lines 480 – 540 carry out the selection of the 15 random numbers. Subroutine 3000 – 3170 is the sorting routine which is the SHELL SORT given in Section T. (A fast sort is needed as at a later stage we are sorting nearly 100 numbers.)

Subroutine 3500 – 3560 puts the numbers into the appropriate array.

1.4 This subroutine (lines 1600 – 1650) displays the numbers on the cards in a tabular form.

2.1/2.2 <u>Display caller's numbers and interrupt if 'House' is called</u>

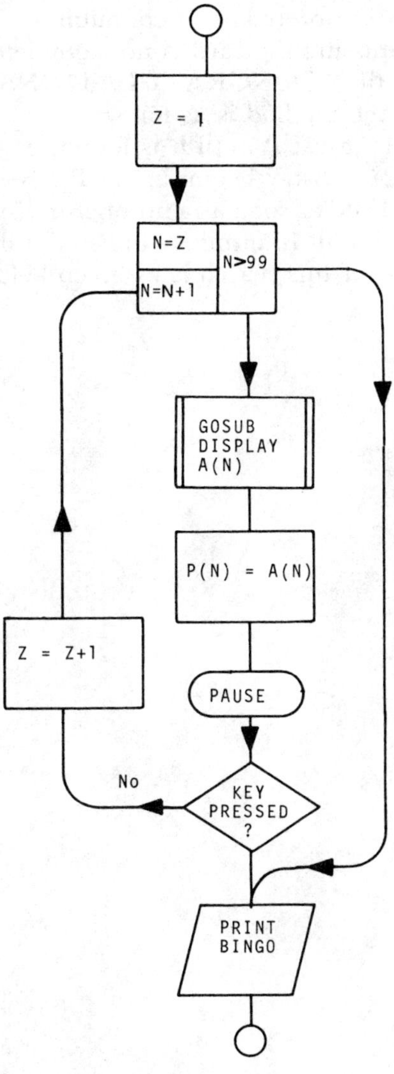

This subroutine takes numbers generated and (in FAST mode on the ZX81) displays them 16 times their normal size and places them in an array P. Variable Z counts the number of numbers called. At the end of this subroutine the numbers called have been put into the array P (which will contain Z numbers).

3.1 This repeats step 1.4.

3.2 This routine (lines 960 – 1070) calls a sort subroutine at line 3000 which sorts the list P (Z) into numerical order and prints them out on the screen.

3.3 This subroutine (lines 4000 – 4260) has two parts.

(1) Select the 'winning' card and arrange for the 'winning' list of numbers to be put in the array V(15) (lines 4000 – 4120)

(2) Check the numbers on the 'winning' card. It is necessary to search the ordered list P containing Z numbers for the numbers in the ordered list V containing 15 numbers. If any number is missing the card is not complete. If all numbers are present then CONGRATULATIONS is printed.

The quickest search method is as follows:

Search for V(1) in list P until it is found, say P(12).

Search for V(2) in list P beginning at P(13) etc.

The search will end as soon as a number in list V is not in list P but will continue for all 15 numbers in list V if they appear in list P. The flowchart for this search is as given below:

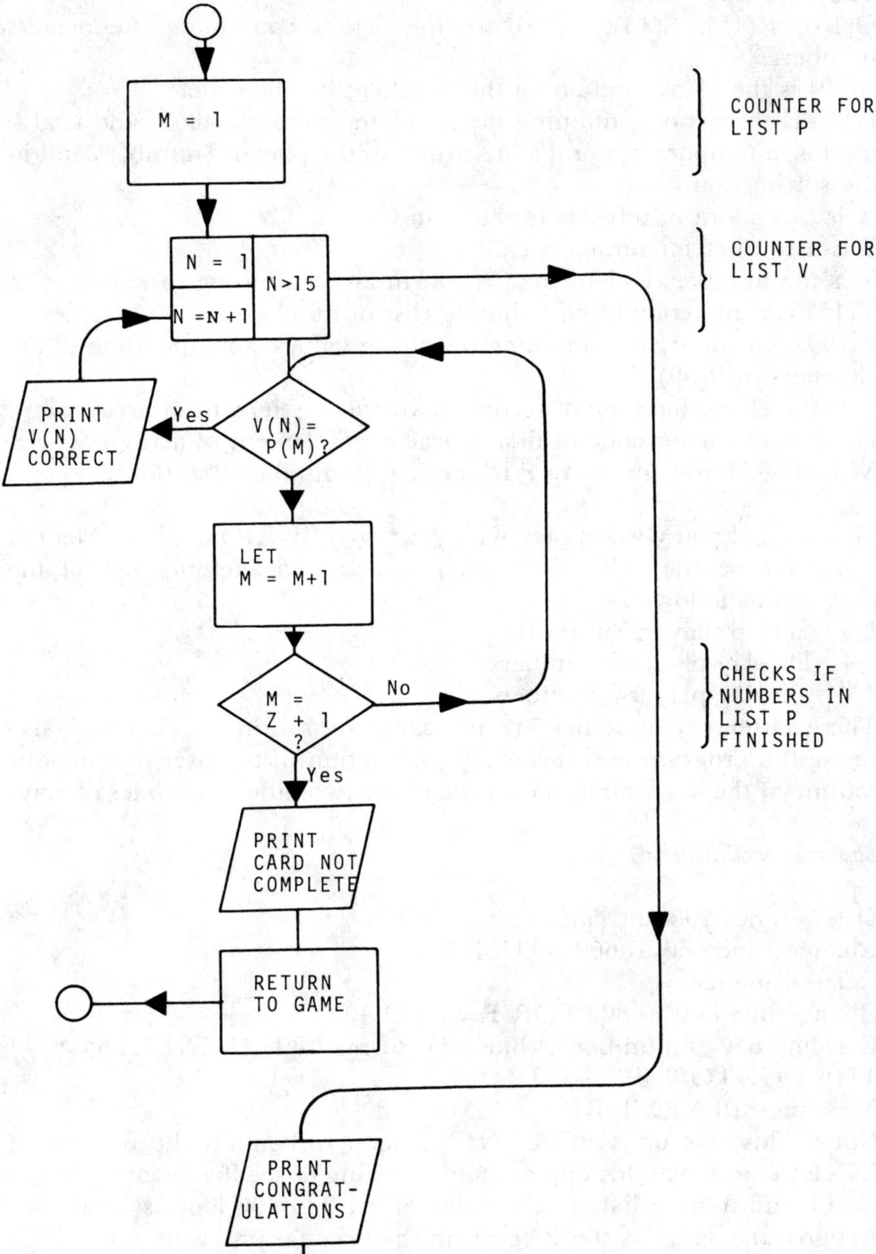
M = 1
COUNTER FOR LIST P
N = 1
N = N + 1
N>15
COUNTER FOR LIST V
PRINT V(N) CORRECT
Yes
V(N)= P(M)?
LET M = M+1
M = Z + 1 ?
No
Yes
CHECKS IF NUMBERS IN LIST P FINISHED
PRINT CARD NOT COMPLETE
RETURN TO GAME
PRINT CONGRAT-ULATIONS
STOP

Data Table

The following variables are used:
Q(15), R(15), S(15), T(15) are the arrays containing the players numbers.
A(99) is the array containing the numbers for the caller.
P(99) is the array containing the numbers actually called, and is also used as a temporary storage in setting up the players' numbers and in the sorting routine.
X is a random number between 1 and 99.
Z is a counter for numbers called.
Y is the number of elements present in an array to be sorted.
V(15) is array containing 'winning' list of numbers.
B$(99,2) is an array containing the string values corresponding to the elements in P(99).
C is the character code of second character in element of array B$.
D is the character code of first character in element of array B$.
M is the counter for array P in the 'check numbers' section.

Comments: If you wish to play with your own BINGO cards and let the computer be the caller only, then you can delete modules of the program as follows:
1.3 Set up players' numbers
1.4 Display players' numbers
3.1 Display players' numbers
These latter two modules are the same subroutine. You could also revise the program and include, as an option in the user instructions routine at the beginning, the choice of the two different modes of play.

Spectrum modifications:

Delete Lines 29Ø and 585.
Change Line 66Ø to 66Ø PAUSE Ø
Delete Line 83Ø
Change line 8ØØ to 8ØØ FOR F = 1 TO 4ØØ
Edit line 81Ø, renumber as line 8Ø5, to read 8Ø5 IF INKEY$<>" " THEN GOTO 83Ø
New line 81Ø NEXT F
Note: This sets up a FOR – NEXT loop to contain the reading of INKEY$, to make this operation of checking to see if someone's bingo card is full more reliable. The delay of a 1 TO 4ØØ loop is about two seconds, the same as the PAUSE in the original program.
Edit line 835, renumber as line 83Ø, to read 83Ø CLS
Delete line 835
Change line 98Ø to PAUSE Ø
Delete line 1ØØ5
Delete line 1Ø25
Delete line 5Ø1Ø

Change line 5Ø7Ø to 5Ø7Ø LET E = PEEK (1536Ø + 8*C + R)
Change line 52ØØ to 52ØØ LET F = PEEK (1536Ø + 8*D + R)

Flowchart 'BINGO'

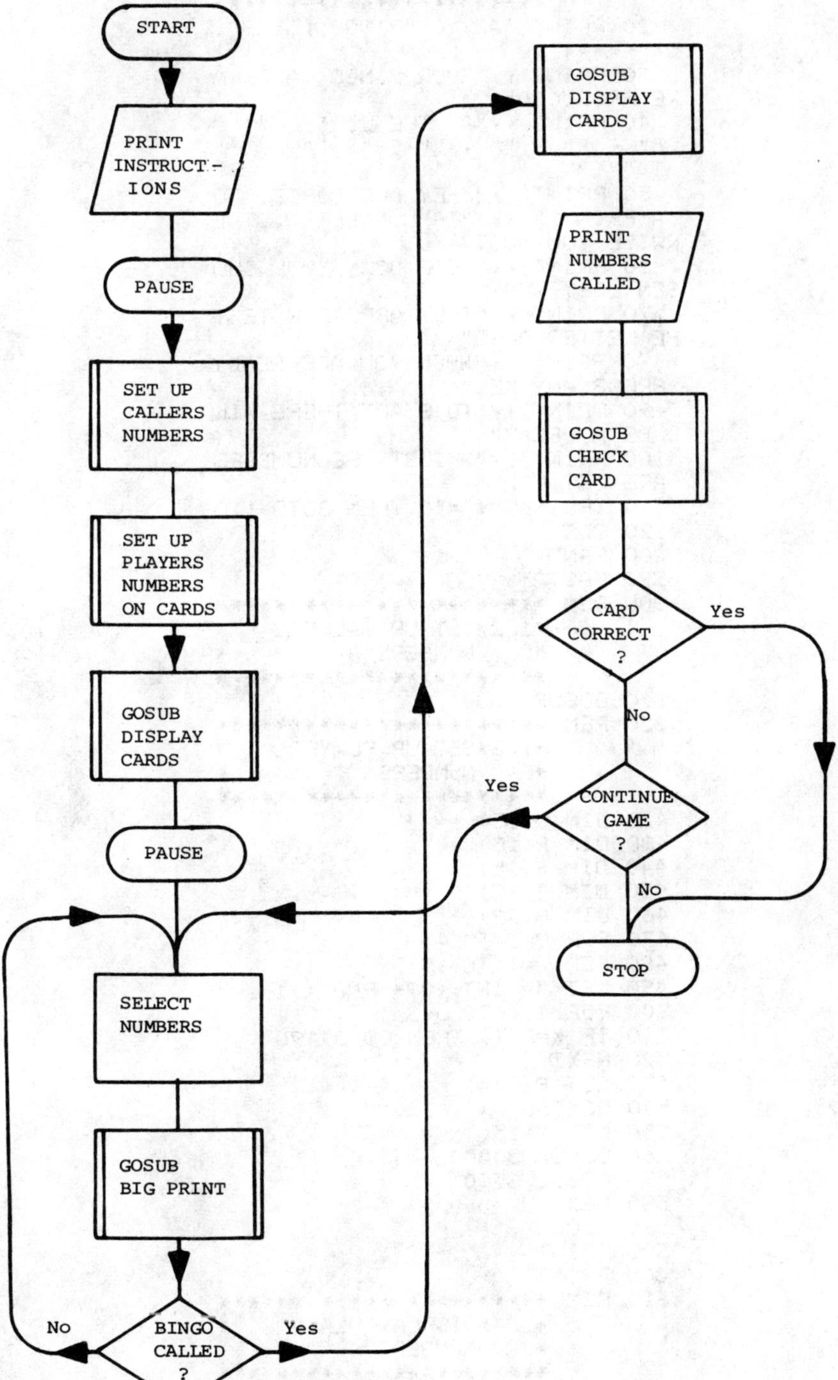

Program Listing

```
   5 REM "BINGO"
  10 REM ***********************
         *1.1*INSTRUCTIONS     *
         ***********************
  20 PRINT TAB 10;"BINGO"; TAB 1
0;"*****"
  30 PRINT ,,"FOUR BINGO CARDS A
RE PRODUCED"
  40 PRINT ,,"AS THE LISTS  "" Q
 "" , "" R "" , "" S ""  AND  ""
 T "" "
  50 PRINT ,,"THEY ARE COPIED TO
 A PRINTER",,,"IF CONNECTED.OTHE
RWISE YOU MUST"
  60 PRINT ,,"NOTE DOWN YOUR CHO
SEN LIST WHEN"
  70 PRINT ,,"THEY APPEAR.NOTE T
HE LETTER ALSO"
  80 PRINT ,,"WHEN YOU ARE READY
 PRESS ANY KEY"
  90 PRINT ,,"TO START.THERE WIL
L BE A DELAY"
 100 PRINT ,,"WHILST THE NUMBERS
 ARE SET UP."
 110 IF INKEY$ ="" THEN GOTO 110
 120 CLS
 200 RAND
 290 FAST
 300 REM ***********************
         *1.2*SET UP CALLERS   *
         *    NUMBERS          *
         ***********************
 310 GOSUB 2500
 320 REM ***********************
         *1.3*SET UP PLAYERS   *
         *    NUMBERS          *
         ***********************
 420 DIM Q(15)
 430 DIM R(15)
 440 DIM S(15)
 450 DIM T(15)
 460 DIM P(99)
 470 FOR U=1 TO 4
 480 FOR J=1 TO 15
 490 LET X= INT (99* RND )+1
 500 FOR I=1 TO J-1
 510 IF X=P(I) THEN GOTO 490
 520 NEXT I
 530 LET P(J)=X
 540 NEXT J
 550 LET Y=15
 560 GOSUB 3000
 570 GOSUB 3500
 580 NEXT U
 585 SLOW
 590 PRINT
 600 PRINT
 610 REM ***********************
         *1.4*DISPLAY PLAYERS  *
         *    NUMBERS          *
         ***********************
 620 GOSUB 1600
```

```
 630 REM **LIST COPIED IF     **
        ** PRINTER            **
 640 COPY
 650 PRINT ,,"PRESS ANY KEY TO P
ROCEED"
 660 IF INKEY$ ="" THEN GOTO 660
 670 CLS
 680 PRINT "THE CALLER WILL GIVE
 THE NUMBERS ONE AT A TIME"
 690 PRINT
 700 PRINT "WHEN YOUR CARD IS CO
MPLETE PRESSANY KEY WHEN NUMBER
IS ON SCREEN"
 710 PRINT
 720 PRINT "PRESS ANY KEY TO PRO
CEED"
 730 IF INKEY$ ="" THEN GOTO 730
 735 CLS
 740 REM **********************
        *2.1* PRINT OUT CALLS *
        **********************
 745 LET Z=1
 750 DIM B$(99,2)
 755 CLS
 760 PRINT "  PRESS ANY KEY WHEN
 YOUR CARD          IS COMPLETE"
 770 FOR N=Z TO 99
 780 GOSUB 5000
 790 LET P(N)=A(N)
 795 PAUSE 200
 800 REM **********************
        *2.2*PLAYER INTERRUPT *
        **********************
 810 IF INKEY$ <> "" THEN GOTO 8
30
 815 LET Z=Z+1
 820 NEXT N
 830 SLOW
 835 CLS
 840 FOR N=1 TO 10
 850 PRINT TAB N;"<*BINGO*><*BIN
GO*>"
 860 NEXT N
 870 PRINT ,,"CHECK YOUR CARDS"
 880 REM **********************
        *3.1*DISPLAY PLAYERS  *
        *    NUMBERS          *
        **********************
 890 PAUSE 100
 900 CLS
 910 LET Y=Z
 920 PRINT "YOUR NUMBERS WERE"
 930 PRINT
 935 REM **********************
       *PRINT OUT CARD NUMBERS*

 940 GOSUB 1600
 945 REM
 950 REM **********************
        *3.2*DISPLAY NUMBERS  *
        *    CALLED           *
        **********************
```

```
 960 PRINT "PRESS ANY KEY TO GET
 LIST OF","THE NUMBERS CALLED."
 970 PRINT "THERE WILL BE A SHOR
T DELAY FOR SORTING."
 980 IF INKEY$ ="" THEN GOTO 980
 990 CLS
1005 FAST
1010 GOSUB 3000
1020 CLS
1025 SLOW
1030 PRINT "CALLERS LIST"
1040 PRINT
1050 FOR N=1 TO Z
1060 PRINT P(N);" ";
1070 NEXT N
1080 PRINT
1085 REM ***********************
         *3.3*CHECK WINNING    *
         *     CARD            *
         ***********************
1090 GOSUB 4000
1100 LET Z=Z+1
1110 PRINT ,,"DO YOU WISH TO CON
TINUE THE GAME? (Y/N)"
1120 INPUT C$
1130 IF C$="N" THEN STOP
1140 IF C$="Y" THEN GOTO 755
1150 PRINT "INPUT Y OR N ONLY,PL
EASE"
1160 GOTO 1120

1190 REM ***********************
         * END PROGRAM         *
         ***********************
1200 STOP

1210 REM

1580 REM ***********************
         * SUBROUTINES         *
         ***********************
1590 REM
1600 REM ***********************
         **SUBROUTINE TO PRINT *
         **OUT PLAYERS CARDS   *
         ***********************
1610 PRINT "Q"; TAB 6;"R"; TAB 1
2;"S"; TAB 18;"T"
1620 FOR J=1 TO 15
1630 PRINT Q(J); TAB 6;R(J); TAB
 12;S(J); TAB 18;T(J)
1640 NEXT J
1650 RETURN

1660 REM **  ENDSUB          **
         ***********************
2490 REM
2500 REM ***********************
         **SUBROUTINE TO SET  **
         **CALLERS NUMBERS    **
         ***********************
2530 DIM A(99)
2540 FOR N=1 TO 99
```

```
2550 LET X= INT (99* RND )+1
2560 IF A(X) <> 0 THEN GOTO 2550
2570 LET A(X)=N
2580 NEXT N
2590 RETURN

2600 REM **  ENDSUB             **
         ***********************

2990 REM ***********************
         **SORT SUBROUTINE     **
         ***********************
3000 LET S=Y
3010 LET S= INT (S/2)
3030 IF S >= 1 THEN GOTO 3050
3040 GOTO 3170

3050 FOR K=1 TO S
3060 FOR A=K TO Y-S STEP K
3070 LET B=A
3080 LET T=P(A+S)
3090 IF T >= P(B) THEN GOTO 3130
3100 LET P(B+S)=P(B)
3110 LET B=B-S
3120 IF B >= 1 THEN GOTO 3090
3130 LET P(B+S)=T
3140 NEXT A
3150 NEXT K
3160 GOTO 3010

3170 RETURN

3180 REM **  ENDSUB             **
         ***********************

3190 REM
3490 REM ***********************
         **SUBROUTINE FOR FOUR**
         **NUMBER ARRAYS       **
         ***********************
3500 FOR J=1 TO 15
3510 IF U=1 THEN LET Q(J)=P(J)
3520 IF U=2 THEN LET R(J)=P(J)
3530 IF U=3 THEN LET S(J)=P(J)
3540 IF U=4 THEN LET T(J)=P(J)
3550 NEXT J
3560 RETURN

3570 REM **  ENDSUB             **
         ***********************

3580 REM
3990 REM ***********************
         **SUBROUTINE TO CHECK**
         **RESULTS             **
         ***********************
4000 PRINT
4010 REM ***********************
         *3.3.1*SELECT WINNING *
         *      CARD           *
         ***********************
4020 PRINT "TYPE WINNING CARD (Q
,R,S,T)"
```

```
4030 INPUT A$
4040 IF A$ <> "Q" AND A$ <> "R"
AND A$ <> "S" AND A$ <> "T" THEN
 GOTO 4020
4050 CLS
4060 DIM V(15)
4070 FOR N=1 TO 15
4080 IF A$="Q" THEN LET V(N)=Q(N
)
4090 IF A$="R" THEN LET V(N)=R(N
)
4100 IF A$="S" THEN LET V(N)=S(N
)
4110 IF A$="T" THEN LET V(N)=T(N
)
4120 NEXT N
4125 REM ***********************
         *3.3.2*CHECK NUMBERS  *
         ***********************
4130 LET M=1
4140 FOR N=1 TO 15
4150 IF V(N)=P(M) THEN PRINT V(N
);" CORRECT"
4160 IF V(N)=P(M) THEN GOTO 4200
4170 LET M=M+1
4180 IF M=Z+1 THEN GOTO 4220
4190 GOTO 4150

4200 NEXT N
4210 GOTO 4245

4220 PRINT "*CARD ";A$;" NOT COM
PLETED*"
4230 PRINT V(N);" NOT CALLED"
4235 REM
      **GOTO RETURN TO CONTINUE

4240 GOTO 4260

4245 PRINT ,, TAB 4;" ** CONGRAT
ULATIONS ** "; TAB 4;"$$$$$$$$$
$$$$$$$$$",,,"GAME ENDED.USE RUN
 TO RESTART"
4250 REM
         ** GOTO PROGRAM END **

4255 GOTO 1200

4260 RETURN

4270 REM **  ENDSUB           **
         ***********************

4900 REM
5000 REM ***********************
         **SUBROUTINE BIG PLOT**
         ***********************
5010 FAST
5020 LET B$(N)= STR$ A(N)
5030 LET C= CODE B$(N)(1 TO 1)
5040 IF LEN B$(N)<2 THEN GOTO 50
60
```

```
5050 LET D= CODE B$(N)(2 TO 2)
5060 FOR R=0 TO 7
5070 LET E= PEEK (7680+8*C+R)
5080 LET W=128
5090 FOR G=0 TO 7
5100 IF E<W THEN GOTO 5150
5110 PRINT AT 2*R+5,2*G+1;"█"
5120 PRINT AT 2*R+6,2*G+1;"█"
5130 LET E=E-W
5140 GOTO 5170

5150 PRINT AT 2*R+5,2*G+1;"  "
5160 PRINT AT 2*R+6,2*G+1;"  "
5170 LET W=W/2
5180 NEXT G
5190 IF LEN B$(N)<2 THEN GOTO 60
20
5200 LET F= PEEK (7680+8*D+R)
5210 LET W=128
5220 FOR H=0 TO 7
5230 IF F<W THEN GOTO 5280
5240 PRINT AT 2*R+5,2*H+16;"█"
5250 PRINT AT 2*R+6,2*H+16;"█"
5260 LET F=F-W
5270 GOTO 6000

5280 PRINT AT 2*R+5,2*H+16;"  "
5290 PRINT AT 2*R+6,2*H+16;"  "
6000 LET W=W/2
6010 NEXT H
6020 NEXT R
6035 SLOW
6040 RETURN

6050 REM **  ENDSUB          **
         **********************

6060 REM
6070 REM **   END PROGRAM LIST**
         **********************
```

3. "REF. INDEX"

Problem: In a laboratory experiment with a spectrometer, a series of measurements are made of the prism angle A and the angle of minimum deviation D for various prisms. The refractive index of each is then determined using the formula:

$$N = \text{Sin}\,\frac{(A + D)}{2} \div \text{Sin}\,\frac{(A)}{2}$$

We require a table of results and an average of the refractive index results for each prism. Six prisms and four measurements for each prism are to be allowed for.

Research the problem: Since we are using up to six prisms and each one can have four readings it is convenient to use nested loops and two-dimensional arrays to store the input. In this way A(3,4) can, for example, represent the third prism, fourth reading of prism angle. We will use lists to refer to the prisms and the quantities associated with the prisms, so that, for example, Z(3) can represent the average refractive index of the third prism.

Angles will be input in degrees. Since the formula for the calculation requires the use of the Sine function SIN, we will need to convert to radians. This will have to be done before the refractive index is calculated. We can provide a simple input check in a subroutine. Zero entries in the input loops will signify end of prisms or end of readings.

Outline Procedure:

1 Input: Data
2 Calculate: Refractive indices and averages
3 Output: Results in suitable tabular form

Detailed Procedure:

1 Input	1.1	Dimension Arrays and Lists
	1.2	FOR each Prism (1 to 6)
	1.3	Set Z as zero
	1.4	Input Prism number
	1.5	If Prism = Ø, GOTO 3.1
	1.6	FOR each Reading (1 to 4)
	1.7	Input Prism Angle
	1.8	If Angle = Ø, GOTO NEXT Prism
	1.9	Input Minimum Deviation
2 Processing	2.1	Convert angle to radians
	2.2	Convert minimum deviation to radians
	2.3	Calculate Refractive Index
	2.4	Round to 3 decimal places
	2.5	Add Refractive Index to Z
	2.6	NEXT Reading
	2.7	Average R.I. = Z divided by number of readings
	2.8	Let Average R.I. = Z(N)
	2.9	NEXT Prism
3 Output	3.1	Print Headings
	3.2	FOR Each Prism
	3.3	FOR Each Reading
	3.4	If Reading not Ø, print Prism, Number, Angle, Minimum Deviation, Refractive Index
	3.5	NEXT Reading
	3.6	NEXT Prism
	3.7	Print Headings
	3.8	FOR Each Prism
	3.9	Print Prism Number, Refractive Index
	3.1Ø	NEXT Prism
4 Correct	4.1	Input null string if error, C if correct

Error Subroutine	4.2	Return

Note: Subroutine called after each input. All entries can be re-input if incorrect. See program listing.

Data Table

P(6)	Prism number
A(6,4)	Four Angles of measurement for each of 6 prisms
D(6,4)	Minimum Deviations, for each value of A(6,4)
N(6,4)	Results of refractive index calculation for each experiment, derived from the values stored in arrays A and D
Z	Variable to store totals of minimum deviations.
Z(6)	Average refractive index for each prism, from the average of the four values stored in array N.
N,M	Used as loop variables for input
X,Y	Used as loop variables for printout
A$	Used as input for error check subroutine. Null string if incorrect, "C" if correct.

Flowchart "REF. INDEX"

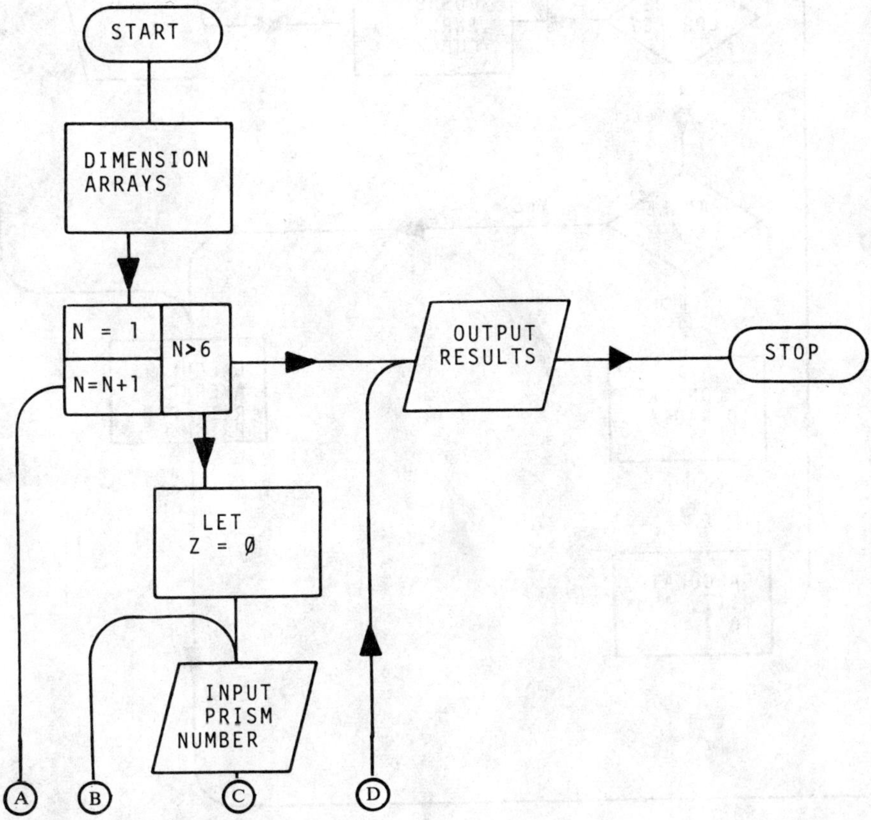

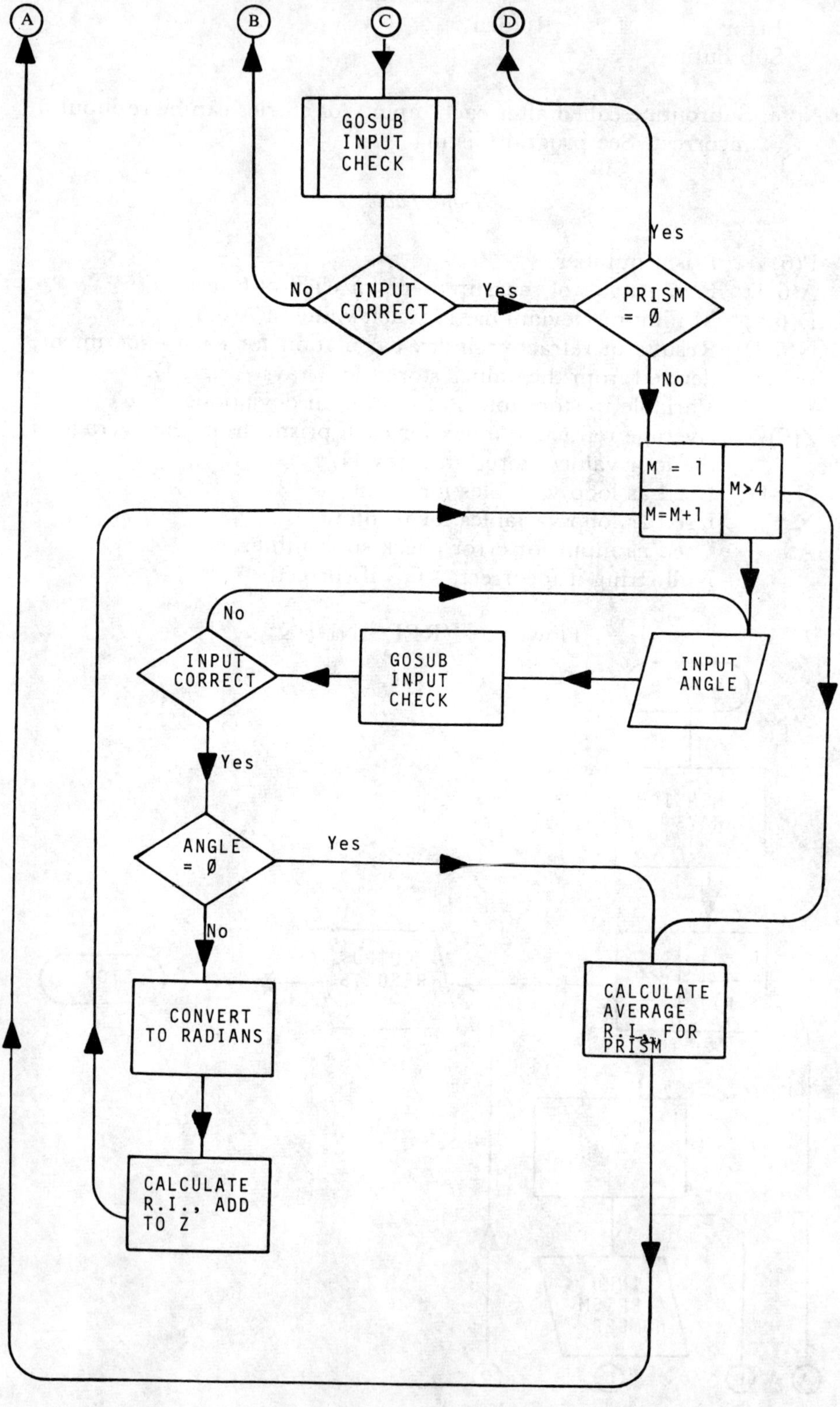
A
B
C
D
GOSUB INPUT CHECK
No
INPUT CORRECT
Yes
PRISM = Ø
Yes
No
M = 1
M=M+1
M>4
No
INPUT CORRECT
GOSUB INPUT CHECK
INPUT ANGLE
Yes
ANGLE = Ø
Yes
No
CONVERT TO RADIANS
CALCULATE R.I., ADD TO Z
CALCULATE AVERAGE R.I., FOR PRISM

Program Listing

```
   5 REM "REF.INDEX"
  10 PRINT "**REFRACTIVE INDEX**
",,,"USING SPECTROMETER"
  20 PRINT ,,"ALLOWS UP TO 6 PRI
SMS AND 4 SETS OF READINGS FOR E
ACH"
  25 REM **AVGE REF.IND.ARRAY**
  30 DIM Z(4)
  35 REM **PRISMS ARRAY**
  40 DIM P(6)
  45 REM **PRISM ANGLE ARRAY**
  50 DIM A(6,4)
  55 REM **MIN.DEV.ARRAY**
  60 DIM D(6,4)
  65 REM **REF.IND.ARRAY**
  70 DIM N(6,4)
  80 REM **********************
  85 REM **INPUT DATA LOOP**

  90 FOR N=1 TO 6
 100 LET Z=0
 110 PRINT "INPUT PRISM NUMBER,I
NPUT 0","TO FINISH"
 120 INPUT P(N)
 130 PRINT "PRISM NUMBER ";P(N)
 140 GOSUB 700
 150 IF A$ <> "C" THEN GOTO 110
 160 IF P(N)=0 THEN GOTO 500
 165 REM **********************
         **START READINGS LOOP**

 170 FOR M=1 TO 4
 180 PRINT "INPUT PRISM ANGLE IN
 DEGREES,    INPUT 0 TO FINISH"
 190 INPUT A(N,M)
 200 PRINT "ANGLE OF PRISM ";A(N
,M)
 210 GOSUB 700
 220 IF A$ <> "C" THEN GOTO 180
 230 IF A(N,M)=0 THEN GOTO 410
 240 PRINT "INPUT MIN.DEV.  IN DE
GREES"
 250 INPUT D(N,M)
 260 PRINT "MIN.DEV.  ";D(N,M)
 270 GOSUB 700
 280 IF A$ <> "C" THEN GOTO 180
 290 REM **CONVERT DEGREES TO**
         **RADIANS           **
 300 LET A=A(N,M)* PI /180
 310 LET D=D(N,M)* PI /180
 320 REM **REFRACTIVE INDEX**
 330 LET N(N,M)=( SIN ((A+D)/2))
 / SIN (A/2)
 340 LET N(N,M)= INT (1000*N(N,M
)+.5)/1000
 350 LET Z=Z+N(N,M)
 360 NEXT M
 370 REM **END READINGS LOOP **
         *********************
 380 REM
 390 REM **AVERAGE TO 2 DEC.**
         **      PLACES     **
```

```
 400 REM
 410 LET Z=Z/(M-1)
 420 LET Z(N)= INT (100*Z+.5)/10
0
 430 NEXT N
 440 REM
 450 REM **END INPUT LOOP   **
 460 REM ********************
 470 REM
 480 REM ********************
 490 REM **    PRINT OUT    **
 495 REM
 500 PRINT "PRISM * ANGLE * MIN.
DEV * RF.IN.*******************
************"
 510 FOR Y=1 TO N-1
 520 FOR X=1 TO 4
 530 IF A(Y,X)=0 THEN GOTO 550
 540 PRINT P(Y); TAB 6;"* ";A(Y,
X); TAB 14;"* ";D(Y,X); TAB 24;"
* ";N(Y,X)
 550 NEXT X
 560 NEXT Y
 570 PRINT "*******************
************"
 580 PRINT
 590 PRINT ,,"AVERAGE REFRACTIVE
 INDICES"
 600 PRINT "*******************
************"
 610 PRINT "PRISM","REF.IND."
 620 FOR X=1 TO N-1
 630 PRINT P(X),Z(X)
 640 NEXT X
 650 PRINT
 660 PRINT "*******************
************"
 670 GOTO 770

 680 REM
 690 REM *********************
 695 REM
 700 REM **CORRECT ERRORS SUB**
 710 PRINT
 720 PRINT "INPUT C IF CORRECT,O
THERWISE","PRESS NEWLINE"
 730 INPUT A$
 740 CLS
 750 RETURN

 760 REM
        **END SUBROUTINE**
        ******************

 770 STOP

 780 REM ** END **
```

Sample Printout:

```
PRISM    *   ANGLE    *    MIN.DEV    * RF.IN.
************************************
1        * 59.8       *     4Ø.5      * 1.54
1        * 6Ø.1       *     4Ø.2      * 1.533
2        * 61.2       *     45.3      * 1.574
2        * 62         *     45.1      * 1.562
2        * 62.5       *     45.4      * 1.558
************************************

AVERAGE REFRACTIVE INDICES
************************************
PRISM                 REF.IND.
1                       1.54
2                       1.56

************************************
```

Comments: Note the importance of a check subroutine in this type of multiple-entry program. It gives the user the chance to verify that the input data is correct. It might have been better to have written a program to deal with any number of prisms and any number of readings. Consider what changes this would make to the program.

There are many other physics experiments which may be treated in a similar way. For example:

(i) The value of the gravitational constant, g, by simple pendulum, using the time period equation $T = 2\pi\sqrt{\frac{l}{g}}$ for experiments with pendula of various lengths l to determine the average value of g resulting.

(ii) The determination of the velocity of sound, using a resonance tube to find the 1st and 2nd resonance lengths (L1 and L2 respectively) and using the equation $V = 2f(L2 - L1)$, where f = frequency of the sound, and V the velocity.

4. "SERIES"

Problem: We are asked to sum the series that gives us the value of e raised to the power x. This is:

$e^x = 1 + x + \frac{x^2}{2!} + \frac{x^3}{3!} + \ldots \frac{x^n}{n!} + \ldots$ for any value of x, with an accuracy

of 1 part in 1ØØ,ØØØ (i.e. $1Ø^{-5}$, .ØØØØ1).

Research the problem: This is the EXP function on your computer, evaluated as a series. The resulting value of, e.g., e^3, will be approximately the value of EXP 3 if you used it on the computer. This is a *convergent* series, the value of each term gets smaller. For example, if we take $x = 2$, $\frac{x^2}{2!}$ is $\frac{4}{2x1} = 2$, whilst $\frac{x^3}{3!} = \frac{8}{3x2x1} = 1.333\ldots$. At a certain point, the effect of adding the value of another term is to increase the sum by less than the accuracy we require. The summing is then finished.

Procedure: This requires a procedure which allows any term in the series to be calculated from the previous term. This is the basic *algorithm* for summing many series.

At this stage we need to consider if it is a specific problem or whether we could extend it to deal with other similar series-sum problems. It is important to make this decision before the program is written as it is often very time consuming to modify a program at a later stage. The answer is yes. We can then restate the problem as: a program is required which will sum a convergent series to any desired accuracy (subject to the limitations of the computer's arithmetic), provided that any term may be expressed as a function of the previous term, with the information needed being the first term and the common ratio. The common ratio is the equation that enables us to calculate any term from the previous one.

For our problem: take the exponential series:

$$e^x = 1 + x + \frac{x^2}{2!} + \ldots . + \underbrace{\frac{x^{n-1}}{(n-1)!}}_{n^{th}\ \text{term}} + \ \ldots$$

In this series the first term is 1.

The common ratio = $\frac{n^{th}\ \text{term}}{(n-1)^{th}\ \text{term}}$. The nth term is $\frac{x^{n-1}}{(n-1)!}$ and the $(n-1)^{th}$ term is $\frac{x^{n-2}}{(n-2)!}$. The ratio is $\frac{x^{n-1}}{(n-1)!} \cdot \frac{(n-2)!}{x^{n-2}} = \frac{x}{n-1}$.

We require an accuracy of one part in 100,000 (10^{-5}). When the effect of adding another term increases the sum by less than this, the program should stop processing and output the result.

Outline Procedure:

1 *Input* necessary information
2 *Sum* series term by term
3 *Compare* sum with previous value
4 *Print* out result when sums differ by less than required value

Detailed Procedure:

1 Input 1.1 Common Ratio – may be easiest to have a replaceable line in program.

		1.2	First term – easily input
		1.3	Accuracy – easily input
		1.4	Value of X – easily input
2	Sum	2.1	Initialisation – set 1st term equal to given value which in turn is the sum of the series at this stage.
		2.2	Next term – may be calculated by multiplying first term by common ratio.
		2.3	Sum – may be calculated by adding this term to previous sum
3	Comparison	3.1	Compare this sum with previous value then EITHER go to 4.1 if the difference is *less* than that required or go back to 2.2 if difference is *more* than that required.
4	Output Results	4.1	Name of series
		4.2	Accuracy
		4.3	First term
		4.4	Value of X
		4.5	Sum of series
		4.6	Number of terms

Variables Table

Input	
A$	Name of Series
A	Value of first term in series
X	Value of X
D	Accuracy required (difference between terms, such that program terminates when difference smaller than this).
Processing and Output	
T	Value of current term being processed
N	Number of terms
S1	Value of Sum of series of N – 1 terms.
S	Value of Sum of series to N terms.
S1 – S	Difference between the sums of the series to the Nth and (N – 1)th terms, checked against value of D.
T = T*X/(N – 1)	Calculates value of next term in series from current term.

The common ratio is set in line 26Ø. This line must be changed for different series. Spectrum users could use the DEF FN instruction in initialisation, and the FN instruction to evaluate the expression in line 26Ø. Try this when you have familiarised yourself with this function.

Flowchart "SERIES"

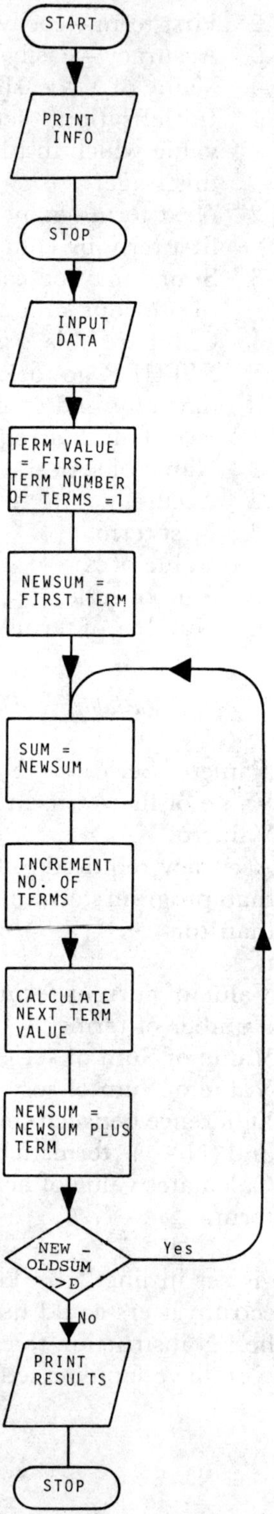

```
  10 REM "SERIES"
  20 PRINT " ** SERIES ** ",,,,"
THIS PROGRAM SUMS ANY SERIES"
  30 PRINT ,,"WHICH IS CONVERGEN
T AND WHERE"
  40 PRINT ,,"ANY TERM MAY BE CA
LCULATED FROM",,,"THE PREVIOUS T
ERM"
  50 PRINT ,,"REPLACE LINE 260 A
S APPROPRIATE"
  60 PRINT ,,"HIT A KEY TO START
"
  65 REM **PAUSE 0 FOR SPECTRUM
       **IN LINE 70        **
  70 PAUSE 40000
  80 CLS
  90 PRINT "INPUT NAME OF SERIES
"
 100 INPUT A$
 110 PRINT "INPUT VALUE OF FIRST
 TERM"
 120 INPUT A
 130 PRINT "INPUT VALUE OF X"
 140 INPUT X
 150 PRINT "INPUT ACCURACY REQUI
RED"
 160 INPUT D
 165 REM
 170 REM **FIRST TERM**
 175 REM
 180 LET T=A
 185 REM
 190 REM **NUMBER OF TERMS**
 195 REM
 200 LET N=1
 205 REM
 210 REM **SUM S,NEW SUM S1**
 215 REM
 220 LET S1=A
 230 LET S=S1
 235 REM
 240 REM **CALCULATE NEXT TERM**
 245 REM
 250 LET N=N+1
 255 REM **SPECTRUM USERS CAN **
         **USE DEF FN HERE     **

 260 LET T=T*X/(N-1)
 265 REM
 270 REM **CALCULATE NEW SUM**
 275 REM
 280 LET S1=S1+T
 285 REM
 290 REM **COMPARE S AND S1**
 295 REM
 300 IF ABS (S1-S)>D THEN GOTO 2
30
 310 CLS
 315 REM **OUTPUT RESULTS**

 320 PRINT "SUM OF ";A$;" SERIES
"
```

```
 330 PRINT "********************
***********"
 340 PRINT "TO AN ACCURACY OF ";
D
 350 PRINT
 360 PRINT "FIRST TERM=";A; TAB
0;"VALUE OF X=";X
 370 PRINT
 380 PRINT "SUM ";S1;" NO. OF TE
RMS ";N
 390 STOP

 400 REM **END PROGRAM**
```

Sample printout:

```
SUM OF EXPONENTIAL SERIES
*********************************
TO AN ACCURACY OF .00001
FIRST TERM=1
VALUE OF X=1
SUM 2.7182815 NO. OF TERMS 10
```

Comment: Typical examples of other series that could be summed using the same program are given below:

$$S = 1 + x + x^2 + x^3 + \ldots\ldots x^n \ldots \text{ if } x<1$$

$$\text{Cos } x = 1 - \frac{x^2}{2!} + \frac{x^4}{4!} \ldots (-1)^n . \frac{x^{2n}}{(2n)!} \text{ for all } x$$

$$\text{Sin } x = x - \frac{x^3}{3!} + \frac{x^5}{5!} \ldots\ldots (-1)^n . \frac{x^{2n+1}}{(2n-1)!} \text{ for all } x$$

$$S = 1 - x + x^2 - x^3 + \ldots\ldots \text{ if } x<1$$

Now consider how you might improve upon this program. Ideally this should have been considered at the planning stage and not *after* coding. We should perhaps include a subroutine to correct the sum to the appropriate number of decimal places or routines to enable the user to check that input data is correct. We could LPRINT directly to the printer for our hard copy printout, to avoid using COPY.

5. "GRAPH"

Problem: To produce a useful hard-copy graph of various functions (Y = function X) in the positive quadrant (X and Y positive), with titles and scales included.

Research the problem: The program must allow a variety of functions to be plotted. Thus there must be an input or a line of the program to be altered, according to the function which is to be plotted.

Titles are to be printed, as are scale values. Hence we need to know the area of the screen in which we are to plot, and define the plotting routine so that it keeps within this area. Indications of the scales should be visible on the plot screen, to enable approximate values to be read off. This will require inputs.

Scale factors must be established so that the points to be plotted are within the defined area and good use is made of the available area, so that the graph is not cramped. The capacity to calculate the values of the dependent variable Y for a chosen range of X will be needed. Alterations of the values of X, so that the derived range of Y may be altered if necessary, should be possible within the program.

As in all graphing programs, some degree of inspection and choice is required. In this case the requirement for scales to be printed requires the input of suitable intervals to make the graph functional.

The program will hence require the following modules:

1 Input and calculation of function to be plotted. Revision of X values and re-calculation if required.
2 Input of X, Y scale values and calculation of scale factors. Printing of graph surround, titles, scale values.
3 Plotting of function.

Outline procedure:

Module 1:	1	Input:	Function to be calculated. Values of X to define range of X required.
	2	Calculation:	Calculate and store in array values of Y. Find maximum and minimum values of Y. Scale factor for X axis.
	3	Output:	Maximum and minimum values of Y for specified range of X.
	4	Repeat 1 – 3 if required. User input to decide if required.	
Module 2:	1	Input:	Low and High X, Y values. Scale values for X and Y axis divisions. X, Y axis titles. Graph titles.
	2	Calculate:	Scale factor for Y.
	3	Output:	Print titles, scale values, major scale intervals.
Module 3:	1	Input:	Values of Y stored in array.
	2	Calculate:	X, Y plot values, in accordance with scale factors.
	3	Output:	Plot of function in specified area of screen.

Detailed Procedure

The descriptive algorithm (with user notes) for obtaining the best possible plot within defined scales is as follows. The user must be presented with the information required to make decisions as to suitable values for the X and Y axis scales.

1 Define range of values of X for which values of Y are to be obtained.
1.1 Input minimum value of X (MINX).
1.2 Input maximum value of X (MX).

Note: Values of X should be chosen such that the scale divisions correspond to values of X that will fit the defined purpose of the graph (range of X required). Thus the range of X would be chosen to suit the major scale divisions of the 'graph paper' drawn by the program. We would choose X to be plotted on a scale running from Ø to 5, to give scale divisions of:

Ø 1 2 3 4 5

along the X axis, even though we were primarily interested in the plot of Y with X in the range, say, Ø.5 to 3.9, adapting the X values to the constraints of the graph scales drawn on the screen. (See the sample printout for these.) Similarly, we might choose X axis scale values of

Ø.4 Ø.5 Ø.6 Ø.7 Ø.8 Ø.9

to fit within the constraints of the display, even when the prime concern was the plot of Y when X runs from Ø.5 to 7.9.

1.3 The scale factor for X (DX) to be used in the calculation loop to derive values of Y is then (Number of points to be plotted on X axis/(Maximum X – Minimum X)). DX = 5Ø/(MX – MINX) for the ZX81 and 2ØØ/(MX – MINX) for the Spectrum.
2 Calculate values of Y for each value of X.
2.1 Set X equal to minimum value of X (MINX). Start calculation loop.
2.2 FOR each plot division on X axis (1 to 5Ø on ZX81, 1 to 2ØØ on Spectrum).
2.3 Calculate Y = (Function of X). Use VAL to calculate value of function input as string.
2.4 Store value in array N (N(F) = Y).
2.5 Increment X for next plot point (X = X + DX).
2.6 NEXT plot point on X axis. End of calculation loop.

Note: The values of Y are now stored in array N. We now require to know the minimum and maximum values of Y that have been produced by the calculation. We must search the array N for these values.

3 Search Array for Maximum and Minimum values of Y.
3.1 Set Maximum value and Minimum value variables (MAXY and MINY) equal to first Array element. (MINY = N(1),MAXY = N(1)). Start search loop.
3.2 FOR each element in array (N(2) to N(End)).
3.3 If array value is less than minimum value variable (N(F) < MINY) then set minimum Y variable equal to array element (MINY = N(F)).
3.4 If array value more than maximum value variable, set this variable equal to array element (MAXY = N(F)).
3.5 NEXT array element.
4 Inspect Range of Y.
4.1 Print maximum, minimum Y values (MAXY,MINY).
4.2 Present menu choice of: (i) Recalculating for a different range of X. Program returns to 1.1 if selected.
(ii) Choosing Y axis values.

Note: The user must now select the scale values for a range of Y such that all values of Y are within the range chosen and maximum vertical spread of plot points is achieved to avoid a cramped plot. This latter is the same decision as was made for the X axis values. A suitable scale must be chosen to conform with the scale divisions presented on the screen. The Y axis has three scale sections, requiring four scale values at the vertical divisions of the graph.

If MINY were Ø.12 and MAXY were 3.6 for a given range of X, for example, we might choose to set the minimum scale value for Y as Ø, and the maximum as 4.5, allowing intermediate values of 1.5 and 3.Ø, which correspond to the scale divisions, so that the Y axis will be labelled:

4.5
3.Ø
1.5
Ø

This gives the maximum vertical spread of plot points.

Having made this decision, the user can input the maximum and minimum Y axis values. The decision can also be made to return to the start of the first module and re-define the values of X, choosing a different range (choosing to calculate for X = 1.5 to 7.5, for example, rather than the original choice of Ø to 6 for the range). This re-calculation can be done repeatedly until the best possible Y values for placing on the graph have been found, within the constraints of the ranges of X that are acceptable.

5 Derive scale factor for Y axis.
5.1 Input minimum Y for scale (Y1).
5.2 Input maximum Y for scale (Y2).

Note: These values are the same as will be inserted as scale values in string form for printing on the display.

5.3 Scale value for Y plot is number of plot points on Y axis divided by maximum Y minus minimum Y. This is (DY = 3Ø/(Y2 – Y1) for ZX81, 12Ø/(Y2 – Y1) for Spectrum.)

Note: Next module of program inputs scale values as strings and the strings for titles to be printed to the screen.

6 Input scale values and titles.
6.1 Input Minimum Y.
6.2 FOR each remaining Y axis scale division (2 to 4).
6.3 Input scale value to be printed.
6.4 NEXT Y axis scale division.
6.5 Print maximum and minimum X value (MINX and MX) as reminder of X axis values.
6.6 FOR each X axis scale division (1 to 6).
6.7 Input scale value to be printed.
6.8 NEXT X axis division.
6.9 Input Graph title, Function or subtitle, X axis and Y axis titles.

This algorithm is coded in the program as the subroutine (lines 1ØØØ to 168Ø), called after initialisation of the arrays (lines 5Ø – 8Ø). On return, all necessary data has been input or calculated. The main program prints the scale divisions on the 'graph paper' area of the screen, using two sets of nested loops (lines 13Ø – 23Ø). Note the bypass condition in line 2ØØ to prevent unwanted horizontal lines being printed.

Scales and titles are then printed to the appropriate screen locations (lines 25Ø – 34Ø).

The plotting routine (lines 35Ø to 38Ø) takes each value from the array N, finds the difference between this value and the defined minimum Y value (Y1), and multiplies by the scale factor to get the Y axis plot position. Plot position is adjusted by the addition of constants to the X,Y values to be plotted, to place plot points within the graph paper area. These are:

X axis: 1Ø on ZX81, 4Ø on Spectrum
Y axis: 13 on ZX81, 52 on Spectrum

The printout is obtained using COPY.

Variables Table

X$(6,4)	Array to store X axis scale values (Input)
Y$(4,5)	Array to store Y axis scale values (Input)
T$(4,25)	Array for X, Y axis titles, graph titles (Input)
N(5Ø)	Array to store calculated Y values
F	Loop variable

L	Loop variable
F$	Function input as string
X	Value of X
MINX	Minimum value of X (Input)
MX	Maximum value of X (Input)
DX	Step value for X value in calculation
Y	Value of Y calculated. Each value stored in Array N(5Ø)
MAXY	Maximum value of Y
MINY	Minimum value of Y
M$	Menu choice (Input)
Y1	Minimum value of Y axis scale (Input)
Y2	Maximum value of Y axis scale (Input)
DY	Scale factor for plot of Y values

Flowchart "GRAPH"

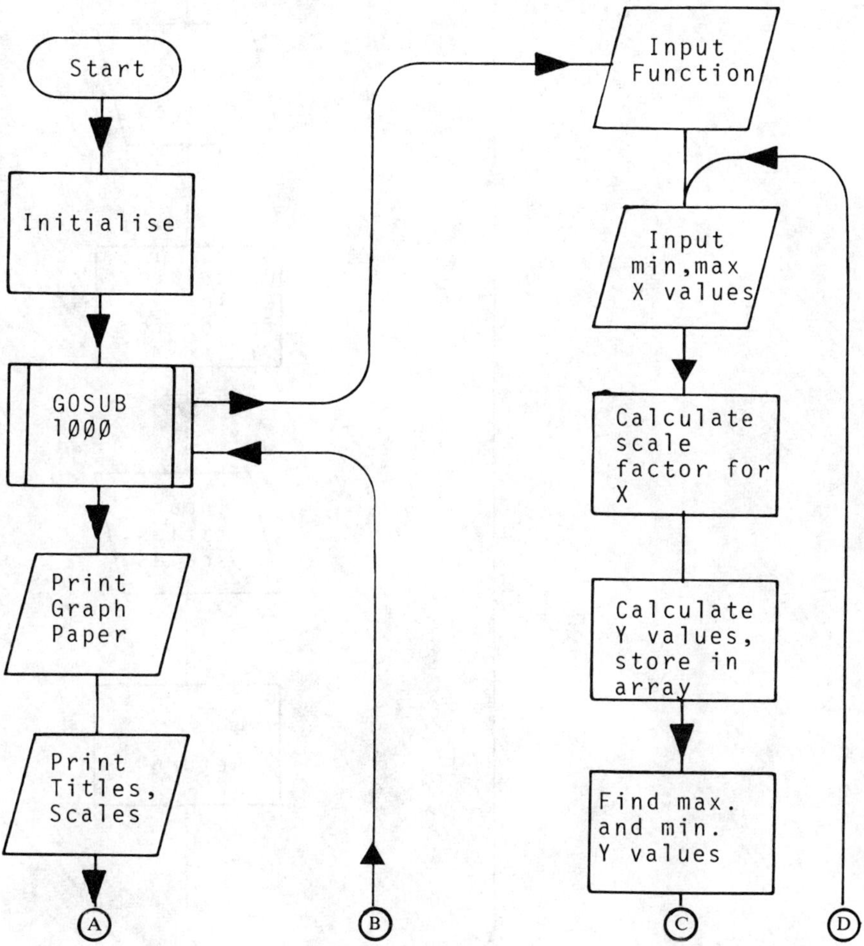

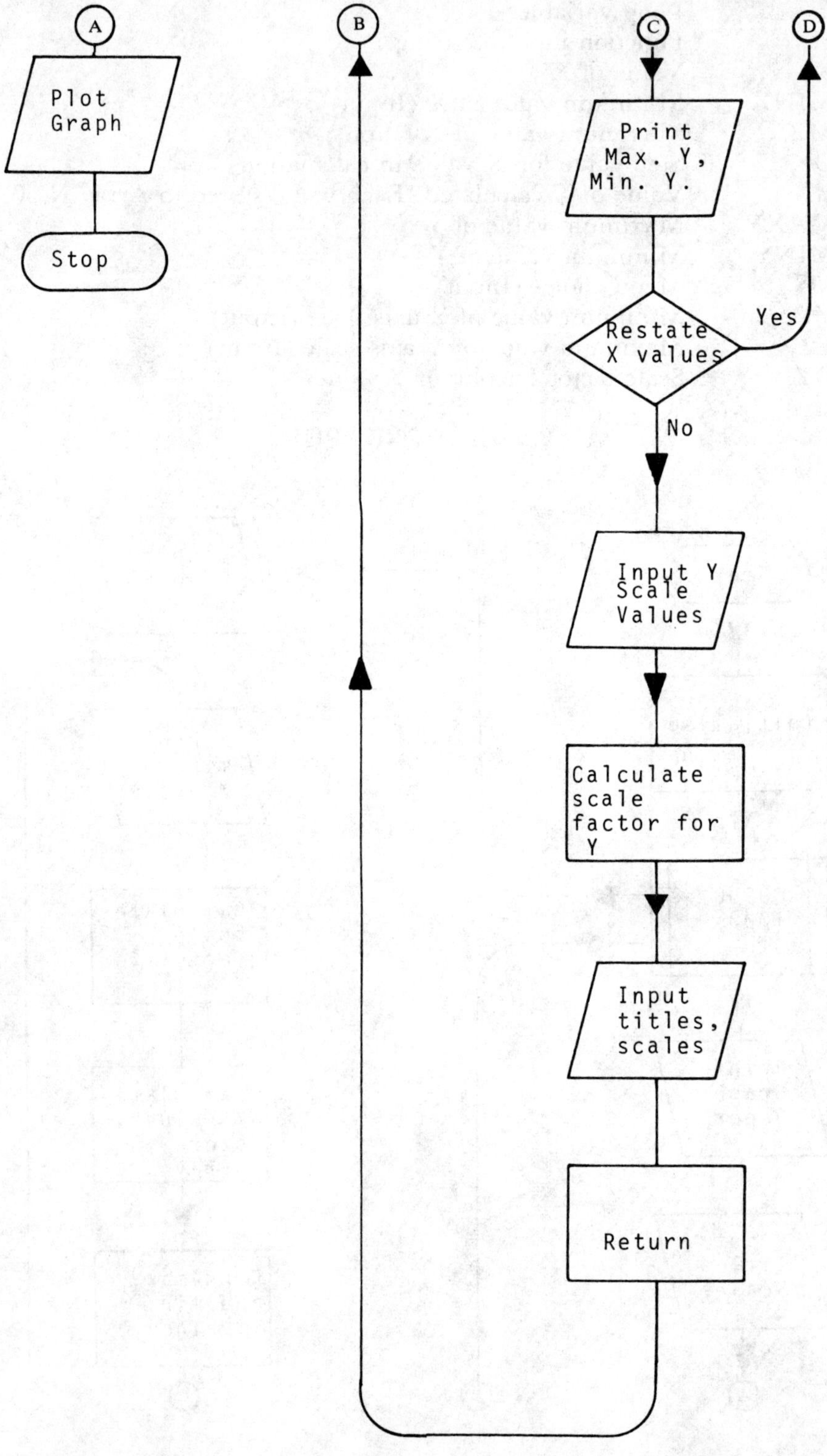
A
Plot
Graph
Stop
B
C
D
Print
Max. Y,
Min. Y.
Restate
X values
Yes
No
Input Y
Scale
Values
Calculate
scale
factor for
Y
Input
titles,
scales
Return

Spectrum modifications:

The different plot screen of the Spectrum must be taken into account. This affects scale factors and the actual plot routine, and requires a larger array for the data (values of Y for the function of X).

In the same area of the screen, where the ZX81 has 5Ø X axis plot points, the Spectrum has (4 × 5Ø), 2ØØ. The array N must thus be initialised as N(2ØØ). The scale factors for Y and X also need to be calculated according to this changed plot resolution. Line changes needed are as follows:

```
  8Ø   DIM N(2ØØ)
 36Ø   FOR F = 1 TO 2ØØ
 37Ø   PLOT F + 4Ø, (N(F) – Y1)*DY + 52
112Ø   LET DX = 2ØØ/(MX – MINX)
Delete lines 1135 and 1265
115Ø   FOR F = 1 TO 2ØØ
123Ø   FOR F = 2 TO 2ØØ
138Ø   LET DY = 12Ø/(Y2 – Y1)
139Ø   Delete 3Ø, Insert 12Ø
152Ø   Delete 3Ø, Insert 2ØØ
```

Spectrum users can also use the DEF FN and FN instructions to define the function to be plotted (in line 1Ø5Ø) and to evaluate the function within the calculation loop (line 116Ø). Revise the program to utilise these functions when they have been dealt with in Section W.

Sample printout

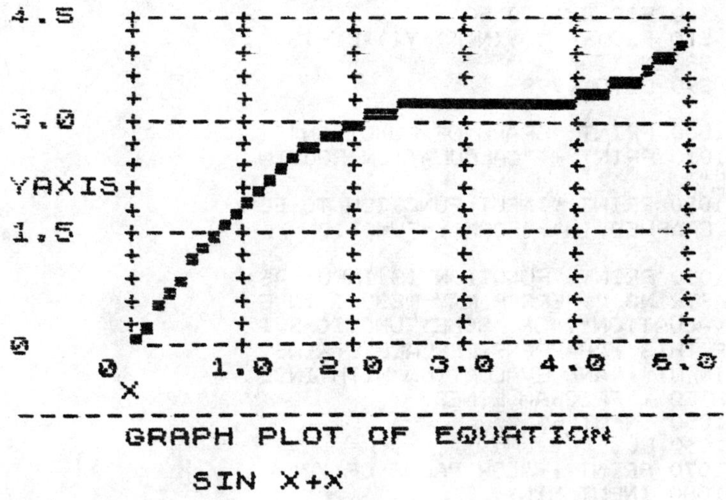

Program listing

```
10 REM "GRAPH"
20 REM *PRODUCES GRAPH OF
30 REM *FUNCTION WITH TITLES
40 REM *AND SCALES FOR +VE
       *QUADRANT
```

```
  50 DIM X$(6,4)
  60 DIM Y$(4,5)
  70 DIM T$(4,25)
  80 DIM N(50)
  90 REM **GOSUB INPUTS**
 100 GOSUB 1000
 110 CLS
 120 REM **PRINT PAPER**
 130 FOR F=5 TO 30 STEP 5
 140 FOR L=0 TO 15
 150 PRINT AT L,F;"+"
 160 NEXT L
 170 NEXT F
 200 FOR L=0 TO 15 STEP 5
 205 FOR F=6 TO 29
 206 IF F/5= INT (F/5) THEN NEXT
 F
 210 PRINT AT L,F;"-"
 220 NEXT F
 230 NEXT L
 240 REM **TITLES**
 250 FOR F=1 TO 6
 260 PRINT AT 16,(F*5-1);X$(F)
 270 NEXT F
 280 FOR F=1 TO 4
 290 PRINT AT 20-F*5,0;Y$(F)
 300 NEXT F
 310 PRINT AT 17,5;T$(3)
 320 PRINT AT 18,0;"------------
--------------------"
 330 PRINT AT 19,5;T$(1); AT 21,
8;T$(2)(1 TO 20)
 340 PRINT AT 8,0;T$(4)(1 TO 5);
 TAB 0;T$(4)(6 TO 10)
 350 REM **PLOT FROM ARRAY **
 360 FOR F=1 TO 50
 370 PLOT F+10,(N(F)-Y1)*DY+13
 380 NEXT F
 390 GOTO 9999

1000 PRINT "GRAPH OF FUNCTION"
1010 PRINT ,,"CALCULATION ROUTIN
E"
1020 PRINT "INPUT FUNCTION TO BE
 GRAPHED,IN","FORM Y=FUNCTION X.
"
1030 PRINT "FUNCTION IS INPUT AS
 STRING. ","ERROR MAY RESULT IN E
VALUATION","OF  SOME FUNCTIONS.I
F THIS","HAPPENS,REPLACE STRING
INPUT","AND EVALUATION WITH INSE
RTED","PROGRAM LINES"
1050 INPUT F$
1060 CLS
1070 PRINT ,,"LOW VALUE OF X?"
1080 INPUT MINX
1090 PRINT ,,"HIGH VALUE OF X?"
1100 INPUT MX
1110 REM **SCALE FACTOR X**
1120 LET DX=50/(MX-MINX)
1130 REM **CALCULATE **
1135 FAST
1140 LET X=MINX
```

```
1150 FOR F=1 TO 50
1160 LET Y= VAL F$
1170 LET N(F)=Y
1180 LET X=X+(1/DX)
1190 NEXT F
1200 REM **GET MAX,MIN Y**
1210 LET MAXY=N(1)
1220 LET MINY=N(1)
1230 FOR F=2 TO 50
1240 IF N(F)<MINY THEN LET MINY=
N(F)
1250 IF MAXY<N(F) THEN LET MAXY=
N(F)
1260 NEXT F
1265 SLOW
1270 PRINT "MINIMUM VALUE FOR Y
IS:",MINY
1280 PRINT "MAXIMUM VALUE FOR Y
IS:",MAXY
1290 PRINT ,,"CHOOSE SUITABLE VA
LUES FOR Y ";"AXIS (Y) OR RESTAT
E RANGE OF X ","(X)? INPUT X OR
Y."
1300 INPUT M$
1310 CLS
1320 IF M$="X" THEN GOTO 1070
1330 REM **SCALE FACTOR Y**
1340 PRINT "INPUT NUMERIC VALUE
OF MIN.Y","( <= ";MINY;")FOR SCA
LE"
1350 INPUT Y1
1360 PRINT "INPUT NUMERIC VALUE
OF MAX.Y","( >= ";MAXY;")"
1370 INPUT Y2
1380 LET DY=30/(Y2-Y1)
1385 REM ** Y AXIS SCALES **
1390 PRINT "Y AXIS HAS 3 SCALE D
IVISIONS,","AND 30 PLOT POINTS."
1400 PRINT "INPUT THE 4 SCALE VA
LUES FOR Y","AXIS.MAX 5 CHRS."
1410 PRINT "NEWLINE FOR BLANK."
1420 PRINT "MINIMUM(1)?"
1430 INPUT Y$(1)
1440 FOR F=2 TO 4
1450 PRINT "VALUE ";F;"?"
1460 INPUT Y$(F)
1470 NEXT F
1480 CLS
1485 REM **X AXIS SCALES**
1490 PRINT "INPUT X AXIS SCALES"
1500 PRINT "LOW X IS ";MINX
1510 PRINT "HIGH X IS ";MX
1520 PRINT ,,"6 SCALE DIVISIONS,
50 PLOT POINTSON X AXIS."
1530 PRINT "SCALE VALUES MAX.4 C
HRS.","FIRST INPUT IS LOW VALUE.
"
1540 FOR F=1 TO 6
1550 PRINT"SCALE VALUE ";F;"?"
1560 INPUT X$(F)
1570 NEXT F
1580 REM **TITLES**
1590 CLS
```

```
1600 PRINT "INPUT GRAPH TITLE (M
AX 25 CHRS)"
1610 INPUT T$(1)
1620 PRINT "INPUT FUNCTION OR SU
BTITLE(20","CHRS MAX)"
1630 INPUT T$(2)
1640 PRINT "INPUT X AXIS TITLE (
20 CHRS MAX)"
1650 INPUT T$(3)
1660 PRINT "INPUT Y AXIS TITLE(2
*5 CHRS)"
1670 INPUT T$(4)
1680 RETURN

9990 REM **END**
9999 STOP
```

6. "ELEMENT"

Problem: To calculate for a chemical compound: (i) Percentage elemental composition and molecular weight *or* (ii) molecular formula from inputs of, for (i), Number of atoms each element and for (ii) Percentages of each element. These are complementary calculations.

Research Problem: We require a program that performs two separate operations. The common requirements will be the Element names, symbols and molecular weights. We choose to input and store these as data in arrays on the computer. This will require an input routine that is not used every time the program is run, and could be edited out. The elements involved should be capable of being changed to facilitate different analyses, and this must be allowed for in our program. This is an advantage over the alternatives of either defining all data with LET statements or the use of DATA and READ (which are only available on the Spectrum).

The program must be split into two processing sections. The first of these (percentage elemental composition and molecular weight) requires an input for the number of atoms of each element. We can use a loop for this, using the loop variable to access the stored element names. Molecular weight equals the number of atoms of each compound multiplied by the atomic weight. This can be calculated within the input loop. Molecular formulae are then derived from the atomic symbol, plus the number of atoms, for each of the elements concerned.

Percentage composition for each element is the number of atoms of the element, times the atomic weight of the element, divided by the molecular weight.

The second section of the program requires an input loop for the percentage of each element. The proportion of atoms of each element will then be the percentage divided by atomic weight. This can be calculated within the input loop. To calculate the molecular formula, we require to know the minimum (to give us the smallest number of atoms of any of the elements) elemental proportion. We can check this through another loop. The number of atoms of each element is then the proportion of each element divided by the smallest proportion. We could round this to integers, but will do so to two decimal places because the actual molecular formula may be a multiple of the derived formula. We should also indicate this possibility to the user.

Zero inputs will be required when elements do not occur in the compound concerned.

For a common organic analysis the following data will be stored via the input routine:

HYDROGEN	H	1.008
CARBON	C	12.01
NITROGEN	N	14.008
OXYGEN	O	16.00
PHOSPHOROUS	P	30.98
SULPHUR	S	32.06
CHLORINE	CL	35.457
BROMINE	BR	79.916

The data entry module is keyed in and the data input as above. The lines 15 to 160 could then be deleted if required, leaving the data stored in the arrays and available for access, as long as RUN is not used (or CLEAR). Spectrum users should replace line 3000 with: 3000 SAVE "ELEMENT" LINE 3010. The program is then SAVEd to tape by using GOTO 3000, when it stops at line 1990, or run again by keying in GOTO 200 as a command.

You may like to derive an additional user dialogue to ask if the user wishes to SAVE or re-run the program, and according to the response, send control to the relevant line number. The procedure for the program is given below.

Detailed Procedure:

1 Data Entry Module
- 1.1 Dimension arrays for data: Element Names, Element Symbols, Atomic Weights
- 1.2 FOR each input (1 to 8)
- 1.3 Input Name, Symbol, Atomic Weight
- 1.4 GOTO subroutine to justify atomic weight (5 below)
- 1.5 NEXT input
- 1.6 Print user warning about the use of RUN

2 Menu
- 2.1 Print Instructions and Menu
- 2.2 If second calculation required, GOTO 4
- 2.3 If first calculation required, proceed to 3

3 Percentage Element Calculation

3.1 Input:

3.1.1 Reference for compound

3.1.2 Initialise arrays, molecular weight variable

3.1.3 FOR each Element (1 to 8)

3.1.4 Input number of atoms present

3.1.5 Calculate total molecular weight (Molecular weight plus (number of atoms * atomic weight))

3.1.6 NEXT Element

3.2 Processing/Output:

3.2.1 Print Reference, Molecular Weight

3.2.2 FOR each Element (1 to 8)

3.2.3 Print Symbol, number of atoms

3.2.4 NEXT Element

3.2.5 FOR each Element (1 to 8)

3.2.6 If no atoms present, GOTO 3.2.10

3.2.7 Calculate percentage as (Number of atoms times atomic weight) divided by molecular weight of compound, times 100

3.2.8 GOSUB (5) for rounding and justification of results

3.2.9 Print Element symbol, percentage

3.2.10 NEXT Element

4 Molecular Formula Calculation

4.1 Input:

4.1.1 Reference for compound

4.1.2 Initialise Arrays

4.1.3 FOR each Element (1 to 8)

4.1.4 Input percentage present

4.1.5 Calculate proportion of Element as percentage present divided by atomic weight

4.1.6 NEXT Element

4.2 Processing/Output:

4.2.1 Print reference

4.2.2 Set C = 100 for percentage calculation

4.2.3 FOR each Element (1 to 8)

4.2.4 If proportion is zero, GOTO 4.2.6

4.2.5 If proportion less than current value of C, then let C equal proportion of element

4.2.6 NEXT Element

4.2.7 FOR each Element (1 to 8)

4.2.8 If proportion is zero, GOTO 4.2.12

4.2.9 Number of atoms equals proportion divided by smallest proportion present, C

4.2.10 GOSUB (5) for rounding and justification to 2 d.p.

4.2.11 Print Symbol, number of atoms

4.2.12 NEXT Element

4.2.13 Print user warning that multiples of this calculated formula may be the actual formula

5 Subroutine to Round and Justify

(Input of number of decimal places (P) and number to be justified (N) from data defined in main program modules)

5.1 X$ set to contain P zeros

5.2 Integer value set as XN

5.3 Decimal value set as XD

5.4 Define X$ as rounded number string

5.5 X$ returned to main modules for printing

6 Auto-run. An automatic RUN routine using GOTO 200 is used to prevent the user entering RUN accidentally after LOADing

Variables Table

1) Input and main program sections:

E$(8,10)	Holds element names
S$(8,2)	Holds element symbol
M(8)	Holds atomic weight
E	Loop variable in main program
X	Loop variable in input routine
A$	Menu choice
R$	Reference for compound
MOLWT	Molecular weight
A(8)	Holds input of number of atoms of element
P(8)	Holds input or calculated percentage of element
N(8)	Holds calculated number of atoms of element
C	Constant for calculating percentages

2) Round and justify subroutine:

N	Holds number for operation of subroutine
X$	Holds string form of number returned by subroutine
XN	Holds integer value of N
XD	Holds decimal value of N
F	Loop variable in subroutine

Flowchart "ELEMENT"

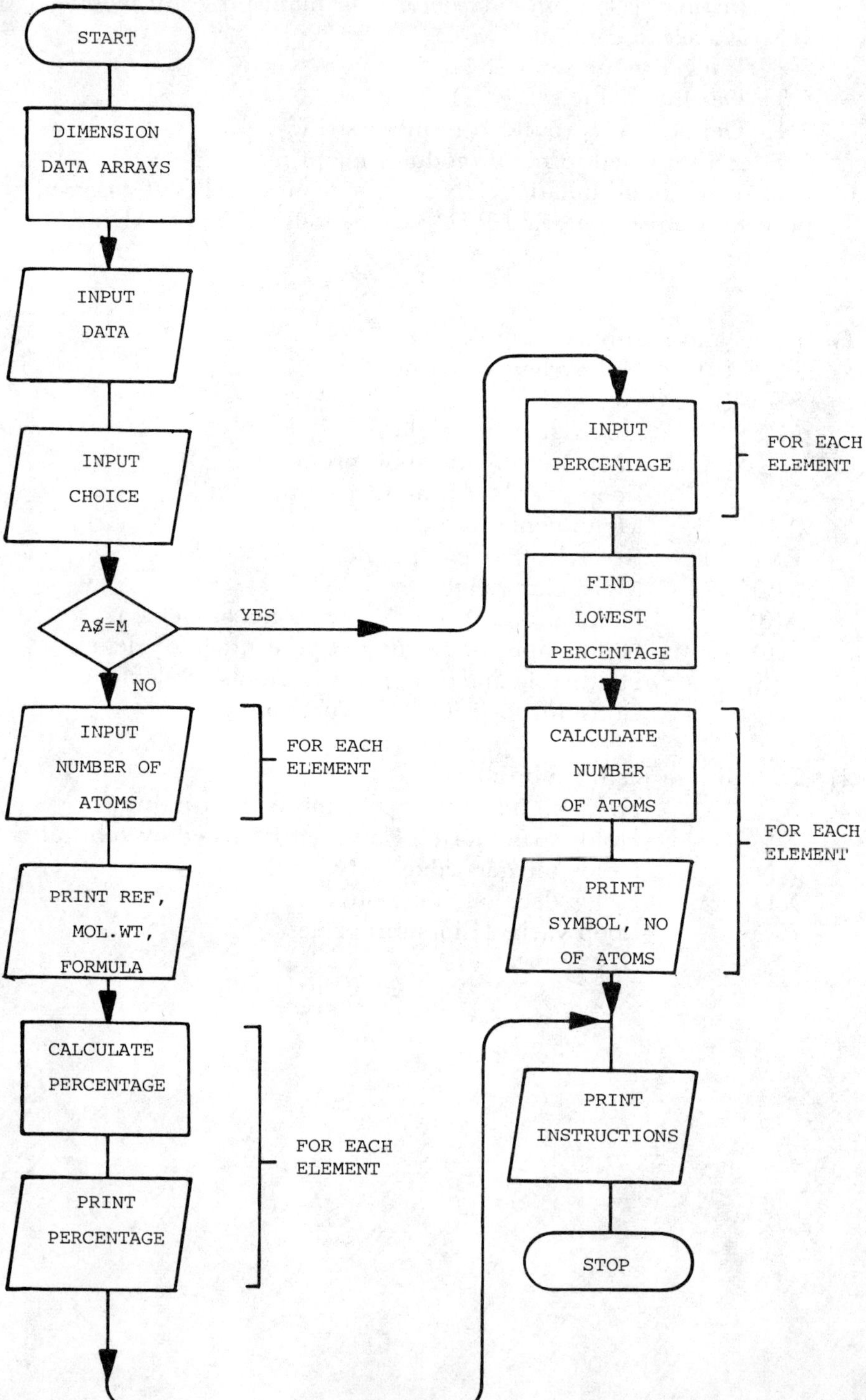

```
 10 REM "ELEMENT"
 15 REM ***********************
        1.DATA ENTRY.  ROUTINE
        CAN BE DELETED WHEN
        ENTRY COMPLETE.
        ***********************

 20 DIM E$(8,10)
 30 DIM S$(8,2)
 40 DIM M(8)
 50 PRINT "   ELEMENT   SYMBOL
 MOL.WT."
 55 PRINT
 60 FOR X=1 TO 8
 65 REM ** ELEMENT NAME **
 70 INPUT E$(X)
 75 REM ** ELEMENT SYMBOL **
 80 INPUT S$(X)
 85 REM ** ATOMIC WEIGHT **
 90 INPUT M(X)
 95 REM *INITIALISE FOR GOSUB**
100 LET P=3
110 LET N=M(X)
120 GOSUB 2000
130 PRINT X; TAB 3;E$(X); TAB 1
4;S$(X); TAB (27- LEN X$);X$
140 PRINT
150 NEXT X
160 REM
    **LINES 15 TO 160 CAN BE
    DELETED AFTER DATA ENTRY
    AND REST OF PROGRAM ENTERED
    MUST USE *GOTO 200* TO USE
    PROGRAM,NOT RUN,TO PRESERVE
    DATA.

170 REM **END 1.             **
        ***********************
180 REM
200 REM ***********************
        2. PROGRAM MENU TO
           CHOOSE CALCULATION
        ***********************

210 PRINT "CHOOSE CALCULATION R
EQUIRED:-"
220 PRINT
230 PRINT "TO INPUT NUMBER OF A
TOMS AND GETPERCENTAGE ELEMENT C
OMPOSITION AND MOLECULAR WEIGHT
INPUT E"
240 PRINT
250 PRINT "TO INPUT PERCENTAGE
ELEMENT ANA-LYSIS AND GET MOLECU
LAR FORMULA INPUT M"
260 INPUT A$
270 IF A$ <> "E" AND A$ <> "M"
THEN GOTO 260
280 CLS
290 IF A$="M" THEN GOTO 1000
```

```
 295 REM ** END 2.           **
     ************************

     ************************
     3.PERCENT ELEMENT
     ************************

 300 PRINT "ENTER REFERENCE FOR
THE COMPOUND"
 310 INPUT R$
 320 REM ** INITIALISE **
 330 DIM A(8)
 340 LET MOLWT=0
 350 DIM P(8)
 360 FOR E=1 TO 8
 370 PRINT "NUMBER OF ATOMS OF "
;E$(E);"?"
 380 INPUT A(E)
 390 LET MOLWT=MOLWT+(A(E)*M(E))
 400 NEXT E
 410 CLS
 420 REM **CALCULATE AND PRINT**
      **RESULTS              **

 430 PRINT "MOLECULAR WEIGHT AND
 COMPOSITION*******************
************"
 440 PRINT
 450 PRINT "REF:";R$
 460 PRINT
 470 PRINT "MOL.WEIGHT= ";MOLWT
 480 PRINT
 490 PRINT "MOL.FORMULA: ";
 500 FOR E=1 TO 8
 510 IF A(E)>1 THEN PRINT S$(E);
A(E);
 520 IF A(E)=1 THEN PRINT S$(E);
" ";
 530 NEXT E
 540 PRINT ".",,,
 550 FOR E=1 TO 8
 560 IF A(E)=0 THEN GOTO 620
 565 REM *CALCULATE PERCENTAGES*

 570 LET P(E)=A(E)*M(E)/MOLWT*
     100
 575 REM *INITIALISE FOR ROUND**
      **SUBROUTINE           **
 580 LET N=P(E)
 590 LET P=2
 600 GOSUB 2000
 610 PRINT "PERCENT ";S$(E); TAB
 (18- LEN X$);X$
 620 NEXT E
 625 REM **COPY HERE FOR PRINTED
      **RESULTS              **

 630 GOTO 1800
```

```
 640 REM ** END 3.              **
     ************************

 650 REM
 990 REM ************************
         4. MOLECULAR FORMULA
         ************************

1000 PRINT "ENTER REFERENCE FOR
COMPOUND"
1010 INPUT R$
1020 REM **DIM ARRAYS**
1030 DIM P(8)
1040 DIM N(8)
1050 PRINT
1060 REM **INPUT PERCENTAGES**

1070 FOR E=1 TO 8
1080 PRINT "PERCENT OF ";E$(E);"
 ?"
1090 INPUT P(E)
1095 REM **CALCULATE PROPORTION*

1100 LET N(E)=P(E)/M(E)
1110 NEXT E
1120 CLS
1130 REM **CALCULATE AND PRINT**
         **RESULTS              **

1140 PRINT "*MOLECULAR FORMULA*"
; TAB 0;"*******************"
1150 PRINT
1160 PRINT "REF:";R$
1170 PRINT
1175 REM **CALCULATE MINIMUM   **
         **PROPORTION ELEMENT **

1180 LET C=100
1190 FOR E=1 TO 8
1200 IF N(E)=0 THEN GOTO 1220
1210 IF N(E)<C THEN LET C=N(E)
1220 NEXT E
1225 REM **DERIVE FORMULA      **

1230 FOR E=1 TO 8
1240 IF N(E)=0 THEN GOTO 1290
1250 LET P=2
1260 LET N=N(E)/C
1270 GOSUB 2000
1280 PRINT S$(E); TAB 8- LEN X$;
X$
1290 NEXT E
1295 REM **COPY HERE FOR PRINTED
         **RESULTS              **

1300 PRINT ,,"MULTIPLES OF THIS
FORMULA MAY","BE THE ACTUAL FORM
ULA IF AT ","LEAST 2 ATOMS OF EA
CH ELEMENT","PRESENT"
```

```
1320 REM
        ** END 4.          **
        ***********************

1780 REM
1790 REM
       **ENDRUN INSTRUCTIONS**

1800 PRINT AT 20,0;"USE GOTO 200
 TO RUN AGAIN.","USE GOTO 3000 T
O SAVE"
1810 STOP

1820 REM
       **** END PROGRAM    ****
1830 REM

2000 REM ***********************
        5.SUBROUTINE TO ROUND
          AND JUSTIFY
        ***********************

2010 LET X$=""
2020 FOR F=1 TO P
2030 LET X$=X$+"0"
2040 NEXT F
2050 LET XN= INT N
2060 LET XD= INT (10 ** P*(N-XN)
+0.5)
2070 LET X$= STR$ XN+"."+(X$(1 T
O P- LEN STR$ XD)+ STR$ XD+X$)(1
 TO P)
2080 RETURN

2090 REM **    END SUB       **
        **********************
2980 REM
2990 REM ***********************
          AUTO-RUN ROUTINE
        ***********************

3000 SAVE "ELEMENT"
3010 GOTO 200

3020 REM **  END PROGRAM LIST **
```

7. "CASSFILE"

Problem: To write a program which will store and manipulate the data concerned with cassette program listings and print out lists of these files. The data must be able to be updated. Cassette labels should be printed out, taking advantage of the fact that the Sinclair printer paper is the correct width for this.

Research the problem: The program must have data entry and and storage for relevant data. This data must be displayed on screen and printed out if required. There must be a facility to add, delete and revise each portion of data separately. Data must be stored in string and numeric arrays, and there should be protection from accidental clearing of the stored data by the use of RUN. However, since more data may be required to be stored than will fit in one set of arrays, there should be also a facility to clear the file data arrays deliberately, to allow a new file system to be set up. Any other variables must be defined by LET statements, and all variables re-initialised after CLEAR has been used.

The best method of setting up a structure for this type of program is to have a *menu* presented to the user. From the menu, control can be passed to a separate module of the program which will perform the appropriate manipulations. After each set of operations have been performed, control will pass back to the menu module, which is the main program, looping back after each call (via a GOSUB or GOTO instruction) of the other program modules.

Outline Procedure:

1 Initialise storage arrays, variables, strings.
2 Present menu options.
3 Pass control to selected area of program.
4 Required are program modules to:
    Input data (create a file)
    Print a file (screen and printer)
    Revise a file
    Delete a file
    Print cassette label
    Erase all files
Control returns to (2) on completion of each operation.
5 Adding a Save files procedure will enable an auto-run system to avoid the risk of using RUN, and wiping out data.

Detailed Procedure:

1 Define the data to be held, its form, variables needed in the program, and strings to be used by one or more program sections to print titles for data. Initialise arrays, variables, strings. (See data table below.) This module is processed only once for each file system.

2.1 Present Menu: 1 Create File
    2 View/Print File
    3 Revise File
    4 Delete File
    5 Print Cassette Label
    6 Save Files
    7 Erase all Files

2.2 Loop back to start of Menu. If CLEAR has been used in 4.7, loop to (1).

3 Go to chosen program section. Use subroutines unless this causes problems.

4.1 Create File.

- 4.1.1 Define file number (existing files + 1)
- 4.1.2 Input data
- 4.1.3 Increment file count
- 4.1.4 Sub-menu: View created file (GOSUB 4.2)
Create another file (GOSUB 4.1)
Menu (RETURN)
- 4.1.5 Return to Menu

4.2 View/Print File

- 4.2.1 Get file number to view
- 4.2.2 Print file contents on screen
- 4.2.3 Sub-menu: Print file to printer (COPY)
View next file (GOSUB 4.2)
Menu (RETURN)
- 4.2.4 Return to Menu

4.3 Revise File

- 4.3.1 Get file number to revise
- 4.3.2 Print each item on screen
- 4.3.3 Input new data if required, leave if correct
- 4.3.4 Print new data if input
- 4.3.5 Return to Menu

4.4 Delete File

- 4.4.1 Get file number to delete
- 4.4.2 Print basic file data (name, reference)
- 4.4.3 Confirm deletion
- 4.4.4 Delete file contents
- 4.4.5 Swap data from files of higher number to maintain file numbering as sequence
- 4.4.6 Print new file numbers and basic data (reference and name)
- 4.4.7 Sub-menu: Copy new file listing (COPY)
Menu (RETURN)
- 4.4.8 Return to Menu

4.5 Print Cassette Label

- 4.5.1 Get file number
- 4.5.2 Print file contents on printer in suitable form
- 4.5.3 Return to Menu

4.6 Save Files

- 4.6.1 Allow revision of program name (string)
- 4.6.2 Allow return to menu if error
- 4.6.3 Stop program until cassette ready
- 4.6.4 Save 'program name string'
- 4.6.5 GOTO Menu (prevent use of RUN)

Note that this module cannot be a subroutine. Auto-run routines on the ZX81 do not operate from within subroutines properly, so control must be passed with GOTO instructions. This procedure is modified for the Spectrum (see notes below).

4.7 Delete all files
  - 4.7.1 Confirm deletion
  - 4.7.2 Use CLEAR to delete data
  - 4.7.3 Set marker for re-initialisation of variables on Return to Menu
  - 4.7.4 Return

  This cannot be a subroutine on the Spectrum (see notes below). The marker informs the main program loop that control must be passed to module (1) for re-initialisation.

Each section of the program must then have the detailed procedures, including input checks, defined. Each area of the program can be treated as a program module for coding purposes. The sections must operate on the same data structures, so the first task is to define the arrays for the data, variables required, and strings for printing, so that a table of these may be used in developing each section of program.

Data Table

C$(10,4)	Holds cassette reference (any four characters)
N$(10,15)	Holds cassette name (15 characters)
P$(10,10,15)	Holds for each cassette file 10 program names (15 characters)
T(10,10,2)	Holds for each program on each cassette tape counter readings (Start and Finish, numbers assumed to be in range 0 – 999)
F	File number of file being manipulated in processing
TF	Total number of files (up to 10)
M$	String input from menus
M	Numeric input from menus
S$	Current file program name
N,L	Used as loop control variables
E$	Set as empty string for overprinting
A$,B$,F$,G$	
H$,I$,X$,Y$,Z$	Used as string literals for printing
X	Marker to show CLEAR has been used and hence that re-initialisation of variables and arrays is required.

Another consideration is whether recursive or nested subroutines should be used. Care must be taken in the use of these facilities, and unnecessary complication should be avoided, since all control is passed back to the Menu, from which all modules can be accessed. However, in the program recursion is used in the Create File routine to allow a sequence of data entries to be made (Line 128Ø), and (Line 23ØØ) in the View File routine to allow stepping through the files.

The View File routine is also available as a nested subroutine from the Create File routine to allow a newly created file to be viewed (Line 2Ø2Ø). Apart from these instances a simple GOSUB – RETURN pattern of control has been followed, and the control flow in the Save Files routine has the same structure, but using GOTO instructions for the reason stated above. The different action of the CLEAR instruction on the Spectrum requires a GOTO instruction for the Erase All Files module (see below).

Ten files are set up and manipulated in this program. Reference to the way variables are stored (Section T) will enable you to discover the memory required for this. The same section has the PEEK routine to discover program size. Work these out. You will find that the program could in fact store and manipulate up to 3Ø such files on the ZX81. Display file size will restrict the 16k Spectrum user to ten files, as in the program.

The main program flow is illustrated in the first flowchart. The nested and recursive structures in the program are illustrated in the second, with the sub-menu control structures also shown. Sub-menus include a "Return to Main Menu" option.

Flowchart "CASSFILE"

1. Main Program Flowchart

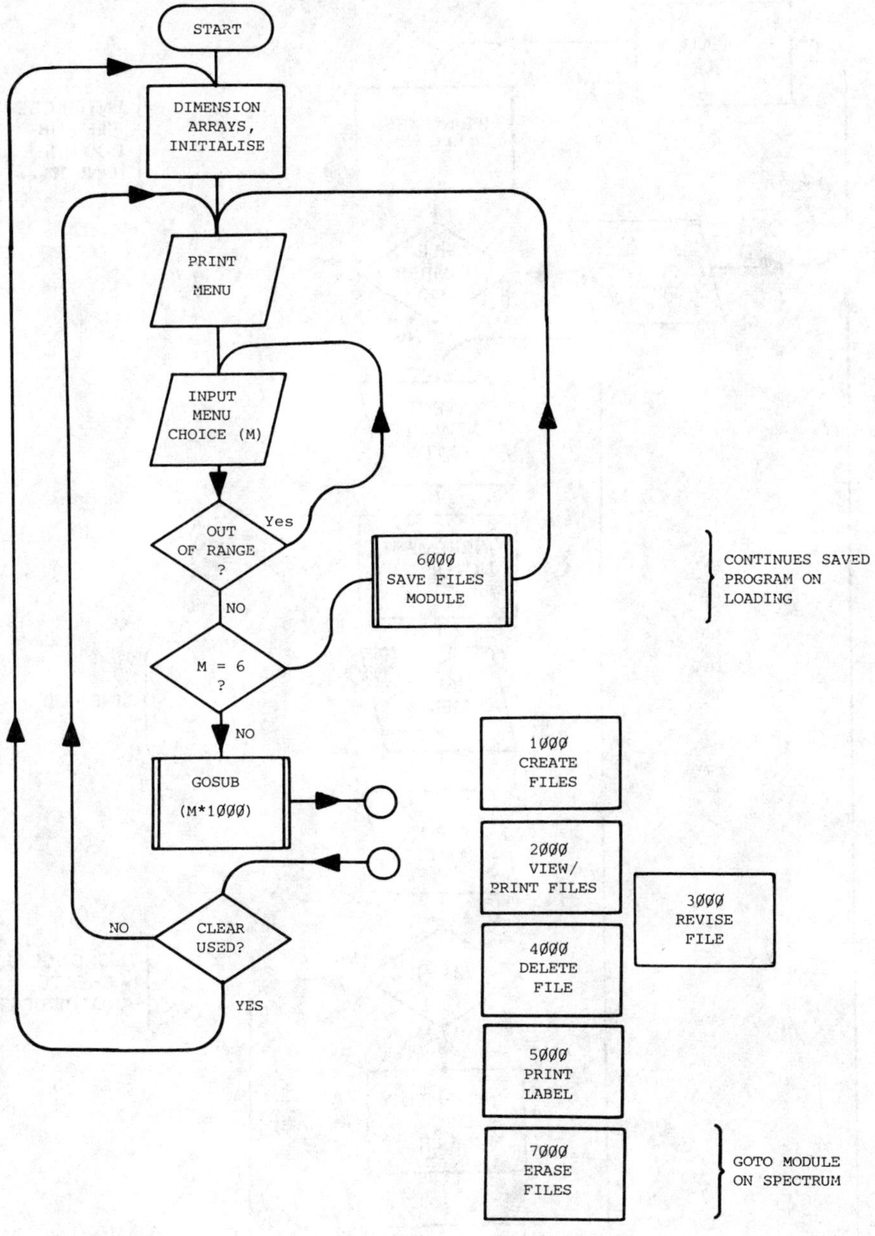

2. Recursion and Nesting the Create File and View File Subroutine

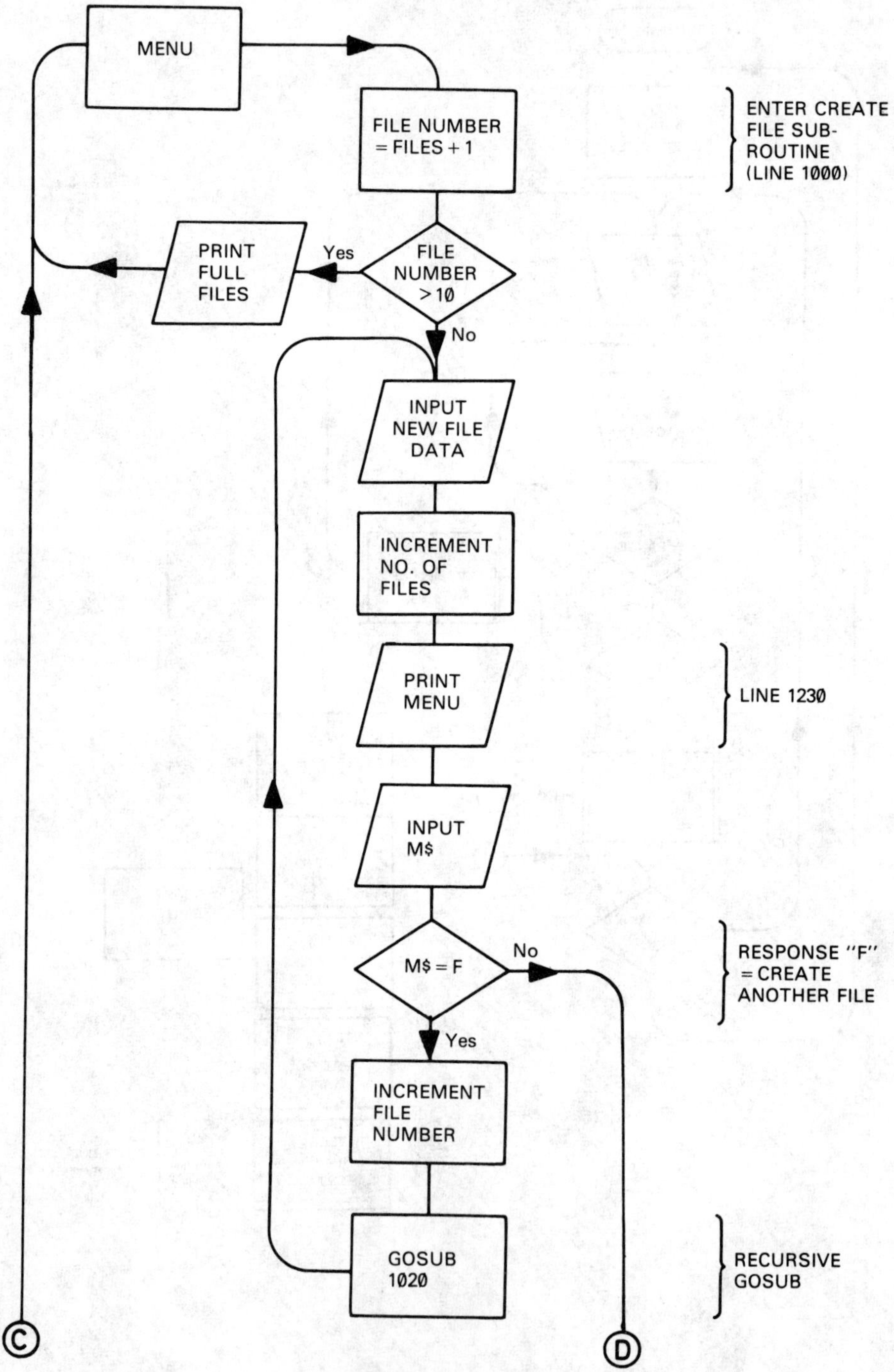

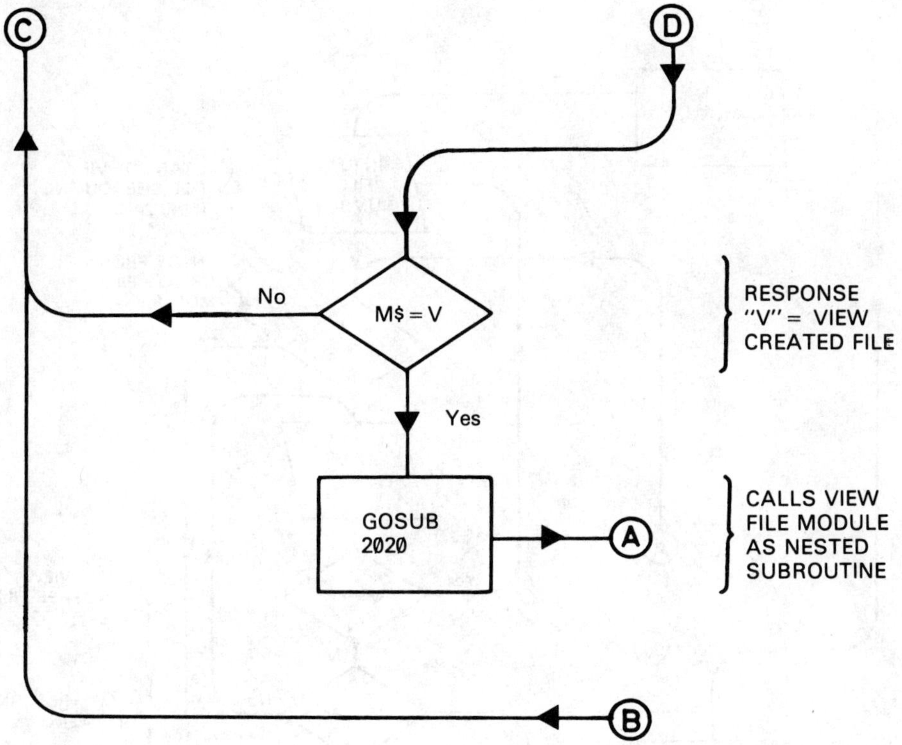
C
D
No
M$ = V
Yes
GOSUB
2020
A
B
RESPONSE
"V" = VIEW
CREATED FILE
CALLS VIEW
FILE MODULE
AS NESTED
SUBROUTINE

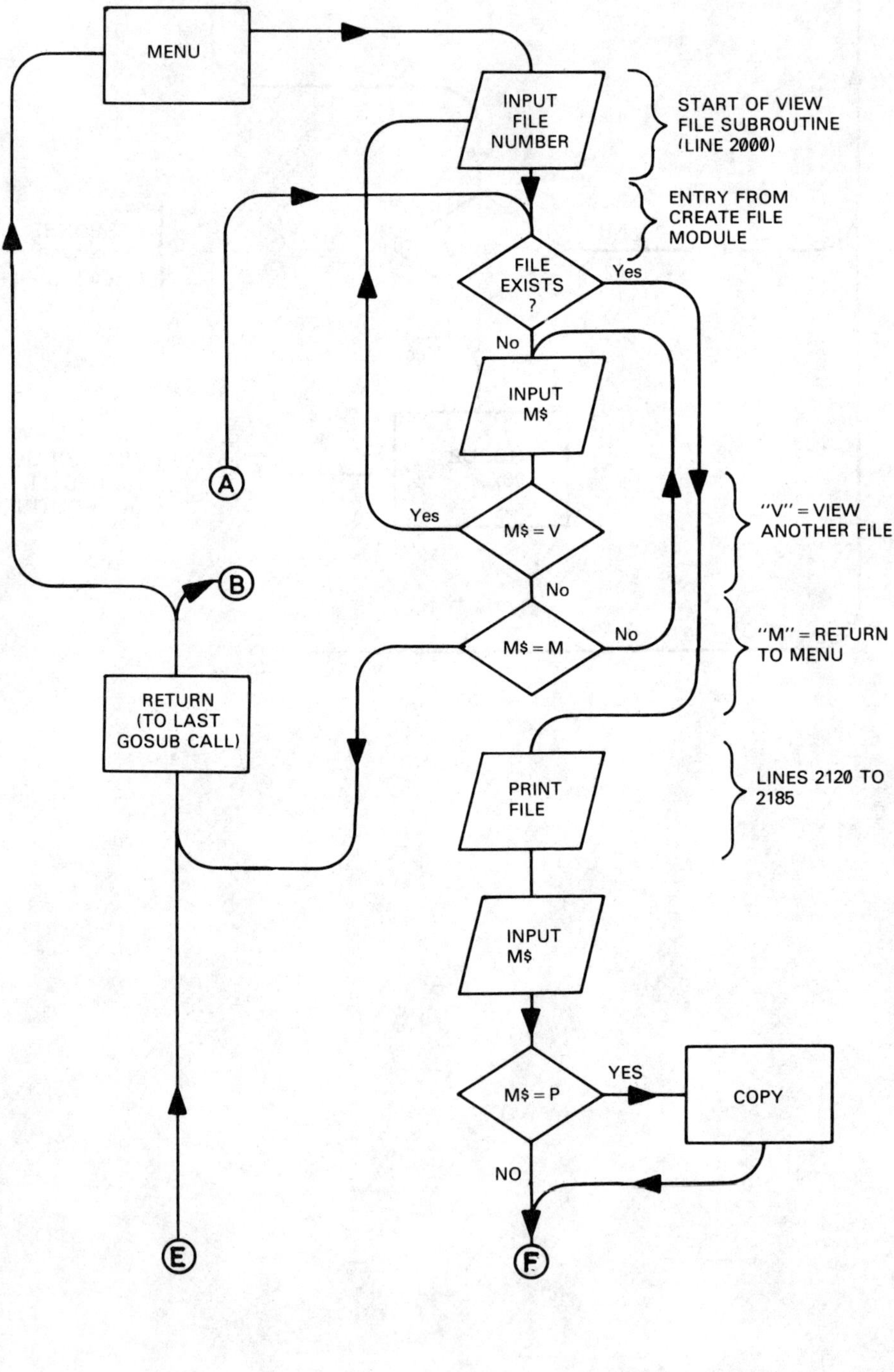
MENU
INPUT FILE NUMBER
START OF VIEW FILE SUBROUTINE (LINE 2000)
ENTRY FROM CREATE FILE MODULE
FILE EXISTS ?
Yes
No
INPUT M$
A
Yes
M$ = V
"V" = VIEW ANOTHER FILE
No
B
M$ = M
No
"M" = RETURN TO MENU
RETURN (TO LAST GOSUB CALL)
PRINT FILE
LINES 2120 TO 2185
INPUT M$
M$ = P
YES
COPY
NO
E
F

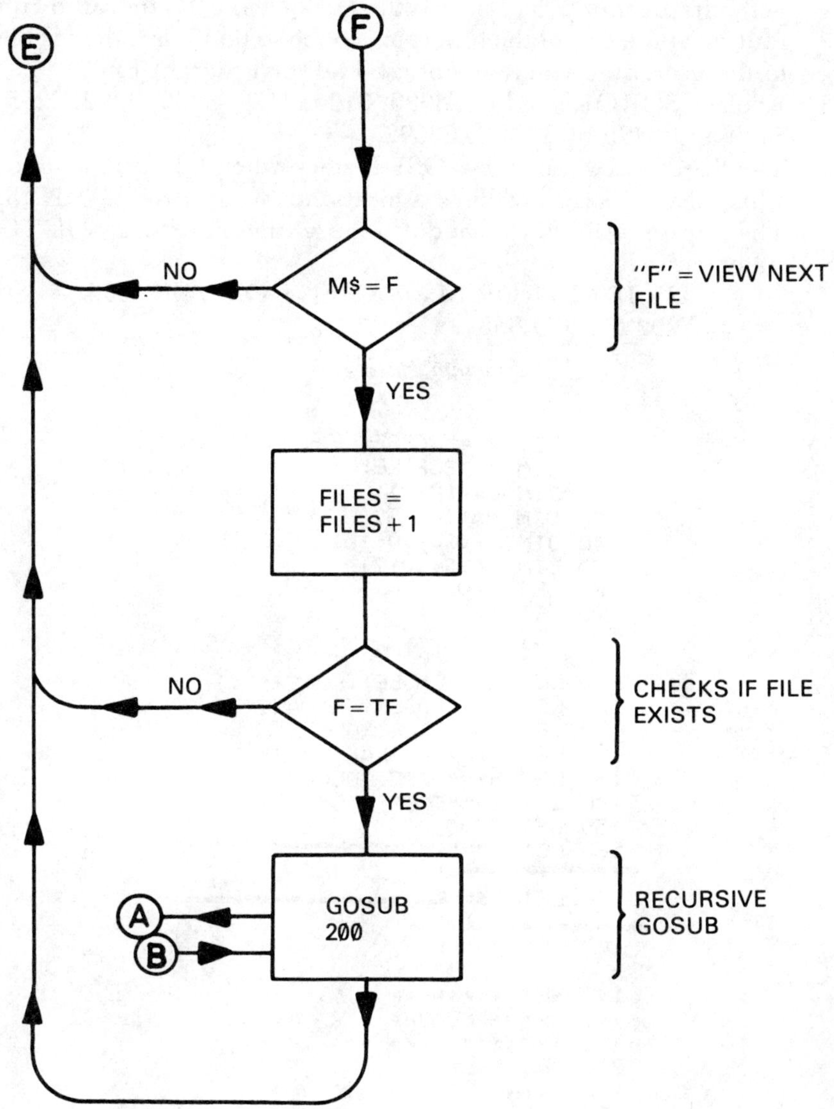

Spectrum Modifications:

1 The Spectrum has a simplified auto-run procedure and printing the prompts is done automatically. Make the following line changes:

```
9950 PRINT "PRESS A KEY FOR SAVE ROUTINE"
9960 PAUSE 0
9970 SAVE S$ LINE 9980
```

This whole module (lines 6000 onwards) *could* be a subroutine on the Spectrum (unlike the ZX81, it will SAVE from a subroutine), but it should then be a self-contained subroutine, without the jump at line 61ØØ. The placing of the auto-run routine at the end of the program is done so that it is more visible to the user, since there is not a STOP or Program End.

2 Replace SCROLL in lines 3Ø9Ø, 315Ø, 317Ø, 323Ø, 325Ø, 3265, 342Ø and 3495 by POKE 23692, – 1.

3 The Spectrum wipes the GOSUB stack when CLEAR is used. This means it will not have a location stored to RETURN to. The Erase All Files module must therefore use GOTO statements:

```
325 IF M = 6 OR M = 7 THEN GOTO M*1ØØØ
7Ø9Ø GOTO 35Ø
```

Program Listing

```
  5 LET S$="CASSFILE*1"
 10 REM "CASSFILE"
 20 DIM C$(10,4)
 30 DIM N$(10,15)
 40 DIM P$(10,10,15)
 50 DIM T(10,10,2)
 60 LET X=0
 70 LET F=0
 80 LET E$="
           "
 90 LET A$="CASSETTE REF:"
100 LET B$="CASSETTE NAME"
110 LET F$="FILE NO. "
120 LET G$="PROGRAM NAME"
130 LET H$="TAPE COUNT"
140 LET I$="FROM  TO"
150 LET TF=0
160 LET X$="▛▀▀▀▀▀▀▀▀▀▀▀▀▀▀▀▀▀▀▀▀▀
▀▀▀▀▀▀▀▀▀▀▀▀▀▀▀▀▀▀▀▀▀▜"
170 LET Y$="▙▄▄▄▄▄▄▄▄▄▄▄▄▄▄▄▄▄▄▄▄▄
▄▄▄▄▄▄▄▄▄▄▄▄▄▄▄▄▄▄▄▄▄▟"
180 LET Z$="▌
           ▐"
190 REM ********
191 REM **MENU**
192 REM ********
200 PRINT S$
210 PRINT TAB 10; "MENU"
220 PRINT
230 PRINT "1. CREATE FILE"
240 PRINT ,,"2. VIEW/PRINT FILE
"
250 PRINT ,,"3. REVISE FILE"
260 PRINT ,,"4. DELETE FILE"
270 PRINT ,,"5. PRINT CASSETTE
LABEL"
280 PRINT ,,"6. SAVE FILES"
290 PRINT ,,"7. ERASE ALL FILES
"
300 PRINT ,,"INPUT YOUR CHOICE"
310 INPUT M
320 IF M<1 OR M>7 THEN GOTO 300
325 IF M=6 THEN GOTO 6000
330 CLS
340 GOSUB M*1000
```

```
 350 CLS
 355 IF X=1 THEN GOTO 20
 360 GOTO 210

 990 REM *********************
        ** CREATE FILE SUB  **
        *********************
1000 LET F=TF+1
1010 IF F <= 10 THEN GOTO 1020
1015 PRINT "**NO SPACE FOR ANOTH
ER FILE**",,,"ON RETURN TO MENU
CHOOSE SAVE","OPTION TO KEEP CUR
RENT FILES","THEN ERASE FILES AN
D START NEW","FILE ARRAY."
1016 PAUSE 300
1017 RETURN

1020 PRINT "READY TO CREATE FILE
 NO. ";F
1030 PRINT AT 2,0;"INPUT CASSETT
E REF.(4 CHRS MAX)"
1040 INPUT C$(F)
1050 PRINT AT 2,0;E$; AT 2,0;B$;
"?(15 CHRS MAX)"
1060 INPUT N$(F)
1070 PRINT AT 2,0;E$; AT 2,0;"IN
PUT PROG.NAMES AND TAPE COUNTS"
1080 PAUSE 300
1090 FOR N=1 TO 10
1100 PRINT AT 4,0;"PROGRAM ";N
1110 PRINT G$;" ? (15 CHRS MAX)"
1120 INPUT P$(F,N)
1130 PRINT AT 5,0;E$; AT 5,0;H$;
" FROM ?"
1140 INPUT T(F,N,1)
1150 PRINT AT 5,11;"TO ?    "
1160 INPUT T(F,N,2)
1170 PRINT AT 5,0;E$; AT 5,0;"AN
OTHER PROGRAM ?(Y/N)"
1180 INPUT M$
1190 IF M$="N" THEN GOTO 1220
1200 IF M$ <> "N" AND M$ <> "Y"
THEN GOTO 1170
1210 NEXT N
1220 CLS
1225 LET TF=TF+1
1230 PRINT "CREATE ANOTHER FILE
(F),VIEW","CREATED FILE (V) OR M
ENU (M)?","INPUT F,V OR M."
1240 INPUT M$
1250 IF M$ <> "F" THEN GOTO 1290
1260 LET F=F+1
1270 CLS
1280 GOSUB 1020
1290 CLS
1295 IF M$="V" THEN GOSUB 2020
1300 RETURN

1980 REM ********************
1990 REM *** VIEW FILE SUB ** *
1991 REM ********************
2000 PRINT "WHICH FILE NUMBER?"
2010 INPUT F
```

```
2015 REM **ENTRY FROM OTHER SUBS
**
2020 CLS
2030 IF TF <> 0 AND F <= TF AND
F >= 1 THEN GOTO 2110
2040 PRINT "NO FILE WITH THAT NU
MBER"
2050 PRINT "MENU (M) OR VIEW OTH
ER FILE (V)"
2060 INPUT M$
2070 IF M$="V" THEN GOTO 2000
2080 IF M$="M" THEN RETURN
2090 PRINT "FOLLOW INSTRUCTIONS
PLEASE."
2100 GOTO 2050

2110 CLS
2120 PRINT F$;F
2130 PRINT ,,A$;C$(F)
2140 PRINT "********************
************"
2150 PRINT G$; TAB 20;H$; TAB 20
;I$
2160 PRINT "--------------------
------------"
2170 FOR N=1 TO 10
2180 PRINT N;".";P$(F,N); TAB 20
;T(F,N,1); TAB 26;T(F,N,2)
2185 NEXT N
2190 PRINT AT 21,0;"PRINT(P),NEX
T FILE(F),OR MENU(M)"
2200 INPUT M$
2210 PRINT AT 21,0;E$
2220 IF M$="P" THEN COPY
2230 IF M$ <> "F" THEN GOTO 2310
2240 LET F=F+1
2250 IF F <= TF THEN GOTO 2300
2255 CLS
2260 PRINT "**NO FILE OF HIGHER
NUMBER**"
2270 PAUSE 150
2280 CLS
2290 GOTO 2310

2300 GOSUB 2020
2310 RETURN

2980 REM ******************
2990 REM **REVISE FILE SUB**
2995 REM ******************
3000 PRINT "WHICH FILE TO REVISE
 ?(1 TO 10"
3010 INPUT F
3020 IF F <= TF THEN GOTO 3060
3030 PRINT "NO SUCH FILE"
3040 PAUSE 150
3050 RETURN

3060 CLS
3070 PRINT "FILE ";F;" DETAILS W
ILL BE PRINTED.",,,"PRESS NEWLIN
E IF CORRECT","INPUT NEW DETAILS
 IF REQUIRED."
```

```
3080 PAUSE 150
3090 SCROLL
3100 PRINT A$;C$(F)
3110 INPUT M$
3120 IF M$="" THEN GOTO 3170
3130 LET C$(F)=M$
3140 CLS
3150 SCROLL
3160 PRINT "NEW ";A$;C$(F)
3170 SCROLL
3180 PRINT B$;" ";N$(F)
3190 INPUT M$
3200 IF M$="" THEN GOTO 3265
3210 LET N$(F)=M$
3220 CLS
3230 SCROLL
3240 PRINT A$;C$(F)
3250 SCROLL
3260 PRINT "NEW CASS. NAME ";N$(F
)
3265 SCROLL
3270 FOR N=1 TO 10
3380 PRINT "PROG. ";N;" NAME ";P$
(F,N)
3390 INPUT M$
3400 IF M$ <> "" THEN LET P$(F,N
)=M$
3410 PRINT AT 21,0;"PROG. ";N;" N
AME ";P$(F,N)
3420 SCROLL
3430 PRINT AT 21,0;"TAPE FROM:";
T(F,N,1)
3440 INPUT M$
3450 IF M$ <> "" THEN LET T(F,N,
1)= VAL M$
3460 PRINT AT 21,0;"TAPE FROM:";
T(F,N,1);"   TO:";T(F,N,2)
3470 INPUT M$
3480 IF M$ <> "" THEN LET T(F,N,
2)= VAL M$
3490 PRINT AT 21,0;"TAPE FROM:";
T(F,N,1);"   TO:";T(F,N,2)
3495 SCROLL
3500 NEXT N
3510 RETURN
3990 REM ********************
4000 REM **DELETE FILE SUB**
4001 REM ********************
4010 PRINT "WHICH FILE DO YOU WI
SH TO","DELETE ? (1 TO 10)"
4020 INPUT F
4030 IF F <= TF AND F >= 1 THEN
GOTO    4070
4040 PRINT "**NO FILE OF THAT NU
MBER**"
4050 PAUSE 150
4060 GOTO 4430

4070 PRINT F$;F,,A$;C$(F)
4080 PRINT B$;" ";N$(F)
4090 PRINT AT 10,0;"INPUT D TO C
ONFIRM DELETION",,,"OR M FOR MEN
U."
```

```
4100 INPUT M$
4110 IF M$ <> "D" THEN GOTO 4430
4120 PRINT AT 14,0;"ALL FILES WI
TH NUMBERS >";F,"WILL HAVE THEIR
 FILE NUMBERS","REDUCED BY ONE."
4125 IF F=TF THEN GOTO 4220
4130 FOR N=F TO TF-1
4140 LET N$(N)=N$(N+1)
4150 LET C$(N)=C$(N+1)
4160 FOR L=1 TO 10
4170 LET P$(N,L)=P$(N+1,L)
4180 LET T(N,L,1)=T(N+1,L,1)
4190 LET T(N,L,2)=T(N+1,L,2)
4200 NEXT L
4210 NEXT N
4220 LET C$(TF)=E$
4230 LET N$(TF)=E$
4240 FOR N=1 TO 10
4250 LET P$(TF,N)=E$
4260 LET T(TF,N,1)=0
4270 LET T(TF,N,2)=0
4280 NEXT N
4290 LET TF=TF-1
4300 CLS
4310 PRINT "FILE DELETED"
4320 PRINT ,,"NEW FILE LISTING:"
4330 PRINT
4340 FOR N=1 TO TF
4350 PRINT F$;N;" ";A$;C$(N)
4360 NEXT N
4370 PRINT AT 21,0;"COPY NEW LIS
T (C) OR MENU (M)"
4380 INPUT M$
4390 IF M$ <> "C" THEN GOTO 4430
4400 PRINT AT 21,0;E$
4410 COPY
4420 CLS
4430 RETURN

4990 REM *********************
5000 REM ** PRINT LABEL SUB***
5010 REM *********************
5020 PRINT "WHICH FILE DO YOU WA
NT TO PRINT",,,"AS A CASSETTE LA
BEL?( 1 TO 10 )"
5030 INPUT F
5040 IF F >= 1 AND F <= TF THEN
GOTO 5090
5050 PRINT "**NO FILE OF THAT NU
MBER**"
5060 PAUSE 150
5070 CLS
5080 GOTO 5280

5090 PRINT ,,"FILE ";F;" WILL NO
W BE PRINTED.",,,"CHECK PRINTER,
HIT A KEY TO START"
5100 IF INKEY$ ="" THEN GOTO 510
0
5120 LPRINT X$;"▌";A$;C$(F); TAB
 20;F$;F; TAB 31;"▌"
5130 LPRINT Z$;"▌";B$;" ";N$(F);
 TAB 31;"▌"
```

```
5140 LPRINT Z$;X$;"▌";G$; TAB 20
;"▌";H$; TAB 31;"▌"
5150 LPRINT "▌"; TAB 20;"▌";I$;
TAB 31;"▌"
5160 LPRINT X$
5170 FOR N=1 TO 6
5180 LPRINT "▌";N;" ";P$(F,N); T
AB 21;T(F,N,1); TAB 25;T(F,N,2);
 TAB 31;"▌";Z$
5190 NEXT N
5200 LPRINT Y$;X$
5210 LPRINT "▌";A$;C$(F); TAB 20
;F$;F; TAB 31;"▌"
5220 LPRINT Z$;"▌";B$;" ";N$(F);
 TAB 31;"▌"
5230 LPRINT Y$;X$
5240 FOR N=7 TO 10
5250 LPRINT "▌";N;" ";P$(F,N); T
AB 21;T(F,N,1); TAB 25;T(F,N,2);
 TAB 31;"▌";Z$
5260 NEXT N
5270 LPRINT Y$
5280 RETURN

5990 REM *********************
6000 REM ** SAVE FILES PROC **
6001 REM *********************
6005 CLS
6010 PRINT "SAVE FILES ON TAPE R
OUTINE"
6020 PRINT ,,"CURRENT PROGRAM NA
ME IS"
6030 PRINT ,," "" ";S$;" "" "
6040 PRINT ,,"INPUT A NEW NAME F
OR THIS ","PROGRAM FILE OR PRESS
 NEWLINE","ONLY TO SAVE WITH CUR
RENT NAME."
6050 PRINT ,,"INPUT M FOR MENU"
6060 INPUT M$
6070 IF M$="M" THEN RETURN
6080 IF M$="" THEN GOTO 9900
6090 LET S$=M$
6100 GOTO 9900

6990 REM ***********************
7000 REM **DELETE ALL FILES SUB*
         ***********************
7010 PRINT "INPUT D TO CONFIRM A
LL FILES","ARE TO BE DELETED."
7020 PRINT ,,"INPUT M TO RETURN
TO MENU."
7030 INPUT M$
7040 IF M$ <> "D" THEN GOTO 7080
7050 CLEAR
7060 PRINT ,,"INPUT NEW NAME FOR
 THIS FILE"
7070 INPUT S$
7080 LET X=1
7090 RETURN

9890 REM *********************
9900 REM ** AUTO-RUN ROUTINE *
9901 REM *********************
```

```
9910 CLS
9920 PRINT "PROGRAM NAME IS "
9930 PRINT " "" ";S$;" "" "
9940 PRINT "**NOTE IT DOWN**"
9950 PRINT ,,"SET CASSETTE TO RE
CORD,AND THEN","PRESS A  KEY TO
SAVE."
9960 IF INKEY$ ="" THEN GOTO 996
0
9970 SAVE S$
9980 CLS
9990 GOTO 200
```

Sample Printout:

```
FILE NO.1

CASSETTE REF:APP1
*********************************
PROGRAM NAME            TAPE  COUNT
                        FROM  TO
---------------------------------
1.GRAPHPLOT             5     25
2.RESIST                35    60
3.STRINGSORT            65    80
4.                      0     0
5.                      0     0
6.                      0     0
7.                      0     0
8.                      0     0
9.                      0     0
10.                     0     0
```

```
CASSETTE REF:APP1  FILE NO.1
CASSETTE NAME APPLICATIONS#1

PROGRAM NAME           TAPE COUNT
                       FROM  TO
1 GRAPHPLOT             5   25
2 RESIST                35  60
3 STRINGSORT            65  80
4                       0   0
5                       0   0
6                       0   0

CASSETTE REF:APP1  FILE NO.1
CASSETTE NAME APPLICATIONS#1

7                       0   0
8                       0   0
9                       0   0
10                      0   0
```

Comments:

This is a fairly long program. Work through the listing, checking you understand the operation of the algorithm within each program module. The individual manipulations of arrays and lists have all been encountered before, and each program module performs a different operation on the arrays and lists holding the data. The program is not by any means 'idiot-proof', although it is reasonably 'user-friendly' and you should note the various input checks used. The program can be crashed by inputs of bad (non-numeric) data into the numeric array holding the tape counter listings, and the main menu. Any file number request is checked.

The input (string or numeric) from menus is checked, in different ways. Either another input is requested, or a default return to the main menu operates. Data correction is dealt with by the View File and Revise File modules.

The program could be improved in two obvious ways. The first improvement would be a search routine to find and display the cassette file containing a desired program. A new module, 8 in the main menu and line 8ØØØ onwards in the program listing, could be added to perform this operation.

The second is that you cannot both print a file (in the View/Print File module) and then step through for the next file, since after printing the program automatically returns to the menu. Consider how you would modify the flow of control in lines 219Ø to 231Ø to allow this.

Notice as a final point that data manipulation programs are long, not necessarily because of the processing manipulations themselves, but due to necessary input checks and user dialogue.

The program can be easily revised for use with your audio cassette library, or other filing purposes.

The program examples included in this Unit have been selected to illuminate the various structured programming techniques discussed in the rest of the book. In order to demonstrate the maximum number of these techniques being used in practice, it proved necessary to give the programs a strong scientific applications bias. Home users will doubtlessly be dismayed to discover that there is little in this part of the book which will be of practical use to them. However, it is important that they understand the principles behind the programs in this Unit, even if they do not actually key them in.

As far as games and home applications programs are concerned, the Program Library at the end of the book (Appendix VI) should provide readers with enough examples to enable them to write their own programs tailor-made to their particular interests.

V4: Games Programming

Games are applications programs which are not of a type which fulfils a specific purpose in a functional context; that is to say they are not written to do a specific scientific, educational or data-manipulation task. This does not mean that, as programming tasks, they are frivolous. The enjoyment of playing the game on or with the computer is the application for which the program is written, but the task of programming a game is often difficult. Games programming is good practice for finding, deriving and coding algorithms and producing efficient and user-friendly programs. Graphics manipulation plays a larger part in games programming than in most applications programs, and such programs are also more interactive, requiring repeated inputs and outputs.

BASIC, an interpreted language, is often slow for games purposes. Fast action graphics games (SPACE INVADERS and their spawn), are written in machine code for speed of operation, as are tactical games where exhaustive exploration of possible moves is required (such as chess). Effective games can be programmed in BASIC, however, if the amount of calculation is not too great.

An area of interaction between Games and Application programming is the question of simulation. A program, given data and rules for manipulating the data, simulates a situation. In a serious application, this would be a real situation, with the manipulations performed as known or hypothesised relations from scientific knowledge. A game simulation would use invented relationships, or perhaps simplified formulae, if it dealt with a 'real' situation. The techniques would be essentially the same, and are used in a program in the same fashion. From the point of view of this book, games may be considered as programming exercises. All the techniques you have learnt can be put to use in writing games programs.

V5: Example Programs

The first program we will examine is a classic computer simulation, or rather implementation, of Life. This is not really a game, but a process that the user sets into operation, and observes. Invented by John Conway, the game simulates a colony of cells, which grows from the initial colony according to three simple rules. Cells are placed on a grid, and in each generation the succeeding generation is determined by the number of neighbouring grid squares which contain a cell. The rules are these:

1 If a cell possesses, in the 8 adjacent grid squares, either two or three neighbour cells, it survives into the next generation.
2 A cell dies (is removed from the grid for the next generation) if it has (i) 4 or more neighbouring cells (overpopulation) or (ii) Ø or 1 neighbours (isolation).
3 Each grid square which is empty, but has exactly three neighbours is a birth cell, and a cell will appear in this position in the next generation.

To implement this on the computer, it is obvious that array manipulation will be involved since a grid is a 2-D array. It is also necessary to have more than one such array, since the grid of Generation (n + 1) is defined from the grid of Generation (n), and none of the cells of Generation (n) can be altered until the checking process is complete.

The array of Generation (n) must have each grid position checked, and the number of neighbours counted. In accordance with the rules, the future of the cell at that position is determined and, if empty, whether a cell will be born. This data is stored in one array, and then the other array is updated to take account of the changes. Spectrum users should delete lines 22Ø and 39Ø.

Program Listing

```
   5 REM "LIFE"
  10 PRINT TAB 12;"*LIFE*"
  20 PRINT
  30 DIM A(16,16)
  40 DIM B(16,16)
  50 DIM A$(6,6)
  60 LET GEN=0
  70 REM *ENTER START COLONY*
  80 PRINT "ENTER START COLONY",
"ON A 6X6 GRID",,,,"INPUT 6 STRI
NGS OF SPACES AND ","ASTERISKS (
*)"
  90 PRINT
 100 FOR F=1 TO 6
 110 PRINT "STRING ";F;
 120 INPUT A$(F)
 130 PRINT " ";A$(F)
 140 NEXT F
 145 REM *PLACE COLONY IN ARRAY*
 150 FOR F=1 TO 6
 160 FOR Z=1 TO 6
 170 IF A$(F,Z)="*" THEN LET B(F
+5,Z+5)=1
 180 NEXT Z
 190 NEXT F
 200 GOSUB 1000
 205 REM *INCREMENT GENERATION*
 210 LET GEN=GEN+1
 220 FAST
 230 FOR X=2 TO 15
 240 FOR Y=2 TO 15
 250 REM *SET COUNTER*
 260 LET C=0
 265 REM *CHECK NEIGHBOUR CELLS*
 270 IF A(X-1,Y)=1 THEN LET C=C+
1
 280 IF A(X-1,Y-1)=1 THEN LET C=
C+1
 290 IF A(X-1,Y+1)=1 THEN LET C=
C+1
 300 IF A(X,Y+1)=1 THEN LET C=C+
1
 310 IF A(X,Y-1)=1 THEN LET C=C+
1
```

```
 320 IF A(X+1,Y-1)=1 THEN LET C=
C+1
 330 IF A(X+1,Y)=1 THEN LET C=C+
1
 340 IF A(X+1,Y+1)=1 THEN LET C=
C+1
 345 REM *DECIDE IF BIRTH*
 350 IF A(X,Y)=0 AND C=3 THEN LE
T B(X,Y)=1
 355 REM *DECIDE IF DEATH*
 360 IF A(X,Y)=1 AND (C>3 OR C<2
) THEN LET B(X,Y)=0
 370 NEXT Y
 380 NEXT X
 390 SLOW
 400 GOTO 200

1000 CLS
1005 PRINT AT 0,1;"GENERATION ";
GEN
1010 FOR X=1 TO 16
1020 FOR Y=1 TO 16
1025 REM *UPDATE ARRAY A*
1030 LET A(X,Y)=B(X,Y)
1035 REM *PRINT ARRAY*
1040 IF A(X,Y)=1 THEN PRINT AT X
+2,Y+6;"*"
1050 IF A(X,Y)=0 THEN PRINT AT X
+2,Y+6;" "
1060 NEXT Y
1070 NEXT X
1080 COPY
1090 RETURN
```

Flowchart of ''LIFE''

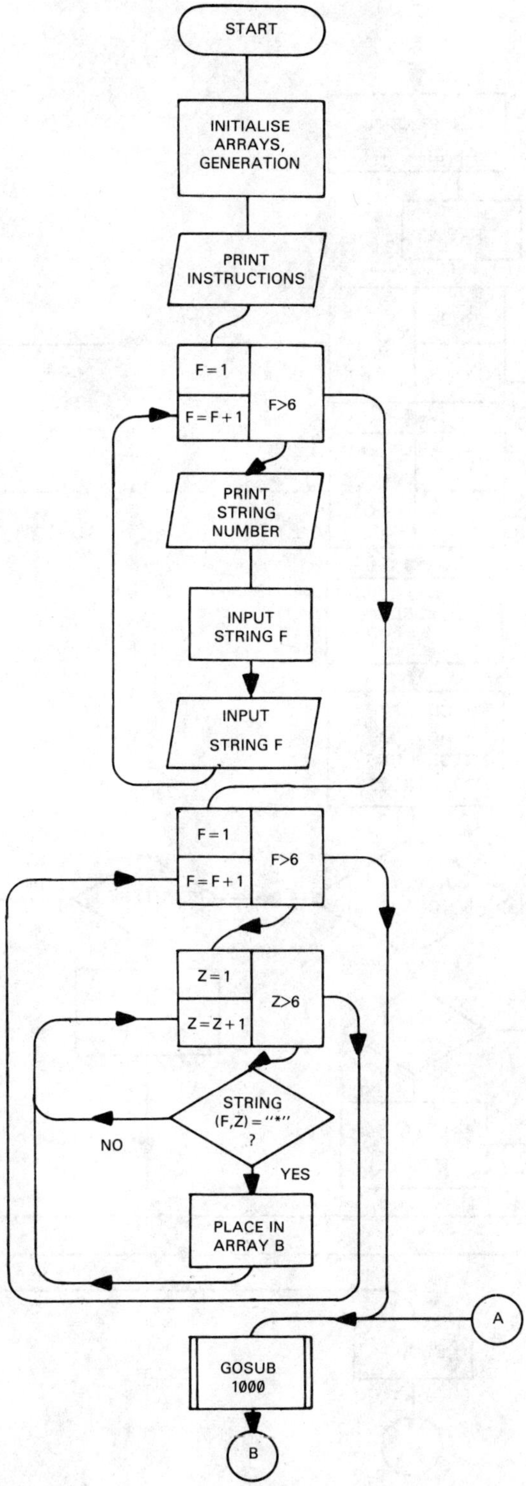

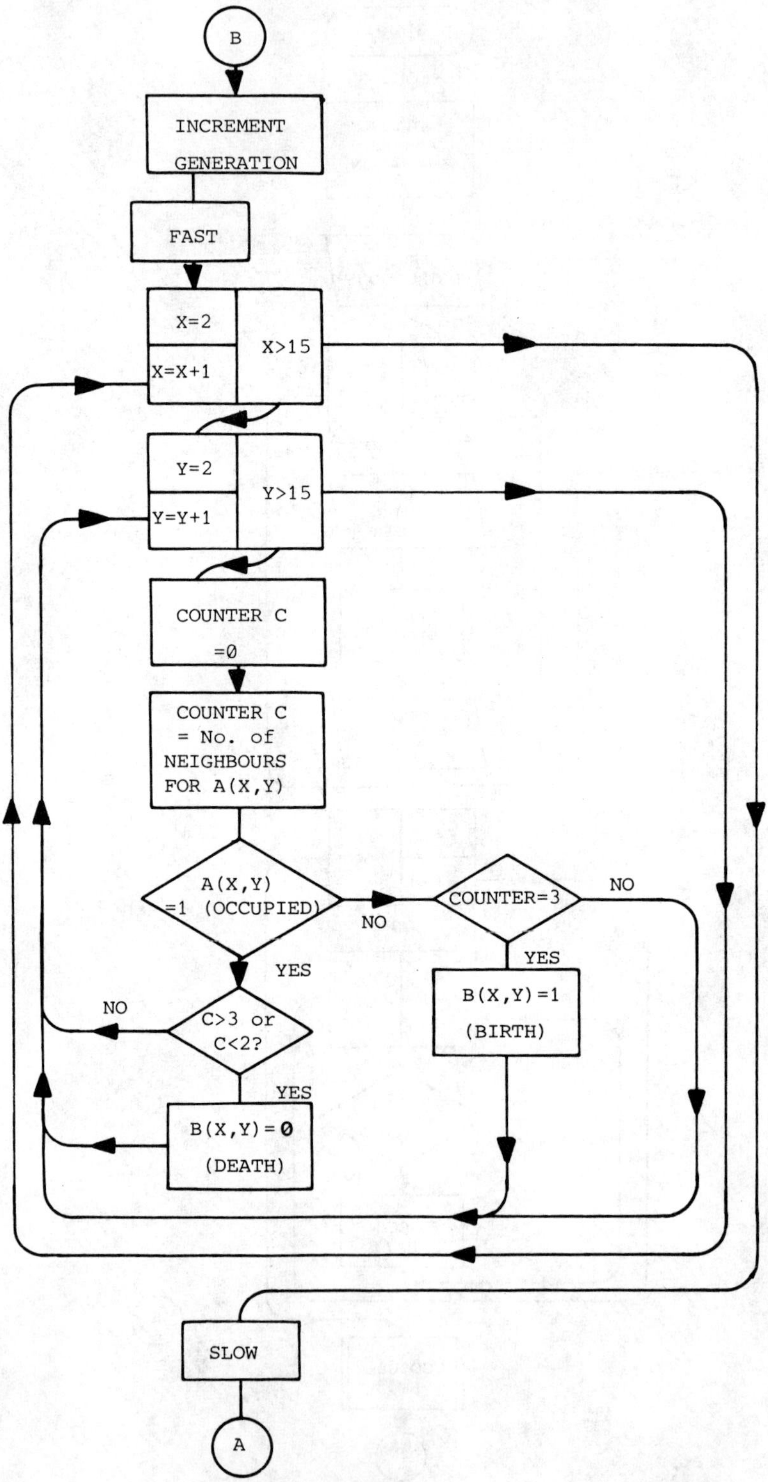
B
INCREMENT GENERATION
FAST
X=2
X=X+1
X>15
Y=2
Y=Y+1
Y>15
COUNTER C =0
COUNTER C = No. of NEIGHBOURS FOR A(X,Y)
A(X,Y) =1 (OCCUPIED)
NO
COUNTER=3
NO
YES
YES
B(X,Y)=1 (BIRTH)
NO
C>3 or C<2?
YES
B(X,Y)=0 (DEATH)
SLOW
A

Flowchart of "LIFE" – Subroutine 1000

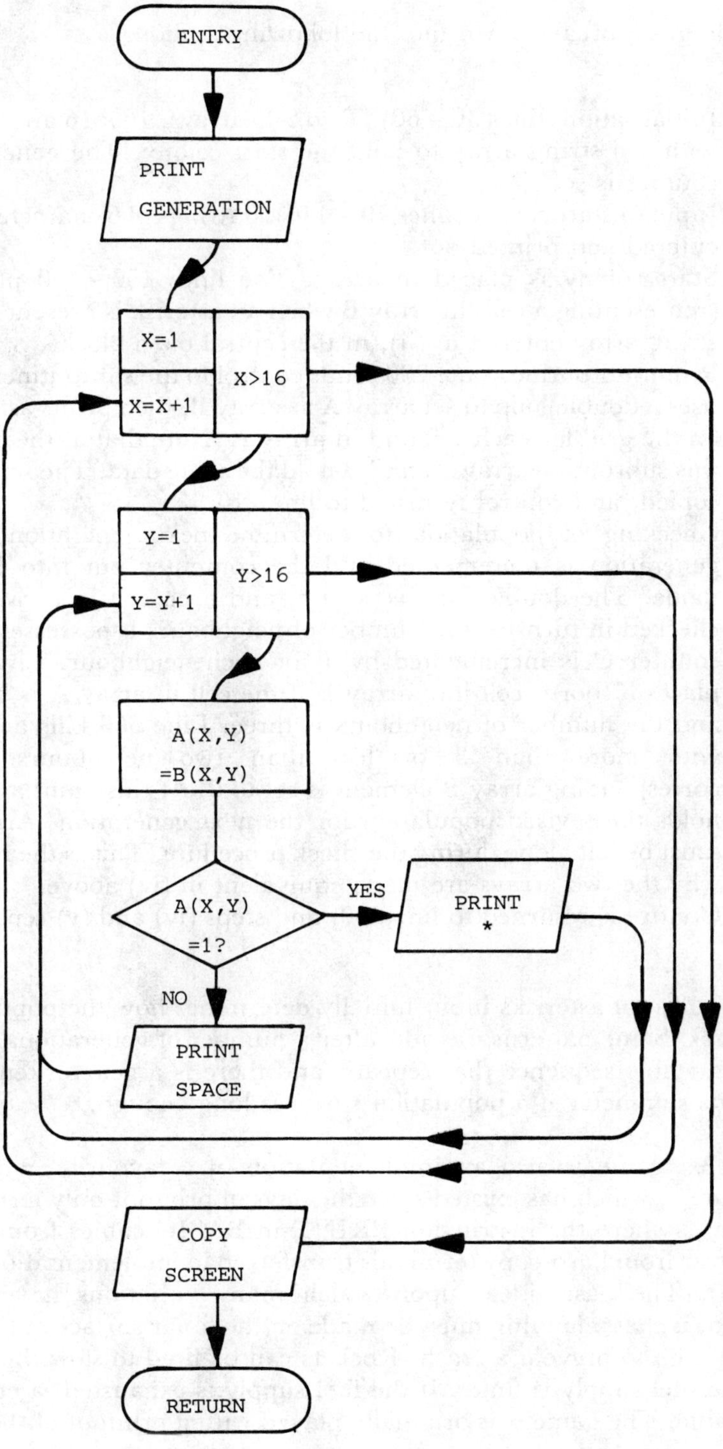

PROGRAM STRUCTURE

The program breaks down into the following sections.

(i) Initialisation (lines 3Ø – 6Ø). Two 2-D arrays, 16 × 16 are set up, with a 6 string array to hold the start colony. The generation counter is set as Ø.
(ii) Input of start colony (lines 7Ø – 14Ø). 6 strings of 6 characters are entered and printed out.
(iii) Start colony is placed in array. The lines 15Ø – 19Ø place 1 (representing a cell) in array B when an asterisk is present in the string array entered in (ii), in the central 6 × 6 block.
(iv) Print Subroutine. Line 2ØØ sends control to the subroutine. This uses a double loop to set array A as array B, then prints asterisks on the grid for each 1 found in array A. Note that at the end of this subroutine arrays A and B hold the same data. The screen is copied, and control returned to line 21Ø.
(v) Checking of population to determine next generation. The generation is incremented and the computer put into FAST mode. The double loop is set up, and each cell in array A is checked in turn for the number of neighbours it possesses. The counter C is incremented by 1 for each neighbour. Line 35Ø places a 'born' cell into array B if the cell in array A is blank, and the number of neighbours is three. Line 36Ø kills any cell with more than 3 or less than two neighbours. The corresponding array B element is set to Ø. At this point array B holds the revised population for the next generation. Array A must be left alone during the check procedure. This is the reason why the two arrays are made equivalent in (iv) above.
(vi) Control is returned to line 2ØØ, and steps (iv) and (v) repeated.

The pattern of asterisks input initially determines how the population develops. Some patterns die out, after a number of generations, some enter a stable sequence that repeats, and there is a general tendency towards symmetry if a population survives long enough.

The next game is also an implementation of a favourite game for computers, which has existed since the days of printout-only terminals (which is where the instruction PRINT in BASIC comes from, as a hangover from hard-copy terminals transferred to implementation on a screen). The basic idea, upon which many variations have been created, is that a landing must be made on the lunar surface at a speed low enough to prevent a crash. Rockets can be fired to slow the craft, but the fuel supply is finite. If the fuel supply is exhausted, a crash is inevitable. The game was originally played with a printout of the data only. This version uses one side of the screen for a graphic display, and prints the data on the other. Spectrum users must replace line 40 with 40 PAUSE 0.

```
   5 REM "LANDER"
  10 PRINT TAB 10;"*LANDER*"; AT
 4,0;"LUNAR LANDING GAME. YOU ARE
 ","INITIALLY 500 METRES ABOVE T
HE","SURFACE OF THE MOON. YOU HAV
E ","100 FUEL UNITS. "
  20 PRINT "PRESS R TO FIRE ROCK
ETS TO SLOW DESCENT. EVERY FIRING
 USES 5 FUEL UNITS. YOU MUST LAND
 SLOWER THAN 8 TO SURVIVE. GOOD L
UCK. "
  30 PRINT ,,"PRESS A KEY TO STA
RT"

  40 PAUSE 40000
  45 REM **INITIALISE**
  50 CLS
  60 PRINT AT 20,15;"┴┴━━━━━━━━━━
┴"
  70 LET F=100
  80 LET H=500
  90 LET S=15
  95 REM **START OF LOOP**
 100 LET V=0
 110 IF H<600 THEN PRINT AT 20-H
/30,20;"   "
 120 PRINT AT 1,0;"FUEL: ";F;" "
; TAB 0;"HEIGHT:";H;" "; TAB 0;"
SPEED:";S;" "
 135 REM **CHECK ROCKETS **
 140 IF INKEY$ ="R" AND F >= 5 T
HEN LET V=5
 150 IF V THEN PRINT AT 21-H/30,
20;"V V"
 160 IF F<5 THEN PRINT AT 1,7;"*
EMPTY*"
 170 LET F=F-V
 180 LET S=S+2-V
 190 PRINT AT 20-H/30,20;"   ";
TAB 20;"   "
 195 REM ** CHECK IF LANDED **
 200 IF H<30 THEN GOTO 230
 210 LET H=H-S
 220 GOTO 100

 225 REM ** LANDING RESULT **
 230 IF S<4 THEN PRINT AT 21,10;
"PERFECT LANDING"
 240 IF S<8 AND S>4 THEN PRINT A
T 21,10;"BUMPY BUT SAFE"
 250 IF S >= 8 THEN PRINT AT 21,
10;"CRASHED AND SMASHED"
 260 PRINT AT 12,0;"ANOTHER GAME
?(INPUT Y OR N)"
 270 INPUT A$
```

```
280 IF A$="Y" THEN GOTO 50
290 REM *END*
```

■■■

Lines 1Ø to 3Ø print instructions, and line 4Ø stops the program until a key is pressed. Lines 5Ø to 9Ø clear the screen, print the 'lunar surface' and set the variables: F is fuel units, H is height above surface, S is speed of descent.

The main program is in the loop between lines 1ØØ and 22Ø. V is set to zero as a flag, and the craft is printed by line 11Ø if the scale set allows it to be on screen. The craft disappears off the top of the screen if the height is greater than 6ØØ since the PRINT AT instruction scales so that 1 print line = 3Ø metres of height. Line 12Ø prints the current data. Note the spaces after the variables to overprint if the values decrease, or in the case of the speed becoming positive after being negative. (Negative descent speed means ascent.)

Line 14Ø checks if the R (for rockets) key is being pressed. If it is, V is set to 5. Line 15Ø prints rocket exhausts below the craft if the R key was pressed (evaluated by V = Ø = False if not pressed, V = 5 = True if pressed). The fuel is checked (line 16Ø) and reduced by the value of V if not empty. The speed is adjusted by increasing it, then reducing it by the value of V if the rockets have been fired. Line 19Ø overprints the craft and rockets, and 2ØØ checks if the surface is near enough for landing to be assumed. If it is, control is transferred to the landing message section. If not, the height is adjusted and the program loops back to repeat the process.

Notice that the variable V is used in three ways within the loop, and that the loop structure, using INKEY$ to see if the player has input instructions, is common in interactive games. It provides a simulation of a real-time process. In this game, the speed is assumed to be metres per second (hence the simple LET H = H – S of line 21Ø). It is actually nominal 'metres' per program loop! Other games can wait for inputs, but the use of a loop allows the inexorable attraction of gravity to go on its way unless the player does something. Spectrum users, with their faster computing, may wish to insert a PAUSE instruction in the loop.

Programming for this type of game can show the programmer that certain structures of programs are inefficient in program execution, since conditional branches to routines requiring calculation will noticeably slow the loop. In the interests of a good game, structured programming practice may be set aside and speed of execution can become a goal in itself. However, remember not to transfer these techniques to serious programs!

Games programming can become extremely complex when we consider the strategy and tactics which must be built into the response from the computer. We have dealt with only the simplest form of game, and have not included any of this type of game. We suggest that you put to work the techniques we have shown you in this text to analyse some of the tactical games in the popular computing magazines, if this area interests you. In order to start learning to appreciate the problems involved, you could start by writing a program to play Noughts and Crosses. You may think this is a very simple game, but it is a surprisingly difficult one to program!

PART FIVE

COVERING THE WHOLE SPECTRUM

SECTION W: THE SPECTRUM

W1: The Spectrum System and Keyboard

This Unit introduces the Spectrum microcomputer system. As a Spectrum user you have been referred to this Unit because, whilst the BASIC language that both the Spectrum and ZX81 use (Sinclair single keystroke BASIC) has only minor differences between the two machines (although the Spectrum has additional features that the ZX81 does not possess, such as colour, high-resolution graphics and sound), there are greater differences in the arrangements of the keyboard. The Spectrum system is also simpler to set up and connect.

After reading this Unit, you should return to the start of Section C (page 19) to start using the BASIC language, once the keyboard and the way to access all the confusing array of characters grouped on and around each key have been explained. Sections A and B are for the ZX81 only, but you will find in this Unit the same information as it applies to the Spectrum. The main text takes you through the Sinclair BASIC language, using the same instructions for the ZX81 and Spectrum, any minor differences being noted. This involves the introduction of a few of the Spectrum's enhanced BASIC instructions, but most of the additional facilities of the Spectrum are covered in the next Units, to be read *after* you have worked through the main text and have learnt the BASIC programming techniques.

SPECTRUM SYSTEM DESCRIPTION

We assume that you have in front of you the components of your Spectrum system.

This consists of:

1 The ZX Spectrum microcomputer.
2 Either 16k of internal RAM or 48k (although nothing in this book demands more memory than 16k).
3 The ZX power supply, with the correct plug attached for the a.c. power sockets you have.
4 The ZX printer and its socket.
5 A domestic TV to act as a display monitor.
6 A mono cassette recorder, with an a.c. supply lead (if not battery powered).
7 The aerial/antenna cable which connects the Spectrum to your TV set. (In the U.S. this is via a switch box.)
8 A pair of cassette recorder leads, fitted with 3.5mm jack-plugs at either end.

These components make up a complete system, the least crucial part of which is the ZX printer. If you do not have a printer then you can ignore the printer-related sections of this book and learn BASIC programming techniques just as well. It is extremely useful, however, to have a printer both for hard-copy printouts of results and, more importantly, for program listings for documentation purposes.

The cassette recorder should preferably be mono, since stereo tape deck recording heads can cause problems, even used on only one channel. The cheaper recorders work somewhat better (due to the less sophisticated audio circuits being better for handling the crude form of the computer's signals) than more expensive ones, but get one with a tape counter, as finding programs without one can be an irritatingly time-consuming process.

FIGURE 3

SPECTRUM SYSTEM DIAGRAM

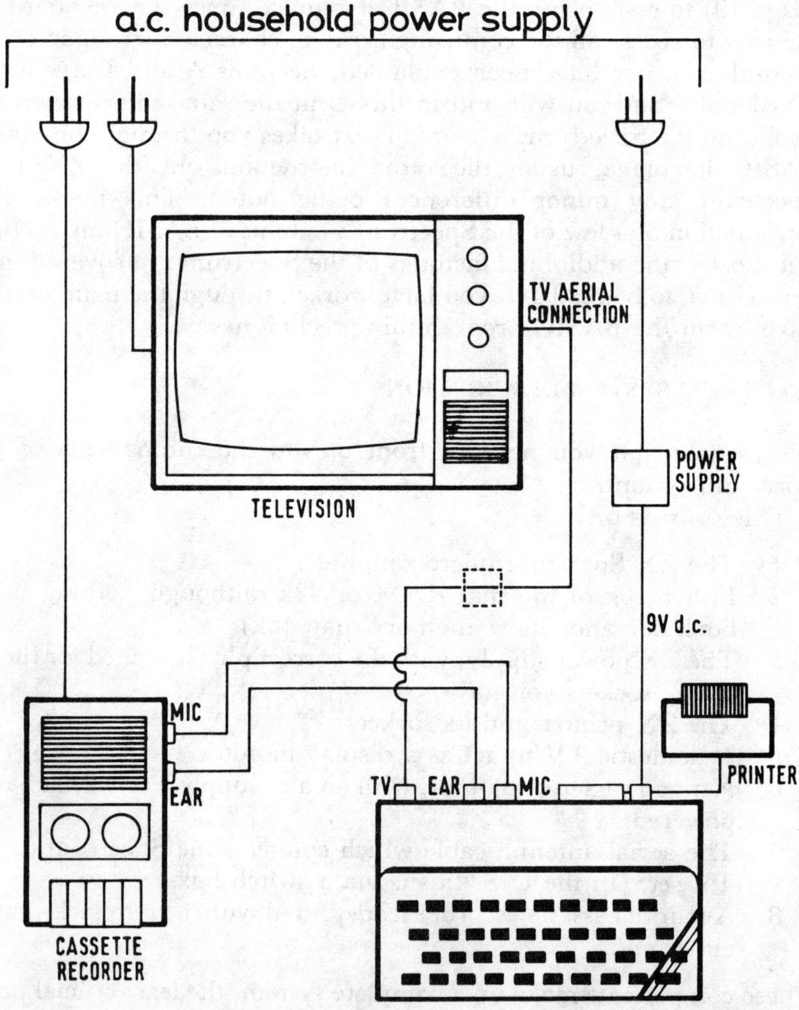

U.S. Users may have antennae on/off switch fitted in aerial lead, shown as dotted box in diagram.

FUNCTION OF COMPONENTS

Here is a brief rundown of the function of each of the components of the Spectrum microcomputer system.

Device	*Function*
Spectrum computer board	Data processing and control of information handling. Input from keyboard or cassette. Output to TV screen and printer. Also holds the 16k or 48k of RAM memory. K stands for kilobyte. One *byte* is eight *bits*, which are the *bi*nary digi*ts* (Ø and 1, represented by on-off switches in the computer) computers work with. A kilobyte is roughly 1ØØØ bytes, hence the name. (It is actually 2^{10}, 1Ø24).
Keyboard	Input of information. Programs, data and commands are keyed in. On-line control.
TV Set	Used as V.D.U. (visual display unit) monitor. Provides on-line output of information – visual display of programs, results (data, graphs, pictures) and control commands.
Cassette recorder	Off-line storage of information Program data are stored (written) as coded electromagnetic impulses on cassette tapes. They can be played back (loaded) at any time for use again. The computer reads the data from the tape. The Spectrum will also be able to use the microdrive, storing the coded impulses on a magnetic-coated disc, when it becomes available.
Printer	Output device, to provide a permanent printed record of the screen display, program listings or information in the computer memory. Prints on electrosensitive paper.
Power Supply	Supplies the d.c. current (9 volts at 1.2 amps) to run the computer, RAM pack and printer, from the household power supply.
Cables	To interconnect the devices which make up the system.

The printed circuit board inside the Spectrum holds and connects the

IC (integrated circuit) microchips which provide the computing facilities. These are:

1 Z80A CPU (Central Processing Unit) microprocessor chip which is the heart of the system. It is used in many other microcomputers, and performs the arithmetic manipulations.
2 ROM (Read Only Memory) chip holds the 16k BASIC interpreter which translates BASIC instructions into the machine-code instructions that the Z80A operates with. The data in this chip is fixed, hence the name, and also stable – it remains when the power is switched off.
3 RAM (Random Access Memory) chips provide the memory store. This is either 16k or 48k, depending on which version of the Spectrum is owned. This memory is *volatile* – the data is stored as electrical impulses and is lost when the power is switched off. This memory stores the BASIC program, the values of variables (including some system variables that the computer uses for to organise its own affairs), a memory picture of the TV screen display, and the stacks which hold the numbers whilst they are being manipulated. The memory organisation is described in Section U.
4 The Logic Chip co-ordinates the operation of the other chips.

Also mounted on the board are the stabiliser for the 5 volt supply the computer takes from the power-supply socket, the colour TV signal encoder and modulator circuits and the sockets for the connecting cables to the TV and cassette recorder. There is also a small speaker for the sound output.

CONNECTING UP

1 Set aside an area to work in and set up your television, Spectrum, cassette recorder, printer (if you have one) and the Spectrum's power supply, as shown in the diagram of the system (Fig. 3).
2 Always remember to connect the printer to the back of the Spectrum *before* you switch the power on for the ZX power supply. With the printer connected, the TV aerial lead connected to the TV socket on the Spectrum, and the 'EAR' and 'MIC' leads correctly set up as below, you can *then* plug into and switch on the a.c. power (household) supply.

   Connect the printer into the socket at the rear of the Spectrum. Make sure the gap in the board at the rear of the Spectrum connects with the plastic piece in the printer socket, then push firmly home.

   Connect one end of the twin cassette leads into the EAR and MIC sockets of the cassette recorder. Push firmly home and twist slightly to get good connections. Take the same colour plug as is in the EAR socket of the cassette recorder and place it in the Spectrum EAR socket. Place the other in the MIC socket.

Inset the jack-plug leading from the power supply into the socket marked 9 V d.c. on the back of the Spectrum. Connect the TV aerial/antenna lead to the aerial socket of the TV.

Your system is now set up. Check the TV is turned off, and no cassette keys are depressed. Plug the ZX power supply and cassette leads into the a.c. (household) power supply sockets, and switch them on if they have switches.

3 Switch on the TV. Choose a channel with the push button or other channel select control, and tune the TV until the display:

© 1982 Sinclair Research Ltd

appears on the screen. Adjust the tuning until the display is clear, and the brightness, contrast and colour (if you're using a colour TV!) controls to get a good picture without it being too bright (since you are going to spend some time looking at it from close up).

Note for U.S. users: In the U.S., the antenna lead connects with standard terminals to the TV. An antenna on/off switch is provided between the computer and the TV. The computer has a channel select switch to select channel 2 or 3. Whichever channel is not transmitting should be selected, and the TV tuned until the computer display is obtained.

4 Press a few keys to get some characters printed on the screen – these should appear at the bottom of the screen. Then press the CAPS SHIFT and 1 (EDIT) keys together, to clear the screen.

5 Press the Z key. The screen will print COPY at the bottom. Then press ENTER. The printer will start operating, feeding paper through. There will be nothing printed on it because there is nothing printed on the screen. Check that the printer paper does not rub against the side of the printer as it is fed through. If it rubs, pull it gently away from the side as the paper is fed through.

You now have an operating microcomputer system. The system needs no maintenance other than the occasional cleaning of the printer and the tape heads on the cassette player. Clean the printer with a small brush to clear away the black dust that accumulates. Be careful not to damage the electrode (a small piece of wire running in the slot visible when the paper carrier is removed). Blow away the dust when you've brushed it from this slot. Keep your cassette tape heads clean and demagnetised.

If the printer doesn't work, first turn off the power. Then remove and re-insert the printer socket. Switch the power on again and try once more. The contacts on the printed circuit boards that the printer socket connects with may need cleaning if the printer doesn't work or prints incorrectly. Clean the contacts with a proprietary contact cleaner or a pencil eraser. DO NOT use abrasives to clean these contacts. These are the only problems you should encounter with your system, as long as all plugs are well seated in their sockets. With the need to remove and re-insert the EAR socket when saving programs on cassette tape, you must take care to always re-insert the jack-plug properly each time.

THE KEYBOARD

The Spectrum keyboard has 4Ø keys arranged in 4 rows of 1Ø. At first sight, it might appear similar to a typewriter keyboard, but on closer inspection you will see that keys have 5 or 6 functions or characters. In fact:

Eight different characters and functions can be obtained with some keys!

The keyboard contains:

1 The digits Ø to 9
2 The letters of the alphabet printed in upper and lower case (capitals)
3 The complete BASIC language:
   - instructions
   - commands
   - arithmetic, conditional and logical operators
   - arithmetic functions
4 Grammatical signs and symbols
5 Special control keys
6 Graphics symbols

These are all called characters, and are on, below or above the keys used to access them.

Notice that words like PRINT, LIST, RUN, etc are all printed on the keyboard and also appear on the screen with a single key press.

The Spectrum's ability to print complete words in the BASIC language at the press of a single key is called:

SINGLE KEYSTROKE BASIC

On most other computers you have to key in each letter of, for example, the instruction PRINT. This is obviously inefficient. The Spectrum is very powerful in this respect. The keyboard contains all the characters in the Spectrum's character set, together with a few special keys. Some 2ØØ or so different characters are available. Some print to the screen, others are non-printing (e.g. DELETE).

Figure 4
SPECTRUM KEYBOARD DIAGRAM

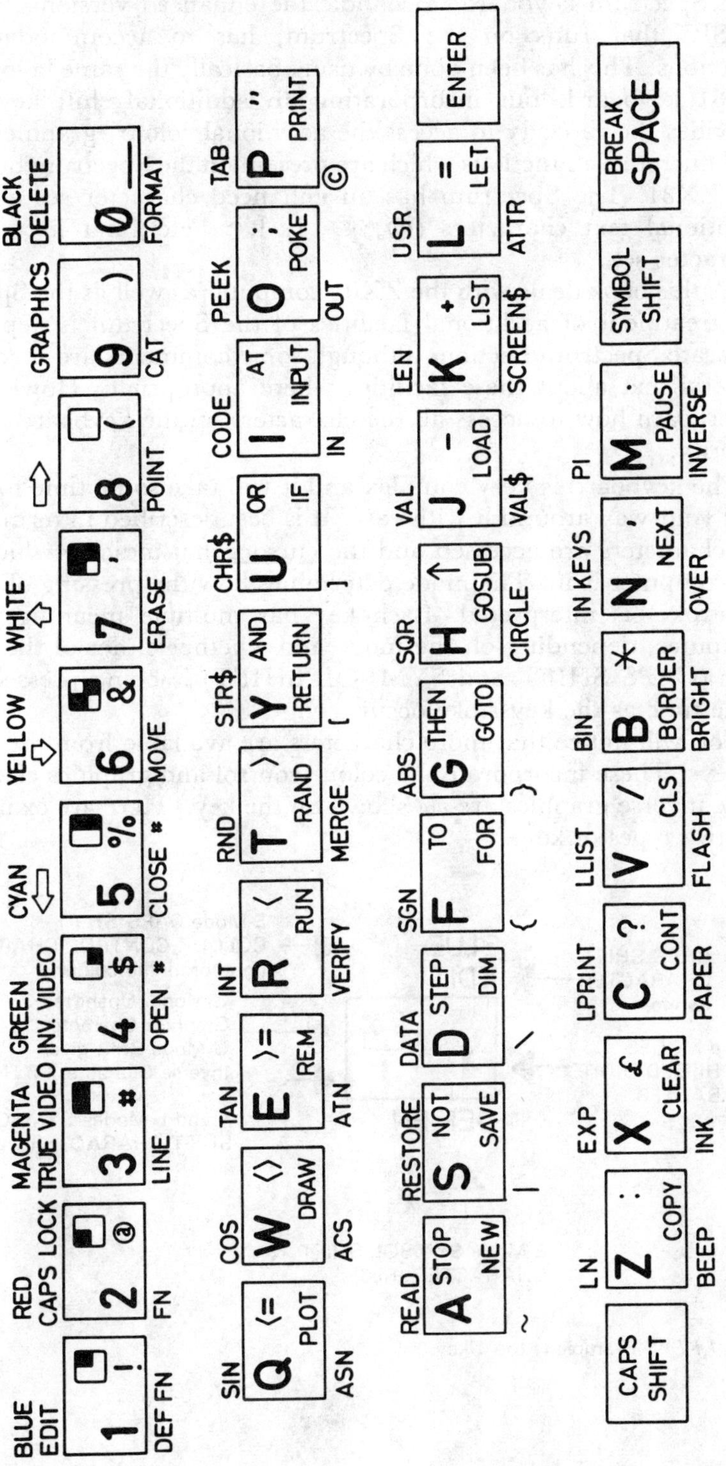

THE CHARACTER TYPES ON THE SPECTRUM KEYS

The Spectrum keyboard, to handle the enhanced version of Sinclair BASIC that runs on the Spectrum, has to accommodate more functions. This has been done by using basically the same layout as the ZX81 keyboard, but incorporating an additional shift key, which provides the capacity to access the additional colour, graphics, sound and microdrive functions which are present on the Spectrum but not on the ZX81. The Spectrum has an enhanced character set also, with additional text characters (@, ©, [,], ~, etc.) not in the ZX81 character set.

As this book deals with the ZX81 computer as well as the Spectrum, the treatment of additional facilities of the Spectrum is kept to this separate Spectrum Section, although some comments are made in the general text about these facilities where appropriate. However, you must learn how to access all the characters on the keyboard as a first priority.

The keyboard is very complex and it will take some time for you to find your way around it with ease. It is best described in terms of how the characters are accessed and the <u>cursors</u> that indicate which <u>mode</u> the computer is in. The mode determines how the pressing of a key (a keystroke) is interpreted. Each key has multiple meanings for the computer, depending on the mode and whether either of the SHIFT keys (CAPS SHIFT and SYMBOL SHIFT) is being pressed at the same time as the keystroke occurs.

You will notice that more characters are available from the top row of keys. These incorporate the colour control and graphics characters. (The inverse graphics are *not* shown on the key.) Here are examples of the two types of key:

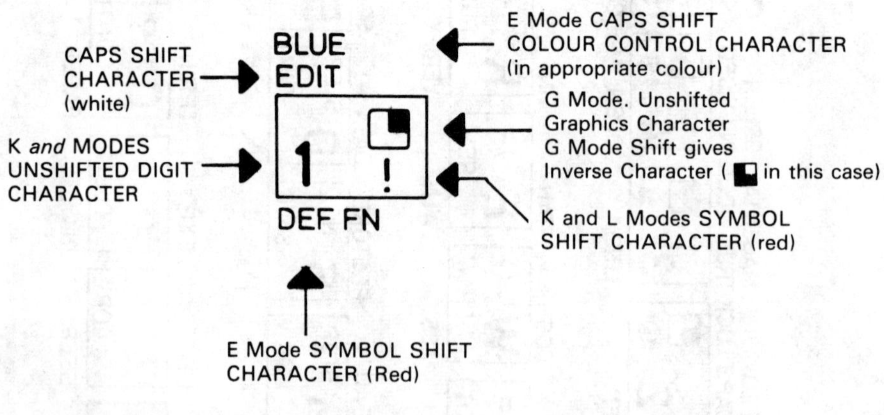

ROW 1 KEYS Example is the 1 key

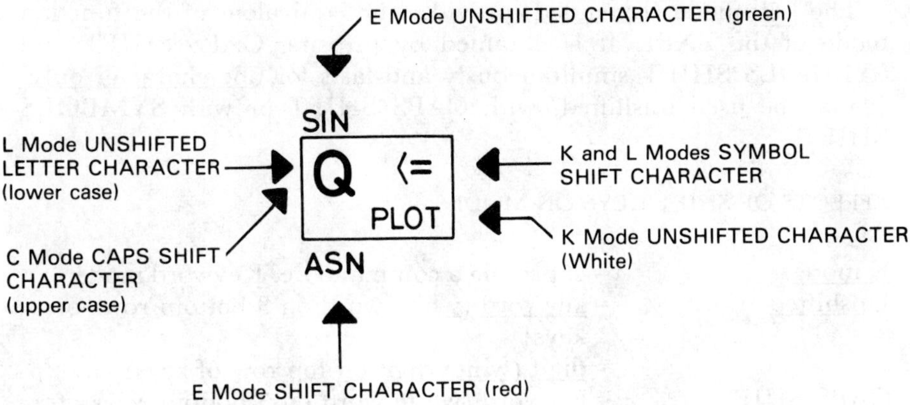

OTHER KEYS Example is Q key

There are also the keys for ENTER, CAPS SHIFT, SYMBOL SHIFT, and the SPACE key (with BREAK printed above SPACE). See the keyboard diagram. We must now describe the modes the computer can be in, and the cursors that indicate the mode. There are also two other cursors which we will deal with here.

MODES

When inputting (keying in) program lines the position for the next entry is indicated by a cursor on the screen. The mode is indicated by the flashing cursors [K] [L] [G] [C] [E] .

The [K] mode (Keywords) and [L] (Letters) may be used unshifted, with CAPS SHIFT or with SYMBOLS SHIFT. Letters of the alphabet are lower case unless the CAPS SHIFT key is used or the [C] mode used. The [C] mode (Capitals) is obtained by pressing CAPS SHIFT and CAPS LOCK simultaneously and is identical to the L mode apart from producing capitals (upper case) instead of lower-case letters. To return to [L] mode press CAPS SHIFT and CAPS LOCK simultaneously. All letter inputs (REM statements, string inputs and assignments) in this text are in Capitals. You must use C-mode exclusively to get listings and printout of letters that correspond to those in this text.

The [G] mode (Graphics) accesses the graphics characters and may be obtained using the GRAPHICS key as an on-off switch. Press CAPS SHIFT and GRAPHICS simultaneously to enter [G] mode. Repeat to cancel.

The [E] mode (Extended) provides the equivalent of the function mode of the ZX81. It is obtained by pressing CAPS SHIFT and SYMBOLS SHIFT simultaneously and lasts for one character only. It may be used unshifted, with CAPS SHIFT or with SYMBOLS SHIFT.

EFFECTS OF SHIFT KEYS ON MODES

K mode	– expecting a command i.e. Keyword mode.
Unshifted	– keyword (white word on 3 bottom rows of keys)
	– digit (white digit on top row of keys)
CAPS SHIFT	– keyword (white word on 3 bottom rows of keys)
	– keyword (white word above top row of keys)
SYMBOLS SHIFT	– keyword or symbol (red symbol or word on key)
L mode	– expecting a letter or a number i.e. Letters mode, giving the lower case letters.
Unshifted	– letter (white letter on 3 bottom rows of keys)
	– digit (white digit on top row of keys)
CAPS SHIFT	– letter (capitals) (white letter on 3 bottom rows of keys)
	– keyword (white word above top row of keys)
SYMBOLS SHIFT	– keyword or symbol (red symbol or word on key)
C mode	– identical with L mode but Capital letters are obtained with Unshifted letter keys.
G mode	– for accessing Graphics symbols.
Unshifted	– graphics character (in grey/white on keys 1 to 8)
	– user defined graphic on keys A through U. (Not shown on keyboard.)
CAPS SHIFT	– inverse graphics character (reverse of symbol on top row of keys)
SYMBOL SHIFT	– same as CAPS SHIFT

User defined graphics are dealt with in Unit W2. They are initially set as the capital letters A to U, which is what appears on the screen.

Note that DELETE works in G mode without CAPS SHIFT being pressed.

E mode	– Extended mode, accessing the function characters in green above the keys in bottom 3 rows, colour control characters on the top row,and the function or symbol characters in red below all keys. E mode lasts for one character only.
Unshifted	– function or symbol (in green above key for 3 bottom rows)
	– colour control (in colour above top row)
CAPS SHIFT	– function or symbol (in red below key for 3 bottom rows)
	– colour control (in colour above key for top row)
SYMBOLS SHIFT	– function or symbol (in red below key for 3 bottom rows)
	– function (in red below key for top row).

The colour control characters print in a program line as the digit of the key that accesses them, i.e. they are coded 1 – 7 and Ø. If they are accessed in E mode without INK or PAPER before them, the effect is to put colour control characters into the display. When unshifted, the colour control characters change the background (PAPER) colour of what is placed on the screen thereafter, and when CAPS SHIFT is pressed, the colour of the character (INK) is changed.

Note: the main body of this text assumes no colours are used, since the ZX81 cannot produce colour. Colour on the Spectrum is dealt with in Unit W3. Experiment with colour all you want, but this text is primarily about BASIC programming, and it doesn't matter what colour is on the screen for this!

Exercise

Access all the modes, i.e. get each different cursor on the screen. Key in all the characters in each mode, first unshifted, then with CAPS SHIFT, and finally with SYMBOL SHIFT. You will have to enter the E mode again after each character. Watch what happens with TRUE VIDEO and INV VIDEO. Notice they reverse each other. Notice you can't see a SPACE. Don't press ENTER, just play around on the bottom lines of the screen. Notice that the line moves up the screen when it is filled. Press EDIT with CAPS SHIFT to clear the screen. You can't harm the computer whatever you enter. Note that two words are abbreviated on the keyboard, but print in full – RAND and CONT.

SYNTAX ERROR CURSOR [?]

This cursor appears flashing in a line input at the bottom of the screen if the computer detects an error in the syntax of the line (i.e. finds an error in the 'grammar' of the BASIC language instruction input). It appears when ENTER is pressed to enter the line of program or the command into memory. The cursor appears before the last error in the line. There may be more than one error, but only one will be indicated at a time. Editing (making any change in the line) causes the cursor to disappear. It will reappear if necessary (error not corrected) when ENTER is pressed once again.

CURRENT LINE CURSOR >

This cursor appears after the line number of the last line entered into a BASIC program (the current line). If EDIT is pressed (CAPS SHIFTed 1) this line is brought down to the bottom of the screen. It can then be edited.

In a program listing of the lines of a program displayed on the screen, the cursor may be moved to point to different lines by using the (CAPS SHIFTed 6) and (CAPS SHIFTed 7) keys to move it down or up a program line. This is used to select a line for editing.

An important point to note with regard to the keyboard is that the Spectrum has a repeat key action on all keys. If any key is held down, after a short time it will automatically repeat.

We now give a table of the characters accessible on the Spectrum keyboard. Ignore the CODE information for now. This will be dealt with later. This table is the Spectrum equivalent of Appendix III, which deals with the ZX81.

CHARACTER SET AND CODES TABLE

This table, which is in alphabetical order, will enable the Spectrum user to quickly reference any character for:

- its position on the keyboard in terms of a row and column 'parent key' address (e.g. A is in the third row and first column of keys (3,1))
- the mode in which the function may be used (indicated by the flashing cursor on the screen)
- which keys to press to obtain the function (here SHIFT means that *either* the CAPS SHIFT or the SYMBOL SHIFT key will give the character)
- the CODE of the character.

Character	Position on Keyboard Row, Column	Mode(s)	To Obtain Press		Code
A	3,1	L	CAPS SHIFT	A	65
		C		A	
a	3,1	L		A	97
ABS	3,5	E		G	189
ACS	2,2	E	SHIFT	W	182
AND	2,6	K L C	SYMBOL SHIFT	Y	198
ASN	2,1	E	SHIFT	Q	181
AT	2,8	K L C	SYMBOL SHIFT	I	172
ATN	2,3	E	SHIFT	E	183
ATTR	3,9	E	SHIFT	L	171
B	4,6	L	SHIFT	B	66
		C		B	
b	4,6	L		B	98
BEEP	4,2	E	SHIFT	Z	215
BIN	4,6	E		B	196
BORDER	4,6	K		B	213
BREAK	4,10		CAPS SHIFT SPACE		–
BRIGHT	4,6	E	SHIFT	B	220
C	4,4	L	SHIFT	C	67
		C		C	
c	4,4	L		C	99
CAPS LOCK	1,2	L	CAPS SHIFT	Z	–
CAPS SHIFT	4,1	all	CAPS SHIFT		
CAT	1,9	E	SYMBOL SHIFT	9	207
CHR$	2,7	E		U	194
CIRCLE	3,6	E	SHIFT	H	216
CLEAR	4,3	K		X	253
CLS	4,5	K		V	251
CODE	2,8	E		I	175
CONTinue	4,4	K		C	232
COPY	4,2	K		Z	255
COS	2,2	E		W	179
D	3,3	L	CAPS SHIFT	D	68
		C		D	
d	3,3	L		D	100
DEF FN	1,1	E	SYMBOL SHIFT	1	206
DELETE	1,10	K L C G	CAPS SHIFT	0	12
		C G		0	
DIM	3,3	K		D	233
DRAW	2,2	K		W	252
E	2,3	L	CAPS SHIFT	E	69
		C		E	
e	2,3	L		E	101
EDIT	1,1	K L C	CAPS SHIFT	1	7
ENTER	3,10		ENTER		13
ERASE	1,7	E	SYMBOL SHIFT	7	210
EXP	4,3	E		X	185

Character	Position on Keyboard Row, Column	Mode(s)	To Obtain Press		Code
F	3,4	L	CAPS SHIFT	F	70
		C		F	
f	3,4	L		F	102
FLASH	4,5	E	SHIFT	V	219
FN	1,2	E	SYMBOL SHIFT	2	168
FOR	3,4	K		F	235
FORMAT	1,10	E	SYMBOL SHIFT	0	208
G	3,5	L	CAPS SHIFT	G	71
		C		G	
g	3,5	L		G	103
GOSUB	3,6	K		H	237
GOTO	3,5	K		G	236
GRAPHICS	1,10	K L C	CAPS SHIFT	0	–
H	3,6	L	CAPS SHIFT	H	72
		C		H	
h	3,6	L		H	104
I	2,8	L	CAPS SHIFT	I	73
		C		I	
i	2,8	L		I	105
IF	2,7	K		U	250
IN	2,8	E	SHIFT	I	191
INK	4,3	E	SHIFT	X	217
INKEY$	4,7	E		N	166
INPUT	2,8	K		I	238
INT	2,4	E		R	186
INVERSE	4,8	E	SHIFT	M	221
J	3,7	L	CAPS SHIFT	J	74
		C		J	
j	3,7	L		J	106
K	3,8	L	CAPS SHIFT	K	75
		C		K	
k	3,8	L		K	107
L	3,9	L	CAPS SHIFT	L	76
		C		L	
l	3,9	L		L	108
LEN	3,8	E		K	177
LET	3,9	K		L	241
LINE	3,9	K		L	202
LIST	1,3	K		K	240
LLIST	4,5	E		V	225
LN	4,2	E		Z	184
LOAD	3,7	K		J	239
LPRINT	4,4	E		C	224
M	4,8	L	CAPS SHIFT	M	77
		C		M	
m	4,8	L		M	109

Character	Position on Keyboard Row, Column	Mode(s)	To Obtain Press		Code
MERGE	2,5	E	SHIFT	T	213
MOVE	1,6	E	SYMBOLSHIFT	6	209
N	4,7	L	CAPS SHIFT	N	78
		C		N	
n	4,7	L		N	110
NEW	3,1	K		A	230
NEXT	4,7	K		N	243
NOT	3,2	K L C	SYMBOLSHIFT	S	195
O	2,9	L	CAPS SHIFT	O	79
		C		O	
o	2,9	L		O	111
OPEN	1,4	E	SYMBOLSHIFT	4	211
OR	2,7	K L C	SYMBOLSHIFT	U	197
OUT	2,9	E	SHIFT	O	223
OVER	4,7	E	SHIFT	N	222
P	2,10	L	CAPS SHIFT	P	80
		C		P	
p	2,10	L		P	112
PAPER	4,4	E	SHIFT	C	218
PAUSE	4,8	K		M	242
PEEK	2,9	E		O	190
PI	4,8	E		M	167
PLOT	2,1	K		Q	246
POINT	1,8	E	SYMBOLSHIFT	8	169
POKE	2,9	K		O	244
PRINT	2,10	K		P	245
Q	2,1	L	CAPS SHIFT	Q	81
		C		Q	
q	2,1	L		Q	113
R	2,4	L	CAPS SHIFT	R	82
		C		R	
r	2,4	L		R	114
RANDomise	2,5	K		T	249
READ	3,1	E		A	227
REM	2,3	K		E	234
RESTORE	3,2	E		S	229
RETURN	2,6	K		Y	254
RND	2,5	E		T	165
RUN	2,4	K		R	247
S	3,2	L	CAPS SHIFT	S	83
		C		S	
s	3,2	L		S	115
SAVE	3,2	K		S	248
SCREEN$	3,8	E	SHIFT	K	170
SGN	3,4	E		F	188
SIN	2,1	E		Q	178
SPACE	4,10		SPACE		32

Character	Position on Keyboard Row, Column	Mode(s)	To Obtain Press		Code
SQR	3,6	E		H	187
STEP	3,3	K L C	SYMBOL SHIFT	D	2Ø5
STOP	3,1	K L C	SYMBOL SHIFT	A	226
STR$	2,6	E		Y	193
SYMBOL SHIFT	4,9		SYMBOL SHIFT		
T	2,5	L	CAPS SHIFT	T	84
		C		T	
t	2,5	L		T	116
TAB	2,1Ø	E		P	173
TAN	2,3	E		E	18Ø
THEN	3,5	K L C	SYMBOL SHIFT	G	2Ø3
TO	3,4	K L C	SYMBOL SHIFT	F	2Ø4
U	2,7	L	CAPS SHIFT	U	85
		C		U	
u	2,7	L		U	117
USR	3,9	E		L	192
V	4,5	L	CAPS SHIFT	V	86
		C		V	
v	4,5	L		V	118
VAL	3,7	E		J	176
VAL$	3,7	E	SHIFT	J	174
VERIFY	2,4	E	SHIFT	R	214
W	2,2	L	CAPS SHIFT	W	87
		C		W	
w	2,2	L		W	119
X	4,3	L	CAPS SHIFT	X	58
		C		X	
x	4,3	L		X	12Ø
Y	2,6	L	CAPS SHIFT	Y	59
		C		Y	
y	2,6	L		Y	121
Z	4,2	L	CAPS SHIFT	Z	9Ø
		C		Z	
z	4,2	L		Z	122
Ø	1,1Ø	K L C		Ø	48
1	1,1	K L C		1	49
2	1,2	K L C		2	5Ø
3	1,3	K L C		3	51
4	1,4	K L C		4	52
5	1,5	K L C		5	53
6	1,6	K L C		6	54
7	1,7	K L C		7	55
8	1,8	K L C		8	56
9	1,9	K L C		9	57

Character	Position on Keyboard Row, Column	Mode(s)	To Obtain Press		Code
!	1,1	K L C	SYMBOL SHIFT	1	33
‘‘	2,1Ø	K L C	SYMBOL SHIFT	P	34
#	1,3	K L C	SYMBOL SHIFT	3	35
$	1,4	K L C	SYMBOL SHIFT	4	36
%	1,5	K L C	SYMBOL SHIFT	5	37
&	1,6	K L C	SYMBOL SHIFT	6	38
‘	1,7	K L C	SYMBOL SHIFT	7	39
(	1,8	K L C	SYMBOL SHIFT	8	4Ø
)	1,9	K L C	SYMBOL SHIFT	9	41
*	4,6	K L C	SYMBOL SHIFT	B	42
+	3,8	K L C	SYMBOL SHIFT	K	43
,	3,6	K L C	SYMBOL SHIFT	H	44
–	3,7	K L C	SYMBOL SHIFT	J	45
.	4,8	K L C	SYMBOL SHIFT	M	46
/	4,5	K L C	SYMBOL SHIFT	V	47
:	4,5	K L C	SYMBOL SHIFT	Z	58
;	2,9	K L C	SYMBOL SHIFT	O	59
<	2,4	K L C	SYMBOL SHIFT	R	6Ø
=	3,9	K L C	SYMBOL SHIFT	L	61
>	2,5	K L C	SYMBOL SHIFT	T	62
?	4,4	K L C	SYMBOL SHIFT	C	63
@	4,2	K L C	SYMBOL SHIFT	Z	64
(	2,6	E	SHIFT	Y	91
)	2,7	E	SHIFT	U	93
\	3,3	E	SHIFT	D	92
↑	3,6	K L C	SYMBOL SHIFT	H	94
—	1,1Ø	K L C	SYMBOL SHIFT	Ø	95
£	4,3	K L C	SYMBOL SHIFT	X	96
{	3,4	E	SHIFT	F	123
}	3,5	E	SHIFT	G	125
|	2,3	E	SHIFT	S	124
~	3,1	E	SHIFT	A	126
©	2,1Ø	E	SHIFT	P	127
<=	2,1	K L C	SYMBOL SHIFT	Q	199
>=	2,3	K L C	SYMBOL SHIFT	E	2ØØ
<>	2,2	K L C	SYMBOL SHIFT	W	2Ø1
←	1,5	K L C	CAPS SHIFT	5	8
→	1,8	K L C	CAPS SHIFT	8	9
↓	1,6	K L C	CAPS SHIFT	6	1Ø
↑	1,7	K L C	CAPS SHIFT	7	11
□ (space)	1,8	G		8	128
█	1,8	G	SHIFT	8	143
▝	1,1	G		1	129
▙	1,1	G	SHIFT	1	142
▘	1,2	G		2	13Ø
▟	1,2	G	SHIFT	2	141
▀	1,3	G		3	131
▄	1,3	G	SHIFT	3	14Ø
▗	1,4	G		4	132
▛	1,4	G	SHIFT	4	139
▐	1,5	G		5	133
▌	1,5	G	SHIFT	5	138
▚	1,6	G		6	134

Character	Position on Keyboard Row, Column	Mode(s)	To Obtain Press		Code
▞	1,6	G	SHIFT	6	137
▜	1,7	G		7	135
▖	1,7	G	SHIFT	7	136

Colour control characters have no special codes. They have the codes of, and print as, the digit of the key that accesses them.

They are on keys 1 to 7 and Ø.

TRUE VIDEO	is on key 1,3. This gives INK on PAPER colours (black on white on switch-on).
INV. VIDEO	is on key 1,4. This gives INVERSE, i.e. PAPER colour on INK colour background (white on black if not coloured). These use CODE 2Ø (a *control code*), and swap the current INK and PAPER colours.

Other control codes are as follows:

Control Character	Code
Comma for print spacing	6
Number (in memory)	14
Ink control	16
Paper control	17
Flash control	18
Bright control	19
Inverse control	2Ø
Over control	21
Print At control	22
Print Tab control	23

These control characters are used to store required information in the attribute file (colour commands and characteristics of screen display), and the display file. They are followed by the values they take.

User-defined graphics have codes 144 to 164 inclusive, and are set, unless redefined, as the capital letters A to U in sequence. See Unit W3 for more information on this.

W2: Additional Spectrum BASIC Functions

This Unit covers the additional instructions and functions that are available in the Spectrum superset of Sinclair BASIC. First we will indicate the major differences.

SUMMARY OF ADDITIONAL SPECTRUM FACILITIES

The following are the significant differences between the ZX81 and the Spectrum which have not been dealt with in the main body of the text:

(i) The Spectrum gives a colour signal to the TV – see COLOUR in Section W3. Of course, it is still possible to use the machine on a black and white TV, where different shades of grey will be obtained when the colour commands are used.

(ii) The Spectrum's character set differs from that of the ZX81 and includes lower case as well as capital letters – see CHARACTER SET and USER DEFINED GRAPHICS.

(iii) The Spectrum's keyboard has additional characters and functions. You should now be familiar with the functions treated in the main text. Extended functions are dealt with a little later in this Unit.

(iv) Simple sound production is available using the Spectrum's BEEP command – see SOUND in Section W3.

(v) The tape storing facilities represent a considerable improvement on those offered by the ZX81 – see TAPE STORAGE below. The tape LOAD and SAVE speed is roughly 16k words in 100 seconds, and there is a facility to merge a program stored on tape with one in memory using MERGE. The VERIFY facility can be used to check that a program has saved correctly, as has been noted.

(vi) Disc storage and file-handling capability with the microdrive will eventually be available on the Spectrum, loading 16k words per second – see OTHER KEYS below.

(vii) Additional graphics commands are available to enable straight lines, arcs and circles to be drawn simply – see GRAPHICS in Section W3.

(viii) The INPUT statement has additional features and instructions. READ, DATA and RESTORE are added – see below: PUTTING DATA INTO PROGRAMS.

(ix) On the Spectrum it is possible to define your own numeric and string functions in a program – see USER DEFINED FUNCTIONS below.

(x) The Spectrum operates in a 'fast mode' at all times and is roughly four times faster than the ZX81.

(xi) Multiple statements on a line are possible on the Spectrum with a colon(:) as a statement separator. For example:

```
10  LET X = 4: LET Y = 6: LET Z = 8
```

Whilst this is a useful addition, multiple line statements can also be very confusing and their use should be minimised. This said, they can be useful for additional REM statements, assignments of related variables and conditional program sequences, and for the combination of graphics and colour commands.

The facility of being able to place a sequence of instructions after a conditional test is valuable. The sequence of BASIC instructions following an IF...THEN will be executed IF the condition is TRUE. Control passes directly to the next *line* of the program if the condition is false. We can write:

```
1Ø  INPUT a
2Ø  IF a<1 OR a>9 THEN PRINT "Out of Range":
    GOTO 1Ø
3Ø  PRINT a
```

It is important to remember that you can only GOTO a line number and start at the beginning of that line. You cannot access the second or subsequent statements of a line with multiple statements.

(xii) There is no SCROLL key on the Spectrum, but scrolling is done automatically by pressing any key (except N, STOP, BREAK) when 'Scroll?' appears on the screen. Making the Spectrum SCROLL in the same way as the ZX81 SCROLL command has been covered in the text.

(xiii) It is important to note that CLEAR operates differently on the Spectrum than on the ZX81. CLEAR not only erases all variables in memory, but also resets RAMTOP and RESTOREs as well as clearing the GOSUB stack. In fact you can use CLEAR on the Spectrum to reserve protected memory space above RAMTOP: using a command like CLEAR 238ØØ sets RAMTOP to 238ØØ. This cannot be done on the ZX81.

You have seen the modifications required for the ZX81 programs to run on the Spectrum. Here is a summary for reference, to convert any programs you may come across in books or magazines. All programs in the text and the program library (Appendix VI) are annotated with any required Spectrum changes.

ZX81 TO SPECTRUM PROGRAM CONVERSION

There are relatively few things to bear in mind when converting a ZX81 program for the Spectrum. Of course, the ZX81 will not have included colour or sound in the programs, and these are aspects you can add for yourself. Note that ZX81 programs SAVEd on cassette will not load into the Spectrum, even if no ZX81 specific commands have been used.

Perhaps the first thing to note is that you must be in CAPS mode to produce listings and programs which are identical to those of the ZX81. (Use CAPS SHIFT with CAPS LOCK to stay in this mode when you switch on.)

PLOT plots in high resolution – 256 × 176 pixels – whereas on the ZX81 the resolution was only 64 × 44. Thus as a general rule you can simply multiply by a factor of four to any PLOTted points in a ZX81 program to obtain a working Spectrum version. Hence PLOT 4,10 on the ZX81 becomes PLOT 16,40 on the Spectrum.

The Spectrum has no FAST and SLOW modes, as it runs in the equivalent of the SLOW mode all the time (always a screen display) but at the speed of a fast mode. Just omit program lines that contain the instructions FAST or SLOW.

The Spectrum does not have SCROLL as a program instruction as the ZX81 does. To SCROLL the screen in a Spectrum program you need to POKE the location 23692 with a number greater than 1, or with −1. This temporarily disables the 'SCROLL?' request, and when followed by PRINTing AT the last line (line 21) on the screen the display will SCROLL.

Thus the ZX81 line:

```
200 SCROLL
```

is replaced by

```
200 POKE 23692, - 1 : PRINT AT 21,0;
```

Raising a number to a power on the ZX81 uses the symbol '**' whereas on the Spectrum we use '↑'. RAND in ZX81 programs is that instruction on the Spectrum keyboard, but prints as RANDOMISE.

POKEing to the display file cannot be easily done, and the same is true of PEEK used to identify a character on the screen. To get around this we recommend using PRINT AT instead of POKEing the display, and SCREEN$ to replace PEEKing the display. Hence you will have to calculate what character cell position corresponds to any address in the ZX81's display file which is used in a program. Read the description of the ZX81 display file in Unit Q4 in order to find out how to do this.

PEEKing the character table in RAM is done equally simply on the Spectrum, with the start of the character table being given by the following PEEKs, *plus* 256:

```
PEEK 23606 + 256*PEEK 23607
```

This is usually set at 15360 – but you can POKE these addresses and change the location at which the character table starts in memory. You can therefore create an entirely new character set in RAM and have the CHARS variable (stored in the locations above) point to 256 bytes *below* it. All other system variables on the ZX81 have equivalents on the Spectrum. This text has the system variables for both machines listed in Appendix V.

Because of the amount of memory (6.5k) taken up for graphics on the Spectrum, you will find that a large program for the 16k ZX81 (of 10k or so), will not fit into a 16k Spectrum. 48k Spectrum owners will of course have no problems with this, but if contemplating keying in a long program with the smaller machine it is worth making a crude estimate of the program length, if the information is not given in the documentation. The number of lines in the listing (total, not numbered lines only), multiplied by 15 will give you a reasonable estimate (biased on the high side) of the program length in bytes.

We will now go on to cover the additional Spectrum facilities and functions, other than those connected with Colour, Graphics and Sound, which are treated in Unit W3.

TAPE STORAGE

New keywords: **VERIFY and MERGE.**
Associated new keywords: **LINE, DATA, SCREEN$**

(i) SAVING Information on Tape

The SAVE key is used to save information on tape. This can be: (a) program and variables, (b) arrays, (c) bytes of memory (memory contents)

When saving information on tape it is essential that the EAR piece jack-plug is removed from the tape recorder.

(a) *Programs and Variables*
SAVE "filnam" – saves programs and variables.
SAVE "filnam" LINE 1Ø – saves programs and variables and when loaded next automatically runs itself from the given line number.

(b) *Arrays*
SAVE "alpha" DATA a() – saves the numeric array a specified under the name alpha.
SAVE "beta" DATA b$() – saves the string array b$ specified under the name beta.

(c) *Bytes*
SAVE "gamma" CODE 16384, 6912 – saves the bytes specified. The first figure (in this case 16384) is the address of the first byte to be saved and the second figure (in this case 6912) is the number of bytes to be saved.

The particular bytes specified above will save the TV picture, but a special key SCREEN$ is available to do this:

SAVE "gamma" SCREEN$

(ii) VERIFICATION of Information on Tape

The VERIFY key is used to check the information saved on the tape against the information in the computer.

VERIFY "filnam" – checks programs and variables

VERIFY "alpha" DATA a() – checks numeric array specified

VERIFY "beta" DATA b$() – checks string array specified

VERIFY "gamma" CODE 16384, 6912 – checks bytes specified (first number – address of first byte, second number – number of bytes).

(iii) LOADING Information from Tape

The LOAD key is used to load new information from the tape, deleting any old information in the memory.

LOAD "filnam" – loads program and variables specified (and automatically runs the program if the SAVE and LINE instructions were used to save the program).

LOAD "alpha" DATA a() – loads numeric array specified by alpha as array a in memory.

LOAD "beta" DATA b$() – loads string array specified by beta as array b$ in memory.

(N.B. If insufficient memory is available, an error message occurs and the old information in memory is *not* deleted.)

LOAD "gamma" CODE 16384, 6912 loads the bytes specified (first number is the address of the first byte, second number is the number of bytes).

LOAD "gamma" SCREEN$ is an alternative for the particular bytes specified above which contain the TV picture.

(iv) MERGING Programs

The MERGE key is used to combine a program already in memory with a program on tape (it may *not be used* on arrays or bytes).

MERGE "delta" – adds the program delta (stored on tape) to the program already in memory, overwriting any program lines and variables in memory which are at the same line numbers or have the same variable name as those on tape. For example:

Program in memory:

```
10  PRINT "hello"
20  PRINT
30  PRINT "goodbye"
40  PRINT
50  PRINT "end"
```

Program "delta" on tape:

```
10  PRINT "no"
20  PRINT "yes"
60  PRINT "repeat"
```

MERGE "delta" results in the program:

```
10  PRINT "no"
20  PRINT "yes"
30  PRINT "goodbye"
40  PRINT
50  PRINT "end"
60  PRINT "repeat"
```

Note the restriction on the use of MERGE. It can only be used for numbered program lines. These can have defined arrays or variables that are transferred with the program, but direct data (array values or bytes) is not MERGEable. See Units T11 and T12 for storing data, and remember that as long as there is one program line, MERGE will work.

PUTTING DATA INTO PROGRAMS

New keywords: **READ, RESTORE and DATA**
Extended function for INPUT key

(i) <u>INPUT Statement</u>

10 INPUT A$	allows input of one string
20 INPUT A,B,C,D	allows input of four numbers
30 INPUT "Enter your name", N$	allows the part within inverted commas to be printed at the bottom of the screen.

If we key in:

```
10  LET M$ = "SPECTRUM"
20  INPUT ("I am";m$;"."); "Your name?", y$
```

these two lines will produce at the bottom of the screen: I am SPECTRUM. Your name? " cursor "

It is also possible to use INPUT AT in a similar way to PRINT AT:

```
10  DIM a$(5)
20  INPUT AT 0,0; a$(1); AT 1,0; a$(2); AT 2,0; a$(3); AT
    3,0; a$(4); AT 4,0; a$(5).
```

This will result in the inputs being placed on separate lines (note what these co-ordinates mean). The lower part of the screen will move up to allow all input lines to be on screen. (The upper part remains unaltered until the lower part would start to write on the same line – the upper part then starts to scroll.)

10 INPUT LINE a$ allows input of a string without the computer inserting quotes around the cursor.

(ii) READ and DATA

These keys allow data to be stored internally within the program. For example:

```
10  READ a,b,c
20  PRINT a,b,c
30  DATA 10,20,30
```

The computer looks at all lines containing DATA statements and puts them sequentially into a data bank. A pointer is associated with the data bank and is initially set to the first item.

```
10    20    30
↑
```

When the program reaches a line with a READ statement, the first data item is allocated to the variable (i.e. a = 10) and the pointer moves to the second item and so on. So b = 20 and c = 30.

Note (i) DATA items are separated by commas
(ii) variables in READ statements are separated by commas
(iii) string data items must be in inverted commas

For example:

```
10  READ a$,b,c$,d
20  PRINT a$,b,c$,d
30  DATA "smith", 90
40  DATA "jones", 60
```

(iii) RESTORE

The RESTORE statement may be used to alter the position of the pointer. For example:

```
10  READ a$,b
20  RESTORE
30  READ c$,d
```

```
40  PRINT a$,b,c$,d
50  DATA "smith", 90, "jones", 60
```

The effect of line 20 is to reset the pointer to the first item. Thus a$ = "smith", b = 90, c$ = "smith", d = 90. It is also possible to use RESTORE with a line number in which case the pointer is reset to the first item of the data statement of that line (or following lines). For example:

```
 10  READ a$,b
 20  RESTORE 100
 30  READ c$,d
 40  PRINT a$,b,c$,d
 50  DATA "smith", 90, "jones", 60
100  DATA "brown", 100, "white", 120
200  DATA "black", 8, "yellow", 6
```

This will allocate a$ = "smith", b = 90 and c$ = "brown", d = 100 (whereas 20 RESTORE gives c$ = "smith", d = 90 and 20 RESTORE 200 gives c$ = "black", d = 8).

If CLEAR is used on the Spectrum, it also does a RESTORE on the data.

USER DEFINED FUNCTIONS

New keywords: **DEF FN** and **FN**

The user can define up to 26 numeric and 26 string functions in any program.

A numeric function is named FN followed by a single letter – e.g. FN Z.

A string function is named FN followed by a single letter and $ – e.g. FN A$.

It is necessary to define the function using a DEF FN statement (i.e. by pressing the DEF FN key). For example:

```
10  DEF FN a(x) = x ↑ 3
20  PRINT FN a(3)
```

Line 10 defines the function and line 20 would give $3^3 = 27$. For strings:

```
10  DEF FN q$(a$) = a$ (2 to 6)
20  PRINT FN q$("harrison")
```

Line 10 defines a string function and line 20 would give 'arris'.

You may also use functions with several variables:

```
 5  LET a = 1Ø: LET b = 2Ø
1Ø  DEF FN p(x,y,z) = a*x↑2 + b*y↑2 + z
2Ø  PRINT FN p(1,2,3)
3Ø  PRINT
4Ø  PRINT FN p(3,2,1)
```

Note that any constants occurring (in this case a,b) are not included in the FN; only the variable values are specified (in this case x, y and z). Thus line 2Ø gives 93 and line 4Ø gives 171.

CHARACTER SET AND USER DEFINED GRAPHICS

(i) *Character Set*

The character set consists of 256 characters each having a code between Ø and 255. The set consists of:

Control characters (code Ø to 31)
ASCII characters (plus the non-standard £ and ©)
Spectrum graphics symbols
User-defined graphics

The program given below will print out the complete character set (excluding the control characters):

```
1Ø  FOR n = 32 TO 255: PRINT CHR$ n; : NEXT n
```

(ii) *User defined graphics*

These are the letters A to U in graphics mode. They initially print as these letters (in capitals), until defined. They enable one to print a given shape in a character cell by pressing a single key. EXAMPLE: Fill the screen with dogs. Begin by producing a dog shape which fills a character cell when GRAPHICS D is pressed and then display the dogs across the screen.

(i) Fill in appropriate squares in 8 by 8 cell
(ii) Allow 1 for ink, Ø for paper
(iii) Put appropriate numbers in data statements

								Binary	Decimal
x	x	x					x	111ØØØØ1	225
x	x	x				x		111ØØØ1Ø	226
x	x	x	x	x	x			111111ØØ	252
		x	x	x	x			ØØ1111ØØ	6Ø
		x	x	x	x			ØØ1111ØØ	6Ø
		x	x	x	x			ØØ1111ØØ	6Ø
		x			x			ØØ1ØØ1ØØ	36
		x			x			ØØ1ØØ1ØØ	36

```
   10 REM user defined graphics
   20 REM definadog
   30 FOR n=0 TO 7
   40 READ x
   50 POKE USR "D"+n,x
   60 NEXT n
   70 DATA 225,226,252,60,60,60,3
6,36
   80 REM screenful of dogs
   90 BORDER 4: PAPER 6: INK 0: C
LS
  100 FOR l=0 TO 20 STEP 2
  110 FOR c=0 TO 30 STEP 2
  120 PRINT AT l,c;"D"
  130 NEXT c
  140 NEXT l
```

The **BIN** key allows you to enter binary numbers – i.e. BIN 11100001 is equivalent to 225 in the DATA statement (line 65). The plot of the user-defined graphic in the 8 × 8 grid, expressed in binary form, can thus be centred directly with the use of BIN into the DATA statement:

70 DATA BIN 11100001, BIN 11100010, etc.

OTHER KEYS

The following keys will only operate when the Sinclair microdrive and the RS 232 (standard printer) interface become available:

OPEN # , CLOSE # , MOVE, ERASE, CAT and FORMAT.

The keys IN and OUT are associated with I/O ports (input and output ports) and enable the SPECTRUM to communicate with peripheral devices. The equivalent commands used by the operating system run the ZX Printer. They are beyond the scope of the present text. The use and format of these instructions will be specified in the documentation of any equipment using them.

W3: Colour, Graphics and Sound

COLOUR

(i) *BORDER AND PAPER*

The screen is divided into two areas referred to as:
BORDER (the outer part) and PAPER (the central area). (24 lines of 32 characters.)
The instructions **BORDER** and **PAPER** are used to define the colours of the areas.

The following colours are available:

0 black
1 blue

2 red
3 magenta
4 green
5 cyan
6 yellow
7 white

Magenta is a purple colour, and cyan is light blue.

Unless otherwise specified, both BORDER and PAPER are white. The colour of border and paper can be changed to any of the eight normal colours. For example:

BORDER 4: the border becomes green on pressing the ENTER key

PAPER 2: no change occurs on pressing the ENTER key (it merely cancels PAPER command already existing). Press the ENTER key again and the centre becomes red.

(On a black and white TV the above numbers correspond to the order of brightness).

Both instructions can be used in programs:

```
10  BORDER 2: PAPER 6
```

These are global commands defining the whole border and paper areas. PAPER may be used as a specific command (see below).

(ii) *PICTURE*

The picture area affected by the global PAPER instruction consists of 24 lines each of 32 positions, i.e. $24 \times 32 = 768$ character cells. The screen that can normally be printed to is 22 lines of 32 character cells. The character cells have printing characteristics (attributes) which may be specified.

Each character cell consists of 8×8 dots and has two colours associated with it:

INK (foreground colour)
PAPER (background colour)

Normally each character cell has black ink and white paper.

In addition, each character cell also has a brightness attributed with **BRIGHT** (normal or extra-bright) corresponding to BRIGHT Ø and BRIGHT 1 and the attribute **FLASH** with the possibility of no-flash or flash corresponding to FLASH Ø and FLASH 1. For example:

```
10  PAPER 3 : INK 6 : BRIGHT Ø : FLASH 1
```

would result in background magenta, foreground yellow, normal brightness and flashing. Flashing characters alternate the ink and paper colours. In addition, 8 can be used with all four statements meaning transparent (i.e. left as previous); 9 can be used with PAPER and INK meaning contrast. PAPER will be dark (black) if INK is specified as a light colour (colours Ø to 3), light (white) if INK specified as a dark colour (colours 4 to 7). INK produces contrasting PAPER in the same way.

(iii) *INVERSE, OVER AND ATTR*

The statements **INVERSE** and **OVER** may also be used to control the dot pattern printed in the character cells.

inverse or normal i.e.	INVERSE 1 (inverse video) or INVERSE Ø (normal video)
over or normal i.e.	OVER 1 (overprints the new character on top of the old) OVER Ø (normal)

All the statements in (ii) and (iii) may be used in conjunction with PRINT and INPUT commands and also with graphics commands such as PLOT and DRAW. For example:

```
10  INPUT INK 2; FLASH 1; "What is your name?"; N$
20  PRINT PAPER 6; N$
```

which will result when run in 'What is your name?' flashing in red and white and the name input (in black and white) is then printed out in black on yellow. If not specified, the PAPER instruction assumes the contrasting INK, FLASH Ø and BRIGHT Ø.

The attributes of any character cell (i.e. PAPER, INK, BRIGHT and FLASH) on the screen may be determined using the **ATTR** key, which returns a number made up as follows:

FLASH on (128), normal (Ø) +
BRIGHT on (64), normal (Ø) +
PAPER (8*colour) +
INK (colour)

Thus, 1Ø PRINT ATTR (19,2Ø) would give the number 162 if the character cell at (19,2Ø) is flashing (128), normal (Ø), green paper (32) and cyan ink (2).

The **TRUE VIDEO** instruction gives the INK colour on PAPER colour background. This may be changed to **INV.VIDEO** (PAPER colour on INK colour). All succeeding printed character squares have the attributes shifted as if INVERSE had been used.

EXAMPLE 1

This is a simple program to display the colours available and to show the effect of the transparency and contrast commands.

```
  5 REM colours
 1Ø FOR n=1 TO 22: FOR p=Ø TO 7
 2Ø PAPER P: PRINT "    ";
 3Ø NEXT p: NEXT n
 4Ø PAUSE 1ØØ
 45 REM transparency and contra
    st
 5Ø INK 9: PAPER 6: PRINT AT Ø,
    Ø;
 6Ø FOR n=1 TO 66: PRINT "colou
    rings";: NEXT D: PRINT
 7Ø PAPER 7: INK Ø: BRIGHT Ø
 8Ø PAUSE 1ØØ
```

EXAMPLE 2

This is a simple program drawing coloured straight lines with different separations.

Line 3Ø – gives a black border.

Line 32Ø – gives paper and ink colours (selected at random, excluding black and white).

Line 2ØØ – resets paper and border to white, ink to black for listing etc. after program has been run.

Notice how colours are <u>character cell dependent</u> not <u>pixel dependent</u>. This program clearly shows this effect.

```
 3Ø BORDER Ø
 4Ø FOR x=Ø TO 254 STEP 2
 5Ø PLOT 128,88: DRAW -127+x,-8
    7
 6Ø NEXT x
 65 GO SUB 3ØØ
 7Ø FOR y=Ø TO 174 STEP 3
 8Ø PLOT 128,88: DRAW 127,-87+y
 9Ø NEXT y
 95 GO SUB 3ØØ
1ØØ FOR z=Ø TO 254 STEP 2
11Ø PLOT 128,88: DRAW 127-z,87
12Ø NEXT z
125 GO SUB 3ØØ
13Ø FOR a=Ø TO 174 STEP 3
14Ø PLOT 128,88: DRAW -127,87-a
15Ø NEXT a
2ØØ PAPER 7: INK Ø: BORDER 7
21Ø STOP
3ØØ LET i=(5*RND+1): LET p=INT
    (5*RND)+1
31Ø IF i=p THEN GO TO 1Ø
32Ø PAPER p: INK i
33Ø RETURN
```

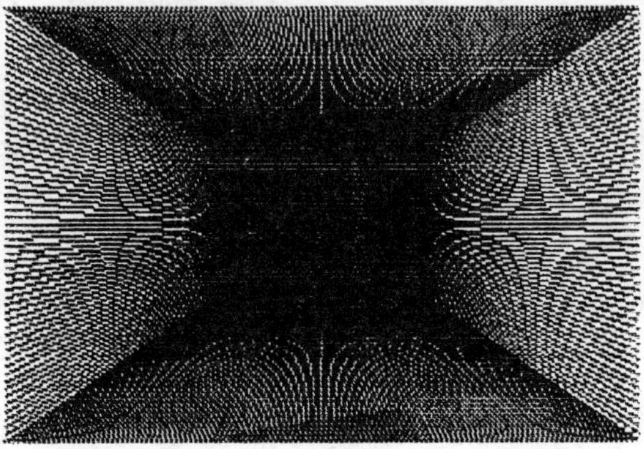

GRAPHICS

New keywords: **DRAW, CIRCLE, POINT**

The screen is 22 lines by 32 columns – i.e. 7Ø4 character cells for graphics use. Each character cell consists of 8 by 8 dots (called *pixels*). Thus the *pixel co-ordinates* go from (Ø,Ø) bottom left-hand corner to (255, 175) the top right-hand corner.

Colour Graphics

You can do graphics in colour but remember that the pixels in any one character cell can only be either of the two colours corresponding to the current ink and paper values for the character cell.
For example, let's attempt to draw three circles one black, one blue and one red:

```
10  INK 2 : CIRCLE 40,40,30      (red circle)
20  INK 1 : CIRCLE 60,60,40      (blue circle)
30  INK 0 : CIRCLE 50,50,40      (black circle)
```

This example shows that colour graphics is possible but can only be handled with great care. It is important to be clear about *character cells* as opposed to *pixels*. For example, you can draw three circles one black, one blue and one red:

```
10  INK 2 : CIRCLE 70,70,70      (red circle)
20  INK 4 : CIRCLE 70,70,50      (blue circle)
30  INK 0 : CIRCLE 70,70,30      (black circle)
```

Graphics Commands

PLOT X,Y – inks in the pixel at the point (X,Y)
DRAW X1,Y1 – inks in the line from the point specified previously to

the point X1 pixels to the right and Y1 pixels up from it. For example:

```
10  PLOT 20,30   – plots point (20,30)
20  DRAW 50,60   – draws line from point (20,30)
                   to the point (20 + 50,30 + 60),
                   i.e. (70,90).
```

DRAW X2,Y2,A – draws an arc of a circle from the previously specified point to the point X2 pixels to the right and Y2 pixels up from it with an angle A radians (anticlockwise). For example:

```
10  PLOT 30,30
20  DRAW 60,60
30  DRAW 80,80, PI
```

CIRCLE X,Y,A draws a circle centre (X,Y) and radius A
POINT (X,Y) will give 0 if pixel at (X,Y) is paper colour and 1 if ink.
For example:

```
10  CIRCLE 40,40,30        – draws circle centre (40,40) and radius 30
20  PRINT POINT (40,40)– pixel paper – 0
30  PRINT POINT (70,70)– pixel ink  – 1
```

The commands INVERSE and OVER may be used with the graphics commands. For example:

PLOT INVERSE 1	will put paper colour at pixel
PLOT OVER 1	will change ink to paper at pixel

There is no UNPLOT on the Spectrum. We must use INVERSE or OVER. PLOT OVER 1 or PLOT INVERSE 1 effectively unplot the pixel. DRAW OVER 1 may be used to rubout a line while preserving the original information; compare result of program 1 with that of program 2.

```
  10 FOR n=1 TO 22
  20 PRINT "[block graphics]"
  30 NEXT n
  40 PLOT 0,0: DRAW 255,175
  45 STOP
  50 PLOT 0,0: DRAW INVERSE 1;25
5,175
```

```
  10 FOR n=1 TO 22
  20 PRINT "[block graphics]"
  30 NEXT n
  40 PLOT 0,0: DRAW 255,175
  45 STOP
  50 PLOT 0,0: DRAW INVERSE 1;25
5,175
```

Try this one-line program:

```
10  PLOT 65,27: DRAW OVER 1; 120,120,49*3*PI
```

Try different values in place of 49.

EXAMPLES

1 *Use of PLOT and DRAW commands* (straight lines)
This program makes use of these statements to draw a histogram by drawing a series of rectangles.

Lines 70 and 80 produce a rectangle as shown:

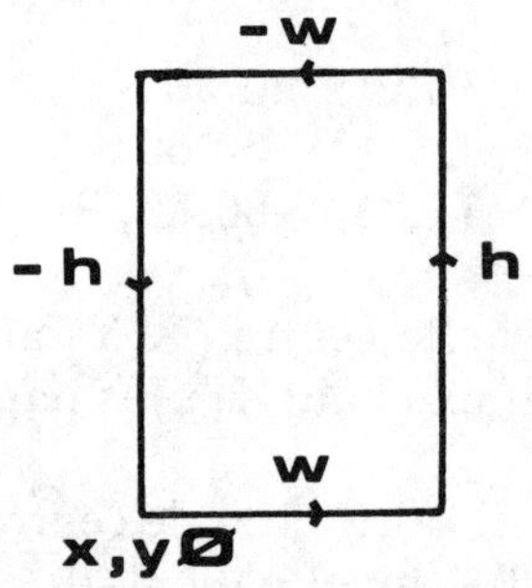


```
 10 REM Histogram using DRAW
 20 READ x0,y0: LET x=x0
 25 REM Coordinates of LHS
 30 READ w,n
 35 REM Width and number of uni
    ts
 40 FOR j=1 TO n
 50 READ h
 60 REM Unit height
 70 PLOT x,y0
 80 DRAW w,0: DRAW 0,h: DRAW -w
    ,0: DRAW 0,-h
 90 LET x=x+w
100 NEXT j
105 DATA 5,5,20,12
110 DATA 12,45,67,98,134,167,17
    0,136,124,87,46,20
```

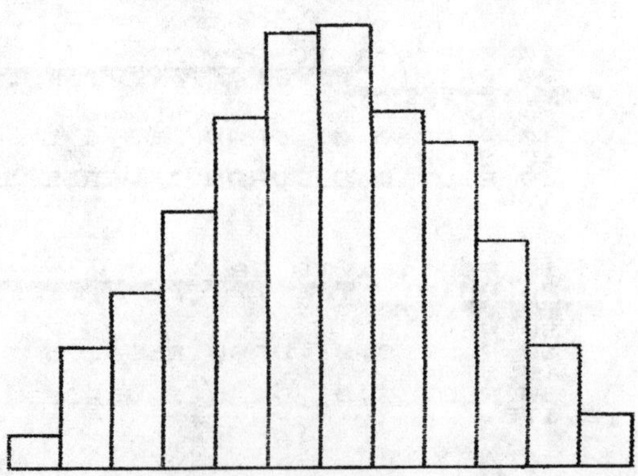

2 *Use of DRAW command* (arcs of circles)
This program produces a pattern by drawing four sets of semicircles. The basic plotting line is illustrated by the diagram of the effect of line 4Ø. This is repeated within a series of four loops.

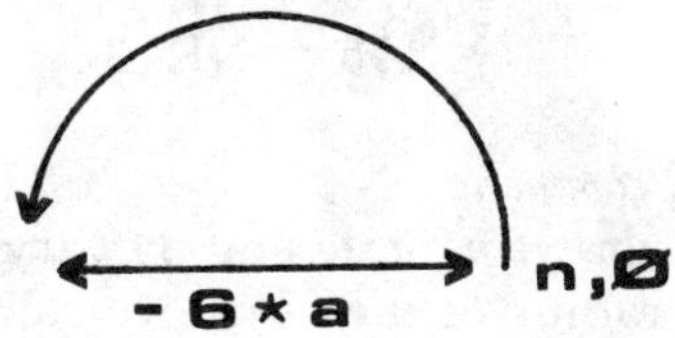


```
 1Ø LET a=Ø
 2Ø FOR n=129 TO 254 STEP 3
 3Ø LET a=a+1
 4Ø PLOT n,Ø: DRAW -6*a,Ø,PI
 5Ø NEXT n
 6Ø LET b=Ø
 7Ø FOR n=129 TO 254 STEP 3
 8Ø LET b=b+1
 9Ø PLOT n,175: DRAW -6*b,Ø,-PI
1ØØ NEXT n
11Ø LET c=Ø
12Ø FOR n=9Ø TO 174 STEP 3
13Ø LET c=c+1
14Ø PLOT Ø,n: DRAW Ø,-6*c,-PI
15Ø NEXT n
16Ø LET d=Ø
17Ø FOR n=9Ø TO 174 STEP 3
18Ø LET d=d+1
19Ø PLOT 255,n: DRAW Ø,-6*d,PI
2ØØ NEXT n
```

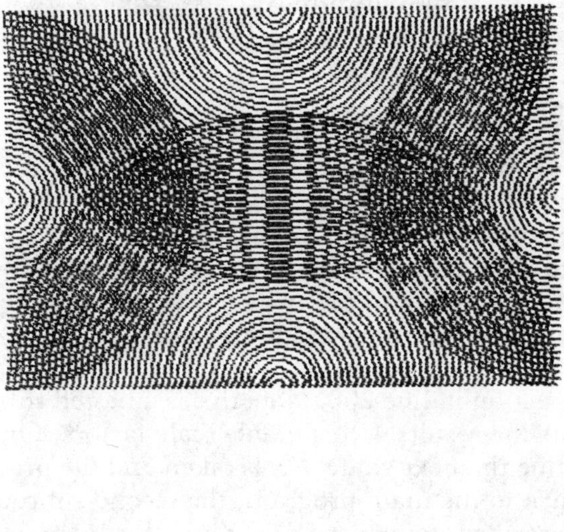

Try inserting the following lines to see the effect of colour (note graphics is pixel but colour is character cells).

```
  5  INK 2
 55  INK 5
105  INK 6
155  INK 3
```

3 *Use of CIRCLE command*

This command draws a circle and by varying the position of the centre and the radius of the circle we can obtain an acceptable drawing of a cone:

```
  5 REM Draw a cone
 10 READ i,p,b
 15 REM ink,paper,border
 20 READ cr
 25 REM radius of cone
 30 CLS : INK i: BORDER b: PAPE
    R p: CLS
 40 LET x=50
 50 FOR r=cr TO 1 STEP -1
 60 CIRCLE x,90,r
 70 LET x=x+3
 80 NEXT r
 90 DATA 1,4,6
100 DATA 50,3
```

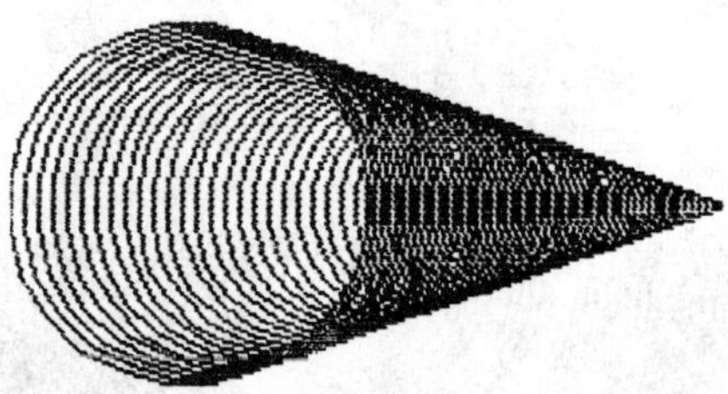

4 *Use of user-defined functions for graph plotting*

The program below illustrates the use of the DEF FN and FN instructions in plotting graphs. Line 5 defines the function. Line 10 bypasses the subroutines (lines 20 to 100) and the main program first defines a = 5 (line 120), then calls the first plot subroutine (lines 20 to 50), which uses a loop to define values of x. Line 30 makes the variable b equal to COS x and passes control to the subroutine at line 200 to evaluate y using the FN (y) instruction in line 200. Note this is a nested subroutine. Line 210 plots the results with suitable scale factors. On return to the subroutine the next value of x is taken and the process repeated. On return to the main program, the second subroutine, lines 70 to 100, is called, to plot the SIN x function by making b = SIN x.

The variable a is redefined to equal 15 in line 150 on completion of the first two plots, and the subroutines are called in sequence again. Note the capability to define a function using variables, and then define the values of the variables as appropriate. In this case, two values (COSx and SINx) are given to b, and the amplitude a is defined as first 5, then 15. Four plots are produced from the one user-defined function of line 5.

```
  5 DEF FN y(x)=b*a
 10 GO TO 120
 14
 15 REM **FUNCTION ONE PLOT **
        **SUBROUTINE        **
 16
 20 FOR x=0 TO 25 STEP .1
 30 LET b=COS x: GO SUB 200
 40 NEXT x
 50 RETURN
 55 REM **END FN ONE SUB      **
        ************************
 56
 57
 60 REM **FUNCTION TWO PLOT **
        **SUBROUTINE        **
 61
 70 FOR X=0 TO 25 STEP .1
 80 LET b=SIN x: GO SUB 200
 90 NEXT x
100 RETURN
105 REM **END FN TWO SUB      **
        ************************
106
110 REM ***********************
        **MAIN PROGRAM        **
120 LET A=5
130 GO SUB 20
140 GO SUB 70
150 LET a=15
160 GO SUB 20
170 GO SUB 70
180 STOP
185 REM **END MAIN PROGRAM**
        *********************
186
190 REM *SUBROUTINE-CALCULATE**
       **USING FN AND PLOT    **
200 LET y=FN y(x)
210 PLOT x*10,y*3+80
220 RETURN
225
230 REM **ENDSUB FUNCTION USE**
        ************************
```

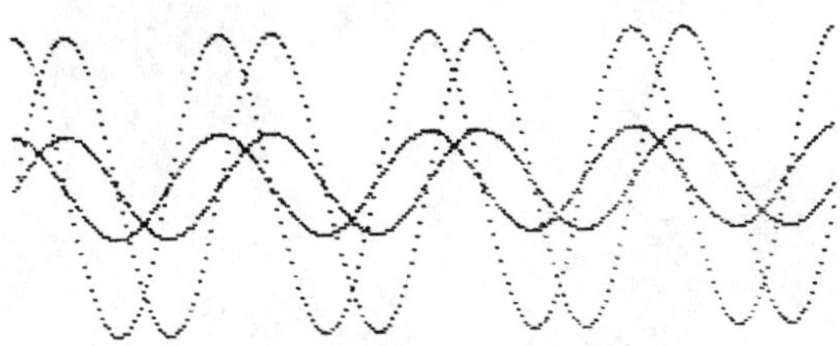

SOUND

New keyword: **BEEP**

BEEP 6, 2 produces a note of *duration* 6 seconds and a *pitch* 2 semitones above middle C. The sound is fairly quiet; however fractional changes in pitch are available and it is possible to tune it to different instruments. To obtain the even-tempered scale of C major:

```
BEEP 1,0 : BEEP 1,2 : BEEP 1,4 : BEEP 1,5 : BEEP 1,7:
BEEP 1,9 : BEEP 1,11 : BEEP 1,12
```

The short program below gives some idea of the useful musical range and how it may be used for sound effects.

```
  5 REM Musical range
 10 READ p1,p2
 15 REM lowest and highest freq
 20 FOR n=p1 TO p2
 30 BEEP .5,n
 40 PRINT AT (13-n/3),(n+1/2);"
▒"
 50 NEXT n
 55 DATA -25,30
 60 PAUSE 200: CLS
 70 REM sound effect
 80 LET x=.1
 90 FOR n=60 TO 20 STEP -1
 95 PRINT AT (30-n/2),12;"▞"
100 BEEP .05,n
110 LET x=x-1
120 NEXT n
130 BEEP .05,-25: BEEP .1,30
```

APPENDIX I

ZX81 BASIC Summary

CONVENTIONS

n or m or p	numeric expression
s	string expression
e	expression (string or numeric)
V	variable name
<s>	statement
[]	indicates an optional item
$	indicates a string instruction

Numeric variables are first character a letter, then any alphanumeric characters.
String variables are A to Z, followed by $.

OPERATING COMMANDS

LOAD s	Load a program from tape. String may be null ("") (Loads first program)
SAVE s	Save a program on tape
RUN [n]	Run program [starting at line n]
CLEAR	Resets all variables in program
NEW	Clears out program and variables
STOP	Stops program execution
CONT	Starts execution after BREAK or STOP
FAST	Screen not displayed until end, PAUSE, INPUT, SLOW. Computes only.
SLOW	Screen displayed continuously, whilst computing

INPUT/OUTPUT INSTRUCTIONS

INPUT V	Input numeric or string variable from keyboard
INKEY$	Reads current input character. Does not wait for key to be pressed.
LIST [n]	Displays program [starting from line n]
PRINT [e][,e][;e][AT n,m;][TABn;]	Print on screen
CLS	Clears the screen
PLOT m,n	Plot ¼ graphic char. } Ø< = m< = 63 horizontal
UNPLOT m,n	Unplot pixel } Ø< = n< = 43 vertical
LLIST [n]	List program on printer [starting from line n]
LPRINT [e][,e][;e][TAB n;]	Print on line printer
COPY	Print a copy of screen on printer

OTHER INSTRUCTIONS

POKE n,m	Store the value m in memory location n. O< = m< = 255.
PEEK n	Returns the value stored in memory location n
PAUSE n	Halts program for n/5Øseconds (n/6Ø in U.S.). If n>32767 then pauses until key pressed. (n<65535)
REM	REMARK – comments. Ignored in program execution.
LET V[$] = e	Assigns the value of e to V

DIM V[$] (n[,m])	Dimensions array n by m (numeric), n strings of length m if string
RAND [n]	Random number seed
RND	Function returns a random number n. Ø< = n<1
GOTO n	Transfers control to line n
GOSUB n	Go to Subroutine at line n
RETURN	Return from subroutine to line after last GOSUB
IF e THEN <s>	If e is true THEN statement s is done, if e is false then s is not done. For e see expressions. Evaluates as TRUE = 1, FALSE = Ø
FOR V = n TO m [STEP p]	V is any single letter control variable.
<s>	m,n,p any numeric expressions. STEP 1 is
[<s>]	assumed if STEP not specified
NEXT V	Increments V by STEP. Goes to next line if V>m (m>n) or V<m (n>m).

TRIG FUNCTIONS

SIN n	Sine n
COS n	Cosine n
TAN n	Tangent n
ASN n	Arc Sine n (ARCSIN on keyboard)
ACS n	Arc Cosine n (ARCCOS on keyboard)
ATN n	Arc Tangent n (ARCTAN on keyboard)
	n evaluated as radians

NUMERIC FUNCTIONS

EXP n	Exponent n or e^n
LN n	Log$_e$ n or ln n
SQR n	Square root of n
INT n	Integer of n (rounds down)
ABS n	Absolute value of n
SGN n	1 if n is positive, Ø if zero, – 1 if negative
PI (π)	3.1415927

STRING FUNCTIONS

LEN s	Length of string s
CHR$ n	Character of code n (single character string)
CODE s	Code of first character in string s
STR$ n	Convert numeric expression to String
VAL s	Convert string to numeric expression
+	String concatenation

EXPRESSIONS
PRIORITY

12 ()	bracketed expressions
11 any function	functions
1Ø **	exponentiation
9 – s	unary minus
8 *	multiplication
7 /	division
6 + –	addition & subtraction
5 = ,<>,<,>,< = ,> =	equality & inequality

4 NOT	logical inversion
3 AND	logical AND
2 OR	logical OR

ZX Spectrum Basic Summary

CONVENTIONS

n, m or p	numeric expressions
s	string expression
e	expression (string or numeric)
V	variable name
<s>	statement
[ ]	indicates an optional item

Numeric variables are first character a letter then any alphanumeric characters. String variables are a letter followed by $.

OPERATING COMMANDS

BREAK	interrupts operation e.g. execution, printer
CLEAR	clears variables
CLEAR n	changes position of RAMTOP
CONT	continues execution after BREAK or STOP
DELETE	allows deletion of character
EDIT	allows editing of current line
ENTER	line entered into program
GRAPHICS	puts into graphics mode
LOAD s	clears program and existing variables and loads program specified from tape. (string may be "" in which case the first program is loaded)
LOAD s CODE n,m	loads m bytes into memory starting at address n
LOAD s DATA V()	loads specified array (string or numeric) into memory
MERGE s	merges program s with the one already in memory
NEW	clears program and variables
RUN [n]	runs program [starting at line n]
SAVE s	Saves program and variables on tape
SAVE s LINE n	saves program so that a LOAD is automatically followed by a GOTO n
SAVE s CODE n,m	saves m bytes starting at address n
SAVE s SCREEN $	saves the picture on tape
SAVE s DATA V()	saved specified array (string or numeric) on tape
STOP	stops program execution
VERIFY s	verifies that program specified has been saved on tape
VERIFY s CODE n,m	verifies bytes specified have been saved on tape
VERIFY s DATA V()	verifies array specified has been saved on tape

OTHER INSTRUCTIONS

BIN n	puts binary number n into decimal
:	separates multiple statements on a line
DATA e1, e2, ...	gives data items within a program
DEF FN	user-defined function definition. It must be

	followed by the name (single letter) of the string or numeric function and the definition – e.g. FNa(x,y,z) = x ↑ 3 + y ↑ 4 + z ↑ 5
FN	calls up the user-defined function. Arguments enclosed in brackets – e.g. FNa(3,5,7)
DIM V[$](n[,m])	dimensions array V. Numeric arrays of n rows [and m columns]. String array of n strings each of length m characters. Multi-dimension arrays possible
FOR V = n TO m [STEP p]	V a single letter, initiates a loop
NEXT V	V a single letter, completes loop
GOSUB n	go to subroutine at line n
RETURN	returns from subroutine to main program
GOTO n	transfers control to line n
IF e THEN <s>	executes statement when the condition is met. (There may be several numeric and logical conditions)
IN n	returns the byte read from I/O port n
OUT n,m	writes value m to I/O port n
LET V[$] = e[$]	assigns value e to variable V
PAUSE n	makes program wait a specified time (n = Ø waits for ever, n = 1 to 65535 waits n/5Ø seconds in UK and n/6Ø seconds in US)
PEEK n	returns the value stored in the memory location n
POKE n,m	stores value m in memory location n
READ V1[$], V2[$], ...	allocates variables the values specified in DATA statements.
USR n	calls the machine-code routine starting address n

GRAPHICS

22 lines with 32 columns available.
Each character cell consists of 8 by 8 pixels.
256 horizontal points and 176 vertical points.

CIRCLE n,m,p	draws a circle centre (n,m) and radius p
DRAW n,m[,p]	draws line [arc] from previous specified point to a point *relative* n horizontal and m vertical [turning through angle p radians (anticlockwise if p positive)]
PLOT n,m	Plots a pixel Ø< = n< = 255 horizontal Ø< = m< = 175 vertical
POINT (n,m)	returns Ø (paper colour) or 1 (ink colour) of the pixel (n,m)

COLOURS:

Ø – black
1 – blue
2 – red
3 – magenta
4 – green
5 – cyan
6 – yellow
7 – white

Picture is divided into 768 (24 lines of 32 columns) character cells.

ATTR (n,m)	gives colour attributes of the character cell (n,m) Ø<=n<=23 lines Ø<=m<=31 columns
BORDER n	makes border specified colour (n=Ø to 7)
BRIGHT n	controls brightness (n=Ø normal, n=1 bright, n=8 transparent)
FLASH n	controls flashing (n=Ø normal, n=1 flash, n=8 no change)
INK n	makes ink (foreground) specified colour (n=Ø to 7, n=8 transparent, n=9 contrast)
INVERSE n	controls dot pattern (n=Ø normal, n=1 inverse)
OVER n	controls overprinting (n=Ø normal, n=1 mixing)
PAPER n	makes paper (background) specified colour (n=Ø to 7, n=8 transparent, n=9 contrast)

SOUND

BEEP n,m	produces sound of duration n seconds and pitch m semitones above (or below) Middle C.

INPUT/OUTPUT INSTRUCTIONS

CLS	clears the screen
COPY	prints out copy of screen on the printer
INKEY$	reads current input character. Does not wait for key to be pressed.
INPUT V[$]	input numeric [or string] variable from keyboard
INPUT LINE V$	allows string variable to be input without quotes
LIST [n]	displays program [starting from line n]
LLIST [n]	lists program on printer [starting from line n]
LPRINT [e][,e][;e][TAB n]	prints out on line printer
PRINT [e][,e][;e][ATp,m][TAB m]	prints on screen 22 lines Ø<=p<=21 32 columns Ø<=m<=31

TRIG FUNCTIONS

ACS n	Arc cosine n
ASN n	Arc sine n
ATN n	Arc tangent n
COS n	Cosine n
SIN n	Sine n
TAN n	Tangent n

(n evaluated in radians)

NUMERIC FUNCTIONS

ABS n	absolute value of n
EXP n	exponential n (i.e. e^n)
INT n	integer of n (rounds down)

LN n	natural logarithm of n (i.e. log n or ln n)
PI	π, 3.1415927
RAND [n]	random number seed
RND	function returns a random number between Ø and 1
SGN n	returns 1 if n is positive, Ø if zero, – 1 if negative
SQR n	square root of n

STRING FUNCTIONS

CHR$ n	character of code n
CODE s	code of first character of string s
LEN s	returns length of string s
STR$ n	converts numeric expression into string
VAL s	converts string expression into numeric
VAL$ s	converts s to a string expression (strips off quotes)

PRIORITY see table for ZX81.

APPENDIX II

ZX81 Error Codes

Code	*Meaning*	*Situations*
Ø	Successful completion, or jump to line number bigger than any existing. A report with code Ø does not change the line number used by **CONT**.	Any
1	The control variable does not exist (has not been set up by a **FOR** statement) but there is an ordinary variable with the same name.	**NEXT** Jumping into a loop.
2	An undefined variable has been used. For a simple variable this will happen if the variable is used before it has been assigned to in a **LET** statement. For a subscripted array variable it will happen if the variable is used before it has been dimensioned in a **DIM** statement. For a control variable this will happen if the variable is used before it has been set up as a control variable in a **FOR** statement, when there is no ordinary simple variable with the same name. For a numeric **INPUT**, will occur if non-numeric input received.	Any
3	Subscript out of range. If the subscript is negative, or bigger than 65535 then error B will result.	Subscripted variables (Lists and arrays) Substrings
4	Not enough room in memory. Note that the line number in the report (after the /) may be incomplete on the screen, because of the shortage of memory: for instance, 4/2Ø may appear as 4/2.	**LET, INPUT, DIM, PRINT, LIST, PLOT, UNPLOT, FOR, GOSUB**. Sometimes during function evaluation.
5	No more room on the screen. **CONT** will make room by clearing the screen.	**PRINT, LIST**.
6	Arithmetic overflow: calculations have led to a number greater than about $1Ø^{38}$.	Any arithmetic. Division by zero is common cause.
7	No corresponding **GOSUB** for a **RETURN** statement.	**RETURN**. No **STOP** statement before subroutine is common cause.
8	You have attempted **INPUT** as a command (not allowed).	**INPUT**
9	**STOP** statement executed. **CONT** will not try to re-execute the **STOP** statement, but continues from next line.	**STOP**
A	Invalid argument to certain functions.	**SQR, LN, ASN, ACS, VAL**
B	Integer out of range. When an integer is required, the floating point argument is rounded to the nearest integer. If this is outside a suitable range then error B results.	**RUN, RAND, POKE, DIM, GOTO, GOSUB, LIST, LLIST, PAUSE, PLOT, UNPLOT, CHR$, PEEK, USR**

C	The text of the (string) argument of **VAL** does not form a valid numerical expression.	**VAL**
D	(i) Program interrupted by **BREAK**.	At the end of any statement as the program runs or in **LOAD, SAVE, LPRINT, LLIST** or **COPY**.
	(ii) The **INPUT** line starts with **STOP**.	**INPUT**
F	The program name provided is the empty string.	**SAVE**

Spectrum Error Codes

The report has a code number or letter (so that you can refer to the following table), a brief message explaining what happened and the line number and statement number within that line where it stopped. (A command is shown as line Ø. Within a line, statement 1 is at the beginning, statement 2 comes after the first colon or **THEN**, and so on.)

The behaviour of **CONTINUE** depends very much on the reports. Normally, **CONTINUE** goes to the line and statement specified in the last report, but there are exceptions with reports Ø, 9 and D.

Here is a table showing all the reports. It also tells you in what circumstances the report can occur.

Code	*Meaning*	*Situations*
Ø	OK Successful completion, or jump to a line number bigger than any existing. This report does not change the line and statement jumped to by **CONTINUE**.	Any
1	NEXT without FOR The control variable does not exist (it has not been set up by a **FOR** statement), but there is an ordinary variable with the same name.	**NEXT** Jumping *into* a loop is a common cause.
2	Variable not found For a simple variable this will happen if the variable is used before it has been assigned to in a **LET**, **READ** or **INPUT** statement, loaded from tape or set up in a **FOR** statement. For a subscripted variable it will happen if the variable is used before it has been dimensioned in a **DIM** statement or loaded from tape.	Any
3	Subscript wrong A subscript is beyond the dimension of the array, or there are the wrong number of subscripts. If the subscript is negative or bigger than 65535, then error B will result.	Subscripted variables (arrays), Substrings
4	Out of memory There is not enough room in the computer for what you are trying to do. If the computer really seems to be stuck in this state, you may have to clear out the command line using **DELETE** and then delete a program line or two (with the intention of putting them back afterwards) to give yourself room to manoeuvre with – say – **CLEAR**.	**LET**, **INPUT**, **FOR**, **DIM**, **GO SUB**, **LOAD**, **MERGE**. Sometimes during expression evaluation.

Code	Meaning	Situations
5	Out of screen An **INPUT** statement has tried to generate more than 23 lines in the lower half of the screen. Also occurs with **PRINT AT** 22,...	**INPUT, PRINT AT**
6	Number too big Calculations have led to a number greater than about $1Ø^{38}$.	Any arithmetic. Division by zero is common cause.
7	RETURN without GO SUB There has been one more **RETURN** than there were **GO SUB**s.	**RETURN**. No STOP statement before a subroutine is common.
8	End of file	Microdrive, etc, operations only.
9	STOP statement After this, **CONTINUE** will not repeat the **STOP,** but carries on with the statement after, or next line after, STOP.	**STOP**
A	Invalid argument The argument for a function is no good for some reason.	**SQR, LN, ASN, ACS, USR** (with string argument)
B	Integer out of range When an integer is required, the floating point argument is rounded to the nearest integer. If this is outside a suitable range then error B results.	**RUN, RANDOMIZE, POKE, DIM, GO TO, GO SUB, LIST, LLIST, PAUSE, PLOT, CHR$, PEEK, USR** (with numeric argument)
C	Nonsense in BASIC The text of the (string) argument does not form a valid expression.	**VAL, VAL$**
D	BREAK – CONT repeats **BREAK** was pressed during some peripheral operation. The behaviour of **CONTINUE** after this report is normal in that it repeats the statement. Compare with report L.	**LOAD, SAVE, VERIFY, MERGE, LPRINT, LLIST, COPY**. Also when the computer asks **scroll?** and you type
E	Out of DATA You have tried to **READ** past the end of the **DATA** list.	**READ**
F	Invalid file name **SAVE** with name empty or longer than 1Ø characters.	**SAVE**
G	No room for line There is not enough room left in memory to accommodate the new program line.	Entering a line into the program
H	STOP in INPUT Some **INPUT** data started with **STOP**, or – for **INPUT LINE – BREAK** was pressed. Unlike the case with report 9, after report H **CONTINUE** will behave normally, by repeating the **INPUT** statement.	**INPUT**
I	FOR without NEXT There was a **FOR** loop to be executed no times (e.g. **FOR** n = 1 **TO** Ø) and the corresponding **NEXT** statement could not be found.	**FOR**

Code	*Meaning*	*Situations*
J	Invalid I/O device	Microdrive, etc., operations only
K	Invalid colour The number specified is not an appropriate value.	**INK, PAPER, BORDER, FLASH, BRIGHT, INVERSE, OVER**; also after one of the corresponding control characters
L	BREAK into program **BREAK** pressed, this is detected between two statements. The line and statement number in the report refer to the statement before **BREAK** was pressed, but **CONTINUE** goes to the statement after (allowing for any jumps to be done), so it does not repeat any statements.	Any
M	RAMTOP no good The number specified for RAMTOP is either too big or too small.	**CLEAR**; possibly in **RUN**
N	Statement lost Jump to a statement that no longer exists.	**RETURN, NEXT, CONTINUE**
O	Invalid stream	Microdrive, etc, operations only
P	FN without DEF User-defined function	**FN**
Q	Parameter error Wrong number of arguments, or one of them is the wrong type (string instead of number or vice versa).	**FN**
R	Tape loading error A file on tape was found but for some reason could not be read in, or would not verify.	**VERIFY, LOAD** or **MERGE**

APPENDIX III

ZX81 Character Codes by Keyboard Arrangement

Note: Character codes for both the ZX81 and the Spectrum are listed in order of code number in Section P, and an alphabetic list for the Spectrum is included in Unit W-1.

1. KEYBORD CHARACTERS

	CHARACTER	CODE
	PLOT	246
	UNPLOT	252
	REM	234
	RUN	247
LINE 2	RAND	249
	RETURN	254
	IF	250
	INPUT	238
	POKE	244
	PRINT	245

	CHARACTER	CODE
	NEW	230
	SAVE	248
	DIM	233
	FOR	235
LINE 3	GOTO	236
	GOSUB	237
	LOAD	239
	LIST	240
	LET	241

	CHARACTER	CODE
	COPY	255
	CLEAR	253
	CONT	232
	CLS	251
LINE 4	SCROLL	231
	NEXT	243
	PAUSE	242
	BREAK	—

TOTAL 26 Characters.
May be entered when [K] mode cursor appears.
Obtained by pressing desired key.

2. SHIFT CHARACTERS

	CHARACTER	CODE
	EDIT	117
	AND	218
	THEN	222
	TO	223
LINE 1	←	114
	↓	113
	↑	112
	→	115
	GRAPHICS	116
	RUBOUT	119

	CHARACTER	CODE
	“ ”	192
	OR	217
	STEP	224
	<=	219
LINE 2	<>	221
	>=	220
	$	13
	(	16
	)	17
	“	11

	CHARACTER	CODE
LINE 3	STOP	227
	LPRINT	225
	SLOW	228
	FAST	229
	LLIST	226
	**	216
	–	22
	+	21
	=	2Ø
	FUNCTION	121

	CHARACTER	CODE
LINE 4	:	14
	;	25
	?	15
	/	24
	*	23
	<	19
	>	18
	,	26
	£	12

TOTAL 39 Characters.
Obtained by pressing [SHIFT] and [CHARACTER] keys together.

3. LETTER CHARACTERS

	CHARACTER	CODE
LINE 1	1	29
	2	3Ø
	3	31
	4	32
	5	33
	6	34
	7	35
	8	36
	9	37
	Ø	28
LINE 2	Q	54
	W	6Ø
	E	42
	R	55
	T	57
	Y	62
	U	58
	I	46
	O	52
	P	53

	CHARACTER	CODE
LINE 3	A	38
	S	56
	D	41
	F	43
	G	44
	H	45
	J	47
	K	48
	L	49
	NEWLINE (ENTER)	118
LINE 4	SHIFT	
	Z	63
	X	61
	C	4Ø
	V	59
	B	39
	N	51
	M	5Ø
		27
	SPACE	Ø

TOTAL 39 Characters.
May be entered when [L] mode cursor appears.
Obtained by pressing the desired key.

4. GRAPHICS CHARACTERS

	CHARACTER	CODE
LINE 1		1
		2
		135
		4
		5
		131
		3
		133
LINE 2		129
		13Ø
		7
		132
		6
		134
	inverse $	141
	inverse (	144
	inverse)	145
	inverse "	139

	CHARACTER	CODE
LINE 3		8
		1Ø
		9
		138
		137
		136
	inverse –	15Ø
	inverse +	149
	inverse =	148
LINE 4	inverse :	142
	inverse ;	153
	inverse ?	143
	inverse /	152
	inverse *	151
	inverse <	147
	inverse >	146
	inverse ,	154
	inverse £	14Ø

TOTAL 36 Characters.
Entered in [G] mode, obtained by pressing [SHIFT] [GRAPHICS] keys.
Character obtained by pressing [SHIFT] [CHARACTER]

5. INVERSE GRAPHICS CHARACTERS

	INVERSE CHARACTER	CODE
LINE 1	1	157
	2	158
	3	159
	4	16Ø
	5	161
	6	162
	7	163
	8	164
	9	165
	Ø	156

	INVERSE CHARACTER	CODE
LINE 2	Q	182
	W	188
	E	17Ø
	R	183
	T	185
	Y	19Ø
	U	186
	I	174
	O	18Ø
	P	181

	INVERSE CHARACTER	CODE
	A	166
	S	184
	D	169
	F	171
LINE 3	G	172
	H	173
	J	175
	K	176
	L	177

	INVERSE CHARACTER	CODE
	Z	191
	X	189
	C	168
	V	187
LINE 4	B	167
	N	179
	M	178
	.	155
	(SPACE)	128

TOTAL 38 Characters.
May be entered in [G] mode obtained by [SHIFT] [GRAPHIC] keys.
Obtained by pressing desired keys.

6. FUNCTION CHARACTERS

	CHARACTER	CODE
LINE 2	SIN	199
	COS	200
	TAN	201
	INT	207
	AND	64
	STR$	213
	CHR$	214
	CODE	196
	PEEK	211
	TAB	194
LINE 3	ARCSIN	202
	ARCCOS	203
	ARCTAN	204
	SGN	209
	ABS	210
	SQR	208
	VAL	197
	LEN	198
	USR	212

	CHARACTER	CODE
LINE 4	LN	205
	EXP	206
	AT	193
	INKEY$	65
	NOT	215
	π(PI)	66

TOTAL 25 Characters.
May be entered in [F] mode obtained by pressing [SHIFT] [FUNCTION] key.
Characters obtained by pressing desired character key.
The [F] mode operates for only one character input.

APPENDIX IV

Use of Cassette Tapes

The following information concerns the use of cassette tapes for program storage and retrieval. Other details of personal tape library practice can be found in the main text.

1 New tapes: Always 'fast forward' and 'rewind' a tape completely before use for program storage. This ensures an even winding and tension. If you have the patience, running the tape one way in 'play' mode after fast forward and reverse is desirable.

2 Do not use the first 15 or 20 seconds of any tape. Most tape problems of coating loss and stretch occur in this portion of the tape.

3 Always rewind tapes fully after use, so as to not leave tape with program data exposed. Never touch the surface of the tape. Before inserting a tape in the cassette player, take up the slack in the tape (using a finger or a pencil) by turning one drive wheel until the other moves.

4 Always replace tapes in the correct library boxes immediately after use. Leave the label side (if only one label) showing.

5 Tapes with programs meant to be permanent should have the tags removed to prevent accidental erasure. The holes can always be covered with sticky tape if you decide in the future to record over a program.

6 Clean the tape-recorder heads after 2 or 3 hours' running time with a head cleaner cassette or head cleaner fluid. De-magnetise heads every 10 or 12 hours' running.

7 Leave long gaps (at least 20 seconds) between programs, if more than one program is on a tape. Note the tape counter readings for beginning and end of each program. Remember that the tape counter is not highly accurate. You can use the TV screen to find a gap between programs, watching for the thick black lines of a program load display change to the thin diagonal lines of a 'blank tape' display.

8 *Loading problems.* These are notes for the ZX81 user. No problems should be encountered with the Spectrum in this respect. For each individual ZX81/cassette system, no problems should be encountered with **SAVE**ing and **LOAD**ing programs with the TONE control set high, and the VOLUME at 3/4 volume. The characteristics of tape recorders vary somewhat, however, and problems may be encountered in LOADing programs which have been SAVEd on a different recorder. Here is a sequence to be followed if a program proves difficult to LOAD.

A Set the TONE control for maximum treble ('High').

B Set the VOLUME to about three-quarters of the maximum.

C Rewind tape to the beginning.

D Type: LOAD "A" – i.e. any letter/word except the program name.
Press PLAY on the cassette, then NEWLINE (ENTER) on the ZX81.
When the thin, slightly sloping black lines change to the programs' typical thick black and white lines, with approximately equal black and white bands, with the white crossed by vertical black lines:
(a) DECREASE THE VOLUME until this changes back to the THIN lines.
(b) Now INCREASE THE VOLUME, noting where the THICK black and white program lines eventually seem to become more unsettled or predominantly black.
Also if you listen to the recording you may be able to notice when the volume is too high and causes distortion.

E Set the VOLUME midway between these two points (a) and (b).
Rewind tape.
Type: LOAD "(The program name)".
Press PLAY on the cassette, then NEWLINE (ENTER) on the ZX81.
If the screen suddenly clears before the program should end, this may mean volume is still too low.

The ZX81 may need to be re-set by pulling out the d.c. supply plug and re-inserting it if the cursor does not return to the screen, either by itself or when BREAK is used.

LOAD again, *slightly* increasing the volume, after rewinding the tape.

If you cannot get a definite, THICK black and white line pattern even at full volume then your recorder may not be powerful enough to load from the signal strength on this specific tape. Test this by using another recorder, or recorder/ZX system. Once the program has LOADed, SAVE it on to a tape in your own recorder.

Turn off cassette recorder and take the EAR/MIC leads out of the ZX81 before swapping recorders, or else you may cause the system to crash whilst taking out and re-inserting the plugs.

9 *NEVER* place a tape on top of the TV monitor. This can affect the signals stored on the tape because of the electromagnetic field generated by the TV.

APPENDIX V

System Variables – ZX81

Notes:

X The system may crash if the variable is poked.
N Poking the variable will have no lasting effect.
S The variable is saved by SAVE.

The number in column 1 is the number of bytes storing the variable. For two bytes, the first one is the less significant byte. To poke a value M to a two-byte variable at address N use:

```
POKE N (M – 256*INT(M/256))
POKE N + 1, INT M/256
```

To peek its value, use the expression

PEEK N + 256***PEEK**(N + 1)

Notes	*Address*	*Name*	*Contents*
1	16384	ERR_NR	1 less than the report code. Starts off at 255 (for – 1), so **PEEK** 16384, if it works at all, gives 255. **POKE** 16384, N can be used to force an error halt: N < = 14 gives one of the usual reports, 15 < = N< = 34 or 99 < = N<127 gives an non-standard report, and 35 < = N < = 98 may disrupt the display file.
X1	16385	FLAGS	Various flags to control the BASIC system.
X2	16386	ERR_SP	Address of first item on machine stack (after **GOSUB** returns).
2	16388	RAMTOP	Address of first byte above BASIC system area. You can poke this to make **NEW** reserve space above that area or to fool **CLS** into setting up a minimal display file. Poking RAMTOP has no effect until one of these two is executed.
N1	1639Ø	MODE	Specified K, L, F or G cursor.
N2	16391	PPC	Line number of statement currently being executed. Poking this has no lasting effect except in the last line of the program.
S1	16393	VERSN	Ø Identifies ZX81 BASIC in saved programs.
S2	16394	E_PPC	Number of current line (with program cursor).
SX2	16396	D_FILE	See Unit Q4.
S2	16398	DF_CC	Address of **PRINT** position in display file. Can be poked so that **PRINT** output is sent elsewhere.
SX2	164ØØ	VARS	See Unit U2.
SN2	164Ø2	DEST	Address of variable in assignment.
SX2	164Ø4	E_LINE	See Unit U2.
SX2	164Ø6	CH_ADD	Address of the next character to be interpreted: the character after the argument of **PEEK**, or the **NEWLINE** (ENTER) at the end of a **POKE** statement.

S2	16408	X_PTR	Address of the character preceding the S marker.
SX2	16410	STKBOT	See Unit U2.
SX2	16412	STKEND	
SN1	16414	BERG	Calculator's b register.
SN2	16415	MEM	Address of area used for calculator's memory. (Usually MEMBOT, but not always.)
S1	16417	not used	
SX1	16418	DF_SZ	The number of lines (including one blank line) in the lower part of the screen. See Unit Q4.
S2	16419	S_TOP	The number of the top program line in automatic listings.
SN2	16421	LAST_K	Shows which keys pressed.
SN1	16423		Debounce status of keyboard.
SN1	16424	MARGIN	Number of blank lines above or below picture: 55 in Britain, 31 in America.
SX2	16425	NXTLIN	Address of next program line to be executed.
S2	16427	OLDPPC	Line number to which **CONT** jumps.
SN1	16429	FLAGX	Various flags.
SN2	16430	STRLEN	Length of string type destination in assignment.
SN2	16432	T_ADDR	Address of next item in syntax table (very unlikely to be useful).
S2	16434	SEED	The seed for **RND**. This is the variable that is set by **RAND**.
S2	16436	FRAMES	Counts the frames displayed on the television. Bit 15 is 1. Bits 0 to 14 are decremented for each frame sent to the television. This can be used for timing, but **PAUSE** also uses it. **PAUSE** resets to 0 bit 15, and puts in bits 0 to 14 the length of the pause. When these have been counted down to zero, the pause stops. If the pause stops because of a key depression, bit 15 is set to 1 again.
S1	16438	COORDS	x-coordinate of last point **PLOT**ted.
S1	16439		y-coordinate of last point **PLOT**ted.
S1	16440	PR_CC	Less significant byte of address of next position for **LPRINT** to print at (in PRBUFF).
SX1	16441	S_POSN	Column number for **PRINT** position.
SX1	16442		Line number for **PRINT** position.
S1	16443	CDFLAG	Various flags. Bit 7 is on (1) during compute and display mode.
S33	16444	PRBUFF	Printer buffer (33rd character is **NEWLINE**).
SN30	16477	MEMBOT	Calculator memory area; used to store numbers that cannot conveniently be put on the calculator stack.
S2	16507	not used	

System Variables – Spectrum

Notes:
X The system may crash if the variable is poked.
N Poking the variable will have no lasting effect.

The number in column 1 is the number of bytes in the variable. For two bytes, the first one is the less significant byte. To poke a value M to a two-byte variable at address N use

POKE N(M – 256* INT(M/256))
POKE N + 1, INT M/256

and to peek its value, use the expression

POKE N + 256*PEEK (N + 1)

Notes	*Address*	*Name*	*Contents*
N8	23552	KSTATE	Used in reading the keyboard.
N1	2356Ø	LAST K	Stores newly pressed key.
1	23561	REPDEL	Time (in 5Øths of a second – in 6Øths of a second in N. America) that a key must be held down before it repeats. This starts off at 35, but you can **POKE** in other values.
1	23562	REPPER	Delay (in 5Øths of a second – in 6Øths of a second in America) between successive repeats of a key held down: initially 5.
N2	23563	DEFADD	Address of arguments of user-defined function if one is being evaluated; otherwise Ø.
N1	23565	K DATA	Stores 2nd byte of colour controls entered from keyboard.
N2	23566	TVDATA	Stores bytes of colour, **AT** and **TAB** controls going to television.
X38	23568	STRMS	Addresses of channels attached to streams.
2	236Ø6	CHARS	256 less than address of character set (which starts with space and carries on to the copyright symbol). Normally in ROM, but you can set up your own in RAM and make CHARS point to it.
1	236Ø8	RASP	Length of warning buzz.
1	236Ø9	PIP	Length of keyboard click.
1	2361Ø	ERR NR	1 less than the report code. Starts off at 255 (for – 1) so **PEEK 2361Ø** gives 255.
X1	23611	FLAGS	Various flags to control the BASIC system.
X1	23612	TV FLAG	Flags associated with the television.
X2	23613	ERR SP	Address of item on machine stack to be used as error return.
N2	23615	LIST SP	Address of return address from automatic listing.
N1	23617	MODE	Specifies K, L, C, E or G cursor.
2	23618	NEWPPC	Line to be jumped to.
1	2362Ø	NSPPC	Statement number in line to be jumped to. Poking first NEWPPC and then NSPPC forces a jump to a specified statement in a line.
2	23621	PCC	Line number of statement currently being executed.

Notes	Address	Name	Contents
1	23623	SUBPPC	Number within line of statement being executed.
1	23624	BORDCR	Border colour * 8; also contains the attributes normally used for the lower half of the screen.
2	23625	E PPC	Number of current line (with program cursor).
X2	23627	VARS	Address of variables.
N2	23629	DEST	Address of variable in assignment.
X2	23631	CHANS	Address of channel data.
X2	23633	CURCHL	Address of information currently being used for input and output.
X2	23635	PROG	Address of BASIC program.
X2	23637	NXTLIN	Address of next line of program.
X2	23639	DATADD	Address of terminator of last DATA item.
X2	23641	E LINE	Address of command being typed in.
2	23643	K CUR	Address of cursor.
X2	23645	CH ADD	Address of the next character to be interpreted: the character after the argument of **PEEK**, or the **NEWLINE** (ENTER) at the end of a **POKE** statement.
2	23647	X PTR	Address of the character after the Syntax error marker.
X2	23649	WORKSP	Address of temporary work space.
X2	23651	STKBOT	Address of bottom of calculator stack.
X2	23653	STKEND	Address of start of spare space.
N1	23655	BREG	Calculator's b register.
N2	23656	MEM	Address of area used for calculator's memory. (Usually MEMBOT, but not always.)
1	23658	FLAGS2	More flags.
X1	23659	DF SZ	The number of lines (including one blank line) in the lower part of the screen.
2	23660	S TOP	The number of the top program line in automatic listings.
2	23662	OLDPPC	Line number to which **CONTINUE** jumps.
1	23664	OSPCC	Number within line of statement to which **CONTINUE** jumps.
N1	23665	FLAGX	Various flags.
N2	23666	STRLEN	Length of string type destination in assignment.
N2	23668	T ADDR	Address of next item in syntax table (very unlikely to be useful).
2	23670	SEED	The seed for **RND**. This is the variable that is set by **RANDOMIZE**.
3	23672	FRAMES	3 byte (least significant first), frame counter. Incremented every 1/50th second (U.K.) or 1/60th second (U.S.).
2	23675	UDG	Address of 1st user-defined graphic.
1	23677	COORDS	x-coordinate of last point plotted.
1	23678		y-coordinate of last point plotted.
1	23679	P POSN	33-column number of printer position.
1	23680	PR CC	Less significant byte of address of next position for **LPRINT** to print at (in printer buffer).

Notes	*Address*	*Name*	*Contents*
1	23681		Not used.
2	23682	ECHO E	33-column number and 24-line number (in lower half) of end of input buffer.
2	23684	DF CC	Address in display file of **PRINT** position.
2	23686	DFCCL	Like DF CC for lower part of screen.
X1	23688	S POSN	33-column number for **PRINT** position.
X1	23689		24-line number for **PRINT** position.
X2	23690	SPOSNL	Like S POSN for lower part.
1	23692	SCR CT	Counts scrolls: it is always 1 more than the number of scrolls that will be done before stopping with **scroll?**
1	23693	ATTR P	Permanent current colours, etc. (as set up by colour statements).
1	23694	MASK P	Used for transparent colours, etc. Any bit that is 1 shows that the corresponding attribute bit is taken not from ATTR P, but from what is already on the screen.
N1	23695	ATTR T	Temporary current colours, etc (as set up by colour items).
N1	23696	MASK T	Like MASK P, but temporary.
1	23697	P FLAG	More flags.
N30	23698	MEMBOT	Calculator's memory area; used to store numbers that cannot conveniently be put on the calculator stack.
2	23728		Not used.
2	23730	RAMTOP	Address of last byte of BASIC system area.
2	23732	P-RAMT	Address of last byte of physical RAM.

APPENDIX VI

PROGRAM LIBRARY

This appendix contains applications and utility programs and routines, and games. Some of these have been referred to in the main text. Due to lack of space, the programs are not fully documented.

1. Polar

Program produces a polar coordinate graph of the function entered as A\$. This must be an expression using A as the dependent variable. Since a common cause of failure of the VAL function (giving the error code A) on the ZX81 is the exponentiation function, this is noted and a way of avoiding it given. The angle increment (in *radians*) is entered as DA. The appropriate scale factor can be experimented with. If you get a small cramped plot (or even a single pixel), increase the scale factor. If the plot goes off the screen, you are informed that the scale factor needs reducing (line 25Ø). Polar coordinate plots can be thought of as an X,Y plot with the X axis bent into a circle, and the Y axis plot point defined as a distance R (radius) away from the centre point. Y is then positioned by the COS and SIN functions in lines 19Ø and 2ØØ.
Spectrum: For use on the Spectrum change ** to ↑ in line 3Ø, and delete line 16Ø. Change line 7Ø to read 7Ø PAUSE Ø. In lines 19Ø and 2ØØ the centre point must be set as plot co-ordinates 84, 82, with LET X = 84 + (R*COS A*SC) and LET Y = 82 + (R*SIN A * SC). Line 21Ø must have the limits of X and Y set at 255 and 176 respectively. Line 27Ø should read PAUSE Ø. The program will then run, but you can also modify it to use the DEF FN and FN instructions: Define the function in line 5Ø, with a DEF FN a() = SIN A * 3 or whatever the derived function is, and use LET R = FN a() in line 18Ø. Change the instructions in line 4Ø to suit.

```
  10 REM "POLAR"
  20 PRINT TAB 8;"*POLAR PLOT*";
TAB 8;"************"
  30 PRINT ,,"PLOT ROUTINE FOR P
OLAR","COORDDINATES.ENTER FUNCTI
ON TO","BE PLOTTED WITHOUT USE O
F **","(RAISED TO POWER) FUNCTIO
N.USE","SIN*SIN*SIN,NOT SIN**3,F
OR","EXAMPLE.USE A FOR ANGLE.","
YOU MUST ALSO ENTER SCALE ","FAC
TOR AND ANGLE INCREMENT."
  40 PRINT ,,"ENTER EXPRESSION T
O BE PLOTTED"
  50 INPUT A$
  60 PRINT "ENTER ANGLE INCREMEN
T"
  70 INPUT DA
  80 PRINT "ENTER SCALE FACTOR"
  90 INPUT SC
 100 CLS
 109 REM *PRINT AXES AND PLOT
    INFORMATION*
 110 FOR F=1 TO 20
 120 PRINT AT 11,F;"."
 130 PRINT AT F,10;":"
 140 NEXT F
 150 PRINT AT 0,12;A$;AT 1,18;"S
.F.=";SC;TAB 18;"ANGLE INC.=";DA
 160 FAST
 169 REM *ROUND THE CIRCLE,STEP
ANGLE*
 170 FOR A=0 TO 2*PI STEP DA
 179 REM *EVALUATE FUNCTION*
 180 LET R=VAL A$
 189 REM *NEXT LINES GET X,Y
CONVERTED TO POLAR(COS AND SIN)
COORDINATES,TIMES SCALE FACTOR,
AND SET WITH CENTRE AT 20,20*
 190 LET X=20+(R*COS A*SC)
 200 LET Y=20+(R*SIN A*SC)
 210 IF X>60 OR X<0 OR Y>43 OR Y
<0 THEN GOTO 250
 220 PLOT X,Y
```

```
 230 NEXT A
 240 GOTO 290
 250 PRINT AT 19,0;"OUT OF PLOT
RANGE.REDUCE SCALE","FACTOR."
 260 PRINT "PRESS A KEY,THEN ENT
ER NEW S.F."
 270 PAUSE 4E4
 280 GOTO 90
 290 REM *FINISH*
```

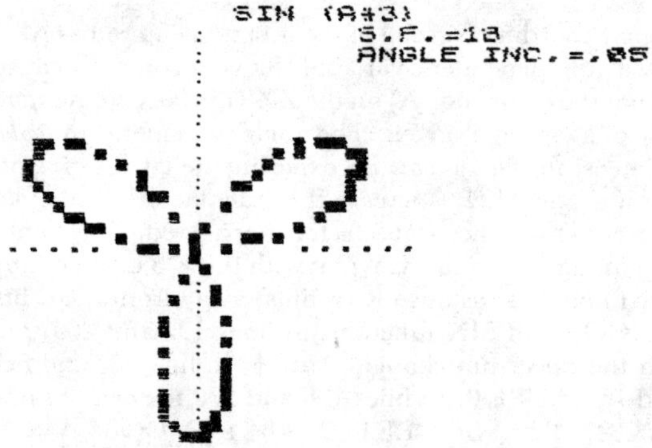

2. Home Accounts

Program allows household expenses for each day for a month to be entered under various headings, which may of course be changed to suit your needs. Income is entered, and credits may also be input under any heading. After entries have been made, a statement of account is derived, which may be printed out. A breakdown of account by heading can also be printed, and the program and data saved to tape so that future entries may be added.

The data is stored in string arrays, and these could be increased up to the limits of memory if a longer period were to be catered for. The program is menu-driven, and all inputs allow the user to check for errors and re-enter if necessary.

```
  5 REM "HOME ACCOUNTS"
 10 REM *INITIALISATION*
 20 LET TOTAL=0
 30 LET I=1
 40 LET C=0
 50 LET Z$="END    "
 61 REM *ARRAY DECLARATION*
 62 DIM D$(31,6)
 63 DIM I$(31,1)
 65 DIM A(31)
 66 DIM A$(10)
 67 DIM C$(6,1)
 68 DIM K$(6,15)
 69 GOSUB 170
 70 REM *MAIN MENU*
 73 CLS
 75 PRINT AT 0,8;"HOME ACCOUNTS
"
 77 PRINT AT 1,8;"---- --------
"
 80 PRINT AT 4,10;"*MAIN MENU*"
 81 PRINT AT 5,11;"---- ----"
```

```
  82 PRINT AT 7,2;"A"; AT 7,10;"
TO ADD AN ENTRY"
  83 PRINT AT 9,2;"S"; AT 9,10;"
FOR ACCOUNT STATEMENT"
  84 PRINT AT 11,2;"C"; AT 11,10
;"FOR CODE BREAKDOWN"
  85 PRINT AT 13,2;"X"; AT 13,10
;"TO EXIT"
  86 PRINT AT 15,8;"OPTION ?"
  87 INPUT Q$
  88 IF Q$="A" THEN GOTO 310
  89 IF Q$="S" THEN GOTO 610
  90 IF Q$="C" THEN GOTO 805
 100 IF Q$="X" THEN STOP
 120 PRINT AT 15,8;"UNKNOWN OPTI
ON: ";Q$
 130 PAUSE 100
 140 PRINT AT 15,8;"
        "
 150 GOTO 85

 160 REM **EXPENSE CODE       **
         **INITIALISATION     **
 170 LET C$(1)="G"
 180 LET K$(1)="GROCERY"
 190 LET C$(2)="P"
 200 LET K$(2)="PETROL"
 210 LET C$(3)="C"
 215 LET K$(3)="CAR REPAIRS"
 220 LET C$(4)="R"
 230 LET K$(4)="RATES"
 240 LET C$(5)="M"
 250 LET K$(5)="MISCELLANEOUS"
 260 LET C$(6)="I"
 270 LET K$(6)="INCOME"
 280 RETURN

 300 REM *INPUTTING DATA*
 310 CLS
 320 PRINT AT 0,8;"HOME ACCOUNTS
"
 330 PRINT AT 1,8;"---- --------
"
 350 PRINT AT 5,5;"             "
 360 PRINT AT 4,2;"ENTER DATE (E
G. 25 NOV, OR      "" END ""  TO
FINISH)"
 370 INPUT D$(I)
 380 IF D$(I)="" THEN GOTO 370
 387 PRINT AT 4,2;"

 "
 388 IF D$(I)=Z$ THEN GOTO 570
 390 PRINT AT 5,5;"DATE: ";D$(I)
 392 PRINT AT 10,5;"CORRECT (Y/N
)?";
 394 INPUT Q$
 395 IF Q$="N" THEN GOTO 350
 396 IF Q$ <> "Y" THEN GOTO 394
 398 PRINT AT 10,5;"
  "
 399 PRINT AT 11,5;"
    "
```

```
 410 GOSUB 1000
 420 PRINT AT 16,5;"EXPENSE CODE
?";
 430 INPUT I$(I)
 431 IF I$(I)="" THEN GOTO 430
 434 GOSUB 2000
 436 FOR J=1 TO 6
 437 IF I$(I)=C$(J) THEN GOTO 44
2
 438 NEXT J
 439 PRINT AT 7,5;"UNKNOWN EXPEN
SE CODE: ";I$(I)
 440 PAUSE 100
 441 GOTO 410

 442 PRINT AT 7,5;"EXPENSE CODE:
 ";K$(J)
 444 PRINT AT 11,5;"CORRECT (Y/N
)?"
 446 INPUT Q$
 447 PRINT AT 11,5;"
   "
 448 IF Q$="N" THEN GOTO 410
 449 IF Q$ <> "Y" THEN GOTO 444
 460 PRINT AT 13,5;"
  "
 470 PRINT AT 9,5;"AMOUNT (- FOR
 EXPENSE) ?"
 480 INPUT A$
 485 IF A$="" THEN GOTO 480
 487 PRINT AT 9,5;"
            "
 490 PRINT AT 9,5;"AMOUNT: ";A$
 500 PRINT AT 13,5;"CORRECT (Y/N
)?";
 510 INPUT Q$
 520 IF Q$="N" THEN GOTO 460
 530 IF Q$ <> "Y" THEN GOTO 510
 532 PRINT AT 13,5;"
  "
 534 PRINT AT 9,5;"
                 "
 536 PRINT AT 7,5;"
                "
 538 LET A(I)= VAL A$
 540 LET I=I+1
 550 LET C=C+1
 560 GOTO 350

 570 PRINT AT 10,3;"DO YOU WISH
TO SAVE THESE"; AT 11,2;"ENTRIES
 (Y/N) ?"
 575 INPUT Q$
 580 IF Q$="N" THEN GOTO 73
 585 IF Q$ <> "Y" THEN GOTO 575
 590 PRINT AT 10,2;"SET UP CASSE
TTE RECORDER, WHEN READY PRESS A
NY KEY"
 595 IF INKEY$ ="" THEN GOTO 595
 598 SAVE "HOME ACCOUNTS"
 599 GOTO 73

 600 REM *STATEMENT OF ACCOUNT*
```

```
 610 CLS
 620 PRINT TAB 5;"STATEMENT OF A
CCOUNT"
 630 PRINT TAB 5;"-------- -- --
------"
 640 PRINT
 650 PRINT "DATE"; TAB 8;"TYPE";
 TAB 15;"CR"; TAB 25;"DB"
 660 PRINT "----"; TAB 8;"----";
 TAB 15;"--"; TAB 25;"--"
 670 FOR I=1 TO C
 680 PRINT D$(I); TAB 8;I$(I);
 690 IF A(I)>0 THEN GOTO 720
 700 PRINT TAB 25; ABS A(I)
 710 GOTO 730

 720 PRINT TAB 15;A(I)
 730 LET TOTAL=TOTAL+A(I)
 740 PRINT
 750 NEXT I
 753 PRINT TAB 20;"------"
 755 PRINT "BALANCE"; TAB 20;TOT
AL
 766 PRINT AT 21,2;"COPY TO PRIN
TER (Y/N) ?"
 767 INPUT Q$
 768 IF Q$="N" THEN GOTO 73
 769 IF Q$ <> "Y" THEN GOTO 767
 770 PRINT AT 21,2;"SET UP PRINT
ER AND PRESS A KEY"
 773 IF INKEY$ ="" THEN GOTO 773
 775 PRINT AT 21,2;"
                    "
 780 COPY
 790 GOTO 73

 800 REM **BREAKDOWN OF       **
         **ACCOUNT BY CODE    **
 805 CLS
 810 PRINT "STATEMENT OF ACCOUNT
 BY CODE"
 820 PRINT "--------- -- -------
-- ----"
 830 PRINT "CODE"; TAB 15;"TOTAL
"
 840 PRINT
 850 LET J=1
 855 LET TOTAL=0
 860 FOR I=1 TO C
 870 IF I$(I)=C$(J) THEN LET TOT
AL=TOTAL+A(I)
 880 NEXT I
 890 PRINT K$(J); TAB 15;TOTAL
 900 LET J=J+1
 910 IF J <= 6 THEN GOTO 855
 926 PRINT AT 21,2;"COPY TO PRIN
TER (Y/N) ?"
 927 INPUT Q$
 928 IF Q$="N" THEN GOTO 73
 929 IF Q$ <> "Y" THEN GOTO 927
 930 PRINT AT 21,2;"SET UP PRINT
ER AND PRESS A KEY"
 940 IF INKEY$ ="" THEN GOTO 940
```

```
 950 PRINT AT 21,2;"
                   "
 960 COPY
 990 GOTO 73

1000 REM ********************
        **EXPENSE CODE MENU**
        **SUBROUTINE       **
        *********************
1020 PRINT AT 7,5;"*EXPENSE CODE
 MENU*         "
1030 PRINT AT 8,5;" ------- ----
 ----"
1050 PRINT AT 9,5;"G"; AT 9,15;"
GROCERY"
1060 PRINT AT 10,5;"P"; AT 10,15
;"PETROL"
1070 PRINT AT 11,5;"C"; AT 11,15
;"CAR REPAIRS"
1080 PRINT AT 12,5;"R"; AT 12,15
;"RATES"
1090 PRINT AT 13,5;"M"; AT 13,15
;"MISCELLANEOUS"
1100 PRINT AT 14,5;"I"; AT 14,15
;"INCOME"
1110 RETURN

2000 PRINT AT 16,5;"
  "
2010 PRINT AT 14,5;" "; AT 14,15
;"      "
2020 PRINT AT 13,5;" "; AT 13,15
;"             "
2030 PRINT AT 12,5;" "; AT 12,15
;"      "
2040 PRINT AT 11,5;" "; AT 11,15
;"           "
2050 PRINT AT 10,5;" "; AT 10,15
;"      "
2060 PRINT AT 9,5;" "; AT 9,15;"
       "
2070 PRINT AT 8,5;"
           "
2080 PRINT AT 7,5;"
           "
2090 RETURN
```

3. Resval

Program derives the preferred resistor value (i.e. the closest standard resistance) from inputs of the voltage and current required in a circuit. From these inputs (in volts and amps) the actual resistance is calculatead by Ohms Law (R = V/I). This value, rounded to two significant figures, is then used to calculate the value L, 1Ø to the power L being the multiplier for the resistor value. The values stored in the array X(13), entered as shown in the first program, are then compared with the calculated resistance. The first value stored in the array which gives a value greater than R is then used to print out the preferred value for the component. The current and power using a resistor of this value are then printed. The user may then choose to run the calculation again with different inputs until the best solution is achieved. This illustrates the basic principle of computer-aided design (CAD) of circuits, where the derived theoretical values are modified to suit the actual components available.

The array creation program and data values (of resistors with ±1Ø% tolerance) are given below. This program is then edited out, and RESVAL entered. Alternatives to storing the data in an array would be to assign each value of the array X with a LET statement, or, if using a Spectrum, to place the values in a DATA statement. Both these methods would eliminate the problem of avoiding the use of RUN.

Spectrum: Change ** to ↑ in lines 22Ø, 24Ø and 27Ø.
Change line 34Ø to read 34Ø SAVE "RESVAL" LINE 1Ø
Delete line 35Ø
As noted, the program could be modified to use the DATA and READ statements. Insert a line 34Ø with the data as given below, and insert 215 READ X. Change X(N) to X in lines 22Ø and 24Ø.

```
  10 REM **RESISTOR VALUES INTO
ARRAY**
  20 REM **LINES EDITED OUT AFTE
R ENTRY OF VALUES**
  30 REM **THEN RESVAL PROGRAM E
NTERED**
  40 DIM X(13)
  50 LPRINT "ARRAY VALUE"
  60 LPRINT
  70 FOR L=1 TO 13
  80 LPRINT "X(";L;")";
  90 INPUT X(L)
 100 LPRINT TAB 7;X(L)
 110 NEXT L
```

```
ARRAY VALUE

X(1)    10
X(2)    12
X(3)    15
X(4)    18
X(5)    22
X(6)    27
X(7)    33
X(8)    39
X(9)    47
X(10)   56
X(11)   68
X(12)   82
X(13)   100
```

```
  10 REM *RESVAL*
  20 PRINT "RESVAL"
  30 PRINT
  40 PRINT "PROGRAM DERIVES PREF
ERRED VALUE";TAB 0;"OF RESISTOR
FROM INPUT";TAB 0;"VOLTAGE AND C
URRENT VALUES"
  50 PRINT
  60 PRINT "PREFERRED VALUES STO
RED IN ";TAB 0;"ARRAY.DO NOT RUN
 PROGRAM.USE";TAB 0;"GOTO 100."
  70 PRINT "SAVE WITH GOTO 340."
  80 PAUSE 800
  90 CLS
 100 PRINT "VOLTAGE ?";
 110 INPUT V
 120 PRINT TAB 12;V;" VOLTS"
 130 PRINT
 140 PRINT "CURRENT ?";
 150 INPUT I
 160 PRINT TAB 12;I;" AMPS"
 170 LET R=INT (V*100/I)/100
 180 PRINT
 190 PRINT "ACTUAL RESISTANCE ";
R;" OHM"
 200 LET L=INT (LN R/2.303)-1
 210 FOR N=1 TO 13
 220 IF R<=X(N)*10**L THEN GOTO
240
 230 NEXT N
 240 LET X=X(N)*10**L
 250 PRINT "PREFERRED RESISTOR:
";X;" OHM"
 260 PRINT "GIVES CURRENT ";INT
(V*100/X)/100;" AMP"
```

```
 270 PRINT "AND ";INT (V**2*100/
X)/100;" WATTS"
 280 PRINT
 290 PRINT "AGAIN?(Y/N)"
 300 INPUT Q$
 310 IF Q$="N" THEN STOP
 320 CLS
 330 GOTO 100
 340 SAVE "RESUA█"
 350 GOTO 10
```

4. Matmult

Program multiplies two square matrices. A two-dimensional matrix is stored as a two-dimensional array, with the size input. Matrix multiplication requires the number of columns in one matrix to be equal to the number of rows in the other. The matrices are set up as square arrays of equal size in this program, and nonsquare mtrices may be multiplied by entering Ø for the elements of a row or column which is unused. Users familiar with matrix arithmetic will be able to derive from this program the routines to handle other matrix operations. The method involves nested FOR-NEXT loops, in conjunction with three arrays in this program, the third array holding the resultant matrix.

Other points to be noted are the input and error routines. The input routine prompts for inputs by row and column number, and when all elements have been entered the error check subroutine is called, so that the user can check the whole matrix at once. This avoids the possibility of confusion over row/column numbers.

```
   5 REM "MATMULT"
   6 REM *BETTER IN FAST*
   7 FAST
  10 PRINT "2D MATRIX MULTIPLICA
TION","************************"
  20 PRINT AT 3,0;"MULTIPLIES SQ
UARE MATRICES.";AT 5,0;"TO USE F
OR NONSQUARE MATRICES","ENTER MA
TRIX SIZE TO ACCOMODATE","AND EN
TER ZEROES.E.G TO MULTIPLY",,"(1
 2 3)   BY","(4)",,"(5)",,"(6)"
  30 PRINT "USE 3 AS MATRIX SIZE
.ENTERING","1 COLUMN AND 1 ROW O
NLY,REST 0.",,,"ENTER MATRICES R
OW BY ROW."
  40 LET A$="
                               "
  50 PAUSE 200
  60 PRINT AT 21,0;"**ENTER MATR
IX SIZE**"
  70 INPUT S
  80 REM *DIMENSION 1ST,2ND  AND
 RESULT MATRICES*
  90 DIM A(S,S)
 100 DIM B(S,S)
 110 DIM C(S,S)
 120 CLS
 130 PRINT "ENTER MATRIX 1",,"EN
TER 0 FOR UNUSED ELEMENTS"
 140 FOR F=1 TO S
 150 FOR N=1 TO S
 160 PRINT AT 21,0;"ROW ";F;" CO
LUMN ";N;" ?"
 170 INPUT A(F,N)
 180 PRINT AT F*3,N*6-6;A(F,N)
 190 NEXT N
 200 NEXT F
 210 REM *M IDENTIFIES MATRIX FO
R SUBROUTINE*
 220 LET M=1
 230 GOSUB 500
 240 CLS
 250 PRINT "MATRIX 2"
 260 FOR F=1 TO S
 270 FOR N=1 TO S
 280 PRINT AT 21,0;"ROW ";F;" CO
LUMN ";N;" ?"
 290 INPUT B(F,N)
 300 PRINT AT F*3,N*6-6;B(F,N)
 310 NEXT N
 320 NEXT F
 330 LET M=2
```

```
340 GOSUB 500
350 CLS
360 PRINT "MATRIX 1 * MATRIX 2
GIVES:-"
370 FOR F=1 TO 5
380 FOR N=1 TO 5
390 FOR L=1 TO 5
400 LET C(F,N)=C(F,N)+A(F,L)*B(
L,N)
410 LET C(F,N)=INT (C(F,N)*1E5+
.5)/1E5
420 PRINT AT F*3,N*6-6;C(F,N)
430 NEXT L
440 NEXT N
450 NEXT F
460 PRINT AT 21,0;"INPUT C(COPY
),R(RUN) OR E(END)"
470 INPUT Z$
480 IF Z$="C" THEN COPY
490 IF Z$="R" THEN RUN
495 GOTO 700
499 REM *ERROR SUBROUTINE*
500 PRINT AT 21,0;A$
510 PRINT AT 20,0;"ARE ALL ENTR
IES CORECT ?(Y OR N)"
520 INPUT B$
530 IF B$="Y" THEN RETURN
540 PRINT AT 21,0;"HOW MANY INC
ORRECT ENTRIES?"
550 INPUT EN
560 FOR F=1 TO EN
570 PRINT AT 20,0;A$;AT 21,0;A$
;AT 21,0;"ERROR ";F;"; ROW ?"
580 INPUT R
590 PRINT AT 21,7;"COLUMN ?"
600 INPUT C
610 PRINT AT 21,0;A$;AT 21,0;"E
NTER CORRECT NUMBER     "
620 INPUT N
630 IF M=1 THEN LET A(R,C)=N
640 IF M=2 THEN LET B(R,C)=N
650 PRINT AT R*3,C*6-6;"      "
;AT R*3,C*6-6;N
660 NEXT F
670 PRINT AT 21,0;A$
680 GOTO 510
700 REM *END*
```

```
ENTER MATRIX 1
ENTER 0 FOR UNUSED ELEMENTS

1     2     3

0     0     0

0     0     0


MATRIX 2

0     0     4

0     0     5

0     0     6


MATRIX 1 * MATRIX 2 GIVES:-

0     0     32

0     0     0

0     0     0


 INPUT C(COPY),R(RUN) OR E(END)
```

5. Fruit

Program simulates a fruit machine. The program allows you to continue playing until your money runs out (which it will eventually) and you can then "borrow" more. Points to be noted in the program are the overprinting of a string to simulate the spinning of the wheels (lines 200 to 230), and the logic used to check wins and amount (if any) won, in lines 250 and 260. The program loops back from line 290 to line 140 unless the money has all gone.

Spectrum: Change line 60 to read 60 PAUSE 0.

```
  10 REM "FRUIT"
  20 PRINT "ONE-ARMED BANDIT"
  30 PRINT ,,"YOU HAVE £2 TO GAM
BLE.","EACH ROLL COSTS 10 PENCE.
"
  40 PRINT ,,"PAYOUTS:2 THE SAME
 PAYS 10P";TAB 8;"3 THE SAME PAY
S 40P";TAB 8;"EXCEPT ***,WHICH P
AYS £1"
  50 PRINT ,,"PRESS A KEY TO STA
RT"
  60 IF INKEY$="" THEN GOTO 60
  70 CLS
  74 REM
  75 REM **INITIALISE/PRINT**
  76 REM
  80 LET C$="£2.00"
  90 LET A$="*█▛▒+$"
 100 PRINT "ONE-ARMED BANDIT"
 110 PRINT AT 3,0;"YOU HAVE ";C$
 120 PRINT AT 8,12;"███████";TAB
12;"█£█£█£█";TAB 12;"███████"
 130 PRINT AT 19,0;"PRESS S TO S
PIN"
 140 IF INKEY$<>"S" THEN GOTO 14
0
 141 REM
 142 REM **SET WIN LINE**
 143 REM
 145 LET B$=""
 150 FOR F=1 TO 3
 160 LET A=INT (RND*6)+1
 170 LET B$=B$+"█"+A$(A)
 180 NEXT F
 184 REM
 185 REM **SPIN WHEELS**
 186 REM
 190 LET F$="█*█▛█+█$█▒█▖"
 200 FOR F=1 TO 10
 210 PRINT AT 9,12;F$(1 TO 6)
 220 LET F$=F$(3 TO )+F$(1 TO 2)
 230 NEXT F
 234 REM
 235 REM **PRINT WIN LINE**
 236 REM
 240 PRINT AT 9,12;B$
 245 REM **CHECK WINS**
 250 LET W=(B$(2)=B$(4))+(B$(2)=
B$(6))+(B$(4)=B$(6))
 254 REM
 255 REM **AMOUNT WON**
 256 REM
 260 LET C=(.10 AND W=1)+(.40 AN
D W=3)+(1.0 AND W=3 AND B$(2)="*
")
 270 LET C$=C$(1)+STR$ (VAL C$(2
TO )+C-.10)
 274 REM
 275 REM **CHECK IF SOLVENT**
 276 REM
 280 PRINT AT 3,9;C$
 290 IF VAL C$(2 TO )>=.10 THEN
GOTO 140
 294 REM
 295 REM **MONEY SPENT**
 296 REM
 300 PRINT AT 3,0;"*YOU ARE BROK
E.* ";TAB 0;"BORROW £2 ?(Y OR N)
"
 310 INPUT M$
 320 CLS
 330 IF M$="Y" THEN GOTO 80
 340 PRINT "BETTER LUCK NEXT TIM
E"
 999 STOP
```

6. Lissajous

A program to produce the intricate, interesting and delightful patterns, named after the mathematician who discovered the equation that produces them. You merely enter the values of A, B and C in response to the prompts and watch the patterns develop. Spectrum users can generate more complex patterns than ZX81 users, because of the higher resolution PLOT screen.

Spectrum: Change line 8Ø to read 8Ø FOR F = Ø TO 2ØØ STEP 2. This defines the number of points to be plotted. You can experiment with different values for STEP if you want more or fewer points plotted. Line 9Ø needs the two 3Øs changing to 12Ø, and line 1ØØ the two 2Øs changing to 8Ø. A and B can both be input with values up to about 1Ø on the Spectrum, so change the Input prompts to suit.

```
   1 REM *LISSAJOUS*
   2 REM PLOTS LISSAJOUS PATTERN
S
   3 REM A IS RELATIVE FREQUENCY
 Y,B IS REL. FREQ. X,C IS Y PHAS
E  OF PI.
  10 PRINT "INPUT A (INTEGER 1 T
O 5)"
  20 INPUT A
  30 PRINT "INPUT B (INTEGER 1 T
O 5)"
  40 INPUT B
  50 PRINT "INPUT C (ANY NUMBER
0 TO 3)"
  60 INPUT C
  70 CLS
  80 FOR F=0 TO 200
  90 LET Y=30+30*SIN (C+A*PI*F/1
00)
 100 LET X=20+20*SIN (B*PI*F/100
)
 110 PLOT Y,X
 120 NEXT F
```

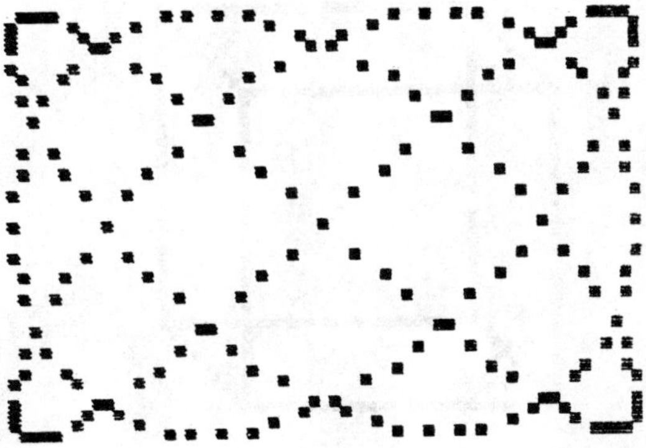

7. Line

This program gives the computer the capacity to draw a line between specified plot co-ordinates. The Spectrum possesses a LINE instruction that does this automatically, but Spectrum users may be interested in the method, which is the way the LINE instruction automatically calculates the points to plot. The program will run on the Spectrum if line 85 is deleted. As it stands, the program prompts for two sets of X, Y points, giving an error message if the points are out of range. Lines 11Ø and 12Ø calculate the X and Y axis differences between the specified points. Line 13Ø defines the variable A as the greater of these. DX and DY are the increments added to the values of X(1) and Y(1) for plotting. In the loop (F = 1 to ABS A, since A may be negative) DX and DY are decremented or incremented (as X and Y are positive or negative) by the distance to be covered between points, divided by the number of steps needed. The program will accept further inputs as required, but does not provide input prompts (lines 21Ø to 28Ø).

```
   5 REM "LINE"
  10 REM DRAWS LINE BETWEEN POIN
T,(X(1),Y(1))AND POINT (X(2),Y(2
))
  20 DIM X(2)
  25 DIM Y(2)
  30 FOR F=1 TO 2
  40 PRINT "COORDINATES POINT ";
F
  50 PRINT ,,"X VALUE ?"
  60 INPUT X(F)
  70 PRINT ,,"Y VALUE ?"
  80 INPUT Y(F)
  85 IF X(F)>63 OR Y(F)>43 THEN
PRINT "ERROR RUN PROGRAM AGAIN "
  90 NEXT F
 100 CLS
 110 LET X=X(2)-X(1)
 120 LET Y=Y(2)-Y(1)
 130 LET A=(X AND ABS X>=ABS Y)+
(Y AND ABS X<ABS Y)
 140 LET DX=0
 150 LET DY=0
 160 FOR F=1 TO ABS A
 170 PLOT DX+X(1),DY+Y(1)
 180 LET DX=DX+X/ABS A
 190 LET DY=DY+Y/ABS A
 200 NEXT F
 210 REM *FOR OTHER LINES*
 220 REM *****************
 230 INPUT X(1)
 240 INPUT Y(1)
 260 INPUT X(2)
 270 INPUT Y(2)
 280 GOTO 110
```

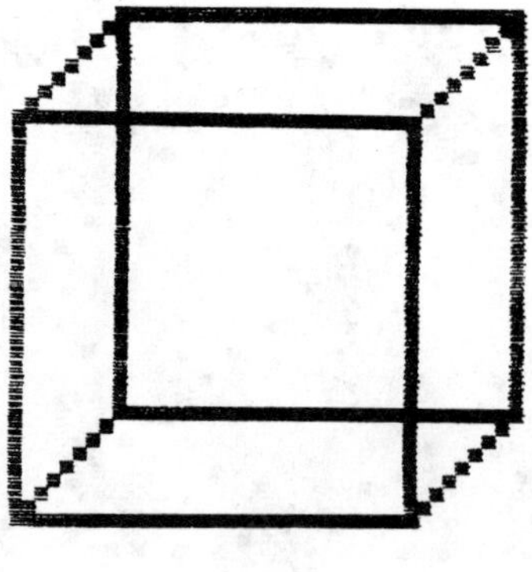

8. Reverse

The computer jumbles up a sequence of 9 numbers, and prints these (subroutine line 5ØØ) after giving the instructions, by calling subroutine 1ØØØ. After each input by the player the subroutine at line 3ØØ is called to print the altered sequence and check if the ordering is complete. If the sequence is correct, control is passed to line 2ØØØ for the end routine, which gives the option of playing again.

```
10 REM "REVERSE"
20 PRINT TAB 10;"*REVERSE*"
30 GOSUB 1000
40 CLS
45 DIM A(9)
50 PRINT TAB 10;"*REVERSE*"
60 PRINT AT 5,5;
```

```
  70 GOSUB 500
  80 LET GOES=0
  90 PRINT AT 15,0;"INPUT NUMBER
TO REVERSE ?"
 100 INPUT R
 110 IF R<1 OR R>9 THEN GOTO 100
 120 GOSUB 300
 130 REM **LOOP NEXT GO**
 140 GOTO 100
 150 REM ********************
 160 REM
 300 REM **REVERSE AND CHECK**
 310 REM **SEQUENCE         **
 315 REM
 320 FOR F=1 TO INT (R/2)
 330 LET T=A(F)
 340 LET A(F)=A(R-F+1)
 350 LET A(R-F+1)=T
 360 NEXT F
 370 LET CORRECT=0
 380 PRINT AT 5,5;
 390 FOR F=1 TO 9
 400 PRINT A(F);" ";
 410 IF A(F)=F THEN LET CORRECT
   =CORRECT+1
 420 NEXT F
 430 LET GOES=GOES+1
 440 IF CORRECT=9 THEN GOTO 2000
 450 RETURN
 460 REM *********************
 470 REM
 500 REM **SET SEQUENCE**
 505 REM
 510 LET A(1)=INT (RND*9)+1
 520 FOR F=2 TO 9
 530 LET A(F)=INT (RND*9)+1
 540 FOR N=F-1 TO 1 STEP -1
 550 IF A(F)=A(N) THEN GOTO 530
 560 NEXT N
 570 NEXT F
 580 FOR F=1 TO 9
 590 PRINT A(F);" ";
 600 NEXT F
 610 RETURN
 620 REM **************
 630 REM
1000 REM **INSTRUCTIONS**
1010 REM
1020 PRINT ,,"COMPUTER GENERATES
 JUMBLED","SEQUENCE OF DIGITS 1
TO 9."
1030 PRINT "YOU MUST INPUT A NUM
BER 1 TO 9,"
1040 PRINT "AND THIS NUMBER OF D
IGITS,","STARTING FROM THE LEFTM
OST,","WILL REVERSE.YOU MUST GET
 THE"
1050 PRINT "DIGITS IN ORDER LEFT
 TO RIGHT."
1060 PRINT ,,"PRESS A KEY TO STA
RT."
1070 PRINT ,,"THERE WILL BE A DE
LAY WHILE","SEQUENCE IS CREATED.
"
1080 PAUSE 40000
1090 RETURN
1100 REM ********************
1110 REM
2000 REM **END ROUTINE**
2005 REM
2010 PRINT AT 20,0;"**SUCCESS IN
 ";GOES;" GOES**","ANOTHER GO?(Y
 OR N)"
2020 INPUT M$
2030 IF M$<>"Y" THEN GOTO 2050
2040 GOTO 40
2050 CLS
2060 PRINT "PLAY AGAIN SOMETIME.
BYE....."
9999 STOP
```

9. Tools

The program shows the principle of a programmer's toolkit program containing useful program modules. You should add to this basic version any further subroutines or modules you want to have available. The inclusion of the BLOCKDEL program makes editing out any modules not required for a specific program very easy. You may wish to add, for example, a round/justify subroutine for numbers, or a sorting subroutine. Note the **mnemonic** for the error subroutine line number. When you add modules, however, use variable names that you are unlikely to use in the program you are developing. Load the program before starting a program on the ZX81.

Spectrum: For the Block delete module see BLOCKDEL. For Renumber module and Memory left see Section U of the text. Remember you can use MERGE to enter this program at any point (hence the high line numbers).

```
   1 REM "TOOLS"
   2 REM **ILLUSTRATES TOOLKIT**
   3 REM **LOAD BEFORE START**
         **INPUTTING PROGRAM**
   4 REM **GOSUB ERROR FOR ERROR
         **MESSAGE             **
   5 REM **GOTO 9500 FOR BLOCK**
       **DELETE                **
   6 REM **GOTO 9700 FOR RENUM*
   7 REM **GOTO 9450 FOR MEMORY
         **LEFT
   8 REM **ADD YOUR OWN ROUTINES
         **********************
   9 LET ERROR=9400
9400 REM **ERROR MESSAGE SUB**
9410 REM ********************
9420 PRINT TAB 7;"***INPUT ERROR
***";TAB 7;"****************"
9430 PAUSE 120
9440 RETURN
9450 REM **MEMORY LEFT **
9460 REM ********************
9470 CLS
9480 PRINT "MEMORY LEFT=";PEEK 1
6386+256*PEEK 16387-PEEK 16412-2
56*PEEK 16413;" APPROX."
9490 STOP
9500 REM **BLOCK DELETE**
9505 REM ****************
9510 PRINT "FIRST LINE TO DELETE
?"
9520 INPUT ST
9530 PRINT "LAST LINE TO BE DELE
TED?"
9540 INPUT END
9550 LET RAM=16509
9560 LET LNUM=256*PEEK RAM+PEEK
(RAM+1)
9570 IF LNUM=ST THEN LET LRAM=RA
M+2
9580 LET LLEN=PEEK (RAM+2)+256*P
EEK (RAM+3)
9590 IF LNUM=END THEN GOTO 9620
9600 LET RAM=RAM+4+LLEN
9610 GOTO 9560
9630 LET LLEN=RAM+LLEN+2-LRAM
9640 POKE LRAM+1,INT (LLEN/256)
9650 POKE LRAM,LLEN-256*PEEK (LR
AM+1)
9660 PRINT "INPUT FIRST,N/L TO D
ELETE BLOCK"
9670 STOP
9700 REM **RENUMBER**
9710 REM ************
9720 LET RAM=16509
9730 LET LINE=10
9740 LET STEP=10
9750 POKE RAM,INT (LINE/256)
9760 POKE RAM+1,(LINE-256*PEEK R
AM)
9770 LET RAM=RAM+1
9780 IF PEEK RAM<>118 THEN GOTO
      9770
9790 LET RAM=RAM+1
9800 IF 256*PEEK RAM+PEEK (RAM+1
)=9000 THEN GOTO 9830
9810 LET LINE=LINE+STEP
9820 GOTO 9750
9830 PRINT "RENUMBERED.NOW DO GO
SUB,GOTO","LINES."
9840 STOP
```

10. Blockdel

Program enables blocks of program lines to be deleted by a single line entry after the line numbers of the first and last lines of the block (ST and END) to be deleted have been entered (the program can also delete itself!). This is done by taking (line 955Ø) the start address of the program storage area (RAM) then finding (line 956Ø) the line number of the first line (LNUM). If this is the line number of the start line, the address of the first byte of the line length storage bytes (= RAM + 2) is stored as LRAM (line 957Ø). The line length bytes are then PEEKed (line 958Ø) to find the line length in bytes (LLEN), *before* the line number is checked in line 959Ø to see if it is the last line to be deleted. If it is, control is passed to line 962Ø. If it is not, RAM is incremented by the line length and four bytes for the program length and line number bytes, to get the address of the start of the next line stored in the memory, and the process is repeated. When the end line number has been located and control passes to 962Ø, the line length variable LLEN is made equal to the number of bytes between the first and last lines for deletion (this is why LLEN was found before checking if the current line was the last of the block) by setting RAM to be RAM + LLEN, i.e. the address of the end byte of the last line to be deleted. This value, less the address of the line length byte of the first line (stored as LRAM), plus 2 for the program line number bytes of the last line gives the number of bytes to be inserted by the POKEs of lines 963Ø and 964Ø as the new line length of the first line requiring deletion. The computer now thinks that the lines for deletion are all one huge line, and keying in this line number and pressing NEWLINE (ENTER) will delete the whole block. The program should be loaded for use on a ZX81 from tape *before* you start working on a program. Spectrum users can use MERGE.

Spectrum: Line 955Ø (giving the start of the program area) must be changed to read:

955Ø LET RAM = PEEK 23635 + 256*PEEK 23636

```
  10 REM "BLOCKDEL"
9500 REM **BLOCK DELETE**
9505 REM ****************
9510 PRINT "FIRST LINE TO DELETE
?"
9520 INPUT ST
9530 PRINT "LAST LINE TO BE DELE
TED?"
9540 INPUT END
9550 LET RAM=16509
9560 LET LNUM=256*PEEK RAM+PEEK
(RAM+1)
9570 IF LNUM=ST THEN LET LRAM=RA
M+2
9580 LET LLEN=PEEK (RAM+2)+256*P
EEK (RAM+3)
9590 IF LNUM=END THEN GOTO 9620
9600 LET RAM=RAM+4+LLEN
9610 GOTO 9560
9620 LET LLEN=RAM+LLEN+2-LRAM
9630 POKE LRAM+1,INT (LLEN/256)
9640 POKE LRAM,LLEN-256*PEEK (LR
AM+1)
9650 PRINT "INPUT FIRST,N/L TO D
ELETE BLOCK"
9660 STOP
```

```
  10 REM "BLOCKDEL"
9500 REM **BLOCK DELETE**
9505 REM ****************
9510 PRINT "FIRST LINE TO DELETE
?"
9520 INPUT ST
9530 PRINT "LAST LINE TO BE DELE
TED?"
9540 INPUT END
9550 LET RAM=16509
```

```
9560 LET LNUM=256* PEEK RAM+ PEE
K (RAM+1)
9570 IF LNUM=ST THEN LET LRAM=RA
M+2
9580 LET LLEN= PEEK (RAM+2)+256*
 PEEK (RAM+3)
9590 IF LNUM=END THEN GOTO 9620
9600 LET RAM=RAM+4+LLEN
9610 GOTO 9560

9630 LET LLEN=RAM+LLEN+2-LRAM
9640 POKE LRAM+1, INT (LLEN/256)
9650 POKE LRAM,LLEN-256* PEEK (L
RAM+1)
9660 PRINT "INPUT FIRST,N/L TO D
ELETE BLOCK"
9670 STOP
```

11. Coder

The computer chooses a four digit code sequence comprised of the digits 1 to 6. You input your guess for this code sequence. The computer prints your guess, checks for the number of digits in the correct place which correspond to the code, storing this as AST (for asterisk), and then checks through the remaining digits for numbers which occur in the code sequence, but are not in the correct place (DOLLAR). These values are then printed. This information helps you to refine your next guess. 15 goes are allowed, and if you haven't got the code in 15 tries, it is printed out for you. The program is structured with a sequence of calls to subroutines. Note that the code can include repeated digits, and analyse the checking procedures to see how this is dealt with.

```
  5 REM "CODER"
 10 GOSUB 1000
 20 REM **INITIALISE AND**
        **CHOOSE CODE   **
 30 LET GUESS=0
 40 LET C$=""
 50 LET N$="123456"
 60 FOR F=1 TO 4
 70 LET C$=C$+N$(INT (RND*6)+1)
 80 NEXT F
 90 CLS
100 PRINT "INPUT YOUR GUESS";
    TAB 0;"GUESS  * $"
110 INPUT G$
120 LET MARK=0
130 GOSUB 400
140 IF MARK=1 THEN GOTO 110
150 LET GUESS=GUESS+1
160 PRINT AT GUESS+2,1;G$;TAB
    7;
170 GOSUB 500
180 GOSUB 600
190 PRINT AST;TAB 9;DOLLAR
200 REM **SEE IF 15 TRIES **
        **OR  CODE CRACKED**
210 IF AST=4 OR GUESS=15 THEN
    GOTO 2000
220 REM **LOOP TO NEXT GUESS**
230 GOTO 110
240 REM **********************
250 REM
260 REM
400 REM **CHECK INPUT**
405 REM
410 FOR F=1 TO LEN G$
420 IF CODE G$(F)>34 OR CODE
    G$(F)<29 THEN LET MARK=1
430 NEXT F
440 IF LEN G$<>4 THEN LET MARK
    =1
```

```
450 IF NOT MARK THEN RETURN
460 PRINT AT GUESS+3,0;
    "WHAT? ";G$;"? TRY AGAIN."
470 PAUSE 100
480 PRINT AT GUESS+3,0;"
                          "
490 RETURN
495 REM ****************
496 REM
500 REM **FIND * NUMBER**
505 REM
506 LET A$=C$
510 LET AST=0
520 FOR F=1 TO 4
530 IF A$(F)<>G$(F) THEN GOTO
    570
540 LET AST=AST+1
550 LET G$(F)="0"
560 LET A$(F)="X"
570 NEXT F
580 RETURN
590 REM ***************
595 REM
600 REM **FIND $ NUMBER**
610 REM
620 LET DOLLAR=0
630 FOR F=1 TO 4
640 FOR N=1 TO 4
650 IF A$(F)<>G$(N) THEN GOTO
    690
660 LET DOLLAR=DOLLAR+1
670 LET A$(F)="X"
680 LET G$(N)="0"
690 NEXT N
700 NEXT F
710 RETURN
720 REM ***************
730 REM
1000 REM **INSTRUCTIONS**
1010 REM
1020 PRINT TAB 12;"*******",TAB
12;"*CODER*";TAB 12;"*******"
1030 PRINT ,,"COMPUTER CHOOSES A
 SEQUENCE OF","4 NUMBERS.THIS IS
 MADE UP OF","ANY OF THE DIGITS
1 TO 6","INCLUSIVE.DIGITS MAY BE
 REPEATEDSO THAT SEQUENCE COULD
BE 1663,",,"FOR EXAMPLE."
1040 PRINT ,,"YOU INPUT SEQUENCE
S TO TRY AND","MATCH THE CODE."
1050 PRINT ,,"COMPUTER WILL PRIN
T NUMBER OF *,SIGNIFYING CORRECT
 DIGIT IN","RIGHT POSITION,AND N
UMBER OF $, MEANING A DIGIT IN G
UESS WHICH "
1060 PRINT "OCCURS IN THE COMPUT
ERS CODE,","BUT IS NOT IN THE RI
GHT PLACE."
1070 PRINT ,,"PRESS A KEY TO PLA
Y"
1080 IF INKEY$="" THEN GOTO 1080
1090 RETURN
1100 REM ***************
1110 REM
2000 REM **END ROUTINE**
2010 REM
2020 IF AST=4 THEN GOTO 2050
2030 PRINT "15 TRIES AND NO SUCC
ESS.CODE","WAS ";C$
2040 GOTO 2060
2050 PRINT "<SUCCESS IN ";GUESS;
" TRIES>"
2060 PRINT "ANOTHER GAME?(INPUT
Y OR N)"
2070 INPUT M$
2080 IF M$="Y" THEN GOTO 30
2090 CLS
3000 PRINT "OK,BYE."
9980 REM
9990 REM *****END*****
9999 STOP
```

```
INPUT YOUR GUESS
GUESS      *  $

 1122      1  1
 2345      0  3
 1345      0  3
```

```
5432   1 2
2342   1 1
6122   1 1
3162   2 1
1353   0 3
6132   1 2
1362   1 2
4632   1 1
5332   1 2
4352   1 2
3342   2 0
3512   4 0
(SUCCESS IN 15 TRIES)
ANOTHER GAME?(INPUT Y OR N)
```

12. Plot

A simple program to plot a graph of data points, with X and Y values input on the screen. Prompts for X and Y axis minimum and maximum values are made, and string inputs for the axis titles. These are then printed, and the data input is prompted. X and Y values for each data point are entered, which is then plotted, and more data is requested.

Spectrum: Change line 310 to read PLOT 12 + 244 * (X – A)/(B – A), 12 + 156 * (Y – C)/(D – C)

```
   1 REM **PLOT**
  10 PRINT TAB 6;"GRAPHPLOTTER"
  20 PRINT
  30 PRINT "SET AXIS RANGES"
  40 PRINT "INPUT X AXIS MIN.VAL
UE ";
  50 INPUT A
  60 PRINT A
  70 PRINT "INPUT X AXIS MAX.VAL
UE ";
  80 INPUT B
  90 PRINT B
 100 PRINT "INPUT Y AXIS MIN.VAL
UE ";
 110 INPUT C
 120 PRINT C
 130 PRINT "INPUT Y AXIS MAX.VAL
UE ";
 140 INPUT D
 150 PRINT D
 160 PRINT "INPUT X AXIS TITLE "
;
 170 INPUT X$
 180 PRINT X$
 190 PRINT "INPUT Y AXIS TITLE "
;
 200 INPUT Y$
 210 PRINT Y$
 220 CLS
 230 PRINT AT 21,6;X$
 240 FOR I=1 TO LEN Y$
 250 PRINT AT I+5,0;Y$(I)
 260 NEXT I
 270 PRINT AT 0,0;"INPUT X"
 280 INPUT X
 290 PRINT AT 0,0;"INPUT Y"
 300 INPUT Y
 310 PLOT 2+61*(X-A)/(B-A),2+39*
(Y-C)/(D-C)
 320 GOTO 270
```

13. and 14. Bidec

Program converts binary numbers to their decimal equivalents. Two programs are given, differing in the conversion procedure applied to the binary number, which is input as a string. The algorithm of BIDEC*2 is more transparent than that of BIDEC. Spectrum users have the facility to input binary numbers directly (using BIN), but this

cannot handle numbers input in the course of a program, or generated by a program, in which case a routine of this type is required.
BIDEC*2

Spectrum: ↑ not ** in line 5Ø.

```
  1 REM *BIDEC*
  2 REM CONVERTS BINARY NUMBERS
 INTO DECIMAL
100 PRINT "ENTER BINARY FORM"
110 INPUT A$
120 PRINT
130 PRINT A$;" IN BINARY IS"
140 LET A=LEN A$
150 LET N=VAL A$(1)
160 FOR F=2 TO A
170 LET N=2*N+VAL A$(F)
180 NEXT F
190 PRINT
200 PRINT N;" IN DECIMAL"
```

```
  5 REM "BIDEC*2"
 10 PRINT "INPUT BINARY NUMBER"
 20 INPUT B$
 30 LET N=0
 40 LET P=0
 50 FOR F=LEN B$ TO 1 STEP -1
 60 LET N=N+VAL B$(F)*2**P
 70 LET P=P+1
 80 NEXT F
 90 PRINT B$;"=DECIMAL ";N
```

15. Hexdec

Program converts hexadecimal numbers up to FFFF (65534 decimal) into decimal. As with DECHEX, the straightforward conversion of a character code to a decimal value which is possible on the ZX81 is more complex on the Spectrum. Line 13Ø in the ZX81 version uses the value of the loop variable K directly to get the decimal value from the character code. On the Spectrum a counter loop is set up to hold and increment the value of K, and a new variable Z is used to hold the number by which K is to be reduced to give the correct decimal value from the hexadecimal character.

Spectrum: Line 5Ø needs ↑ , not **
Insert 55 PRINT " LETTERS MUST BE CAPITALS."
Insert 115 LET K = 48: LET Z = 48
Change 12Ø to read 12Ø FOR Y = Ø TO 15
Change 13Ø to read 13Ø IF A(F) = K THEN LET N = ((K – Z)*X) + N
Insert 135 LET K = K + 1
Insert 136 IF K = 58 THEN LET K = 65:LET Z = 55
Change 14Ø to read 14Ø NEXT Y

```
  1 REM *HEXDEC*
 10 DIM A(4)
 20 LET N=0
 30 PRINT "HEXADECIMAL TO DECIM
AL"
 40 PRINT
 50 PRINT "ENTER HEXADECIMAL NO
."
 60 PRINT
 70 INPUT H$
 80 PRINT H$;
 90 FOR F=1 TO LEN H$
100 LET A(F)=CODE H$(F)
110 LET X=16**(LEN H$-F)
120 FOR K=28 TO 43
130 IF A(F)=K THEN LET N=((K-28
)*X)+N
140 NEXT K
150 NEXT F
160 PRINT " IS ";N;" IN DECIMAL
"
```

```
170 PRINT
180 PRINT "AGAIN?(N OR Y)"
190 IF INKEY$="Y" THEN GOTO 30
200 STOP
```

16. Dechex

Program converts decimal (base 1Ø) numbers up to 65534 to their four-figure hexadecimal/(base 16) equivalents. Hexadecimal numbers use the digits Ø to 9 plus the letters A to F. This requires a means of deciding which character is to be printed, after the decimal number has been broken down. On the ZX81 this is simple, since the (capital) letters A to F follow directly after the digits in the character code sequence. This is not the case on the Spectrum, and the gap in the sequence must be bypassed. CHR$ can then be used to change the decimal values (Ø to 15), into which lines 12Ø to 17Ø break down the input number, to the appropriate character.

Spectrum: Change 19Ø to read 19Ø LET X = 48
Insert 2Ø5 IF X = 58 THEN LET X = 65

```
  1 REM DECHEX
 10 DIM A(4)
 20 DIM A$(4)
 30 PRINT "DECIMAL BASE TO HEXA
DECIMAL BASENUMBER CONVERSION"
 40 PRINT
 50 PRINT "NUMBERS <65535 ONLY"
 60 PAUSE 350
 70 CLS
 80 PRINT "INPUT DECIMAL VALUE"
 90 INPUT N
100 PRINT
110 PRINT N;
120 LET A(1)=INT (N/4096)
130 LET B=N-A(1)*4096
140 LET A(2)=INT (B/256)
150 LET C=B-A(2)*256
160 LET A(3)=INT (C/16)
170 LET A(4)=C-A(3)*16
180 FOR F=1 TO 4
190 LET X=28
200 FOR Y=0 TO 15
210 IF A(F)=Y THEN LET A$(F)=CH
R$ X
220 LET X=X+1
230 NEXT Y
240 NEXT F
250 PRINT " IS ";A$;" IN HEX"
260 PRINT AT 12,0;"HIT NEWLINE
TO RUN AGAIN"
270 INPUT B$
280 GOTO 70
```

17. Gridhunt

The computer hides itself on an 8 by 8 grid, which is displayed on the screen. You input your guesses of the co-ordinates, the guessed square is marked, and if not correct the computer gives a prompt for its direction from this square, using compass directions.

```
  1 REM *GRIDHUNT*
 10 PRINT "GRIDHUNT"
 30 FOR X=2 TO 16 STEP 2
 34 IF X/2=9 THEN GOTO 40
 35 PRINT AT 2,X+1;X/2;AT X+2,1
;X/2
 40 PRINT AT 3,X;"+";AT 19,X;"+
"
 45 PRINT AT X+1,2;"+";AT X+1,1
8;"+"
 50 NEXT X
 60 LET E=INT (RND*8)+1
 70 LET N=INT (RND*8)+1
 80 LET G=(E-1)*8+N
 90 LET M=0
```

```
 100 PRINT AT 3,20;"YOUR GUESS:-
";AT 5,20;"ACROSS?"
 110 INPUT A
 120 PRINT AT 5,26;" ";A;AT 7,20
;"DOWN?"
 130 INPUT D
 131 FOR X=1 TO 5
 132 PRINT AT 2+D*2,1+A*2;"▛"
 133 PRINT AT 2+D*2,1+A*2;"▙"
 134 NEXT X
 135 PRINT AT 2+D*2,1+A*2;"*"
 140 PRINT AT 7,24;" ";D;AT 9,20
;
 145 LET M=M+1
 150 LET C=(A-1)*6+D
 160 IF C=G THEN GOTO 300
 165 PRINT "I AM ";
 170 IF N=D THEN GOTO 210
 190 IF N>D THEN PRINT "S";
 200 IF N<D THEN PRINT "N";
 210 IF E>A THEN PRINT "E";
 220 IF E<A THEN PRINT "W";
 230 PRINT " ";TAB 52;"OF YOU"
 240 PAUSE 200
 250 FOR X=3 TO 10
 260 PRINT AT X,20;"           "
 270 NEXT X
 280 GOTO 100
 290 STOP
 300 PRINT "GOT ME";TAB 52;"IN "
;M;" MOVES"
 310 PRINT AT 20,0;"PRESS A KEY
TO PLAY"
 320 IF INKEY$="" THEN GOTO 320
 330 PRINT AT 20,0;"
        "
 340 CLS
 350 GOTO 10
```

18. Rescode

Program calculates resistor values from inputs of the colour bands on the resistor. Three bands are input, end band first, using the abbreviations given. The first two bands define the basic value and the third the multiplier.

```
  10 REM RESCODE
  20 PRINT "ENTER COLOUR BANDS,E
NDBAND FIRST"
  30 PRINT
  40 PRINT "USE CODES AS BELOW:"
  50 PRINT TAB 6;"RED      RE";TAB
 6;"BLACK  BL";TAB 6;"BROWN  BR"
;TAB 6;"ORANGE OR";TAB 6;"YELLOW
 YE";TAB 6;"GREEN  GR";TAB 6;"BL
UE   BL";TAB 6;"VIOLET VI";TAB 6
;"GREY    GY";TAB 6;"WHITE   WH";T
AB 6;"GOLD    GO";TAB 6;"SILVER S
I"
  60 FOR A=1 TO 3
  70 PRINT "COLOUR ";A;"?  ";
  80 INPUT C$
  90 PRINT C$
 100 IF C$="BK" THEN LET V=0
 110 IF C$="BR" THEN LET V=1
 120 IF C$="RE" THEN LET V=2
 130 IF C$="OR" THEN LET V=3
 140 IF C$="YE" THEN LET V=4
 150 IF C$="GR" THEN LET V=5
 160 IF C$="BL" THEN LET V=6
 170 IF C$="VI" THEN LET V=7
 180 IF C$="GY" THEN LET V=8
 190 IF C$="WH" THEN LET V=9
 200 IF C$="GO" THEN LET V=10
 210 IF C$="SI" THEN LET V=100
 220 IF A=1 THEN LET F=V
 230 IF A=2 THEN LET F=F*10+V
 240 NEXT A
 250 PRINT "RESISTANCE VALUE IS
";
 260 IF V>9 THEN GOTO 360
 270 PRINT F;
 280 FOR A=1 TO V
 290 PRINT "0";
 300 NEXT A
```

```
310 PRINT " OHMS"
320 STOP
360 PRINT F/V;
370 PRINT " OHMS"
```

19. Marker

Program produces a marksheet for the pupils in a class after exam results are entered in five subjects, set in this program as English, Maths, French, Computing and Biology. The average mark for each pupil is calculated, and a grade breakdown of the results is printed, giving the total number of pupils in each grade. The grades are defined as:

45% or less	FAIL
45 to 75%	PASS
More than 75%	DISTINCTION

As initialised, the program allows up to ten pupils in each class. A pupil name is entered with the results in each of the subjects, and the average calculated. When all entries have been made, END is entered and the subjects, results and grades for each pupil are printed. The grade breakdown is then given of the number of pupils in each grade for each subject.

```
  1 REM "MARKER"
  5 LET T1=0
  6 LET T2=0
  7 LET T3=0
  8 LET Z$="END
"
 10 DIM A$(10,20)
 20 DIM A(10)
 25 DIM D(5)
 26 DIM P(5)
 27 DIM F(5)
 30 DIM S$(5,10)
 40 DIM M(10,5)
 50 PRINT "MARK SHEET"
 60 PRINT "**********"
 70 PRINT ""
 80 PRINT ""
100 LET I=1
110 LET C=0
120 LET S$(1)="ENGLISH"
130 LET S$(2)="MATHS"
140 LET S$(3)="FRENCH"
150 LET S$(4)="COMPUTING"
160 LET S$(5)="BIOLOGY"
200 PRINT "ENTER NAME (ENTER EN
D TO FINISH): ";
210 INPUT A$(I)
220 PRINT A$(I)
230 IF A$(I)=Z$ THEN GOTO 500
240 GOSUB 1000
250 LET I=I+1
252 LET C=C+1
253 COPY
255 CLS
260 GOTO 200
500 REM CALC AVERAGES
501 COPY
505 CLS
510 FOR I=1 TO C
520 FOR J=1 TO 5
530 LET A(I)=M(I,J)+A(I)
540 NEXT J
550 NEXT I
600 FOR I=1 TO C
610 PRINT "NAME :";A$(I)
615 PRINT ""
620 PRINT "SUBJECT";TAB 15;"MAR
K";TAB 20;"GRADE"
625 PRINT "--------------------
-----------"
630 FOR J=1 TO 5
635 IF M(I,J)>75 THEN GOSUB 200
0
636 IF M(I,J)>45 AND M(I,J)<=75
THEN GOSUB 2200
637 IF M(I,J)<=45 THEN GOSUB 24
00
```

```
 640 PRINT S$(J);TAB 15;M(I,J);T
AB 20;G$
 650 NEXT J
 665 PRINT ""
 666 PRINT "AVERAGE= ";A(I)/5
 667 PAUSE 500
 668 COPY
 669 CLS
 670 NEXT I
 700 PRINT "GRADE BREAKDOWN BY S
UBJECT"
 710 PRINT "--------------------
-----------"
 720 PRINT "SUBJECT";TAB 15;"DIS
T.";TAB 22;"PASS";TAB 27;"FAIL"
 725 PRINT ""
 730 FOR J=1 TO 5
 740 PRINT S$(J);TAB 15;D(J);TAB
 22;P(J);TAB 27;F(J)
 750 LET T1=T1+D(J)
 760 LET T2=T2+P(J)
 770 LET T3=T3+F(J)
 800 NEXT J
 810 PRINT ""
 820 PRINT "TOTAL";TAB 15;T1;TAB
 22;T2;TAB 27;T3
 830 COPY
 850 STOP
1000 REM INPUT DATA
1040 FOR J=1 TO 5
1050 PRINT "SUBJECT ";S$(J);" MA
RK: ";
1060 INPUT M(I,J)
1070 PRINT M(I,J)
1080 NEXT J
1100 RETURN
2000 REM DISTINCTION
2010 LET G$="DISTINCTION"
2020 LET D(J)=D(J)+1
2030 RETURN
2200 REM PASS
2210 LET G$="PASS"
2220 LET P(J)=P(J)+1
2230 RETURN
2400 REM FAIL
2410 LET G$="FAIL"
2420 LET F(J)=F(J)+1
2430 RETURN
```

20. Indate

Program is a date entry routine, with the input subroutine starting at line 1Ø, and, nested within this, an error notice subroutine at line 25Ø. On running the program, control passes to line 3ØØ, which has a short example of the manner of use of the subroutines. Subroutines are usually grouped at the end of a program, but they can equally well be put at the beginning, as shown here. With long programs, using the subroutines repeatedly, this can speed execution, since the computer counts from the start of a program to find the line number corresponding to a GOSUB or GOTO destination.

```
   1 REM "INDATE"
   2 REM *DATE INPUT ROUTINES
   3 REM *DATE ENTRY/CHECK SUBRO
UTINES.ENTRY GOSUB 10,ERROR MESS
AGE GOSUB 250*
   5 GOTO 300
   8 REM *********************
   9 REM **DATE ENTRY SUB**
  10 PRINT "ENTER DATE"
  20 PRINT "DAY?"
  30 INPUT D
  40 IF D>=1 AND D<=31 THEN GOTO
 70
  50 GOSUB 250
  60 GOTO 20
  70 PRINT "MONTH?(1 TO 12)"
  80 INPUT M
  90 IF M>=1 AND M<=12 THEN GOTO
 120
 100 GOSUB 250
 110 GOTO 70
 120 PRINT "YEAR?(AS LAST 2 DIGI
TS)"
```

```
 130 INPUT Y
 140 IF Y>10 AND Y<99 THEN GOTO
170
 150 GOSUB 250
 160 GOTO 120
 170 REM *CHECK DAY VS MONTH*
 180 REM *LEAP YEAR*
 190 IF INT ((Y+1900)/4)<>(Y+190
0)/4 AND M=2 AND D=29 THEN GOTO
220
 200 REM *SHORT MONTHS*
 210 IF NOT ((M=2 AND D>29) OR (
(M=4 OR M=6  OR M=9 OR M=11) AND
 D=31)) THEN GOTO 240
 220 GOSUB 250
 230 GOTO 10
 240 RETURN
 248 REM *********************
 249 REM **ERROR NOTICE SUB**
 250 PRINT "***INPUT ERROR***","
PLEASE FOLLOW INSTRUCTIONS","RE-
INPUT REQUESTED DATA."
 260 PAUSE 180
 270 CLS
 280 RETURN
 300 REM ***PROGRAM HERE TO USE
     INPUT ROUTINES***
 310 REM *EXAMPLE*
 320 PRINT "YOUR BIRTHDAY"
 330 GOSUB 10
 340 LET BD=D
 350 LET BM=M
 360 LET BY=Y
 370 CLS
 380 PRINT "BIRTHDATE:";BD;"/";B
M;"/19";BY
```

21. Headliner

Program prints banner headlines on the printer, using the character arrays stored in ROM. As listed, the program allows the inverse characters of the ZX81 to be used, accessing the normal character (line 130) to get the pattern of bits, but reversing this (i.e. swapping black for white) for printing (line 560). This procedure is not possible on the Spectrum, since the inverse forms are not included in the character set. The basis of the program is the reading of the character arrays (as with the BIGPRINT program in Unit U3 of the main text), but with the additional complication of reading the first bit of each byte, then the second bit of each byte, and so on, in order to print a character with a sequence of printer lines.

Spectrum: Delete lines 40, 120. 130, 550, 560
Change line 160 to read: 160 LET L = PEEK (15360 + C + 8 * CODE L$)

```
   1 REM *HEADLINER*
  10 PRINT TAB 8;"HEADLINES";TAB
 8;"---------"
  20 PRINT ,,;"PROGRAM TO PRODUC
E LARGE PRINT","AS HEADLINES ALO
NG PRINTER PAPER"
  30 PRINT ,,;"INPUT ANY LENGTH
STRING."
  40 PRINT ,,;"YOU MAY USE ALL L
ETTERS,NUMBERS","AND GRAPHICS."
  50 REM DIM ARRAY TO STORE LETT
ER
  60 DIM A(64)
  70 INPUT U$
  80 FAST
  90 FOR F=1 TO LEN U$
 100 REM TAKE LETTER
 110 LET L$=U$(F)
 120 REM IF CHR INVERSE THEN
SWAP FOR NORMAL FORM
 130 IF CODE L$>63 THEN LET L$=C
HR$ (CODE U$(F)-128)
 140 REM GET ROM CODES
 150 FOR C=0 TO 7
 160 LET L=PEEK (7680+C+8*CODE L
$)
```

```
 170 REM GET BINARY INTO ARRAY
 180 FOR B=1 TO 8
 190 IF L-2*INT (L/2)=1 THEN GOT
O 220
 200 LET A(8*C+B)=0
 210 GOTO 230
 220 LET A(8*C+B)=1
 230 LET L=INT (L/2)
 240 NEXT B
 250 NEXT C
 260 GOSUB 500
 270 NEXT F
 280 STOP
 500 REM PRINT SUBROUTINE
 510 REM REVERSE LOOPS
 520 FOR X=8 TO 1 STEP -1
 530 LET A$=""
 540 FOR Y=7 TO 0 STEP -1
 550 REM REVERSE IF CHR INVERTED
BEFORE
 560 IF CODE U$(F)>63 THEN LET A
(Y*8+X)=NOT A(Y*8+X)
 570 REM PUT ONE ROW OF CHR INTO
A$
 580 IF A(Y*8+X)=1 THEN LET A$=A
$+"████"
 590 IF A(Y*8+X)=0 THEN LET A$=A
$+"    "
 600 NEXT Y
 610 LPRINT A$
 620 LPRINT A$
 630 NEXT X
 640 RETURN
```

22. Input

Program checks a number input as a string. This is a useful way to input numbers, as an error will not cause a program halt, as will happen, for instance, if a numeric input contains more than one decimal point. The program is listed as an input check for decimal currency, but is easily modified to suit any numeric input of a known form.

The string input is checked by the subroutine at line 200, each character in turn being checked by means of its code to ensure it is either a digit or a decimal point. To check for multiple d.p.'s the counter S is incremented each time one is encountered. M is set equal to the number of digits before the d.p. A check is then made for S being greater than 1 (non-numeric character or more than one decimal place), 0 (no d.p.), and for more than two digits after the d.p. Any error sends control to the error subroutine at line 400. This requests a re-input the number. The error check subroutine is then called recursively to check this input. A correct input will pass control back to the main program, where the user is given the opportunity to check that the input value is correct.

```
   1 REM "INPUT"
   5 REM STRING INPUT CHECKED AS
NUMBER
   9 REM *MARKERS*
  10 LET S=0
  15 LET M=0
  19 REM *EMPTY LINE*
  20 LET E$="
                    "
  30 PRINT "ENTER AMOUNT.ENTER P
OUNDS,","FULLSTOP,PENCE:- 99.99"
  40 INPUT N$
  50 GOSUB 200
  59 REM *OFFER VALUE CHECK*
  60 PRINT AT 20,0;"ENTRY VALID.
ENTRY WAS £";N$,"INPUT C TO CONF
IRM,E TO RE-ENTER"
  70 INPUT A$
  80 IF A$="C" THEN GOTO 170
  90 IF A$="E" THEN GOTO 120
 100 PRINT AT 20,0;"FOLLOW INSTR
UCTIONS.     "
 110 GOTO 70
 120 PRINT AT 20,0;E$;AT 21,0;E$
 130 PRINT AT 20,0;"ENTER CORREC
T VALUE."
 140 INPUT N$
 150 PRINT AT 20,0;E$;E$
```

```
 160 GOSUB 200
 170 CLS
 180 PRINT "END OF PROGRAM"
 190 GOTO 999
 199 REM *ERROR CHECK*
 200 LET L=LEN N$
 210 FOR F=1 TO L
 219 REM *CHECK NON-NUMERIC CHRS
*
 220 IF CODE N$(F)<27 OR CODE N$
(F)>37 THEN LET S=2
 229 REM *CHECK FULLSTOP*
 230 IF N$(F)="." THEN LET S=S+1
 240 IF N$(F)="." THEN LET M=F
 250 NEXT F
 260 IF L-M<>2 OR S>1 OR S=0 THE
N GOSUB 400
 270 RETURN
 399 REM *ERROR FOUND*
 400 PRINT AT 21,0;"*INPUT INVAL
ID*RE-ENTER VALUE"
 410 INPUT N$
 411 LET S=0
 412 LET M=0
 420 GOSUB 200
 430 RETURN
 999 REM *END*
```

23. Asteroids

The program puts you at the helm of a Mars shuttle disguised as an asterisk. Avoiding the Nova Heat you have to weave through the strangely square low albedo asteroids that look surprisingly like inverse squares. Your controls are fairly minimal – not much money on the Mars run smuggling algae these days, so you have a button marked 1 to go left and one marked Ø to go right.

The program cannot be simply modified for the Spectrum so this listing applies to the ZX81 only.

```
   5 REM "ASTEROIDS"
  10 PRINT "**ASTEROIDS**"
  20 PRINT
  30 PRINT "AVOID BLACK ASTEROID
S"
  40 PRINT "YOU STEER YOUR SHIP
(*)"
  50 PRINT "BY PRESSING 1 TO GO
LEFT"
  60 PRINT "AND 0 TO GO RIGHT"
  70 PAUSE 400
  80 CLS
  90 POKE 16418,8
 100 LET S=0
 110 LET C=10
 120 SCROLL
 130 PRINT AT 5,C;
 140 IF PEEK ( PEEK 16398+256* P
EEK 16399)=128 THEN GOTO 250
 150 PRINT "*"
 160 LET L=C
 170 IF INKEY$ ="" THEN GOTO 190
 180 LET C=C-(C>1 AND INKEY$ ="1
")+(C<19 AND INKEY$ ="0")
 190 PRINT AT 8, RND *20;"■"
 200 LET S=S+1
 210 PRINT AT 5,L;" "
 220 GOTO 120
```

```
250 PRINT S
260 PAUSE 250
270 CLS
280 PRINT "PRESS NEWLINE FOR"
290 PRINT "ANOTHER GAME"
300 INPUT A$
310 IF A$="" THEN GOTO 80
```

Peter Morse is Professor and Head of Computer Science at the Polytechnic of Central London. He has wide ranging teaching, research and consultant activities in the fields of digital systems, software engineering and computer education.

Ian Adamson is an educational consultant active in the design of technical and scientific courses, and the associated buildings, laboratories and equipment, working mainly on overseas projects.

Ben Anrep is a Senior Programmer working on microprocessor system development and software with the Computer Centre of the PCL.

Brian Hancock is Senior Lecturer in Computer Science. His teaching and research activities include programming methods and the operation of computer courses for schoolteachers.